Readings in
LABOR ECONOMICS
and
LABOR RELATIONS

Readings in
LABOR ECONOMICS
and
LABOR RELATIONS

LLOYD G. REYNOLDS
Yale University

STANLEY H. MASTERS
Notre Dame University

COLLETTE MOSER
Michigan State University

PRENTICE-HALL, INC., *Englewood Cliffs, New Jersey*

Library of Congress Cataloging in Publication Data

REYNOLDS, LLOYD GEORGE , comp.
Readings in labor economics and labor relations.

Includes bibliographical references.
1. Labor economics—Addresses, essays, lectures.
2. Industrial relations—Addresses, essays, lectures.
I. Masters, Stanley,   joint comp. II. Moser,
Collette,   joint comp.   III. Title.
HD4901.R474   331   74-3270
ISBN 0-13-761551-5

PRENTICE-HALL INTERNATIONAL, INC., *London*
PRENTICE-HALL OF AUSTRALIA, PTY. LTD., *Sydney*
PRENTICE-HALL OF CANADA, LTD., *Toronto*
PRENTICE-HALL OF INDIA PRIVATE LIMITED, *New Delhi*
PRENTICE-HALL OF JAPAN, INC., *Tokyo*

Contents

v

II
LABOR MARKETS AND UNEMPLOYMENT 45

III
WAGE RATES 127

Money Wages, Phillips Curves, and Incomes Policy 149

IV

DISCRIMINATION AND POVERTY 177

Discrimination 179

Poverty 211

VII
SPECIAL TOPICS 363

Preface

The literature of labor economics is rich and varied. Students in graduate courses are exposed to this literature, gaining a sense of its historical development and of the frontiers of current research. But the undergraduate usually has access to it only indirectly through a textbook, in which knowledge necessarily appears more definite than it actually is.

We believe that students can gain much by reading the original works of leading scholars in labor economics and industrial relations; we have tried to assemble as rich a menu as possible within reasonable space limitations. The general organization follows that of Reynolds' *Labor Economics and Labor Relations,* but these readings could form a useful supplement to any labor text.

In addition to setting high quality standards, two principles have governed the content of the book. First, we have chosen excerpts that are long enough to give the full flavor of an author's thought, rather than a larger number of shorter pieces. Second, we have tried to achieve a balanced coverage of both labor economics and industrial relations, rather than focusing primarily on one area or the other.

Thanks are due to the authors who have given permission for this reprinting of their work. Although many people have assisted us in the preparation of this book, we would like to express special appreciation to Deborah Johnson and Jeanette Barbour at Michigan State University.

CREDITS

The editors would like to acknowledge the following for their generosity in allowing them to use this material:

1. E. H. Phelps-Brown, *The Economics of Labor* (New Haven, Conn.: Yale University Press, 1962), Chap. 1. Reprinted with permission of Yale University Press.

2. Glen G. Cain, *Married Women in the Labor Force* (Chicago: University of Chicago Press, 1966), Chaps. 1, 2, and 4. ©1966 by the University of Chicago Press. Reprinted with permission.

3. Richard A. Easterlin, "Population," in *Contemporary Economic Issues,* Neil W. Chamberlain, ed. (Homewood, Ill.: Richard D. Irwin, Inc., 1969). Reprinted with permission.

4. Gary S. Becker, *Human Capital—A Theoretical and Empirical Analysis, With Special Reference to Education,* Chap. 2. Copyright 1964 by National Bureau of Economic Research. Reprinted with permission.

5. William G. Bowen, "Assessing the Economic Contribution of Education," in *The Robbins Report on Higher Education,* CMND 2154. Used with the permission of the Controller of Her Britannic Majesty's Stationery Office.

7. Alfred Marshall, *Principles of Economics,* 8th ed. (New York: The Macmillan Company, 1936), Book VI, Chaps. 3-5.

8. Clark Kerr, "The Balkanization of Labor Markets," in *Labor Mobility and Economic Opportunity,* E. Wight Bakke. Reprinted by permission of the Technology Press of Massachusetts Institute of Technology and John Wiley and Sons, Inc.

9. Albert Rees, "Information Networks in Labor Markets," *American Economic Review,* Vol. 56, No. 2 (May, 1966). Reprinted by permission of the *American Economic Review.*

10. Charles C. Holt, "Improving the Labor Market Trade-off between Inflation and Unemployment," *American Economic Review,* Vol. 59, No. 2 (May, 1969). Reprinted by permission of the *American Economic Review.*

11. Robert E. Hall, "Why Is the Unemployment Rate So High at Full Employment?" in *Brookings Papers on Economic Activity 1970:3,* Arthur M. Okun and George L. Perry, eds. ©1971, The Brookings Institution, Washington, D.C.

12. Charles C. Killingsworth, "Unemployment: A Fresh Perspective," a prepared statement given on August 6, 1971, before the Joint Economic Committee, U. S. Congress. Reprinted with permission of the U. S. Government Printing Office.

13. Sar A. Levitan and Garth L. Mangum, *Federal Training and Work Programs in the Sixties* (Ann Arbor, Mich.: Institute of Labor and Industrial Relations, 1969), Chap. 1.

14. With the assistance of Robert A. Levine, "Job Creation," in *Setting National Priorities: The 1972 Budget,* by Charles L. Schultze, Edward F. Fried, Alice M. Rivlin, and Nancy H. Teeters. ©1971, The Brookings Institution, Washington, D. C.

15. Sar A. Levitan and Robert Taggart, "The Emergency Employment Act: An Interim Assessment," *Monthly Labor Review,* Vol. 95, No. 6 (June, 1972). Prepared by the authors under a grant from the National Manpower Policy Task Force.

16. Beatrice Reuben, *The Hard-to-Employ: European Programs,* Chap. 14. ©1970 by Columbia University Press. Reprinted with permission.

17. H. Gregg Lewis, *Unionism and Relative Wages in the United States* (Chicago: University of Chicago Press, 1963), Chap. 1. ©1963 by the University of Chicago Press. Reprinted with permission.

18. Albert Rees, "The Effects of Unions on Resource Allocation," 6 *J. Law & Econ.* 69 (1963). ©1966. Reprinted by permission of the University of Chicago Law School.

19. Robert Ozanne, "Impact of Unions on Wage Levels and Income Distribution," *The Quarterly Journal of Economics,* Vol. 73, No. 2 (May, 1959). Reprinted with permission of *The Quarterly Journal of Economics.*

20. John T. Dunlop, "Guideposts, Wages, and Collective Bargaining," in *Guidelines: Informal Controls and the Marketplace,* George P. Schultz and Robert A. Aliber, eds. ©1966 by the University of Chicago Press. Reprinted with permission.

21. Lloyd Ulman, "Cost-Push and Some Policy Alternatives," *Industrial Relations Research Association Proceedings* (24th Annual Winter Proceedings). Reprinted with permission of the Industrial Relations Research Association.

22. William Poole, "Thoughts on the Wage-Price Freeze," *Brookings Papers on Economic Activity 1971:2,* Arthur M. Okun and George L. Perry, eds. ©1971, The Brookings Institution, Washington, D. C.

23. James Tobin, "Inflation and Unemployment," *American Economic Review,* Vol. 62, No. 1 (March, 1972). ©by the American Economic Association. Reprinted with permission of the *American Economic Review.*

24. Gary S. Becker, *The Economics of Discrimination* (Chicago: University of Chicago Press, 1971), Chaps. 1 and 2. ©1971 by the University of Chicago Press. Reprinted with permission.

25. Michael Reich, "The Economics of Racism," in *Problems in Political Economy: An Urban Perspective,* David M. Gordon, ed. (Lexington, Mass.: D. C. Heath and Co., 1970). ©1970 by Michael Reich; reprinted with his permission.

26. Francine D. Blau, " 'Women's Place' in the Labor Market," *American Economic Review,* Vol. 62, No. 2 (May, 1972). Reprinted by permission of the *American Economic Review.*

27. Juanita Kreps, *Sex in the Marketplace* (Baltimore, Md.: The Johns Hopkins University Press, 1971). Copyright ©1971 by The Johns Hopkins University Press.

29. Michael Harrington, *The Other America* (New York: Macmillan Publishing Co., 1969). Copyright ©Michael Harrington, 1962, 1969. Reprinted with permission of Macmillan Publishing Co., Inc.

30. Reprinted from *The Poor Ye Need Not Have with You* by Robert A. Levine by permission of the M.I.T. Press, Cambridge, Mass. ©1970 by the M.I.T. Press, Cambridge, Mass.

31. James Tobin, "On Improving the Economic Status of the Negro," *Daedulus,* Vol. 94, No. 4 (Fall, 1965). Reprinted by permission of *Daedulus.*

32. Earl R. Rolph, "The Case for a Negative Income Tax Device," *Industrial Relations,* Vol. 6, No. 2 (February, 1967). Copyright 1967 by the Regents of the University of California, Berkeley. Reprinted with permission of *Industrial Relations.*

34. Thomas I. Ribich, *Education and Poverty.* ©1968, The Brookings Institution, Washington, D. C.

35. Jacob J. Kaufman and Terry G. Foran, "The Minimum Wage and Poverty," in *Towards Freedom from Want,* Sar A. Levitan, *et al.,* eds. Reprinted by permission of Industrial Relations Research Association.

36. Philip Taft, "Theories of the Labor Movement," in *Interpreting the Labor Movement,* George W. Brooks, *et al.,* eds. Reprinted by permission of the Industrial Relations Research Association.

37. Selig Perlman, *A Theory of the Labor Movement* (New York: The Macmillan Company, 1928). Reprinted with permission of the author.

38. Everett M. Kassalow, "The Development of Western Labor Movements: Some Comparative Considerations," in *Labor: Readings on Major Issues,* Richard A. Lester, ed. (New York: Random House, 1965).

39. Walter Galenson, "Why the American Labor Movement Is Not Socialist," *American Review,* Vol. 1, No. 2 (Winter, 1961). Reprinted with permission of the author.

40. Harry Shulman and Neil W. Chamberlain, "The Process of Bargaining," *Cases on Labor Relations* (Mineola, New York: The Foundation Press, 1949). Reprinted with permission.

41. Albert Rees, *The Economics of Trade Unions* (Chicago: University of Illinois Press, 1962), Chap. 2. ©1962 by the University of Chicago Press. Reprinted with permission.

42. Excerpted from Chapter 17, "Government Regulation or Control of Union Activities," by Charles Gregory in *Labor in a Changing America,* edited by William Haber, ©1966 by Basic Books, Inc.

43. Clark Kerr, "Industrial Relations and the Liberal Pluralist," Presidential address, *Industrial Relations Research Association Proceedings,* Vol. 7 (1954). Reprinted with the permission of the Industrial Relations Research Association.

44. Clark Kerr, *Unions and Union Leaders of Their Own Choosing* (Santa Barbara, Calif.: The Center for the Study of Democratic Institutions, 1958).

45. From pp. 6-18 in *Goals and Strategy in Collective Bargaining* by Frederick H. Harbison and John R. Coleman. Copyright 1951, by Harper and Row, Publishers, Inc. By permission of the publisher.

46. Abridged from *Collective Bargaining* by Neil W. Chamberlain and James W. Kuhn. Copyright ©1965 by McGraw-Hill, Inc. Used with permission of McGraw-Hill Book Company.

47. Clark Kerr, "Industrial Conflict and Its Mediation," *The American Journal of Sociology,* Vol. 60, No. 3 (November, 1954). ©1954 by the University of Chicago Press.

48. Paul E. Sultan, "The Union Security Issue," in *Public Policy and Collective Bargaining,* Shister, *et al.,* eds. (Industrial Relations Research Association, 1962). Reprinted with permission of the Industrial Relations Research Association.

49. and 60. Derek C. Bok and John T. Dunlop, *Labor and the American Community* (New York: Simon & Schuster, 1970). Copyright ©1970 by The Rockefeller Bros. Fund, Inc. Reprinted by permission of Simon & Schuster, Inc.

50. W. Willard Wirtz, "The 'Choice-of-Procedures' Approach to National Emergency Disputes," in *Emergency Disputes and National Policy,* Irving Bernstein, *et al.,* eds. Reprinted by permission of Industrial Relations Research Association.

51. Carl M. Stevens, "Is Compulsory Arbitration Compatible with Bargaining?" *Industrial Relations,* Vol. 5, No. 2 (February, 1966). Reprinted by permission of *Industrial Relations.*

52. Everett M. Kassalow, "Trade Unionism Goes Public," *The Public Interest,* No. 14 (Winter, 1969). Copyright © National Affairs, Inc., 1969.

53. Harry H. Wellington and Ralph K. Winter, Jr., "The Limits of Collective Bargaining in Public Employment," reprinted by permission of The Yale Law Journal Company and Fred B. Rothman & Company from *The Yale Law Journal,* Vol. 78, pp. 1111, 1112-24, 1126-27.

54. John F. Burton, Jr., and Charles Krider, "The Role and Consequences of Strikes by Public Employees," reprinted by permission of The Yale Law Journal Company and Fred B. Rothman & Company from *The Yale Law Journal,* Vol. 79.

55. Myron Lieberman, "Professors, Unite!" *Harper's Magazine* (October, 1971). Copyright ©1971 by Minneapolis Star and Tribune Co., Inc. Reprinted from the October 1971 issue of *Harper's Magazine* by permission of the author.

56. Joan London and Henry Anderson, *So Shall Ye Reap* (New York: Thomas Y. Crowell Company, Inc., 1970). Copyright ©1970 by Joan London and Henry Anderson. With permission of the publisher, Thomas Y. Crowell Company, Inc.

57. Herbert Hill, National Labor Director of the NAACP and Professor at Princeton University and the New School for Social Research, "Black Protest and the Struggle for Union Democracy," *Issues in Industrial Society,* Vol. 1, No. 1 (Cornell University, 1969). Reprinted with permission of *Issues in Industrial Society* and the author.

58. Orley Ashenfelter, "Discrimination and Trade Unions," in Orley Ashenfelter and Albert.Rees, *Discrimination in Labor Markets* (Princeton, N. J.: Princeton University Press, 1973). Reprinted with the permission of Princeton University Press.

59. Reprinted from "Women and American Trade Unions" by Alice H. Cook, January 1968 issue of *The Annals of The American Academy of Political and Social Science.* ©1968 by The American Academy of Political and Social Science.

61. Jack Barbash, *Trade Unions and National Economic Policy* (Baltimore, Md.: The Johns Hopkins University Press, 1972). ©1972 by Jack Barbash. Reprinted with permission of The Johns Hopkins University Press.

L. G. Reynolds
S. H. Masters
C. H. Moser

LABOR MARKETS

I

LABOR SUPPLY

Labor Supply

The introductory essay by E. H. Phelps-Brown discusses how labor economics relates to other branches of economics and to other social sciences. While labor can be studied simply as a factor of production, labor economists devote much of their attention to the unique features of labor markets, including such important institutions as trade unions. Since there is little that is unique regarding the demand for labor, labor economics has emphasized issues pertaining to labor supply.

The supply of labor has many different aspects, including the amount of hours people want to work, the skills they bring to the job, and their attitudes toward work, (e.g., dependability, cooperativeness and initiative). In addition, we can look at the supply of labor at different levels of aggregation: the economy; the industry, occupation, or region; and the firm.

Our first selection on labor supply is taken from Glen Cain's analysis of *Married Women in the Labor Force.* He is interested primarily in explaining why there has been a marked increase over time in the percentage of married women who desire market work while the corresponding labor force participation rates have declined for most other demographic groups. His empirical work, based on a wide variety of different kinds of data, suggests that for wives the substitution effect of a wage increase is often larger than the income effect. Since real wages have been rising over time, a positive net wage effect provides a partial explanation for the increase in the labor force participation rate of married women.

The aggregate labor supply depends not only on the labor force participation rate, the percentage of the population that is over sixteen and wants to work, but also on the total size of this population. For many years economists simply accepted the size of the total population as determined by noneconomic forces. With the increase in availability and popularity of various birth control techniques in recent years, family size has become more the result of conscious decisions and less of random chance. Consequently economists have begun to apply the standard tools of economic analysis to explain changes in the birth rate, the most important determinant of population changes in our society. The essay by Richard Easterlin provides an interesting example of such analysis.

5

From an economic point of view, labor supply depends on the quality as well as the quantity of labor. Differences in quality depend partly on differences in innate ability, but they also depend on the amount of economic resources that has been invested in different individuals. Expenditures to improve the health, education, or training of individuals so that they may earn a higher future income are often called investments in human capital. The theory of human capital is developed in the selection from Gary Becker's pioneering book, *Human Capital—A Theoretical and Empirical Analysis.*

While Becker's theoretical analysis is concerned primarily with on-the-job training, much of the work on human capital has focused on the effects of schooling on earnings. The essay by William Bowen summarizes the conceptual issues involved and presents some of the empirical results that economists have obtained in attempting to assess the economic effects of education. While education has other important effects in addition to increasing labor-market productivity, the evidence suggests that it does yield significant economic rewards. This finding is still generally valid today, although in the last few years the demographic changes discussed by Easterlin have sharply reduced the rate of return to some kinds of education, especially the education of teachers.

1. The Economist's Study of Labor

E. H. Phelps-Brown

The tools of his trade that the economist applies to labor are the same as those he would bring to any other subject in his field. They consist of micro- and macroeconomic theory, and a stock of information about institutions and magnitudes. The theory gives the economist a framework within which to arrange his observations and direct his inquiries: it suggests where causes and consequences are to be looked for, it traces the network of interdependence, and it guards against pitfalls in reasoning. The information provides a diagram, roughly to scale, of the whole mechanism of which the particular element studied forms one working part.

Applied to labor as a factor of production, these tools quickly yield an answer to a first question, why the rates of pay for different kinds of labor are what they are. These rates appear as one set of prices, simultaneously determined with all others, whether of factors or of final products, through the interplay between demand and scarce resources in the pricing system. Any one rate has to equilibrate the number of applicants coming forward for a job with the number of vacancies offered. There is a supply curve of applicants, whose form depends in part on what alternative demands there are for that kind of labor. The vacancies are given by a curve of derived demand, i.e., the demand for one of several collaborating factors, derived from the demand for their joint product.

But this is only common form: we may have called the factor "labor," but the argument would be much the same if we spoke of land or equipment. Only when we bring in more particular circumstances do we develop a theory specific to labor. We do this when, for instance, we allow that how much work a man will do depends on his relative valuation of monetary income and leisure; or recognize the imperfections of the labor market, and apply the theories of market forms such as monopoly and oligopoly; or ask what obstacles prevent some men from earning as much as others, and on what conditions some remain unemployed. In such ways as these the methods of economic analysis are applied to situations which, though still generalized, are specified in sufficient detail to be characteristic of labor markets.

Such applications yield insights, but into possibilities rather than actualities. There has to be a running interaction between analysis and field work. Analysis there must be to start with, for facts do not speak for themselves, and the meaning that those we gather have for us depends on the framework within which we arrange them. But given an informative arrangement, it is only through the patient study of the facts that we can reach the actual causes of particular states of affairs. Much more than this, the framework of analysis itself bends or breaks as new facts are brought into it, and it has to be designed anew. Gathering information does not merely give body to established relations, but questions existing hypotheses and suggests new ones.

A great part of the economics of labor consists accordingly of information about those institutions and procedures through which the labor force is nurtured and trained, deployed between occupations and industries, and organized and directed at the place of work; and those through which its rates of pay are administered and negotiated. This information is not merely factual. It has life: it is physiology, so to speak, and pathology, as well as anatomy. It shows us how things seem to work; it suggests what can or cannot be done about them. It also reveals an amazing variety. Everywhere men have to work to get their living, but the arrangements they work under have been and are extraordinarily divergent: techniques differ, but also there is a range of striking contrasts in the relations between the worker, the community he lives in, the consumer of his product, and the hirer of his work. . . . When we find the day's work organized in so many different ways, when the same effect arises from different causes or the same cause is followed by different effects, we recognize the interplay of more factors than we had seen at first.

In the study of labor, these additional factors include some that lie beyond the usual beat of the economist. Labor is a factor of production—but the worker is a human being, and his work involves social as well as technical relations. Work is not merely the way to get a living, but a way of life, a game or a thralldom, a field of conflicts and loyalties, anxieties and reassurances, prestige and humiliation. The propensities of human nature that suffice to actuate a pricing system are limited, but the student of labor who does not go beyond the "economic man" leaves out much that is indispensable to his own etiology. The quality of the labor force depends on inheritance and upbringing. The occupational and social structures are interlocked. How much work any one man will do depends on his motivation—on his household, the standards of the group he works in, and the goals inculcated by his community. The application of labor requires direction: some workers are self-directed, but most come under management, and the relations between employer and employed affect both produc-

tivity and the satisfactions of the working life. They also affect pay. Though pay is arrived at in a market, it depends not only on the impersonal balance of supply and demand but also on custom, notions of equity, and the balance of power between groups and classes. At these and many other points the economist who has set out simply to study labor as a factor of production, and pay as a price, will find his attention drawn inescapably to matters commonly pertaining to psychology and sociology.

If this is true of the attempt to understand why things are what they are at any one time, it is even more true of the study of why things change. Such questions as why the differential for skill has generally diminished in Western countries over the last fifty years, or why real wages in Western Europe fell greatly during the sixteenth century but have risen greatly during the twentieth, can fairly be put to the labor economist; but when he tackles them he finds that what he has to try to understand is history. The growth of population, the stagnation of technique or its rapid development, the opening up of new natural resources and new channels of trade, the extension of literacy, the rise and fall of principles of public policy—he cannot explain what has happened in the labor market without going to some extent into such questions as these. In part, of course, he can take them as given, and look simply at what goes on within the setting that they from time to time impose. But he cannot ignore the interaction between his own subject matter and the setting. This is evident in questions of economic growth: in the setting of a given achieved technique and stock of capital a certain distribution of the product between labor and capital will work itself out, but this distribution will react on the rate of accumulation, and this in turn on the technique and capital stock of the future. There is a similar interaction with the social setting: a higher general level of real wages enables wage earners' children to defer their entry into full-time employment and get more training meanwhile; the consequent change in the supplies of different kinds of labor reacts on their relative pay; this in turn reacts on social structure and attitudes, and these affect trade unionism. The test of the labor economist's ability to stop short at the boundary of someone else's field is his capacity to advise. What will he point to, for instance, if he is asked how an underdeveloped country can raise the productivity of its labor force? If he seeks the understanding that is effective operationally, he must study the labor market in its setting of economic growth and social change.

But in the division of labor among the social sciences he does not cease to be an economist, and economics proper has its distinctive contribution to make. In some studies of wages, it is true, the influence of such factors as convention and bargaining power have seemed so paramount that economic analysis has been dismissed, its services no longer required. But this has been too hasty. What stands out in particular transactions is often peculiar to them: the course of events in the aggregate is influenced more by forces that may be secondary in any one case but work in the same direction in all. The forces of demand and supply are of that kind. The actual course of pay, country by country and period by period, shows uni-formities that can be anticipated on the grounds with which the economist works, but would be surprising on others. Whatever their causes, the movements of the labor market are knit up with those of prices, incomes, and output generally, in a system whose static and dynamic connections have been explored only by economic analysis. If a textbook of that analysis is read as a description of what the investigator will find when he goes into the field, it will appear to leave out so much of practical importance that it may seem far removed from reality; but the forces it has lifted out for separate scrutiny are really at work, and policy will flounder if it neglects them. Nonetheless, the economist who studies labor needs to recognize that his own quest for causes leads him within the scope of other disciplines, from which he must get all the help he can.

2. Married Women in the Labor Force

Glen G. Cain

INTRODUCTION

. . . The rise over time in the work rates of wives has been impressive. The labor force participation rate of married women in the United States more than doubled from 1900 to 1940 and then doubled again from 1940 to 1960. Although the hours worked per day have decreased over time, the large rise in participation rates ensures that market work by married women has increased substantially over time. In sharp contrast are the participation rates and, more definitely, total hours of work of single women and males. Both have declined over this 60-year period, and the trends continue as of 1964 (see Table 1).

In recent years, moreover, the principal change in the composition of the labor force and the most important source of its growth has been the increased participation of married

Table 1

Trend in Labor Force Participation Rates of the Adult Population by Sex and Marital Status

	1964[a]	Comparison I[b] 1960	Comparison I[b] 1940	Comparison II[c] 1940	Comparison II[c] 1900
Married Women	34	31	15	14	6
Single Women	41	44	48	53	46
Males	75	78	80	80	86
All Women	36	35	27	27	21
Both Sexes	55	56	54	55	52

[a]Women and men, 14 years and older. Source: U.S. Department of Labor, Bureau of Labor Statistics, "Special Labor Force Report, No. 50," Reprint No. 2457, p. 1.
[b]Women and men, 14 years and older. Source: U.S. Department of Labor, Bureau of Labor Statistics, "Special Labor Force Report, No. 13," Reprint No. 2364, p. 3.
[c]Women, 16 years and older; men, 14 years and older. Source: Clarence Long, The Labor Force under Changing Income and Employment, National Bureau of Economic Research (Princeton: Princeton University Press, 1958), pp. 292 and 297.

women. Between 1940 and 1960, the labor force increased by 14.4 million. The category, "married female, husband present," accounted for slightly more than 56 percent (8.1 million) of this increase. Between 1950 and 1960 this category comprised nearly 60 per cent of the labor force growth.[1] The labor force behavior of married women over time presents a challenging problem for analysis.

There are insufficient observations from the time series, however, for statistical research, and the investigator is compelled to utilize the more plentiful cross-section data. But the economist who looks at cross-section and time series data on this problem soon recognizes a striking contradiction. First, over time the rise in income of families has been accompanied by a rise in work rates of married women, but the cross-section data show that increased income is associated with a decline in work rates. A second contrast concerns the influence of children. The most rapid increase in work rates of wives has come since 1940, during a period when birth rates have risen sharply,[2] but the cross-section relationship between the presence of children and work rates is consistently negative. . . .

THE MODEL AND A REVIEW OF THE LITERATURE

The Underlying Concepts

The study of labor force participation is a study of labor supply. The theory of labor supply is one of an individual making choices among alternative uses of his time. For present purposes it will suffice to consider two categories, work and leisure, as an exhaustive description of the choices. Work, however, may take place in the market for a money wage or in a non-market sector like the home or school. If we restrict the discussion to adults, then we might consider homework as the principal type of non-market work, and we can think of some non-money wage rate that applies to this work[3]

For a male, homework will be a negligible part of his activities over the span of his adult life for biological and cultural reasons. The opportunity cost of not working—the price of his leisure—will then be represented solely by his market wage rate. Wage rate changes will carry both income and substitution effects on labor supplied. An increase in wages will have an income effect that is negative, since leisure is a superior good and a higher income implies that more of it will be bought, or alternatively, less time will be spent at work. The substitution effect of a wage increase will be positive since leisure time becomes more expensive relative to the alternative of work, and less leisure would be purchased.

The secular decrease in time devoted to work by males, which has been substantial, implies that the income effects have outweighed the substitution effects, given small influences from changes in institutions (like legislation), tastes, and relative prices among goods complementary to and substitutable with leisure. Furthermore, since the rises in income over time have stemmed mainly from wage and salary gains, a reasonable generalization is that the (negative) income effects of the increases in wages have swamped their (positive) substitution effects. Thus, the time series suggests that the supply curve of labor is negatively sloped.[4] This hypothesis was tested and confirmed with cross-section data in several careful studies: first by Paul Douglas and his associates, later by Clarence Long and T. Aldrich Finegan, and most recently by Marvin Kosters.[5] The "back-

[1] U.S. Department of Labor, Bureau of Labor Statistics, "Special Labor Force Report, No. 13," Reprint No. 2364, p. 3.

[2] The number of children ever born per 1,000 women (aged 15 to 44) ever married rose from 1.9 in 1940 to 2.3 in 1959, and the rate rose for each age group of wives up to 40 years of age and older. *Statistical Abstract*, 1962, Table 61, p. 60.

[3] In this book homework is defined as cleaning house, raising children, and preparing meals. Child care, food preparation, and housekeeping, then, may be considered home goods.

[4] For a more complete theoretical statement of these matters see H. G. Lewis, "Hours of Work and Hours of Leisure," *Proceedings of the Industrial Relations Research Association*, 1957.

[5] The classic work is Erika H. Schoenberg and Paul H. Douglas, "Studies in the Supply Curve of Labor," *The Journal of Political Economy*, XLV (1937), 45-79, reprinted in *Landmarks in Political Economy*, eds. Earl H. Hamilton, Harry G. Johnson, and Albert Rees (Chicago: University of Chicago Press, 1962), Vol. I. A summary statement of Long's research is given in Clarence Long, *The Labor Force under Changing Income and Employment*, National Bureau of Eco-

ward bending" supply curve of labor has proved to be a rather remarkably consistent aspect of behavior. Its theoretical explanation, which entails impressive empirical support, has been a noteworthy achievement of economics.

When we turn to the analysis of the labor supply of married women, the assumption that market work is the main alternative to leisure becomes inappropriate. Cultural and biological factors in this case make homework the most important type of work for the wife over most of her married life. We need to view the wife within her family context where she specializes in the production of home goods. Within this context the market and home productivities and tastes of each family member, along with the family income status, will determine the allocation among market work, homework, and leisure among all members.[6] From this point of view, let us examine the implications of the conventional theory, which had been previously applied to the individual.

For the family a rise in income should reduce the work and increase the leisure of the family members. But while the husband reduces only his market work (on the simplifying assumption that he engages in no homework), the wife reduces her homework as well. Indeed, our knowledge of the respective income elasticities of market goods and home goods suggests that homework should have declined more than market work over the long run.

The effect of changes in market wage rates— the substitution effect—should also be different for wives. In general, the substitution effect will be small and the supply of labor inelastic if good substitutes for one's working time are lacking. But although the substitute of leisure is available to husbands (or single men and

women) and wives, the responsibilities of homework are a much more important substitute for the wife's time than for other adults. For married women, then, we should expect a relatively high elasticity for their supply curve of labor; in other words, the substitution effect should be relatively large.

The generalization that the substitution effect is large for wives and small for husbands is meant to apply to work choices in the context of a lifetime. At a particular moment in time the generalization may not hold. When young children are present, for example, the wife's time will not be easily substitutable for market work, given prevailing standards for the care of children. At other times the presence of older children or other adults besides the husband and wife, who may be productive as either home or market workers, will influence the work decisions of the wife. An even more temporary event is unemployment of the husband. This will tend to make homework a relevant alternative use for his time. But if we do summarize the lifetime experience of the family and suppress the life-cycle events or transitional situations, the generally greater area of choice between work alternatives (home and market) for wives than for husbands does imply a larger substitution effect for wives.

Herein lies the foundation of Mincer's reconciliation on theoretical grounds of the time-series differences in market labor supplied by wives and other adults. For the latter group the income effect exceeds the substitution effect, but for wives the reverse is eminently reasonable. In the face of rising incomes and rising wages market work declines for males and single women and their leisure increases, while homework declines for wives and their leisure and their market work both increase. . . .

nomic Research (Princeton: Princeton University Press, 1958), pp. 3-7. Also, T. Aldrich Finegan, "Hours of Work in the United States: A Cross-Sectional Analysis," *The Journal of Political Economy,* Vol. LXX (October, 1962). The work of Marvin Kosters is contained in an unpublished Ph.D. dissertation, "Income and Substitution Parameters in a Family Labor Supply Model" (University of Chicago, 1966).

[6]The following two paragraphs in the text draw freely on the analysis of Jacob Mincer, "Labor Force Participation of Married Women," in *Aspects of Labor Economics, A Conference of the Universities.* National Bureau of Economic Research (Princeton: Princeton University Press, 1962).

RESULTS

This study of the labor force participation of married women builds upon an impressive foundation of prior research. The works of Jacob Mincer and Marvin Kosters in particular provided models that, with slight modifications, I applied to a wider range of data than heretofore examined. The sources of data for statistical analyses were ample.

The over-all problem is one of explaining labor force participation of married women. At the center is the challenge of explaining the increase in participation over time. We began with two basic propositions from price theory on the effects of income and of wages on the supply of labor. An economic model was set up to deal with two types of available data. The first type consisted of aggregative data, and the model incorporated market variables—average labor force participation rates, average income, average wages, and so on. These market variables correspond to the observations we have in mind when discussing the time series increase. An advantage of the data in this form is that the wide variations in preferences or tastes for and against market work among women can be greatly reduced in the process of averaging. The principal disadvantage is the "identification problem"—the danger that responses in labor force participation rates to changes in wage rates engender feed-back effects that modify the wage and thereby cloud the interpretation of the statistical results.

The second application of the model was with disaggregated data. Here we are given almost no information on market variables but instead work with the personal characteristics of the subject. The troublesome problem lies in distinguishing between the effects of variables that impinge upon the wife's decisions from those that merely reflect her decisions—perhaps via some factor like tastes that is common to both the decision and to the variable in question. The low multiple correlations common to regressions with survey data may not be cause for alarm, but they do tell us that there are missing variables that could greatly add to the explanatory power of the relation. We hope, but we cannot feel sure, that these omitted variables are uncorrelated with the included variables.

The economic model was, thus, made to do double duty, handling market data in one case and individual or personal data in another. Although specific criteria for judgment are lacking, I believe the agreement of the results between the two applications was considerable. Indeed, there was about as much agreement between the results from the regression analysis with aggregated and disaggregated data as there was among different samples within each of the two types of data. Confining our attention to results with total or white wives, recall that the elasticities (or logarithmic coefficients) of variables representing the wife's wage with aggregated data varied from about 1.0 (with SMA's in 1950) to around .4 or .5 (with aggregated

data from the 1955 GAF sample, cities in 1940, and SMA's in 1960). From the disaggregated data the approximations of the wage elasticity varied from around .8 (the GAF sample) to .5 (the 1-in-1,000 sample).

Income elasticities based on the logarithmic coefficients of either the husband's earnings or family income (excluding the wife's earnings) were remarkably stable from sample to sample. The coefficients of husband's income were about −.4 to −.6 for each of the samples of aggregative data—1940 cities, 1950 and 1960 SMA's, and the "cluster points" with the 1955 GAF survey data. The elasticities computed with disaggregated data ranged between −.3 and −.7.

One of the principal issues in the explanation of the increase in work rates by wives over time involves the comparative sizes of the elasticities of wages and income. Since the earnings of females and males have been rising by about the same rate over time, an explanation for the secular increase in work rates is that the positive effect on the labor supply of the rise in wages outweighs the negative effects of the rise in incomes. The major finding made by Mincer was that, for wives, the positive wage effect exceeds the absolute value of the negative income effect. This finding was weakened by my research but not overturned. The result held for 1950 with the aggregative data that were essentially the same as Mincer used, but in 1940 and 1960 the income elasticity was sometimes larger than the wage elasticity. With disaggregated data the wage elasticity was larger than the income elasticity in each of the two samples used, but the estimation procedures for the wage effect were, by necessity, quite rough.

Lower wage elasticities relative to income elasticities indicate that less of the time series increase in work rates of married women can be explained by these two variables.[7] Nevertheless, the positive direction of change in the time series agrees with that generally predicted by the cross-section results for wage and income effects. The findings about female educational attainment add supporting evidence of two sorts. First, a positive effect of education on

[7]See Mincer's application of cross-section coefficients of income and wages to time series data from 1900-1950. Jacob Mincer, "Labor Force Participation of Married Women," in *Aspects of Labor Economics, A Conference of the Universities*, National Bureau of Economic Research (Princeton: Princeton University Press, 1962), p. 93.

the labor force participation of wives was established with cross-section data, and the increase of both education and participation over time is consistent with this finding. Second, the hypothesis of a large wage effect for wives is supported since education is a variable that partly captures the non-pecuniary returns to labor—fringe benefits, pleasant working conditions, and so forth. . . .

The time series increase in work by married women remains only partially explained. A more complete explanation requires more information about the interrelations of work, wage rates, and fertility, about changes in work in the home, about the non-pecuniary aspects of market work, and about changes in attitudes (or tastes). . . .

The analysis made of the labor force behavior of nonwhite wives showed similar patterns to those for white (or "total") wives, although there were differences between the two color groups that called for special attention. Over time, work rates of white wives have increased more rapidly than those of nonwhite wives. On this point I noted the large proportion of the nonwhite female labor force in domestic service, the declining trends of this occupation, and the impact this would have on the time series of participation rates of nonwhite wives. In addition we can point to the findings from regression analyses of larger income effects relative to wage effects for nonwhite wives in comparison with white wives. These were consistent with the slower rate of increase in work rates of nonwhite wives over time. The explanation for the differences in wage and income effects is not, however, evident.

At a moment-in-time we consistently observe two related differences in the labor force behavior of nonwhite and white wives: higher levels of labor force participation over-all among nonwhite wives, and higher work rates for nonwhite mothers of young children. Four explanations of these differences were suggested, each along with some supporting empirical evidence.

(1) The simplest point is that labor force participation *rates* overstate the amount of labor supplied by nonwhite wives compared with white wives, since the latter are more likely to be working more hours per week or weeks per year if working at all. Nonwhite females are disproportionately represented in service occupations, particularly domestic service, that involve part-time work. Their occupational characteristics in turn reflect relatively low educational attainments, lesser training, and market discrimination.

(2) Poorer housing conditions, smaller dwelling units, and more doubling up of families among nonwhites are all generally conducive to more market work and less homework by wives.

(3) Relative instability of nonwhite families leads the wife to maintain closer ties to the labor market. This tendency is reinforced by her typically low income status and limited chances of obtaining alimony or adequate financial support for her children.

(4) Finally, the nonwhite husband may face greater discrimination in the labor market than the wife, leading to some substitution in market work between them. It is unlikely that this disadvantage to the male would be entirely captured in the measures of his earnings and unemployment experience that were included in my analyses.

Two points are noteworthy about the foregoing list. One is that they are interrelated and reinforcing. The second is that all of them contribute to explaining both the higher levels of participation among nonwhite wives *and* the lesser importance of children as a deterrent to work. In fact, I should say that in explaining the second question you explain the first. . . .

Some Implications

I will conclude by pointing to a few implications of this study for some current theoretical and policy issues. Married women have become so important a segment of the labor force that attention to their work patterns is necessary for a full understanding of many important economic problems: economic growth and the cyclical behavior of national income, the personal distribution of income, the effects of income taxes on labor supply, and birth rates.

Consider first the effect of unemployment conditions on labor force participation. It was noted many times that the elasticity of the supply of labor will be relatively high for wives and, probably, for other secondary workers who similarly possess good alternatives to leisure and market work. Decreases in the wage rate are likely to result in relatively large decreases in the quantity of labor supplied. This prediction is consistent with the result in cross-sections of a reduction in labor supplied for areas of depressed business conditions or high unemployment. If these results apply to the time series, the rather high national rates of unemployment of recent years (1958-63) may, therefore, be an important cause of the decline in labor force participation of several groups of secondary workers.[8] This decline in participation, moreover, is surely part of the explanation of the slow-down in the rate of growth of the Gross National Product during these years. Now, a decline in GNP is not necessarily a decline of equal magnitude in the well-being of the population, particularly when unmeasured homework (or school work) may be increasing. Nevertheless, the withdrawal from the labor force of secondary workers in the face of high unemployment can be the source of economic hardship, particularly in depressed areas.[9]

Renewed interest in the question of the distribution of income in general and the problem of low incomes in particular calls for special attention to the role of secondary workers like wives. At the upper end of the income distribution, we see that 64 per cent of families in 1960 earning $10,000 or more had two or more earners.[10] At the other end of the income scale where unemployment is an important cause of low income, secondary workers often provide the means for economic solvency. Referring to a survey of families with the head of the household unemployed 5 weeks or more in 1961, Ewan Clague, former Commissioner of Labor Statistics, stated:

> Additional workers in the family constitute the greatest single bulwark against poverty through unemployment. . . . Most of these families had

some nonwage income, but the amounts were small in relation to the wage and salary incomes of family workers.[11]

Another important issue concerns the effect of the personal income tax on the household's work decisions. The economist's analysis of this problem calls for determining whether the substitution effect of the tax on work reduces the supply of labor more or less than the income effect of the tax increases the supply of labor. The impression obtained from prior research is that the income tax does not reduce the quantity of labor supplied, but the evidence pertains mainly to primary earners.[12] Wage or substitution effects are expected to be small among primary earners, but not for secondary workers, so the effects of taxation may be different for the latter. Indeed, on the basis of the evidence at hand, the substitution effect appears to outweigh the income effect of the tax, and a net deterrence to work is implied. One qualification, however, is that the suggested special importance of non-pecuniary aspects of employment for wives and, perhaps, other secondary workers provides a means of avoiding the incidence of the tax, since payment for work in this form is not taxed. These remarks are highly tentative, however. More information on the impact of various marginal rates of the progressive income tax is needed, and more

[8]See the discussion of this decline in the Report of the President's Committee to Appraise Employment and Unemployment Statistics, *Measuring Employment and Unemployment* (Washington, D.C.: Government Printing Office, 1963), pp. 69-72.

[9]See the findings of Martin Segal and Richard B. Freeman, *Population, Labor Force, and Unemployment in Chronically Depressed Areas* (U.S. Department of Commerce, Economic Analysis Division, Office of Planning and Research, Area Redevelopment Administration, 1964).

[10]U.S. Census of Population, 1960, Subject Reports, "Sources and Structure of Family Income," Table 1, p. 1.

[11]Ewan Clague, "Anatomy of Unemployment," speech before the Conference of Business Economists, New York, May 8, 1964, unpublished. The survey referred to by Clague is described in U.S. Department of Labor, Bureau of Labor Statistics, "Special Labor Force Report No. 37," Reprint No. 2430. Table B on page A-8 of this report showed that among the families surveyed, the median earnings of family members other than the head of the household contributed 26 per cent ($1,564) of total family income; that nonwage sources (like unemployment compensation) added 16 per cent; and the rest was the earnings of the head during the period when he was not unemployed. The wife was most likely to be the supplementary earner in these families.

[12]See Marvin Kosters, "Income and Substitution Parameters in a Family Labor Supply Model" (Ph.D. dissertation, University of Chicago, 1966) for a brief review of the literature and for his estimates of wage effects on the labor supply of males aged 50-64, which support the conclusion that the substitution effect for males is small.

precise estimates of income and substitution effects than those offered in this study are called for.

Finally, the relation between female wages, work rates, and birth rates needs to be explored much more fully to determine the partial effect of changes in wages on fertility. Advances in the means of birth control will permit greater personal choice in decisions about family size and, I would argue, more scope for the influence of economic variables. At the same time there is a growing concern over the size and density of the population. It is not necessary to dwell on the importance of these issues.

3. Population

Richard A. Easterlin

The subject of population is an increasing source of uneasiness to economists. In the half century or so before World War II, it was considered off limits, and happily left to demographers and sociologists.[1] But as so often happens, the pressure of events is forcing reconsideration of accepted views. At home, there has been the unexpected swing in fertility since World War II, with its manifest impact on the economy. In less developed countries the population explosion—population growth rates rapidly rising as mortality declines sharply and fertility remains relatively constant—has engendered concern about the possibility of economic growth in less developed areas—indeed, about the adequacy of the earth to support prospective levels of population.

The questions raised by these developments are challenging and disturbing. But the plain truth is that economists—indeed, social scientists generally—do not have reliable answers. Only in the past decade or so has the subject of population started to be considered seriously by economists, and even this is a peripheral development. Contrast this with the long record of scholarship underlying the policy prescrip-

tions on business cycles offered by economists today.

Nor is the situation better in sister disciplines. Demography, the scientific study of population, is a creature of the 20th century. The great bulk of work to date has aimed to establish the *facts* of population change—an essential first step in any field of science. But work on the causes and effects of population change is still in a very early stage. It is chastening to recognize, for example, that while the historical record of fertility has now been established for a number of countries for the last half century or more, there exists not a single widely accepted and empirically tested explanation of the experience of any one of these countries. . . .

RECENT AMERICAN EXPERIENCE

The Record

Figure 1 presents two measures of the course of American fertility since World War 1.[2] Two

[1] The works of Joseph S. Davis and Alvin Hansen were early and outstanding exceptions to this generalization.

[2] Definitions appear at the foot of the figure. The age-adjusted rate eliminates the effect on the fertility measure of changes over time in the proportion of

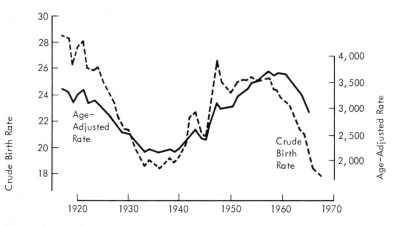

Figure 1

**United States Fertility Rates, Annually, 1917-1965
(rate per 1,000)**

Source [14]: The age-adjusted rate is the total fertility rate per 1,000 women, computed by summing age-specific rates for 5-year age groups of women from 15-19
through 40-44, and multiplying the result by 5. The crude birth rate is total births
divided by the total population.

aspects are of immediate interest. First, there is
the abrupt rise in fertility following World War
II. When it first occurred, this was interpreted
as the usual surge in births which follows a war,
but as the birth rate remained at high levels into
the 1950's, it became increasingly apparent that
a new and wholly unexpected phenomenon in
fertility behavior was taking place. Second,
beginning in the late fifties fertility starts to
drop off, at first slowly and then much more
precipitously. The abrupt decline was as unexpected as the postwar baby boom. The
steeper decline in the crude birth rate than in
the age-adjusted fertility curve reflects that a
decline was taking place in the proportion of
women of child-bearing age in the total population—a negative influence on the birth rate
which was foreseen. But an important part of
the decline is due to the age-adjusted rate—a
movement not anticipated. The upsurge in
fertility since the thirties and the subsequent
decline has generated a corresponding wave of
population growth, described in one comprehensive study of the postwar economy as

"perhaps the most unexpected and remarkable
social feature of the time" [11, pp. 161-62].

Causes of the Fertility Swing

Before suggesting a possible interpretation of
this experience, it is necessary first to develop
the relevant economic theory.[3] The standard
analysis of household consumption choices
takes as given three sets of data—preferences,
income, and product prices—and poses the
question: How will the household allocate its
expenditure among the variety of commodities
available to it? Household preferences are represented by an indifference map, which expresses
the degree of satisfaction the household attaches to every possible combination of commodities—the more there is of everything, the
greater the satisfaction. Since household
income is limited, and each commodity can be
obtained only through purchase at some given
price, there is one set of commodity combinations constituting the upper limit of those

women at various child-bearing ages in the population.
Thus, it relates births directly to those capable of bearing children.

[3]The presentation here is highly simplified. A fuller
exposition is given in [8]. Writings of special interest
on the economic theory of fertility are [1, 2, 3, 9, 10,
12, 15, 16, 17].

within financial reach of the household. The particular combinations contained in this set, represented by a budget line, depend on the size of the household's income and the structure of product prices with which it is confronted. The household is then seen as choosing from among this set of combinations just within financial reach that which will maximize its satisfaction, according to its subjectively determined preferences.

Thus, the decision-making process involves a balancing of subjectively determined preferences or tastes against externally determined constraints in the form of income and prices so as to maximize satisfaction. Changes in the basic data will alter the choice. An increase in income will normally lead to an increase in the amount of each good chosen, though not necessarily in the same proportion. If the relative prices of certain commodities decline, their proportion in the combination will rise. If consumer preferences change, the relative worth of certain goods rising in the household's subjective evaluation, the combination purchased will alter correspondingly. Typically, this last possibility receives little attention in economic analysis; attempts to explain changes in behavior focus on the possible influence of income and price changes.

At first thought, it may seem strange to view household decisions about having children in terms of this type of calculation. But further consideration suggests a certain plausibility to the approach. First, with regard to commodity purchases themselves, economic theory does not assert that households actually go through such precise calculations. Rather, the point is that purchase decisions do involve a rough weighing of preferences against constraints of the type spelled out rigorously in the formal theory, and if the constraints or preferences change, behavior will change. Thus confronted with higher prices for certain goods, a typical household will substitute other goods to some extent. Again, if the household's income rises, it will feel freer to expand its purchases generally. While typically there are no actual calculations—indeed, reactions may be in a sense automatic rather than the product of conscious deliberation—behavior does change in a way implying the type of subjective balancing of preferences against constraints envisaged by the theory.

To turn to the question of having children, they, like commodities, are a source of satisfaction. Indeed, just as one observes that one household differs from another with regard to the intensity of its desire for a given good, say, a vacation trip abroad, so, too, we detect differences in the strength of desires or tastes for children. Moreover, children, like commodities generally, are not costless. From prenatal medical expenses through college education, a child involves a long succession of outlays, of which the typical household is painfully aware. Finally just as different commodities compete with one another for the household's dollar, so, too, do children compete with goods. Having another child this year may mean sacrificing a new car or a long-awaited month at the shore. Perhaps, then, there is some plausibility to supposing that decisions about having children may involve a rough balancing of preferences and constraints, maybe largely subconscious, of the type described in the economic theory of household commodity purchases.

This is what was argued by Gary S. Becker, the Columbia University economist who pioneered in the extension of consumption theory to fertility behavior [2]. Suppose, he said, one thinks of children by analogy with economic goods. Then, we may envisage an indifference map, expressing the household's estimation of the degree of satisfaction attaching to alternative combinations of children and commodities. One can think, too, of a price tag attaching to children, the discounted cost of the various expense items required to have and raise them. Together with product prices and household income, this establishes a budget line constraint. The interaction of this externally determined constraint with the subjectively determined indifference map determines the combination of goods and children chosen. If the relative price of children increases, because the prices of the relevant expense items rise more than the average of goods generally, the combination chosen would shift toward more goods and fewer children. If, subjectively, the attractiveness of commodities rises relative to that of children, a similar shift would occur. Finally—and this is the analytical point Becker himself especially emphasized—if the level of household income were higher, both more children and more goods would be chosen (though the increase would not necessarily be proportionate). Thus, the number of children people have would be expected to vary direc' with household income and with the pric goods relative to children, and inversel the strength of desires for goods relative to children.

Before exploring the relevance of this theory to the interpretation of the observed fertility movement, it is necessary first to consider another frequently mentioned possibility— namely, the recent fertility decline is attributable to the growing use of the contraceptive pill. While the economic analysis of fertility control methods needs fuller development [8], it does not seem that an explanation in these terms will suffice. The decline in fertility started in 1957, while the earliest date at which the pill could have a detectable influence was 1962. An assessment in [14, p. 12] concludes that as of 1965 "even if a generous allowance were made for the amount of the overall decline that might be attributed solely to the use of the pill, it would probably not exceed half of the decline that has taken place." It should be noted, too, that a major advance in contraceptive knowledge took place during World War II when indoctrination in birth control methods was widely provided for those in the armed forces. Following the war, however, fertility rose to high levels rather than declining as one might have expected on the basis of the change in contraceptive knowledge.

But can the economic framework above explain, at least in part, the fertility swing in Figure 1? The answer is no, if, as is usually the case in economics, the explanation is sought entirely in price and income movements, with tastes being assumed to remain constant. While no thorough study has been made of the trend in the price of goods relative to children in the last three decades, it is implausible to suppose that it has undergone the kind of gyrations necessary to produce the striking shifts in fertility displayed in Figure 1. As for income, it is true that in the 1940's and most of the 1950's the labor market for young adults and, consequently, their income experience was especially favorable. The marked rise in fertility observed at this time is consistent with an explanation emphasizing income experience. But the recent fertility decline cannot be explained on these grounds. While the labor market for young adults has slackened in the last decade, nevertheless, the average income of young adults in the late 1960's is above that of their counterparts in the late fifties. The number of children they are having is, however, substantially lower.

Those who have been critical of economic interpretations of the postwar baby boom have been quick to note this last point [4]. But an economic interpretation need not place exclusive reliance on income—though the attention Becker himself devoted to this in his pioneering article may have misguided some on this score. In particular, if the possibility of taste changes is admitted, with fertility behavior reflecting the shifting balance between income and taste movements, an interpretation in keeping with the preceding framework may be developed.

Figure 2 presents an idealized sketch of one possibility—idealized because only fragmentary data are actually available (cf. [7, Part II]), and the primary purpose here is to illustrate an analytical model based on the foregoing economic theory, not to offer a definitive explanation (which no one has). In keeping with this purpose, highly simplified assumptions have been made.

The upper and lower *solid* lines in Figure 2 represent the presumptive path of the average income of household heads aged, respectively, 35-44 and 20-24. The movement of the curves through time conforms in general to the actual state of the economy. The curve for the older household heads lies above that for the younger in keeping with reality. The differential between the curves is assumed constant; this assumption is contrary to experience but is made for simplicity. With regard to fertility behavior, it is the heavier curve, portraying the income experience of younger households, that is of central importance, since the decisions of young adults dominate observed fertility experience.

To interpret fertility decisions, however, account must be taken not only of actual income but of subjective preferences, and it is in this respect that the curve for older adults is of interest. As has been noted, economists characteristically take tastes as given and are reluctant to explain changes in behavior in terms of changes in tastes. There is, however, one widely accepted propostion relating to the determinants of preferences: of two families with equal current income, if one income was previously higher than at present that family would be expected to spend proportionately more on consumption in order to maintain a standard of living to which it had become adjusted. In other words, *experience* with previous higher income levels alters tastes and thereby consumption behavior [5, 6, 13].

This line of reasoning may be transferred with some modification to the present problem. Young adults today were, a few years back,

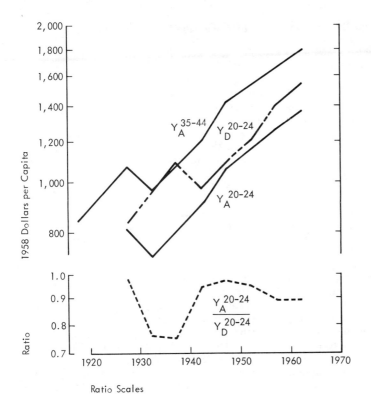

Figure 2

**Illustrative Model of Shifting Balance between Actual
and Desired Income of Young Adults, Aged 20-24,
United States, 1925-1965**

Legend:

$Y_A 25\text{-}44$ =   actual income of households with head aged 35-44.

$Y_A 20\text{-}24$ =   actual income of households with head aged 20-24.

$Y_D 20\text{-}24$ =   desired income of households with head aged 20-24.

     (= $Y_A 35\text{-}44$ 10 years earlier).

dependent members in their parents' households. It seems plausible to argue that the
consumption levels experienced in the parents'
households served, among other things, to
shape their current preferences for material
goods. Specifically, let us make the highly
simplified assumption that the consumption
level to which they aspire today corresponds to
the actual income level of their parents 10 years
ago when the parents were, say, in the 35-44
age bracket. On this assumption, the *desired*
income level of households aged 20-24 in 1930
would equal the *actual* income level of households 35-44 in 1920, and so on year by year
down to the present, with desired income of
young adults today equaling that actually received a decade ago by those aged 35-44.
Graphically, this amounts to saying that by
shifting forward one decade in time the curve
representing the actual income of households
35-44, one can obtain a new curve portraying
the desired consumption level of young adults
at each date, the curve represented by the
dashed line in Figure 2.

We now have two curves for young adults—
one showing the course of their subjective

preferences for consumption goods and one that of their actual income. The second, of course, governs the degree to which preferences can be realized. If for each date the ratio of the two curves is computed and the results plotted, one obtains the dotted curve at the bottom of Figure 2, showing how the ability of young adults to realize their consumption aspirations varied during this period. It is the *pattern of change* depicted by this curve that is central to the present model; the *level* of the curve, and correspondingly of those from which it is derived, is not essential.

What does this curve show? That young adults in the postwar period were in a much better position to fulfill their goods aspirations than were their predecessors in the thirties. This is not only because their income situation improved drastically over that of their predecessors but also because their desired consumption levels, shaped so largely during the economic stagnation of the thirties, advanced relatively little over their predecessors. Comparing young adults in the 1960's with their predecessors in the post-World War II period, the reverse is found to be so. Actual income of the first grew at a slower rate, while desired consumption levels advanced more rapidly, reflecting the

Effects of the Fertility Swing

Age structure. A great swing in fertility of the type experienced in the United States results in striking differences in the rate at which various age groups of the population grow at any given time. The following are the prospective percent changes of young age groups according to the current series D projections of the Bureau of the Census [18, p. 7]. Short of a major catastrophe, the projections in the first two columns can be accepted with substantial confidence; those in the second two columns rest on less certain assumptions.

Compare the prospective growth rates between 1965 and 1975 of 18-24-year-olds with those aged 5-13. Whereas young adults increase during the decade by over a third, the younger group actually declines in absolute size. That this difference stems directly from the swing in fertility can be quickly seen by comparing the birth years of the two age groups at successive dates. The 5- to 13-year-olds of 1965 were born in 1952-60; those of 1970, in 1957-65; and of 1975, in 1962-70. Thus, this age group at quinquennial dates from 1965 through 1975

Age Group	1965 to 1970	1970 to 1975	1975 to 1980	1980 to 1985
5 to 13 years	+ 3.7	− 8.1	−4.4	+ 9.9
14 to 17 years	+12.0	+ 6.9	−5.3	−10.4
18 to 24 years	+21.8	+12.0	+7.5	− 4.0

effect on their tastes of the material affluence resulting from the long postwar economic boom during which they were brought up.

The foregoing, while highly simplified, may indicate the general manner in which factors important to young adults' fertility decisions have been shifting over the past four decades. The relative ease with which postwar adults could fulfill their consumption desires left them in a much better position to enjoy larger families than could their predecessors in the thirties. Correspondingly, the severer financial constraint felt by young adults today compared with the postwar generation may account for the reversal in fertility behavior.

hails from periods in which the birth rate was successively lower. The impact of this on the size of this group over time is correspondingly reflected in the net decline projected for it. The opposite is true for the 18-24-year-olds. Those who will be in this age group during the decade 1965-1975 come from the period of rising and high fertility of the 1940's and 1950's, and this

Age Group	1965	1970	1975
5 to 13 years	1952-60	1957-65	1962-70
18 to 24 years	1941-47	1946-52	1951-57

group's size is accordingly growing markedly in the current decade. Thus, the historical turn-around in fertility in the late 1950's leaves its imprint currently on the population in the form of differing magnitudes and even directions of growth for virtually adjacent age groups.

The age structure effects of the fertility swing, in turn, have further consequences on the economy. Consider, for example, the area of education. The age groups selected above correspond roughly to those at three different levels of schooling—elementary, secondary, and higher education. Through 1975, there will be little need for additional facilities or teachers at the elementary level, aside from needs associated with changes in population distribution. In secondary and higher education, however, requirements will be rising noticeably. But, if the projection above proves correct, by 1980-85 this situation will have been reversed; at that time, pressures on elementary school will be rising, while at the other two levels they will be declining. Clearly, the adjustments necessitated by fertility swings call for a flexible and adaptable economic system.

REFERENCES AND SUGGESTIONS FOR FURTHER READING

1. Adelman, Irma. "An Econometric Analysis of Population Growth," *American Economic Review,* LIII, 31 (June, 1963), pp. 314-39.

2. Becker, Gary S. "An Economic Analysis of Fertility," in Universities—National Bureau Committee for Economic Research, *Demographic and Economic Change in Developed Countries* (Princeton: Princeton University Press, 1960).

3. ———. "A Theory of the Allocation of Time," *Economic Journal,* LXXV, 299 (September, 1965), pp. 493-517.

4. Blake, Judith. "Income and Reproductive Motivation," *Population Studies,* XXI, 3 (November, 1967), pp. 185-206.

5. Brady, Dorothy S., and Rose D. Friedman. "Savings and the Income Distribution," in Conference on Research in Income and Wealth, *Studies in Income and Wealth,* X (New York: National Bureau of Economic Research, 1947), pp. 247-65.

6. Duesenberry, James E. *Income, Saving, and the Theory of Consumer Behavior* (Cambridge, Mass.: Harvard University Press, 1952).

7. Easterlin, Richard A. *Population, Labor Force, and Long Swings in Economic Growth: The American Experience* (New York: Columbia University Press, 1968).

8. ———. "Towards a Socio-Economic Theory of Fertility: A Survey of Recent Research on Economic Factors in American Fertility," in *Fertility and Family Planning: A World View* (Ann Arbor: University of Michigan Press, 1969), pp. 127-56.

9. Freedman, Deborah. "The Relation of Economic Status to Fertility," *American Economic Review,* LIII, 3 (June, 1963), pp. 414-26.

10. Freedman, Ronald, and Lolagene Coombs. "Economic Considerations in Family Growth Decisions," *Population Studies,* XX, 2 (November, 1966), pp. 197-222.

11. Hickman, Bert G. *Growth and Stability in the Postwar Economy* (Washington: Brookings Institution, 1960).

12. Mincer, Jacob. "Market Prices, Opportunity Costs, and Income Effects," in *Measurement in Economics: Studies in Mathematical Economics and Econometrics in Memory of Yehuda Grunfeld* (Stanford: Stanford University Press, 1963).

13. Modigliani, Franco. "Fluctuations in the Savings-Income Ratio: A Problem in Economic Forecasting." *Conference on Research in Income and Wealth,* Studies in Income and Wealth, XI (New York: National Bureau of Economic Research, 1949), pp. 371-443.

14. National Center for Health Statistics. *Natality Statistics Analysis: United States—1963 and 1964* (Washington: U.S. Government Printing Office, 1966).

15. Okun, Bernard. *Trends in Birth Rates in the United States Since 1870* (Baltimore: Johns Hopkins Press, 1958).

16. Silver, Morris. "Births, Marriages, and Business Cycles in the United States," *Journal of Political Economy,* LXXIII, 3 (June, 1965), pp. 237-55.

17. Spengler, Joseph J., "Values and Fertility Analysis," *Demography,* 3, 1 (1966), pp. 109-30.

18. U. S. Bureau of the Census, *Current Population Reports. Population Estimates,* "Summary of Demographic Projections," Series P-25,388 (March 14, 1968).

4. Human Capital—A Theoretical and Empirical Analysis

Gary S. Becker

INTRODUCTION

Some activities primarily affect future well-being; the main impact of others is in the present. Some affect money income and others psychic income, that is, consumption. Sailing primarily affects consumption, on-the-job training primarily affects money income, and a college education could affect both. These affects may operate either through physical resources or through human resources. This study is concerned with activities that influence future monetary and psychic income by increasing the resources in people. These activities are called investments in human capital.

The many forms of such investments include schooling, on-the-job training, medical care, migration, and searching for information about prices and incomes. They differ in their effects on earnings and consumption, in the amounts typically invested, in the size of returns, and in the extent to which the connection between investment and return is perceived. But all these investments improve skills, knowledge, or health, and thereby raise money or psychic incomes.

Recent years have witnessed intensive concern with and research on investment in human capital, much of it contributed or stimulated by T. W. Schultz. The main motivating factor has probably been a realization that the growth of physical capital, at least as conventionally measured, explains a relatively small part of the growth of income in most countries. The search for better explanations has led to improved measures of physical capital and to an interest in less tangible entities, such as technological change and human capital. Also behind this concern is the strong dependence of modern military technology on education and skills, the rapid growth in expenditures on education and health, the age-old quest for an understanding of the personal distribution of income, the recent growth in unemployment in the United States, the Leontief scarce-factor paradox, and several other important economic problems.

The result has been the accumulation of a tremendous amount of circumstantial evidence testifying to the economic importance of human capital, especially of education. Probably the most impressive piece of evidence is that more highly educated and skilled persons almost always tend to earn more than others. This is true of developed countries as different as the United States and the Soviet Union, of underdeveloped countries as different as India and Cuba, and of the United States one hundred years ago as well as today. Moreover, few, if

24

any, countries have achieved a sustained period of economic development without having invested substantial amounts in their labor force, and most studies that have attempted quantitative assessments of contributions to growth have assigned an important role to investment in human capital. Again, inequality in the distribution of earnings and income is generally positively related to inequality in education and other training. To take a final example, unemployment tends to be strongly related, usually inversely, to education.

Passions are easily aroused on this subject and even people who are generally in favor of education, medical care, and the like often dislike the phrase "human capital" and still more any emphasis on its economic effects. They are often the people who launch the most bitter attacks on research on human capital, partly because they fear that emphasis on the "material" effects of human capital detracts from its "cultural" effects, which to them are more important. Those denying the economic importance of education and other investments in human capital have attacked the circumstantial evidence in its favor. They argue that the correlation between earnings and investment in human capital is due to a correlation between ability and investment in human capital, or to the singling out of the most favorable groups, such as white male college graduates, and to the consequent neglect of women, drop-outs, non-whites, or high-school graduates. They consider the true correlation to be very weak, and, therefore, a poor guide and of little help to people investing in human capital. The association between education and economic development or between inequality in education and income is attributed to the effect of income on education, considering education as a consumption good, and hence of no greater causal significance than the association between automobile ownership and economic development or between the inequality in ownership and incomes.

This study hopes to contribute to knowledge in this area by going far beyond circumstantial evidence and analysis. . . .

. . . [T] he attention paid to the economic effects of education and other human capital in this study is not in any way meant to imply that other effects are unimportant, or less important than the economic ones. . . .I would like to urge simply that the economic effects are important

and they have been relatively neglected, at least until recently. . . .

EFFECTS ON EARNINGS

1. On-the-Job Training

Theories of firm behavior, no matter how they differ in other respects, almost invariably ignore the effect of the productive process itself on worker productivity. This is not to say that no one recognizes that productivity is affected by the job itself; but the recognition has not been formalized, incorporated into economic analysis, and its implications worked out. I now intend to do just that, placing special emphasis on the broader economic implications.

Many workers increase their productivity by learning new skills and perfecting old ones while on the job. Presumably, future productivity can be improved only at a cost, for otherwise there would be an unlimited demand for training. Included in cost are the value placed on the time and effort of trainees, the "teaching" provided by others, and the equipment and materials used. These are costs in the sense that they could have been used in producing current output if they had not been used in raising future output. The amount spent and the duration of the training period depend partly on the type of training since more is spent for a longer time on, say, an intern than a machine operator. . . .

. . . In the following sections two types of on-the-job training are discussed in turn: general and specific.

General training. General training is useful in many firms besides those providing it; for example, a machinist trained in the army finds his skills of value in steel and aircraft firms, and a doctor trained (interned) at one hospital finds his skills useful at other hospitals. Most on-the-job training presumably increases the future marginal productivity of workers in the firms providing it; general training, however, also increases their marginal product in many other firms as well. Since in a competitive labor market the wage rates paid by any firm are determined by marginal productivities in other firms, future wage rates as well as marginal products would increase in firms providing general training. These firms could capture some of the return from training only if their marginal product rose by more than their wages. "Perfectly general" training would be equally useful in many firms and marginal products would rise by the same extent in all of them. Consequently, wage rates would rise by exactly the same amount as the marginal product and the firms providing such training could not capture any of the return.

Why, then, would rational firms in competitive labor markets provide general training if it did not bring any return? The answer is that firms would provide general training only if they did not have to pay any of the costs. Persons receiving general training would be willing to pay these costs since training raises their future wages. Hence it is the trainees, not the firms, who would bear the cost of general training and profit from the return.[1] . . .

Income-maximizing firms in competitive labor markets would not pay the cost of general training and would pay trained persons the market wage. If, however, training costs were paid, many persons would seek training, few would quit during the training period, and labor costs would be relatively high. Firms that did not pay trained persons the market wage would have difficulty satisfying their skill requirements and would also tend to be less profitable than other firms. Firms that paid both for training and less than the market wage for trained persons would have the worst of both worlds, for they would attract too many trainees and too few trained persons.

These principles have been clearly demonstrated during the last few years in discussions of problems in recruiting military personnel. The military offers training in a wide variety of skills and many are very useful in the civilian sector. Training is provided during part or all of the first enlistment period and used during the remainder of the first period and hopefully during subsequent periods. This hope, however,

is thwarted by the fact that re-enlistment rates tend to be inversely related to the amount of civilian-type skills provided by the military.[2] Persons with these skills leave the military more readily because they can receive much higher wages in the civilian sector. Net military wages for those receiving training are higher relative to civilian wages during the first than during subsequent enlistment periods because training costs are largely paid by the military. Not surprisingly, therefore, first-term enlistments for skilled jobs are obtained much more easily than are re-enlistments.

The military is a conspicuous example of an organization that both pays at least part of training costs and does not pay market wages to skilled personnel. It has had, in consequence, relatively easy access to "students" and heavy losses of "graduates." Indeed, its graduates make up the predominant part of the supply in several civilian occupations. For example, well over 90 per cent of United States commercial airline pilots received much of their training in the armed forces. The military, of course, is not a commercial organization judged by profits and losses and has had no difficulty surviving and even thriving.

What about the old argument that firms in competitive labor markets have no incentive to provide on-the-job training because trained workers would be bid away by other firms? Firms that train workers are supposed to impart external economies to other firms because the latter can use these workers free of any training charge. An analogy with research and development is often drawn since a firm developing a process that cannot be patented or kept secret would impart external economies to competitors. This argument and analogy would apply if firms were to pay training costs, for they would suffer a "capital loss" whenever trained workers were bid away by other firms. Firms can, however, shift training costs to train-

---

[1] Some persons have asked why any general training is provided if firms do not collect any of the returns. The answer is simply that they have an incentive to do so wherever the demand price for training is at least as great as the supply price or cost of providing the training. Workers in turn would prefer to be trained on the job rather than in specialized firms (schools) if the training and work complemented each other (see the discussion in section 2 on p. 31).

[2] See *Manpower Management and Compensation*, report of the Cordiner Committee, Washington, 1957, Vol. I, Chart 3, and the accompanying discussion. The military not only wants to eliminate the inversion relation but apparently would like to create a positive relation because they have such a large investment in heavily trained personnel. For a recent and excellent study, see Gorman C. Smith, "Differential Pay of Military Technicians," unpublished Ph.D. dissertation, Columbia University, 1964.

ees and have an incentive to do so when faced with competition for their services.[3]

The difference between investment in training and in research and development can be put very simply. Without patents or secrecy, firms in competitive industries cannot establish property rights in innovations, and these innovations become fair game for all comers. Patent systems try to establish these rights so that incentives can be provided to invest in research. Property rights in skills, on the other hand, are automatically vested, for a skill cannot be used without permission of the person possessing it. The property right of the worker in his skills is the source of his incentive to invest in training by accepting a reduced wage during the training period and explains why an analogy with unowned innovations is misleading.

Specific training. Completely general training increases the marginal productivity of trainees by exactly the same amount in the firms providing the training as in other firms. Clearly some kinds of training increase productivity by different amounts in the firms providing the training and in other firms. Training that increases productivity more in firms providing it will be called specific training. Completely specific training can be defined as training that has no effect on the productivity of trainees that would be useful in other firms. Much on-the-job training is neither completely specific nor completely general but increases productivity more in the firms providing it and falls within the definition of specific training. The rest increases productivity by at least as

much in other firms and falls within a definition of general training. A few illustrations of the scope of specific training are presented before a formal analysis is developed.

The military offers some forms of training that are extremely useful in the civilian sector, as already noted, and others that are only of minor use to civilians, i.e., astronauts, fighter pilots, and missile men. Such training falls within the scope of specific training because productivity is raised in the military but not (much) elsewhere.

Resources are usually spent by firms in familiarizing new employees with their organization,[4] and the knowledge thus acquired is a form of specific training because productivity is raised more in the firms acquiring the knowledge than in other firms. Other kinds of hiring costs, such as employment agency fees, the expenses incurred by new employees in finding jobs, or the time employed in interviewing, testing, checking references, and in bookkeeping do not so obviously increase the knowledge of new employees, but they too are a form of specific investment in human capital, although not training. They are an investment because outlays over a short period create distributed effects on productivity; they are specific because productivity is raised primarily in the firms making the outlays; they are in human capital because they lose their value whenever employees leave. In the rest of this section reference is mostly to on-the-job specific training even though the analysis applies to all on-the-job specific investment.

Even after hiring costs are incurred, firms usually know only a limited amount about the ability and potential of new employees. They try to increase their knowledge in various ways—testing, rotation among departments, trial and error, etc.—for greater knowledge permits a more efficient utilization of manpower. Expenditures on acquiring knowledge of employee talents would be a specific investment if the knowledge could be kept from other firms, for then productivity would be raised more in the firms making the expenditures than elsewhere.

The effect of investment in employees on

---

[3]Sometimes the alleged external economies from on-the-job training have been considered part of the "infant industry" argument for protection (see J. Black "Arguments for Tariffs," *Oxford Economic Papers,* June 1959, pp. 205-206). Our analysis suggests, however, that the trouble tariffs are supposed to overcome must be traced back to difficulties that workers have in financing investment in themselves—in other words, to ignorance or capital market limitations that apply to expenditures on education, health, as well as on-the-job training. Protection would serve the same purpose as the creation of monopsonies domestically, namely, to convert general into specific capital so that firms can be given an incentive to pay for training (see the remarks on specific training below). Presumably a much more efficient solution would be to improve the capital market directly through insurance of loans, subsidies, information, etc.

[4]To judge from a sample of firms recently analyzed, formal orientation courses are quite common, at least in large firms (see H. F. Clark and H. S. Sloan, *Classrooms in the Factories,* New York, 1958, Chap. IV).

their productivity elsewhere depends on market conditions as well as on the nature of the investment. Very strong monopsonists might be completely insulated from competition by other firms, and practically all investments in their labor force would be specific. On the other hand, firms in extremely competitive labor markets would face a constant threat of raiding and would have fewer specific investments available.

These examples convey some of the surprisingly large variety of situations that come under the rubric of specific investment. This set is now treated abstractly in order to develop a general formal analysis. Empirical situations are brought in again after several major implications of the formal analysis have been developed.

If all training were completely specific, the wage that an employee could get elsewhere would be independent of the amount of training he had received. One might plausibly argue, then, that the wage paid by firms would also be independent of training. If so, firms would have to pay training costs, for no rational employee would pay for training that did not benefit him. Firms would collect the return from such training in the form of larger profits resulting from higher productivity, and training would be provided whenever the return—discounted at an appropriate rate—was at least as large as the cost. Long-run competitive equilibrium requires that the present value of the return exactly equals costs. . . .

. . . But could not one equally well argue that workers pay all specific training costs by receiving appropriately lower wages initially and collect all returns by receiving wages equal to marginal product later? . . . Is it more plausible that firms rather than workers pay for and collect the return from training?

An answer can be found by reasoning along the following lines. If a firm had paid for the specific training of a worker who quit to take another job, its capital expenditure would be partly wasted, for no further return could be collected. Likewise, a worker fired after he had paid for specific training would be unable to collect any further return and would also suffer a capital loss. The willingness of workers or firms to pay for specific training should, therefore, closely depend on the likelihood of labor turnover.

To bring in turnover at this point may seem like a *deus ex machina* since it is almost always

ignored in traditional theory. In the usual analysis of competitive firms, wages equal marginal product, and since wages and marginal product are assumed to be the same in many firms, no one suffers from turnover. It would not matter whether a firm's labor force always contained the same persons or a rapidly changing group. Any person leaving one firm could do equally well in other firms, and his employer could replace him without any change in profits. In other words, turnover is ignored in traditional theory because it plays no important role within the framework of the theory.

Turnover becomes important when costs are imposed on workers or firms, which are precisely the effects of specific training. Suppose a firm paid all the specific training costs of a worker who quit after completing it. According to our earlier analysis, he would have been receiving the market wage and a new employee could be hired at the same wage. If the new employee were not given training, his marginal product would be less than that of the one who quit since presumably training raised the latter's productivity. Training could raise the new employee's productivity but would require additional expenditures by the firm. In other words, a firm is hurt by the departure of a trained employee because an equally profitable new employee could not be obtained. In the same way an employee who pays for specific training would suffer a loss from being laid off because he could not find an equally good job elsewhere. To bring turnover into the analysis of specific training is not, therefore, a *deus ex machina* but is made necessary by the important link between them.

Firms paying for specific training might take account of turnover merely by obtaining a sufficiently large return from those remaining to counterbalance the loss from those leaving. (The return on "successes"—those remaining— would, of course, overestimate the average return on all training expenditures.) Firms could do even better, however, by recognizing that the likelihood of a quit is not fixed but depends on wages. Instead of merely recouping on successes what is lost on failures, they might reduce the likelihood of failure itself by offering higher wages after training than could be received elsewhere. In effect, they would offer employees some of the return from training. Matters would be improved in some respects but worsened in others, for the higher wage would make the supply of trainees greater than the demand, and rationing would be required. The final step would be to shift some training costs as well as returns to employees, thereby bringing supply more in line with demand. When the final step is completed, firms no longer pay all training costs nor do they collect all the return but they share both with employees.[5] The shares of each depend on the relations between quit rates and wages, layoff rates and profits, and on other factors not discussed here, such as the cost of funds, attitudes toward risk, and desires for liquidity.[6]

If training were not completely specific, productivity would increase in other firms as well, and the wage that could be received elsewhere would also increase. Such training can be looked upon as the sum of two components, one completely general, the other completely specific; the former would be relatively larger, the greater the effect on wages in other firms relative to the firms providing the training. Since firms do not pay any of the completely general costs and only part of the completely specific costs, the fraction of costs paid by firms would be inversely related to the importance of the general component, or positively related to the specificity of the training. . . .

Employees with specific training have less incentive to quit, and firms have less incentive to fire them, than employees with no training or general training, which implies that quit and layoff rates are inversely related to the amount of specific training. Turnover should be least

for employees with extremely specific training and most for those receiving such general training that productivity is raised less in the firms providing the training than elsewhere (as, say, in schools). These propositions are as applicable to the large number of irregular quits and layoffs that continually occur as to the more regular cyclical and secular movements in turnover; in this section, however, only the more regular movements are discussed.

Consider a firm that experiences an unexpected decline in demand for its output, the rest of the economy being unaffected. The marginal product of employees without specific training—such as untrained or generally trained employees—presumably equaled wages initially, and their employment would now be reduced to prevent their marginal productivity from falling below wages. The marginal product of specifically trained employees initially would have been greater than wages. A decline in demand would reduce these marginal products too, but as long as they were reduced by less than the initial difference with wages, firms would have no incentive to lay off such employees. For sunk costs are sunk, and there is no incentive to lay off employees whose marginal product is greater than wages, no matter how unwise it was, in retrospect, to invest in their training. Thus workers with specific training seem less likely to be laid off as a consequence of a decline in demand than untrained or even generally trained workers.[7]

If the decline in demand were sufficiently great so that even the marginal product of specifically trained workers was pushed below wages, would the firm just proceed to lay them off until the marginal product was brought into equality with wages? To show the danger here, assume that all the cost of and return from specific training was paid and collected by the firm. Any worker laid off would try to find a new job, since nothing would bind him to the old one.[8] The firm might be hurt if he did find

---

[5]A. Marshall (*Principles of Economics*, 8th ed., New York, 1949, p. 626) was clearly aware of specific talents and their effect on wages and productivity: "Thus the head clerk in a business has an acquaintance with men and things, the use of which he could in some cases sell at a high price to rival firms. But in other cases it is of a kind to be of no value save to the business in which he already is; and *then his departure would perhaps injure it by several times the value of his salary,* while probably he could not get half that *salary elsewhere.*" (My italics) However, he overstressed the element of indeterminacy in these wages ("their earnings are determined . . . by a bargain between them and their employers, the terms of which are theoretically arbitrary") because he ignored the effect of wages on turnover.

[6]The rate used to discount costs and returns is the sum of a (positive) rate measuring the cost of funds, a (positive or negative) risk premium, and a liquidity premium that is presumably positive since capital invested in specific training is very illiquid.

[7]A very similar argument is developed by Walter Oi in "Labor as a Quasi-fixed Factor of Production," unpublished Ph.D. dissertation, University of Chicago, 1961. Also, see his article with almost the same title in *Journal of Political Economy,* December 1962.

[8]Actually one need only assume that the quit rate of laid-off workers tends to be significantly greater than that of employed workers, if only because the opportunity searching for another job is less for laid-off workers.

a new job, for the firm's investment in his training might be lost forever. If specifically trained workers were not laid off, the firm would lose now because marginal product would be less than wages but would gain in the future if the decline in demand proved temporary. There is an incentive, therefore, not to lay off workers with specific training when their marginal product is only temporarily below wages, and the larger a firm's investment the greater the incentive not to lay them off.

A worker collecting some of the return from specific training would have less incentive to find a new job when temporarily laid off than others would: he does not want to lose his investment. His behavior while laid off in turn affects his future chances of being laid off, for if it were known that he would not readily take another job, the firm could lay him off without much fear of losing its investment. . . .

The analysis can easily be extended to cover general declines in demand; suppose, for example, a general cyclical decline occurred. Assume that wages were sticky and remained at the initial level. If the decline in business activity were not sufficient to reduce the marginal product below the wage, workers with specific training would not be laid off even though others would be, just as before. If the decline reduced marginal product below wages, only one modification in the previous analysis is required. A firm would have a greater incentive to lay off specifically trained workers than when it alone experienced a decline because laid-off workers would be less likely to find other jobs when unemployment was widespread. In other respects, the implications of a general decline with wage rigidity are the same as those of a decline in one firm alone.

The discussion has concentrated on layoff rates, but the same kind of reasoning shows that a rise in wages elsewhere would cause fewer quits among specifically trained workers than among others. For specificially trained workers initially receive higher wages than are available elsewhere and the wage rise elsewhere would have to be greater than the initial difference before they would consider quitting. Thus both the quit and layoff rate of specifically trained workers would be relatively low and fluctuate relatively less during business cycles. These are important implications that can be tested with the data available.

Although quits and layoffs are influenced by considerations other than investment costs, some of these, such as pension plans, are more strongly related to investments than may appear at first blush. A pension plan with incomplete vesting privileges[9] penalizes employees who quit before retirement and thus provides an incentive—often an extremely powerful one—not to quit. At the same time pension plans "insure" firms against quits for they are given a lump sum—the nonvested portion of payments—whenever a worker quits. Insurance is needed for specifically trained employees because their turnover would impose capital losses on firms. Firms can discourage such quits by sharing training costs and the return with employees, but they would have less need to discourage them and would be more willing to pay for training costs if insurance were provided. The effects on the incentive to invest in one's employees may have been a major stimulus to the development of pension plans with incomplete vesting.[10]

An effective long-term contract would insure firms against quits, just as pensions do and also insure employees against layoffs. Firms would be more willing to pay for all kinds of training—assuming future wages were set at an appropriate level—since a contract, in effect, converts all training into completely specific training. A casual reading of history suggests that long-term contracts have, indeed, been primarily a means of inducing firms to undertake large investments in employees. These contracts are seldom used today in the United States,[11] and while they have declined in importance over time, they were probably always the exception here largely because courts have considered them a form of involuntary servitude. Moreover, any enforcible contract could at best specify the hours required on a job, not the quality of performance. Since performance can vary widely, unhappy workers could usually "sabotage" operations to induce employers to release them from contracts.

[9]According to the National Bureau study of pensions, most plans have incomplete vesting.

[10]This economic function of incomplete vesting should caution one against conceding to the agitation for more liberal vesting privileges. Of course, in recent years pensions have also been an important tax-saving device, which certainly has been a crucial factor in their mushrooming growth.

[11]The military and the entertainment industry are the major exceptions.

Some training may be useful not in most firms nor in a single firm, but in a set of firms defined by product, type of work, or geographical location. For example, carpentry training would raise productivity primarily in the construction industry, and French legal training would not be very useful in the United States. Such training would tend to be paid by trainees, since a single firm could not readily collect the return,[12] and in this respect would be the same as general training. In one respect, however, it is similar to specific training. Workers with training "specific" to an industry, occupation, or country are less likely to leave that industry, occupation, or country than other workers, so their industrial, occupational, or country "turnover" would be less than average. The same result is obtained for specific training, except that a firm rather than an industry, occupation, or country is used as the unit of observation in measuring turnover. An analysis of specific training, therefore, is helpful also in understanding the effects of certain types of "general" training. . . .

Earnings might differ greatly among firms, industries, and countries and yet there might be relatively little worker mobility. The usual explanation would be that workers were either irrational or faced with formidable obstacles in moving. However, if specific training were important, differences in earnings would be a misleading estimate of what "migrants" could receive, and it might be perfectly rational not to move. For example, although French lawyers earn less than American lawyers, the average French lawyer could not earn the average American legal income simply by migrating to the United States, for he would have to invest in learning English and American law and procedures.[13]

In extreme types of monopsony, exemplified by an isolated company town, job alternatives for both trained and untrained workers are nil, and all training, no matter what its nature, would be specific to the firm. Monopsony combined with control of a product or an occupation (due, say, to antipirating agreements) converts training specific to that product or occupation into firm-specific training. These kinds of monopsony increase the importance of specific training and thus the incentive to invest employees.[14]. . .

2. Schooling

A school can be defined as an institution specializing in the production of training, as distinct from a firm that offers training in conjunction with the production of goods. Some schools, like those for barbers, specialize in one skill, while others, like universities, offer a large and diverse set. Schools and firms are often substitute sources of particular skills. This substitution is evidenced by the shift over time, for instance, in law from apprenticeships in law firms to law schools and in engineering from on-the-job experience to engineering schools.[15]. . .

3. Other Knowledge

On-the-job and school training are not the only activities that raise real income primarily by increasing the knowledge at a person's command. Information about the prices charged by different sellers would enable a person to buy from the cheapest, thereby raising his command over resources; information about the wages offered by different firms would enable him to work for the firm paying the highest. In both examples, information about the economic system and about consumption and production possibilities is increased, as distinct from knowledge of a particular skill. Information about the political or social system—the effect of different parties or

[12]Sometimes firms cooperate in paying training costs, especially when training apprentices (see *A Look at Industrial Training in Mercer County, N. J.,* Washington, 1959, p. 3).

[13]Of course, persons who have not yet invested in themselves would have an incentive to migrate, and this partly explains why young persons migrate more than older ones. For a further explanation, see the paper by L. Sjaastad, "The Costs and Returns of Human Migration," *Investment in Human Beings,* pp. 80-93.

[14]A relatively large difference between marginal product and wages in monopsonies might measure, therefore, the combined effect of economic power and a relatively large investment in employees.

[15]State occupational licensing requirements often permit on-the-job training to be substituted for school training (see S. Rottenberg, "The Economics of Occupational Licensing" *Aspects of Labor Economics,* pp. 3-20).

social arrangements—could also significantly raise real incomes.[16]

Let us consider in more detail investment in information about employment opportunities. A better job might be found by spending money on employment agencies and situation wanted ads, by using one's time to examine want ads, by talking to friends and visiting firms, or in Stigler's language by "search."[17] When the new job requires geographical movement, additional time and resources would be spent in moving.[18] These expenditures constitute an investment in information about job opportunities that would yield a return in the form of higher earnings than would otherwise have been received. . . .

4. Productive Wage Increases

One way to invest in human capital is to improve emotional and physical health. In Western countries today earnings are much more closely geared to knowledge than to strength, but in an earlier day, and elsewhere still today, strength had a significant influence on earnings. Moreover, emotional health increasingly is considered an important determinant of earnings in all parts of the world. Health, like knowledge, can be improved in many ways. A decline in the death rate at working ages may improve earning prospects by extending the period during which earnings are received; a better diet adds strength and stamina, and thus earning capacity; or an improvement in working conditions—higher wages, coffee breaks, and so on—may affect morale and productivity.

Firms can invest in the health of employees through medical examinations, lunches, or avoidance of activities with high accident and death rates. An investment in health that

[16]The role of political knowledge is systematically discussed in A. Downs, *An Economic Theory of Democracy,* New York, 1957, and more briefly in my "Competition and Democracy," *Journal of Law and Economics,* October 1958.

[17]See G. J. Stigler, "Information in the Labor Market," *Investment in Human Beings,* pp. 91-105.

[18]Studies of large geographical moves—those requiring both a change in employment and consumption—have tended to emphasize the job change more than the consumption change. Presumably money wages are considered to be more dispersed geographically than prices.

increased productivity to the same extent in many firms would be a general investment and would have the same effect as general training, while an investment in health that increased productivity more in the firms making it would be a specific investment and would have the same effect as specific training. Of course, most investments in health in the United States are made outside firms, in households, hospitals, and medical offices. A full analysis of the effect on earnings of such "outside" investment in health is beyond the scope of this study, but I would like to discuss a relation between on-the-job and "outside" human investments that has received much attention in recent years.

When on-the-job investments are paid by reducing earnings during the investment period, less is available for investments outside the job in health, better diet, schooling, and other factors. If these "outside" investments were more productive, some on-the-job investments would not be undertaken even though they were very productive by "absolute" standards.

Before proceeding further, one point needs to be made. The amount invested outside the job would be related to current earnings only if the capital market was very imperfect, for otherwise any amount of "outside" investment could be financed with borrowed funds. The analysis assumes, therefore, that the capital market is extremely imperfect, earnings and other income being a major source of funds.

A firm would be willing to pay for investment in human capital made by employees outside the firm if it could benefit from the resulting increase in productivity. The only way to pay, however, would be to offer higher wages during the investment period than would have been offered since direct loans to employees are prohibited by assumption. When a firm gives a productive wage increase—that is, an increase that raises productivity—"outside" investments are, as it were, converted into on-the-job investments. Indeed, such a conversion is a natural way to circumvent imperfections in the capital market and the resultant dependence of the amount invested in human capital on the level of wages. . . .

The effect of a wage increase on productivity depends on the way it is spent, which in turn depends on tastes, knowledge, and opportunities. Firms might exert an influence on spending by exhorting employees to obtain good food, housing, and medical care, or even by requiring purchases of specified items in company stores. Indeed, the company store or truck system in nineteenth century Great Britain has been interpreted as partly designed to prevent an excessive consumption of liquor and other debilitating commodities.[19] The prevalence of employer paternalism in underdeveloped countries has frequently been accepted as evidence of a difference in tempera-

ment between East and West. An alternative interpretation suggested by our study is that an increase in consumption has a greater effect on productivity in underdeveloped countries, and that a productivity advance raises profits more there either because firms have more monopsony power or because the advance is less delayed. In other words "paternalism" may simply be a way of investing in the health and welfare of employees in underdeveloped countries.

[19]See C. W. Hilton, "The British Truck System in the Nineteenth Century," *Journal of Political Economy,* April 1957, pp. 246-247.

5. Assessing the Economic Contribution of Education

William G. Bowen

Of late, economists have been spending considerable time attempting to assess the economic contribution of education, and one of the hallmarks of the burgeoning literature is the variety of approaches that have been employed. The variety of tacks taken can, I suppose, be regarded as a tribute to the inventiveness of the profession, as an index of the complexity of the problem(s), or as an indicator of the fact that we simply don't know as yet how best to proceed. . . .

The following discussion is couched mainly in analytical terms, although references to data problems and to actual findings are interspersed throughout. The focus is on major approaches, not on individual studies.[1] . . .

I. THE SIMPLE CORRELATION APPROACH

In the generic sense, this approach consists of correlating some overall index of educational activity with some index of the level of economic activity.

Inter-country Comparisons (Cross-sectional)

Inter-country correlations at a fixed point in time constitute one well-known member of this group. Svennilson, Edding, and Elvin, for example, have correlated enrollment ratios and GNP *per capita*, and have found that there is indeed a positive relationship, although there is also considerable dispersion, particularly among the countries falling in the middle range.[2]

Comparisons of this kind serve a number of useful purposes. For one thing, they enable countries to see their own educational efforts in the perspective of what is being done elsewhere, and thus can serve to disturb complacency. Comparisons between countries in similar economic circumstances may also provide at

---

[1] For a more broadly-gauged and comprehensive survey of work in the area of the economics of education, see Alice Rivlin's paper in *Economics of higher education,* (ed.) Selma J. Mushkin (U.S. Dept. of Health, Education, and Welfare, Office of Education, 1962); Seymour Harris' study, *Higher education, resources, and finance, 1962,* (McGraw-Hill) includes a wealth of material and references germane to the problems of planning and financing higher education. John Vaizey's recent book, *The economics of education,* Faber and Faber, 1962, contains discussions of many of the topics treated below.

[2] *Targets for education in Europe in 1970,* paper prepared for Washington Conference of the O.E.C.D., 1961, p. 75.

least a rough idea of what is possible, with "possible" defined in terms of actual educational outlays in countries having an approximately equal GNP *per capita.* Comparisons between countries at different stages of economic development may provide the less-advanced countries with a rough notion of what general level of educational activity is associated with a more advanced stage of economic development—so long as one remembers that standards in this respect, as in so many others, have a habit of changing rapidly.

The construction of meaningful inter-country comparisons is, of course, beset by many practical problems. We can leave aside the problem of obtaining comparable GNP figures—provided we realize that we are leaving aside a subject to which a whole segment of professional literature has been devoted. Finding comparable indices of educational activity (or attainment) is no less difficult, given the pronounced inter-country variations in educational systems.[3] If expenditure data are used, it is essential that cognizance be taken of the opportunity costs (foregone output) involved in having students attend school rather than work.[4] It is also necessary to recognize that equal resource expenditures in two countries imply equal educational output only if resources are used with the same degree of efficiency in both countries—and we know astonishingly little about how efficiency is to be

defined and measured, in spite of a recent upsurge of interest in the subject.

The practical problems of constructing indices can no doubt be solved to a tolerably satisfactory extent, and emphasis ought not to be placed here. It is the more basic question of what cause and effect relationship is bound up in education—GNP correlations[5] that deserves emphasis. A positive correlation can be viewed as evidence in support of the proposition that spending money on education is an important way of raising a country's GNP. But the same correlation can also be viewed as evidence in support of the proposition that education is an important consumer good on which countries elect to spend more as their GNP rises.[6]

The trouble is that these propositions are almost certainly both true *to some extent*—and, in the absence of other information, we have no way of disentangling the two relationships. The inescapable conclusion is that simple education—GNP correlations, in and of themselves, cannot tell us anything about the quantitative dimensions of the contribution that education makes to economic growth.[7]

Inter-temporal Correlations

A second basic variant of the simple correlation approach consists of correlating education and GNP within a given country over time.

---

[3]The debate in the British House of Commons on the Government's policies toward university education illustrates beautifully the way in which different measures of educational activity can lead to radically different conclusions. Mr. Gaitskell, leading off for the Opposition, cited estimates of total university students as a proportion of the total population in various countries to show how far Britain was lagging behind other countries. Mr. Henry Brooke, replying for the Government, cited percentages of the relevant age group *graduating* from universities to show that in fact Britain was doing better than many of the same Western European countries mentioned by Mr. Gaitskell. (See *Hansard,* vol. 657, no. 91 (5 April 1962), pp. 719 ff., and especially pp. 726, 734–36.)

[4]In the case of the United States, T. W. Schultz ("Capital formation by education," *Journal of Political Economy,* December 1960, p. 582) has estimated that opportunity costs were equal to about three-fifths of the total costs of high school and college education in 1956.

[5]From here on, all general references to correlations between education and GNP should be interpreted to mean correlations between *relative* measures of educational activity (e.g., proportions of the total population in school or fractions of the total GNP spent on education) and GNP *per capita.*

[6]This assumes that the income-elasticity of demand for education is greater than unity and that any negative substitution effect, arising as a consequence of the (likely) possibility that the price of education will go up relative to other prices, will be swamped by the positive income effect. These assumptions seem reasonable.

[7]There are, of course, many other considerations in addition to the two-way causation problem that make it difficult to interpret cross-sectional correlations between education and GNP. Apart from the universal problem of holding other things constant, there are time-lag and external economies problems, both of which will be discussed below in other contexts.

Schultz has recently made a correlation of this type for the U.S. over the period 1900 to 1956, and, treating education solely as a consumer good, he found that the income-elasticity of demand for education was 3.5.[8] But treating education solely as a consumer good begs the question of course (as Schultz is the first to admit), and one must conclude that here again the two-way causation problem makes it impossible to give a satisfactory interpretation to the figures.

Attempts at inter-temporal correlations also highlight the time-lag problem that plagues many approaches. Education is a long-lived asset, in that an educated man presumably contributes more on account of his education, not just one year after his graduation, but for much of the rest of his life. If a country doubled its expenditure on education in year t, the positive economic effects ought not to be looked for in year t's GNP figures (which actually will be lower because students who would have worked are now in school), but in the figures for all the years from, say, $t + 4$ on.[9] . . .

II. THE RESIDUAL APPROACH

In general terms, this approach consists of taking the total increase in economic output of a country over a given period of time, identifying as much of the total increase as possible with measurable inputs (capital and labour being the two measurable inputs usually chosen) and then saying that the residual is attributable to the unspecified inputs. It is because education and advances in knowledge are usually regarded as the most important of the unspecified inputs that this approach deserves to be discussed in the context of the contribution-of-education question. . . .

The residual, as usually measured, no doubt embodies the results of some secular improvement in the quality of capital assets; it also encompasses changes in output attributable to economies of scale, to improvements in the health of the labour force, to informal as well as formal education, to changes in the product mix, to reorganizations of the economic order, and to who knows what else. Moses Abramovitz has called it a "measure of our ignorance."[10] The heterogeneity of the elements that go to make up the residual means, of course, that a large residual cannot safely be interpreted as a mandate for more spending on any particular project, whether it be a massive research and development effort or better school lunches.

However, the size of the residual certainly does serve as a mandate to explore in detail the economic effects of activities often neglected. It seems clear that the simple accumulation of physical capital, in and of itself, has not played the dominant role in economic growth sometimes ascribed to it.

III. THE DIRECT RETURNS-TO-EDUCATION APPROACH

An obvious way of studying the economic consequences of education is by contrasting the lifetime earnings of people who have had "more" education with the lifetime earnings of people who have had "less" education. The difference in lifetime earnings can then be expressed as an annual percentage rate of return on the costs involved in obtaining the education.[11] Actually, as the following discussion is

---

[8]T. W. Schultz, "Education and economic growth," in *Yearbook of the National Society for the Study of Education,* 1961, p. 60; Seymour Harris, in *The market for college graduates,* Harvard University Press, 1949, pp. 160-72, has also made correlations of this kind.

[9]The best way of surmounting this problem is by measuring the total *stock* of education at different points in time, not just the current level of educational activity. (For a recent attempt at this, see Schultz's paper in the 1961 *Education and economic growth* volume, pp. 64 ff. Note, however, that in some of his work Schultz suggests the desirability of calculating a kind of present value of the stock by weighting younger persons more heavily than older persons; this makes good sense if one wants to know what the economic worth of the stock is, but not if one just wants to relate current educational attainments to current economic output.) Stock measurements are also better than flow measurements, in the case of cross-sectional inter-country comparisons, for exactly the same reasons.

[10]*Resources and output trends in the United States since 1870,* Occasional Paper 52, New York, National Bureau of Economic Research, 1956, p. 11. It is to the great credit of the authors of the estimates of the residual that without exception they have repeatedly emphasized this aspect of its character.

[11]For references to some early studies of this kind, see J. R. Walsh, "The capital concept applied to man,"

likely to make painfully clear, this approach, like so many others, is deceptively simple.

At the outset it is useful to distinguish two ways of looking at direct returns to education: (a) the personal profit orientation; (b) the national productivity orientation.

The "personal profit orientation" consists of looking at differences in the net earnings of people with varying amounts of education as evidence of the amount of personal financial gain that can be associated with the attainment of a given level of education. This is, of course, the relevant orientation for the individual trying to make private calculations (in a country where students pay a substantial share of educational costs), and it can also be argued that evidence of this kind is germane to a country's decision as to what fraction of the costs of education should be borne by the students themselves.

The "national productivity orientation" consists of looking at education-related earnings differentials as partial evidence of the effects of education on the output of the country, and is based on the premise that in a market economy differences in earnings reflect differences in productivity.This orientation is relevant to the question of whether society as a whole is investing the right share of its resources in education.

From the standpoint of procedures and problems, these two ways of looking at direct returns to education are sufficiently similar to allow us to discuss them together, although there are also differences which will require comment from time to time. Right here it is worth noting that in calculating rates of return the relevant concept of educational cost depends on the investigator's orientation (only private costs, including opportunity costs, are relevant to an assessment of the private rate of return, whereas all costs, including public subsidies, are relevant to the measurement of direct social returns) as does the relevant concept of earnings (after tax in the private returns case, before tax in the social returns case). Other differences will be touched on in due course.

So far we have spoken of two groups of persons: a group having "more" education and a group having "less" education. When it comes to calculating actual rates of return, however, this vague dichotomy will not do, and many of the recent studies have calculated separate rates of return for each stage of the educational process. While there is obviously much to be said for dividing education into stages, the results can be misleading if looked at in isolation from one another. Calculating the rate of return on primary education by comparing the net earnings of persons who have completed just the primary grades with the net earnings of persons who have not had even this much education is bound to produce an erroneously low result in that no account is taken of the fact that primary education is a stepping stone to secondary and college education. The value of the option to continue one's education ought to be included in the rate of return on both primary and secondary education, and the value of this option obviously depends on the rate of return to be had from the higher levels of education and on the probability that the option will be exercised. Education must be viewed as a series of related steps. Weisbrod has made this point quite clearly, and, to illustrate the order of magnitude involved, has shown that recognizing the value of the option to obtain additional education raises the expected 1939 rate of return on grade school education from a previous estimate of 35 per cent to 52 per cent.[12]

Separate rates of return can also be calculated for males and females, for persons of different races, and so on. One of Becker's most interesting (and disturbing) findings is that whereas the rate of return on the cost of college education was 9 per cent for urban white males in the United States as of 1950, the comparable rate of return for non-whites was about two percentage points lower than this—presumably because of greater job discrimination against college-educated non-whites than against other non-whites.[13]

The rate-of-return approach has many attractions, not the least of which is that educational benefits are related to educational costs in a way that holds out the hope of providing useful information concerning the adequacy of the

Quarterly Journal of Economics, February 1935, p. 235. Among the more recent studies, Gary Becker's work has received by far the most attention from professional economists, although only a preliminary report on his research has been published so far ("Underinvestment in college education?" *American Economic Review,* May 1960, pp. 346-54.)

[12]Burton A. Weisbrod, "Education and investment in human capital," *The Journal of Political Economy,* October 1962, pp. 106-23.

[13]Becker, *op. cit.,* pp. 347-48.

overall level of investment in education and the extent to which economic benefits accrue directly to private individuals. But, the implementation of this approach is also subject to many difficulties, which must be examined in some detail if we are to minimize the risk of misinterpreting results.

The "Holding Other Things Constant" Problem

Unfortunately for purposes of analysis, groups with differing amounts of education tend to differ systematically in terms of other attributes which are also likely to influence relative earnings. An oft-quoted (and justifiable) criticism of many studies purporting to show that a person could add "X" thousand dollars to his lifetime income by going to college is that they attribute results to education which were caused, *in part*, by differences in intelligence, ambition, family connections, and so on. At the same time, it must be emphasized that this problem has been recognized by the investigators themselves and that attempts have been made to adjust for differences in factors such as ability and family background.[14]

No one would claim that the efforts to date have been entirely satisfactory, and one of the reasons is the difficulty of obtaining satisfactory measures of such elusive variables as ability and motivation. (It is much easier to adjust for differences in mortality rates and unemployment experience.) We also need to

[14]Becker has standardized his data for differences in ability on the basis of test score information, and for differences in unemployment and mortality as well. He reports (*op. cit.*, p. 349) that adjusting for differential ability reduces the rate of return on a college education by about two percentage points (from 11 to 9 per cent). Results of detailed case-study type inquiries into the education–ability-earning relationship have been reported by Wolfle and Bridgman in the volume of papers edited by Seymour Harris, *Higher Education in the United States; the economic problems*, Harvard University Press, 1960, pp. 178-79 and pp. 180-84. Denison, in his C.E.D. study of the sources of economic growth, has reduced actual earnings differentials by one-third in order to take account of the effects of characteristics correlated with education (especially ability), but he acknowledges in a very forthright fashion that this adjustment represents nothing more than a rough guess on his part as to the quantitative importance of differences in ability and in other associated factors. (op. cit., pp. 69-70.)

know more than we do at present about the relationship between different *levels* of ability and differences in earnings associated with varying amounts of formal education. The results of a questionnaire study reported by Bridgman suggest that differences in earnings (between college graduates and "comparable" high school graduates) were greatest for those of highest ability.[15] The relation between levels of intellectual ability and the likelihood that one will profit economically from higher education deserves much more study, particularly in the context of discussions concerning the extension of higher education to a larger proportion of a given population.

Do Earnings Measure Productivity?

The question of whether differences in relative earnings reflect differences in productivity does not arise so long as one looks at returns to education solely from the personal profit point of view. But, if we wish to interpret rates of return on education as indicative of over- or under-investment in education from the national productivity point of view, then this question becomes very important indeed.

In general, in an economy where relative earnings are subject to the push and pull of market forces, we should certainly expect to find relatively high earnings accruing to persons possessing special skills which enable them to make a greater economic contribution than the average person. However, there are also reasons for thinking that earnings differentials may not always be an accurate reflection of differences in marginal productivities, and the likely effects of these other considerations on rates of return figures must be examined carefully.

"Conspicuous Production" and "Tradition-bound" Wage Structures

The link between relative wages and marginal productivities will be weakened to the extent that employers do not set wages so as to maximize their profits. The phrase "conspicuous production" refers to the possibility that some employers may choose to hire college graduates (and pay them "college graduate" salaries) for jobs which do not really require college training. Instances of this type can no doubt be found in a country such as the United States,

[15]*Op. cit.*, p. 178.

but I suspect that we tend to exaggerate the frequency with which bosses insist on paying extra for unnecessary qualifications.[16]

The phrase "tradition-bound wage structures" refers to what may well be a more important variant of non-profit-maximizing behaviour. Persons who have studied the so-called "underdeveloped countries" have noted a tendency to continue paying relatively high salaries to educated persons in, for example, the Government service, when such a salary policy is no longer necessary from a recruitment standpoint.[17] In countries where the salary structure is rigid because of status overtones, calculations of monetary returns to education can be very misleading as a guide to educational policy.

The Non-monetary Attractions of Jobs Open to Graduates

All occupations have their non-monetary plusses and minuses, and the wage structure presumably adjusts accordingly—occupations which are dirty, hard, or unpleasant in any respect will be characterized by higher earnings than those which require the same kinds of qualifications but which are cleaner, easier, more interesting, have a higher status appeal, and so on. There would be no need to dwell on the existence of these non-monetary attractions if they were of roughly the same order of importance in the case of jobs open to highly-educated persons and jobs open to persons with less education. In actual fact, however, it seems clear that non-monetary attractions are much greater in the case of the usual jobs filled by college graduates; hence, non-monetary con-

siderations cannot be dismissed as a neutral factor.[18]...

The important question is: how (if at all) should one adjust rates of return to take account of differences in non-monetary advantages? This is a very troublesome question at the conceptual level, as well as at the empirical level, and part of the explanation is that the answer depends on whether one is looking at returns to education from the personal profit or national productivity point of view.

From the standpoint of the individual gain from education (personal profit), it seems clear that we ought to add in a sum approximating the dollar equivalent of the non-monetary advantages. Non-monetary advantages certainly do accrue to the individuals concerned and increase their welfare. At the moment, quantitative estimates are lacking, but my guess is that taking account of this consideration would increase the calculated rate of return on higher education (and especially on graduate education) to a very marked extent.

From the national productivity standpoint, one might think at first that a similar upward adjustment is required.[19] But, to the extent that the non-monetary aspects of employment are purely a supply-side phenomenon (that is, affect only the willingness of individuals to take

---

[16]It may well be that as a higher proportion of the people in a country receive a college education, employers, in order to recruit people possessing a certain level of ability, will find themselves forced to recruit college graduates—even though college training may be unnecessary for the job. However, this situation ought not to be confused with the "conspicuous production" case. To the extent that these people are paid higher salaries solely because of their basic ability, employers cannot be accused of nonprofit-maximizing behaviour. Actually this kind of situation affords an excellent illustration of the need to avoid attributing higher salaries due to ability differentials to education (as discussed above), but it is quite different from a situation in which an employer pays more to a college graduate holding a particular job just because he is a college graduate.

[17]See, for example, the paper prepared by F. H. Har-

bison for the O.E.C.D. Conference on Education held in Washington in the fall of 1961.

[18]I grant that attitudes toward the non-monetary attractions of certain jobs vary significantly from one person to the next; and I also grant that my own preferences no doubt influence my judgement on this point. But it still seems safe to say that, if salaries were the same and if qualifications were not a constraint, most people would prefer the kinds of jobs that are in fact open only (or mainly) to holders of degrees. Studies that have been made of popular attitudes towards various vocations support this position. (A poll conducted for the President's Commission on Higher Education and cited by Harris [*The market for college graduates,* 1949, p. 7] showed that, with regard to prestige, virtually all occupations ranked in the top twenty-five by a cross-section of Americans would normally require a college education but most others would not.)

[19]This seems to be Villard's position (see his criticism of Becker's work in the *American Economic Review*, May 1960, p. 376). Many other writers have said essentially the same thing, and I should add that at one point I too shared this position. As the rest of this discussion indicates, I have now revised my views; I have Ralph Turvey to thank for forcing me to think this problem through more fully.

jobs at alternative rates of pay and not the costs incurred by employers in hiring additional men), this is not so. The greater the non-monetary attractions of any occupation, the greater the number of people who will be willing to enter the occupation at a given wage and thus the greater the ability of the employer to hire a given number of people at a lower rate of pay. The extent of non-monetary attractions determines the position of the supply curve of labour, but this does not alter the fact that the employer will still pay that money wage which will equal the value of the marginal product produced by the last man hired. . . .

The above line of argument holds only to the extent that non-monetary attractions are truly "non-monetary" and do not cost the employer anything. This is generally true of such attractions as prestige, but it may not be true of attractions such as subsidized housing, subsidized travel, and long, paid vacations. . . .

There is one final point—the argument presented here is based on the assumption that persons interested in rates of return on education, from what we have called the "national productivity" standpoint, are concerned solely with the effects of education on the nation's GNP. If one wishes to work from a broader national frame of reference and look at the effects of education on the total "welfare" of the citizenry, then once again, as in the case of the personal profit orientation, a full adjustment for non-monetary attractions is in order since such attractions most certainly do contribute to the aggregate welfare of the populace.

External Economies, Indirect Benefits, or Social Benefits

Anyone using direct returns to education as a guide to the proper level of spending must recognize that rates of return based on the relative earnings of groups of individuals will never reflect the external economies (or indirect benefits, or social benefits, depending on one's terminological preferences) generated by education. By definition, external economies consist of those benefits which are not confined to individual economic units—and thus do not show up in the relative earnings of identifiable groups—but which "spill-over" to the economy as a whole, raising the level of real income and welfare generally.

While external effects are by no means con-

fined to education, education is probably more likely to generate indirect benefits than any other single activity of comparable scope. Without pretending to present anything resembling a complete catalogue, it may be useful to mention a few of the main kinds of external effects.

As everyone knows, the educational process is intimately related to advances in knowledge, and it is equally clear that advances in knowledge can have important economic effects. Yet, because new ideas are not used up by being understood, and because the results of basic research are rapidly disseminated free of charge (over the entire world in many cases), the economic contribution of basic research will not be fully reflected in the relative earnings of the producers of this new knowledge.[20] Nor is it just research in natural science that has important economic consequences—it would be interesting to know the magnitude of the increase in real incomes that has stemmed from our improved understanding of how to prevent large-scale unemployment.

There are also, of course, important social and political benefits of education which accrue to the populace as a whole—a better informed electorate, more culturally alive neighbourhoods, a healthier and less crime-prone population, and so on. What is not always recognized is that these social and political consequences may in turn have significant economic effects— the efficiency with which goods are exchanged is obviously enhanced by general literacy. To the extent that education reduces crime (even if only by keeping children off the streets during the day) the country can shift resources that would have had to be used for the police function to other ends, and so on.

While education could conceivably entail social costs as well as social benefits (for instance by producing a class of unemployed, unproductive, frustrated, and socially-destructive intellectuals), there is no doubt that on balance the positive benefits are paramount. However, it is one thing to be able to say that external benefits are obviously very important and quite another to know what order of magnitude to attach to the word "very." I think that most people who have worked actively on the problem of estimating national returns to edu-

[20]W. Leontief presents a lucid discussion of the underlying reasons why advances in knowledge have the attributes of indirect benefits in his preface to Leonard Silk's *The research revolution,* McGraw-Hill, 1960.

cation are agreed that this is the biggest unsolved riddle of all. At the present time all we
know is that estimates of direct returns ought
to be adjusted upward to take account of external economies—we do not know how much
of an adjustment to make or even how to go
about finding out how much of an adjustment
to make.[21]

Collective Power

Finally, it is worth noting that the existence
of collective power in certain sectors may influence relative earnings. It has been argued, for
example, that some part of the relatively high
earnings enjoyed by doctors in the United
States should be attributed directly to the
effectiveness of the American Medical Association in limiting entry and keeping fees
high.[22]

In interpreting the implications for educational policy of an "artificially" high rate of
return of this kind, it is necessary to be very
careful indeed. While the wage will be higher
than under competitive conditions, so will
marginal productivity (because of a smaller
active labour input), and therefore an increased
investment in this particular type of activity
would be called for. The fact that in cases of
this type relatively high rates of return have
been caused in part by organized power groups
(rather than solely by ignorance, underestimates of returns by policy makers, or imperfections in the capital market) makes no difference at all to the basic conclusion—that the
relatively high rates of return imply under-
investment and a mis-allocation of resources.
But, the cause of the relatively high rate of
return has, of course, important implications
for the selection of the most appropriate
remedial policy measure—a relatively high rate

of return attributable to the exercise of market
power may be best treated by trying to eliminate the source of the market imperfection.[23]

The Consumption Versus Investment Problem

Critics of the direct returns to education
approach have repeatedly emphasized that such
calculations ignore the so-called "consumption"
or "cultural" contributions of education. The
point is that education presumably has purposes besides that of increasing a person's
potential economic productivity—yet it is only
his economic productivity (and in fact only
that part of his economic productivity which
passes through the market mechanism)[24] that
enters into the measurement of returns to
education.

Thus, no account is taken of the value of the
current consumption enjoyed by the student
who may say that his college years were "the
best years of his life." (True, there may be some
students who regard education as a painful
process to be endured for the sake of future
gain, but such students would no doubt turn
out to be in the minority, especially if forced to
contrast the net attractions of being a student
with the net attractions of what in fact they
would be doing if they were not students rather
than with the attractions of what they would
like to be doing.) In the case of primary education, parents no doubt derive immediate
pleasure from having the children in school
rather than at home, apart from that felt by the
children.

It is also generally agreed that education
confers long and lasting benefits of a consumption variety by extending the range of activities
which a person is able to enjoy during his leisure hours. For many people, education has no
doubt awakened interests which have been a
source of pleasure over an entire lifetime. In

---

[21]Some progress can be reported, however, Weisbrod,
in his *Journal of Political Economy* paper (October
1962, pp. 106-23), has suggested ways of estimating
the value of savings in terms of certain "avoidance
costs" (i.e., costs that, were it not for education, we
would have had to incur for, say, added police protection). Others have attempted direct assessments of the
economic value of various kinds of basic research. But
all would agree that there is room for much more
work on this problem.

[22]The classic is by M. Friedman and S. S. Kuznets,
Income from independent professional practice,
National Bureau of Economic Research, 1946.

[23]I am indebted to Thomas Ribich for helpful comments on the subject-matter of this paragraph.

[24]The importance of non-market production furth-
ered by education is illustrated by Weisbrod's estimate
that the annual value of services performed by persons
who fill out their own income tax returns has
amounted to about 66 million dollars, which is almost
1 per cent of elementary school costs. Were this
service provided through the market it would, of
course, be priced and included in the national income.
(This estimate comes from the paper by Weisbrod
cited in footnote 21.)

this sense, education can be thought of as conferring a durable consumer good of great value.

The important question is not whether education is a source of present and future pleasure—unquestionably it is, quite apart from its effects on one's ability to obtain a satisfying and productive job—but how, if at all, estimates of the direct monetary returns to education should be adjusted to take account of such considerations.

Certainly the individual trying to decide whether or not to continue his education will want to add his own estimate of "consumption" values to his estimate of job-related values in coming to a decision. . . .

[From the societal viewpoint,] the logical way to proceed is to make an explicit evaluation of the worth of the consumption contributions of education to society (expressed in dollar terms), next add this sum to the monetary returns from education, and then compare the total benefits to the total costs in order to see if the undertaking as a whole is sufficiently worthwhile to merit devoting more resources to it. The evaluation of the consumption component depends, of course, on society's preferences and cannot be deduced in a mechanical way from any known set of figures. This is also true of parks and many other things, and the difficulties involved in making this kind of evaluation certainly do not justify the easy escape of ignoring the value of the consumption benefits altogether.[25]

The Discount Rate (or "Other" Rate of Return) Problem

Since the monetary benefits of education accrue over time, it is necessary to use some discount factor to take account of the fact that a dollar earned tomorrow is less valuable than a dollar earned today, and computations of the present value of the future stream of benefits to be expected from education are, of course, very sensitive to the discount factor used. Houthakker has made some calculations (based on 1950 census data for the U.S.) which indicate that the capital value (present value) at age 14 of before-tax lifetime income associated with four or more years of college, ranged from a

figure of $280,989 if a zero discount rate is used to $106,269 at a 3 per cent rate of discount, to $47,546 at 6 per cent and to $30,085 at 8 per cent.[26] Unfortunately, there is no simple answer to the question of what is the right discount factor, and this question has in fact been the subject of considerable debate. . . .

Some authors have used 4 per cent as the discount factor (or the other rate of return) on the ground that this is roughly the long-term rate of interest and represents the cost that the government itself must incur in borrowing money. To the extent that one is prepared to assume that in fact it is going to be the government that will be providing any additional funds for education, there is much to be said for using a figure of this kind.

However, if we assume that individual students (or their families) are the ones contemplating investing in education, then a higher rate is surely appropriate, partly to take account of the greater risk involved in financing a single (typical) individual than in financing a large group. An individual would find it simply impossible to borrow educational funds on the private market at anything like 4 per cent interest.[27]

Becker[28] has made use of a comparative rate of return in the neighbourhood of 9-10 per cent, on the ground that this is roughly the average rate of return on private investment in the United States—businesses would certainly be reluctant to undertake any project that did not promise to yield at least this high a rate of return. The argument is, of course, that if we can earn 9-10 per cent on alternative investments, a purely economic case for investing relatively more in education would have to be based on at least as high a rate of return on education.

From the standpoint of the large private

---

[25]It may be noted in passing that the existence of a significant *personal* consumption component in the educational benefit stream also raises some nice questions germane to the issue of who should pay for education.

[26]H. S. Houthakker, "Education and income,"*Review of Economics and Statistics,* February 1959, Table 2, p. 26.

[27]It is true that individual universities, charitable groups, and some governments will make loans at lower rates of interest. The individual with access to such sources should, of course, calculate accordingly. However, since special terms of this sort do not reflect current market demands for loanable funds, they are of limited use as a guide to social policy (they in turn already reflect social policy).

[28]*Op. cit.,* pp. 348-49.

investor, the logic of this argument is unassailable, provided that there are no appreciable differences in the degree of risk involved (and whether this proviso holds I do not know). But, whether this is the appropriate rate for the purposes of government policy can be questioned on the ground that, for a host of primarily political reasons (and this does not mean they are bad reasons), the actual alternative investment opportunities open to the government may not be nearly so lucrative. (In the U.S. economy at any rate, there is a strong presumption that public funds will not be invested in such commercially profitable fields as chemicals, applied electronics, soft drink production and the like but rather, in such activities as running the post office and supporting agricultural prices, as well as in research and development and education.). . .

Danger of Extrapolating the Past

The rates of return that I have been discussing are, of course, *average* rates of return for *past* periods, and so the question naturally arises: are there any particular cautions that must be borne in mind when using such rates of return as a guide to future actions?

The first answer to this question is that we should, of course, prefer to have a *marginal* rate of return figure rather than an average figure, since we are especially interested in the consequences of marginal changes in educational expenditures. Unfortunately, no direct way of estimating a marginal rate of return has as yet been found, and so we are forced to address ourselves to the question of whether we might expect the marginal figure to differ from the average figure in any systematic way. If we make the usual assumption that the conditions of a competitive market equilibrium obtained at the time the earnings and cost measurements were taken, then it follows that the average value can be regarded as equal to the marginal value, and this problem of the relationship between average and marginal values can be disposed of accordingly. Actually, this is taking too easy a way out in that the profit-maximization considerations which push industries to the equilibrium level of output are presumably less operative in the education field. Nonetheless, for want of a better assumption, we must act as if the past average rate of return were equal to the marginal rate of return. . . .

Predicting the future rates of return that will be associated with possible expansions in education is likely to be more difficult than making similar predictions for other activities, for three main reasons: (a) so much depends on the quality of the additional students, a factor which is variable and hard to judge—when one is considering whether or not to produce more shoes, it can be safely assumed that the extra shoes produced will be much like their predecessors, but in education the extra student may turn out to be an academic failure or an Einstein; (b) the future educational requirements of a country will depend to a substantial degree on future discoveries and advancements in knowledge—which are almost impossible to foresee; (c) education is such a long process, and education once acquired is such a long-lived asset, that educational decisions must be based on an unusually long time-horizon.

In any case there is no avoiding the necessity of predictions—and past experience, modified by our understanding of trends and new developments, is likely to provide a better basis for decisions than implicit guesses predicated on unstated assumptions.

It is hoped that the above discussion has helped to clarify some of the reasons why various users of the direct returns approach have drawn somewhat different conclusions from their work. Procedural choices and decisions have to be made at many steps in the analysis, and personal judgments and value preferences inevitably enter in.

Nonetheless, the results obtained for the U.S. economy offer rather consistent (some might say surprisingly consistent) support for the notion that education, on the average, has paid significant financial as well as non-financial rewards. The evidence is quite strong that individuals with the requisite ability have been well advised to continue their education through university level—and there is no reason to think that this pattern will not continue.

The difficulties involved in identifying earnings differentials with productivity differentials force one to be somewhat more cautious in drawing sweeping conclusions as to the effects of education on national output. However, here too the burden of proof is surely on those who would play down the economic importance of education. The likely existence of obscured relationships between ability and earnings constitutes the main reason for supposing that rate of return figures have an upward bias, and even after allowing (as best he could) for this cross-relation, Becker still obtained a 9 per cent per annum figure. When we then recognize that on top of this 9 per cent one surely must make some allowance for external benefits, and for the non-pecuniary contributions of education (if one wishes to think in terms of total welfare and not just in terms of GNP figures), the grounds for thinking that past investments in education have paid handsome returns to the nation as a whole are quite impressive.

It would be utter folly to pretend that the rate-of-return approach is free of troublesome difficulties or that it can be relied on to prove conclusively to a staunch unbeliever that investing resources in education makes good eco-nomic sense. But this approach does have three rather important appeals: (a) it enables us to obtain results in a form which permits compari-sons of costs with benefits; (b) it permits us, in making calculations, to examine the quantita-tive effect on our results of alternative assump-tions about such things as the proper discount rate and the effect of ability differentials on earnings differentials; and (c) as I hope the above discussion and the references to work in progress have shown, this approach is suscept-ible to further refinement and holds out the possibility that further research will remedy some of the present difficulties.

II

LABOR MARKETS AND UNEMPLOYMENT

Labor Market Theory and Practice

The operation of markets, in which buyers and sellers exchange commodities or services at a price, is central to the study of economics. The hiring of labor at a specified price (wage rate) is a market transaction. Economists have always recognized, however, that a worker selling labor is differently situated from a shoe merchant selling shoes.

One difference is that the worker delivers himself as part of the bargain. So, in choosing among occupations, the agreeableness or disagreeableness of the work is an important consideration. The worker will also consider such things as the cost of training for the occupation, the chances of success in it, and the regularity of employment. Given full information and freedom of choice, the market will operate to equalize *not* the wage rate for different occupations, but their total attractiveness to workers on the margin of decision. Jobs that cost much to learn, involve disagreeable work, or offer only irregular employment, will pay a higher wage to offset these disadvantages.

These principles were first stated two hundred years ago in Adam Smith's *Wealth of Nations*. It is a mark of Smith's genius that later writers have not been able to improve very much on his original statement. Note also that Smith recognized the important restrictions on free choice that existed in his day, which prevented the market from equalizing the advantages of different occupations.

Alfred Marshall, the great Cambridge University economist of the period 1880-1920, analyzed labor markets in a way that, while consistent with Smith, goes beyond him in several respects. He noted, first, that workers differ in efficiency. Thus a competitive labor market will not equalize the wage rates of workers in the same occupation, but rather the ratio of their wage rates to their efficiency—what Marshall termed their *efficiency earnings*. He then proceeded to explore several "peculiarities" in the operation of labor markets. Of these, the most interesting are:

47

1. Parents who invest in the education and training of their children do not receive the future monetary rewards. Parents in the lower occupational grades, he thought, will have neither the resources nor the foresight to invest much in training; and this is an important factor perpetuating inequality from generation to generation.

2. Workers are under greater pressure than employers to conclude an employment bargain quickly, because they must have income to live. This fact, Marshall believed, placed them at a bargaining disadvantage and tended to drive down wages. This provides an argument for trade union organization in order to "equalize bargaining power."

3. Since training for the higher occupations takes a long time, supply responds only slowly to changes in earnings. Thus at any moment the market for such occupations is likely to be out of equilibrium. The "long run," in which competition would equalize the total attractiveness of occupations, must be interpreted as a long period of calendar time.

Restrictions on free choice of occupation have concerned economists from Adam Smith to the present. Clark Kerr argues that, instead of the completely open market of pure competition, actual labor markets are highly compartmentalized ("Balkanized") by employer and union rules. In unionized craft occupations, entrance to and exit from the market occurs only *via* the union. In manufacturing industries, workers are hired from the outside only at a few "ports of entry" to the company. Most jobs are filled by promotion from inside—the "internal" labor market—with seniority the dominant principle. This channeling of labor mobility by institutional rules, Kerr argues, makes actual wage decisions quite different from those pictured in simple supply-demand models.

The information sources available to workers and employers can be divided into two channels: formal, such as local offices of the state employment service; and informal, such as tips from friends and relatives. Economists concerned with improvement of information have tended to urge greater use of formal channels. Albert Rees, on the basis of research in the Chicago labor market, points out that informal channels have certain advantages to both employers and workers and often work better than has been supposed. He suggests that formal information networks may be most useful for specialized managerial, professional, and technical jobs, where matching vacancies and applicants may require search over a wide geographical area.

48

6. The Wealth of Nations

Adam Smith

Of Wages and Profit in the Different Employments of Labour and Stock

The whole of the advantages and disadvantages of the different employments of labour and stock must, in the same neighbourhood, be either perfectly equal or continually tending to equality. If in the same neighbourhood, there was any employment evidently either more or less advantageous than the rest, so many people would crowd into it in the one case, and so many would desert it in the other, that its advantages would soon return to the level of other employments. This at least would be the case in a society where things were left to follow their natural course, where there was perfect liberty, and where every man was perfectly free both to choose what occupation he thought proper, and to change it as often as he thought proper. Every man's interest would prompt him to seek the advantageous, and to shun the disadvantageous employment.

Pecuniary wages and profit, indeed, are everywhere in Europe extremely different, according to the different employments of labour and stock. But this difference arises partly from certain circumstances in the employments themselves, which either really, or at least in the imaginations of men, make up for a small pecuniary gain in some, and counterbalance a great one in others; and partly from the policy of Europe, which nowhere leaves things at perfect liberty.

The particular consideration of those circumstances and of that policy will divide the chapter into two parts.

PART I

Inequalities Arising from the Nature of the Employments Themselves

The five following are the principal circumstances which, so far as I have been able to observe, make up for a small pecuniary gain in some employments, and counterbalance a great one in others: First, The agreeableness or disagreeableness of the employments themselves; Secondly, The easiness and cheapness, or the difficulty and expense of learning them; Thirdly, The constancy or inconstancy of employment in them; Fourthly, The small or great trust which must be reposed in those who exercise them; and, Fifthly, The probability or improbability of success in them.

First, the wages of labour vary with the ease or hardship, the cleanliness or dirtiness, the honourableness or dishonourableness of the employment. Thus in most places, take the year round, a journeyman tailor earns less than a journeyman weaver. His work is much easier. A

journeyman weaver earns less than a journeyman smith. His work is not always easier, but it
is much cleanlier. A journeyman blacksmith,
though an artificer, seldom earns so much in
twelve hours as a collier, who is only a labourer,
does in eight. His work is not quite so dirty, is
less dangerous, and is carried on in day-light,
and above ground. Honour makes a great part
of the reward of all honourable professions. In
point of pecuniary gain, all things considered,
they are generally underrecompensed, as I shall
endeavour to show by and by. Disgrace has the
contrary effect. The trade of a butcher is a
brutal and an odious business; but it is in most
places more profitable than the greater part of
common trades. The most detestable of all
employments, that of public executioner, is, in
proportion to the quantity of work done,
better paid than any common trade whatever. . . .

Disagreeableness and disgrace affect the
profits of stock in the same manner as the
wages of labour. The keeper of an inn or tavern,
who is never master of his own house, and who
is exposed to the brutality of every drunkard,
exercises neither a very agreeable nor a very
creditable business. But there is scarce any common trade in which a small stock yields so great
a profit.

Secondly, the wages of labour vary with the
easiness and cheapness, or the difficulty and
expense of learning the business.

When any expensive machine is erected, the
extraordinary work to be performed by it before it is worn out, it must be expected, will
replace the capital laid out by it, with at least
the ordinary profits. A man educated at the
expense of much labour and time to any of
those employments which require extraordinary dexterity and skill, may be compared to
one of those expensive machines. The work
which he learns to perform, it must be expected, over and above the usual wages of common labour, will replace to him the whole expense of his education, with at least the ordinary profits of an equally valuable capital. It
must do this too in a reasonable time, regard
being had to the very uncertain duration of
human life, in the same manner as to the more
certain duration of the machine.

The difference between the wages of skilled
labour and those of common labour, is founded
upon this principle. . . .

Thirdly, the wages of labour, in different
occupations vary with the constancy or inconstancy of employment.

Employment is much more constant in some
trades than in others. In the greater part of
manufactures, a journeyman may be pretty sure
of employment almost every day in the year
that he is able to work. A mason or bricklayer,
on the contrary, can work neither in hard frost
nor in foul weather, and his employment at all
other times depends upon the occasional calls
of his customers. He is liable, in consequence,
to be frequently without any. What he earns,
therefore, while he is employed, must not only
maintain him while he is idle, but make him
some compensation for those anxious and
desponding moments which the thought of so
precarious a situation must sometimes occasion.
Where the computed earnings of the greater
part of manufacturers, accordingly, are nearly
upon a level with the day wages of common
labourers, those of masons and bricklayers are
generally from one half more to double those
wages. Where common labourers earn four and
five shillings a week, masons and bricklayers
frequently earn seven and eight; where the
former earn six, the latter often earn nine and
ten; and where the former earn nine and ten, as
in London, the latter commonly earn fifteen
and eighteen. No species of skilled labour,
however, seems more easy to learn than that of
masons and bricklayers. Chairmen in London,
during the summer season, are said sometimes
to be employed as bricklayers. The high wages
of those workmen, therefore, are not so much
the recompense of their skill, as the compensation for the inconstancy of their employment.

A house carpenter seems to exercise rather a
nicer and more ingenious trade than a mason.
In most places, however, for it is not universally
so, his day-wages are somewhat lower. His
employment, though it depends much, does not
depend so entirely upon the occasional calls of
his customers; and it is not liable to be inter-
rupted by the weather. . . .

Fourthly, the wages of labour vary according
to the small or great trust which must be reposed in the workmen.

The wages of goldsmiths and jewellers are
everywhere superior to those of many other
workmen, not only of equal, but of much
superior ingenuity; on account of the precious
materials with which they are intrusted.

We trust our health to the physician; our
fortune, and sometimes our life and reputation,

to the lawyer and attorney. Such confidence could not safely be reposed in people of a very mean or low condition. Their reward must be such, therefore, as may give them that rank in the society which so important a trust requires. The long time and the great expense which must be laid out in their education, when combined with this circumstance, necessarily enhance still further the price of their labour. . . .

Fifthly, the wages of labour in different employments vary according to the probability or improbability of success in them.

The probability that any particular person shall ever be qualified for the employment to which he is educated, is very different in different occupations. In the greater part of mechanic trades, success is almost certain; but very uncertain in the liberal professions. Put your son apprentice to a shoemaker, there is little doubt of his learning to make a pair of shoes: but send him to study the law, it is at least twenty to one if ever he makes such proficiency as will enable him to live by the business. In a perfectly fair lottery, those who draw the prizes ought to gain all that is lost by those who draw the blanks. In a profession where twenty fail for one that succeeds, that one ought to gain all that should have been gained by the unsuccessful twenty. The counsellor at law who, perhaps, at near forty years of age, begins to make something by his profession, ought to receive the retribution, not only of his own so tedious and expensive education, but of that of more than twenty others who are never likely to make any thing by it. How extravagant soever the fees of counsellors at law may sometimes appear, their real retribution is never equal to this. . . .The lottery of the law, therefore, is very far from being a perfectly fair lottery; and that, as well as many other liberal and honourable professions, are, in point of pecuniary gain, evidently under-recompensed.

Those professions keep their level, however, with other occupations, and, notwithstanding these discouragements, all the most generous and liberal spirits are eager to crowd into them. Two different causes contribute to recommend them. First, the desire of the reputation which attends upon superior excellence in any of them; and, secondly, the natural confidence which every man has, more or less, not only in his own abilities, but in his own good fortune.

To excel in any profession, in which but few arrive at mediocrity, is the most decisive mark of what is called genius or superior talents. The public admiration which attends upon such distinguished abilities, makes always a part of their reward; a greater or smaller in proportion as it is higher or lower in degree. It makes a considerable part of that reward in the profession of physic; a still greater perhaps in that of law; in poetry and philosophy it makes almost the whole. . . .

The five circumstances above mentioned, though they occasion considerable inequalities in the wages of labour and profits of stock, occasion none in the whole of the advantages and disadvantages, real or imaginary, of the different employments of either. The nature of those circumstances is such, that they make up for a small pecuniary gain in some, and counterbalance a great one in others.

In order, however, that this equality may take place in the whole of their advantages or disadvantages, three things are requisite, even where there is the most perfect freedom. First, the employments must be well known and long established in the neighbourhood; secondly, they must be in their ordinary, or what may be called their natural state; and, thirdly, they must be the sole or principal employments of those who occupy them.

First, this equality can take place only in those employments which are well known, and have been long established in the neighbourhood.

Where all other circumstances are equal, wages are generally higher in new than in old trades. When a projector attempts to establish a new manufacture, he must at first entice his workmen from other employments by higher wages than they can either earn in their own trades, or than the nature of his work would otherwise require, and a considerable time must pass away before he can venture to reduce them to the common level. Manufactures for which the demand arises altogether from fashion and fancy, are continually changing, and seldom last long enough to be considered as old established manufactures. Those, on the contrary, for which the demand arises chiefly from use or necessity, are less liable to change, and the same form or fabric may continue in demand for whole centuries together. The wages of labour, therefore, are likely to be higher in manufactures of the former, than in those of the latter kind. Birmingham deals chiefly in manufactures of the former kind; Sheffield in those of the latter; and the wages of labour in those two different places, are said to be suitable to this difference in the nature of their manufactures. . . .

Secondly, this equality in the whole of the advantages and disadvantages of the different employments of labour and stock, can take place only in the ordinary, or what may be called the natural, state of those employments.

The demand for almost every different species of labour is sometimes greater and sometimes less than usual. In the one case the advantages of the employment rise above, in the other they fall below the common level. The demand for country labour is greater at hay time and harvest than during the greater part of the year; and wages rise with the demand. In time of war, when forty or fifty thousand sailors are forced from the merchant service into that of the king, the demand for sailors to merchant ships necessarily rises with their scarcity; and their wages upon such occasions commonly rise from a guinea and seven-and-twenty shillings, to forty shillings and three pounds a month. In a decaying manufacture, on the contrary, many workmen, rather than quit their old trade, are contented with smaller wages than would otherwise be suitable to the nature of their employment. . . .

Thirdly, this equality in the whole of the advantages and disadvantages of the different employments of labour and stock, can take place only in such as are the sole or principal employments of those who occupy them.

When a person derives his subsistence from one employment, which does not occupy the greater part of his time, in the intervals of his leisure he is often willing to work at another for less wages than would otherwise suit the nature of the employment. . . .

PART II

Inequalities Occasioned by the Policy of Europe

Such are the inequalities in the whole of the advantages and disadvantages of the different employments of labour and stock, which the defect of any of the three requisites above mentioned must occasion, even where there is the most perfect liberty. But the policy of Europe, by not leaving things at perfect liberty, occa-

sions other inequalities of much greater importance.

It does this chiefly in the three following ways. First, by restraining the competition in some employments to a smaller number than would otherwise be disposed to enter into them; secondly, by increasing it in others beyond what it naturally would be; and, thirdly, by obstructing the free circulation of labour and stock, both from employment to employment, and from place to place.

First, the policy of Europe occasions a very important inequality in the whole of the advantages and disadvantages of the different employments of labour and stock, by restraining the competition in some employments to a smaller number than might otherwise be disposed to enter into them.

The exclusive privileges of corporations are the principal means it makes use of for this purpose.

The exclusive privilege of an incorporated trade necessarily restrains the competition, in the town where it is established, to those who are free of the trade. To have served an apprenticeship in the town, under a master properly qualified, is commonly the necessary requisite for obtaining this freedom. The bylaws of the corporation regulate sometimes the number of apprentices which any master is allowed to have, and almost always the number of years which each apprentice is obliged to serve. The intention of both regulations is to restrain the competition to a much smaller number than might otherwise be disposed to enter into the trade. The limitation of the number of apprentices restrains it directly. A long term of apprenticeship restrains it more indirectly, but as effectually, by increasing the expense of education. . . .

Secondly, the policy of Europe, by increasing the competition in some employments beyond what it naturally would be, occasions another inequality of an opposite kind in the whole of the advantages and disadvantages of the different employments of labour and stock.

It has been considered as of so much importance that a proper number of young people should be educated for certain professions, that sometimes the public and sometimes the piety of private founders have established many pensions, scholarships, exhibitions, bursaries, &c. for this purpose, which draw many more people into those trades than could otherwise pretend to follow them. In all Christian countries, I believe, the education of the greater part of churchmen is paid for in this manner. Very few of them are educated altogether at their own expense. The long, tedious, and expensive education, therefore, of those who are, will not always procure them a suitable reward, the church being crowded with people who, in order to get employment, are willing to accept of a much smaller recompence than what such an education would otherwise have entitled them to; and in this manner the competition of the poor takes away the reward of the rich. It would be indecent, no doubt, to compare either a curate or a chaplain with a journeyman in any common trade. The pay of a curate or chaplain, however, may very properly be considered as of the same nature with the wages of a journeyman. They are, all three, paid for their work according to the contract which they may happen to make with their respective superiors. . . .

In professions in which there are no benefices, such as law and physic, if an equal proportion of people were educated at the public expense, the competition would soon be so great, as to sink very much their pecuniary reward. It might then not be worth any man's while to educate his son to either of those professions at his own expense. They would be entirely abandoned to such as had been educated by those public charities, whose numbers and necessities would oblige them in general to content themselves with a very miserable recompence, to the entire degradation of the now respectable professions of law and physic.

That unprosperous race of men, commonly called men of letters, are pretty much in the situation which lawyers and physicians probably would be in upon the foregoing supposition. In every part of Europe the greater part of them have been educated for the church, but have been hindered by different reasons from entering into holy orders. They have generally, therefore, been educated at the public expense, and their numbers are everywhere so great, as commonly to reduce the price of their labour to a very paltry recompence. . . .

Thirdly, the policy of Europe, by obstructing the free circulation of labour and stock both from employment to employment, and from place to place, occasions in some cases a very inconvenient inequality in the whole of the advantages and disadvantages of their different employments.

The statute of apprenticeship obstructs the free circulation of labour from one employment to another, even in the same place. The exclusive privileges of corporations obstruct it from one place to another, even in the same employment.

It frequently happens that while high wages are given to the workmen in one manufacture, those in another are obliged to content themselves with bare subsistence. The one is in an advancing state, and has, therefore, a continual demand for new hands: the other is in a declining state, and the superabundance of hands is continually increasing. Those two manufactures may sometimes be in the same town, and sometimes in the same neighbourhood, without being able to lend the least assistance to one another. The statute of apprenticeship may oppose it in the one case, and both that and an exclusive corporation in the other. In many different manufactures, however, the operations are so much alike, that the workmen could easily change trades with one another, if those absurd laws did not hinder them. The arts of weaving plain linen and plain silk, for example, are almost entirely the same. That of weaving plain woollen is somewhat different; but the difference is so insignificant, that either a linen or a silk weaver might become a tolerable workman in a very few days. If any of those three capital manufactures, therefore, were decaying, the workmen might find a resource in one of the other two which was in a more prosperous condition, and their wages would neither rise too high in the thriving, nor sink too low in the decaying manufacture. . . .

The obstruction which corporation laws give to the free circulation of labour is common, I believe, to every part of Europe. That which is given to it by the poor laws is, so far as I know, peculiar to England. It consists in the difficulty which a poor man finds in obtaining a settlement, or even in being allowed to exercise his industry in any parish but that to which he belongs. It is the labour of artificers and manufacturers only of which the free circulation is obstructed by corporation laws. The difficulty of obtaining settlements obstructs even that of common labor. . . .

To remove a man who has committed no misdemeanour from the parish where he chooses to reside, is an evident violation of natural liberty and justice. The common people of England, however, so jealous of their liberty, but like the common people of most other countries, never rightly understanding wherein it consists, have now for more than a century together suffered themselves to be exposed to this oppression without a remedy. Though men of reflection, too, have sometimes complained of the law of settlements as a public grievance, yet it has never been the object of any general popular clamour, such as that against general warrants, an abusive practice undoubtedly, but such a one as was not likely to occasion any general oppression. There is scarce a poor man in England of forty years of age, I will venture to say, who has not in some part of his life felt himself most cruelly oppressed by this ill-contrived law of settlements.

7. Principles of Economics

Alfred Marshall

It is commonly said that the tendency of competition is to equalize the earnings of people engaged in the same trade or in trades of equal difficulty; but this statement requires to be interpreted carefully. For competition tends to make the earnings got by two individuals of unequal efficiency in any given time, say, a day or a year, not equal, but unequal; and, in like manner, it tends not to equalize, but to render unequal the average weekly wages in two districts in which the average standards of efficiency are unequal. Given that the average strength and energy of the working-classes are higher in the North of England than in the South, it then follows that the more completely "competition makes things find their own level," the more certain is it that average weekly wages will be higher in the North than in the South.[1]

Cliffe Leslie and some other writers have naively laid stress on local variations of wages as tending to prove that there is very little mobility among the working-classes, and that the competition among them for employment is ineffective. But most of the facts which they quote relate only to wages reckoned by the day or week: they are only half-facts, and when the missing halves are supplied, they generally support the opposite inference to that on behalf of which they are quoted. For it is found that local variations of weekly wages and of efficiency generally correspond: and thus the facts tend to prove the effectiveness of competition, so far as they bear on the question at all. We shall however presently find that the full interpretation of such facts as these is a task of great difficulty and complexity.

The earnings, or wages, which a person gets in any given time, such as a day, a week, or a year, may be called his *time-earnings,* or *time-wages*: and we may then say that Cliffe Leslie's instances of unequal time-wages tend on the whole to support, and not to weaken, the presumption that competition adjusts earnings in

---

[1] About fifty years ago correspondence between farmers in the North and the South of England led to an agreement that putting roots into a cart was an excellent measure of physical efficiency: and careful comparison showed that wages bore about the same proportion to the weights which the labourers commonly loaded in a day's work in the two districts. The standards of wages and of efficiency in the South are perhaps now more nearly on a level with those in the North than they were then. But the standard trade union wages are generally higher in the North than in

the South: and many men, who go North to reach the higher rate, find that they cannot do what is required, and return.

occupations of equal difficulty and in neighbouring places to the efficiency of the workers.

But the ambiguity of the phrase, "the efficiency of the workers," has not yet been completely cleared away. When the payment for work of any kind is apportioned to the quantity and quality of the work turned out, it is said that uniform rates of *piece-work* wages are being paid; and if two persons work under the same conditions and with equally good appliances, they are paid in proportion to their efficiencies when they receive piece-work wages calculated by the same lists of prices for each several kind of work. If however the appliances are not equally good, a uniform rate of piece-work wages gives results disproportionate to the efficiency of the workers. If, for instance, the same lists of piece-work wages were used in cotton mills supplied with old-fashioned machinery, as in those which have the latest improvements, the apparent equality would represent a real inequality. The more effective competition is, and the more perfectly economic freedom and enterprise are developed, the more surely will the lists be higher in the mills that have old-fashioned machinery than in the others.

In order therefore to give its right meaning to the statement that economic freedom and enterprise tend to equalize wages in occupations of the same difficulty and in the same neighbourhood, we require the use of a new term. We may find it in *efficiency-wages,* or more broadly *efficiency-earnings*; that is, earnings measured, not as time-earnings are with reference to the time spent in earning them; and not as piece-work earnings are with reference to the amount of output resulting from the work by which they are earned; but with reference to the exertion of ability and *efficiency* required of the worker.

The tendency then of economic freedom and enterprise (or, in more common phrase, of competition), to cause every one's earnings to find their own level, is a tendency to equality of efficiency-earnings in the same district. This tendency will be the stronger, the greater is the mobility of labour; the less strictly specialized it is, the more keenly parents are on the lookout for the most advantageous occupations for their children, the more rapidly they are able to adapt themselves to changes in economic conditions, and lastly the slower and the less violent these changes are. . . .

§1. The action of demand and supply with regard to labour was discussed in the last chapter. . . .But some peculiarities in this action remain to be studied. We shall find that the influence of many of them is not at all to be measured by their first and most obvious effects: and that those effects which are cumulative are generally far more important in the long run than those which are not, however prominent the latter may appear.

The problem has thus much in common with that of tracing the economic influence of custom. For it has already been noticed, and it will become more clear as we go on, that the direct effects of custom in causing a thing to be sold for a price sometimes a little higher and sometimes a little lower than it would otherwise fetch, are not really of very great importance, because any such divergence does not, as a rule, tend to perpetuate and increase itself; but on the contrary, if it becomes considerable, it tends itself to call into action forces that counteract it. Sometimes these forces break down the custom altogether; but more often they evade it by gradual and imperceptible changes in the character of the thing sold, so that the purchaser really gets a new thing at the old price under the old name. These direct effects then are obvious, but they are not cumulative. On the other hand, the indirect effects of custom in hindering the methods of production and the character of producers from developing themselves freely are not obvious; but they generally are cumulative, and therefore exert a deep and controlling influence over the history of the world. If custom checks the progress of one generation, then the next generation starts from a lower level than it otherwise would have done; and any retardation which it suffers itself is accumulated and added to that of its predecessor, and so on from generation to generation.[2]

And so it is with regard to the action of demand and supply on the earnings of labour. If at any time it presses hardly on any indi-

[2]It ought, however, to be remarked that some of the beneficial effects of custom are cumulative. For among the many different things that are included under the wide term "custom" are crystallized forms of high ethical principles, rules of honourable and courteous behaviour, and of the avoidance of troublesome strife about paltry gains; and much of the good influence which these exert on race character is cumulative. Compare [ii.], 2.

viduals or class, the direct effects of the evils are obvious. But the sufferings that result are of different kinds: those, the effects of which end with the evil by which they were caused, are not generally to be compared in importance with those that have the indirect effect of lowering the character of the workers or of hindering it from becoming stronger. For these last cause further weakness and further suffering, which again in their turn cause yet further weakness and further suffering, and so on cumulatively. On the other hand, high earnings, and a strong character, lead to greater strength and higher earnings, which again lead to still greater strength and still higher earnings, and so on cumulatively.

§ 2. The first point to which we have to direct our attention is the fact that human agents of production are not bought and sold as machinery and other material agents of production are. The worker sells his work, but he himself remains his own property: those who bear the expenses of rearing and educating him receive but very little of the price that is paid for his services in later years.

Whatever deficiencies the modern methods of business may have, they have at least this virtue, that he who bears the expenses of production of material goods, receives the price that is paid for them. He who builds factories or steam-engines or houses, or rears slaves, reaps the benefit of all net services which they render so long as he keeps them for himself; and when he sells them he gets a price which is the estimated net value of their future services; and therefore he extends his outlay until there seems to him no good reason for thinking that the gains resulting from any further investment would compensate him. He must do this prudently and boldly, under the penalty of finding himself worsted in competition with others who follow a broader and more far-sighted policy, and of ultimately disappearing from the ranks of those who direct the course of the world's business. The action of competition, and the survival in the struggle for existence of those who know best how to extract the greatest benefits for themselves from the environment, tend in the long run to put the building of factories and steam-engines into the hands of those who will be ready and able to incur every expense which will add more than it costs to their value as productive agents. But the investment of capital in the rearing and early training of the workers of England is limited by the resources of parents in the various grades of society, by their power of forecasting the future, and by their willingness to sacrifice themselves for the sake of their children.

This evil is indeed of comparatively small importance with regard to the higher industrial grades. For in those grades most people distinctly realize the future, and "discount it at a low rate of interest." They exert themselves much to select the best careers for their sons, and the best trainings for those careers; and they are generally willing and able to incur a considerable expense for the purpose. The professional classes especially, while generally eager to save some capital *for* their children, are even more on the alert for opportunities of investing it *in* them. And whenever there occurs in the upper grades of industry a new opening for which an extra and special education is required, the future gains need not be very high relatively to the present outlay, in order to secure a keen competition for the post.

But in the lower ranks of society the evil is great. For the slender means and education of the parents, and the comparative weakness of their power of distinctly realizing the future, prevent them from investing capital in the education and training of their children with the same free and bold enterprise with which capital is applied to improving the machinery of any well-managed factory. Many of the children of the working-classes are imperfectly fed and clothed; they are housed in a way that promotes neither physical nor moral health; they receive a school education which, though in modern England it may not be very bad so far as it goes, yet goes only a little way; they have few opportunities of getting a broader view of life or an insight into the nature of the higher work of business, of science or of art; they meet hard and exhausting toil early on the way, and for the greater part keep to it all their lives. At least they go to the grave carrying with them undeveloped abilities and faculties; which, if they could have borne full fruit, would have added to the material wealth of the country—to say nothing of higher considerations—many times as much as would have covered the expense of providing adequate opportunities for their development.

But the point on which we have specially to insist now is that this evil is cumulative. The worse fed are the children of one generation, the less will they earn when they grow up, and the less will be their power of providing adequately for the material wants of their children; and so on to following generations. And again, the less fully their own faculties are developed, the less will they realize the importance of developing the best faculties of their children, and the less will be their power of doing so. And conversely any change that awards to the workers of one generation better earnings, together with better opportunities of developing their best qualities, will increase the material and moral advantages which they have the power to offer to their children: while by increasing their own intelligence, wisdom and forethought, such a change will also to some extent increase their willingness to sacrifice their own pleasures for the wellbeing of their children; though there is much of that willingness now even among the poorest classes, so far as their means and the limits of their knowledge will allow. . . .

§ 5. The next of those characteristics of the action of demand and supply peculiar to labour, which we have to study, lies in the fact that when a person sells his services, he has to present himself where they are delivered. It matters nothing to the seller of bricks whether they are to be used in building a palace or a sewer: but it matters a great deal to the seller of labour, who undertakes to perform a task of given difficulty, whether or not the place in which it is to be done is a wholesome and a pleasant one, and whether or not his associates will be such as he cares to have. In those yearly hirings which still remain in some parts of England, the labourer inquires what sort of a temper his new employer has, quite as carefully as what rate of wages he pays.

This peculiarity of labour is of great importance in many individual cases, but it does not often exert a broad and deep influence of the same nature as that last discussed. The more disagreeable the incidents of an occupation, the higher of course are the wages required to attract people into it: but whether these incidents do lasting and widespreading harm depends on whether they are such as to undermine men's physical health and strength or to lower their character. When they are not of this sort, they are indeed evils in themselves, but they do not generally cause other evils beyond themselves; their effects are seldom cumulative.

Since however no one can deliver his labour in a market in which he is not himself present, it follows that the mobility of labour and the mobility of the labourer are convertible terms: and the unwillingness to quit home, and to leave old associations, including perhaps some loved cottage and burial-ground, will often turn the scale against a proposal to seek better wages in a new place. And when the different members of a family are engaged in different trades, and a migration, which would be advantageous to one member would be injurious to others, the inseparability of the worker from his work considerably hinders the adjustment of the supply of labour to the demand for it. But of this more hereafter.

§ 6. Again, labour is often sold under special disadvantages, arising from the closely connected group of facts that labour power is "perishable," that the sellers of it are commonly poor and have no reserve fund, and that they cannot easily withhold it from the market.

Perishableness is an attribute common to the labour of all grades: the time lost when a worker is thrown out of employment cannot be recovered, though in some cases his energies may be refreshed by rest. It must however be remembered that much of the working power of material agents of production is perishable in the same sense; for a great part of the income, which they also are prevented from earning by being thrown out of work, is completely lost. There is indeed some saving of wear-and-tear on a factory, or a steam-ship, when it is lying idle: but this is often small compared with the income which its owners have to forego: they get no compensation for their loss of interest on the capital invested, or for the depreciation which it undergoes from the action of the elements or from its tendency to be rendered obsolete by new inventions.

Again, many vendible commodities are perishable. In the strike of dock labourers in London in 1889, the perishableness of the fruit, meat, etc., on many of the ships told strongly on the side of the strikers.

The want of reserve funds and of the power of long withholding their labour from the market is common to nearly all grades of those whose work is chiefly with their hands. But it is especially true of unskilled labourers, partly because their wages leave very little margin for saving, partly because when any group of them suspends work, there are large numbers who are capable of filling their places. . . .

But these statements do not apply to all kinds of labour. . . .

It is . . . certain that manual labourers as a class are at a disadvantage in bargaining; and that the disadvantage wherever it exists is likely to be cumulative in its effects. For though, so long as there is any competition among employers at all, they are likely to bid for labour something not very much less than its real value to them, that is, something not very much less than the highest price they would pay rather than go on without it; yet anything that lowers wages tends to lower the efficiency of the labourer's work, and therefore to lower the price which the employer would rather pay than go without that work. The effects of the labourer's disadvantage in bargaining are therefore cumulative in two ways. It lowers his wages; and as we have seen, this lowers his efficiency as a worker, and thereby lowers the normal value of his labour. And in addition it diminishes his efficiency as a bargainer, and thus increases the chance that he will sell his labour for less than its normal value.

§ 1. The next peculiarity in the action of demand and supply with regard to labour, which we have to consider, is closely connected with some of those we have already discussed. It consists in the length of time that is required to prepare and train labour for its work, and in the slowness of the returns which result from this training.

This discounting of the future, this deliberate adjustment of supply of expensively trained labour to the demand for it, is most clearly seen in the choice made by parents of occupations for their children, and in their efforts to raise their children into a higher grade than their own. . . .

§ 2. Not much less than a generation elapses between the choice by parents of a skilled trade for one of their children, and his reaping the full results of their choice. And meanwhile the character of the trade may have been almost revolutionized by changes, of which some probably threw long shadows before them, but others were such as could not have been foreseen even by the shrewdest persons and those best acquainted with the circumstances of the trade.

The working classes in nearly all parts of England are constantly on the look-out for advantageous openings for the labour of themselves and their children; and they question friends and relations, who have settled in other districts, as to the wages that are to be got in various trades, and as to their incidental advantages and disadvantages. But it is very difficult to ascertain the causes that are likely to determine the distant future of the trades which they are selecting for their children; and there are not many who enter on this abstruse inquiry. The majority assume without a further thought that the condition of each trade in their own time sufficiently indicates what it will be in the future; and, so far as the influence of this habit extends, the supply of labour in a trade in any one generation tends to conform to its earnings not in that but in the preceding generation. . . .

§ 4. Let us now revert to the principle that the income derived from the appliances for the production of a commodity exerts a controlling influence in the long run over their own supply and price, and therefore over the supply and the price of the commodity itself; but that within short periods there is not time for the exercise of any considerable influence of this kind. And let us inquire how this principle needs to be modified when it is applied not to the material agents of production, which are only a means towards an end, and which may be the private property of the capitalist, but to human beings who are ends as well as means of production and who remain their own property.

To begin with we must notice that, since labour is slowly produced and slowly worn out, we must take the term "long period" more strictly, and regard it as generally implying a greater duration, when we are considering the relations of normal demand and supply for labour, than when we are considering them for ordinary commodities. There are many problems, the period of which is long enough to enable the supply of ordinary commodities, and even of most of the material appliances required for making them, to be adjusted to the demand; and long enough therefore to justify us in regarding the average prices of those commodities during the period as "normal," and as equal to their normal expenses of production in a fairly broad use of the term; while yet the period would not be long enough to allow the supply of labour to be adjusted at all well to the demand for it. The average earnings of labour during this period therefore would not be at all certain to give about a normal return to those who provided the labour; but they would rather have to be regarded as determined by the available stock of labour on the one hand, and the demand for it on the other. . . .

To conclude this part of our argument. The market price of everything, *i.e.,* its price for short periods, is determined mainly by the relations in which the demand for it stands to the available stocks of it; and in the case of any agent of production, whether it be a human or a material agent, this demand is "derived" from the demand for those things which it is used in making. In these relatively short periods fluctuations in wages follow, and do not precede, fluctuations in the selling prices of the goods produced.

But the incomes which are being earned by all agents of production, human as well as material, and those which apppear likely to be earned by them in the future, exercise a ceaseless influence on those persons by whose action the future supplies of these agents are determined. There is a constant tendency towards a position of normal equilibrium, in which the supply of each of these agents shall stand in such a relation to the demand for its services, as to give to those who have provided the supply a sufficient reward for their efforts and sacrifices. If the economic conditions of the country remained   stationary sufficiently long, this tendency would realize itself in such an adjustment of supply to demand, that both machines and human beings would earn generally an amount that corresponded fairly with their cost of rearing and training, conventional necessaries as well as those things which are strictly necessary being reckoned for. But conventional necessaries might change under the influence of non-economic causes, even while economic conditions themselves were stationary: and this change would affect the supply of labour, and would lessen the national dividend and slightly alter its distribution. As it is, the economic conditions of the country are constantly changing, and the point of adjustment of normal demand and supply in relation to labour is constantly being shifted.

8.   The Balkanization of Labor Markets

Clark Kerr

Labor markets are more talked about than seen, for their dimensions most frequently are set by the unknown and, perhaps, mystic ideas in people's minds. A worker wishes to be employed in a certain area and at a certain type of job, and an employer wants employees drawn from certain groups and possessing certain characteristics. Unless it is said that each worker always has his own market area and each employer his,[1] there must be some adding of worker and employer preferences to get designated "markets."

[1] If this is said, then the term "market," with all it implies, might better be dropped. Instead, attention should be directed to the scales of preference of individual workers and individual employers. This approach might very well constitute a gain for realism and for precision but a loss for comprehension. It probably is true that no two people are alike, and for some purposes this is the relevant generalization; but it is also probably true that all people need to eat, and for other purposes this is the relevant generalization. The use of the term "labor market" implies that there is enough uniformity of behavior among certain workers and among certain employers to warrant generalizations about the actions of each as a group. Thus it might be said that the labor market for waitresses in Oakland is characterized (among other things) by sellers who want part-time employment and buyers who prefer married women, or by high turnover, or by a lack of formal structure.

These preferences vary from person to person and from time to time for the same person, and when they are totaled the "market" that they constitute has vague and varying contours but no ultimate limits short of those for American society itself. For example, there is said to be a market for waitresses in Oakland with certain women normally attached to it and certain employers hiring from it. Since, however, a woman need not always be a waitress once having been one and a woman never having been one can become one and since a restaurant employer can hire a girl from San Francisco as well as from Oakland, the market is by no means a self-contained one with precise limits. Preferences of workers and employers are also relative to time. In a depression, a "waitress" may consider herself also available for work in a laundry, and a restaurant employer in wartime may be willing to hire former laundry workers to serve as waitresses.

Most labor markets are similarly indefinite in their specification of the sellers and the buyers. Such a labor market is merely an area, with indistinct geographical and occupational limits within which certain workers customarily seek to offer their services and certain employers to purchase them. But any single worker or any single employer may decide to go elsewhere. This might be identified as the "free choice" market or the "natural market,"[2] for which the individual and changing preferences of workers and employers set the hazy limits.

THE INSTITUTIONAL MARKET

An increasing number of labor markets, however, are more specifically defined at any moment of time and have their dimensions less constantly changed over time. These are the "institutional markets." Their dimensions are set not by the whims of workers and employers but by rules, both formal and informal. These rules state which workers are preferred in the market or even which ones may operate in it at all, and which employers may or must buy in this market if they are to buy at all. Institutional rules take the place of individual preferences in setting the boundaries. Such institutional rules are established by employers' associations, by the informal understandings of employers among each other (the "gentlemen's agreement"), by companies when they set up their personnel policies, by trade unions, by collective agreements, and by actions of government. They contrast with the independent preferences of the individuals who are directly involved.

Economists once spoke of *the* labor market. Each worker competed with all other workers for jobs, and each employer with all other employers for workers. Cairnes, however, early saw there were noncompeting groups:[3]

> No doubt the various ranks and classes fade into each other by imperceptible gradations, and individuals from all classes are constantly passing up or down; but while this is so, it is nevertheless true that the average workman, from whatever rank he be taken, finds his power of competition limited for practical purposes to a certain range of occupations, so that, however high the rates of remuneration in those which lie beyond may rise, he is excluded from sharing them. We are thus compelled to recognize the existence of noncompeting industrial groups as a feature of our economy.

[2] See Clark Kerr, "Labor Markets: Their Character and Consequences," *Papers and Proceedings,* American Economic Association, May 1950.

[3] J. E. Cairnes, *Political Economy,* Harper, New York, 1874, pp. 67-68.

Cairnes used the word "compelled" advisedly. For the existence of "noncompeting" groups adds both complications to economic analysis and impediments to the maximization of welfare. Economic society would be both simpler to understand and closer to the economist's prescription if there were only one labor market.

In the long run, perhaps over several generations, it may be correct to talk about *the* labor market. Unless society has a hereditary class system, social mobility over time will permit, if not all, at least many individuals or their descendants to prepare themselves for any specific line of work. But a medical practitioner of today can hardly be said to be competing in the market with the unborn son of a pipe fitter. Yet in the long run, defined as the time it takes for the greatest occupational shift to work itself out, *the* labor market may be said to exist.

In the long run all families may compete with all other families, but in the short run most individuals are not in competition with each other. In fact, at any instant of time the standard case is one man faced by one job—this one job is available to only this one man, and this man has only this one job available to him. We are more concerned, however, with labor markets in the short run when several men and several jobs, rather than all men and all jobs or one man and one job, may face each other. In the short run a worker can make himself available for several jobs, according to his preferences, and an employer can make a job available to several workers, according to his preferences.

The noncompeting groups of Cairnes were the several socio-economic classes (manual, white-collar, professional workers, and so forth). We have found, however, that each of these classes is composed in turn of many largely noncompeting groups. Painters do not compete with bricklayers, or typists with accountants, or doctors with lawyers; nor individuals in Portland, Maine, with those in Portland, Oregon (except perhaps in certain professions). Barriers to movement are set up by the skill gaps between occupations and the distance gaps between locations. Beyond the specificity of skills and the money costs of physical transfer, lie such various but no less important impediments to competition as lack of knowledge, the job tastes of workers, their inertia and their desire for security, and the personal predilections of employers. The competitive market areas within which somewhat similar men look for somewhat similar jobs, and within which somewhat similar employers try to fill somewhat similar jobs, are normally quite restricted. It has even been suggested that the only meaningful definition of a labor market is one which calls each place of employment a separate market[4] and, perhaps, beyond that, each separate class of work at each such place. More commonly, it is said that a labor market covers the several employers in the same industry in the same area. Thus there are markets and submarkets, all more or less interrelated with each other. The introduction of institutional rules, as we shall see presently, generally creates a larger number of such markets and universally makes them less interrelated.

Institutional rules put added structure into labor markets. Lloyd Fisher has lucidly described the "structureless market" for harvest labor in California.[5] The characteristics of this market serve as a point of contrast for the market types to be described later. The structureless market, according to Fisher, has five conditions: (1) there are no unions with seniority and other rules, (2) the relation between the employee and the employer is a transitory, impersonal one, (3) the workers are unskilled, (4) payment is by unit of product, and (5) little capital or machinery is employed. The employer prefers one worker to another only if he accepts a lower piece rate and the worker one employer over another only if he will pay a higher piece rate. Rates vary greatly over time, but at any moment of time are uniform over space. There are no structural barriers to the mobility of workers and to the fluidity of rates. The only nexus is cash.

Structure is introduced into labor markets even without institutional rules. Many workers have skills which restrict the occupational area in which they seek work, and the number of these skills limits the supply to the employer. Moreover, workers and employers form attachments for each other which neither like to break lightly—"You must realize that the labor market is like the marriage market"[6]—and separation is for cause only. Thus most jobs, even without institutional rules, belong to single workers or to small groups of workers. The craft exists without the craft union, and informal job ties exist without formal seniority rules. Institutional rules, however, add new rights and new preferences and strengthen the old ties.

Institutional labor markets create truly noncompeting groups. Markets are more specifically delimited, and entrance into them, movement within them, and exit from them more precisely defined. Such labor markets find their definition not in the composite of individual preferences but in precise rules. "Natural" frictions are replaced by institutional ones; the free and ignorant man by the exclusive and knowledgeable group. Market forces, seemingly impersonal in the aggregate but exceedingly personal in individual situations, give way to personnel rules which may seem exceedingly impersonal when applied to specific workers. Fraternity triumphs over liberty as "no trespassing" signs are posted in more and more job markets.

The sources of this enclosure movement are not far to seek. Employing units are larger, and bureaucratic rules take the place of individual judgments. These rules accept or reject classes of people, instead of the single individuals who met or failed to meet the tests of judgment or the prejudices of the small employer or the foreman. Workers have organized into unions which seek to establish sovereignty over a "job territory." Within this job territory work the citizens who belong to this private government; outside are the noncitizens without rights. The demands of all citizens will be met before the petitions of the aliens are considered. The institutionalization of labor markets is one aspect of the general trend from the atomistic to the pluralistic, and from the largely open to the partially closed society.

---

[4]"There are as many labor markets as there are employers of labor." (Gordon F. Bloom and Herbert R. Northrup, *Economics of Labor and Industrial Relations,* Blakiston, Philadelphia, 1950, p. 265.) Lloyd G. Reynolds states: "The firm is the hiring unit and . . . each company employment office is really a distinct market for labor." (*The Structure of Labor Markets,* Harper, New York, 1951, p. 42.)

[5]Lloyd H. Fisher, "The Harvest Labor Market in California," *Quarterly Journal of Economics,* Nov. 1951.

[6]Kenneth Boulding, *The Impact of the Union,* ed. David McCord Wright, Harcourt, Brace and Co., New York, 1951, p. 254.

TYPES OF INSTITUTIONAL MARKETS

Many barriers divide the totality of employment relationships into more or less distinct compartments. These barriers have five sources: (1) the preferences of individual workers, (2) the preferences of individual employers, (3) the actions of the community of workers, (4) the actions of the community of employers, and (5) the actions of government. The controls on movement flowing from the last three are defined as institutional rules, whether they are written or merely understood, as compared with the "free choices" flowing from the first two.

The institutional rules of employers, workers, and government are enormously varied, reflecting as they do a diversity of environments and desires, and consequently it is difficult to generalize about them. There are, however, two general systems of rules, each with important subtypes. We shall discuss here only the two broad systems and not all the variations of each, significant as they are. The two systems are the communal-ownership approach of craft groups and the private-property method of industrial workers.

Communal ownership. The craft union asserts proprietorship on behalf of its members over the jobs falling within a carefully defined occupational and geographical area. Employers needing the specified occupational skill in that area must hire union members or take the consequences. The building, printing, maritime, and teamster trades illustrate this type of arrangement.

Workers enter the market through the unions; and the unions have preferences just as do employers. They may be in favor of or against Negroes, or women, or students, or Communist party members, and these preferences will show up in the labor supply made available.[7] Entrance is sometimes through closely supervised apprenticeship systems[8]

[7]Thus the "membership function" of the union, because of its restrictive preferences, may lie to the left of the "market-supply function." (See John T. Dunlop, *Wage Determination under Trade Unions,* The Macmillan Co., New York, 1944, p. 33.) The employer may also, however, because of his preferences, draw from less than the total supply of efficient workers potentially available to him.

[8]The classic discussion of apprenticeship, as of other union rules, is by Sumner H. Slichter, *Union Policies*

which require the worker to choose his specific occupation early in life and make initial sacrifices in order to gain admittance. These apprenticeship programs are usually pursued with government aid. Admission may also be by transfer card from another local. Occasionally, as in the case of the typographical workers, the man with a transfer card has equal rights with some local members. More frequently, however, he must go to the end of the list and wait until all local members are employed. The transfer card gives him preference only over new applicants for membership. When work is abnormally plentiful, some unions issue work permits, analogous to visas, which entitle outsiders to temporary employment. When employment returns to normal, they lose their privileges. They are renters, not owners.

Once fully in the market, the craft worker can move anywhere within it. Sometimes, when there is a hiring hall with rotation of work, as for longshoremen on the Pacific Coast, he may move throughout the market. Inside the market, wages, working conditions, and job requirements are equalized, and the worker has an unusual knowledge of conditions and job opportunities. Sometimes worker performance is standardized also,[9] so that no employer need prefer any worker any more than any worker need prefer any employer. Though the men within the market are equal with each other, they are unequal with others outside the market. A little equalitarian island has been created in the midst of a sea of inequality.

Movement of workers is vitally affected. Occupational identification is unchanging and, largely because of this, other types of movement are encouraged—from one plant to another and even one industry or one locality to another. Since some fluidity is necessary in a progressive society, a tight tie to occupation forces a looser tie to employer, industry, and locality. Movement is primarily horizontal in the craft market. The worker gets his security not from the individual employer but from his skill, the competitive supply of which is controlled by his union; and he is known as a carpenter and not as an employee of a certain

and Industrial Management, Brookings Institution, Washington, 1941.

[9]When it is not standardized, competition among workers is by degree of skill. The more skilled workers are in greater demand.

company. Just as the worker is free to move from employer to employer, so also are employers free to encourage such movement. "Gentlemen's agreements" against "pirating" are not the mark of the craft trades.

Ejection from the market is controlled by the union. An employer can discharge a man from a specific job but not from the market. Few discharge grievances are filed in craft markets because the man gets his security from union control of the market and not from the employer. The union, however, may eject a man, but its reasons are not normally the same as those actuating employers. Political sins are given a higher order of value as compared with the economic sins which an employer is more apt to punish. Union ejections, which are infrequent, are not so subject to appeal to third parties as are employer discharges. . . .

Private property. In the industrial enterprise, the central rule is to each man one job and to each job one man. The typical market consists of one job for which one man is available. This is an exaggerated description of the average situation, for ability usually counts as well as seniority, but since the trend is toward strict seniority provisions it may stand as a statement of the central tendency. The man on the job (given good behavior) is the only man eligible for it, and when he leaves the next man on the seniority list (given minimum ability to perform the task) is the only eligible candidate. The market has been reduced to the irreducible minimum.

The production contract does not define the occupation. It sets forth the plant or company or industry. The plant or company or industry is the market. New workers are hired by the company,[10] not the union, but the union may impose its scale of preferences on the employer. It may, for example, refuse to accept Negroes or it may, alternatively, prohibit the employer from discriminating against Negroes. Bargained rules, however, usually first become operative once the employee is hired. The union then seeks to set a rising scale of jobs and a rising hierarchy of workers. As jobs open up, the workers move up in order; and as they close they move down in order. The worker temporarily laid off still holds his place on the seniority roster. For each job there is a worker and

thus a whole series of submarkets where one job and one man are paired.

Two important qualifications must be entered here. First, many contracts do not provide for straight seniority but for some combination of seniority and ability. Jobs are posted and all men who claim the necessary qualificiations may compete. But this is still an internal submarket to which persons outside the plant have little or no access. Second, usually there are several families of jobs—production, maintenance, sales, white-collar—each with a contact point with the outside world and with an internal hierarchy of men and jobs related to each other. These families of jobs constitute noncompeting classes within the plant.

The employer, and occasionally the union (for nonpayment of dues or some other offense against the union), can separate the man from the market, usually subject to appeal to a third party. Institutional rules, set forth in a contract, often specify the proper causes for discharge—inefficiency, insubordination, and so forth.

The worker is held within this marketing apparatus not alone by prospects of advancement within the plant. He may be tied to it by a pension plan as well. More important, perhaps, is what would happen to him if he wished to leave. First of all, he would need to quit his job before finding another one since other employers, under the customary gentlemen's agreement against pirating, would be reluctant to hire him away from his firm;[11] and, second, in most cases, he would need to start again at the bottom of the seniority ladder in some other plant with lower status and income.

Movement, as in the craft case, is affected, but in a reverse fashion. Movement to another employer is greatly discouraged but change of occupation is almost automatic.[12] The important market for the worker is the internal plant market with its many submarkets spelled out in great detail. Movement is vertical in the

---

[10]For a study of employer hiring preferences, see E. William Noland and E. Wight Bakke, *Workers Wanted,* Harper, New York, 1949.

[11]For a discussion of the importance of "gentlemen's agreements," see Charles A. Myers and W. Rupert Maclaurin, *The Movement of Factory Workers,* The Technology Press and John Wiley & Sons, New York, 1943, p. 39.

[12]Most labor market studies find the worker's chief attachment is to his occupation, yet the essence of the seniority approach is to create an employee largely devoid of narrow occupational attachment.

plant instead of horizontal as in the craft market; and workers fight over seniority rights instead of unions over craft jurisdictions. The "haves" are separated from the "have-nots" not by a union card, but by a place on the seniority roster. When the "haves" compete among themselves, it is more in relation to the accumulation of seniority than in relation to the possession of skill.

Governmental policy supports both the communal-ownership and the private-property systems. Apprenticeship programs bolster the former; unemployment compensation rules, since they do not require an employee to leave his accustomed occupation or place of residence to accept work as a condition for the receipt of benefits, help hold workers available for openings in the same craft[13] or the same plant. These rules accept worker attachment to craft and to employer,[14] and support a pool of workers in slack times into which the union or employer can dip.

Neither the craft nor the industrial institutional rules are completely new departures. Even without formal contracts, the craft worker holds to his craft, and the industrial worker to his plant. Employers hired craft workers for craft jobs and promoted from within before closed shops and seniority clauses tightened the rules. The institutional rules, however, do match men and jobs more precisely in the craft case, and the man and the job in the industrial case, than was done informally before their introduction.[15]

---

[13]In some states, unemployed workers report to the union hiring hall to demonstrate their availability for work rather than to the employment service.

[14]A study in Nashua, New Hampshire, found, however, that many workers took lower-paid jobs in preference to staying on unemployment compensation. But this was a situation where a large plant had ceased operation and would not reopen. (Charles A. Myers and George P. Shultz, *Dynamics of a Labor Market,* Prentice-Hall, New York, 1951, p. 100.)

[15]The case of the operating crafts in the railroad system is an interesting one, for it has elements of both the craft and industrial patterns. Normally, craft workers can obtain transfer cards, but production workers cannot transfer seniority from one plant to another. On the railroads, seniority rights are rigidly defined but employees do have the right to take their seniority to another location and "bump" less senior men there.

INSTITUTIONAL LABOR MARKETS IN OPERATION

Ports of entry. Not all jobs are open at all times to all bidders except in the structureless market. Even in the absence of institutional rules, most employers consider a job not open for bid so long as the incumbent fills it satisfactorily; and employers generally prefer to promote from within to canvassing the outside market. Institutional rules, however, set sharper boundaries between the "internal" and "external" markets and define more precisely the points of entrance.[16] In the craft case, the internal market is the area covered by the jurisdiction of the local union, and in the industrial case it is the individual plant. The port of entry in the former instance is the union office, and union membership (achieved through apprenticeship, transfer, or application) provides access to all the jobs on the inside. In the latter

---

[16]Labor markets are of two broad types: (1) the structureless and (2) the structured. In the structureless market, there is no attachment except the wage between the worker and the employer. No worker has any claim on any job and no employer has any hold on any man. Structure enters the market when different treatment is accorded to the "ins" and to the "outs." In the structured market there always exists (1) the internal market and (2) the external market. The internal market may be the plant or the craft group, and preferment within it may be based on prejudice or merit or equality of opportunity or seniority or some combination of these. The external market consists of clusters of workers actively or passively available for new jobs lying within some meaningful geographical and occupational boundaries, and of the port or ports of entry which are open or are potentially open to them. It may happen that some such markets have only one port of entry, but this can hardly be the standard case as Northrup and Reynolds state (Northrup, *op. cit.,* p. 265, and Reynolds, *op. cit.,* p. 42). They may be right where certain large manufacturing plants are involved, but more commonly such a cluster of workers will face several ports of entry. The extreme cases would be (*a*) one worker facing one port of entry and (*b*) large numbers of workers facing a large number of ports of entry. The more structured the market, the more precise will be the rules on allocation of opportunity within the internal market and the fewer will be the ports of entry and the more rigid will be the requirements for admission. Institutional rules do not usually introduce structure into a market—it often arises from the individual preferences of workers and employers—but they uniformly add to it.

case, there are usually several ports of entry (each reached through the company personnel office)—common labor for production workers, lower clerical occupations for the white-collar workers, and junior posts for sales and executive personnel, among others—although if qualified candidates are not available almost any job on an *ad hoc* basis may be opened to outsiders.[17] The external market is the totality of the labor force outside this one market or submarket, or at least that part of it which potentially might like to gain entry.

Thus the internal market has points of contact with the external market rather than interconnections all along the line-up of jobs. Workers inside the market, though they may compete with each other in a limited way, are not in direct competition with persons outside. Outside workers compete directly with each other, not with the inside workers, to gain admittance.

At these ports of entry, the individuals are selected who may enter. Employers have their hiring preferences which are usually dominant when it comes to hiring into the plant, although unions can and do affect these preferences; and the unions have theirs[18] which determine who gains access to the craft, although employers can and do affect them also.

The process of selection is also the process of rejection. Decisions are made in favor of certain individuals but at the same time against others. The individuals and groups which control these ports of entry greatly affect the distribution of opportunities in economic society. The rules that they follow determine how equitably opportunity is spread and the characteristics for which men are rewarded and for which they are penalized. The controlling individuals and groups may and do choose between prospective efficiency and prospective social acceptability. Since labor resources are being distributed, as well as individual opportunities, the comparative emphasis on efficiency and on acceptability affects the productivity of the economic system. When men fail to find jobs, it may be because there are not enough jobs to go around, or because they do not know about the

jobs which do exist or do not think such jobs fit their expectations, or because they do not meet the specifications set by employers and unions. In the last case, as the specifications become more formal and cover more jobs, determination of the specifications becomes of increasing concern to persons in the external market who are universally unrepresented in the councils which set the specifications. For society to remain free and open, many ports of entry should exist and the immigration barriers should not hold outside the able and the willing. . . .

All societies are stratified to a degree, although the degrees vary enormously, and a key element in any society is the character and the intensity of stratification. For our purposes here we shall designate three systems of organization: the "open," the "guild," and the "manorial." The pre-Cairnes classical version of the labor market was of the truly open type—all workers competed for all jobs all of the time. The guild system stratifies the labor force horizontally. Walter Galenson has described such a "closed labor market" under the control of craft unions as it operates in Denmark.[19] The manorial system places its emphasis not on skill but on attachment to the place of work and thus on vertical stratification. The industrial worker may demonstrate (albeit for somewhat different reasons) the same perpetual adherence to the plant as the serf did to the soil of the estate, although he does have opportunities for upward movement unknown to the serf.

The institutional rules we have been discussing move the labor force farther away from the open system of the classical economists which never, however, was as open as they thought it was or hoped it might be. But as it moves toward the guild and manorial systems, which will predominate? For they follow quite different principles of societal organization. The conflict in the United States evidences itself in the conflict between craft and industrial unions over the representation of skilled workers in industrial plants, in the effort of skilled workers in such plants to have their own job families and seniority lists, in the insistence of craft workers that their wages follow the

---

[17]Thus there are more ports of entry in a period of prosperity than in a period of depression.

[18]For a discussion of union preferences, see Clyde Summers, "Admission Policies of Labor Unions," *Quarterly Journal of Economics,* Nov. 1946.

[19]Walter Galenson, *The Danish System of Labor Relations,* Harvard University Press, 1952, pp. 195-200. See also remarks by Gladys Palmer on European labor markets in a paper presented to the Industrial Relations Research Association, May 1952.

market rather than the dictates of a job evaluation plan dedicated to internal consistency. In Denmark, the guild system is dominant; in Germany, with all the paternalistic devices of large employers and the life-long attachment of the worker to his plant, the manorial system, and this is one source of the union insistence on codirection at the plant level.

The stratification of the labor force affects the worker as citizen. Is he a free-roving mobile person ranging widely horizontally and vertically and probably having a middle-class outlook,[20] is he a carpenter, or is he a UAW-GM man? How he is located economically will affect his view of society and his personal identification with society and its constituent groups, and thus his political behavior.

Institutional rules and wage setting. "Potential mobility," Hicks noted, "is the ultimate sanction for the interrelations of wage rates."[21] Other sanctions do exist and many times are the more important, but the less the potential mobility of workers the less the economic pressures that relate wage rates to each other. Institutional rules, to the extent that they reduce mobility, also lessen the economic pressures. As we have seen, some internal markets are quite isolated from their external markets by the working of these rules, and the interrelatedness of wage rates may be traced more to political, ethical, or operational than to labor market considerations. How do the rules we have been discussing impinge on the wage-setting process?

Extensive discussions with craft union leaders and the employers dealing with them in the San Francisco Bay area indicate that these unions do not generally use their control over the supply of labor to force up wage rates. They employ it rather to adjust supply to demand once the wage has been fixed.[22] If the supply falls too far short of demand, the employers are encouraged to introduce machinery or look to another craft for workers or even to

non-union men. If the supply is too great, some union members are unemployed. This is politically uncomfortable for the union leaders and may require the members to undertake some work-sharing device. Further, employers may point to this unemployed group at the next wage negotiations and the members may be less willing to support wage demands with an effective strike threat. All in all, it is better to adjust supply to demand as closely as possible. This is done by controlling the flow of new members and by issuing work permits.

In neo-classical wage theory, supply (which is assumed to be relatively fixed in the short run) and demand are the independent variables which simultaneously determine the wage and the volume of employment. The standard craft market process runs instead along these lines: (1) the wage is set by collective bargaining in response to many considerations (including economic ones) and usually for a one-year duration; (2) demand which changes constantly determines the amount of employment at the fixed rate; and (3) supply is constantly adjusted by the union to keep close contact with the changing volume of jobs offered by the employers.[23] Control over supply is used more to preserve the integrity of the wage rate rather than to create it.[24] The wage rate determines supply more than supply the wage rate. Demand itself is subject to some control (foremen are limited in the work they may perform; one man may handle only so many machines; certain work must be reserved for a certain craft, and so forth). Demand, the wage rate, and supply all respond to more or less control by the bargaining institutions.

The production case is a different one. Industrial unions cannot control the supply of workers. Their attention is turned rather to stabilizing the demand for labor so that all workers with seniority rights may have assured employment, for example, by introducing the

---

[20]S. M. Lipset and Joan Gordon, "Mobility and Trade Union Membership," in *Class, Status and Power,* ed. R. Bendix and S. M. Lipset, The Free Press, Glencoe, Ill., 1953, p. 498.

[21]J. R. Hicks, *The Theory of Wages,* The Macmillan Co., New York, 1935, p. 79.

[22]"The jobs must be rationed among the seekers for jobs. And this is the important economic function which so-called restrictive practices play." (Milton Friedman in *Impact of the Union,* p. 213.)

[23]The supply curve may be shown as a straight line which stops at or shortly before the volume of jobs normally expected at the fixed wage rate. If demand moves to the right temporarily, the supply line can be temporarily extended by the issuance of work permits, which can be cancelled if it moves again back toward the left.

[24]This sets the craft groups apart from certain professional groups. These professional groups do not control the wage (the fee) and so they influence it by control of supply.

guaranteed wage or heavy dismissal bonuses.[25] These devices have no appeal to the craft unions. But, for the industrial union, the supply of workers with seniority rights is fixed, and this makes it more conscious of the impact of fluctuating demand. Institutional rules have two further wage results. Since seniority ties workers to the plant, the industrial union must be more concerned with the effect of a negotiated wage rate on employment. Were it not for seniority rules, wage rates probably could not have deteriorated comparatively so greatly for telegraph and railroad employees during the past quarter of a century. The seniority tie to the industry has reduced the minimum price which would hold the workers in the industry. Industrial unions, also, are more willing than are craft unions to make exceptions to the common rate to meet the necessities of the individual company and its employees. Further, institutional rules by reducing the contact points with the external markets encourage formal or informal job evaluation plans as a means of setting rates acceptable in the internal market.

Under both systems of rules, wage rates are less effective in allocating labor (just as the movement of labor is less potent in setting wage rates) than they are in less structured labor markets.

The locus of control. This reconstitution of labor markets reflects the shift in locus of control from the individual entrepreneur to the bureaucratic manager and to the work group. And with this shift goes a change in values. The entrepreneur felt personally the pressure for efficiency and expressed personally his prejudices, sometimes quite violent, about men. The hired manager and the work group both respond more to considerations of security, of order, and of certainty—and, in the case of the craft group, of preservation of the all-around skilled worker. By making men alike and jobs alike and placing each in a certain order, decisions are more or less automatically made by the rules rather than by individual men;[26] but

these rules can reflect prejudice just as men in their actions can evidence it. These prejudices may be the same (racial) or different (seniority, instead of merit), but prejudices, or perhaps better, value judgments, they remain. The rule of law is still the rule of men—once removed.

A further shift in locus of control may lie in the future. If the laws of the private governments of industry and labor fail by too great a margin to meet the definition of welfare as conceived by the public at large, then government may enter the labor market and try to impose its set of values. For example, in Denmark there is agitation against the closed labor market; and in the United States against discriminatory practices.* The "planned labor market" may succeed the institutional market.[27]

CONCLUSION

Institutional rules in the labor market, as we have seen, establish more boundaries between labor markets and make them more specific and harder to cross. They define the points of competition, the groups which may compete, and the grounds on which they compete. The study of the import of these rules,[28] though less exciting than the examination of wage policies, is more needed. It is debatable whether wage policies of unions and employers have much impact on wage determination. It is not debatable that institutional rules in the labor market do have substantial effects on the performance of our economic system. These rules increasingly affect both the opportunities held open to workers and the contributions which they can make to the national product.

When private functional governments establish rules which so affect the unrepresented worker and the unrepresented consumer, the cry for public intervention is not long in being sounded even though it may not be very loud.

[25]Once the wage has been set, the craft union tries to adjust supply to demand; the industrial union, demand to supply.

[26]The rules are a method of settling the intense disputes between men over job preferment. While the rules settle the individual disputes, they are themselves subject to dispute. See, for example, Leonard R.

Sayles, "Seniority: An Internal Union Problem," *Harvard Business Review,* Jan.-Feb. 1952.

Editor's note: Ten years after this was written, the Civil Rights Act of 1964 outlawed labor market discrimination on the basis of race, color, religion, sex, or national origin.

[27]See Kerr, "Labor Markets: Their Character and Consequences," *op. cit.*

[28]For a list of research suggestions see Gladys L. Palmer, *Research Planning Memorandum on Labor Mobility,* Social Science Research Council, 1947.

Sir William Beveridge has called for "organized mobility" in the labor market,[29] as have others. This cannot be accomplished mainly as a consequence of guaranteeing full employment, as he claims, although full employment does reduce some barriers; for craft unions will want to control entrance to the craft, and industrial unions to provide for seniority rights, regardless of how full employment may be. Nor may the market be made much more fluid by

[29]William H. Beveridge, *Full Employment in a Free Society,* W. W. Norton, New York, 1944, p. 172.

other governmental actions. Seniority rules probably restrict the freedom of the worker and retard his efficiency more than the craft rules which are the customary target of criticism, yet government is not going to do much about them. At most, governmental policy can make more equitable the rules affecting entrance at those points of entry left open by the private agencies. Security will not be taken away from those who own the jobs, but nonowners can be placed on a more equal footing one against another in contesting for the vacancies.

9. Information Networks in Labor Markets

Albert Rees

This paper is not concerned with the information about the labor market provided by labor statistics. Rather it deals with the information that participants in the market have about one another—with the ways in which job seekers find jobs and employers find employees. I shall draw heavily on a study of the Chicago labor market now in progress in which my associates are George P. Shultz, Joseph C. Ullman, David P. Taylor, and Mary Hamilton.[1] The focus of the paper is accordingly on local rather than national markets.

We may divide information networks in the labor market into two groups: formal and informal. The formal networks include the state employment services, private fee-charging employment agencies, newspaper advertisements, union hiring halls, and school or college placement bureaus. The informal sources include referrals from employees, other employers, and miscellaneous sources, and walk-ins or hiring at the gate.

The literature stresses the great importance of the informal channels, and our study of the Chicago labor market offers additional support for this emphasis. In the four white-collar occu-

pations under study, informal sources account for about half of all hires; in the eight blue-collar occupations, informal sources account for more than four-fifths of all hires.

Economists have traditionally taken a dim view of informal networks of labor market information. The typical discussion of channels of employment begins with an analogy between the public employment service and stock or commodity exchanges. To be sure, various reasons are given why the analogy is imperfect and a "grain exchange for labor" cannot be established. But in the end, the disorganization of the labor market is deplored and suggestions are made for the improvement of the employment service.

For example, a recent textbook in labor economics starts a discussion of the effectiveness of the labor market by using the New York Stock Exchange as a model of efficiency. It notes that formal intermediaries in the labor market are not widely used, and concludes that "the worker who sets out to find employment very likely goes through a process of chasing down vague rumors or leads." "All too frequently," it adds, "the buyers and sellers, blindfolded by a lack of knowledge, simply grope about until they bump into each other."[2] I

[1] I am indebted to these associates and to George J. Stigler and Arnold R. Weber for helpful comments on a draft of this paper. I am also indebted to the Ford Foundation for its generous support of this study.

[2] Sanford Cohen, *Labor in the United States* (Charles E. Merrill, 1960), p. 351.

shall argue here that the analogies with commodity and security markets, even when qualified, are mischievous and misleading and that the effectiveness and advantages of informal networks of information have been too little appreciated.

The search for information in any market has both an extensive and an intensive margin. A buyer can search at the extensive margin by getting a quotation from one more seller. He can search at the intensive margin by getting additional information concerning an offer already received. Where the goods and services sold are highly standardized, the extensive margin is the more important; when there is great variation in quality, the intensive margin moves to the forefront. This point can be illustrated by considering the markets for new and used cars. Since there is relatively little variation in the quality of new cars of the same make and model and since the costs of variation are reduced by factory guarantees, the extensive margin of search is the important one. A rational buyer will get quotations from additional dealers until the probable reduction in price from one additional quotation is less than the cost of obtaining it.[3]

In used cars of the same make, model, and year much of the variation in asking prices reflects differences in the condition of the cars, and this calls for a substantial change in the strategy of the rational buyer. He will invest less in obtaining large numbers of offers and much more in examining each car. For example, he may have each car he seriously considers inspected by a mechanic. He may want information on the history of the car as a substitute for the direct assessment of condition and will pass up a used taxi in favor of the car owned by the proverbial little old lady who drives only to church. It will not be irrational for him to pay a relatively high price for a car owned by a friend if he has favorable information about his friend's habits as a car owner.

Organized commodity and security exchanges deal in highly standardized or perfectly uniform contracts, where the intensive margin of search is effectively eliminated. One is entirely indifferent as to whether one buys 100 shares of General Motors from a taxi company, a little old lady, or Alfred P. Sloan, though much search may enter into the decision to buy

General Motors rather than some other security. Organized exchanges perform a highly effective job of widening the extensive margin of search and need to transmit only a few bits of information (the name of the contract, the quantity, and the price) to conclude a transaction. Labor markets lie as far from this pole as used car markets, and a grain exchange for labor is about as possible as a contract on the Chicago Board of Trade for 1960 Chevrolet sedans.

The large variance of wages within narrowly defined occupations in particular local markets affords some evidence of the variance in the quality of labor and in the attractiveness of jobs, though it has other sources as well. For example, in our sample of maintenance electricians in the Chicago area we found a range of hourly earnings in June, 1963, of from $1.75 to $4.75 an hour. Their formal educations ranged from less than four years of schooling to some college. They worked in places ranging from spotless modern plants in pleasant suburbs to old loft buildings in central city slums.

Variation in the quality of applicants in many dimensions is one reason why employers invest so much in the selection of new employees. A second is that present seniority arrangements, both contractual and traditional, mean that in a large number of occupations an employee who survives the probationary period is likely to be with the firm for many years. The total of his wages over this period will run to tens of thousands of dollars. The hiring of an employee is a transaction analogous in size to the purchase of a car or even a house by a consumer and justifies substantial costs of search.

It is therefore not surprising to find employers using many different selection devices. An applicant for employment may be examined in several or in extreme cases all of the following ways: a written application for employment, an interview, paper and pencil tests, work sample tests, a medical examination, a check of credit standing, a check of school and employment references, and even police record checks. The problem facing the employer is not to get in touch with the largest possible number of potential applicants; rather it is to find a few applicants promising enough to be worth the investment of thorough investigation. This is particularly true since in general the buyer and not the seller in labor markets quotes the starting wage. The employer usually has little in-

[3]See George J. Stigler, "The Economics of Information, " *J.P.E.*, June, 1961.

terest in discovering applicants willing to work at less than the prevailing rate; if he is covered by a union contract, he has none at all.

Many employer hiring standards can be viewed as devices to narrow the intensive field of search by reducing the number of applicants to manageable proportions. Within the narrowed field defined by hiring standards, extensive search can be conducted through the most appropriate channels. Thus we encounter such rules as the following: clerical workers must be high school graduates; material handlers must weigh at least 150 pounds; janitors must have lived a year in the metropolitan area; employees who use public transportation must not need to make more than two transfers. Each of these rules has some relevance to job performance, but lack of the qualities specified could be compensated for by the presence of others. Such rules are often relaxed if there is a shortage of applicants who can meet them. This flexibility is illustrated by a large Chicago area manufacturing establishment whose newspaper ads for blue-collar workers when the market is loose specify, "Must be high school graduate"; when the market tightens, this is replaced by, "Average piece rate earnings $3.19 an hour." In addition to formal hiring standards, employers have a still more flexible set of preferences among job applicants, such as the preference for married men for unskilled work because they are thought to have lower quit rates.

Most employers have a strong preference for using informal information networks, for a variety of reasons. Employee referrals—the most important informal channel—usually provide good screening for employers who are satisfied with their present work force. Present employees tend to refer people like themselves, and they may feel that their own reputation is affected by the quality of the referrals. Informal sources also tend to provide applicants from the neighborhood in which the establishment is located; this is particularly important for female employees in reducing turnover, absenteeism, and tardiness resulting from transportation difficulties. Moreover, informal channels are usually costless to the employer, though we have found a few cases in which bonuses are paid for employee referrals that result in hires. Of course, some formal channels such as the state employment service are also costless. The few employers who deliberately avoid informal sources are either those who are seeking to upgrade their work force or those who have had bad experience with nepotism or cliques.

The informal sources also have important benefits to the applicant. He can obtain much more information from a friend who does the kind of work in which he is interested than from an ad in the paper or a counselor at an employment agency, and he places more trust in it. He can ask the counselor about the fairness of supervision in a factory, but he cannot often get an informed or reliable answer. If informal sources result in a placement in the applicant's home neighborhood, he minimizes transportation costs, both in time and in direct outlay. Finally, the presence of a friend in the plant may be an important "fringe benefit," making the job more attractive to the worker at no cost to the employer.

The fact that employers generally prefer informal sources does not mean they are always able to use them. As George Stigler has pointed out, high wages and high search costs are substitutes for an employer; low-wage employers are therefore forced to use high-cost information channels, such as newspaper advertising and private employment agencies.[4] This hypothesis receives strong support from the findings of Joseph C. Ullman, who has analyzed the Chicago market for two female clerical occupations: typists and keypunch operators. Ullman reports significant negative relationships between wages and the proportion of clerical workers hired through newspaper advertising and private agencies.[5]

The literature on formal information networks is uniformly hostile to private employment agencies. One of the leading scholars in the field, E. Wight Bakke, speaks of unemployed workers "falling into the clutches of exploiting fee-charging agencies, who took from ignorant people in desperate need of jobs a big toll from their pay for providing a very poor labor broker service.."[6] Many employers also have little use for private agencies, or "flesh

[4]See George J. Stigler, "Information in the Labor Market," *J.P.E.*, Oct. 1962, Sup.

[5]Joseph C. Ullman, "Inter-firm Differences in the Cost of Search for White Collar Workers" (unpublished doctoral dissertation, Graduate School of Business, Univ. of Chicago, 1965).

[6]E. Wight Bakke, *A Positive Labor Market Policy* (Charles E. Merrill, 1960), p. 15.

peddlers." Some complain of pirating—attempts by agencies to hire away people they have previously placed in order to earn another fee—and many complain of being pestered by phone calls from agency counselors. Some agencies do a poor screening job because of the high turnover of counselors. Since there are many agencies and there is vigorous competition among them, employers who complain about the practices of a particular agency often shift their business to a competing agency rather than turning to an alternative type of hiring channel.

Despite complaints from professors and employers, private agencies have been growing rapidly. Between 1943 and 1958 the number of private employment agencies in the United States increased from 2,200 to 3,900, their receipts tripled, and their payrolls quadrupled.[7] One is forced to at least grudging admiration of an industry that can thrive on selling at substantial fees a service that the government provides gratis.

In fact, our employer interviews reveal that many employers are well satisfied with private agencies. This is especially true in the clerical market, where Chicago employers typically pay agency fees of 60 or 72 percent of a month's salary. There is some tendency for the firms that use agencies extensively to be smaller than average, with fewer facilities in their own personnel departments, which suggests the presence within limits of economies of scale in hiring. The most satisfactory relationships are often with agencies that are specialized in terms of occupation, industry, or location, and involve dealings over a prolonged period with a particular counselor who knows the employer's needs.

The number of employers in our sample who make frequent use of the Illinois or Indiana Employment Services and are well satisfied with them is considerably smaller than the number who report good results from private agencies. Private agencies placed from 10 to 32 percent of the workers in the four white-collar occupations we studied; the state employment services placed only from 1 to 3 percent. In the eight blue-collar occupations, private agencies were more important than the employment services in three and less important in three

others; in no case were hires through the state employment services more than 4 percent of the total.

The highest level of satisfaction with the state employment services was reported by employers who deal with suburban offices rather than central city offices. In these cases they often mentioned regular contact with the same counselor as the key factor in good service.

We encountered some employers who object on principle to the government running an employment service, and several who avoid the employment service because, despite Fair Employment Practices Acts, they do not hire Negroes. However, such cases were clearly not the main source of dissatisfaction or nonuse in our sample. The most frequent complaints against the employment service are slowness and poor screening. Some respondents gave specific examples, such as this one from a branch store of a large department store chain: "A year or so ago we placed an order with the Employment Service for a couple of high school graduates for openings in the credit department. We didn't care too much about experience, and would take trainees. They sent over fourty applicants and about half weren't high school graduates. Most of the rest were overqualified and wouldn't accept the jobs. I finally hired a couple of people, but it just wasn't worth the effort to talk to them." Stories such as this suggest that the number of referrals is a very poor yardstick for evaluating an employment service—the number of placements is a better one, and the ratio of placements to referrals may be better still.

A manufacturing firm that has employed Negro blue-collar workers for many years stated that it does not use the employment service because "instead of trying to meet our qualifications, they just send over people who have trouble finding jobs, and they aren't the best people." Such employer reactions suggest the strong tension between the employer objective of getting the best for his money and the objectives of agencies that seek to promote social welfare by referring the workers whose needs are greatest. Unfortunately, referrals alone do not alleviate need—only placements do.

Chicago area employers use newspaper advertising extensively in recruiting white-collar workers (from 14 to 23 percent of all hires in four occupations) and to a smaller but still

---

[7]See Eaton Conant, "An Evaluation of Private Employment Agencies as Sources of Job Vacancy Data," in *The Measurement and Interpretation of Job Vacancies* (N.B.E.R., 1966).

significant extent for blue-collar workers (1 to 13 percent of hires in eight occupations). In no occupation was the employment service more important than newspaper advertising. Many employers prefer neighborhood to metropolitan papers. In some cases this is again a device for racial screening, but more often it is intended to minimize transportation costs and thus to cut turnover and encourage attendance. Trade papers and foreign language papers are important in some industries, such as men's clothing.

The preceding discussion fails to suggest the rich variety of hiring channels in a metropolitan labor market. Referrals from unions are important in trucking and in the printing trades, as well as in construction, which was excluded from our sample. Referrals from one employer to another occur in cases of layoffs and plant shutdowns. Public utilities recruit clerical workers extensively from high schools; private vocational schools are important in the data processing occupations; and college recruiting is important for professional and managerial jobs. Some of the hiring channels we discovered do not fit any of the usual categories. One manufacturer hires truck drivers through a large trucking firm located across the street; another employer hires accountants through the public accounting firm that audits its books. A large distributor of furniture and home appliances hires warehousemen from moving and storage companies, whose slack season coincides with this employer's peak season. Such arrangements seem untidy in terms of the design of an orderly information network; yet they may nonetheless be highly effective.

In some cases matching an opening with an applicant requires search over a wide geographical area. Such cases arise largely for a few highly skilled crafts and for specialized managerial and professional jobs. The employer with a sudden need for a bassoon player, a deep sea diver, or a specialist in the chemistry of fluorine compounds might be willing to recruit from across the country or around the world. Such needs are served in part by the professional office network of the United States Employment Service and in part by the private executive recruiting or "head hunting" agencies. Search at long distances is also indicated when there are serious local imbalances between supply and demand. The employer will engage in long-distance search in cases of excess demand and the employee in cases of excess supply.

It is in such cases that direct communications networks connecting widely separated locations make the most sense. A highly sophisticated network would enable the university in New England with a vacancy for a mathematical economist to call the nearest professional office of the employment service, which through its link to a computer in Washington would discover in microseconds a well-trained mathematical economist on the Pacific Coast dissatisfied because he had been passed over for promotion. Yet even a system with such capabilities would have to struggle for users against the network of personal contacts built up within industries and professions. It is quite possible that the department chairman in New England would prefer, even in making his initial list of prospects, to phone or write to one or two senior mathematical economists whose judgment he has learned to trust.

For the major portion of the market, the crucial characteristic of an effective formal information system is not the length or the number of interconnections between geographical locations or the number of applications and openings that can be brought together at one place. Rather, it is the richness and reliability of the information carried over each link. The crucial component of such a system will not in our life-times be built by I.B.M. or Western Electric. It is the experienced employment service counselor who is a good judge of applicants and of their records and who knows thoroughly and respects the requirements of a small number of employers he has served for a long time. This in turn implies a compensation system in which such skill and experience are well rewarded.

Unemployment and Manpower Programs

Probably the best known and perhaps the most important difficulty with the operation of labor markets is the problem of unemployment. Charles Holt discusses the structure of labor turnover and how it is related to changes in aggregate demand for goods and services in the economy. While unemployment can be reduced simply by increasing aggregate demand, this approach may lead to excessive inflation. Consequently Holt proposes a series of manpower-type policies that should reduce unemployment without contributing to inflationary pressures.

The selection by Robert Hall investigates why the unemployment rate is so high at full employment. Hall analyzes both the structural and search theories of unemployment and discusses the difficulties involved in defining unemployment. He concludes that the problem of hard-core unemployment is not so much that there are individuals who are permanently out of work as that there are many workers, especially blacks and women, who move frequently from job to job without advancing their careers. Therefore, although Hall is in agreement with Holt's emphasis on the labor turnover aspect of unemployment, he is skeptical whether Holt's manpower proposals would get at the root of our unemployment problems.

A given level of unemployment appears to be associated with inflation more now than in the 1960s (i.e., the Philips curve has shifted to the right). Although there are many possible explanations, the selection by Charles Killingsworth emphasizes labor market factors, including the reduction in the armed forces, massive layoffs in defense plants, and the reduced expansion of government manpower programs. Like Holt, Killingsworth argues for more emphasis on manpower programs, as a means of combatting unemployment.

During the 1960s there was an enormous increase in federal manpower programs. These new programs are discussed in the selection by Sar Levitan and Garth Mangum. In their view the manpower focus shifted during this period from the former emphasis of the employment service on matching the best man with an existing job to a new emphasis on providing a suitable job for each man (or else equipping the man to fill a suitable job). As Killingsworth indicates, manpower expenditures have

not increased very much under the Nixon administration. Instead the main thrust has been to shift control of the programs to state and local governments.

As unemployment increased in the early 1970s, job creation became a primary manpower issue. The selection by Charles Schultze and his associates discusses some of the issues involved in assessing the desirability of job creation programs. The Emergency Employment Act of 1971 did establish a large-scale Public Employment Program. Under this act, the federal government creates public-sector jobs at the state and local level for certain categories of disadvantaged workers. This Public Employment Program is analyzed in the selection by Sar Levitan and Robert Taggert.

While the United States has greatly increased its manpower activities since 1960, our programs are still quite small and relatively unsophisticated compared with those of many European countries. The selection by Beatrice Reuben discusses the European experience. Unemployment rates in Europe generally have been much lower than in the United States, an occurrence that Reuben attributes partly to a stronger demand for labor and partly to the greater European emphasis on manpower and other social programs.

10. Improving the Labor Market Trade-off between Inflation and Unemployment*

Charles C. Holt

I. INTRODUCTION[1]

The work on the Phillips curve has been predominantly empirical, but policy intervention designed to decrease both inflation and unemployment requires a better theoretical understanding of the determinants of this relation. This paper attempts to sketch out the basic labor market relationships that appear to the author to account largely for the Phillips relation and then to consider the kinds of policy measures that this analysis suggests are relevant for moving the Phillips curve. . . .

The emphasis in this paper is on the atomistic operation of the labor market because it appears sufficient to generate the Phillips relation, but we do not deny that union bargaining and price dynamics may also be involved to some degree.

This paper concentrates on conceptual issues. Continuing research will be devoted to the statistical measurement of relationships.

*The research reported here was conducted under Contract 82-09-68-44 for the Manpower Administration, U.S. Department of Labor, under the authority of the Manpower Development and Training Act. Researchers undertaking such projects under the government sponsorship are encouraged to express their own judgment. The author expresses appreciation for helpful comments received from Harvey Garn, Ralph Smith, Richard Wertheimer, and C. Duncan McRae.

[1] Due to space restrictions the original, "How Can the Phillips Curve Be Moved to Reduce Both Inflation and Unemployment?" could not be included in the *Proceedings.* Consequently this paper has summarized the conclusions of its technical analysis and has incorporated additional material, especially in Sections II, VI, and the appendix. The original paper will appear in *Micro-economic Foundations of Employment and Inflation Theory,* Edmund S. Phelps, ed. (W. W. Norton, 1969).

II. THE STRUCTURE OF THE LABOR MARKET

Since unemployment is viewed as a transitory state through which most workers pass rather- than an experience suffered only by some particular kinds of people, it is relevant to examine the tremendous turnover of workers that keeps the labor market in a continual state of flux. Figure 1 shows various flows and stocks in the labor market that we shall discuss, giving rough numerical magnitudes.

The balance of this section is devoted essentially to an explication of this figure.

Starting at the bottom of the diagram, aggregate demand, which is influenced by monetary and fiscal policy, etc., when combined with

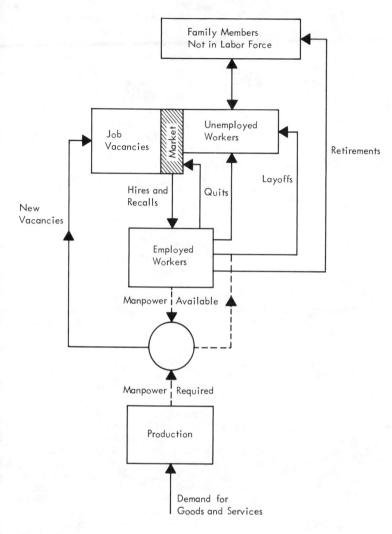

Figure 1

Flows and Stocks of Workers and Jobs

product prices, determines the real demand for goods and services and, in turn, production which generates manpower requirements. If these exceed the manpower available from the current stock of employed workers, new job vacancies are created which add to the stock of unfilled job vacancies. If manpower requirements fall short of available manpower, layoffs occur and workers flow from the category of employed to unemployed, reducing one stock and increasing the other. Vacancies and unemployment influence hires and recalls.

Worker decisions to leave employment also account for labor turnover flows by (1) searching for better jobs while still employed and then quitting to change jobs without being unemployed, (2) quitting and engaging in unemployed job search, and (3) retiring from the labor force. For various domestic and educational reasons family members are continually entering and leaving the labor force.

The following rough and rounded figures will give an impression of the magnitudes of the stocks, flows, durations, and probabilities involved in this system. In the United States currently there are about 80 million employed workers, 3 million unemployed workers, and probably a comparable number of vacancies, but data on this are inadequate. Employment durations for all accessions average roughly 2.7 years. Unemployed workers and vacancies wait roughly a month on the average before finding work or employees. The total flow of quits and layoffs amounts to roughly 30 million per year. Some workers even travel the hire and quit or layoff loop several times in a year. Turnover rates of the order of 3 or 4 percent a month account for this tremendous flow. The stock of unemployed workers is replaced every month on the average. Offsetting this flow from the stock of employed workers is a roughly equal flow of accessions. Employers have to recruit continually in order to hold a constant work force. The probability that an unemployed worker will find a job is roughly 20 percent per week and gives a long-tailed exponential distribution of unemployment duration.

Now consider a cyclical fluctuation in which production increases by an arbitrary amount, say 3 percent. Labor productivity of the existing work force then increases by about 1 percent through reducing slack time, etc. To recruit the larger work force that is now needed, new vacancies are generated, which when matched with workers, reduce the unemployment rate roughly 1 percent. The increased vacancies and reduced unemployment encourage family members to increase their labor market participation so the labor force increases by about 1 percent. Ultimately the vacancies are matched with workers so that the 3 percent increase in production leads to an employment increase of approximately 2 percent and an unemployment reduction of about 1 percent.

The average duration of vacancies is increased and the duration of unemployment is decreased. Workers encouraged by the increased vacancies and decreased duration of unemployment increasingly engage in on-the-job search for better jobs and quit when they find them or, alternatively, quit first and then search. Employers, finding recruiting more difficult and quit rates increased, respond by reducing the flow of layoffs. The total turnover flow changes little because the changes in layoffs and quits largely cancel.

Through the process of quitting and finding better jobs, workers are able to improve their money wages. Relatively low-wage employers suffer relatively high quit rates and long va-

cancy durations; and, in order to hold their work forces, are under increased pressure to raise money wages for their employees or to lower their quality standards in recruiting—this is equivalent to offering higher money wages. This process tends to force the laggard employers to change their wages in line with wage changes generated in the labor market.

Taken together these mechanisms can produce an upward creep of money wages.

The opposite effects, of course, occur for reduced demand. When unemployment is high enough, money wages fall steadily.

Thus, high turnover initiated by both employers and workers coupled with the heterogeneity of jobs and workers leads to the time-consuming search for new matches that accounts for stocks of unemployed workers and unfilled vacancies and continuing changes in the level of money wages....

Without going into detail, we can simply list the changes that could be influenced by policy actions to reduce unemployment (and vacancies) without increasing inflation:

1. Improving the information, search processes, and counseling of workers and employers would speed up the search[2] and reduce the average time to arrange fruitful interviews.

2. Decreasing the segmentation of the market that is not necessitated in terms of production requirements, regionally, occupationally, racially, sexually, etc., will increase economic opportunities for both workers and employers.

3. Imbalances between labor market segments can be partially offset in the placement of government orders, stimulants to plant location decisions, the subsidy of geographic and occupational mobility by workers, and the restructuring of jobs to better fit worker abilities.

4. Interviews are more likely to result in placements, . . .if the initial wage aspirations of workers and employers are set realistically close to the prevailing opportunities in the market. This should be improved by better information and counseling. Also, the faster workers and employers adjust their wage aspirations, the shorter their market searches will tend to be.

[2]With aid from electronic computers the duration of search by unemployed workers should be reduced, but in so doing it is important not to stimulate the turnover rate. If the offices of the U.S. Employment Service were kept open in the evenings, perhaps more of the job search could be done while workers are still employed but again the turnover caution applies. Efforts to reduce search costs need to be accompanied by efforts to make better placements that will have longer employment durations.

5. Employers can reduce their contribution to labor turnover by lowering their layoff rates through better sales forecasting, production, and employment planning, including seasonal smoothing, and through improved internal channels for promotion.

6. Workers can reduce their contribution to labor turnover by reducing their quit rates and reduce their unemployment by searching while still employed.

The high turnover rates[3] account for high training and other transition costs and undoubtedly could be greatly reduced before one need be concerned about excess rigidity in the economy. Making jobs more satisfying and improving the means of learning about jobs short of taking them could reduce turnover, but this important area is not well understood and requires much more research.

7. Since wage and price expectations can contribute to the inflation process, counseling efforts to reduce inflation expectations that are unrealistically high could be useful.

Although the above actions are oriented toward lowering unemployment and vacancies, they can be converted into reducing inflation by adjusting aggregate demand to change the vacancy-unemployment ratio.

VI. CONCLUSION

The foregoing policy recommendations are hardly surprising, but hopefully further quantitative research will contribute to our understanding of the relative benefits from the various alternatives.

Such manpower programs need to be coordinated with aggregate income policies, since manpower programs with no increase in demand are likely simply to redistribute jobs rather than reduce unemployment.

Manpower programs of the above type operate in the United States, but on a small scale. What are the arguments for increasing government resources in this area? The answer lies in the presence of externalities, equity objectives, institutional limitations, and economies of scale.

[3]Since 5 and 6 depend directly on private decisions, they can be influenced by government only indirectly. However, government leadership on the highest level may be helpful in getting employers to recognize that their individual decisions collectively have important national implications. Also, through counseling and computer aides, workers might be helped to find jobs that would satisfy them longer.

Most of the costs of labor turnover are not borne by the party that incurred them. When workers quit, employers must recruit and train replacements, often at higher wages. More than half of the quitting workers go directly to new jobs without any intervening unemployment to inhibit their moves. When employers lay off workers, they lose income while searching for new jobs. Government action is needed to minimize these serious external costs that are suffered involuntarily by both employers and employees.

Workers, in order to reach their maximum production potentials, particularly in a period of rapid changes in the structures and locations of jobs, require costly investments in education, training, job search, retraining, and relocation. Unfortunately, many do not have the money to make these investments themselves. Their employers may not make investments in training because the expected durations of employment are short.[4] Financial institutions typically refuse unsecured loans for such manpower investments by families because the risk is excessive, as there is no tangible asset that can be sold in case of default. Consequently, many socially and privately desirable human investments are not made, especially in disadvantaged workers, unless governmental action is taken. The inability to borrow to finance human investments may partially inhibit such investments for all except high-income families. The additional equity justification can be used for low-income families.

In the job and worker information area much of the cost is in obtaining the information in the first place rather than in its manipulation and dissemination. This is especially true where electronic computers are involved. There appear to be strong economies of scale that support the development of a small number of large efforts and in the extreme case lead to a natural monopoly as the most efficient form of organization. A strong case can be made for upgrading the resources, quality, scope, and computerization of the United States Employment Service.

Manpower programs offer the prospect not only of decreasing frictions and increasing efficiency of those directly involved but also may

[4]Some training costs are, of course, shifted to workers in the form of lower wages during training periods, but some workers may not be able to afford such jobs even though their long-term payoffs are high.

make it possible to increase production by increasing aggregate demand, decreasing unemployment, increasing labor market participation, and increasing the productivity of the whole employed work force—all of these are possible without contributing to inflation. Such programs seem to have significant potential for large-scale payoffs that can justify substantial increases in resources devoted to them. . . . A lower level of unemployment should have the additional benefit of stimulating productivity gains by increasing technological innovation and capital investment.

These policy implications are sufficiently important that continuing research is needed to test fully the view that the Phillips relation largely reflects the micro-dynamics of the labor market and to determine the specific effects of various manpower programs.

11. Why Is the Unemployment Rate So High at Full Employment?

Robert E. Hall *

The outstanding problem of contemporary macroeconomic policy in the United States is the unfavorable trade-off that exists between unemployment and inflation. Many economists have studied this phenomenon in detail,[1] and there is practically universal agreement that low unemployment rates imply high rates of wage and price inflation, or, equivalently, wage and price stability requires a high rate of unemployment. In short, the Phillips curve has an unfavorable location in the unemployment-inflation diagram, passing far above and to the right of the point of low unemployment and wage stability. There are many interesting ways to examine this problem; my purpose in this paper is to study it only in the way suggested by the title. That is, I will look into the nature of the unemployment that remains when labor mar-

kets are reasonably tight and the economy seems to be at full employment. Most of my data are observations on individuals, collected in a variety of surveys, rather than macroeconomic aggregates.

Throughout the paper, I will occasionally refer to the notion of the equilibrium level of unemployment. I use this term more or less synonymously with "full employment unemployment" to mean the level that, if maintained permanently, would produce a steady rate of inflation of 3 or 4 percent per year.[2] Most economists agree that this is somewhere between 4 and 5 percent unemployment.[3]

*This paper draws on research supported by a grant from the Manpower Administration, U.S. Department of Labor, under provisions of the Manpower Development and Training Act of 1962. Earlier work was supported by the Office of Economic Opportunity. The author is solely responsible for the opinions expressed.

[1]In particular, see Robert J. Gordon, "The Recent Acceleration of Inflation and Its Lessons for the Future," *Brookings Papers on Economic Activity* (1:1970), pp. 8-41; and George L. Perry, "Changing Labor Markets and Inflation," *Brookings Papers on Economic Activity* (3:1970), pp. 411-41.

[2]There is nothing special about this rate of inflation. In general, the optimal rate of inflation depends on the relative social costs of unemployment and inflation. This rate is merely illustrative and does not play an important role in what follows.

[3]Milton Friedman, Edmund Phelps, and a number of other economists have argued that the equilibrium rate defined in this way is a fixed, "natural" rate, independent of the steady-state rate of inflation. If so, my definition of full employment unemployment is unambiguous; otherwise, it depends, probably not very sensitively, on the rate of inflation. See, for example, Milton Friedman, "The Role of Monetary Policy," in *American Economic Review*, Vol. 58 (March 1968), pp. 1-17; and Edmund S. Phelps, "The New Microeconomics in Inflation and Employment Theory," in American Economic Association, *Papers and Proceed-*

Further, to forestall misunderstanding, I should say something about the relevance of my study to contemporary macroeconomic problems. Nothing in this paper directly concerns the state of the economy at the end of 1970 with 6.0 percent unemployment, surely above the equilibrium level at current rates of inflation of 4 to 6 percent per year. Rather, the paper concerns current problems of macroeconomic policy in the sense that it suggests why it would not be possible to reach and maintain, in a year or two, a level of unemployment of, say, 3 percent, through the application of even the most intelligently conceived fiscal and monetary policy.

The body of the paper begins with a discussion of the problem of defining and measuring unemployment. Definition derives from theory. In this case the theory underlying most macroeconomic thinking about unemployment is that of Keynes. Keynes believed that a certain level of frictional unemployment was characteristic of all labor markets, but that, in addition, involuntary unemployment could arise when a condition of disequilibrium existed in labor markets, with supply exceeding demand. Involuntary unemployment, then, is the difference between supply and demand. Further, as Keynes emphasized, the forces causing movement toward aggregate equilibrium in the labor market are weak, so unemployment will persist in the absence of active policy—indeed, even in its presence, as this paper seeks to explore.

Keynes proposed an elaborate and frequently misunderstood definition of involuntary unemployment to accompany his theory. For my purposes, his definition can be put in the following simple way: A person is unemployed if he offers his labor at its market price but is unable to find a buyer. Keynes explicitly distinguished this kind of unemployment from frictional unemployment, which he believed arose in the normal operation of the labor market. From the start, government agencies have had to use a single definition to measure all unemployment, and problems of measurement have caused the definition used in the United States to evolve toward one more appropriate for measuring frictional unemployment. The next section discusses the implications of this change, and concludes with a warning about the unreliability of all data on unemploy-

ment. The reader will note that the warning is largely unheeded in the rest of the paper. Unemployment is too important a problem to be ignored by empirical economists on the grounds of unsatisfactory data. . . .

DEFINING AND MEASURING UNEMPLOYMENT

The problem of defining and measuring unemployment has concerned economists since the Great Depression, when it became clear that unemployment was the single most important indicator of economic distress in an industrial economy. The simple disequilibrium view has dominated thinking about the definition of unemployment since then, even in periods like the late 1960s when aggregate excess supply plainly did not exist in the labor market. The major debate of the late 1950s and early 1960s between advocates of the structural and deficient-aggregate-demand views of the prevailing high rates of unemployment was carried out largely within the definition implicit in the disequilibrium theory. According to that definition, unemployment is the difference between the supply and demand for labor at the prevailing rigid wage. An unemployed person is one who is willing to work at a wage currently being paid to other individuals like himself, but who finds no job available. This definition is purely subjective—there is no objective way to distinguish between an individual who is unemployed and one who has decided not to work.

Early attempts to measure unemployment involved simply asking a representative group of individuals whether they were working, and if not, whether they thought they were unemployed. Doubts about this procedure led to the use of a more behavioral definition. The celebrated report of the Gordon Committee, *Measuring Employment and Unemployment,* laid down as its first general rule that "each concept should correspond to objectively measurable phenomena and should depend as little as possible on personal opinion or subjective attitudes." [4] The objectively measurable phenomenon underlying the measure of unemployment currently in use in the United States is "specific job-seeking activity within the past

ings of the Eighty-first Annual Meeting, 1968 (American Economic Review, Vol. 59, May 1969), pp. 147-60.

[4]President's Committee To Appraise Employment and Unemployment Statistics, *Measuring Employment and Unemployment* (1962), p. 43.

four weeks."[5] It would be natural to expect that many individuals who were unemployed in the sense of the original definition would not be recorded as unemployed according to this criterion. The disequilibrium theory of unemployment does not suggest that a rational person would continue to search for work after discovering the existence of excess supply for labor.

The Gordon Committee recommended that the household survey be extended to identify "discouraged workers" who had stopped looking for work. The extension was carried out starting in January 1967, and quarterly data have been published since December 1969. They show that there are very few discouraged workers when the labor market is tight. In the second quarter of 1969, there were 149,000 men and 386,000 women who had not looked for work in the past four weeks who still desired it but reported that they were unable to find it. By contrast, there were 1,254,000 men and 1,288,000 women unemployed in April 1969 according to the official definition. These results suggest that no major error is caused by using a strict definition of unemployment in terms of recent activity in seeking jobs. I will argue later in the paper that there is a different sense in which many individuals out of the labor force might be classified as unemployed. . . .

GEOGRAPHICAL VARIATIONS IN UNEMPLOYMENT

A conventional view among economists about the persistence of unemployment when the economy is at full employment can be put in the following way: There are many different labor markets, distinguished by geographical location and the skills and other characteristics of the participants. Workers cannot move easily from one market to another since it is expensive to move their households or to acquire a new set of skills. At any point in time, some of the markets will be in equilibrium (involving, of course, frictional unemployment, as noted earlier), some will have shortages of workers, and some will have excess workers and hence unemployment. If demand begins to expand in all of the markets more or less uniformly, then the labor shortages will become more severe, and some of the markets that had unemployment before will develop shortages themselves. But even if demand rises to the point that shortages are widespread and wages are rising briskly, so that the economy appears to be at full employment, some markets will still have unemployment. To put it another way, there are bottlenecks that prevent output from rising enough to reduce unemployment to minimal frictional levels in every market.

Two forces tend to bring about the gradual elimination of the kind of imbalance just described. First, in the longer run workers may move from a market with excess labor supply to one with a labor shortage, either by relocating geographically or by offering a different skill. Second, the wage level may fall (at least relative to other wages) in markets with unemployment, stimulating demand for labor in those markets, and eventually putting the unemployed to work. Economists continue to disagree about the strength of these two equilibrating forces. Pessimists believe that they are so weak that there are markets—for unskilled workers in depressed regions, for example— where unemployment above frictional levels is virtually permanent in spite of the most energetic expansionary policy for aggregate demand. This is the hypothesis of structural unemployment.[6] A more optimistic view holds that under conditions of stable demand, the equilibrating forces of labor mobility and changes in relative wages could eventually eliminate unemployment and labor shortage in every labor market, but that the process is thwarted by continual shifts in the composition of demand. According to this view, high unemployment at full employment is simply a reflection of the fact that, at any moment in time, some unlucky workers will find themselves in markets where the demand for labor has just fallen relative to the supply, creating unemployment.

I propose to examine these hypotheses in terms of the conditions in the labor markets of

[5]U.S. Bureau of Labor Statistics and U.S. Bureau of the Census, "Concepts and Methods Used in Manpower Statistics from the Current Population Survey," BLS Report 313 and Census Bureau, *Current Population Reports,* Series P-23, No. 22 (1967), p. 5.

[6]My characterization of the problem of structural unemployment follows Robert M. Solow, *The Nature and Sources of Unemployment in the United States* (Stockholm: Almqvist and Wiksell, 1964).

twelve large cities in the United States, without trying to distinguish the various markets in each city for skills of different types. By any measure of unemployment, there are substantial variations among cities in their rates of unemployment. Table 1 presents estimates prepared

tional unemployment rate. Moreover, they seem to support the hypothesis of long-term structural unemployment. They show little evidence that the equilibrating forces have much effect over the four-year span of the data. The scatter diagram of Figure 1 demonstrates this

Table 1

Unemployment Rates in Twelve Cities, Annual Averages, 1965-69

City	1965	1966	Percent[a] 1967	1968	1969
Baltimore	3.8	2.9	2.8	2.9	2.8
Chicago	3.0	2.6	2.7	2.7	2.5
Cleveland	3.1	2.6	2.8	2.5	2.3
Detroit	3.5	3.3	4.2	3.9	3.7
Houston	3.?	2.4	2.1	1.9	2.2
Los Angeles	5.7	4.5	4.5	4.2	4.1
New York	4.5	4.2	3.7	3.3	3.2
Philadelphia	4.3	3.3	3.2	3.1	3.0
Pittsburgh	3.6	3.0	3.1	2.8	2.5
St. Louis	3.5	3.3	3.4	3.5	3.5
San Francisco	5.0	4.4	4.4	4.0	3.9
Washington, D.C.	2.2	2.4	2.3	2.2	2.2

Source: *Manpower Report of the President* (March 1970). Prepared by the U.S. Department of Labor (1970), Table D-8, pp. 284-86.
[a]Annual averages of total unemployment as percent of total work force.

for the Manpower Administration of average annual rates of unemployment for the twelve cities.[7] In 1965, a year of 4.5 percent national unemployment, the highest rate was considerably more than twice the lowest rate. Four years later, in 1969, when the national unemployment rate was 3.5 percent, the rates still show a great deal of dispersion; further, there seems to have been a general tendency for the rates to fall more or less uniformly.

These data seem to support the conventional view that a few markets with excess supply of labor contribute disproportionately to the na-

graphically. Except for Detroit and St. Louis, the cities fall along a smooth curve: Those that had high unemployment in 1965 still suffered it in 1969 and those with low rates in earlier years continued to experience them. Before embracing the structural hypothesis, however, I think it is appropriate to consider alternative explanations of the persistent differentials in the unemployment rates of these cities.

In the first place, the unemployment rate for each city represents an average over the rates of disparate groups in the labor force. For example, teenagers invariably have high rates of unemployment, so if a city has an unusually large fraction of teenagers, its unemployment rate will be high relative to those of other cities even though neither its rate for adults nor its rate for teenagers is high. An adjustment for the varying composition of the labor forces of the twelve cities appears necessary before any meaningful conclusion can be drawn about the persistence of differentials in unemployment rates. . . .

Important as this kind of adjustment is in

[7]This is the only set of estimates of unemployment by city available annually for years before 1968. They are prepared from data on claims for unemployment insurance, payrolls, and various other sources. The Bureau of Labor Statistics has recently published estimates of unemployment rates by city from the household survey averaged over 1969. See Paul O. Flaim and Paul M. Schwab. "Geographic Aspects of Unemployment in 1969," *Employment and Earnings,* Vol. 16 (April 1970), pp. 5-6, 16-22.

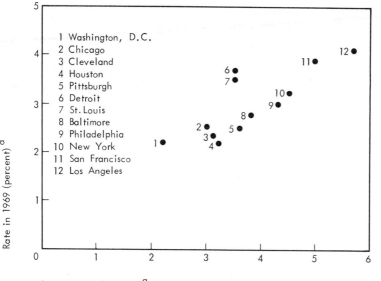

Figure 1

**Relation between Unemployment Rates in 1965
and 1969 in Twelve Cities**

Source: Table 1.

ªAnnual average of total unemployment as percent of total work force.

principle, it turns out to make remarkably little difference in this case. . . .

Thus we can rule out the simple explanation that the persistent differentials in unemployment by city are the result of corresponding differences in the composition of the labor forces of the cities. The structural hypothesis seems to be the winner. Must optimists now abandon their view that, left to themselves, the equilibrating forces of labor mobility and changes in relative wages will gradually eliminate differentials in unemployment rates? Perhaps so. I offer here a distinctly tentative hypothesis that might explain the apparent weakness of the equilibrating forces in terms that should not be offensive to economists who have a basic faith in the efficacy of the price system.

In the data from the SEO, there is a positive association between average weeks of unemployment for men and average wages among the twelve cities.[8] High-wage cities, notably San

Francisco and Los Angeles, have high rates of unemployment, and low-wage cities tend to have low rates of unemployment. The data for white males are presented in Figure 2. If there is a general tendency for cities with high wages to have high unemployment rates, then there is no longer a presumption that geographical mobility of labor will act to reduce unemployment. The attraction of high wages may cancel or even outweigh the discouraging effect of unemployment.[9] A rational worker might decide to move from Cleveland to Los Angeles even though it is much harder to find a job in California, precisely because wages are significantly higher there. In this situation, geographical mobility of labor may not function at all as

They are presented in Robert E. Hall, "Wages, Income, and Hours of Work in the U.S. Labor Force," Working Paper 62 (Massachusetts Institute of Technology, Department of Economics, August 1970; processed).

[9]Unemployment does not necessarily exert its discouraging effect directly. Rather, high unemployment may be a sign of low rates of job vacancies.

[8]The wage rates used here are also adjusted for variations in the composition of the labor force by city.

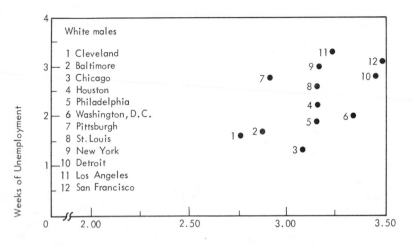

Figure 2

**Relation between Average Wages and Weeks of Unemployment
in Twelve Cities by Race and Sex, 1966***

Source: Wages—Robert E. Hall, "Wages, Income, and Hours of Work in the U.S.
Labor Force," Working Paper 62 (Massachusetts Institute of Technology, Depart-
ment of Economics, August 1970; processed), p. 25; Weeks of unemployment—
Table 2.

*Editor's note: The author finds a similar negative relation for black males, white
females, and black females.

an equilibrating force. If the decisions of most
families about their locations are influenced
mainly by consideration of the husband's employment, then the relationship between unemployment and wages should be stronger for
men than for women.

What about the other main equilibrating
force, changes in relative wages? Deeply embedded in modern economic thought is the idea
that excess supply of labor in a market should
drive down the wage, at least relative to the
average wage in all markets. It is, for example,
the explanation of the Phillips curve. The basic
mechanism that economists usually have in
mind is that in a market where unemployment
is high, employers find it possible to hire at
slightly lower wages, or at least they need not
keep up with wage increases in other markets in
order to fill their jobs. In this view, the pool of
unemployment consists of workers who are
increasingly desperate for work, and who will
take somewhat lower wages than they had originally expected. I have suggested above, however, that those unemployed in a city with high
wages may have a rather different attitude:

They may be in the market precisely because
they are willing to pay the price of a spell of
unemployment in order to locate a high-paying
job. If so, there is no reason to expect this kind
of unemployment to exert a downward pressure on wages. The employer who offered a job
at a slightly reduced wage to an unemployed
worker would simply be refused.

One final question needs to be answered to
complete this explanation. Why do employers
hire in cities with high wages rather than relocating in low-wage areas? In the long run, one
might expect the mobility of employers to
bring about equalization of wages, even if the
other forces were not acting to do so.[10] However, the existence of unemployment in his

[10]Of course, other factors as well determine the geographical pattern of wages. In an ideal set of labor
markets, one would expect uniformly low unemployment rates and differences in wages that reflected only
these other determinants. Climate is the obvious example of such an influence. By equalization, then, I
really mean equalization after taking these other determinants into account.

labor market is a distinct advantage to the employer. It acts to stabilize his work force, reducing his hiring costs and permitting him to capture the benefits of training that his workers acquire on the job. The existence of a high level of unemployment imposes a substantial price on workers who change jobs, and materially reduces the frequency with which workers do so voluntarily. The prospective employer, deciding where to locate, can buy stability in his work force by locating in a high-wage, high-unemployment city.

Taken together, these arguments suggest that there can be an indeterminacy of the equilibrium in the labor market of a city. There may be a whole set of unemployment-wage combinations each of which represents equilibrium in the sense that it can be maintained indefinitely. None of the combinations is really satisfactory, and it would be unfortunate to suppose that the goal of manpower policy should be to try to move to a position of low unemployment and accept the consequent low wage. If some other means, less costly than unemployment, could be found to reduce turnover, then the equilibrium could be at high wages and low unemployment.

IS THERE A SUBSTANTIAL AMOUNT OF CHRONIC UNEMPLOYMENT AT FULL EMPLOYMENT?

Popular accounts of unemployment often seem to suggest that full employment leaves behind a residual group of chronically unemployed workers who are unable to find work over long periods of time. I interpret the notion of chronic unemployment to refer to individuals who are literally unable to find a job after looking for six months or more. This is a very stringent definition (some might say it is a caricature of the usual idea of chronic unemployment); I use it because there is still a very large difference between having difficulty finding a job (spending up to six months searching), and not being able to find a job at all. Nothing in my definition is intended to suggest that there is not a great deal of hardship in four or five months of joblessness. I wish to suggest only that it is misleading to label a spell of unemployment of this length as chronic unemployment, in which the same individuals remain unemployed month after month, and unemployment involving continual, even if relatively slow, turnover among the unemployed.

The first place to evaluate the importance of chronic unemployment is in the data on the duration of unemployment. Table 2 presents these data for April 1969, a month of high employment. About half of those unemployed in that month had become so within the previous four weeks. Only a very small fraction had been unemployed for six months or more: in the case of adult men, 7.4 percent of the total, or about 70,000 individuals. If chronic unemployment is a major social problem when the economy is at full employment, that fact is not revealed in the data on unemployment from the household survey. Those data show that individuals leave the status of unemployment relatively rapidly; very few of them are reported as unemployed for long periods.

The definition of unemployment used in the survey practically guarantees that little chronic unemployment will be reported. If an individual is unable to find work after searching for several months, he may well not take the trouble to engage in specific job-seeking activities in the four weeks preceding the survey. In an earlier section I discussed the new data on

Table 2

Percentage Distribution of Unemployment in Sex and Age Groups, by Duration, April 1969

Sex and age	Weeks of unemployment			
	0–4	5–14	15–26	27 or more
Both sexes, 16-19 years	60.1	25.6	7.3	7.0
Male, 20 years and over	47.9	26.2	18.4	7.4
Female, 20 years and over	55.1	25.6	14.5	4.9

Source: *Employment and Earnings,* Vol. 15 (May 1969), Table A-13, p. 39.

individuals not in the labor force who nonetheless desire a job or would normally be in the labor force. It is now useful to take a second look at this group, which is not very large compared with total unemployment, but is certainly large enough so that if it comprised mainly those permanently out of work, it would indicate that chronic unemployment was a major problem. In February 1967, the Bureau of the Census carried out a follow-up survey of men aged 20 through 64 who were reported as not in the labor force in the regular monthly survey one week earlier.[11] Most of them were sick or disabled (59.0 percent) or retired (10.7 percent). Almost 700,000 men, however, were out of the labor force for unusual reasons—that is, for reasons other than poor health or retirement. Might not some fraction of these be chronically unemployed? The survey seems to rule this out almost completely. Astonishingly enough, just under half of those who had been out of the labor force the previous week were back in it by the time the follow-up survey was made. . . .

. . . Most of those who did not work at all probably looked for work only a small part of the year.

Taken together, the evidence on the duration of unemployment and on individuals who are not in the labor force suggests rather strongly that chronic inability to find a job is not a problem faced by a significant number of people when the economy is at full employment. The real problem is that many workers have frequent short spells of unemployment. This is the topic of the next section.

FRICTIONAL UNEMPLOYMENT AND TURNOVER IN THE LABOR FORCE

Economists have generally recognized that a certain amount of unemployment will always arise in the normal operation of a labor market. Especially when unemployment is defined in terms of activity in looking for a job, a certain fraction of the nonworking population will be searching for work whenever the household survey is conducted, and will be measured as unemployed. At full employment, in fact, a good fraction of those unemployed are at natural transition points in their careers where it is normal to be looking for jobs; those who have just finished school or have just been discharged from the military are the obvious examples. In April 1969, individuals with no previous work experience constituted over 11 percent of total unemployment and reentrants to the labor force constituted another 30 percent. Experienced workers may seek new jobs, either because they have exhausted the possiblities for training and advancement in their old jobs, or because technical progress or shifts in the composition of demand have eliminated their previous jobs. Unemployed individuals who are changing jobs may have been laid off, or they may have quit in the belief that more favorable opportunities exist elsewhere. These two sources accounted for 43 and 16 percent, respectively, of total unemployment in April 1969. Unemployment that arises from any of these sources need not be a subject of social concern if the unemployed find jobs reasonably rapidly; in fact, labor markets could not function efficiently if workers did not spend some fraction of their time searching for the best possible jobs.

This observation has led some economists to adopt normal turnover as a unitary explanation of unemployment. The resulting doctrine is rather loosely called the Search Theory of Unemployment.[12] It emphasizes that it is rational for an unemployed worker not to take the first job available, but to wait long enough to get a particularly good job. This incentive to remain unemployed operates even when the demand for labor is exceedingly strong, so there is a level of frictional unemployment that is the irreducible minimum that can be achieved by expansionary fiscal and monetary policy.

In the search theory, unemployment is a transitory experience, generally associated with voluntary or involuntary changes in jobs. The appropriate policy for reducing unemployment, then, is to eliminate some of the friction in the labor market. The policy conclusions of the search theory are typified by Charles C. Holt's

---

[11]Vera C. Perrella and Edward J. O'Boyle, "Work Plans of Men Not in the Labor Force," *Monthly Labor Review,* Vol. 91 (August 1968), pp. 8-14.

[12]Many interesting papers on the search theory and related topics appear in Edmund S. Phelps and others, *Microeconomic Foundations of Employment and Inflation Theory* (Norton, 1970).

ingenious suggestion that the offices of the U.S. Employment Service should be kept open at night so that workers can search for new jobs before quitting their old ones.[13] To practical economists, something is missing here. In the course of providing a firm logical foundation for the traditional notion of frictional unemployment, the search theory seems to claim that all unemployment is frictional, that every person who reports himself as out of work is spending a few weeks between jobs in the normal advancement of his career. In his discussion of Holt's and Phelps' work, Otto Eckstein puts this point forcefully: ". . . the central employment problem of our society today is the disparity of employment opportunities among blacks and whites, among skilled and unskilled, among young and experienced. . . . We are in danger of devising a labor market theory which is as remote from the central employment problem of our times as the classical theory was in the 1930's."[14]

In the previous section I tried to show that chronic unemployment is not the central employment problem of our time, either. Whatever the merit of Eckstein's criticism, it does not appear that the search theorists are wrong in looking at the problem of unemployment from the point of view of turnover in the labor force. The central problem seems to be that some groups in the labor force have rates of unemployment that are far in excess of the rates that would accord with the hypothesis that the unemployed are making a normal transition from one job to another. Some groups exhibit what seems to be pathological instability in holding jobs. Changing from one low-paying, unpleasant job to another, often several times a year, is the typical pattern of some workers. The resulting unemployment can hardly be said to be the outcome of a normal process of career advancement. The true problem of hard-core unemployment is that certain members of the labor force account for a disproportionate share of unemployment because

they drift from one unsatisfactory job to another, spending the time between jobs either unemployed or out of the labor force. The most compact evidence supporting the existence of such a group is provided by the data on the number of spells of unemployment experienced by the labor force. Among those who were unemployed at some time in 1968, 69 percent had only one spell of unemployment, 15 percent had two spells, and 16 percent had three or more.[15] The overall unemployment rate in 1968 was 3.6 percent, and the average unemployed person required about one month to find a new job. The implied average duration between spells of unemployment was about twenty-seven months. In order to have two, much less three, spells of unemployment in the same twelve months, an individual could hardly be making normal changes in jobs. Yet almost a third of those unemployed at all in 1968—more than 3 million individuals—had two or more spells. The existence of this group is surely a matter of social concern.

In order to identify groups in the labor force who suffer from excess unemployment at full employment, it is necessary to make a crude guess about the amount of unemployment that arises from normal turnover. I have done this by making a set of assumptions about the time required to find a job and the frequency with which individuals of various ages change jobs.[16] From this I have calculated the implied rates of unemployment by age groups, as shown in Table 3. The assumptions are as follows: (1) An individual looking for his first job requires, on the average, two months to find it, but he requires only one month to find subsequent jobs; (2) teenagers change jobs every year, young adults every two years, and adults (age 25 and over) every four years; (3) the pattern of entry into the labor force yields the distribution between inexperienced and experienced members shown in columns 1 and 3 of Table 3. The resulting hypothetical normal rates of unemployment appear in column 6 of the table. With

[13]"Improving the Labor Market Trade-off between Inflation and Unemployment," in American Economic Association, *Papers and Proceedings of the Eighty-first Annual Meeting, 1968, American Economic Review,* Vol. 59 (May 1969), p. 142.

[14]"Discussion," in American Economic Association, *Papers and Proceedings* (May 1969), p. 163.

[15]Vera C. Perrella, "Work Experience of the Population," *Monthly Labor Review,* Vol. 93 (February 1970), Table 2, p. 57.

[16]These are purely assumptions and are not drawn from any data. Actual data would, of course, include the effects of the abnormal unemployment I am trying to distinguish.

Table 3

Comparison of Hypothetical Normal Rates of Unemployment and Actual Rates, by Age Group, April 1969

| | | | | | | Actual rates | | | |
| | | | | | | Males | | Females | |
Age	*Percent looking for or holding first job* (1)	*Percent looking for first job*[a] (2)	*Percent looking for or holding subsequent job* (3)	*Years per job* (4)	*Percent looking for subsequent job*[b] (5)	*Hypothetical normal unemployment rate* (6)	*White* (7)	*Black* (8)	*White* (9)	*Black* (10)
16-17 years	75	13	25	1	2	15	11.1	18.0	12.9	22.8
18-19 years	38	6	62	1	5	11	7.0	19.0	9.1	23.3
20-24 years	6	1	94	2	4	5	3.8	8.6	4.8	13.0
25 years and over	0	0	100	4	2	2	1.6	2.7	2.7	5.5

Sources: Columns 1, 3, and 4—author's assumptions; column 2—one-sixth of column 1; column 5—one-twelfth of (column 3 divided by column 4); column 6—column 2 plus column 5; actual rates—*Employment and Earnings*, Vol. 15 (May 1969), Table A-3, pp. 31, 32.

a Assumes that two months are required to find first jobs.
b Assumes that one month is required to find subsequent jobs.

the distribution of the labor force among age groups prevailing in 1969, the overall normal unemployment rate would be 3.3 percent, not a great deal below the actual rate of 3.5 percent. The last four columns show why this is so. White males, the largest of the four sex-race groups, actually had unemployment rates below the hypothetical normal rates in every age group in April 1969. This probably demonstrates that the assumptions used in making the calculations are a little pessimistic, although it should be kept in mind that April 1969 was a month of over-full employment and not one of equilibrium as I defined it at the beginning of the paper. It is important to note that if my assumptions are anywhere near the truth, the differentials between the unemployment rates of teenagers and adults among white males are a normal consequence of the process of looking for jobs and are not an indication of a special problem for teenagers. For black males, the situation is altogether different. Rates of unemployment are about 35 percent greater among adult black males than the hypothetical values, and are even higher for 18- and 19-year-olds. Nothing in the theory of turnover or frictional unemployment seems capable of explaining this extraordinary discrepancy. Blacks are poorly educated and poorly trained in comparison to their white counterparts, and they suffer from discrimination as well, but those facts do not adequately explain why they should take longer to find a job or why they should change jobs more often. In the framework of the search theory, a satisfactory explanation would involve demonstrating that it is in the interest of disadvantaged workers to search for jobs more often and for longer periods. I shall have a little more to say about this matter in a later section, but it remains an urgent unsolved problem of modern economic research.

White females have unemployment rates somewhat below the hypothetical levels in all but the highest age group. These and other data suggest that the main problems experienced by white females in the labor force arise not in their early years in the labor force, but after age 25. For example, as I shall show in the next section, wages paid to white females are almost as high as those paid to white males up to age 25, but after that age wages paid to men rise steadily while those paid to women remain at essentially the level of age 25.

Finally, black females suffer the largest discrepancy of all between actual and hypothetical unemployment rates. In fact, they suffer more than doubly for being black and for being women: In every category their unemployment rate exceeds the rate of white females by more than the difference between black and white males.

I conclude, then, that only among white males is normal turnover a satisfactory unitary explanation of the observed levels of unemployment by age groups. Signs of pathological excess unemployment appear in the data for women and blacks. Even for white males, unemployment is distributed unevenly between high- and low-paid workers, as I will show in the next section.

WORKERS WHO ARE UNEMPLOYED FREQUENTLY

Earlier in this paper I have argued that the problem of hard-core unemployment at full employment is not so much that there are individuals who are permanently out of work as that there are many workers who move frequently from job to job without advancing their careers. Further study of the problem ought logically to be carried out with data on the experience over time of a representative sample of members of the labor force. The existence of groups with unstable work histories could be confirmed and the nature of the problem examined more deeply with such data. The only data available, however, give information about the status of individuals only for a single year. This makes it necessary to infer conclusions about the experience of an individual over time from the status of similar individuals of different ages at the same point in time.

To an economist, the natural way to measure the progress of an individual worker is by his wage. As he accumulates experience and specialized training on the job, his hourly wage should rise year by year. At a point in time, then, the age profile of wages should rise smoothly with age, provided that an appropriate adjustment is made for the fact that older workers tend to have less formal education and may tend to live in areas with lower wages. From the data in the Survey of Economic Opportunity, I have made estimates of the pure age profile of hourly wages, incorporating adjustments for years of education, loca-

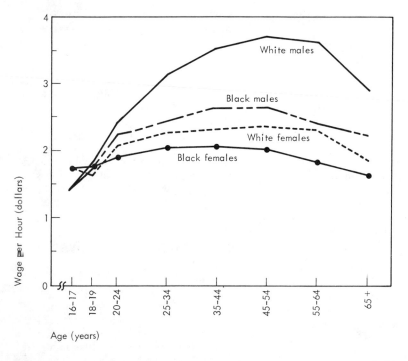

Figure 3

Age Profile of Wages by Sex and Race, 1966

Source: Hall, "Wages, Income, and Hours of Work," Table 2-2, p. 23.

tion, union membership, health, and country of birth. The results are presented in Figure 3. They suggest that the whole notion of a career with steady advancement is relevant only for white males, whose wages rise through ages 45 to 54. Black males, and women of both races, make progress only through ages 20 to 24. From ages 25 to 34 onward, their wage profiles are practically flat.

From data on the status of a sample of individuals at a single point in time, something can be inferred about the proportion of time that individuals with various characteristics spend looking for work, although there is no way to tell if a high proportion is the result of many short spells or a few long ones. Within each of the four sex-race groups in the SEO sample, unemployment is very unevenly distributed. In general, workers with few skills are much more likely to be unemployed than others. Once again, to an economist, the natural overall measure of an individual's level of skill is the wage he earns, or would earn if he were working. To adjust for the tendency for well-paid

workers to live in cities where unemployment rates are high, and for other related effects, it is necessary again to use estimates of the pure effects obtained by regression. These are presented in Table 4 and incorporate adjustments for age, marital status, number of children, income, and location.

White males in the lower wage groups experience unemployment of moderate length; the length declines to the relatively low rate of 1.4 weeks per year in the highest wage group. Black males, in contrast, have much longer periods than whites in the lower wage groups, and shorter ones in the higher groups.[17] I offer the following tentative explanation for this difference: Whites are willing to work steadily at low-paying jobs because they are aware that they can start up a job ladder by establishing a stable employment record. Blacks, on the other hand, do not seem to have this opportunity,

[17]The negative value for the highest wage group for black males serves as a reminder that these results are subject to a certain amount of statistical variation.

Table 4

Estimates of Weeks of Unemployment, by Race, Sex, and Wage Groups, 1966

Hourly wage in dollars	Men		Women	
	White	Black	White	Black
0-1.50	4.3	9.4	1.3	1.0
1.50-1.75	2.8	8.3	1.1	1.3
1.75-2.00	2.8	4.9	1.0	1.6
2.00-2.50	3.0	2.7	0.8	1.2
2.50-3.00	2.0	0.0	0.9	0.3
3.00 or more	1.4	1.0	0.0	0.6

Source: Derived from regression estimates for married individuals, aged 20 through 59, with no children, living in the New York Standard Metropolitan Statistical Area, and with family incomes between $3,750 and $4,500 per adult per year.

and therefore are likely to leave a low-paying job within a few months or a year. Thus trainees in banks and workers in service stations receive about the same hourly wages, but the trainees have an incentive to work hard and steadily that is absent for the service station men. A few blacks accomplish what is routine for whites, however, so in the higher wage groups there is much more selection of the most stable workers among blacks than among whites.

Racial differences among women are not as pronounced, perhaps because women of both races are generally excluded from the job ladder. Note that although women have higher unemployment rates than men, as reported in the household survey, they have fewer weeks of unemployment per year. The unemployment rate in a group is, roughly speaking, the ratio of weeks of unemployment to weeks in the labor force, and women tend to spend substantially fewer weeks in the labor force than men.

Economists are occasionally tempted to speculate about another source of unemployment: For many people only low-paying, unpleasant jobs are available, either because of lack of skills or because of discriminatory exclusion. If they have income from sources other than their own work, they might work only part time, or more likely, part of the year, and enjoy leisure (which is cheap for them) the rest of the time. Moving in and out of the labor force would cause them to be recorded as unemployed frequently. Further, a person who feels guilty about not working might report himself as unemployed even though he was not

actually interested in taking the kind of job he could get. Both of these kinds of unemployment are voluntary in that they are different from the unemployment suffered by a person who is simply unable to find a job despite serious effort. One implication of this argument seems to be that unemployment ought to be positively associated with income from sources other than an individual's own work. In the regressions ... discussed above, I have controlled for income as well as wages, using a comprehensive measure of income that includes the nonwage income of the family and estimates of the wage income of other members of the family. It also includes the value of the individual's own time, but this does not affect the interpretation, since his wage is included separately. Income does not include the individual's actual wage income, of course, since that depends on his amount of unemployment. The income effects in all four regressions are quite small, and generally have signs that are the opposite of those predicted by the theory just mentioned. If anything, individuals in a given wage group tend to have more unemployment if their families are poor. There is no evidence whatever in favor of the hypothesis that unemployment is voluntary in the sense defined above.

Earlier sections of the paper have suggested how these data on individuals at a single point in time ought to be interpreted. They show who is likely to become unemployed for a spell one or more times during a year, not who is likely to remain permanently out of a job. Blacks and women seem to be excluded from work that offers an incentive to stay with a job permanently, and spend much larger fractions of their time in the labor force looking for new jobs than do white males. Within each group, the lower-paid members spend many more weeks looking for work than do the higher-paid ones. Finally, even with the wage level held constant, higher income seems to reduce weeks of unemployment.

12. Unemployment: A Fresh Perspecti

Charles C. Killingsworth

98   Unemployment: A F
counted as unem
participants in
rary progra
ployed." T
soundne
impo
the

INTERPRETING THE 1960's

There has developed what may fairly be called a "conventional wisdom" concerning what happened to unemployment in the 1960's.   . . .Even after recovery from the 1960-61 recession the national unemployment rate remained at the excessively high level of 5.5 to 6.0 percent. Most economists attributed this "prosperity" unemployment to a chronic insufficiency of aggregate demand, produced by "fiscal drag" in the Federal revenue system. If aggregate demand were sufficiently stimulated by massive tax cuts, it was argued, unemployment would fall at least to the 4 percent level. In 1964, there was a huge reduction in personal and business income taxes, and further cuts were made in 1965. Then, also in 1965, defense expenditures moved sharply upward, providing further fiscal stimulus. The unemployment rate fell below 4 percent in 1966 and continued down to roughly 3.5 percent, which prevailed through most of 1968 and 1969. The conventional wisdom sees a simple cause and effect relationship at work here: the great tax cut, followed by great increases in defense expenditures, fully remedied the earlier insufficiency of aggregate demand and solved the problem of excessive unemployment. The policy conclusion, which is heard constantly today, is that sufficiently strong application of

fiscal and monetary policy, *without anything else,* is capable of reducing unemployment to the 3.5 percent level. Any unemployment rate higher than that is clear evidence of an insufficiency of aggregate demand *and nothing else.* Most economists today accept this conventional wisdom as fully proven by the experience of the 1960's.

In my view, the conventional wisdom rests squarely on the *post hoc, ergo propter hoc* fallacy. It implicitly assumes that the only factor which reduced the reported unemployment rate was the rapid growth of aggregate demand in the later 1960's. This assumption is demonstrably contrary to the facts of the matter. Undeniably, the expansion of aggregate demand created more jobs in the 1960's and was partially responsible for the lower unemployment rates. But there were other factors at work which, in combination, accounted for more of the decline in unemployment than did the growth of demand.

First, there were two significant changes in the definition of unemployment. In 1965, government technicians decided that they would no longer count as "unemployed" the participants in certain work-relief programs—notably the Neighborhood Youth Corps and the College Work-Study Program, and some other smaller ones. In the 1930's, participants in the CCC, NYA, and WPA program had been

ployed; but starting in 1965,
the fairly comparable contempo-
ns have been counted as "em-
here is no point now in debating the
ss of that change in definition. What is
tant is that it contributed significantly to
lowering of the reported unemployment
te. By a very conservative method of calculation, it can be shown that by 1969, the national
unemployment rate was 0.5 percent lower than
it would have been under the pre-1965 definition. Another set of definition changes was
made effective in 1967. One of the important
changes was a tightening of the "seeking work"
test. The net effect of these changes, according
to the Bureau of Labor Statistics, was to reduce
the reported unemployment rate by about 0.2
percent under the conditions prevailing in
1966. (I suspect that the effect might be somewhat greater under the higher unemployment
levels of today.) The combined effect of the
1965 and 1967 definition changes, then, was a
reduction of at least 0.7 percent in the unemployment rate.

Second, the expansion of the Armed Forces
which began in 1965 withdrew a total of about
900,000 young men from civilian life at the
peak (in late 1968). Most of these young men
would have been in the labor force if they had
not been in the military. Only a minor fraction
would have been unemployed; but the jobs
filled by those who were employed obviously
would have been unavailable to those who
actually held them. After making a generous
allowance for new entries to the labor force
induced by the greater availability of jobs, it
seems reasonable to estimate that the expansion
of the Armed Forces and the resulting shrinkage of the civilian labor force reduced the
reported unemployment rate by 450,000, or
0.6 percent.

The national unemployment rate fell from
about 5.5 percent in early 1964 to about 3.5
percent in 1969. The two factors just discussed
accounted for a total of 1.3 percentage points,
or roughly three-fifths of the decline. At the
risk of some oversimplification, it might be said
that if demand expansion had been the *only*
factor affecting the unemployment rate, it
probably would have fallen no lower than
about 4.8 percent.

I trust that the fallacy in the conventional
wisdom now stands exposed. But there is more
that must be said. There was a *third* factor,
other than "pure" demand expansion, which

contributed to lower unemployment in the late
1960's. This factor was the nature of defense
spending increases. Most of the defense work
went to manufacturing industries, and in those
industries a disproportionately large number of
the new jobs were filled by bluecollar workers.
In the 1950's and early 1960's, bluecollar jobs
in manufacturing had been subject to a disproportionately high rate of attrition, and defense
spending patterns temporarily reversed this
trend. There is no obvious way to quantify the
effect of this factor in the national unemployment rate, but it must have made some contribution.

There was also a *fourth* factor. Even during
the great economic expansion of the middle
1960's, there was a continued growth of hidden
unemployment among men with less-than-
average education. Even in the years from 1962
to 1967, there was a net increase of more than
700,000 men who must be counted among the
hidden unemployed, according to my estimates.
In these years, even among men in the prime
working ages but with less-than-average education, there was a persistent and pervasive decline in labor force participation rates. The
basic reason for this continuing phenomenon,
in my judgment, was a continuing scarcity of
jobs for low-skilled and poorly-educated workers. It is true that millions of new jobs were
created in the 1960's; but my calculations show
that about 97 percent of the gross increase in
jobs for men went to those with average or
better-than-average education. The employment
of men with 8 or fewer years of schooling
actually declined from 1962 to 1969—by more
than 2.5 million. Some of the job loss was
offset by deaths and retirements in this group,
but hundreds of thousands of less-educated
men simply stopped looking for work. Since
those not actively seeking employment are not
counted among the unemployed, these drop-
outs made some further contribution to the
lowering of the reported unemployment rate.

THE RECENT RISE IN UNEMPLOYMENT

The conventional wisdom has no difficulty
in explaining the rise in unemployment that
began late in 1969. The level of unemployment
is determined by the state of aggregate demand,
says this school of thought; and, it argues, the
experience of the 1960's is clear proof that any
level of unemployment above 3.5 percent is

conclusive evidence of insufficient aggregate demand. If our only domestic goal is full employment, this school says, we can readily achieve it by fiscal and monetary policies directed to the expansion of demand. In this view, the real obstacle in the road to full employment is inflation: a policy of strong stimulation of aggregate demand would defeat the effort to bring inflation under control. Therefore, it is obvious to this school that the restoration of price stability must be given priority over the restoration of full employment. (Unless, of course, political necessities dictate an economically irrational reversal of these priorities.)

In my view, the linkages between inflation, aggregate demand and unemployment are considerably looser and less direct than the conventional wisdom assumes. Perhaps it is hardly necessary to do more than to point to our recent experience with sustained high levels of unemployment, large amounts of unused industrial capacity, and continued high rates of price increases in order to make the basic point. But I think it can also be shown that, even in the absence of a recession, we would have had a substantial rise in reported unemployment. In other words, some part—but only a part—of the recent rise in unemployment rates was caused by the economic slowdown; and faster economic growth will remedy part—but only part—of our excessive unemployment.

Three major factors in addition to the recession have contributed to higher unemployment rates in the past two years. The first and most obvious is the reduction in the size of the Armed Forces. Current reports indicate a reduction by mid-1971 of about 800,000 men from the peak strength reached late in 1968; the present level is only about 100,000 men above the pre-Vietnam level. Obviously, not all of the men returned to civilian life are in the labor force, nor are all of those in the labor force unemployed; but unemployment rates for Vietnam-era veterans are running substantially above the national average, and the jobs now held by veterans are obviously unavailable to the unemployed workers who might have filled them if the veterans were still withheld from the labor force. In other words, the reduction in the size of the Armed Forces has contributed to the growth of the civilian labor force and has increased the competition for jobs.

The second obvious factor is massive layoffs and dismissals from defense plants as a result of spending cutbacks. I have not succeeded in finding any up-to-date figures that I regard as reliable, but it seems likely that a substantial part of the 2.2 million job loss in manufacturing must be attributed to this factor.

A third, less obvious, factor is slower or zero growth of the manpower programs that were expanding in the mid-1960's. In their expansionary years, these programs were drawing off into "employment" a growing percentage of designated groups with high unemployment rates. Many of these groups have continued to grow, but the manpower programs stopped growing (or greatly slowed their growth rates) some time ago.

I emphasize these factors because I believe that many analysts have ignored or underrated their significance. Let me also emphasize that in my view the recession, and the weakening in aggregate demand which it brought, have contributed to the rise in unemployment. It would be clearly contrary to the evidence to deny that. But it is equally contrary to the evidence to assert that all of the rise in unemployment is the result of the recession (as conventionally defined).

HIDDEN UNEMPLOYMENT

I have already referred briefly above to the concept of "hidden unemployment." Almost by definition, hidden unemployment cannot be counted as accurately as officially-defined unemployment. And the basic assumption of the official definitions is that if a man (or woman) is not actively looking for work, his desire for it is at least questionable. Yet we know from a number of technical studies that the percentages of certain groups that get counted as being "in the labor force" change considerably as their reported unemployment rate rises and falls. We do have fairly elaborate reporting of labor force participation rates, and the study of these rates can give us some fairly strong clues to the approximate size and distribution of hidden unemployment. The Government has now adopted the concept of the "full employment budget," which sometimes turn deficits into surpluses; and I think that labor market analysts should give more attention to the idea of an unemployment measure calculated on the basis of a "full employment participation rate." Unfortunately, the kinds of data that I regard as most meaningful in the calculation of a reasonable estimate of "hidden unemployment" are gathered only once a year and are not available to the public for many months after they have been gathered. Therefore, I have not been able to update to 1971 my own detailed estimates of hidden unemployment. There is every reason to expect, however, given the level of reported unemployment, that the calculated figure for hidden unemployment in early 1971 will exceed 1,000,000 persons.

There is one aspect of hidden unemployment which deserves special attention at this hearing today. As the Committee undoubtedly knows, considerable attention has recently been directed to the nonwhite-white unemployment rate ratio. Since 1954, the nonwhite unemployment rate has consistently been at least twice the white unemployment rate. In recent months, however, that ratio has declined. In 1970, for the first time since the early 1950's, the ratio was below 2.0 for the entire year. This fact has repeatedly been cited as a bright area in a generally gloomy unemployment picture. Even though nonwhite unemployment rates were going up, it has been said, the fact that they were rising less rapidly than white rates meant that this long-established racial inequity was finally being reduced. Unhappily, further analysis shows that this optimistic interpretation is unjustified.

The reduction in this unemployment ratio is more than accounted for by a rise in hidden unemployment among nonwhites. Especially

since 1967, nonwhite males in virtually all age groups have had declining labor force participation rates, and the rate of decline has, in general, substantially exceeded declines in the comparable white age groups. The aggregate participation rate for nonwhite females has remained essentially unchanged in recent years, while the participation rate for white females has steadily risen. We can calculate what the nonwhite unemployment rate would have been if male and female participation rates had changed in the same way and by the same proportion as the participation rate changes for white males and females. (This would mean declining participation rates for nonwhite males, but at a slower rate; it would mean rising, instead of static, participation rates for nonwhite females.)

This seems to me to be a reasonably conservative method of calculating a "real" unemployment rate for nonwhites—that is, adding into the official count a realistic estimate of the *recent* increases in hidden unemployment in this group. Table 1 presents the reported figures for 1966 through 1970, the ratios, and the revised unemployment rates and ratios for nonwhites in 1970. When recent additions to hidden unemployment are taken into account, the nonwhite unemployment rate for 1970 increases by nearly half; and the nonwhite-white ratio rises from the widely-publicized 1.8 to 2.6.

In other words, the apparent reduction in this racial inequity is entirely attributable to the economic forces that produced a relatively

Table 1

Unemployment Rates for Persons Age 16 and Older, by Sex and Color, Annual Averages, 1966-70, and Nonwhite/White Ratio

| | | *Unemployment rates* | | | | | | | |
| | | *White* | | | *Nonwhite* | | *Nonwhite/White Ratio* | | |
	Total	*Male*	*Female*	*Total*	*Male*	*Female*	*Total*	*Male*	*Female*
Year:									
1966	3.3	2.8	4.3	7.3	6.3	8.6	2.2	2.3	2.0
1967	3.4	2.7	4.6	7.4	6.0	9.1	2.2	2.2	2.0
1968	3.2	2.6	4.3	6.7	5.6	8.3	2.1	2.2	1.9
1969	3.1	2.5	4.2	6.4	5.3	7.8	2.1	2.1	1.9
1970	4.5	4.0	5.4	8.2	7.3	9.3	1.8	1.8	1.7
1970R*	4.5	4.0	5.4	12.0	9.5	14.8	2.6	2.4	2.7

*Nonwhite unemployment rates based on revised labor force participation rates by methods summarized in test.

rapid shrinkage in the nonwhite male labor force and a lack of growth in the nonwhite female labor force at a time of relatively rapid growth in the white female labor force. The "better" figures for nonwhites are not attributable to more jobs, or more success in holding on to jobs, but rather to delayed entry to or induced departure from the labor force.

POLICY CONCLUSIONS

I have imposed upon the patience of the Committee enough, or perhaps too much already. The purpose of this discussion has obviously been diagnosis rather than prescription. Yet I hope that I may offer a few concluding words on the implications of my diagnosis for public policy. In particular, I want to draw attention to two currently popular lines of policy that are, in my judgment, traps for the unwary.

Passivity in employment policy has gained a degree of acceptance in high circles, it appears. It is true that the President ultimately accepted a Public Service Employment program, but not until the Congressional proposals had been considered watered down under threats of another veto. The Administration has proposed a new Manpower bill; but its chief purpose appears to be the tidying-up of organization and flow charts, with only a modest increase in funding. It is fair to say, I think, that these measures would be just as appropriate at a 4.5 percent level of unemployment as they are today. In other words, they are not really responsive to the degree of excess unemployment that we are presently experiencing. The basic assumption in the Administration appears to be that "natural forces" will clear away the excess unemployment if we just wait long enough; the unemployed veterans and the displaced defense workers will be "absorbed" in a year or two. Obviously, not all are likely to be permanently unemployed. However, many of these long-term unemployed may drop out of the unemployment reports and into the limbo of hidden unemployment, as so many nonwhites have recently. And that kind of statistical improvement is hardly a solution to either the economic or the human problems that are really involved.

There is always a temptation to postpose action until next month's report or next quar-ter's index figure is available. There are also those who will argue that "benign neglect" is the best treatment for some problems, because they will go away if you wait long enough. There were some who so argued with regard to the teen-age unemployment problem of the 1960's. Wait until the teen-agers get a little older, and their apparent unemployment problem will moderate greatly, it was argued. And that was partly true. In the current recession, the teen-age unemployment rate went up at a substantially slower rate than the national rate (about a 40 percent rise versus about a 70 percent rise). The catch—so often there is a catch!—is that the teen-age problem of the 1960's, which was treated in part with benign neglect, has now matured into a young adult unemployment problem. The unemployment rate for workers in ages 20 to 24 rose substantially faster than the national rate during the recession; and the May 1971 rate of 11.1 percent for this group has been exceeded only once in the past 25 years: at the bottom of the 1957-58 recession. Time does not really solve most problems, at least in the labor market; it only makes them older and makes us more complacent about them.

The second policy trap is the belief that we have now discovered and tested the ultimate weapon against unemployment—sufficiently vigorous fiscal and monetary policy—and the only thing wrong with it is that we can't use it right now. As I have demonstrated, this belief rests squarely on a fallacy. Yet we must not underestimate its influence. This belief does not induce action, in the present circumstances; its real utility today is as another justification for passivity in employment policy. But so long as the inflation threat prohibits the use of this putative weapon, it is the practical equivalent of no weapon at all. And, in any event, a proper reading of the experience of the 1960's shows that the reputed power of this ultimate weapon is grossly exaggerated.

Fiscal and monetary policy have an important role to play in controlling unemployment. I argued in 1963, however, and continue to argue today that it is a serious mistake to make fiscal and monetary policy the "centerpiece" of employment policy. It would be an equally serious mistake to make manpower retraining, or public service employment, or any other one program the "centerpiece" of employment policy. Medical men today generally accept the idea that cancer is really a whole family of diseases which must be fought with a variety of treatments. Similarly, we need to see that unemployment is a complex of problems for which we lack a sovereign remedy. Economic growth will cure some cases while leaving others untouched. Retraining is best for some, but useless for others, and many cases will need subsidized employment of one kind or another. Various combinations of remedies may be needed for some types of unemployment.

The greatest weakness of our array of manpower programs at present is that all, without any exception known to me, provide "slots" for only a pitifully small fraction of those eligible under the terms of the programs. This weakness is especially apparent in the newly-enacted Public Service Employment Program. This new program will provide a maximum of about 173,000 slots in this fiscal year; several million workers will be eligible for them. . . .

. . . I suggest that the trouble today with the rules of economics is that we have tried to apply the unchanged rules of the past to a greatly changed world. I suspect that J. M. Keynes himself would protest against some of the applications of his doctrines today. Even 35 years ago, Keynes had a keener appreciation of the limitations of his analysis and policy prescriptions than some of his recently-converted disciples of today.

13. Federal Training and Work Programs in the Sixties

Sar A. Levitan

Garth L. Mangum

A $2.2 BILLION PACKAGE

The federal government has become deeply committed to manpower programs to enhance the employment prospects and employability of individuals. Manpower policy—as contrasted with fiscal and monetary policies which affect total levels of employment—is an integral component of federal economic policy. Federally-supported manpower programs, mostly devoted to aiding the unemployed and the inadequately educated, carried in 1968 an annual price tag of $2.2 billion, a ninefold increase since 1961.

An intricate, but far from comprehensive, federal manpower policy has been emerging from the variety of programs created piecemeal during the present decade to meet separate but related needs. The goals are noble in purpose, but the terrain is new and difficult. The range of undertaking is impressive, but the distribution of effort is not well balanced and the administrative machinery seems unduly complex.

Though the progress in federal manpower policy has been notable, it is inaccurate to speak of federal manpower programs. Of the total manpower budget, only about one of every ten federal dollars is spent on programs operated by agencies of the federal government. The rest is expended through grants-in-aid, contracts and grants to encourage and assist state and local governments and private institutions to provide employment-related services. . . .

THE EMERGENCE OF NEW PROGRAMS

Two major developments combined to generate federal support for training and rehabilitating the unemployed and disadvantaged. First was the sustained high level of unemployment experienced during the latter part of the 1950's and persisting into the mid-1960's. The second development, and perhaps the more significant in the long-run, was the civil rights movement.

The concern with unemployment prompted attack on two fronts: (1) stimulation of total demand for goods and services with a consequent increase in employment levels; and (2) lowering of geographical, age, skill, and racial barriers which prevented many individuals from competing effectively for existing jobs.

The civil rights movement initially focused upon civil and political rights of Negroes, particularly school integration, voting rights, and equal access to public facilities. It soon became clear, however, that Negroes and other deprived minorities could not compete on an equal footing in American life without special economic assistance. As President John F. Kennedy stated: "Employment opportunities play a major role in determining whether [civil] rights are meaningful. There is little value in a Negro's obtaining the right to be admitted to hotels and restaurants if he has no cash in his pocket and no job."[1] With that diagnosis, the solutions appeared the same as for general unemployment—more jobs and more training—but there was an essential difference. Without the civil rights movement and the attention it focused upon poverty, reduction of unemployment could have dissolved effective support for continuing public manpower efforts. More recently, riots in the nation's urban slums, stemming from the unrest among minorities, have, while antagonizing some voters, added the impetus of fear for others. As a result, falling unemployment has brought the problem of competitive disadvantage in the job market into sharper relief.

Both demand-stimulating measures and manpower programs have contributed in varying degrees to declining unemployment but with an essential difference. Once monetary and fiscal policy decisions were made, their administration involved relatively few problems. This is not true of the manpower programs, where political decision was only the first step. Success or failure depended upon innovation in the creation of a viable administrative structure.

THE NEW DIMENSION

Although the federal government is no novice in affecting manpower utilization, the emphasis during the sixties has changed radically. The traditional concern of federal manpower policy was the supply of labor, both skilled and unskilled. Early examples are the land-grant college system established during the Civil War period of agricultural expansion and early industrialization, and matching grants for vocational education as industrialization entered a more sophisticated stage. Even the federally-financed state employment services have been primarily concerned with filling job orders. Only during the depression of the 1930's did manpower policy efforts shift to the demand side in financing public works and work-relief jobs.

During World War II the federal impact upon

[1] Civil Rights Message, June 19, 1963.

manpower was all pervading. Not only were millions of persons drafted into the armed forces, but vast numbers were also trained and retrained for war production. Wage policies also were utilized to channel labor into defense industries. The G.I. Bill of Rights, following World War II, had a significant impact upon manpower development by providing education and training to 7.8 million veterans.

During the fifties, federal manpower policies focused upon expanding the supply of highly skilled and professional labor. The establishment of the National Science Foundation and the passage of the National Defense Education Act were illustrative of the new interests.

During the sixties, these efforts have continued but a new dimension has been added. No longer is the emphasis on matching the best man with an existing job, but on providing a suitable job for each man or equipping the man to fill a suitable job.

Serving the undereducated, the undermotivated, and victims of discrimination demanded not only reorientation in the values of existing manpower agencies but also a whole set of closely interwoven new functions. The agencies neither generated nor sought this reorientation, but new functions have been thrust upon them by changing public attitudes and new government commitments.

The new measures for the competitively disadvantaged which have emerged from the experiments of recent years are broad in scope but the machinery for implementing them is cumbersome. One present challenge is to build a balanced and orderly vehicle to administer the new programs without losing the stimulus to continuing innovation. Another is to expand the manpower services to a reasonable relation with need.

THE FEDERALLY-SUPPORTED MANPOWER PROGRAMS

The complexity of current manpower policy can be traced to the rapid development of the new programs and their interaction at the federal, state, and local levels (Table 1).

The first of the new programs aimed at reducing the competitive disadvantage of individuals and groups was the Area Redevelopment Act of 1961. Its target was the unemployment concentrated in depressed areas and its intent was to attract industry and jobs to those

Table 1

Funding Federally-Supported Manpower Programs Fiscal Years 1961-1968 (Millions of Dollars)

	1961	1962	1963	1964	1965	1966	1967	1968
TOTALS	245	296	402	499	1377	1926	2162	2184
DEPARTMENT OF LABOR								
United States Employment Service	112	144	162	173	182	226	277	296
Bureau of Apprenticeship and Training	4	5	5	5	6	7	8	8
Bureau of Labor Statistics (Manpower Statistics)	4	5	5	6	7	8	9	9
Manpower Development and Training Act	–	–	70	130	397	435	421	416
DEPARTMENT OF HEALTH, EDUCATION AND WELFARE								
Vocational Education	50	54	57	57	187	261	285	296
Vocational Rehabilitation	75	88	103	128	146	231	328	387
Adult Basic Education	–	–	–	–	19	36	29	39
OFFICE OF ECONOMIC OPPORTUNITY								
Neighborhood Youth Corps	–	–	–	–	132	272	373	281
Job Corps	–	–	–	–	183	310	211	285
Work Experience and Training	–	–	–	–	112	112	100	45
Operation Mainstream	–	–	–	–	–	–	36	36
New Careers	–	–	–	–	–	–	36	36
Special Impact	–	–	–	–	–	–	20	20
CAP Manpower	–	–	–	–	6	28	29	30

Source: Departments of Labor; Health, Education, and Welfare; and Office of Economic Opportunity.

areas. The measure to aid depressed areas received priority, having been twice vetoed by the previous Administration. It had been a political issue in the 1958 and 1960 elections and was ready for passage when President Kennedy assumed office. The program floundered because, given the intransigent forces which had restrained the long-term growth of those areas and the general slack in the total economy, ARA's resources were inadequate to the task and they were frittered away attempting to do too much with too little in too many places.

The next effort was to expand the training of the unemployed which had been a miniscule component of ARA. The Manpower Development and Training Act of 1962 concentrated at first upon the needs of unemployed family heads with a past history—three years or more—of labor force attachment. Emphasis was placed upon institutional training; allowances, linked to the average levels of unemployment compensation in the state, were paid through the network of local employment offices. Also, an experimental effort—Community Work and Training—was started under the Welfare Ad-

ministration designed to let relief recipients (unemployed parents under AFDC-UP) develop work habits and "work off" the aid received.

The following year the emphasis shifted to youth. Unemployment of male adult family heads had dropped sharply, but the level of youth unemployment continued to rise despite overall economic expansion. In 1963, one of every seven white teenagers remained unemployed, and for nonwhites the rate was twice as high. The Youth Employment Act was passed by the Senate, combining the experience of the Civilian Conservation Corps and the National Youth Administration of the 1930's. However the bill was bottled up by the House Committee on Rules which objected to racially integrated camps. Instead, the youth component of MDTA was expanded, raising maximum allowances to youth from five percent of total expenditures to 25 percent of the trainees enrolled. The Vocational Education Act of 1963 quintupled federal support of vocational education over a period of three years hoping at the same time to shift its [focus toward the] expanding secretarial and technical occupations and buy greater attention for those with educational handicaps.

In 1964 President Johnson declared "total war on poverty," but the beginnings were modest. In line with traditional values, the goal was not to lift the needy out of poverty but to open the paths of opportunity and self-help to them. Wrapped in the poverty ribbon of the Economic Opportunity Act was a series of work training programs, some conventional and some new but all directed toward employment as the preferred source of income. After a learning period, the antipoverty budget was expected to increase to a level commensurate with the task at hand, but with subsequent events the needed funding never came.

The pending Youth Employment Bill became the Neighborhood Youth Corps and the Job Corps, the former providing work experience and income to unemployed youth both in and out of school. The Job Corps was designed for those youths whose home environment was the major obstacle to successful education, training, and employment.

Also included in the antipoverty package were funds for basic adult education, a work-experience program which enlarged the earlier Community Work and Training Program designed to offer opportunities to relief recipients and other needy persons, limited loan provisions for self-employed, and the Community Action Program (CAP).

The Community Action Program, based on concepts developed by the Ford Foundation's "gray-areas" program and the Juvenile Delinquency and Youth Offense Control Act of 1961, was the "heart" of the Poverty Act. Practically any project that aimed at reducing poverty in a community could be funded by the Community Action Program, provided only that the poor or their spokesmen participated in the planning and execution of the project, and that racial discrimination was barred. Employment and training efforts approved under the CAP accounted for about a fifth of the total program funds expended during the first three years. Other approvable projects included, but were not limited to, remedial and preschool education, health services, birth control clinics, housing and home management, consumer education, legal aid, social services, and the establishment of neighborhood centers.

While new programs were being introduced, old ones had been expanding, The Vocational Rehabilitation Program had been established in 1920 to qualify the physically and mentally handicapped for productive employment. New legislation, in 1965, authorized the tripling of federal support and the definition of handicapped was broadened administratively to include impairment due to "vocational, educational, cultural, social, environmental, or other factors." The program was further expanded three years later.

The budget of the United States Employment Service was also expanded, though perhaps not commensurately with the added work load imposed by the new manpower programs. As the result of the broadened responsibilities and competition from community action and other agencies, the public employment services became concerned with outreach, training, job development, and supportive services for the disadvantaged. As Frank H. Cassel, USES Director, 1966-67, put it, the mission had changed from "screening out" to "screening in."[2]

The emphasis in 1965 was on education. Federal support for higher education was increased, but far more important was the Elementary and Secondary Education Act of 1965. The largest single commitment of federal aid to education since the G.I. Bill of Rights and the first general federal support to the public schools, it stressed the needs of school districts with concentrations of the poor and the educationally disadvantaged. This was also the year of the Economic Development Act and the Appalachian Regional Development Act, both of which attempted to apply lessons from the ARA experience to generate employment in depressed areas.

The year 1965 proved to be the high tide in manpower policy. Unemployment had been high enough in 1961-63 to affect politically potent segments of society. Civil rights and minority problems were gaining sympathy through 1963-65 and the budgetary environment was permissive. The 1964 tax cut had given an impetus to economic growth and brought unemployment to five percent for the first time in the decade. The fiscal drag propensities of the progressive federal tax structure had been demonstrated. It was recognized that either taxes had to be cut or expenditures increased by five or six billion dollars each year if economic growth were not to be restrained.

[2]Frank H. Cassell, *The Public Employment Service: Organization in Change* (Ann Arbor, Michigan: Academic Publications, 1968), p. 122.

The permissive environment disappeared with the Vietnam escalation in the latter half of the year. Unemployment plunged quickly to 3.6 percent in March 1967—the lowest point since the Korean War. The price level began a warborne escalation of its own. The Administration maintained the country could have guns, and butter too; but its consistent underestimate of this war's cost and the increasingly restrictive tenor of public opinion belied its brave words.

The momentum built up between 1961 and 1965 carried through the following two years but more in new programs than in new money. The Economic Opportunity Act was amended in 1965, 1966, and 1967 adding funds for direct employment of the poor. Under the 1965 amendments, only $13 million was provided for the employment of poor people in conservation and beautification efforts, but this program was expanded sixfold a year later by the Nelson-Scheuer "New Careers" amendment which provided for the creation of subprofessional jobs, and the Kennedy-Javits "Special Impact" amendment which emphasized job creation in areas with concentrations of poverty. Both were in addition to the employment of the poor in community action neighborhood centers.

The 1966 session was not the end of manpower legislation but the climate and impetus were different thereafter. The optimism of 1961-1965 was replaced by frustration. The war dictated other priorities but the growing tempo of ghetto riots screamed for attention. While part of public opinion would not allow withdrawal from the manpower and antipoverty effort, other strong political forces demanded restriction. The reaction of administrators was rapid fire "panacea hopping" in search of a quick and cheap solution. This administrative repackaging added to the plethora of legislated programs.

The antipoverty program appeared to be in real trouble in 1967. The Job Corps residential training program had proven very expensive. More importantly, the community action agencies had proven to be a focal point in many cities for organized opposition to the local political establishment. Yet the fact that the Economic Opportunity Act was renewed and funded at a somewhat higher level than in the previous year was evidence that the programs initiated by EOA were creating their own vested interests and were likely to endure.

The countervailing forces were also apparent in the support and opposition for a multibillion dollar proposal to guarantee employment opportunities for all. As an immediate aftermath of serious riots in Newark and Detroit, Congressman James O'Hara of Michigan had introduced, along with 76 co-signers, a $4 billion bill for emergency public service employment. Senator Joseph S. Clark of Pennsylvania introduced an emergency employment amendment to EOA calling for $3 billion expenditures over two years. The O'Hara bill never came to a vote. The Administration, opposing any budget increase and fearful that the EOA bill might be damaged, pulled out all stops in opposing the Clark proposal and a less costly substitute by Republican Senator Winston L. Prouty of Vermont. The latter was narrowly defeated as a result of Administration opposition. . . .

. . . The growing thrust of the Administration's manpower programs in 1967 and 1968 was to involve . . . private employers in training and employing the disadvantaged.

MDTA was the first to be affected. Early in 1966, the Labor Department made plans to allocate two-thirds of the MDTA budget for training and employing the disadvantaged, raising the quotas of OJT not only to get more trainees from the limited budget (OJT is cheaper for the government than institutional training because income support is not required) but also to make a direct connection between training and jobs with private employers. By reimbursing employers for the cost of on-the-job training, it was anticipated that they would be encouraged to hire the disadvantaged workers they might otherwise have avoided.

It was soon realized that the limited subsidies paid to private employers under MDTA were an inadequate inducement to hire, train, and retain disadvantaged employees. Consequently, during 1967 the Administration embarked upon a series of experimental programs to induce employers to hire poorly educated, unskilled and, especially, Negro workers. The Concentrated Employment Program (CEP) was one major effort. Nearly $100 million allocated to MDTA, Neighborhood Youth Corps, New Careers and Special Impact Programs was put in one package to be concentrated on target areas in nineteen large cities and two rural communities. An important goal was to induce employers to hire the disadvantaged. The selectees from the target areas were to be given a two-week orientation course and then placed on jobs or in training programs. The goal of placing half of them with private employers did not materialize. Nevertheless, plans were made to expand CEP during the subsequent two years from nineteen cities and two rural areas to an intended goal of 146.

In addition to CEP, which concentrated on training and employing unemployed or under-employed workers in slum areas, an effort was initiated in the fall of 1967 aimed at subsidizing employers to bring jobs to the slums. The funds allocated to the program were to be used as a reimbursement to pay employers for the extra cost of hiring the disadvantaged workers. In reality, it was a subsidy to get business firms to locate industrial plants in or near the slums in the selected five cities.

A third experiment was a recognition that if submarginal workers were to be trained and employed the government would have to bear not only the training costs but also the other costs associated with hiring high-risk workers. In December 1967, the Labor Department announced that it was ready to pay an average annual subsidy of $3,500 to employers who would hire disadvantaged workers selected by public employment offices. A month later in January 1968, the President announced in his State of the Union message that government subsidies to employ the disadvantaged would be expanded during the next few years. The goal was to provide jobs in private industry for 500,000 hard-core unemployed during the suc-ceeding three years. While the President in-tended to allocate additional funds for the newly expanded program, an examination of the proposed 1969 budget clearly indicated that part of the subsidies to private industry to employ the disadvantaged would be carried out at the cost of retrenchment of training and work experience programs.

Major expansions of federally-supported manpower programs occurred during fiscal 1965 and 1966. The emphasis since then has been on improving the administration of the programs and developing viable techniques to reach and train the disadvantaged. Though con-cern for manpower shortages arose during 1966 and 1967 as unemployment fluctuated between 3.5 and four percent, federal manpower pro-grams gave priority to improving the employ-ability of those who had not been absorbed in the mainstream of American economic life in preference to upgrading the labor force. A formidable array of manpower programs had been undertaken . . . The numbers enrolled in them were still few, and the objectives and the interrelationships among programs were un-clear. Nonetheless, needy people had been helped, and lessons had been learned—if such lessons could be identified, evaluated and, im-plemented.

14.   Job Creation

Charles L. Schultze

Edward R. Fried

Alice M. Rivlin

Nancy H. Teeters

The argument for job creation as a primary weapon against unemployment is essentially this: Socially useful jobs need to be done; people need to work; it is logical to put the two together. It may be quicker to use public funds to create jobs than to wait for economic policy to stimulate demand. Creating jobs is less risky than training people for jobs that may not exist or in which the newly trained person may simply replace someone else, who then becomes unemployed. Job creation offers a more dignified solution than welfare and is more acceptable to politicians and perhaps also to the unemployed. This general rationale underlay the choice of public employment as a major weapon against unemployment in the 1930s.

More recently, job creation has been defended less as a primary than as a residual strategy against unemployment. It has proved difficult to use monetary and fiscal policy to reduce unemployment much below 4 percent without accelerating inflation. But at this overall level, unemployment rates remain high for some groups (teenagers, blacks, women), and considerable underemployment persists. Unemployment rates by race, age, and sex as of April 1969, when the overall unemployment rate was 3.5 percent, are shown below.[1] Manpower

[1]From Robert E. Hall, "Why Is the Unemployment Rate So High at Full Employment?" *Brookings Papers on Economic Activity*(3:1970), p. 391.

training may help to reduce the inflationary pressure and equalize unemployment rates among groups. Nevertheless, it is difficult and expensive to train many of the unemployed and place them in existing jobs. It may be quicker and cheaper to create jobs that the unemployed could fill, and useful work would be done in the process.

Table 1

Unemployment Rates by Race, Sex, and Age, April 1969

Age	Male White	Male Black	Female White	Female Black
16-17 years	11.1	18.0	12.9	22.8
18-19 years	7.0	19.0	9.1	23.3
20-24 years	3.8	8.6	4.8	13.0
25 years and over	1.6	2.7	2.7	5.5

Opponents argue that job creation programs, without training or career advancement opportunities, result in wasteful padding of private payrolls. The unemployed poor, they maintain, should be provided the skill training and career experience that would enable them to be absorbed by the regular job market. Those who cannot be trained for a regular job should be aided through income maintenance rather than "make-work" employment. . . .

SIX MAJOR QUESTIONS

1. Do we need a job creation program in the 1970s? In the 1930s this question was clearly answered in the affirmative. An extraordinary proportion of the labor force was out of work; from 1931 to 1939 the unemployment rate never dipped below 14 percent, and job creation was seen as a major instrument for returning the economy to full employment. The unemployed were not especially disadvantaged or unskilled. Most of them had worked before and could be expected to work again, but no one knew how to stimulate private demand for such large numbers of workers. Putting them to work doing something useful seemed better than having millions on relief.

By the early 1960s, when public employment once again became a subject of active debate, the economic situation was significantly different. Unemployment was substantial (5½-7 percent) but not massive, and confidence in the efficacy of fiscal and monetary policy to stimulate the economy had greatly increased. At these levels of unemployment, is there still an essential role for job creation?

2. For whom should jobs be created? At low levels of unemployment (in the neighborhood of 4 percent), a public employment program necessarily concentrates on the hard-core unemployed. This is likely to be a continuing requirement. But when unemployment rises to 6 or 7 percent, people with skills and working experience lose their jobs, and a number of them eventually exhaust their unemployment compensation entitlements. Can a program meeting the needs of the latter, more average, group be mounted quickly in a recession and then turned off when full employment is regained?

3. How should the several objectives of job creation be balanced? If the principal objective of job creation is simply to get people to work, then it does not matter much what jobs are done. The objective of employing two men is attained if one digs a hole and the other fills it up. But with so much socially useful work to be done, the creation of useless make-work

projects is wasteful of public funds and demoralizing to those employed. It would be preferable to work toward a second objective: let the job produce something that people want. But can this be done?

The problem is that "useful" jobs, like the construction of schools or dams or the provision of most public services, require a fairly high component of skilled and experienced labor, while the hard-core unemployed are mostly unskilled and inexperienced. Efforts can be made to provide training and simplify job requirements, but these measures increase the cost of the project. In general, the more emphasis that is placed on the utility of the work, the less job creation that can be attained per dollar spent. The question is how much to buy of each.

Moreover, another kind of objective should be considered—to create jobs that will develop skills and lead to advancement into better jobs. Again there is an economic tradeoff. Upgrading the worker's skills is not costless. The more emphasis that is given to training and upward mobility, the fewer the jobs that can be created per dollar spent, and the more difficult it is to mount a large-scale program.

4. Should jobs be created in the public or in the private sector? Job creation is usually associated with public employment, but it is also possible to subsidize private employers to hire additional workers. The choice depends on the priority given to the need for more services in the traditionally public areas, like education and conservation, and the relative cost of the two types of job creation.

5. How attractive should the jobs be? If conditions of work are poor and pay is low in the created jobs, people will not want to hold them, at least not for long. They may consider themselves better off if they are on welfare or are finding sporadic employment in the regular job market. On the other hand, if jobs are created at good wage levels, people will leave other jobs to hold them, and the net increase in employment may be considerably less than the number of jobs created.

6. How large should a job creation program be? The answer to this question depends in part on the answers to the previous ones. It depends also on estimates of the population that might respond to an offer of subsidized work, and on the priority accorded job creation relative to other public objectives.

15. The Emergency Employment Act: An Interim Assessment

Sar A. Levitan

Robert Taggart

The Public Employment Program initiated by the Emergency Employment Act of 1971 represents a major departure in manpower policy. The program is the first large-scale public employment effort since the New Deal. Providing $1 billion in its first year to State and local governments for the hiring of unemployed workers to help meet growing needs for public services, it will account for 15 percent of all manpower expenditures in its first year, equalling the combined outlays for all other work experience and public employment training efforts, including the Neighborhood Youth Corps, Operation Mainstream, Work Incentive, and Public Service Careers programs.

The program is important in the short run because of its impact on the unemployed as well as on State and local governments, and in the long run because of its implications for public policy.

This evaluation relies heavily on case studies of State and local experience, combined with an analysis of legislative and administrative developments at the national level. The areas studied and the investigators—all experienced

This article is based on a more extensive report prepared under a grant from the Ford Foundation to the National Manpower Policy Task Force. The report, together with nine case studies, is being published concurrently by the Senate Subcommittee on Employment, Manpower, and Poverty.

manpower researchers—included Champaign, Decatur, Springfield, and the State of Illinois (Roger Bezdek); Chicago (Myron Roomkin); District of Columbia (Robert Taggart); Houston, Laredo, and the State of Texas (Vernon Briggs); Los Angeles (Walter Fogel); Milwaukee (Peter Kobrak); Missouri (David Stevens); New York City (Marilyn Gittell); and Utah (Garth Mangum). Additional studies are now in progress.

OBJECTIVES

Persistent high unemployment and claims of unmet public sector needs provided the major impetus for the passage of the Emergency Employment Act. A public employment program is the most direct way to alleviate unemployment. At the same time, it can provide personnel for the delivery of vital public services.

The recession in 1970 and 1971 caused a sharp increase in joblessness. The national unemployment rate rose from 3.6 percent in 1968 to 4.9 percent in 1970, and to 5.9 percent in 1971 (Table 1). Moreover, the number of part-time jobholders who would rather work full time increased 1.3 million, so that the total labor force time lost through unemployment or

111

Table 1

Unemployment, Selected Groups, 1968 and
1971 (Percent Distribution)

Group	Average Annual Unemployment Rate	
	1968	1971
Total	3.6	5.9
Whites	3.2	5.4
Blacks	6.7	9.9
Men	2.9	5.3
Women	4.8	6.9
Teenagers	12.8	18.1
Vietnam-war veterans	(*)	8.8
Scientists and engineers	1.6	2.9

*For 1969, the rate was 4.5 percent.

part-time work for economic reasons rose from
4.0 in 1968 to 6.4 percent in 1971.

The impact of rising unemployment was
unevenly distributed geographically, but every
region was affected. Some cities and States
encountered serious problems with falling
defense expenditures. The already severe problems of urban ghetto and rural depressed areas
were intensified.

Given the grave dimensions of the unemployment problem, a public employment program of $1 billion could be expected to have a
limited impact, creating only 140,000 jobs. If
everyone hired under the program had been out
of work and would have otherwise remained
idle, the number of unemployed would have
been reduced by less than 3 percent from the
1971 level, or the aggregate unemployment rate
would have fallen by only 0.2 percentage
points.

There was a possibility, however, that the
program could significantly reduce unemployment of particular groups in the labor force, or
in particular areas of high employment. For
instance, there are roughly 325,000 unemployed Vietnam-era veterans, 75,000 unemployed scientists and engineers, 250,000
unemployed black teenagers, and a total of
500,000 unemployed persons in the poverty
areas of the 100 largest cities. The 140,000 jobs
would have had very significant impact if concentrated on any single group.

PROVISIONS OF THE LAW

The Emergency Employment Act designates
a number of target groups. To be eligible, a
person must be unemployed at least a week,
working part time but seeking full-time work,
or earning insufficient wages to lift his or her
family out of poverty. Vietnam veterans are to
be given preference, and priority is also to be
given to former participants in manpower programs, young persons entering the labor force,
older workers, migrant farmworkers, persons
whose native tongue is not English, welfare
recipients, aerospace and other displaced
workers.

The act states that participants must be
chosen on an "equitable basis" from among the
unemployed, but it does not specify any priorities among the target groups. This scattershot
approach, a result of legislative compromise,
diffuses the act's impact.

The act is also designed to serve areas with
substantial unemployment. Funds are authorized separately under two titles: Section 5 provides $750 million for all areas based on the
extent and severity of unemployment; Section
6 adds $250 million to areas with an unemploy-
ment rate of 6 percent or more for 3 consecutive months, and having sufficient size and
scope to sustain a public employment program.
Section 5 funds are "triggered" by the national
unemployment rate and are available only so
long as it equals or exceeds 4.5 percent; Section
6 or "special employment assistance" monies
are available to high unemployment areas, even
if overall economic conditions improve and the
national unemployment rate falls below 4.5
percent.

The act is also intended to alleviate the reported growing manpower shortages afflicting
State and local governments. However, claims
of shortages must be interpreted with caution:
aggregate employment figures do not suggest
any serious setback in the growth of the public
sector. Despite evidence that some cities and
counties are being forced to lay off workers,
the aggregate statistics belie any massive cutbacks.

All factors considered, the number of readily
available, worthwhile jobs in the public sector is
probably in the hundreds of thousands rather
than in the millions. It is, therefore, a reason-

able expectation that the Emergency Employment Act will have an impact upon public employment in the short run.

TRADE-OFFS

The Emergency Employment Act is the product of compromise. In the effort to achieve consensus, a "little something" was offered for everyone. Potentially troublesome issues were sidestepped through open-ended guidelines, and the law is ambiguous and often contradictory in its goals and substance.

On the broadest scale, the act promises to meet vital public service needs while helping the unemployed. The two goals can be, but are not necessarily, compatible. Quite obviously, lower skilled and less educated workers are overrepresented among the unemployed while public sector needs are concentrated in the more skilled categories. If elected officials are given free rein to fill the jobs they consider most vital, they will surely cream—hire the most qualified from the unemployed. Limiting Federal contributions to annual salaries to $12,000 and allowing professionals to constitute no more than one-third of hires presumably constitute safeguards to assure a "balanced" occupational distribution. However, wide loopholes are open because local funds can be used to supplement the law's salary maximum and because teachers are not included among the professionals, making it possible to hire one-third professionals, two-thirds teachers, and no disadvantaged. The real safeguard is that elected officials shun extremes in hiring even when there is a temptation to fill critical public service needs.

The program is supposed to vest States and local governments with considerable authority, but it allows them paltry funds for administration. Public employee unions are to be allowed to comment on any plans (but States and localities can ignore the comments), and no jobs can displace present public employees. Finally, the Public Employment Program is supposed to open up new careers, yet there is no allowance for advancement within the program, little money for training and education, and no leverage for changing occupational ladders in the

public agencies which might not endorse Emergency Employment Act hires in the first place. The act also proscribes the use of its funds for supplies and equipment, effectively limiting the scope of jobs.

IMPLEMENTING THE PROGRAM

Choosing program agents. Because the Emergency Employment Act is exceptionally vague in determining who will administer the funds and how much they will get, the Department of Labor had to choose program agents and devise a formula for allocation of funds. On August 12, 1971, it apportioned $600 million of Section 5 funds to 50 States, the District of Columbia, Puerto Rico, the territories, Indian tribes, and all cities or counties with a population of 75,000. A total of $425 million was "passed through" to cities or counties or allocated by the States to them to fill State and local jobs.

The States allocated "balance-of-State" funds to cities and counties with populations below 75,000 and acted as program agent for them. The States could select smaller towns, cities, counties, and other units of government as subagents. The guidelines left the State governors relatively free to decide what proportion of funds was to be used for State jobs and what proportion was to be passed down to city and county subagents.

The implementation of the act conformed with the pending manpower reform proposals, providing greater decentralization of decision-making. Federal funds were distributed to State and local governments, who were to decide within broad guidelines how to spend the money. Whether or not this can be called "revenue sharing," it follows many of the same procedures.

Dividing the pie. Once program agents were selected, the Department of Labor adopted a two-part formula for allocation of funds, giving equal consideration to the total number of unemployed persons in a State and the number of unemployed in excess of 4.5 percent relative to the national totals. This formula favored areas with "excess" unemployment. . . .

A SENSE OF URGENCY

Declaring that "America needs jobs and it needs them now," the President launched the Emergency Employment Act in a spirit of urgency. The Federal bureaucracy, under pressure from Congress and the President, moved with uncommon speed to draw up guidelines, distribute funds, and approve local plans. Interest groups, representing either public employees or potential employees claiming special rights to the new jobs, presented few obstacles. By March 10, 1972, more than 140,000 persons had been hired under the program.

Speed was necessary if the Public Employment Program was to be an effective counter-cyclical tool. But speed meant sacrifice of civil service reform, training, and other manpower efforts, and allowed little time for coordination with other manpower programs. The opportunity for labor unions, community groups, and governmental units to contribute to the decisionmaking was all but eliminated; few outside the administrative staffs of the program agents could follow the course of events.

DECENTRALIZATION

The thrust of the Emergency Employment Act guidelines was to encourage States and localities to design and implement programs best suited to their needs, conditions, and capabilities. Program agents, in turn, were to provide maximum flexibility and choice to political subdivisions. Decentralization was, however, far from complete. Federal officials retained many strings because the law still holds them accountable for the expended funds and Federal officials are required to monitor activities of program agents to assure that Federal objectives are met. . . .

The surprising finding is how little—not how much—confusion actually existed. Dealing with entirely new intergovernmental relations, dividing up a great deal of money, and accomplishing this at a rapid pace could be expected to generate many more problems than have come to light thus far. In most cases balance was struck between decentralization of decisionmaking and oversight and control by the Federal Government and program agents.

THE JOB CHOICE

The selection of jobs was perhaps the most important decision made by program agents. The choice determined not only which public service needs were filled, but also the general characteristics of those hired, the likelihood of their learning useful skills while on the job, and the probability of their moving on to permanent payrolls.

A combination of critical needs, expediency, and concern with Emergency Employment Act goals usually governed the choice of jobs, but States and localities varied markedly in the weight given to each of these factors. The larger cities tended to mix their jobs as follows: first, concentrating resources in areas of critical budget needs (especially where there had been lay-offs); second, distributing large shares of the remaining funds among as many agencies as possible for "regular" jobs; third, including a few jobs to serve specific target populations; fourth, creating a number of social service aides or public works slots for the unskilled; and finally, initiating a few innovative and restructured jobs if funds were left. . . .

Smaller cities and counties had a lesser choice of jobs. There were rarely any "new-career-type" positions for the disadvantaged, nor enough slots to spread the wealth. The typical pattern was either to hire workers for regular jobs or to create public works slots for unskilled labor.

At the State level, the jobs were either spread among State agencies according to present employment, as in North Carolina and Missouri, or concentrated in specific fields. California emphasized correctional institutions, while Utah concentrated on law enforcement and public works. Illinois also emphasized public works to create jobs for unskilled welfare recipients. All the above alternatives satisfy the broad aims of the act, but some conclusions about program effectiveness and the choice of jobs can be drawn from the case studies.

First, a mix of jobs sufficient to satisfy the multiple goals in the legislation is appropriate only for large urban areas. Small towns and cities and many States do not deliver extensive social services; to them, hiring the disadvantaged means putting them to work with their hands.

Second, few areas have designed jobs with

much thought of moving participants to permanent payrolls.

Third, program agents created a number of entry level, low-wage jobs which provide little skill training—in fact, nothing more than temporary employment. Jobs leading to "new careers" account for only a small proportion of the total. There is a heavy emphasis on public works projects to help the hardest core, but the bulk of the jobs parallel those on the regular payrolls and were intended for the type of workers who would have been hired anyway.

Fourth, there are some indications that program agents had to be given enough money to fill critical needs, to spread a little wealth, and to satisfy vested interests before they would consider more creative uses of their funds. Even if resources are increased, as under demonstration projects, the temptation to carry on business as usual persists. Increased and especially earmarked funds are apparently necessary for more creative use of limited resources.

PARTICIPANTS

The "typical" person hired under the Emergency Employment Act is a white male high school graduate between 22 and 44 years old, who was unemployed for a month or more (Table 2). Special efforts were made to enroll veterans and members of racial minority groups.

The Labor Department guidelines state that one-third of all participants should be Vietnam-era or special (having served in Southeast Asia) veterans. Within this broad guideline, individual program agents established their own hiring priorities at the outset, whether or not they are articulated. . . . Overall, 29 percent of hires on March 21, 1972, were Vietnam-era veterans, slightly below the target, although nationally, less than 7 percent of the unemployed in 1971 were from this group.

To the extent that preference was given to male veterans of prime working age, younger and older unemployed persons, women, and the disadvantaged had to be deemphasized. A good argument might be made by any of these groups that they were short-changed. Only 12 percent of all Public Employment Program hires were under age 22 or over 65, although they represented 45 percent of the unemployed

Table 2

Characteristics of Public Employment Program Employees, as of March 21, 1972

Characteristic	Percent* Distribution
Age	100
18 or less	1
19-21	11
22-44	71
45-54	11
55-64	5
65 and over	0
Sex	100
Male	72
Female	28
Group	100
White	68
Black	20
American Indian	2
Oriental	1
Spanish American	7
Other	2
Military service status	100
Special veteran**	13
Other Vietnam-era veteran	16
Other veteran	17
Nonveteran	54
Education	100
8 years or less	8
9th-11th	15
12th	45
13th-15th	18
16th and more	15
Weeks unemployed	100
4 or less	32
5-14	27
15 or more	40
Occupational group	100
Professional	6
Teacher	4
Other	89
Labor force status	100
Unemployed	90
Underemployed	10
OTHER CHARACTERISTICS	
Disadvantaged	36
Public assistance recipient	11
Previously employed by agent	11

*Totals may not add to 100 because of rounding.
**Vietnam-era veterans who served in Southeast Asia.

in 1971. Only 28 percent were women, but they constituted two-fifths of the unemployed.

Racial minorities, however, seem to be fairly well represented among program participants. Blacks, who accounted for 18 percent of the unemployed in 1971, constituted 19 percent of the Section 5 and 16 percent of the Section 6 hires. Indians and Spanish-Americans also appear to share proportionally.

Most evidence suggests, however, that the program is not reaching the hardest core of the unemployed. The most significant fact about the hiring practices of program agents is that they generally chose the most qualified from the available unemployed. The Labor Department's presumed target was that one-half of all hires be disadvantaged, that is, unemployed or underemployed, living in poverty, and either a veteran, under age 22, or over 45, a member of a minority group, or a woman. However, only a third of participants were disadvantaged. Similarly, one-tenth were previously on welfare. There was also high educational level among participants; only one-fifth had not completed high school, although dropouts were 45 percent of the unemployed in 1971.

The aggregate data yield little evidence of "paper hires," that is, where workers were laid off the State or local payroll in order to be rehired under the Emergency Employment Act. The Regional Manpower Administrators made it clear they would police against paper hires.

Only 12 percent of all Section 5 participants had been previously employed by the program agent, and probably half of these were teachers. The data also suggest that only a minority of those hired have left a previous job to find a better one under the act: only a tenth were underemployed previously, and among those who were unemployed, two-thirds had been idle 5 weeks or more.

In summary, the program is apparently drawing on a broad range of unemployed. The typical participant is neither extremely disadvantaged nor extremely well qualified. Rather, he is an average worker idle in a 6-percent unemployment economy. To a large extent, this focus was dictated by the priority given to veterans. Clearly, teenagers, the elderly, the disadvantaged, public assistance recipients, and, most of all, women would have benefited more if alternative priorities had been chosen.

The other major dimension of impact is the filling of State and local manpower needs. The act authorized jobs in almost all areas of public service, and the jobs which have been created are addressed to all these needs (Table 3).

There is no way to judge from these aggregate data whether the jobs fill the most "vital" service needs, or even whether they fill productive functions. The whole question of "needs" is ambiguous, and estimates are at best based on guesses about shortages rather than effective demand or actual priorities determinations

Table 3

Distribution of Emergency Employment Act Jobs, as of January 7, 1972 (Percent Distribution)

Job Category	Section 5 (all areas)	Section 6 (areas with severe unemployment)
Total	100	100
Law enforcement	13	10
Education	20	26
Public works and transportation	22	27
Health and hospitals	7	6
Environmental quality	5	5
Fire protection	3	1
Parks and recreation	8	8
Social services	5	4
Other	17	13

made by State, city, and county decision-makers. But overall, there is a larger concentration of slots in public works and transportation than needs surveys or current distribution of jobs in State and local government would indicate. The ability to phase out a project once Federal funds are withdrawn was apparently more important in choosing jobs under the program than filling needs.

It is fairly clear, however, that Public Employment Program jobs are a step up for most participants. Thirty-three percent of hires earned less than $2 an hour in their last job; 12 percent earned less than that under the Public Employment Program (Table 4). Only 10 percent of the slots are for professionals, well within the one-third limit set by Congress, including 4 percent for classroom teachers.

Most of the Public Employment Program jobs, then, are above the minimal entry level, but not far up the job scale. For most of those who were selected, they provided gains in wages and fringe benefits.

wise have been idle. There is little evidence that State and local governments resorted to paper layoffs or of workers quitting other jobs enmasse to get on the Emergency Employment Act payroll. The clientele was apparently creamed, but most areas made an effort to spread jobs among claimant groups. For the most part, jobs filled with Emergency Employment Act funds were vacant because of budget stringencies, and in most areas there was a mixture of professional slots, openings for the unskilled, a few new careers opportunities, and a majority of average middle-level jobs. Although the Labor Department and the President had to prod slow-spenders into action, overall, the States and localities which administered local efforts moved quickly, effectively, and sometimes innovatively to meet the prime Federal guidelines.

The Public Employment Program has been less effective in achieving its secondary goals. The designers of the law envisioned that, in addition to providing "transitional employ-

Table 4

Wages of Participants as of March 21, 1972
(Percent Distribution)

Hourly Wage	Last Previous Job	Public Employment Program Job
Total	100	100
Under $1.60	18	2
$1.60 to $1.99	15	12
$2 to $2.99	33	46
$3 to $3.99	19	27
$4 to $4.99	8	8
$5 and over	7	5

SIZING UP THE PROGRAM

A review of the employment program 8 months after the passage of the Emergency Employment Act indicates accomplishments and shortcomings. The program was intended as an "emergency" measure to combat rising unemployment, and, to some degree, it fulfilled this purpose. One hundred forty thousand persons were employed under the employment act within 7 months after Congress appropriated funds, and most of these persons would other-

ment," the public service program would be combined with "related training and manpower services" to become a useful component of the nation's manpower policy. First, graduates from manpower programs could be placed in Public Employment Program jobs, supplementing their earlier counseling and training with on-the-job experience and preparation for permanent employment. Second, linkages could be established with existing manpower programs so that participants could benefit from the whole range of services available in the community. Third, training and other services would be provided from Emergency Employment Act funds, although expenditures for such purposes were limited by Congressional appropriations to 6.8 percent of apportionments under the general grant for all areas. And fourth, worthwhile on-the-job training could be provided from the 10-percent cash or in-kind share of the program agents. But coordination with manpower programs has been limited, either because program agents looked on the Public Employment Program as an employment and not a training program, or because manpower funds were already committed. Finally, little civil service reform has been associated with the program.

Undoubtedly, it is hard to achieve such diverse goals as civil service reform, job restructuring, and coordination with manpower projects when implementation proceeds at a breakneck pace and when there are few sticks or carrots used to achieve these ends. It is perhaps unrealistic to think that all these things could have been achieved at once, and program agents concentrated on the primary goals. A retrospective assessment of the Public Employment Program will have to determine whether continued progress was made towards these secondary goals, and whether the binding decisions made so far to get the program off the ground quickly were worth the price of contraining progress in other directions.

IMPLICATIONS FOR REVENUE SHARING

More than any other recent manpower program, the Emergency Employment Act and its administrative guidelines decentralized decision-making authority to the State, county, and city level. The administrative arrangements which were adopted, with direct fund allocations to State and local governments, were adapted from manpower reform legislation intended to decentralize control. The State and local program agents were delegated major responsibility for deciding their own needs, choosing jobs, selecting workers, and determining priorities for the other goals of the program. The Federal Government, operating through its 10 Regional Manpower Administration offices, checked applications to make sure that they adhered in a general way to legislative and administrative intents. The guidelines and the act itself, with their sometimes vague wording and multiple

goals, left much leeway to State and local officials. And, finally, the emphasis on speedy implementation placed constraints on the controls that could be exercised by Federal officials, increasing the flexibility of program agents. From the performance of State, county, and city governments, therefore, one might expect some indication of the strengths and weaknesses of decentralized manpower efforts.

Care must be exercised in interpreting the experience of the Public Employment Program and in drawing implications about revenue sharing. For one thing, the program was implemented rapidly, and program agents had hardly enough time to fill out their applications, much less to carry out any thoughtful planning. At best, then, the Public Employment Program suggests what would happen if revenue sharing were implemented at a breakneck pace with no planning or learning period. Obviously, this is not the way revenue sharing should be implemented.

Another problem in trying to draw lessons about revenue sharing from the Public Employment Program is that the program, despite its multiple goals, has a single major thrust—public employment. This is only one component of a comprehensive manpower strategy. The experience with public employment is therefore an inadequate basis for judging whether the same States, counties, and cities can implement all the different manpower components and integrate them into a comprehensive strategy which best serves the needs of their work force.

To complicate matters, administrative flexibility exercised under the Emergency Employment Act varied markedly from area to area. Still, some broad lessons from the Public Employment Program experience are relevant to manpower reform. An important conclusion which emerges from case studies of local experience is that many State, county, and city governments have developed during the past decade the capability to plan and administer manpower programs. The diffusion of competence is notable, and this process will accelerate if money is more flexibly distributed. Another general lesson—which is not likely to surprise anyone—is that decentralized decisionmaking increases adaptability to local conditions, but this is sometimes achieved at cost of national priorities.

In future legislation, funds for public employment will most likely be lumped in with other shared manpower revenues. Based on the experience so far under the Emergency Employment Act, this strategy seems to have many shortcomings. Funds have already been committed without comprehensive manpower planning and they would add little to flexibility. If increased resources are provided for comprehensive manpower programs, the Public Employment Program is likely to absorb most of them even if unemployment eases. Including the Emergency Employment Act among potential strategies would force State and local decisionmakers into a choice between helping the disadvantaged or filling their most vital needs, when the goals of manpower revenue sharing should be to provide the best mix of services to help those who need them most. It makes sense, therefore, to keep the Emergency Employment Act outside the sphere of shared manpower revenues. Other types of public employment serving particular groups of the manpower clientele and offering intensive manpower services might be included, but the Emergency Employment Act should probably be operated as a separate countercyclical program.

As a rough estimate, it is reasonable to assume that the Public Employment Program could be expanded to two or three times its present size without a significant loss in effectiveness or speed of implementation. But whether or not larger scale public employment programs of other types can be effectively implemented remains to be seen. The experience under the Emergency Employment Act does not prove that work relief programs for the structurally unemployed, depressed area employment efforts, or the new careers approach will (or will not) work. Some welfare recipients have been helped, as have a substantial number of disadvantaged. A few high unemployment areas will receive concentrated assistance and a few restructured career job opportunities have been opened. But these accomplishments have been achieved as part of an overall approach that mostly emphasized quick hiring to fill jobs left vacant because of inadequate funding. Whether States and localities could have done as well with a program geared chiefly to another purpose, which would require much more than merely traditional hiring, remains to be seen.

What has been learned, however, is that unless program agents are operating under strictly enforced guidelines, they are likely to go about business as usual—hiring the most qualified workers for the most vital jobs. If a large-scale program is to be implemented, more attention will have to be paid to these guidelines. The legislation should specify more exactly who is to be served; and it should provide incentives for job redesign, civil service reform, extensive training, and use of funds for the purchase of supplies, if these are desired. Congress must specify the type of public employment program it has in mind, rather than passing open-ended legislation which has something for everyone.

16. The Hard to Employ: European Programs

Beatrice Reuben

When one explores the programs of another country for relevance to American problems, it is helpful but not essential if conditions in the foreign nation are closely comparable to ours in nature and scope. We can learn about programs for the integration of minority groups, for example, from countries where minorities are a much smaller part of the population than they are in the United States. And we should not offer our larger and more complicated problems as an excuse for a troublesome backlog of unresolved issues. All the more reason to have initiated earlier and greater preventive and remedial action! A confrontation with alternative sets of values and priorities or with different national styles provides the opportunity to reassess features of one's own country which are generally regarded as fixed and immutable.

The choice of the countries of northwestern Europe as exemplars in a discussion of programs for the hard-to-employ follows a clear but not always acknowledged American pattern. European leadership in social policy, notably in social insurance, has long provided models for the United States. Although our programs have been adopted piecemeal after considerable debate and passage of time, and we have added our own modifications and distinctive features, our debt to western Europe has been great. Since World War II northwestern Europe also has pioneered in the recognition and assistance of the hard-to-employ. While each country has its own strengths and specialities, Sweden's experience commands the greatest attention, not only for its specific programs but also for its supporting institutions and policies.

The experience of western Europe strongly suggests that the maintenance of over-all unemployment rates at 2 percent or less for years at a time may be the single most important factor in minimizing the number of hard-to-employ and motivating a program to seek out the residual group who might appear unemployable in the United States at 4 percent unemployment. From this point of view, American unemployment rates of 3 to 4 percent, though inflationary, may not be low enough, especially if account is taken of the absorption by the armed forces of large numbers of youths who otherwise might have been jobless. . . .

While the reasons for the European ability to achieve much lower unemployment rates than the United States are complex, part of the explanation lies in the deliberate and effective European programs to smooth seasonal and regional variations in employment, resulting in lower over-all unemployment rates and having an anti-inflationary influence as well. The United States has far to go in these fields.

120

Differential unemployment rates, such as those for youths, are also less marked in Europe than in the United States, in part because European institutional arrangements and standards afford an easier transition from school to work. After 8 to 10 years of basic schooling, European youths are accepted directly for training which can lead to skilled status, but those who remain in unskilled jobs are not regarded as deprived. The issue is complicated in the United States by high expectations based on long stays in school, the view that all jobs should have promotional possibilities, and the growing reluctance of youths from the minority groups to accept employment in the low-prestige and low-paid service occupations.

Moreover, the unemployment situation does not permit the United States to import foreign workers for the menial jobs, as labor-short northern Europe has done, thereby upgrading opportunities for its domestic labor force. . . .

Under the pressure of labor shortages and the guidance of advanced social policies, several western European nations have forestalled unemployment and the development of hard-to-employ groups by aiding rural people to adapt to an urban environment and helping foreign workers to adjust to a new country. General manpower programs to match workers and jobs, to train and upgrade the whole labor force, and to aid mobility have reduced unemployment and promoted the placement of the hard-to-employ. Naturally, these efforts are most effective when the demand for labor is strong. By European standards, American programs to date have been underdeveloped and too reliant on private enterprise and nonprofit organizations.

The commitment to full employment is put to a severe test when demand slackens or balance-of-payments problems threaten employment. Unlike some of the other European countries, Sweden continues to give "the individual's right to make a meaningful contribution to production . . . decisive importance for the shaping of policy." Even price and cost stability are secondary objectives so long as international competitiveness and domestic equity can be maintained by productivity gains, taxation policy, and other means.

As unemployment rises, specific measures are initiated in Sweden to maintain or increase employment in the private and public sectors. The Swedish innovation of "investment reserve funds" for private firms is used in such a period. The government's own contracts and orders to private firms are increased by advancing the schedule for placing such orders. In this connection, the United States has only scratched the surface of the possibilities for utilizing government contracts, but also purposive geographical distribution and the potential for aiding specific groups of workers should be explored fully. Sweden also uses its extensive public construction program to influence the volume, location, and timing of employment. Schools and homes for the aged which are scheduled for later construction are started up sooner if the over-all employment situation or the state of the construction industry are weak. These measures to maintain employment are supplemented by the enlargement of existing programs to train workers and offer created jobs of a public works type.

In February-March 1968, it is estimated that about 125,000 Swedish workers were saved from unemployment by these measures; in terms of an American labor force twenty times larger, this would be 2,500,000 persons who otherwise might have swelled the unemployment rolls. Actual unemployment in February 1968, according to the Swedish quarterly labor force sample surveys, was 102,000, or 2,040,000 in the U.S. equivalent. Since seasonally adjusted American unemployment in that month was 2,941,000, it appears that the Swedish countermeasures held the deepest unemployment of their recession at a lower figure than the U.S. did at its full employment level.

While it is difficult in a discussion of the hard-to-employ to over-emphasize the importance of a high demand for labor relative to the supply, it should be noted that the proportion of the population which is hard-to-employ, especially through functional illiteracy, poor motivation, or alienation, is sharply affected by the social standards of the society. If a high place is given to the welfare of all children, if only a narrow gap is permitted between the minimum and the average levels of housing, education, nutrition, health care, social services and recreational facilities, and if equality is sought in legal and civil rights and income distribution, then the proportion who are hard-to-employ for social reasons is apt to be relatively low.

The western European countries which care

most about the human and social aspects, Holland and the Scandinavian countries, have found that a large public role is necessary to achieve these objectives and to provide the required personnel and facilities. . . .

The question arises of how these social measures are financed. An international comparison in 1966 of the proportion of gross national product represented by taxes of every kind shows Sweden with 41.1 percent and the United States with only 28.2 percent; Sweden's per capita GNP is second highest in the world after the United States. Of the eleven European nations in the comparison compiled by the Swedish Ministry of Finance, only Switzerland had a lower proportion of GNP in taxes than the United States.

Not only is the share of GNP taken by government greater in Sweden than in the United States, but the share of governmental expenditures devoted to social programs in Sweden is also larger than in the United States. The central government in Sweden supports social programs both by direct expenditures and by grants-in-aid to the municipal governments which have primary responsibility in some areas. Grants-in-aid constitute about one-sixth of central government expenditures and one-fourth of municipal expenditures, higher proportions than in the United States.

These financial facts underlie the national priorities which Sweden has been quite successful in meeting. But Sweden and other countries in Europe do not share the American faith in the power of money alone or the efficacy of crash programs. Time, careful planning, and long periods for training personnel are allowed. Gradual improvements and expansions of programs are acceptable and they are geared to the possibilities of delivering services.

A combination of tight labor market and effective social programs in several European countries has tended to hold down the number of hard-to-employ, but the variety of types has not diminished. Every kind of difficulty found among the American hard-core can be duplicated in European countries, but in relatively small numbers. In Sweden alcoholics, narcotics addicts, refugees, gypsies, released prisoners, school dropouts, youths from reform schools, and older workers are the main categories of the socially handicapped. Their total number is not staggering, though Sweden uses methods of out-reach which few countries can equal. . . .

The initial elements of the most advanced European programs for the hard-to-employ are the interviewing and screening process and the provision of guidance and counseling services, including the advice of various specialists. A selected group may be sent to other institutions for psychotechnical tests, an assessment of vocational capacity, work experience, vocational training, or further education. The attempt to make placements in the competitive labor market is the culmination of the earlier efforts, and it proceeds either by intensified or special techniques or by approaches to prospective employers through legal compulsion or financial incentives. Finally, those who cannot be placed in open employment may be provided with created jobs outside the usual enterprise structures.

Since many of the European measures exist to some degree in the United States, the novelty is not in their content but in their widespread application throughout a country under uniform standards. It may be easier to bring together the European experience than to collect and present the diverse American practices. Hardly a day goes by but that some American demonstration project, announced as breathtakingly revolutionary, tries out a program which has been well-established in a European country for some time. Some translation of the scope of European programs into American dimensions will be attempted, along with reflections on the aspects of European policy which are suited to American conditions.

Intake procedures are a clue to a program's ability to reach those who need its services. One evidence of success in Sweden is the large number of registrants at the Vocational Rehabilitation Service. The total is approaching 100,000 new cases annually; in terms of an American population 25 times larger, this would be 2.5 million cases handled in a single year. It should be contrasted with the U.S. Rehabilitation Services Administration's report that over 200,000 persons were rehabilitated into employment or self-employment in 1968 and that a backlog of 4 million people in the United States with physical and mental disabilities need rehabilitation services; 450,000 more become disabled each year.

If the millions of socially handicapped who need rehabilitation services are added, the size of the problem emerges, even if it is restricted to the portion requiring vocational rehabilitation only. In Sweden disabled homemakers are eligible for the vocational rehabilitation program and are taught to manage at home with little or no assistance. Adaptation of appliances and surroundings to the disability is part of the service. . . .

Guidance and counseling may be offered to the hard-to-employ by placement officers or counselors who have no placing functions. They may act alone or after conferences with psychologists, psychiatrists, social workers, doctors, vocational guidance specialists, technical advisers, and others who are on the staff or serve as consultants. Whether the counselor refers the worker directly for placement or suggests that further services are desirable, the usefulness of the personal contact and interest of a counselor is gaining acceptance. Counseling of the hard-core has made rapid strides in the United States, particularly in experimental programs. The task is to make the best practices general and expand the number who receive counseling. . . .

A special word should be said about the work experience centers or Industrial Rehabilitation Units, as the British named them. They have enormous potential usefulness for the United States as a means of preparing people for work, increasing their punctuality and work pace, and stimulating the conditions of work. The voluntary efforts of American business to fill this void are inadequate on several counts: the total number of places supplied is unlikely to meet the total need, the worker is readied for whatever work the particular employer happens to be engaged in without regard to the worker's own inclinations and abilities, and the quality of the supervision cannot be verified. . . .

Vocational retraining for the hard-to-employ is most highly developed in Sweden, where over 50 percent of all trainees are disadvantaged in the labor market. Since Sweden's total retraining effort is impressive—2 percent of the labor force annually are retrained at present—the large share of the hard-to-employ is particularly significant. Moreover, high proportions of all retrainees obtain jobs in the occupation for which they trained and at higher wages than they earned previously. In this as in other spheres, the hard-to-employ benefit from the concurrent programs to retrain, upgrade, and improve the utilization of the entire labor force. The substantial increase in the numbers in retraining during the winter months of the 1967-68 recession especially benefited the Swedish hard-to-employ, and is one of the countercyclical policies that bear exploration in the United States.

Since there is considerable interest in skill training within industry for the hard core in the United States, the European experience should be examined. In spite of acceptance of a more active role for employers in the formal training of youth in Europe than in America, European employers have not responded well to subsidies for training the hard-to-employ. Retraining in industry in Sweden has constituted about 15 percent of the total, excluding informal on-the-job training which is not counted in Europe. Employers are a useful source of training in certain occupations, but public courses have had to supply the bulk of the retraining places. A disappointing aspect of training within industry has been the very small fraction of trainees retained by the company as employees. American results should be reviewed after a few years to see whether the Eurpoean pattern is repeated.

Placement is the objective of all the services for the hard-to-employ. Probably every special technique known in Europe has been used in some part of the United States, at least in an experimental or pilot program. One American experiment, genuinely innovative, and which has not been tried in Europe, has been the banding together of corporation representatives to pledge themselves to hire the hard-to-employ out of a sense of social responsibility. When the public relations smoke has cleared, it may be possible to estimate how many vacancies would have been available in any case and how many of those hired might have been chosen without a campaign. Comparisons should be made between participating and nonparticipating firms. To test such a program properly it should be conducted in a period of steady or slack demand and attention should be given to the effects on those just above the hard-core level.

In some European countries, the placement of the hard-to-employ in competitive markets has been promoted by two methods not in fashion in the United States: wage subsidies and legal compulsion. Employers have reacted very poorly to the offer of wage supplements as an inducement to hire the hard-to-employ referred by the Employment Service. There is no requirement that training be given. In Belgium and Sweden, only a few hundred workers are employed under this system, but Sweden has hopes of swelling the number of semisheltered workers, as they call them, to 5,000. Employers seem disinclined to submit to the reporting and supervision involved in obtaining the subsidy.

Legal compulsion on private and public employers to provide jobs for the physically or mentally disabled exists in the larger western European countries. It has been well accepted by employers in Great Britain and West Germany because the quotas are reasonable, active rehabilitation programs are in effect, and specialized officers of the Employment Service make careful placements. In American terms, about 1,500,000 workers would be on the quota system if the proportion in Britain and West Germany prevailed.

Many of those on quota employment in Europe would obtain jobs without legal support, especially when there is a strong demand for labor. For those who might not obtain work and for those who might be the first to be fired, the legal backing is valuable. To the extent that employers create more jobs under the quota than they would otherwise offer, and to the extent that quota workers earn standard wages for lower-than-average output, employers and consumers are absorbing some of the costs that would otherwise be borne by the workers in question and public programs. The quota system in West Germany may provide a job for the kind of severely disabled worker who would not be accepted by Swedish or Dutch employers, but this is difficult to test, as is the quality of the jobs under the quota.

Even if a law to establish a quota system seems a remote possibility, some use of the idea could be made in the United States, perhaps under the Rehabilitation Services Administration. On a voluntary basis, the acceptance of a given quota of referred disabled persons or hard-core unemployed could be proposed to government agencies at all levels and to government contractors. If it proved successful, private employers could be enlisted with credit given for the disabled or hard-core already employed by given firms. The Philadelphia Plan for the employment of minority workers by government contractors is an example of this approach, although the term "quota" is resisted by officials.

Another group which has received attention in western Europe is that we call the hard-to-reemploy. Some employed older workers who never had difficulty in obtaining or keeping jobs would have difficulties if they lost their jobs. Others who are at work have such serious handicaps that they would surely be hard-to-

employ if their present jobs ended. The interest of these groups is to maintain continuity of employment, and various kinds of general manpower measures influence their position. In West Germany, Holland, and France the hard-to-reemploy are aided by general and specific legislation which restricts the freedom of employers to dismiss their workers. Legislation in some countries also provides for work-sharing instead of dismissals, supplementing and reinforcing custom, and trade union agreements.

The general laws concerning dismissals and work-sharing cannot prevent but may delay reductions of staff when an industry-wide or nation-wide slump occurs. The hard-to-reemploy tend to be dismissed first under such conditions, unless they have specific protection under special dismissal laws, which usually are enacted in connection with the quota system for employing the physically or mentally handicapped.

When, as in the United States, strenuous efforts have been made to obtain employment for the handicapped or hard-core unemployed, the entire project may be nullified if the disadvantaged workers are the first to be laid off. But is is doubtful that legislation on dismissals or work-sharing will be enacted in the United States, since there would be severe conflict with trade union seniority rules on lay-off. For informal arrangements, the greatest hope lies in making compensated lay-off so attractive to workers with seniority that they will not object to the hard-core workers being retained. . . .

A final area in which European experience is valuable is that of special job creation for those who temporarily or permanently have difficulty in obtaining or holding employment in the competitive labor market. This activity, which in the United States is called "Government as Employer of Last Resort," has much the same status in Europe; it is suggested only after all other placement possibilities have been considered. Holland and Sweden have developed job creation most extensively and elaborately, but virtually every western European country has some form in operation. However, none would be considered guaranteed employment. . . .

Under European conditions, the job creation programs appear to be free of stigma on the workers or "leaf-raking" charges, perhaps as a result of using private contractors to execute all projects in Holland and considerable numbers in Sweden. A small portion of the projects are carried out on private property, with the owners paying a portion of the costs. These aspects may be important fot the United States, where the old image of the WPA and fears of creeping socialism and the underserving poor may threaten any program entirely operated by government. However, over-all direction and maintenance of standards is a responsibility which government cannot shirk. In any case, a strengthened Employment Service is needed to assist whatever agency is chosen to create the jobs.

III

WAGE RATES

Unionism, Wage Rates, and Resource Allocation

Do unions raise the wages of unionized workers relative to those of non-union workers? To the man in the street, the answer seems self-evident. But economists have a professional distrust of such offhand judgments. Is there solid statistical evidence that unions have raised the relative wages of their members? This is a trickier problem than one might think. It involves comparing something we *can* observe (the wages received by union members) with something we *cannot* observe (what those same workers would have received in the absence of unionism). There are several ways of tackling the problem, but none of them is entirely satisfactory.

H. Gregg Lewis reviews the research studies that had appeared up to 1960 and adds new estimates of his own. He concludes that the impact of unionism on relative wages is moderate, in the order of 10 to 15 percent; but that some unions have gained considerably more than this, while others have gained little or nothing. Another interesting conclusion is that the advantage of unionized workers is greatest in depression and least in periods of high labor demand, when competitive bidding for scarce labor raises non-union wages closer to the union level.

If unionism raises relative wage levels in particular industries, this will tend to reduce employment in those industries and to raise employment in non-union sectors of the economy. This redistribution of employment, most economists have argued, means a less efficient allocation of labor resources and a reduction in national output. Output may be further reduced by union-imposed work rules and manning requirements. Albert Rees tries to estimate the probable size of these effects, concluding that they are small but not insignificant.

Robert Ozanne gets at the problem of union influence by comparing the wage gains of manufacturing workers, relative to the increase in all personal incomes, during two periods: 1923-29, a period of weak unionization, and 1947-57, a period of strong unionization. He finds that manufacturing workers did much better during the second period, and surmises that this was due partly to union influence. His article illustrates the difficulties of statistical analysis in this area and the need for caution in drawing conclusions.

17. Unionism and Relative Wages in the United States

H. Gregg Lewis

I.1. INTRODUCTION

This is an empirical study of labor unions and relative wages in the United States. Its main purpose is to estimate the magnitude of the impact of unionism on percentage (relative) wage differentials among groups of labor. The principal questions for which the study attempts to give quantitative answers are:

By how much has unionism increased the average wage of union labor relative to the average wage of all labor, both union and nonunion? Reduced the average wage of nonunion labor relative to the average wage of all labor?

To what extent has unionism affected, in different proportions, the average wages of different industries?

How variable were the effects of unionism on relative wages from one date to another during the last forty years? How much of this variability can be explained by changes in the rate of inflation of the general price level or general money wage level? By changes in the degree of unionization of the labor force?

How much higher or lower is the relative inequality in average wages among industries than it would be in the absence of relative wage effects of unionism? The amount of relative inequality in the distribution of wages among all workers?

I.2. RELATIVE AND ABSOLUTE WAGE EFFECTS OF UNIONISM

Labor unions may have three different kinds of "wage" effects that are often confused with each other. Unionism may change (a) the economy-wide average or general level of money wages per hour; (b) the economy-wide average or general level of real wages per hour; and (c) relative wages—the ratios of the wages per hour of particular groups of labor to the average wage per hour of all labor. The first two, (a) and (b), are *absolute* wage effects of unionism. This study deals only with (c), the *relative* wage effects of unionism.

Unionism can affect the relative wages of different groups of labor only if it changes the wages of the groups by percentage amounts which differ from one group to another, that is, changes the percentage differences in wages among the groups. Furthermore, neither unionism nor anything else can raise (or, alternatively, lower) the wage of every different group of labor relative to the average wage of all labor. Therefore, all of the following statements have the same meaning:

Unionism has raised the average relative wage of union workers.

Unionism has lowered the average relative wage of nonunion workers.

Unionism has raised the average wage of union workers relative to the average wage of nonunion workers.

Unionism has lowered the average wage of nonunion workers relative to the average wage of union workers.

On the other hand, that unionism has raised the average *relative* wage of union workers—lowered the average *relative* wage of nonunion workers—does not mean that unionism has raised the average *absolute* wage (money or real) of union workers or lowered the average *absolute* wage of nonunion workers or changed in either direction the average *absolute* wage of all workers taken together. The effects of unionism on the general level of either money or real wages cannot be deduced from knowledge only of the *relative* wage effects of unionism. . . .

The effect of unionism on the average relative wage of a particular group of labor (the labor employed in a particular industry, occupation, city, etc.) is a weighted average of corresponding relative wage effects for (a) the union workers and (b) the nonunion workers in the group, where the relative weight for the union workers is the degree of unionization of the group. For example, if the degree of unionization were 50 per cent and if unionism had raised the relative wage of union workers in the group by 10 per cent and lowered the relative wage of the nonunion workers by 2 per cent, the effect of unionism on the average relative wage of the group would be a plus 4 per cent. Thus the differences among groups in the impact of unionism on their relative wages will be larger, the greater are the corresponding differences in degree of unionization and in the effects of unions on the relative wages of union workers and of nonunion workers. . . .

I.3. EMPIRICAL STUDIES OF UNIONISM AND WAGES

Our knowledge of the relative wage impact of unionism in the United States stems almost entirely from research reported in the last decade and a half. Before 1945 there were, to be sure, many serious studies of wages and of unionism containing statements regarding the effects of unions on wage differentials, but in none of these studies, to the best of my knowledge, are there numerical estimates of the relative wage effects of unions. Since World War II, on the other hand, a substantial amount of empirical research on one or another facet of unionism and wages has been performed by economists; the findings given in this study are based chiefly on the evidence presented in twenty of these recent studies.[1]

Twelve of them focus on relatively small segments of the U.S. labor force, ranging from barbers to steel workers. In addition, there are eight global studies dealing with large segments of the labor force. . . . From the evidence presented in each study and from supplementary data, I have drawn estimates of the impact of unionism on the relative wage of the union workers covered in the study. . . .

At first glance the amount of dispersion in the estimates appears to be enormous: the figures range from zero to more than 100 per cent. Bituminous coal mining is the extreme case. The data for this industry indicate that in 1921-22 the wages of coal miners in unionized mines may have been more than twice as high as they would have been in the absence of unionization in coal mining. In contrast, it appears that about 1945 the wages of unionized miners on the average were *no* higher than they would have been in the absence of miner unionization. Neither of these two extremes lasted very long. By the mid-1920's the estimated relative wage effect had fallen to about 50 to 60 per cent. Similarly, after 1945 the relative wage

---

[1]I have endeavored to cover all of the reports of empirical research on unionism and wage differentials from which I could take directly or compute numerical estimates of relative wage effects of unionism or of directions of change in these effects. I have excluded, therefore, a good many studies in which there is evidence that unionism may have caused relative wage changes, but the evidence was of such nature that I could not estimate the size or direction of change of the wage effects. Much of the postwar research on unions and wage differentials has been reported only in unpublished or little-known papers and dissertations, some of which, no doubt, I have not covered simply because they were not known to me.

effect rose to a level in 1956-57 which was about the same as that in 1924-26.

Few of the studies of other groups of union labor, however, yielded estimates above 25 per cent. The relative wage effects of 50 per cent or more observed for union coal miners in part of the 1920's and 1930's and again in recent years, therefore, truly deserve to be called "extremely large." On the other hand, the zero relative wage effect for union coal miners near the end of World War II was not exceptionally low compared to the effects estimated from studies of other industries. Rather, the period was exceptional: during much of 1944-49, unionism apparently had little impact on the U.S. relative wage structure.

I.4. THE IMPACT OF UNIONISM ON THE AVERAGE WAGE OF UNION LABOR RELATIVE TO THE AVERAGE WAGE OF NONUNION LABOR

. . . There is much uniformity in the evidence provided by the studies reviewed . . . that the impact of unionism on the average union/nonunion relative wage varied markedly from one date to another. The peak impact of the last forty years occurred, I judge, about 1932-33, near the bottom of the Great Depression. At the peak, the effect of unionism on the average wage of union workers relative to the average wage of nonunion workers may have been above 25 per cent. In the ensuing inflation the relative wage effect declined sharply to a level between 10 per cent and 20 per cent, I estimate, by the end of the 1930's.

The decline in the average union/nonunion relative wage effect of unionism continued until about 1947 or 1948, near the peak of the inflation immediately following World War II. At the trough, the impact of unionism on the average wage of union labor relative to the average wage of nonunion labor was close to zero—under 5 per cent. (There is much less evidence for the similar period following World War I, but what there is suggests that then, too, the relative wage impact of unionism was unusually low.)

The near-zero relative wage effect of unionism observed shortly after World War II did not

persist, however, through the following decade. I estimate that in recent years the average union/nonunion relative wage was approximately 10 to 15 per cent higher than it would have been in the absence of unionism. During the 1950's, the extent of unionization of the labor force was close to 25 per cent. These figures imply that recently the average wage of union workers was about 7 to 11 per cent higher relative to the average wage of all workers, both union and nonunion, than it would have been in the absence of unionism. Similarly, the average wage of nonunion workers was about 3 to 4 per cent lower relative to the average wage of all workers than in the absence of unionism.

I.5. UNIONISM AND MONEY WAGE RIGIDITY

The finding that the relative wage impact of unionism was greatest near the bottom of the Great Depression and was least during the periods of unusually rapid inflation and low unemployment following both world wars is not new. The authors of several of the studies reviewed in chapters iii and iv noted the phenomenon and commented on it. Albert E. Rees, Milton Friedman, Walter A. Morton,[2] and a number of other economists have attributed the phenomenon to rigidities or lags in the adjustment of money wages introduced by collective bargaining: the collective-bargaining contract running for a year or more, the reluctance of unions to accept wage cuts during periods of deflation lest the deflation not continue, and the similar reluctance of employers of union labor to agree to unusually large money wage

[2]Albert E. Rees, "Postwar Wage Determination in the Basic Steel Industry," *American Economic Review,* XLI, No. 3 (June, 1951), 395-99. Milton Friedman, "Some Comments on the Significance of Labor Unions for Economic Policy," in David McCord Wright (ed.), *The Impact of the Union* (New York: Harcourt, Brace & Co., 1951), pp. 226-31. See also Friedman's "Discussion" in Industrial Relations Research Association, *Proceedings of the Eleventh Annual Meeting* (1958), pp. 212-16. Walter A. Morton, "Trade Unionism, Full Employment and Inflation," *American Economic Review,* XL, No. 1 (March, 1950), 18.

increases during periods of unusually rapid inflation. . . .

I.6. THE EXTENT AND LOCUS OF UNIONISM IN THE UNITED STATES

To a significant extent, the differences among industries in the effects of unionism on their average relative wages stem from corresponding differences in their degree of unionization. . . .

In 1897, eleven years after the founding of the American Federation of Labor, union membership comprised less than 2 per cent of the labor force. By 1904 the proportion had risen to about 7 per cent, where it remained until 1917. From 1917 to 1920, union membership grew rapidly, but the increment in membership was short lived. In 1923 about one-twelfth of the labor force was unionized; a decade later the fraction was almost the same as in 1904.

In the decade beginning in 1935 the degree of unionization of the labor force approximately quadrupled to a level of about 25 per cent in 1945. The percentage rose slightly from 1945 to 1953 and since 1953 has declined by a small amount.

Before 1934 the degree of unionization was appreciable only in coal mining, contract construction, printing, men's and women's outerwear manufacturing, the railroads, local transit and trucking, the stage and theater, and the postal service, yet in 1929 only one-third of the persons engaged in this group of industries were union members. In 1929 these industries employed one-sixth of the U.S. labor force and three-fourths of all union members.

Since 1944 roughly half the work forces in mining, contract construction, manufacturing, and communications and public utilities (except transportation) have been represented by unions in collective bargaining. In transportation the degree of unionization has been about 75 per cent. However, within each of these broad industry divisions there are wide differences in degree of unionization among detailed industries.

Both before and after 1934 the degree of unionization has been close to zero in agriculture, wholesale and retail trade, finance and insurance, and government (except government enterprises). The same is true of the service industries except for hotels and eating and drinking places in large cities, the entertainment industries, and some of the personal service industries. The agriculture, trade, finance, service, and government industry divisions have employed about half the labor force. . . .

I.7. UNIONISM AND THE INTERINDUSTRIAL RELATIVE WAGE STRUCTURE

Chapter viii deals mainly with the relative wage effects of unionism among industries. The studies reviewed earlier provide estimates for various dates of relative wage effects for only a short list of industries. Moreover, it is not possible to deduce from these estimates and from other data presented in this study the relative wage effects, industry by industry, for the rest of the industries in the economy.

Nevertheless, some of the over-all characteristics of the distribution of the relative wage effects of unionism among industries can be gauged from the data on degree of unionization by industry given in chapter vii and the relative wage effect estimates drawn from earlier studies. The majority of workers, I judge, are employed in industries whose average relative wages have been raised or lowered by unionism by no more than about 4 per cent. However, in industries employing a quite small fraction of the labor force—considerably less than 6 per cent—the relative wage effect is 20 per cent or more.

I cannot, for lack of information, give a complete list of the industries in which the relative wage effects recently have been as high as 20 per cent. The studies covered in chapter iii suggest that the list includes bituminous coal mining, some of the building trades in some cities in which the trades are highly unionized, and possibly barbering in a few cities. The inclusion of the building trades, however, rests chiefly on data for 1939 and for both these trades and other industries the estimates of the relative wage effects of unionism may contain substantial errors.

It is likely that the industries which should be added to the list are highly unionized. However, a high degree of unionization does not guarantee that the relative wage effect of unionism is also large. For example, the manufacturing of men's and boys' suits and coats is a highly unionized industry, yet . . . the relative wages of union workers in the industry have been affected very little by unionism since World War II.

Only about 15 per cent of the females in the labor force are union members. The corresponding figures for males is 30 per cent. If there were no differences by sex in the average relative wage effects of unionism among either union workers or nonunion workers, I estimate that in recent years unionism has lowered the average relative wage of females by about 1 to 1.5 per cent and raised that of males by less than 1 per cent. However, in the occupations in which the impact of unionism on relative wages apparently has been greatest—coal miners, airline pilots, skilled building tradesmen, and seamen, for example—the ratio of female to male employees is very close to zero. For this reason, the above figures may underestimate somewhat the difference in relative wage effects by sex. But even if the effect for women were the same as that estimated for *nonunion* workers—a minus 3 per cent to a minus 4 per cent—the corresponding effect for males would be no more than a plus 2 per cent.

I.8.   THE IMPACT OF UNIONISM ON THE DISTRIBUTION OF WAGE AND SALARY INCOME

Unionism has tended to raise relative wages most in industries with above-average relative wages. Therefore, unionism has been a factor making the relative inequality of wages *among industries* greater than it otherwise would be . . . I estimate that in 1958, unionism increased the relative inequality of average wages among industries by about 6 to 10 per cent compared to what the inequality would have been in the absence of relative wage effects of unionism.

It does not follow, however, that unionism must have increased the relative inequality of the distribution of wages *among all individual workers in the labor force.* The latter inequality depends on both (a) the relative inequality of average wages *among* industries and (b) the average relative inequality of wages of individual workers *within* industries. Therefore, unionism could have reduced the all-worker inequality by reducing the average inequality *within* industries by more than enough to offset the increase in inequality *among* industries.

Unfortunately, numerical evidence of the kind and quantity needed to estimate closely the magnitude of the impact of unionism on the average inequality of wages among individual workers within industries is not available. Nevertheless, I think it is improbable that unionism has changed this within-industry inequality by as much as 5 per cent. The majority of employees, I judge, work in industries within which unionism has had a trivial effect on relative wage inequality. The remaining minority of employees are divided in uncertain ratio between industries (a) within which unionism has increased relative wage inequality and industries (b) within which unionism has decreased relative wage inequality. But this implies that the average increase in relative wage inequality within industries (a) or, alternatively, the average decrease in relative wage inequality within industries (b) would have to be quite large in order to change the average within-industry inequality by as much as 5 per cent for all industries taken together.

If unionism has increased the inequality of average relative wages *among industries* by 8 per cent and has changed the average relative wage inequality *among workers within industries* by no more than 5 per cent, then unionism has changed the relative wage inequality *among all workers* by less than 6 per cent.

I conclude tentatively that unionism has had a small impact on the relative inequality of the distribution of wages among all workers. The direction of the effect, on presently available evidence, is ambiguous.

18.   The Effects of Unions on Resource Allocation

Albert Rees

The purpose of this [article] is to suggest in highly condensed form the general order of magnitude of the effects of unions and collective bargaining on the allocation of resources. It is widely accepted that unions have the power to raise wages in the establishments where they have bargaining rights. (The term "wages" should be understood to include fringe benefits.) This power comes from their ability to impose costs on management through strikes, slow-downs, or other pressure tactics which, in the short run, are greater than the costs of the wage increases provided through collective bargaining. By changes in relative wages we shall mean changes in wages in establishments covered by collective bargaining relative to wages elsewhere. For the discussion of resource allocation it is not necessary to specify how much of the relative increase arises from an absolute increase in union wages and how much from any possible decrease in nonunion wages. (Such a decrease could occur if labor were displaced

I am heavily indebted to H. Gregg Lewis for comments on an earlier draft of this paper and for permission to draw freely on two of his works: *Unionism and Relative Wages in the United States* (1963) and *Relative Employment Effects of Unionism*, in Proceedings of Sixteenth Annual Meeting of Industrial Relations Research Association 104 (1964). However, he is in no way responsible for the opinions expressed here or for the dificiencies of my estimates.

from the union sector by rising wages and were therefore in more plentiful supply to the nonunion sector.)

The existence of a relative wage effect implies the existence of a relative employment effect. If blue-collar labor is made more expensive in the union sector, management will have added incentives to save such labor through closer supervision and through the use of additional labor-saving capital equipment. Such substitution will minimize, but not eliminate, the addition to cost created by union wage gains. The remaining addition to average unit costs will tend to increase the price of final products and services produced in the union sector and therefore to reduce their consumption. Relative employment in the union sector should therefore decline for two reasons: (a) the substitution of other factors of production for union labor and (b) the substitution by consumers of cheaper final products and services for the more expensive output of the union sector. Whether these effects are empirically important depends on the size of the relevant elasticities of substitution and of demand.

Empirical estimates of the effect of unions on relative wages and relative employment encounter many difficulties. The basic problem is to correct for factors other than collective bargaining that might have produced differences between the union and nonunion sectors in the movements or levels of wages and employment. The devices used to control for such factors in the estimation of wage effects are discussed in detail in *Unionism and Relative Wages in the United States.*[1]

Lewis' book reviews, criticizes, and amends the previous studies that have estimated union effects on relative wages. In addition, it includes very substantial new work. From all this evidence, Lewis concludes that the effect of unions on relative wages in the late 1950's was about 10-15 per cent (that is, wages of union labor had been raised by unionism 10-15 per cent relative to the wages of nonunion labor). The highest estimate for any part of the period considered is 25 per cent or more at the depth of the Great Depression of the 1930's. In the late 1940's, because of rapid inflation, the union effect is estimated at 5 per cent or less.[2] During rapid inflation, market wages in the nonunion sector tend to rise rapidly, while the rise in union wages is often slowed by rigidities inherent in the bargaining process.

In his paper on *Relative Employment Effects of Unionism,*[3] Lewis estimates that the order of magnitude of the relative employment effect is not significantly different from that of the relative wage effect. In other words, the effect of collective bargaining is to reduce employment in the union sector about 10-15 per cent relative to employment elsewhere. This estimate rests on a less substantial body of work than the estimate of the wage effect.

The effects of unions on resource allocation can be divided into three components: effects via the interindustry wage structure, effects via the intraindustry wage structure, and effects via direct restrictions on output. We shall consider each of these in turn.

Lewis' two works permit us to make a rough estimate of the loss in real output caused by the effects of collective bargaining on the interindustry wage structure. Under certain conventional assumptions, it can be shown that the loss of real output is approximately equal to one-half the product of the wage effect and the employment effect (see Figure 1). I have used

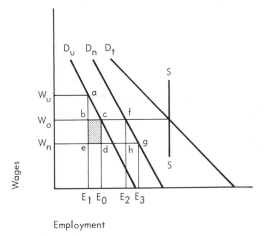

Figure 1

SS is the supply of labor, and D_u, D_n, and D_t are the demand for labor in the union sector, the nonunion sector, and both combined. Before the entry of the union, the wage is W_O. If the union raises the wage in its sector to W_u, employment in the sector declines from E_0 to E_1. This increases the supply of labor to the nonunion sector, raising employment from E_2 to E_3 and forcing the wage down to W_n. The areas under the demand curves are the real net product of labor. The loss in product in the union sector is E_0caE_1, the gain in product in the nonunion sector is E_2fgE_3. *The difference between these areas is the loss of product shown by the shaded rectangle b c d e. This is equal to the change in employment times one-half the differences in wages. In the more general case, where the demand curves in the two sectors are nonlinear or do not have the same slope, the equality will be only approximate.*

this formula to make a rough estimate for 1957, the last nonrecession year covered in Lewis' estimates. This estimated loss turns out to be approximately 600 million dollars. Since gross national product in 1957 was 443 billion dollars, the loss is approximately 0.14 per cent of national output. This welfare loss is of the same general magnitude as that estimated earlier by Arnold Harberger for enterprise monopoly (0.1 per cent).[4] The method used here is an application of that used by Harberger and derived from Harold Hotelling.[5]

---

[1]Lewis, *Unionism and Relative Wages in the United States, op. cit.* A briefer and less technical discussion may be found in Rees, *The Economics of Trade Unions,* (1962), pp. 73-75.

[2]These summary figures appear in Lewis, *Relative Employment Effects of Unionism, op. cit.*

[3]*Ibid.*

[4]Harberger, "Monopoly and Resource Allocation," American Economic Association Papers and Proceedings, *Am. Econ. Rev.* (May, 1954), p. 77.

[5]Hotelling, "The General Welfare in Relation to Problems of Taxation and of Railway Utility Rates," 6 *Econometrica* (1938), p. 242.

The estimated loss is arrived at as follows. Union membership in the United States in 1957 was approximately 17 million. A relative employment effect of 15 per cent implies a transfer of about 1.7 million workers out of the union sector as a result of bargaining, and a relative wage effect of about 700 dollars per worker per year. One-half of 700 dollars times 1.7 million is approximately 600 million dollars.

This calculation assumes that the average compensation of union members is equal to the average compensation of all employees in the highly unionized industry divisions: mining, contract construction, manufacturing, transportation, and communications and public utilities. The last assumption involves offsetting errors. Among production workers, union members in these industry dividions have higher compensation than nonunion workers. However, in manufacturing, which accounts for about 70 per cent of total employment in these divisions, the compensation of nonproduction workers is substantially higher than that of production workers, and nonproduction workers are seldom unionized. Moreover, there are some union members in other industry divisions who will on the average have lower compensation than those in the divisions listed above.

In one very restricted sense, the estimate of 600 million dollars as the interindustry component of welfare loss for 1957 is an upper-limit estimate—it uses the upper limits of the ranges of relative wage effects and relative employment effects estimated by Lewis. Nevertheless, there are other assumptions embodied in the estimate that could lead it to be too low. First, since the estimate of employment effects rests on less evidence than that of wage effects, it is possible that they exceed the upper limit of the estimated range. An alternative method of estimation would be to combine the estimated relative wage effect with an assumed elasticity of demand for labor. This is the method used by Harberger in his study of enterprise monopoly, in which he assumed an average elasticity of demand for products of -1. The assumption of an elasticity of demand for labor of -1 would not change the estimate given above, since this is the elasticity implicit in the estimates used for the wage and employment effects.

The estimate also assumes that the relative wage and employment effects of unions are uniform within the union sector. The more real-istic assumption that the size of these effects varies within the sector will not change the estimate provided that there is no correlation across unionized industries between the size of actual employment and actual wage effects. However, if in general large wage effects are associated with small employment effects, the estimate given above is too high; if large wage effects are associated with large employment effects, the estimate is too low.

In general, it seems reasonable to assume that large wage effects are associated with smaller-than-average employment effects—that is, that unions will raise wages most where the elasticity of demand for labor is smallest and the costs in reduced employment are lowest. There is, however, one important case that does not fit this generalization: the bituminous coal industry, where both the wage effect and the employment effect seem to be unusually large.

The estimated loss under discussion also assumes that no unemployment results from the employment effects of unionization. We should not, of course, charge the unions with the losses arising from general deficiencies in aggregate demand. However, the displacement of labor from one industry to another will give rise to frictional unemployment even under conditions of general prosperity, and the costs of this should be added to the interindustry component of welfare loss. These costs will be smaller if unionization is concentrated in expanding industries, since relative employment effects will then take the form of reducing the rate of hiring rather than requiring the dismissal of present employees. In fact, however, much of the strength of unions has been in contracting or stable industries, so that the unemployment costs of unionization are probably significant.

Professor Lewis has reported to me that he has made an unpublished estimate of the welfare cost of the interindustry component of relative wage and employment effects, using a somewhat more sophisticated method of calculation which allows for the dispersion of the relative wage effect within the union sector. The resulting measure of loss is almost the same as that reported above: 0.15 per cent of national product.

Not much is known about the relative wage effects of unions in particular industries. The available industry studies are summarized by Lewis in *Unionism and Relative Wages in the United States,* chapters iii and v, especially

Table 49. These studies suggest that the unions of the following groups of workers had larger than average effects (20 per cent or more): skilled building craftsmen, bituminous coal miners, commercial airline pilots, and East Coast seamen. These estimates refer to the 1950's except that for building craftsmen, which is for 1939. The studies also show that one union, the Amalgamated Clothing Workers, had no appreciable relative wage effect in the period 1946-57, though it did in the years from 1919 to 1939. This loss of power was associated with declining demand for the product.

The list of cases with very large estimated wage effects includes three for craft unions and one for an industrial union. Economic theory suggests that craft unions will have larger relative wage effects than industrial unions because their wages constitute a smaller portion of total costs, except in the unusual case where there are very good substitutes for union craftsmen in production and the elasticity of demand for the product is low.[6] But this advantage holds only if the craft unions in an industry bargain individually. If they bargain as a group, or wage patterns are transmitted to all the occupations in the industry, the case becomes similar to that of industrial unionism.

It is possible to put together the available industry studies, the relevant economic theory, and data on wage movements to make informed guesses on which unions not mentioned in the preceding paragraphs have larger-than-average relative wage effects. My leading candidates would be the skilled craft unions in railroads, entertainment, and the printing trades; the teamsters; and the steelworkers. A list of candidates for additional unions with less-than-average relative wage effects would include the unions of ladies' garment workers, textile workers, shoe workers, and white-collar government workers. The first is included because of the similarity of the industry to men's clothing. The next two are examples of unions that have incomplete organization of industries with national product markets. The government unions are included because their political power is probably an inferior substitute for the use of the strike.

The relative wage and employment effects considered so far arise from the impact of collective bargaining on the interindustry wage

structure. We turn next to the effects of collective bargaining on the wage structure within industries, which in some cases may be of considerable importance. Geographical wage patterns are one example. In the absence of collective bargaining, manual labor, and particularly unskilled labor, is appreciably cheaper in the South than in other regions. This regional wage differential arises from the more abundant supply of unskilled labor in the South. It tends to be reduced by the migration of labor to the North and of capital to the South, but such movements of resources have not been sufficient to offset the greater rate of natural population increase in the South.

Unions that bargain with multiplant employers or with associations of employers operating both in the South and elsewhere have attempted to eliminate regional wage differentials and frequently have succeeded. The union rate for unskilled labor in the southern operations of these employers is therefore further above the market rate than in their northern and western operations.[7] From this may flow a number of consequences: (1) national employers constructing new facilities both in the South and in the North would normally have an incentive to use somewhat more labor-intensive methods in the South; this incentive is eliminated by the uniform wage; (2) where plant location is oriented toward labor costs rather than access to markets or raw materials, an incentive to locate plants in the South is removed; (3) where plant location has been determined by access to southern markets or raw materials, the national employer may be unable to compete with local nonunion employers able to take advantage of low market rates of wages. Factors of this kind are unlikely to be important in the automobile or steel industries but are of considerable importance in meat packing. The displacement of national by local firms could retard the industrialization of the South to the extent that national firms have access to lower-cost sources of capital, both internal and external.

The elimination of regional wage differentials through collective bargaining benefits the southern workers already employed in the

[6]See Rees, *op. cit.,* at 70-73, and the passages from Marshall and Hicks cited therein.

[7]This is especially true in motor freight, where Hoffa has obtained the same mileage rates from southern as from midwestern truckers, removing traditional differentials. Because of superior weather conditions in the South, these bring higher weekly earnings to southern drivers.

unionized sector. However, it injures those workers, not readily identifiable, who would have been employed in industry had incentives for the expansion of industrial employment in the South not been diminished. Equality is achieved within the union sector at the cost of increased disparity between the union plant in the South and the rest of the southern economy.

Another area in which collective bargaining affects the structure of wages is that of skill differentials. Such effects may be readily apparent to personnel people in industry. However, they have not been much studied by academic economists, and the discussion below is therefore somewhat conjectural. The effects seem from existing literature to be mixed and without a dominant pattern.[8]

In several industries represented by industrial unions, the effect of collective bargaining early in the postwar period appeared to be to compress skill differentials. The compensation of the least skilled workers was raised most by unions, that of the most skilled less or perhaps not at all. Such wage compression could affect resource allocation by reducing incentives to undertake training and could lead to shortages of apprentices for the skilled trades. More recently, such compression has been limited or reversed by the actual or threatened secession of skilled workers to form separate unions of their own and by the operation of percentage wage increases such as annual improvement factors.

An opposite effect on skill differentials can occur under craft unionism if the unions representing the most skilled crafts are stronger than those representing the less skilled. This situation may prevail in portions of the railroad and printing industries. In such cases the effect of unionism is to prevent skill differentials from narrowing as much as would be expected from the general long-run trend; this provides incentives for employers to economize most in the use of skilled labor. However, the ability of employers to substitute other factors for skilled labor may be severely restricted by union rules.

Since union effects on intra-industry wage structures are more difficult to discern than effects on the interindustry structure, the costs of the former are probably less than those of the latter. This would suggest a combined cost

of less than 0.3 per cent of gross national product. If this estimate seems low, it is because the social costs of transferring resources to less productive uses are far less than those of wasting resources altogether. This brings us to the third avenue of union effects on resource allocation: direct restrictions of output through control of manning requirements, the work pace, and work practices, often called "featherbedding." In the course of preparing this paper, I have reached the conclusion that losses of this kind—dead-weight losses—probably exceed the social losses from relative wage effects. Indeed, management in a single industry—railroads— claimed in 1959 that obsolete work rules were costing 500 million dollars a year, or over 0.1 per cent of national product. Although this may be an overestimate, particularly through the inclusions of some costs that are in reality higher compensation for necessary work, the comparison between this amount and those mentioned above suggests something about the general magnitudes involved.

The evidence available is not sufficient to permit any numerical estimate of the total costs of union control of manning practices and work rules. The published accounts suggest that a large part of the costs is concentrated in a few industries, especially railroads, printing, longshoring, entertainment, and some aspects of building construction. Costs are especially high in industries with craft union organization where each piece of work, however small, "belongs" to a particular craft, and a member of that craft must be called to do it. On the railroads such practices can result in the payment of a day's pay for a few minutes' work and sometimes in payment to two men for work done by one.[9]

It should be noted, however, that direct union impact on output is not always restrictive. Under some circumstances, unions have made significant contributions to efforts to raise output or productivity, especially where jobs have been threatened by competition from new products or products produced in other locations.

The practices bearing directly on resouce use include apprenticeship rules, which can affect the number and qualtiy of people trained, either by their effect on the size and nature of the entering group or by their influence on the

---

[8]Reynolds and Taft, *The Evolution of the Wage Structure* (1956), pp. 185-86.

[9]Slichter, Healy, and Livernash, *The Impact of Collective Bargaining on Management* (1960), Ch. 11.

percentage of entrants who complete the program. There seems to be general agreement that the number and quality of apprentices in many trades are inadequate to meet probable future needs. Such an effect could arise in any or all of the following ways: (1) the quality of the entering group can be lowered by nepotism or discrimination in the selection of entrants; (2) the number of apprentices can be limited by rules setting the ratio of apprentices to journeymen—this is the best known, but probably not the most important, of the restrictive devices; (3) the numbers of people entering and completing programs will be held down if the programs are unnecessarily long or if the program content is poor; (4) the number entering and completing will be reduced if the apprentice's wage is too low relative to the journeyman's; (5) conversely, the willingness of employers to train apprentices will be reduced if the apprentice's wage rate is too high relative to the journeyman's. All of these observations apply in principle to training programs operated solely by management. However, when management is in sole control of a training program, it has greater freedom to take prompt corrective action if the number or quality of trainees is inadequate.

Union influence on resource allocation that arises from increases in relative wages works unambiguously in the direction of reducing relative employment. Practices that limit output or require unnecessary numbers of men have an unpredictable effect in the long run. In the short run, the effect may be an absolute increase in the employment of the group that institutes the restrictive practices; in the longer run, such practices may encourage types of substitution that the union is powerless to cope with, which will ultimately reduce employment. For example, an effective full-crew law or rule on railroads will increase the number of operating employees per train but may accelerate the substitution of other forms of transportation for rail transportation. In the long run, the number of jobs lost thorough such accelerated substitution could exceed the number created or preserved by the full-crew rule. The only unambiguous effect is to increase the cost of transportation.

Union restrictions on contracting out work traditionally done in the bargaining unit are less formalized than some other types of restric-

tions, but may be becoming more widespread. If the work can be done at less cost by the outside contractor, there is an obvious adverse effect on efficiency. In cases where the outside contractor also uses union labor (not necessarily from the same union), any shifts in employment arising from restrictions on contracting out will not be caught by estimates of changes in relative employment in the union sector as a whole.

Throughout the preceding discussion, the implicit comparison has been between the relative wages and distribution of employment existing under unionism and those which would exist under perfectly competitive labor markets. Since the allocation of resources by perfectly competitive markets is known to be optimal, by this standard the impact of the union is necessarily adverse. The standard must be modified to the extent that actual nonunion laobr markets are monopsonistic. If nonunion employers, either singly or acting in concert, have the power to hold wages below the levels that would prevail under perfect competition, moderate union effects on relative wages may bring employment closer to an optimal configuration. The scanty available evidence suggests that monopsony power by employers in United States labor markets is small but not nonexistent.[10] However, in some markets where employers have such power (textile-mill towns, for example) there is little unionization, while in others where such power may once have existed (especially coal-mining areas), the union corrective may have gone too far.

If the entire impact of unions on our society could be subsumed under the heading of resource allocation, there would be little difficulty in reading the conclusions that the overall impact is adverse and that union power is excessive. The difficulties for policy explored in Professor Meltzer's paper[11] arise because this is not the case. Important aspects of collective bargaining, such as grievance procedure, have only tangential implications for resource allocation, but strong effects on equity in work situa-

[10]Bunting, *Employer Concentration in Local Labor Markets* (1962).

[11]See Meltzer, "Labor Unions, Collective Bargaining, and the Antitrust Laws," 6 *J. Law & Econ.* (1963), p. 152.

tions and on the meaning and status of manual work. Union representation of workers in political processes is largely noneconomic, yet could be affected by policies designed to deal with problems of resource allocation. The central policy issue is how to design measures that would reduce the adverse effects of collective bargaining on resource allocation while preserving those aspects of bargaining that are socially constructive. There remains much room for debate whether such goals can best be achieved by radical or by cautious measures.

19. Impact of Unions on Wage Levels and Income Distribution

Robert Ozanne

PERIOD COMPARISON METHOD

To avoid the pitfalls of interindustry comparisons, this study uses a period comparison method. In this method wage gains of an industry or group of industries in one period are compared with gains of the same industry or group in a different period. This method involves selecting two presumably comparable periods, one union and the other nonunion. Wage gains in each period are related to per capita income gains in each period. . . .

The periods chosen for this study are the

Table 1

Per Capita Personal Income Gain Per Year, Real Dollars

Period	Per Capital Personal Income Gain Per Year[1] (Per cent)
Post World War I, 1923-29[2]	1.74
Post World War II, 1947-57[3]	2.08

[1] Based on compound interest formula.

[2] National Industrial Conference Board, *The Economic Almanac, 1951-52,* p. 210.

[3] U.S. Congress, Joint Economic Committee, *Economic Indicators* (Sept. 1958), p. 4.

prosperous periods after both world wars, 1923-29 and 1947-57. The post World War I period is the six year period, 1923-29. For the post World War II period as much of the ten year period as possible is used. In some cases wage data are available through 1957, in some cases only through 1955, and productivity data are available only through 1953.

In spite of some differences the two periods are surprisingly similar. Tables 1 through 4 give economic data on the two periods.

In terms of the growth of the economy, Table 1 demonstrates that the rate of growth in the two periods was reasonably similar.

Table 2 above shows productivity somewhat ahead in the post World War I period. While productivity figures are not as precise in their meaning as many of our more common statistics, the figures of Table 2 indicate clearly that the economy in the post World War I period was certainly not less able to support wage increases than in the post World War II period.

The greatest difference in the periods is to be found in price behavior.

The post World War I period was one of rela-

The author is indebted in the preparation of this paper to colleagues in the University of Wisconsin Economics Department for helpful criticisms and to research assistants Joyce Skeels and Karen Kleist.

Table 2

Gain in Physical Output Per Man Hour in Manufacturing

Period	Gain in Physical Output Per Man Hour Per Year, Manufacturing[1] (Per cent)
Post World War I, 1923-29[2]	4.64
Post World War II, 1947-53[3]	3.45

[1]Based on compound interest formula.

[2]U.S. Department of Labor, *Handbook of Labor Statistics*, 1950, p. 168.

[3]*Trends in Output Per Man Hour and Man Hours Per Unit Output, Manufacturing, 1939-53*, Bureau of Labor Statistics Report No. 100, p. 315.

tive price stability. The later period was characterized through 1951 by substantial price increases. Since wages have a tendency to lag behind price increases, the post World War I period was more conducive to real wage increases, especially since in the real increase in per capita income and in productivity, Period I was every bit the equal of Period II.

Table 3

Consumer Prices[1]

Period	Annual Rate of Increase[2] (Per cent)
Post World War I, 1923-29	.09
Post World War II, 1947-57	2.36

[1]Bureau of Labor Statistics consumer price index from *Economic Indicators*.

[2]Based on compund interest formula.

No accurate figures on unemployment were kept in the twenties, and the estimate of unemployment is probably too conservative. But these figures, plus the very considerable farm-city migration in both periods, indicate that in neither period was there a tight over-all labor market. The brief exception would be during the Korean crisis. Here no real shortage of labor developed, but late in 1950 employers did some hoarding of workers in anticipation of a shortage which never developed because of the short duration and limited nature of the Korean War.

While the expanded role of government in the post World War II period as compared with the period of the twenties is often referred to as

a major difference, in its economic effects the role of government is exaggerated. In 1929 government accounted for 6 per cent of the nation's total gross national product.[1] In 1956

Table 4

Unemployment as a Percentage of the Labor Force

Period	Unemployment as a Percentage of the Labor Force, Annual Average
Post World War I, 1923-29	2.9[1] (est.)
Post World War II, 1947-57	4.3[2]

[1]Woytinsky, *Employment and Wages in the United States*, p. 397.

[2]Bureau of Labor Statistics data as reported in *Economic Indicators*.

the government sector had increased to only 10 per cent.[2] Since most of this increase occurred from 1941 to 1945, there is no reason to believe that government activity had a significant effect on the wage patterns of the nation. The exception, again, occurred during the Korean War, when government expenditures for war supplies had an inflationary effect on wages. Since at this time (1950-51) prices rose as fast as wages, the net effect of government expenditures plus government wage controls was to hold down real wages. Except for a few months in late 1950, wage behavior during the Korean War does not appear to have differed fundamentally from the rest of the post World War II period.

In summary, the two periods bear significant resemblances. At least in their wage paying abilities as measured by productivity and national income growth, neither period seems to have much advantage over the other.

WAGE BEHAVIOR IN NONUNION (1923-29) AND UNION (1947-55) PERIODS

The first comparison of wage gains on the period basis is that for manufacturing, which has the advantage of including many industries and a very large segment of wage earners. In 1929 production workers in manufacturing

[1]*Economic Report of the President, 1957*, p. 126.

[2]*Ibid.*

Table 5

Average Hourly Earnings of Production Workers in Manufacturing, Current Prices[1]

	Nonunion Period Average Hourly Earnings	Union Period Average Hourly Earnings	
1923	$.52	$1.24	1947
1924	.55	1.35	1948
1925	.55	1.40	1949
1926	.55	1.47	1950
1927	.55	1.59	1951
1928	.56	1.67	1952
1929	.57	1.77	1953
		1.81	1954
		1.88	1955
		1.98	1956
		2.07	1957
Annual Rate of Increase[2]	1.54%	5.24%	

[1]*Historical and Descriptive Supplement to Economic Indicators* (1955), p. 29, and *Economic Indicators* (Mar. 1958).

[2]Based on compound interest formula.

were only 11 per cent unionized,[3] as compared with 67 per cent in 1956.[4]

The hypothesis we are testing is that the greatly increased proportion of union members in the post World War II period has substantially altered wage patterns from those found in the nonunion twenties, and further, that this altered wage pattern has given the average hourly wage earner in manufacturing a greater share of national income than he received in the twenties. To what extent do available data support the above hypothesis?

Table 5 lists the current average hourly earnings of manufacturing workers in the two periods.

Table 5 reveals a phenomenal change in the wage patterns of the two periods. In the twenties wages remained stationary year after year. In the post World War II period wages moved upward year after year. Since the characteristic of union wage bargaining is to negotiate for annual wage increments, unions are eligible for

[3]Leo Wolman, *Ebb and Flow in Trade Unionism,* National Bureau of Economic Research (New York, 1936), p. 226.

[4]Data from Bureau of Labor Statistics, *Monthly Labor Review* (Oct. 1957), pp. 1208 and 1270.

serious consideration as probable causes of the changed pattern. The twenties with its long period of wage stability appears to be characteristic of wages in a nonunion period.

Are the wage increases of the union period illusory or real? Table 6 converts the data into real terms.

As Table 6 shows, the regular annual increments negotiated by unions are real and substantial. Since they occur in years of stable prices as well as in years of price increases they cannot be attributed to the effects of inflation. If accurate data on fringe benefits were readily available, the rate of increase in the union period would average somewhat higher.

What is the gain in production workers' income compared with that of other groups in the two periods? Table 7A and 7B give comparisons with other groups.

Tables 7A and 7B lead to some very important conclusions:

(1) Average income per full-time employee lagged behind increases in per capita personal income in the nonunion period, but did substantially better than per capita personal income gains in the union period. This supports the probability that gains which went to union workers were not made at the expense of non-

union employees. All employees (No. 2, Table 7A) in the union period received larger average wage increases in relation to per capita personal income gains than in the nonunion period.

(2) White collar workers in manufacturing (No. 3, Table 7A) who fared so well in the nonunion twenties were keeping well ahead of per capita personal incomes in the union period, although they had a better relative position in the twenties.

Table 6

Average Hourly Earnings in Real Dollars for Production Workers in Manufacturing, 1923-1929 and 1947-1957 (Constant Prices)[1]

Post World War I Period	Average Hourly Earnings in Real Dollars		Post World War II Period
1923	$.82	$1.51	1947
1924	.86	1.53	1948
1925	.84	1.60	1949
1926	.83	1.66	1950
1927	.85	1.66	1951
1928	.88	1.71	1952
1929	.89	1.80	1953
		1.83	1954
		1.91	1955
		1.98	1956
		2.00	1957
Annual Rate of Increase[2]	1.375%	2.80%	

[1]*Historical and Descriptive Supplement to Economic Indicators* (1955), p. 29, (1957), p. 31, and *Economic Indicators* (Mar. 1958).
[2]Based on compound interest formula.

Table 7A

Percentage Comparisons of Gains in Average Annual Income[1]

	Nonunion Period 1923-29 (6 years)	Union Period 1947-55 (8 years)
(1) Gain in average annual per capita personal income	100[2]	100[3]
(2) Gain in average annual compensation per full-time employee (all industries)	71[4]	134[5]
(3) Gain in average annual income per white collar worker in manufacturing	157[6]	143[7]
(4) Gain in average annual income per production worker in manufacturing	42[6]	144[7]

[1] Figures are expressed as a per cent of gain in per capita income, constant dollars.
[2]*Economic Almanac, 1951-52*, p. 210.
[3]*Economic Report of the President, 1957*, p. 104.
[4]Simon Kuznets, *National Income and Its Composition, 1919-1933*, pp. 314-15.
[5]*National Income Supplement to the Survey of Current Business, 1954*, p. 201. *Survey of Current Business* (July 1957), Table 27.
[6]*Statistical Abstract of the United States* (1956), p. 791.
[7]U. S. Department of Commerce, *Annual Survey of Manufactures*.

Table 7B

Gains in Average Annual Income[1]

	Nonunion Period 1923-29 (6 years) (Per cent)	Union Period 1947-55 (8 years) (Per cent)
(1) Gain in average annual per capita personal income	1.74	1.98
(2) Gain in average annual compensation per full-time employee (all industries)	1.23	2.66
(3) Gain in average annual income per white collar worker in manufacturing	2.74	2.83
(4) Gain in average annual income per production worker in manufacturing	.73	2.85

[1]Table 7A was constructed from these data. The sources are the same as those for Table 7A. Figures are expressed as an annual rate of increase, based on constant dollars and a compound interest formula.

(3) Production workers in manufacturing (No. 4, Table 7A) showed the most striking gains. In the nonunion twenties the stable wage pattern set by employers left them far behind gains of the population generally, as measured by per capita personal incomes. In the union period the union-established wage pattern of regular annual increases pulled production workers well ahead of per capita income gains and gave them gains equal to those of white collar workers in the same industries.

These conclusions might be said to lend considerable weight to the hypothesis that unions have so changed the wage pattern in American industry that not only are production workers in manufacturing substantially better off relative to per capita personal income, but that all employees as a group, nonunion as well as union, are receiving relatively better annual incomes.

This type of time period comparison has certain advantages over the union-nonunion industry comparison method. The time period method establishes for each time period a benchmark such as per capita personal income against which income behavior of other groups may be measured.

When comparing income gains of one or more groups in different periods the annual rates of gain as shown in Table 7B, Nos. 2, 3, and 4 are not particularly significant. These rates of gain must first be related to the average gain of the entire population in the period under consideration.

Table 7A gives this relationship. The important consideration is not whether produc-

tion workers gained at a higher rate in one period than in another, but how production workers' gains ranked in each period in relation to gains of other groups. Per capita personal income has been used as the benchmark in each period.[5] Thus, white collar workers' incomes went up faster in the 1947-55 period than in the twenties (No. 3, Table 7B). But relative to the gains of other groups, white collar workers did better in the twenties (No. 3, Table 7A). We are here concerned more with relative gains in income captured by various groups in both periods than with whether a group's income rose faster in one period than in the other. Presumably union bargaining might have influenced the relative status of production workers in manufacturing from the twenties to the post World War II period (No. 4, Table 7A).

The data in Tables 5 through 7B all point toward unionism as a possible cause of the increased share of national income received by the average blue collar worker in manufacturing in the 1947-55 period as compared with his share in the 1923-29 period. . . .

[5]There are logically as many reasons for using per capita national income as a benchmark as there are for using per capita personal income. Actually in these two periods the two indices moved so closely that substituting per capita national income for per capita personal income would not noticeably change the results.

Table 8A

Comparison of Income Gains by Distributive Shares, Union and Nonunion Periods[1]

	Income Gains as a Percentage of National Income Gain (Constant Dollars)	
	Nonunion Period 1923-29	Union Period 1947-56
National income, unadjusted	100.0	100.0
Employee compensation	100.7	129.5
Corporate profits before taxes (adjusted for inventory changes)	176.5[2]	106.9[2]
Corporate profits before taxes (unadjusted)	182.4	57.1
Interest	157.3	286.6
Rent	131.6	61.7
Unincorporated enterprise income, adjusted		21.4[2]
Business and professional	72.6[2]	62.7[2]

[1] Simon Kuznets, *National Income and Its Composition, 1919-1938*, pp. 310-19, 900. *Survey of Current Business*, July 1957, p. 16.
[2] Adjusted national income figures used.

Table 8B

Comparison of Income Gains by Distributive Shares, Union and Nonunion Periods[1]

	Income Gains as an Annual Rate of Interest[2] (Constant Dollars)	
	Nonunion Period 1923-29	Union Period 1947-56
National income, unadjusted	3.07	3.73
Employee compensation	3.09	4.83
Corporate profits before taxes (adjusted for inventory changes)	5.42	3.99
Corporate profits before taxes (unadjusted)	5.60	2.13
Interest	4.83	10.69
Rent	4.04	2.30
Unincorporated enterprise income, adjusted		−.08
Business and professional	2.23	2.34

[1] Sources same as for Table 8A.
[2] Based on compound interest formula.

INCIDENCE OF WAGE GAINS

If production workers were doing relatively better in the union post World War II period, it follows that some one or more of the income recipients must have been relatively less well off than in the twenties. Who were they? Tables 8A and 8B showing distributive share changes in the two periods throw some light on this question.

While profits during the union period have held their own in comparison with national income, they have failed to make the relative advance which they made in the nonunion period. Rent and unincorporated income were actual losers. While employee compensation fared better in the union period, referral to Table 7A indicates that all the gains in the 1947-55 period went to the blue collar group. . . .

CONCLUSION

The following comparisons between the non-union period, 1923-29, and the union post World War II period beginning in 1947 are consistent with substantial trade union collective bargaining impact on income distribution:

(1) Real average hourly earnings of production workers in manufacturing in the union period rose over twice as rapidly as in the nonunion period (Table 6), although increase in productivity in manufacturing as measured by change in physical output per man hour was greater in the nonunion period (Table 2).

(2) Average annual compensation per full-time employee (all industries) rose less than per capita personal income in the nonunion period but exceeded gains in per capita personal income in the union period (Tables 7A and 7B).

(3) The rate of increase in average annual incomes of white collar workers in manufacturing far outdistanced that of production workers in the same industries in the nonunion period. In the union period the rate of increase in average annual incomes of production workers slightly exceeded that of white collar workers (Tables 7A and 7B).

(4) In the nonunion period the rate of increase in average annual incomes of production workers lagged well behind the rate of increase in per capita personal income. In the union period the situation was reversed (Tables 7A and 7B). Average hourly earnings of production workers in manufacturing showed the same trends. . . .

The period comparison method will never provide "proof" of anything since the number of periods under observation is always too few to eliminate what the statistician calls "random fluctuations." The limited data here presented, however, seem perfectly consistent with an appreciable degree of trade union influence on income distribution.

If data on 1958 had been included the result would have been to accentuate the role of unions. This is because in 1958 profits dove while wage rates either held their own or continued their upward trend. For unions to maintain the relative income position of workers in the face of simultaneous unemployment and inflation is indeed evidence of some kind of evolutionary change.

To make a prediction, I would suggest that the accumulating bulk of evidence gathered since 1947 will support the notion of businessmen, politicians, and trade unionists—that collective bargaining is more than a ritual.

Money Wages,
Phillips Curves,
and Incomes Policy

An awkward characteristic of the American economy is that the money wage and price level tend to rise quite rapidly whenever full employment is approached. The Phillips curve, picturing an inverse relation between the unemployment rate and the rate of wage-price increase, describes this phenomenon but does not explain it. What is the explanation? To what extent can inflation be controlled by monetary and fiscal policy? Is there a case for supplementing these traditional instruments with direct wage-price controls? Economists are deeply divided on these questions, making them a challenging frontier area in contemporary economics.

The earliest American experiment with peacetime controls was the wage-price "guide-posts" developed by President Kennedy's Council of Economic Advisers in 1962, and implemented by informal "jawboning" in key situations. John Dunlop discusses the shortcomings of this policy and offers positive proposals for the future. He favors concentrating on bottleneck sectors of the economy, and emphasizes the need for industry and labor participation in any viable control program.

The next two readings were stimulated by the controls imposed by the Nixon administration in 1971. Lloyd Ulman examines critically three approaches to inflation control: (a) management of aggregate demand, which tends to mean a "stop-go" policy of periodic deflation to damp down inflationary pressure; (b) structural reform of labor and product markets to strengthen competitive restraints on wage-price increases; and (c) direct restraints through incomes policy. He finds some possibilities in the third approach, but emphasizes the difficulty of winning union support for wage restraint and the deep-rooted reasons for this difficulty.

William Poole considers that the cost of wage and price controls exceeds any possible benefit. He prefers to combine traditional monetary-fiscal instruments with structural reforms in labor and product markets. The Dunlop, Ulman, and Poole readings illustrate the variety of opinions among economists on feasible methods of inflation control.

Turning from practice to theory, some economists doubt the reality of the Phillips curve tradeoff. The economy, they believe, tends toward a "natural rate" of unemployment, which depends on the amount of time workers choose to spend in job search. An increase in aggregate demand can reduce unemployment below the natural level temporarily—but not permanently. James Tobin devoted his presidential address to the American Economic Association, part of which is reproduced here, to a critique of the "natural rate" doctrine and a defense of the Phillips curve approach.

20. Guideposts, Wages, and Collective Bargaining

John T. Dunlop

This [article] is divided into four sections. The first briefly appraises the contribution of the guideposts to economic policy in recent years. The second section states briefly and sharply the major defects of the policy. The third section sets forth some basic problems which every form of wage and price policy must resolve to remain viable in our society, and the final section proposes an alternative or transformed wage and price policy for high levels of utilization. Each section is organized to make a series of points.

I. GIVE CREDIT WHERE CREDIT IS DUE

(1) The guideposts were developed as an integral part of an expansionist policy, to help move the economy toward its full employment potential. They were aimed at "segments of the economy where firms are large or employees well organized or both" and where "there is considerable room for the exercise of private power and a parallel need for the assumption of private responsibility." They were designed to prevent sectors with strong market power from dissipating expansionary measures into wage and price increases while the system as a whole operated with considerable slack.

The guideposts were also formulated to mitigate the fears of conservative elements—in Congress, in the administration, and in the business community—who were not naturally attracted to the analysis of the new economics or its policy prescriptions. Later, the advocacy of a tax cut could point to the guideposts as evidence of a concern for the dangers of inflation. The unwarranted fears of inflation were a major deterrent to expansionist policies. As Mr. Slichter said to a bankers' association in the spring of 1959: "The greatest harm and waste caused by inflation and the fear of inflation is that they have made both government and industry afraid of expansionist policies and have deprived the country of billions of dollars of production and millions of man years of employment which the country could have had if it had not made a fetish of a stable price level."[1] The guideposts were designed to mute some of the opposition to expansionist policies.

(2) The guideposts have probably played a role, on the price side anyway, in mitigating the psychological and speculative elements of inflationary pressures in recent years. Prices are influenced by anticipations and expectations of future prices. A rise in uncertainty over the prospects of holding current prices and an increase in the probabilities of price increases may be an independent factor influencing cur-

[1] *Potentials of the American Economy, Selected Essays of Sumner H. Slichter* (Cambridge, Mass.: Harvard University Press, 1961), p. 149.

rent price stability. The guideposts as popularly conceived, backed by a few cases of dramatic confrontation between the White House and industry, have probably exerted a measure of constraint on these factors influencing prices. The anticipations of inflation, expectations and uncertainty in price making, have been mitigated to a degree, and stability has thereby been enhanced. The guideposts have also helped to educate the community that every rise in wage rates does not provide a justifiable basis for increasing prices by the same percentage or amount. In enterprises that have a measure of control over price, and where price decisions are prominent and publicly exposed, it appears that a degree of additional caution and care, and increased subtlety, has been introduced by the guideposts. My impression is that the guideposts to date probably have constricted price increases to a small degree.

On the wage side, it is my considered judgment that the guideposts probably have had no independent restraining influence on wage changes in private industry. They have been used to insist upon smaller increases for federal government employees than might otherwise have been enacted by Congress; but even here the independent effect of the guideposts is unclear. I know of no person actually involved in wage setting on the side of industry, labor organizations, or as a government or private mediator or arbitrator who thinks that the guideposts have had on balance a constrictive influence; and I have discussed the issue in detail with scores of such persons in the past six months.[2] There have been no confrontations on wages as on prices.[3] The evidence from statistical studies of the Phillips curve, relating wage changes and unemployment, appears to me inclusive both to what has happened and the reasons for any possible change.

(3) The guideposts were adopted in part out of concern with the balance of payments. While international competition has been a factor in particular sectors affecting price and wage making in the United States from colonial times, the guideposts helped to emphasize the interdependence of the economy of the United States with those of other advanced countries. The guideposts helped to popularize the balance of payments factor in the consciousness of many groups and organizations for the first time. The Trade Expansion Act was being discussed at about the same time. Regardless of any constraint the guideposts may have had on wages and prices, these developments required for many some attention to policy changes that might be necessary because wages and prices in the United States are not set in a closed economy. It is a little strange that the balance-of-payments problem has been so little discussed in conjunction with the guideposts in recent years.

(4) The guideposts were in part initiated as economic discussion and education in the community. The 1962 Economic Report of the President stated: "How is the public to judge whether a particular wage-price decision is in the national interest? No simple test exists, and it is not possible to set out systematically all of the many considerations which bear on such a judgment. However, since the question is of prime importance to the strength and progress of the American economy, it deserves widespread public discussion and clarification of the issues. What follows is intended as a contribution to such a discussion." This report proposed no "rule" but a "guide"; the guideposts did not "contribute a mechanical formula for determining whether a particular price or wage decision is inflationary"; they were "general guideposts" to which "specific modifications must be made to adapt them to the circumstances of particular industries." While the guideposts have become a rigid 3.2 formula since 1962, in the views of many newspapers, they started out in part as a contribution to a public dialogue on economic policy. There were many earlier advocates of such an annual discussion of the economic setting and criteria for wage and price decisions.[4]

II. THE BRICKBATS

(1) It is strange that the same policy makers who were so successful in selling the country a major change in fiscal policy should be so un-

[2]At the conference meetings two participants with experience in negotiations volunteered that they thought the wage guideposts had had on balance a slightly constrictive influence, but they cited no specific cases.

[3]I do not exclude the basic steel settlement. The *Newark Operating Engineers* case is a sport.

[4]John T. Dunlop, "Policy Problems: Choices and Proposals" in *Wages, Prices, Profits and Productivity,* edited by C. A. Myers (New York: American Assembly, 1959), pp. 137-60.

successful in securing assent to its guideposts. As I size up the situation, as they relate to wages the guideposts enjoy the active opposition of organized labor, of most business spokesmen, except as they may be advocated to constrict wages, of mediators or arbitrators whether public or private; and they enjoy little respect among industrial relations specialists in universities. It may be said that such a state of affairs should not be surprising since the Council of Economic Advisers is representing public interest against special interests. But in our society, the guideposts must command widespread respect and assent among decision makers—which they do not—to be viable.

The government economic policy makers did not devote much time or energy to sell the guideposts policies. They were understandably preoccupied with fiscal policies which warranted top priority. The guideposts were generally less urgent with underutilized resources and stable prices. The Council was better equipped and staffed to deal with macroeconomic issues than with wage and price decisions in a wide variety of particular sectors. Decision makers on fiscal policy are more prominent and concentrated than those who make wage and price decisions in sectors with substantial market power. When the guidepost policies came to be most needed in 1965 and 1966, they could not be counted an effective policy tool. The superb performance of securing support for the fiscal policy has not been matched in efforts or results in the wage-price area.

(2) The wage and price guideposts are not expressed in criteria that are meaningful to private decision makers. The "trend rate of overall productivity increase" and the relative rate of an industry's increase in productivity compared to the average are scarcely standards which are meaningful to decision makers on wages and prices. These concepts are not congenial or directly applicable in their operating experience. Wage decisions are typically argued in terms of comparative wages, living costs, competitive conditions, labor shortages, ability to pay, specific productivity, job content, and bargaining power. Negotiators and their constituents understand these concepts. Pricing decisions are considered in terms of specific competitive prices, quality, advertising, market prospects, responses to changes in other prices, costs, and the like. The diffuse structure of collective bargaining and pricing makes the

standards of the guideposts appear remote and unrealistic. The guideposts simply "do not come through." The macro-standards not only have no simple application to specific wage or price decisions, they do not appear relevant, controlling or decisive to micro-decision makers. You cannot effectively prescribe micro-decisions with macro-precepts. I suggest that unless guidepost standards are formulated in terms much more directly applicable and specific for decision makers, in terms they ordinarily utilize, the guideposts will command neither respect nor application.

(3) One of the most serious shortcomings of current wage-price policy, as it has been administered, is that the Council of Economic Advisers is being forced reluctantly in the direction of becoming an administrative agency. It is ill equipped for the purpose. There is danger that its concentration on a growing number of wage-price cases may divert it from the formulation of general economic policy which it has performed with great distinction. The Council has a very small staff; the Council and its staff turn over frequently. At the early stages of the expansion, only a few cases were likely to arise. But it is the nature of an economy near full employment that inflationary pressures on wages and prices arise at many points. The Council is not designed or equipped to deal with a substantial volume of actual wage-price decisions. Neither is the White House. The prestige of the President is too valuable an asset to be dissipated in a growing number of wage or price confrontations. As the economy tightens, the present wage-price policy does not appear to be administratively viable.

(4) The actual administration of the guideposts, not in the form of general preachment but rather in the mobilization of governmental pressures in particular cases, raises two groups of questions of deep concern. (a) Why were particular situations selected for confrontation rather than others, and what criteria are to be used in the selection of such cases in the future? (b) What review of the facts and arguments regarding wage and price decisions is to be made, and in what forum, in advance of the conclusion that the "guideposts have been violated" and that a wage or price decision is "against the public interest"? Certainly not all wage increases in excess of 3.2 per cent a year, to use the popular view of the guideposts, or all wage increases that violate the more flexible language of the 1962 guideposts have been

seriously scrutinized. Neither have all prices been reviewed, and those situations in which prices might have been reduced or quality improved pose almost impossible administrative difficulty.

I am personally disturbed by the absence of due process in the administration of the policy. I have looked at thousands of wage decisions in my time and have been involved in such decisions as mediator, arbitrator, fact-finder, or administrator of wartime controls. I am always impressed with how different a case may look after it has been presented in a forum which permits full review of the facts and contending arguments as compared to the reports of government or academic experts. The judgment that a wage or price increase in our economy is violative of the public interest is a serious conclusion that should warrant dispassionate review with full opportunity for the presentation of contesting views. The present policy does not afford this elementary right.

(5) There are a number of questions of analysis that can be raised with the guideposts. The neutrality of the guideposts with respect to the distribution of income does not appear to hold if the requisite price reductions do not take place. It is not clear what is the "general guide" for compensation in the event that the price guideposts are not achieved nor what is the "general guide" for prices if the wage guideposts are not achieved.

The relation of the guideposts to patterns of wages and prices during cyclical fluctuations raises a number of questions. If one starts with an economy moving upward from low levels of utilization to high levels, it appears that average wage or compensation rates increase slowly at first and then more rapidly. Deferred increases and settlements in 1966 continue to show a more rapid rate of increase than in earlier years. Average productivity, in contrast, appears to increase more rapidly during early stages of the upswing than can be sustained over the long pull at peak levels. At present levels of utilization, the further hiring of the unemployed and the large attraction of additional women and youth into the labor force should be expected to accelerate an increase in labor costs. The higher recruitment and training costs and generally lower productivity will increase labor costs and may be expected to offset overhead reductions at peak operations. The consequences of these wage rate, labor cost, and productivity movements is not price stability at sustained high levels of utilization, but rather price

increases. It is by no means clear that some average level of productivity increase over recent years is a reliable measure of the rate of productivity increase at sustained high employment. The relevant question is an old one—how much price drift at sustained high employment?

As an economy approaches any practicable definition of full employment, the relative argument for concentrating wage and price policy on "segments of the economy where firms are large or employees well organized or both" would seem to be less appropriate. The competitive sectors and bottlenecks, generally, in competitive or more concentrated sectors become more significant. The guideposts may be more appropriate to moving toward practical full employment than defining wage and price policies appropriate to sustained full employment.

III. SOME BASIC PROBLEMS

In my view a wage-price or incomes policy does not consist primarily in proclaiming each year the ideal or utopian world in which wages and prices so move that the average level of prices is stable, average wages rise by average productivity, and there are suitable adjustments in the structure of wages and prices. That ideal has been portrayed and preached for many years, and it was popular before the Council existed. A policy is to be judged rather in terms of the implementation of these objectives and in the administrative arrangements suitable and practicable to achieve the goals.

It has been suggested earlier that policies and administrative arrangements suitable during an upswing toward potential output are not necessarily suitable for continuing levels of sustained full employment, defined in practicable terms including "appropriate" regard for other objectives of public policy.[5] It is important now to identify a few of the basic problems of establishing and sustaining wage and price policies for full employment.

(1) Any viable policy must command in our society the respect and allegiance of the leaders of labor organizations and the business community as well as governmental agencies and

[5]These other objectives include economic growth, employment of marginal groups of workers, industrial peace, the absence of formal wage and price controls, distributional equity, price stability, balance-of-payment objectives, and so forth.

the press. In order to secure such consensus it is clear that the policy can only be expressed in rather general terms. But one should not underestimate the significance of such general statements and shared ideas in influencing specific behavior, at least to some degree. The policy statement which was drafted on "Sound Wage and Price Policies" by the President's Committee on Labor-Management Policy[6] in the first part of 1963, but never consummated, would be illustrative of what I have in mind.

Business and labor leaders have little respect for the current guideposts, in part because they had no role in drafting them. This is one of the major defects with the guideposts. In our society interest groups must have a role—not a controlling role—in the formulation of wage-price policy if they are to conform to it. Any new or reformulated wage-price policy must be developed with the active participation of business and labor leaders.

(2) A specific illustration of the significance of participation in policy formulation concerns the use of economic force, the strike and the lockout. A wage policy is not likely to be effective, nor will be related policies concerning price setting, if parties feel no qualms about using force against the policy. The acid test of a wage policy is what happens to a strike in defiance of the policy. In an industrial relations system, such as ours, with decentralized bargaining and with little direct control by confederations of labor and employers over constituents, the difficulties are substantically increased of achieving a viable wage and price policy. The high value placed in the community (and in legislation) on rank and file control is a further significant factor imparting an upward influence on wage settlements. The achievement of consent by leaders of labor and management is indispensable to a viable wage-price policy. Participation in the policy formulation is decisive to consent and to disavowal of economic action against the policy, at least in the absence of legal controls. Any new or reformulated wage-price policy must be prepared to deal with the strike or lockout against the policy.

(3) The federal government is poorly equipped and coordinated to facilitate a viable wage-price policy at high employment. The statistical and other data on price schedules,

[6]See Jack Stieber, "The President's Committee on Labor-Management Policy," *Industrial Relations* (February, 1966), pp. 1-19.

quality, margins, productivity, wage rates, compensation, labor costs, and the like are simply not available by detailed sectors for these policy purposes. Neither are there generally available the experts in government with detailed knowledge of market structures, price schedules, and wage setting in specific sectors adequate to the detailed policy issues. The price and wage sectors, moreover, do not well correspond. The data and expertise required for policy judgments are of a very different order than required for general economic reporting and indicators. Any new or reformulated wage-price policy must give careful attention to more appropriate administrative arrangements.

I trust you are aware that all these questions are not hypothetical. One set of government agencies exists to settle disputes and another to be concerned about stabilization and inflation. They do not speak the same language, and it is difficult to find a basis for any collaboration. In our pluralistic society this state of affairs may not seem unusual or serious. Yet, it is having some dangerous consequences for both collective bargaining and stability. In situations in which employers may fear that settlements are likely to run high, some have rushed to seek the assistance of the White House, the Council of Economic Advisers, or the Secretary of Labor, or all three, "to enforce" the guideposts. The resulting inept private bargaining and strike have frequently produced larger and more unstabilizing settlements. There have also been cases in which a union in a relatively weak bargaining position has sought to interpret the 3.2 figure as one to which it was entitled by government declaration. The guideposts have held out unavailable and ineffectual government assistance in negotiations, resulting in more inflationary capitulations or routes after shutdowns. Any new or reformulated wage-price policy must clarify the relation of mediation and fact-finding to general economic policy.

IV. AN ALTERNATIVE APPROACH

The discussion which follows is concerned with the spectrum of wage-price policy between pure preachment on the one hand and the introduction of wage and price controls on the other. It concerns an economy operating near full employment, however that may be exactly defined.

The terrain of wage-price policy between

formal controls on one side and pure macro-preachment on the other is very large and has been relatively underdeveloped. It is this range of policies which needs formulation if there is to be a lesser degree of price inflation at high utilization. It is also the zone in which there should be identified alternative policies, with greater or lesser degrees of stringency, so that wage-price policies, in addition to fiscal and monetary policies, may be adapted to changes in inflationary pressures.

It may be useful to distinguish at least five types of policy approaches in this vast terrain: (1) Do nothing extraordinary to interfere with the operation of labor and product markets. This approach would not preclude improvements in public and private employment services and more training in the labor market or continued anti-trust policies in product markets. But no accelerated policies are advocated to deal with full employment. (2) Use executive power to pressure particular price or wage decision makers to reduce or rescind increases already made or in prospect. This has been the approach of recent years. (3) Use executive power under established legislation to reduce inflationary pressures by such measures as variations in stockpiles, constriction of expenditures or procurement in sensitive sectors, adjustments in tariff schedules and the like. These methods have recently been utilized in a few situations. (4) The identification of a few major bottleneck sectors and the development with industry and labor of comprehensive programs to reduce price and wage pressures in these sectors. This approach is explored later in this section. (5) The legislative authorization for advance reporting of certain price and wage changes and the establishment of a machinery for pre- or post-review of price and wage situations. This approach has been used abroad and has its advocates here.

There are no doubt other alternatives and variants in this terrain, and social inventiveness to create others is to be encouraged. It is appropriate to hold that the present approaches are to be appraised in terms of alternative policies. But the choice is not wage and price controls or the present policy approach and practices. There are more options, and we need to use our ingenuity to invent even more.

The basic suggestion of this section is that the wage-price policy be reformulated to concentrate private and public policy on expanding supplies (and constricting demands) in a limited number of bottleneck sectors which are likely to contribute most substantially to increases in wage rates and prices. Aside from continuing general preachment, government policy should give up the attempt to review by administrative decision and to pass judgment on various private wage and price decisions and try to compel by administrative pressure changes in those decisions. It should concentrate its energies rather on the problems of a few of the most important bottleneck sectors.

The proposal for the abandonment of the present use of administrative pressure is not derived from any lack of concern with the prospects of inflationary pressures at high utilization nor from an absolute preference for employment compared to stability. My judgment is based rather on the views developed in section II that the present approach is no longer viable administratively or economically, and that some transformation of wage-price policy is urgently needed. Moreover, my judgment is that the vigorous pursuit of the bottleneck approach advocated will yield larger results in constraints on prices and wage rates. The proposed policy transformation should be developed through a reconstituted President's Committee on Labor-Management Policy to secure the requisite consensus.

The major activities of the government in such a bottleneck oriented program would be as follows:

1. The identification in the short run and in the longer period of the major priority bottlenecks in the economy. This process would require both a good deal of technical ingenuity in estimating forward demands and supplies and capacities by time periods, substitution possibilities, and the like, and also the exercise of judgment in the selection of a limited number of priority sectors.

2. The development of detailed private and public policies in the bottleneck sectors to mitigate inflationary pressures by increasing supplies and constricting demands. This policy development would require close collaboration of labor, managements, and operating government agencies at the state and federal level. The government would require interagency task forces or committees to develop and to follow the variety of policies developed for each of the priority sectors. But there must be central direction and authority to resolve conflicting governmental policies, perhaps an office of economic stabilization.

3. The range of policies developed for each bottleneck sector would involve continuing interchange of discussion, statistics and appraisal of the outlook by private parties and government representatives designed to review measures to reduce inflationary pressures, and the prescription of a wide range of private

and public activities. It is clear that the appropriate and practical policy is highly variable and specialized to a sector.

This approach is not inconsistent with the 1966 report of the Council; indeed, it there specified a few "selected problem areas"—food, non-ferrous metals, machinery, construction, and medical services. In my view, this approach requires much higher priority, much more careful formulation, the development of program for each sector with business and labor and operating government agencies, and most of all the establishment of mechanisms to secure the execution of government policies and the cooperation of private policies in each of these critical sectors.

The government is not now organized to effectuate such an approach. A few paragraphs of advice in an annual report to an industry will not produce results; the need in these trouble spots is for detailed studies for working with the sectors, coordinating diffuse and often conflicting government policies, a number of specific administrative or legislative actions, leadership, and a sense of persistence and urgency. Structural changes in organizations, in ways of making decisions, and in criteria of internal success typically come about very slowly, and yet, these institutional changes are likely to be most decisive in achieving greater stability in wages and prices at high degrees of utilization.

The list of the sectors which are likely to be most critical to wage and price stability over the next five years or so, in my view, would include some branches of transportation, medical and hospital services, construction, local government services, certain professional services, and perhaps automobile manufacturing should be added. Most of these trouble spots are not the concentrated sectors which are the focal concern of the guideposts. In each of these sectors detailed, but coordinated, studies should be in process of inflationary pressures and bottlenecks. Consultations on a continuing basis should be under way under coordinate government leadership with business and labor leaders, and a consistent range of policy suggestions should be explored. . . .

If one takes the construction industry as only one example, the scale of the problems and the inadequacy of the government to contribute to the solution of bottlenecks is apparent. I do not wish to excuse the management and labor organizations from failures as well.

There has been no census of construction since 1939. The data are most inadequate on prices, costs, and productivity on an overall basis or by branch of the industry. Regional data are highly inadequate. The general quality of almost all statistics is poor.

Any careful review of the problems of this industry would suggest a need for long-term improvement in the collective bargaining and dispute settling machinery of most branches of the industry to bring more national responsibility to unresolved local issues; a strengthening of the integrity of employer bargaining groups; reforms to make pension and health and welfare benefits transferable from one locality or region to another to improve mobility; improvements in quantity and quality of training programs of many branches of the industry; consensus on estimates of forward manpower needs by categories; changes in tax credits for travel allowances to encourage mobility; greater attention to measures to reduce seasonality; the development of measures to control in some degree the rates of expenditures of governmental agencies on construction in the light of market conditions; the adaptation of credit policies in housing to inflationary pressures; the coordination of the policies of the new HUD department to the major tendencies in construction; the need for greater research and development expenditures, and so forth. I intend no definitive program here, and it should be observed that a number of steps in some of these directions have been advocated and some are under way in consultation between the industry and the Secretary of Labor.

A listing of measures and the preparation of supporting studies (and these do not exist) in each of the bottleneck sectors does not automatically produce results. Where is there responsibility in the federal government to discuss these problems and their solutions on a continuing basis? How is one to unify a highly diffused, feuding, and decentralized labor and management? How should the government be organized to pursue these questions to assist in securing changes in private and public policies to reduce inflationary pressures and achieve higher utilization?

A wage-price policy—between preachment and controls—at high levels of utilization comes down to detailed micro-problems. No general phrasing will substitute. Government leadership which takes the form of conference, persuasion, study, catalyst, and regulation can only be effective through continuing activity related to these problems as a group. No mechanism now exists for such coordinated policy development and implementation in major bottleneck sectors. A wage-price policy for high employment involves the development of programs to break through bottlenecks (and constrict demand) rather than to roll back wages and price changes that may appear to have exceeded a generalized macro-yardstick.

21. Cost–Push and Some Policy Alternatives

Lloyd Ulman

This [article] proceeds first by considering certain aspects of the inflationary potential of market power in connection with certain limitations of monetary policy and demand management generally. It next considers some of the implications of applying the principle of Antitrust in the labor markets. Finally, it turns to incomes policies attempted to date, to suggest some conditions which might possibly be conducive to greater future effectiveness.

MONETARY POLICY AND DEMAND MANAGEMENT

There is both a rather radical and theoretical case for monetary policy and a more pragmatic and traditional case for demand management in general. Advocates of the former either deny the existence of cost-push inflation or claim that it can be quickly made to disappear by appropriate monetary policy. Their own theory of inflation, however, assigns an important role to the expectations of private individuals: although misguided monetary policy is held responsible for arousing inflationary expectations in the first place, the latter, once aroused, can force the monetary authority up against the wall.

Wage increases generated under collective bargaining can exert even greater pressure.

Collective bargaining may operate with a lag in responding to prior price increases (depending in good part on the timing of contract expirations), but, because wage increases under collective bargaining are generated primarily by strikes and the threat of strikes or of union organization, rather than by labor turnover, they can occur more readily and persistently after excess demand has been removed by fiscal-monetary policy. Thus collectively negotiated wage increases—especially those occurring sequentially in a decentralized system of collective bargaining—can be more difficult to damp down by monetary policy alone than can wage increases generated under what used to be known as "individual bargaining."

Moreover, conditions which monetary policy by itself are powerless to prevent can stimulate general wage increases under collective bargaining. People respond to a rise in the cost of living out of a desire to compensate for past or probable adverse effects on their real or relative incomes. Such effects can of course proceed from other causes as well as from increases in the general level of prices. They include changes in conditions of demand or supply for particular types of labor, which by themselves would induce changes in relative wages adverse to groups not directly affected. Such wage changes would not be generally inflationary in themselves except for their tendency to be transmitted to other groups, in excess supply situa-

159

tions, whether by unions or by nonunion employers seeking to maintain union-preventive wage differentials—and associated differentials in productivity. Thus potential changes in relative wages are converted, at least in part, into actual increases in the general level of money wages.

Indeed, a tendency to cost-push would exist even in the absence of any threatened disturbance to the distribution of labor incomes as well as in the absence of any threatened reduction in labor's share of the general income. The fact that potential adverse changes in relative wages can generate cost-push does not imply prior satisfaction on the part of all groups concerned with pre-existing income distributions. On the contrary, there need be no general tendency, even under static conditions, for union groups to cease attempting to improve their real or relative positions by pushing up on money wages, given employer resistance to union demands combined (perhaps in inverse proportion) with employer capacity to pass negotiated wage increases along in the form of price increases. As Samuel Gompers once put it,

> I would not want any man to believe that our movement is satisfied. There is not anything satisfying in what we have accomplished. It is gratifying but simply whets our appetite for better and better and still better things.

In view of this state of equilibrium dissatisfaction, a union can be counted on to maintain or increase its premium over the wage which would be sustained by competitive forces alone, even at some sacrifice of employment opportunity.[1] Two examples merit mention. The first, which seems to have been largely ignored in formal market analysis, consists in the alchemy by which collective bargaining transforms declining demand into rising wages when, as in the case of certain types of technical change, reduction in the level of demand is associated with reduction in labor cost ratios and, to this extent, demand elasticity. Declining

[1] We might assume, as a generalization about actual behavior, a very low marginal rate of substitution between the relative wage and employment, at least down to some critical minimum level of employment usually characterized by a credible threat of permanent establishment closing.

labor cost ratios reduce the potential gain to the employer from taking a strike at the same time that they raise the costs associated with a shutdown. Wages increases directly generated by this process are in real terms, but, to the extent that they preclude price reductions and to the extent that they ripple out to groups unaffected by the technical change in question, they have inflationary consequences.

The second example is provided by the fact that younger employees and members seem generally to have higher reservation prices than their elders. They are more adverse to drudgery, sweat, and imposed discipline; they are better educated and might have higher transfer earnings; and the union means less to them than it does to more senior members. To be responsive to the younger generation of members, the unions will have to try to raise their average wage premiums or to press for productivity-reducing conditions in the work place. This cloud is already bigger than a man's hand; and such by now familiar phenomena as higher frequencies of contract rejections by membership referendum and of electoral defeats of incumbent officers are serious portents. They also testify to the predictive properties of Gompers' statement; the problems posed by a new generation of union members can be viewed in the context of an underlying state of dissatisfaction.

The more pragmatic case for monetary policy and demand management is less ambitious than the monetarist approach. While it holds that the avoidance or elimination of excess demand can mitigate cost-push inflation, the pragmatic approach implicitly acknowledges the existence of causes of cost-push other than prior increases in the cost of living. Thus the pragmatists have tended to regard periodic deflation as the best that demand management alone could do to damp down inflationary pressures. That is what the British have called Stop-Go and what some members of an older generation of economists in this country meant by "creeping inflation."

This alternative has not been too unpalatable in a country where unemployment targets have been more modest than elsewhere. In fact, we seemed to accommodate our two-party system to its requirements, calling in one party when we wanted more price stability and the other when we wanted higher levels of employment.

Moreover, the effectiveness of Stop-Go can be enhanced by the restraining influence of foreign competition in some of the major domains of collective bargaining (although, as the basic steel settlement of 1971 most recently illustrated, this source of restraint can be quite limited in a predominantly "closed" economy). However, there is reason to believe that the time of naked Stop-Go may be running out.

In the first place, repeated recourse to periodic deflation presumptively reduces its effectiveness. As uncertainty concerning official intentions is reduced, firms rationally react to deflation by hoarding labor. This makes for lower productivity and profits, and so, guided by the same set of optimistic expectations, they react to this development by raising prices—which of course helps to touch off wage increases. Such persistent inflation at reduced levels of activity inspires fiscal and monetary caution, which delays the re-attainment of high employment and normal productivity growth. The reduced effectiveness of the "policy recession" in damping down inflation might call for longer or more severe spells of deflation, but this prospect would (as it has done) weaken the resolve of even the political party with the greater willingness to trade off employment and output for price stability.

One reason why Stop-Go should no longer (even if it could) suffice as even a second-best solution is that it tends to saddle the poor, including the non-whites in disproportionate numbers, the unorganized, and the underemployed with a disproportionate share of the task of absorbing the shock of wage and price increases originating in the more protected labor markets. One of the distinguishing characteristics of these unprotected markets is that they cannot so readily react to wage and price increases originating elsewhere with sympathetic wage increases. Lacking the organizational potential of public employees (to whom they stand in vivid contrast) and of workers in protected private product markets, workers in these unprotected markets are more likely to be on the receiving end of the neoclassical adjustment mechanism. For them relative improvement is to be found in sustained high employment and rapid growth which afford escape into higher-paying jobs as well as increased employment opportunities and higher wages in the unprotected markets. But the wage and price increases which are thereby induced in unprotected markets invite wage and price increases elsewhere and help induce deflation.

STRUCTURAL REFORM

It has never been disputed that careful demand management constitutes a necessary condition for the restraint of cost-push inflation by curbing inflationary price movements to which the bargainers would otherwise respond. A similar role might usefully be performed by active labor market policies. On the other hand, the effectiveness of both types of policy is limited; and institutional influences in labor markets, combined with discretionary pricing in product markets, contribute to these limitations. Hence the attraction of other policies designed to restrain discretionary wage and price setting more directly, either by reducing the areas of discretion or by inducing underutilization of private market power. In recent years both types of policy have been subsumed under the heading of "incomes policy," but I shall reserve that label for the second type and designate the first "structural reform."

Structural reform presumably includes measures to reduce concentration of power in both product and labor markets. In the past, this concept has embraced legislation designed to reduce the size of the bargaining unit or otherwise to reduce the power of the national unions; and, as we continue our quest for effective policy instruments, it is not unlikely that proposals of this type will be put forth again. I believe, however, that they are not likely to be effective and, indeed, that they might be counterproductive unless they are accompanied by a degree of decentralization in product markets—which in some cases might be excessive in terms of standard market criteria.

To the extent that decentralization means that one's competitors would continue to operate while he was shut down, it would raise the cost of a strike to the employer. To raise the gains from taking a strike, decentralization would have to reduce the probability that any price increase occasioned by a peacefully negotiated wage increase would be promptly followed by one's competitors. But this, as I have suggested, would require decentralization of product as well as of labor markets and the abandonment of all manner of legal price supports as well as legal wage supports. This in turn would mean that farm price supports, tariffs, tax preferences would also have to go, because the political process required for such dismantling would be roughly analogous to a successful multinational disarmament conference. Such domestic economic disarmament would indeed be effective in reducing inflationary pressures; but it is only natural that elected politicians should have passed up the radical solution of disarmament in favor of a ceasefire. Thus incomes policy—which is designed to induce underutilization, rather than reduction, of market power—has been regarded as the only game in town.

INCOMES POLICY

Incomes policy has enjoyed some success as a limited-duration instrument, mainly under conditions of excess supply and especially in the form of an absolute freeze on wages and prices. It has yet to demonstrate effectiveness in modifying deep-seated propensities that underlie inflationary institutional behavior and thus in bringing about a steady state of full employment. Its failure to date in this more ambitious role has been due in part in insufficient firmness or realism on the part of government but also to the lack of sufficiently effective incentives to self-restraint.

...[Greater wage restraint might be achieved] by adding or increasing legal compulsion, by providing more efficient inducements to the unions to support the policy, or by providing employers with incentives to resist union demands more strongly under given labor market conditions. No one of these approaches can be considered in isolation from the others since compulsion, cooperation, and resistance are strongly interrelated. Thus union cooperation and legal compulsion complement one another. Under a decentralized system of collective bargaining where the cooperation of any particular autonomous group is heavily conditioned on compliance by the others, it must be possible to prod the rogue elephant back into the herd. On the other hand, any set of legal sanctions requires a sufficient degree of popular support to give it effect. Indeed, a policy of increased governmental sanctions can run into an area of

negative returns unless an increased degree of cooperation can also be induced.

One need not be a student of foreign experience to appreciate that the discovery of incentives to union cooperation is not an easy task. However, the experience of other countries which have been experimenting with incomes policy, in most cases longer and more intensively than we have, is obviously relevant to this discussion. I shall hazard a few generalizations from that experience, based largely on research reported in the book *Wage Restraint* by Ulman and Flanagan.[2]

In the first place, persuasive evidence of the imminence or existence of a national emergency has proved to be an effective incentive to union cooperation, but, apart from war, sufficiently persuasive evidence is hard to come by and official appeals to patriotism are not taken at face value. Actual or threatened crises in the balance of payments have on notable occasions served this purpose well, but mainly as a temporarily effective incentive to union cooperation; and even these have been losing potency in recent years. To the extent that exchange rates become more flexible, it might be noted, this incentive to restraint will further diminish in importance.

In addition to furnishing a patriotic incentive to cooperation, the currency crisis has served as an important aid to incomes policy as a pedagogical instrument. It dramatizes and makes more credible the lesson that excessive wage increases will entail a higher rate of unemployment. It also helps incomes policy to get across another lesson: that excessive increases in money wages tend to inhibit economic growth and thus to slow down the rate of increase in real wage incomes. However, the ability of pedagogical effectiveness *per se* to shift Phillips curves (the premise on which the first Kennedy Guideposts were erected) is doubtful. Enlightenment need not bring forth self-restraint. For even if he is persuaded that the anti-inflationary alternative to wage restraint is more unemployment, the probability of job loss for the average union member is likely to be very low. To him, the choice is between a low probability of income loss through unemployment and a high probability

[2] Lloyd Ulman and Robert J. Flanagan, *Wage Restraint: A Study of Income Policies in Western Europe* (Berkeley and Los Angeles: University of California Press, 1971).

of income loss through wage restraint. (Since the probability of loss through self-restraint to any given group is partly determined by the capability for defection by others, the prospects for a policy based on cooperation tend, other things equal, to vary inversely with the degree of decentralization of authority within the union movement.) Nor would the message of growth through wage restraint hold out much appeal to a man, however rational and sophisticated, whom a relatively low level of income has endowed with a high rate of time preference.

Favored treatment of workers at the low end of the pay distribution has been almost invariably a characteristic of incomes policy and has formed the basis of appeals to the egalitarian tradition of trade union movements. The principle of differential treatment has been taken most seriously by the leaders of the central federations who are the guardians of that tradition—and are furthest removed from the rank and file. The latter are not unsympathetic to wage increases for the working poor, but neither are they above demanding and obtaining—often in the form of locally negotiated wage drift—compensatory increases for themselves—to redress inequities, restore traditional differentials, etc.

Indeed, incomes policy has failed to win friends and influence unionists in part because the hoped-for incentives to compliance involved redistribution of income adverse to those groups of wage-earners to whom they have been addressed.[3] Thus the policy itself has threatened to aggravate a problem which, as suggested above, would contribute to cost-push inflation in its absence. One remedy would be to substitute selfish incentives for appeals to the better nature and to make the former more specific and concrete. In the manner of the French, the Dutch, and others, such a policy might promise the unions a specified higher rate of increase in real wages under restraint than they had been able to secure during inflationary "free-for-alls." This would include the approval and even encouragement of cost-of-living guarantees. Among the hoped-for gains from this feature would be not only reduced inflationary hedging on the part of unions but also—assuming that escalation requires some direct price restraint—an increase in the "supply" of employer resistance to wage demands.

[3]*Ibid.*, pp. 224-30.

Another way to secure high rates of increase in real wages is through "pay and productivity bargains" whereby specific union groups, by surrendering restrictive working practices, enable management to realize above-trend increases in productivity. However, while productivity bargaining can contribute to the effectiveness of an overall policy of wage-price restraint, it is obviously subject to abuse in the absence of an effective overall policy, as the British discovered.

Finally, it is becoming increasingly apparent that the effectiveness of wage restraint is dependent on the distributional implications of associated policies of demand management. In particular, it is probable that union leaders will increasingly look outside incomes policy proper for favored treatment of low-income groups; so must the authorities if they wish to hold down wage drift and other forms of wage increases powered by claims of "inequity."

It is thus apparent that the gains from incomes policies associated with more effective incentives to union cooperation and employer resistance will come at a price. To achieve greater wage restraint by unions will cost something in terms of economic growth, social harmony, and possibly industrial peace; and even if the costs are outweighed by the gains from increased effectiveness, the policy will lose some of its political appeal.

The most likely alternative to an incomes policy sufficiently effective to assure a steady state of relatively noninflationary high employment is a policy of short-term effectiveness designed to minimize the amplitude and duration of periodic "policy recessions" (as the latter become less efficient in curbing inflation on their own). . . . The prospect of an infinite series of controlled Stop-Go's is not cheering: it seems to imply incurring the cost of the method of price control without reaping the full benefits in the terms of improving the relative incomes of the unprotected. Yet, just as the laissez-faire policy cycle can breed destabilizing expectations, the price-controlled cycle might generate stabilizing expectations and, in time, less inflationary institutional behavior. But in order to minimize the interval involved, it would be necessary for the policy-makers to run risks and incur costs, as suggested above. It would also be necessary for practitioners and policy-makers in industrial relations together to reappraise some of the inherited rules and customs, as they did in 1935, in 1947, and in

1959. The social costs of an effective incomes policy and of constructive structural reform are not as disparate as policy-makers would like to think: nor are the two approaches mutually exclusive.

22. Thoughts on the Wage–Price Freeze

William Poole

In reading the newspapers since August 15, I have been impressed with the frequency of the arguments that "something" had to be done about the economy and the paucity of the arguments that the program announced by the President will actually accomplish the desired objectives at an acceptable cost. There is no assurance that the new course is better, only that it is different. This paper concentrates on the wage-price controls part of the program which, in my view, raises the most serious issues. . . .

The economists who favor controls generally do so with the idea that they are a lesser evil than inflation accompanied by unemployment. The controls issue is more one of differing empirical judgments about benefits and costs than of differing doctrinal viewpoints. While economists give different weights to various aspects of their ideals of "the good life," most cherish the maximum possible freedom for economic decisions, a reduction of which is one of the costs of controls. But individual decisions, of course, ought to be taken within the context of the full employment economy

The views expressed in this paper are those of the author and do not necessarily reflect those of the Division of Research and Statistics or the Board of Governors. Indeed, to emphasize the personal nature of these views this paper has been written with extensive use of the first person singular.

necessary to provide genuine choices among job opportunities and among investment opportunities, as well as the stable incomes and goods required for a widely shared prosperity.

Economists differ widely in their empirical judgments as to the policies necessary to approach the ideal. I believe that the differences in empirical judgments primarily center around the following aspects of controls: (1) the ease of enforcement; (2) cost; (3) required extent in terms of the number of prices and wages that must be affected; (4) required duration; and (5) efficacy.

These issues are interrelated, and the sections below attempt to untangle them, and then to outline an alternative course of action that could have been pursued instead of a freeze followed by controls of one type or another.

The analysis is based on the assumption that the controls following the freeze will be of the "mild" variety. It is also assumed that the controls will be temporary, that is, of less than three years' duration.

THE COSTS OF WAGE-PRICE CONTROLS

Controls incur three different types of costs. The first is the loss of individual freedom resulting from central control over individual wage and price decisions. The second is the misallocation of resources resulting from controls. And the third is the administrative cost. All these costs are interrelated. For example, if administrative cost is kept low, enforcement of the controls will be weak and will have relatively little effect after a time. Also, it is obvious that the costs of controls are a function of their duration.

The resource allocation and administrative costs of controls are not likely to prove great if the controls last for at most several years, especially if they are of the mild variety and really "buy" lower unemployment and greater price stability. In any event, a rich society can bear these costs. The important issue concerns the costs in individual freedom and the way in which they affect the nature of controls that are politically acceptable. The question is whether temporary mild controls will make any lasting contribution to the goals of full employment and price stability.

Considerable governmental power was applied when the wage-price freeze was put into effect. All contracts voluntarily reached by individuals and firms, with each other and with governmental units, have been suspended insofar as they provide for increases in wages and prices. But the central question about the efficacy of temporary controls is precisely whether they will have any lasting effect if existing contracts are permitted to resume force once the freeze ends. The cost of controls will be high if existing contracts must be rewritten following the freeze. This issue will be examined in the next section.

Several examples may serve to amplify the hitherto vague references to "individual freedom." These examples should not be taken to concern "mere details," for one of the major arguments against controls is that there is no satisfactory way of handling these details. To consider the problems of enforcing wage controls, suppose that a firm wants to increase the pay of an employee to a level above the controlled level, perhaps because he is threatening to take a job with a competitor. An obvious technique is to promote him—indeed, so obvious that one of the first clarifications issued during the current freeze was that wages could be increased only in the event of a "bona fide" promotion.

What is a "bona fide" promotion? One approach is not to allow promotions into newly created positions. A firm is not permitted to create new vice presidents, or new foremen, or

new senior accountants just to have more higher paying slots to put employees in. But clearly this approach to wage control cannot last very long since many firms have valid reasons for creating new positions.

What criteria can the controllers then use to distinguish between bona fide and control-avoidance promotions? Beyond the cases where the issues are clear-cut, many problems will arise, for example, in connection with corporate mergers and reorganizations. To offer another example, how does a government official know how many foremen are needed in a new plant producing a new product?

Comprehensive wage control is no easy matter. Many arbitrary decisions must be made. Wage control will be relatively easy and most complete over standardized types of jobs, including most blue collar and clerical jobs. Managerial and professional jobs, on the other hand, are more varied and more subject to change. The inequities will multiply, and so will the pressure for a more and more elaborate control machinery to limit the inequities by adjusting wages and salaries.

To obtain wage increases some individuals will be forced to change jobs because one firm, though willing, is not permitted to grant an increase in pay, while another obtains permission for a new position, or has a vacancy in an existing position. Excessive job changing is not only inefficient but also tends to break down wage control. To combat this tendency, controls may be imposed on job moves, or directly on the pay of individuals rather than of jobs.

Price control presents problems that are just as serious. How is the price on a new product to be determined? To set the price on the basis of the firm's costs requires the perhaps expensive attempt to understand its cost accounting methods. To set it equal to that of the closest competitive product is unsatisfactory if the new product costs more to produce but has superior characteristics that are not permitted to bring a higher price, or if it has roughly the same performance characteristics but costs less to produce. In the latter case the cost savings are not passed on to the purchasers of the new product.

Another problem arises when firms face cost increases, some of which in practice will prove unavoidable. Is a firm to be permitted to pass these increases on in the form of higher prices? If not, what happens if the firm simply stops production of an unprofitable item? Will a firm be forced to continue production of an item "vital to the national interest"? If cost increases on "vital" products, however defined, are considered a valid reason for price increases, how many officials will be required to administer the price controls?

Product specifications are constantly changing, sometimes reflecting improvement, sometimes deterioration.[1] In comprehensive price control firms have an obvious incentive to reduce the quality of their goods and services. If the inflationary pressures to be suppressed by controls are powerful, control over product specifications will be required.[2]

Although economists disagree as to the severity of these problems, they acknowledge their existence and believe that they will become more apparent with time. As problems appear, some economists will call for an escalation of controls, while others, like me, will argue that there is no natural end to the escalation of controls. How can these administrative problems be handled without a large bureaucracy? Only administrative guidelines that permit individuals, firms, and control administrators to know what changes in wages and prices, and in job and product specifications,

are and are not permitted could make a small bureaucracy feasible. I do not believe such guidelines can be constructed, and, if these matters must be handled on a case-by-case basis, will not the sheer volume of cases overwhelm the control bureaucracy? Will the decisions by controllers be subject to legal appeal, and if so what is the case load likely to be?

Whether controls can work without a large bureaucracy is an empirical question.[3] In my view the issue involved is whether the inflation problem arises primarily from relatively few sources of market power, both on the labor side and the product side, that can be effectively controlled without an elaborate control machinery.

I believe that the economy is far more competitive than surface appearances would indicate. Suppose that, following the freeze, mandatory controls were placed on the wages and prices of the 200 or the 500 largest corporations in the nation. Furthermore, suppose that prices were not permitted to increase at all, and wage increases were limited to the 3.2 percent productivity guideline. Assume, too, that the controls were really strict and all the problems of evasion were handled successfully. How would the experiment work out?

Those who favor this approach would predict that the rate of increase of prices and wages in the whole economy would be drastically slowed. Firms with controlled prices would take business away from those that raised prices and thereby effectively control all prices. Since the prices of uncontrolled firms would in fact be effectively controlled, they would be forced to limit their wage increases. Furthermore, wage demands made to the uncontrolled firms would moderate because the big, visible unions would not be obtaining big wage increases for others to emulate.

Those predicting failure for this approach expect, of course, that some evasion of the controls would take place. To the extent that it is stemmed, the controlled firms would lose their operating flexibility. Their key employees would be bid away, and in some product lines

[1] Product deterioration is not always a bad thing. For example, when clothing styles are undergoing particularly rapid change, reducing costs by a reduction in the durability of the cloth makes perfectly good sense because the clothes won't be worn out anyway.

[2] For a recent example, consider the following quote, "General Motors executives also said that they were making optional some equipment that was to have been standard on 1972 models. The change was made because the company must sell new models at 1971 prices during the Government's 90-day price freeze. . . .

"G.M. officials here made it clear that wherever possible they would pull out items that had been added to the 1972 cars, making the newer models more like the 1971's. For example, the company had planned as standard equipment to have rubber protective guards running along the entire length of the front and rear bumpers. Now they will be optional at $23.

"Also, a larger 400-cubic-inch displacement engine was to be standard on the 1972 Pontiac Catalina, replacing a 350-cubic-inch engine that was standard on the 1971. With the price freeze the 350-inch engine is standard again and the larger engine is optional at $52." ("Pontiac Offering Energy-Absorbing Bumper for '72," *New York Times,* August 31, 1971.)

[3] This sentence should not be interpreted as implying that I believe that controls can work *with* a large bureaucracy. I do not believe that controls of any type can work for very long without moving far in the direction of a centrally planned economy and relying on a degree of compulsion unacceptable in a democracy.

they would find themselves unable to meet the market demand at the prices allowed. Customers, therefore, would turn to uncontrolled firms. Furthermore, the controls and the uncertainty of their application would limit the incentive for large firms to invest in expanded facilities, further eroding their positions. . . .

I predict that in a relatively short space of time competitive forces would be operating so powerfully that the control experiment described above would be dropped or altered to meet the competitive situation. If the controls were altered, the uncontrolled sectors would determine the level of the wage and price controls in the controlled sectors, rather than the controls affecting the level of wages and prices.

These predictions are straightforward, but the experiment is unlikely to be undertaken. It simply is not politically possible to place strict controls on the largest firms. The reason lies beyond the political power they and unions hold and people's strongly held beliefs about equity. Rather, the reason is primarily the severity of the economic dislocations that would ensue from controls. To counter that it is "unrealistic" to set a 3.2 percent limit on wage increases when wages have been rising at two or three times that rate is not sufficient. If wage increases cannot be set at 3.2 percent, the economic realities control the controllers, rather than the other way round.

If mandatory controls on the largest firms and unions won't work, there is, of course, little hope for a voluntary guidelines approach. Voluntary compliance is possible only when the guidelines are very close to what would have happened anyway. . . .

AN ALTERNATIVE PROGRAM

. . . "doing something" is not always better than "doing nothing." I am prepared to defend the basic prefreeze monetary and fiscal policies as superior to those now being followed. But this is not to say that the prefreeze policies were the best of all possible policies. . . .

. . . A strong case can be made for attacking some of the structural causes of high prices and excessive unemployment. It should be emphasized that the word used here is "high" and not "rising." Structural deficiencies in the economy raise the level of unemployment consistent with stability in the rate of inflation, but do not by themselves cause the inflation. But while struc-

tural reforms were being put into effect the result would be downward pressure on some wages and prices. This transitional effect would be most welcome, given the present public concern over inflation, and would help to generate support for the reforms.

Steps could have been taken—through executive action where possible and submission of new legislation where necessary—in at least the following areas: (1) modification or elimination of minimum wage laws; (2) modification of the tax laws to provide for the inclusion of all corporate profits rather than dividends alone in the definition of personal taxable income of common stock shareholders, in order to encourage increased dividend payouts and discourage corporate agglomerations;[4] (3) antitrust action leading to dissolution of large firms in excessively concentrated industries; (4) elimination of farm price supports to reduce the cost of food; (5) elimination of regulation of transportation fares and rates; (6) elimination of tariffs and quotas on imported goods and services; (7) strengthening of retraining programs and employment services, perhaps including subsidies to encourage migration out of labor surplus areas.[5] This list could no doubt be extended, but it is long enough to give the flavor of the reforms I would favor.

At the same time, to ease the burdens of unemployment, unemployment benefits should be extended and the welfare program enacted. In addition, temporary adjustment assistance should be provided to cushion the impact on individuals and firms unduly affected by the structural reforms proposed above.

SOME CONCLUDING COMMENTS

The structural reforms discussed above would generate much political opposition. For this reason many will dismiss them as the equivalent of a "do nothing" program on the grounds that they could never be enacted. I am not optimistic about the chances for large-scale structural reforms, but I believe that some of

[4]The increased revenues from this tax change could be offset by a reduction in personal or corporate tax rates or both.

[5]This program, of course, would not be very important until the recovery starts to produce some areas with labor shortages. But now is the time to initiate it, so that it will be operating when needed.

them might be enacted, given the mood of the nation.

It is a mistake, I believe, to think that controls will be politically viable for very long. The fine reception the freeze received in its first days resulted largely from the failure to comprehend what controls involve. Most people seem to believe that the controls will be more effective on what they buy than on what they sell. My prediction is that the problems with controls will become more and more apparent as time goes on, that mild controls will prove ineffective, and that comprehensive controls will have less long-run political viability than structural reform.

I do not believe, however, that an alternative course of action exists that would ensure a prompt return to both full employment and price stability. It took five years—from 1964 to 1969—for inflation, as measured by the GNP deflator, to climb from 1.5 percent to 5.8 percent at annual rates. I am not optimistic that inflation can be reduced to the 1964 rate in the same length of time while, simultaneously, full employment is maintained.

Following 1964 the inflation rate rose relatively slowly in the face of an overheated economy, because the economy had been well adjusted to a low inflation rate. Now the economy is adjusted to a higher inflation rate, perhaps around 4 percent. This adjustment is not simply a matter of inflationary expectations. It includes countless private contracts and established methods of operation. . . .

Since the economy is so well adjusted to an inflationary environment, the cost of continued inflation at a 3 to 5 percent rate is relatively small. While it is not zero, it is low enough to be much below the cost of attempting to suppress inflation through tighter controls or a prolonged period of high unemployment. I believe that the costs of mild controls or guidelines are greater than their likely contribution, and that the controls should be phased out as soon as possible regardless of whether the inflation rate has declined. The least costly policy, I believe, is to accept the fact that inflation—very moderate inflation by world standards—is here to stay for a while. . . .A conservative policy is in order. If we do not push too hard and if we avoid another inflationary boom caused by overshooting full employment, there is an excellent chance that unemployment and inflation will both decline in the years ahead.

23. Inflation and Unemployment

James Tobin

On this rostrum four years ago, Milton Friedman identified the noninflationary natural rate of unemployment with "equilibrium in the structure of real wage rates." "The 'natural rate of unemployment,' " he said, ". . . is the level that would be ground out by the Walrasian system of general equilibrium equations, provided that there is embedded in them the actual structural characteristics of the labor and commodity markets, including market imperfections, stochastic variability in demands and supplies, the costs of getting information about job vacancies and labor availabilities, the costs of mobility, and so on." Presumably this Walrasian equilibrium also has the usual optimal properties; at any rate, Friedman advised the monetary authorities not to seek to improve upon it. But in fact we know little about the existence of a Walrasian equilibrium that allows for all the imperfections and frictions that explain why the natural rate is bigger than zero, and even less about the optimality of such an equilibrium if it exists.

In the new microeconomics of labor markets and inflation, the principal activity whose marginal value sets the reservation price of employment is job search. It is not pure leisure, for in principle persons who choose that option are not reported as unemployed; however, there may be a leisure component in job seeking.

A crucial assumption of the theory is that search is significantly more efficient when the searcher is unemployed, but almost no evidence has been advanced on this point. Members of our own profession are adept at seeking and finding new jobs without first leaving their old ones or abandoning not-in-labor-force status. We do not know how many quits and new hires in manufacturing are similar transfers, but some of them must be; if all reported accessions were hires of unemployed workers, the mean duration of unemployment would be only about half what it is in fact. . . .

In any event, the contention of some natural rate theorists is that employment beyond the natural rate takes time that would be better spent in search activity. Why do workers accept such employment? An answer to this question is a key element in a theory that generally presumes that actual behavior reveals true preferences. The answer given is that workers accept the additional employment only because they are victims of inflation illusion. One form of inflation illusion is over-estimation of the real wages of jobs they now hold, if they are employed, or of jobs they find, if they are unemployed and searching. If they did not underestimate price inflation, employed workers would more often quit to search, and unemployed workers would search longer.

The force of this argument seems to me diluted by the fact that price inflation illusion affects equally both sides of the job seeker's equation. He over-estimates the real value of an immediate job, but he also over-estimates the real values of jobs he might wait for. . . .

Does the market produce the *optimal* amount of search unemployment? Is the natural rate optimal? . . .

An omniscient and beneficent economic dictator would not place every new job seeker immediately in any job at hand. Such a policy would create many mis-matches, sacrificing efficiency in production or necessitating costly job-to-job shifts later on. The hypothetical planner would prefer to keep a queue of workers unemployed, so that he would have a larger choice of jobs to which to assign them. But he would not make the queue too long, because workers in the queue are not producing anything.

Of course he could shorten the queue of unemployed if he could dispose of more jobs and lengthen the queue of vacancies. With enough jobs of various kinds, he would never lack a vacancy for which any worker who happens to come along has comparative advantage. But because of limited capital stocks and interdependence among skills, jobs cannot be indefinitely multiplied without lowering their marginal productivity. Our wise and benevolent planner would not place people in jobs yielding less than the marginal value of leisure. Given this constraint on the number of jobs, he would always have to keep some workers waiting, and some jobs vacant. But he certainly would be inefficient if he had fewer jobs, filled and vacant, than this constraint. This is the common sense of Beveridge's rule—that vacancies should not be less than unemployment.

Is the natural rate a market solution of the hypothetical planner's operations research problem? According to search theory, an unemployed worker considers the probabilities that he can get a better job by searching longer and balances the expected discounted value of waiting against the loss of earnings. The employed worker makes a similar calculation when he considers quitting, also taking into account the once and for all costs of movement. These calculations are like those of the planner, but with an important difference. An individual does not internalize all the considerations the planner takes into account. The external effects are the familiar ones of congestion theory. A worker deciding to join a queue or to stay in one considers the probabilities of getting a job,

but not the effects of his decision on the probabilities that others face. He lowers those probabilities for people in the queue he joins and raises them for persons waiting for the kind of job he vacates or turns down. Too many persons are unemployed waiting for good jobs, while less desirable ones go begging. However, external effects also occur in the decisions of employers whether to fill a vacancy with the applicant at hand or to wait for someone more qualified. It is not obvious, at least to me, whether the market is biased toward excessive or inadequate search. But it is doubtful that it produces the optimal amount.

Empirically the proposition that in the United States the zero-inflation rate of unemployment reflects voluntary and efficient job-seeking activity strains credulity. If there were a natural rate of unemployment in the United States, what would it be? It is hard to say because virtually all econometric Phillips curves allow for a whole menu of steady inflation rates. But estimates constrained to produce a vertical long-run Phillips curve suggest a natural rate between 5 and 6 percent of the labor force.

So let us consider some of the features of an overall unemployment rate of 5 to 6 percent. First, *about 40 percent of accessions in manufacturing are rehires rather than new hires.* Temporarily laid off by their employers, these workers had been awaiting recall and were scarcely engaged in voluntary search activity. Their unemployment is as much a deadweight loss as the disguised unemployment of redundant workers on payrolls. This number declines to *25-30 percent when unemployment is 4 percent or below.* Likewise, a 5-6 percent unemployment rate means that voluntary quits amount to only about a third of separations, layoffs to two-thirds. The proportions are reversed at low unemployment rates.

Second, the unemployment statistic is not an exhaustive count of those with time and incentive to search. An additional 3 percent of the labor force are involuntarily confined to part-time work, and another 3/4 of 1 percent are out of the labor force because they "could not find job" or "think no work available"— discouraged by market conditions rather than personal incapacities.

Third, with unemployment of 5-6 percent the number of reported vacancies is less than 1/2 of 1 percent. Vacancies appear to be understated relative to unemployment, but they rise to 1½ percent when the unemployment rate is below 4 percent. At 5-6 percent unemployment, the economy is clearly capable of generating many more jobs with marginal productivity high enough so that people prefer them to leisure. The capital stock is no limitation, since 5-6 percent unemployment has been associated with more than 20 percent excess capacity. Moreover, when more jobs are created by expansion of demand, with or without inflation, labor force participation increases; this would hardly occur if the additional jobs were low in quality and productivity. As the parable of the central employment planner indicates, there will be excessive waiting for jobs if the roster of jobs and the menu of vacancies are suboptimal.

In summary, labor markets characterized by 5-6 percent unemployment do not display the symptoms one would expect if the unemployment were voluntary search activity. Even if it were voluntary, search activity on such a large scale would surely be socially wasteful. The only reason anyone might regard so high an unemployment rate as an equilibrium and social optimum is that lower rates cause accelerating inflation. But this is almost tautological. The inferences of equilibrium and optimality would be more convincing if they were corroborated by direct evidence.

WHY IS THERE INFLATION WITHOUT AGGREGATE EXCESS DEMAND?

Zero-inflation unemployment is not wholly voluntary, not optimal, I might even say not natural. In other words, the economy has an inflationary bias: When labor markets provide as many jobs as there are willing workers, there is inflation, perhaps accelerating inflation. Why?

The Phillips curve has been an empirical finding in search of a theory, like Pirandello characters in search of an author. One rationalization might be termed a theory of stochastic macro-equilibrium: stochastic, because random intersectoral shocks keep individual labor markets in diverse states of disequilibrium; macro-equilibrium, because the perpetual flux of particular markets produces fairly definite aggregate outcomes of unemployment and wages. Stimulated by Phillips's 1958 findings, Richard Lipsey proposed a model of this kind in 1960, and it has since been elaborated by Archibald,

Holt, and others. I propose now to sketch a theory in the same spirit.

It is an essential feature of the theory that economy-wide relations among employment, wages, and prices are aggregations of diverse outcomes in heterogeneous markets. The myth of macroeconomics is that relations among aggregates are enlarged analogues of relations among corresponding variables for individual households, firms, industries, markets. The myth is a harmless and useful simplification in many contexts, but sometimes it misses the essence of the phenomenon.

Unemployment is, in this model as in Keynes reinterpreted, a disequilibrium phenomenon. Money wages do not adjust rapidly enough to clear all labor markets every day. Excess supplies in labor markets take the form of unemployment, and excess demands the form of unfilled vacancies. At any moment, markets vary widely in excess demand or supply, and the economy as a whole shows both vacancies and unemployment.

The overall balance of vacancies and unemployment is determined by aggregate demand, and is therefore in principle subject to control by overall monetary and fiscal policy. Higher aggregate demand means fewer excess supply markets and more excess demand markets, accordingly less unemployment and more vacancies.

In any particular labor market, the rate of increase of money wages is the sum of two components, an equilibrium component and a disequilibrium component. The first is the rate at which the wage would increase were the market in equilibrium, with neither vacancies nor unemployment. The other component is a function of excess demand and supply—a monotonic function, positive for positive excess demand, zero for zero excess demand, nonpositive for excess supply. I begin with the disequilibrium component.

Of course the disequilibrium components are relevant only if disequilibria persist. Why aren't they eliminated by the very adjustments they set in motion? Workers will move from excess supply markets to excess demand markets, and from low wage to high wage markets. Unless they overshoot, these movements are equilibrating. The theory therefore requires that new disequilibria are always arising. Aggregate demand may be stable, but beneath its stability is never-ending flux: new products, new processes, new tastes and fashions, new developments of land and natural resources, obsolescent industries and declining areas.

The overlap of vacancies and unemployment—say, the sum of the two for any given difference between them—is a measure of the heterogeneity or dispersion of individual markets. The amount of dispersion depends directly on the size of those shocks of demand and technology that keep markets in perpetual disequilibrium, and inversely on the responsive mobility of labor. The one increases, the other diminishes the frictional component of unemployment, that is, the number of unfilled vacancies coexisting with any given unemployment rate.

A central assumption of the theory is that the functions relating wage change to excess demand or supply are non-linear, specifically that unemployment retards money wages less than vacancies accelerate them. Nonlinearity in the response of wages to excess demand has several important implications. First, it helps to explain the characteristic observed curvature of the Phillips curve. Each successive increment of unemployment has less effect in reducing the rate of inflation. Linear wage response, on the other hand, would mean a linear Phillips relation.

Second, given the overall state of aggregate demand, economy-wide vacancies less unemployment, wage inflation will be greater the larger the variance among markets in excess demand and supply. As a number of recent empirical studies, have confirmed (see George Perry and Charles Schultze), dispersion is inflationary. Of course, the rate of wage inflation will depend not only on the overall dispersion of excess demands and supplies across markets but also on the particular markets where the excess supplies and demands happen to fall. An unlucky random drawing might put the excess demands in highly responsive markets and the excess supplies in especially unresponsive ones.

Third, the nonlinearity is an explanation of inflationary bias, in the following sense. Even when aggregate vacancies are at most equal to unemployment, the average disequilibrium component will be positive. Full employment in the sense of equality of vacancies and unemployment is not compatible with price stability. Zero inflation requires unemployment in excess of vacancies.

Criteria that coincide in full long-run equilibrium—zero inflation and zero aggregate excess demand—diverge in stochastic macro-equilibrium. Full long-run equilibrium in all markets would show no unemployment, no vacancies, no unanticipated inflation. But with unending sectoral flux, zero excess demand spells inflation and zero inflation spells net excess supply, unemployment in excess of vacancies. In these circumstances neither criterion can be justified simply because it is a property of full long-run equilibrium. Both criteria automatically allow for frictional unemployment incident to the required movements of workers between markets; the no-inflation criterion requires enough additional unemployment to wipe out inflationary bias.

I turn now to the equilibrium component, the rate of wage increase in a market with neither excess demand nor excess supply. It is reasonable to suppose that the equilibrium component depends on the trend of wages of comparable labor elsewhere. A "competitive wage," one that reflects relevant trends fully, is what employers will offer if they wish to maintain their share of the volume of employment. This will happen where the rate of growth of marginal revenue product—the compound of productivity increase and price inflation—is the same as the trend in wages. But in some markets the equilibrium wage will be rising faster, and in others slower, than the economy-wide wage trend.

A "natural rate" result follows if actual wage increases feed fully into the equilibrium components of future wage increases. There will be acceleration whenever the non-linear disequilibrium effects are on average positive, and steady inflation, that is stochastically steady inflation, only at unemployment rates high enough to make the disequilibrium effects wash out. Phillips tradeoffs exist in the short run, and the time it takes for them to evaporate depends on the lengths of the lags with which today's actual wage gains become tomorrow's standards.

A rather minor modification may preserve Phillips tradeoffs in the long run. Suppose there is a floor on wage change in excess supply markets, independent of the amount of excess supply and of the past history of wages and prices. Suppose, for example, that wage change is never negative; it is either zero or what the response function says, whichever is algebraically larger. So long as there are markets where this floor is effective, there can be determinate rates of economy-wide wage inflation for various levels of aggregate demand. Markets at the floor do not increase their contributions to aggregate wage inflation when overall demand is raised. Nor is their contribution escalated to actual wage experience. But the frequency of such markets diminishes, it is true, both with overall demand and with inflation. The floor phenomenon can preserve a Phillips tradeoff within limits, but one that becomes ever more fragile and vanishes as greater demand pressure removes markets from contact with the zero floor. The model implies a long-run Phillips curve that is very flat for high unemployment and becomes vertical at a critically low rate of unemployment.

These implications seem plausible and even realistic. It will be objected, however, that any permanent floor independent of general wage and price history and expectation must indicate money illusion. The answer is that the floor need not be permanent in any single market. It could give way to wage reduction when enough unemployment has persisted long enough. But with stochastic intersectoral shifts of demand, markets are always exchanging roles, and there can always be some markets, not always the same ones, at the floor.

This model avoids the empirically questionable implication of the usual natural rate hypothesis that unemployment rates only slightly higher than the critical rate will trigger ever-accelerating deflation. Phillips curves seem to be pretty flat at high rates of unemployment. During the great contraction of 1930-33, wage rates were slow to give way even in the face of massive unemployment and substantial deflation in consumer prices. Finally in 1932 and 1933 money wage rates fell more sharply, in response to prolonged unemployment, layoffs, shutdowns, and to threats and fears of more of the same.

I have gone through this example to make the point that irrationality, in the sense that meaningless differences in money values *permanently* affect individual behavior, is not logically necessary for the existence of a long-run Phillips trade-off. In full long-run equilibrium in all markets, employment and unemployment would be independent of the levels and rates of change of money wage rates and prices. But this is not an equilibrium that the system ever approaches. The economy is in perpetual sectoral disequilibrium even when it has settled into a stochastic macro-equilibrium.

I suppose that one might maintain that asymmetry in wage adjustment and temporary resistance to money wage decline reflect money illusion in some sense. Such an assertion would have to be based on an extension of the domain of well-defined rational behavior to cover responses to change, adjustment speeds, costs of information, costs of organizing and operating markets, and a host of other problems in dynamic theory. These theoretical extensions are in their infancy, although much work of interest and promise is being done. Meanwhile, I doubt that significant restrictions on disequilibrium adjustment mechanisms can be deduced from first principles.

Why are the wage and salary rates of employed workers so insensitive to the availability of potential replacements? One reason is that the employer makes some explicit or implicit commitments in putting a worker on the payroll in the first place. The employee expects that his wages and terms of employment will steadily improve, certainly never retrogress. He expects that the employer will pay him the rate prevailing for persons of comparable skill, occupation, experience, and seniority. He expects such commitments in return for his own investments in the job; arrangements for residence, transportation, and personal life involve set-up costs which will be wasted if the job turns sour. The market for labor services is not like a market for fresh produce where the entire current supply is auctioned daily. It is more like a rental housing market, in which most existing tenancies are the continuations of long-term relationships governed by contracts or less formal understandings.

Employers and workers alike regard the wages of comparable labor elsewhere as a standard, but what determines those reference wages? There is not even an auction where workers and employers unbound by existing relationships and commitments meet and determine a market-clearing wage. If such markets existed, they would provide competitively determined guides for negotiated and administered wages, just as stock exchange prices are reference points for stock transactions elsewhere. In labor markets the reverse is closer to the truth. Wage rates for existing employees set the standards for new employees, too. . . .

Reference standards for wages differ from market to market. The equilibrium wage increase in each market will be some function of past wages in all markets, and perhaps of past prices too. But the function need not be the same in every market. Wages of workers contiguous in geography industry, and skill will be heavily weighted. Imagine a wage pattern matrix of coefficients describing the dependence of the percentage equilibrium wage increase in each market on the past increases in all other markets. The coefficients in each row are nonnegative and sum to one, but their distribution across markets and time lags will differ from row to row.

Consider the properties of such a system in the absence of disequilibrium imputs. First, the system has the "natural rate" property that its steady state is indeterminate. Any rate of wage increase that has been occurring in all markets for a long enough time will continue. Second, from irregular initial conditions the system will move toward one of these steady states, but which one depends on the specifics of the wage pattern matrix and the initial conditions. Contrary to some pessimistic warnings, there is no arithmetic compulsion that makes the whole system gravitate in the direction of its most inflationary sectors. The ultimate steady state inflation will be at most that of the market with the highest initial inflation rate, and at least that of the market with the lowest initial inflation rate. It need not be equal to the average inflation rate at the beginning, but may be either greater or smaller. Third, the adjustment paths are likely to contain cyclical components, damped or at most of constant amplitude, and during adjustments both individual and average wage movements may diverge substantially in both directions from their ultimate steady state value. Fourth, since wage decisions and negotiations occur infrequently, relative wage adjustments involve a lot of catching up and leapfrogging, and probably take a long time. I have sketched the formal properties of a disaggregated wage pattern system of this kind simply to stress again the vast simplification of the one-market myth. . . .

To the extent that one man's reference wages are another man's wages, there is something arbitrary and conventional, indeterminate and unstable, in the process of wage setting. In the same current market circumstances, the reference pattern might be 8 percent per year or 3 percent per year or zero, depending on the historical prelude. Market conditions, unemployment and vacancies and their distributions, shape history and alter reference patterns. But accidental circumstances affecting stragetic wage settlements also cast a long shadow.

Price inflation, is a neutral method of making arbitrary money wage paths conform to the realities of productivity growth, neutral in preserving the structure of relative wages. If expansion of aggregate demand brings both more inflation and more employment, there need be no mystery why unemployed workers accept the new jobs, or why employed workers do not vacate theirs. They need not be victims of ignorance or inflation illusion. They genuinely want more work at feasible real wages, and they also want to maintain the relative status they regard as proper and just.

Guideposts could be in principle the functional equivalent of inflation, a neutral method of reconciling wage and productivity paths. The trick is to find a formula for mutual deescalation which does not offend conceptions of relative equity. No one has devised a way of controlling average wage rates without intervening in the competitive struggle over relative wages. Inflation lets this struggle proceed and blindly, impartially, impersonally, and nonpolitically scales down all its outcomes. There are worse methods of resolving group rivalries and social conflict.

IV

DISCRIMINATION
AND POVERTY

Discrimination

Until the late 1950s economists paid little attention to discrimination. Then Gary Becker showed how discrimination could be incorporated into standard economic theory in his book, *The Economics of Discrimination.* Becker defines discrimination as occurring whenever a person acts "as if he were willing to pay something . . . to be associated with some persons instead of others." He analyzes the economic effects of racial discrimination in terms of two separate societies, one white and one black, which trade with each other. In this model discrimination acts as a barrier to trade and hurts both whites and blacks. Assuming that blacks have a relative abundance of labor and whites of capital, Becker concludes that white labor and black capitalists may gain from economy-wide discrimination, but that their gains will be more than counterbalanced by the losses of white capitalists and black workers.

Radical economists argue that decision-making should be viewed in terms of class interests rather than solely in terms of individual interest as in the Becker model. In contrast to Becker, the radicals conclude that white capitalists may gain from discrimination since they can often use racism to divide the working class and reduce its bargaining power. Michael Reich outlines the radical view and presents some empirical analysis to test the explanatory power of the two competing theories.

In the last several years concern about sexual discrimination has increased dramatically. Francine D. Blau traces the history of women in the labor market in the United States. Although the labor force participation rate of women has increased substantially, most women have always been concentrated in a few occupations, such as household worker and secretary. Blau discusses why such segregation exists and argues that its elimination is essential if women are to attain economic equality.

While Blau argues for desegregating all occupations (e.g., encouraging more men to become secretaries and more women to become electricians), Juanita Kreps puts more emphasis on the extent of earnings differentials by sex within those occupations that do include both men and women. She maintains that the first priority should be to improve the employment opportunities available to highly-educated women. To do so requires not only a reduction in discrimination by employers, but also a change in life styles so that women with young children do not have to significantly interrupt their work lives. Under such conditions, many more women might become interested in pursuing careers.

Labor market discrimination on account of race, color, religion, sex, or national origin was prohibited by Title VII of the Civil Rights Act of 1964. Problems of enforcing this legislation are discussed by Stanley Masters and Collette Moser, who conclude that it may be impossible to eliminate discrimination by trying to force employers to ignore the race and sex of actual or potential employees. Instead it may be necessary for employers to be under some pressure to actually hire significant numbers of blacks, women, and other minority groups, especially for top jobs. As an example of such pressures, the affirmative action requirements imposed on government contractors are discussed.

24.   The Economics of Discrimination

Gary S. Becker

THE FORCES DETERMINING
DISCRIMINATION IN THE MARKET PLACE

In the sociopsychological literature on this subject one individual is said to discriminate against (or in favor of) another if his behavior toward the latter is not motivated by an "objective" consideration of fact.[1] It is difficult to use this definition in distinguishing a violation of objective facts from an expression of tastes or values. For example, discrimination and prejudice are not usually said to occur when someone prefers looking at a glamorous Hollywood actress rather than at some other woman; yet they are said to occur when he prefers living next to whites rather than next to Negroes. At best calling just one of these actions "discrimination" requires making subtle and rather secondary distinctions.[2] Fortunately, it is not

necessary to get involved in these more philosophical issues. It is possible to give an unambiguous definition of discrimination in the market place and yet get at the essence of what is usually called discrimination.

1. The Analytical Framework

Money, commonly used as a measuring rod, will also serve as a measure of discrimination. If an individual has a "taste for discrimination," he must act *as if* he were willing to pay something, either directly or in the form of a reduced income, to be associated with some persons instead of others. When actual discrimination occurs, he must, in fact, either pay or forfeit income for this privilege. This simple way of looking at the matter gets at the essence of prejudice and discrimination.

Social scientists tend to organize their discussion of discrimination in the market place according to their disciplines. To the sociologist, different levels of discrimination against a particular group are associated with different

[1]Many references can be cited for definitions of this kind. In a discussion of the problems involved in defining prejudice, Gordon Allport arrives at this definition: "Ethnic prejudice is an antipathy based upon a faulty and inflexible generalization" (see his *The Nature of Prejudice* [Cambridge, Mass.: Addison-Wesley Press, 1955], p. 9).

[2]The distinction drawn by Allport and others is that those discriminating against Negroes give "erroneous" answers to various questions about Negroes, while those asked about Hollywood actresses do not. Let us waive the problem of determining whether some

answers are erroneous and probe this distinction from another direction. Suppose that the answers given about Negroes violate no known facts, while those given about Hollywood actresses are in blatant conflict with the facts. Would persons drawing this distinction now agree that the preference for whites is not, and that for actresses is, discrimination?

levels of social and physical "distance" from that group or with different levels of socio-economic status; the psychologist classifies individuals by their personality types, believing that this is the most useful organizing principle. The breakdown used here is most familiar to the economist and differs from both of these: all persons who contribute to production in the same way, e.g., by the rent of capital or the sale of labor services, are put into one group, with each group forming a separate "factor of production." The breakdown by economic productivity turns out to be a particularly fruitful one, since it emphasizes phenomena that have long been neglected in literature on discrimination.

By using the concept of a *discrimination coefficient* (this will often be abbreviated to "DC"), it is possible to give a definition of a "taste for discrimination" that is parallel for different factors of production, employers, and consumers. The *money* costs of a transaction do not always completely measure *net* costs, and a DC acts as a bridge between money and net costs. Suppose an *employer* were faced with the money wage rate π of a particular factor; he is assumed to act as if $\pi(1 + d_i)$ were the *net* wage rate, with d_i as his DC against this factor. An *employee,* offered the money wage rate π_j for working with this factor, acts as if $\pi_j(1 - d_j)$ were the net wage rate, with d_j as his DC against this factor. A *consumer,* faced with a unit money price of p for the commodity "produced" by this factor, acts as if the net price were $p(1 + d_k)$, with d_k as his DC against this factor. In all three instances a DC gives the percentage by which either money costs or money returns are changed in going from money to net magnitudes: the employer uses it to estimate his net wage costs, the employee his net wage rate, and the consumer the net price of a commodity.

A DC represents a non-pecuniary element in certain kinds of transactions, and it is positive or negative, depending upon whether the non-pecuniary element is considered "good" or "bad." Discrimination is commonly associated with *dis*utility caused by contact with some individuals, and this interpretation is followed here. Since this implies that d_i, d_j, and d_k are all greater than zero, to the employer this coefficient represents a non-monetary cost of production, to the employee a non-monetary cost of employment, and to the consumer a

non-monetary cost of consumption.[3] "Nepotism" rather than "discrimination" would occur if they were less than zero, and they would then represent non-monetary *returns* of production, employment, and consumption to the employer, employee, and consumer, respectively.

The quantities πd_i, $\pi_j d_j$, and $p d_k$ are the exact money equivalents of these non-monetary costs; for given wage rates and prices, these money equivalents are larger, the larger d_i, d_j, and d_k are. Since a DC can take on any value between zero and plus infinity, tastes for discrimination can also vary continuously within this range. This quantitative representation of a taste for discrimination provides the means for empirically estimating the quantitative importance of discrimination.

2. Tastes for Discrimination

The magnitude of a taste for discrimination differs from person to person, and many investigators have directed their energies toward discovering the variables that are most responsible for these differences. I also attempt to isolate and estimate the quantitative importance of some of these variables; the following discussion briefly describes several variables that receive attention in subsequent chapters.

The discrimination by an individual against a particular group (to be called N) depends on the social and physical distance between them and on their relative socioeconomic status. If he works with N in production, it may also depend on their substitutability in production. The relative number of N in the society at large also may be very important: it has been argued that an increase in the numerical importance of a minority group increases the prejudice against

---

[3]Allport makes a distinction between negative and positive prejudice that is identical with my distinction between a taste for discrimination and a taste for nepotism. He agrees that negative prejudice is usually the motivating force behind behavior considered to be discriminatory (*op. cit.,* pp. 6 and 7). He asserts later (p. 25) that "we hear so little about love [positive] prejudice" because "prejudices of this sort create no social problem." In this he is mistaken, since the social and economic implications of positive prejudice or nepotism are very similar to those of negative prejudice or discrimination.

them, since the majority begins to fear their growing power; on the other hand, some argue that greater numbers bring greater knowledge and that this leads to a decline in prejudice. Closely related to this variable are the frequency and regularity of "contact" with N in different establishments and firms.

According to our earlier definition, if someone has a "taste for discrimination," he must act *as if* he were willing to forfeit income in order to avoid certain transactions; it is necessary to be aware of the emphasis on the words "as if." An employer may refuse to hire Negroes solely because he erroneously underestimates their economic efficiency. His behavior is discriminatory not because he is prejudiced against them but because he is ignorant of their true efficiency. Ignorance may be quickly eliminated by the spread of knowledge, while a prejudice (i.e., preference) is relatively independent of knowledge.[4] This distinction is essential for understanding the motivation of many organizations, since they either explicitly or implicitly assume that discrimination can be eliminated by a wholesale spread of knowledge.[5]

Since a taste for discrimination incorporates both prejudice and ignorance, the amount of knowledge available must be included as a determinant of tastes. Another proximate determinant is geographical and chronological location: discrimination may vary from country to country, from region to region within a country, from rural to urban areas within a region, and from one time period to another. Finally, tastes may differ simply because of differences in personality.

[4]Many prejudiced people often erroneously answer questions about groups they discriminate against; their "ignorance" about these groups, however, is of secondary importance for understanding and combatting their discrimination, since their behavior is independent of all attempts to give them the facts. For a similar observation see *ibid.*, chap. i.

[5]Some advertisements are primarily devoted to spreading knowledge, while others are aimed at changing preferences or prejudices by creating pleasant, although logically irrelevant, associations with their products. Likewise, some organizations try to change tastes for discrimination by creating unpleasant, although similarly irrelevant, associations with discrimination.

3. Market Discrimination

Suppose there are two groups, designated by W and N, with members of W being perfect substitutes in production for members of N. In the absence of discrimination and nepotism and if the labor market were perfectly competitive, the equilibrium wage rate of W would equal that of N. Discrimination could cause these wage rates to differ; the *market discrimination coefficient* between W and N (this will be abbreviated to "MDC") is defined as the proportional difference between these wage rates. If π_w and π_n represent the equilibrium wage rates of W and N, respectively, then

$$\text{MDC} = \frac{\pi_w - \pi_n}{\pi_n}$$

If W and N are imperfect substitutes, they may receive different wage rates even in the absence of discrimination. A more general definition of the MDC sets it equal to the difference between the ratio of W's to N's wage rate with and without discrimination.[6] In the special case of perfect substitutes, this reduces to the simpler definition given previously, because π_w^0 would equal π_n^0.

It should be obvious that the magnitude of the MDC depends on the magnitude of individual DC's. Unfortunately, it is often implicitly assumed that it depends *only* on them; the arguments proceed as if a knowledge of the determinants of tastes was sufficient for a complete understanding of market discrimination. This procedure is erroneous; many variables in addition to tastes take prominent roles in determining market discrimination, and, indeed, tastes sometimes play a minor part. The abundant light thrown on these other variables by the tools of economic analysis has probably been the major insight gained from using them.

The MDC does depend in an important way on each individual's DC; however, merely to use some measure of the average DC does not suffice. The complete distribution of DC's among individuals must be made explicit because the size of the MDC is partly related to individual *differences* in tastes. It also depends on the rela-

[6]That is, $MDC = \pi_w/\pi_n - \bar{\pi}_w^0/\pi_n^0$ where π_w^0 and π_n^0 are the equilibrium wage rates without discrimination.

tive importance of competition and monopoly in the labor and product markets, since this partly determines the weight assigned by the market to different DC's. The economic and quantitative importance of N was mentioned as one determinant of tastes for discrimination; this variable is also an independent determinant of market discrimination. This independent effect operates through the number of N relative to W and the cost of N per unit of output relative to the total cost per unit of output. Both may be important, although for somewhat different reasons, in determining the weight assigned by the market to different DC's. Reorganizing production through the substitution of one factor for another is a means of avoiding discrimination; the amount of substitution available is determined by the production function. . . .

EFFECTIVE DISCRIMINATION

An MDC between any two groups can be defined for a particular labor or capital market or for all markets combined; in the latter, interest would center on the effect of discrimination on the total incomes of these groups. For example, discrimination by whites presumably reduces the income of Negroes, but how does it affect their own incomes? Many writers have asserted that discrimination in the market place by whites is in their own self-interest; i.e., it is supposed to raise their incomes. If this were correct, it would be in the self-interest of Negroes to "retaliate" against whites by discriminating against them, since this should raise Negro incomes. . . . It is shown in the following that discrimination by any group W reduces their own income as well as N's, and thus retaliation by N makes it worse for N rather than better. . . .

1. The Model

New insights are gained and the analysis made simpler if the discussion is phrased in terms of trade between two "societies," one inhabited solely by N, the other by W. Government and monopolies are ignored for the present, as the analysis is confined to perfectly competitive societies. Since our emphasis here is on the over-all incomes of W and N, the multiplicity of factors of production will also be

ignored, and the discussion will be confined to two homogeneous factors in each society—labor and capital—with each unit of labor and capital in N being a perfect substitute in *production* for each unit of labor and capital in W. These societies do not "trade" commodities but factors of production used in producing commodities. Each society finds it advantageous to "export" its relatively abundant factors: W exports capital, and N labor. The amount of labor exported by N at a given rate of exchange of labor for capital is the difference between the total amount of labor in N and the amount used "domestically"; the amount of capital exported by W is derived in a similar manner.

The following conditions would be satisfied in a full equilibrium with no discrimination: (a) payment to each factor would be independent of whether it was employed with N or W; (b) the price of each product would be independent of whether it was produced by N or W; and (c) the unit payment to each factor would equal its marginal value product. If members of W develop a desire to discriminate against labor and capital owned by N, they become willing to forfeit money income in order to avoid working with N. This taste for discrimination reduces the net return[7] that W capital can receive by combining with N labor, and this leads to a reduction in the amount of W capital exported. Since this, in turn, reduces the income that N labor can receive by combining with W capital, less N labor is also exported. In the new equilibrium, then, less labor and capital are exported by N and W, respectively. It can be shown that this change in resource allocation reduces the equilibrium net incomes of both N and W. Since discrimination by W hurts W as well as N, it cannot be a subtle

---

[7]If W wants to discriminate, exported capital must receive a higher equilibrium money return than domestically used capital, to compensate for working with N labor. However, if all W has the same taste for discrimination, the equilibrium net return must be the same for all W capital. Net and money returns to domestic capital are identical, since there are no psychic costs to working with W labor; therefore, the equilibrium money return to domestic capital can be used as the equilibrium net return to all W capital. The money and net returns to all W labor are the same, since it works only with W capital.

means by which W augments its net command of economic goods.[8]

2. Discrimination and Capitalists

Although the aggregate net incomes of W and N are reduced by discrimination, all factor⁻ are not affected in the same way; the return to W capital and N labor decreases, but the return to W labor and N capital actually increases. There is a remarkable agreement in the literature on the proposition that capitalists from the dominant group are the major beneficiaries of prejudice and discrimination in a competitive capitalistic economic system.[9] If W is con-

sidered to represent whites or some other dominant group, the fallacious nature of this proposition becomes clear, since discrimination *harms* W capitalists and benefits W workers. The most serious non sequitur in the mistaken analyses is the (explicit or implicit) conclusion that, if tastes for discrimination cause N laborers to receive a lower wage rate than W laborers, the difference between these wage rates must accrue as "profits" to W capitalists.[10] These profits would exist only if this wage differential resulted from price discrimination (due to monopsony power), rather than from a taste for discrimination.

---

[8]If we compare discrimination with tariffs, we find that, although some of their effects are similar, other effects are quite different. Discrimination always decreases both societies' net incomes, while a tariff of the appropriate size can, as Bickerdike long ago pointed out, increase the levying society's net income. A tariff operates by driving a wedge between the price a society pays for imported goods and the price each individual member pays; it does not create any distinction between net income and total command over goods. Discrimination does create such a distinction and does not drive a wedge between private and social prices. Discrimination has more in common with transportation costs than with tariffs.

[9]Saenger, a psychologist, said: "Discriminatory practices appear to be of definite advantage for the representatives of management in a competitive economic system" (*The Social Psychology of Prejudice* [Harper & Bros., 1953], p. 96). Allport, another psychologist, likewise said: "We conclude, therefore, that the Marxist theory of prejudice is far too simple, even though it points a sure finger at *one* of the factors involved in

prejudice, viz., rationalized self-interest of the upper classes" (*The Nature of Prejudice* [Cambridge, Mass.: Addison-Wesley Press, 1955], p. 210.) Similar statements can be found in A. Rose, *The Costs of Prejudice* (Paris: UNESCO, 1951), p. 7; and throughout O. C. Cox, *Caste, Class, and Race* (Garden City: Doubleday & Co., 1948); J. Dollard, *Caste and Class in a Southern Town* (New Haven: Yale University Press, 1937); C. McWilliams, *A Mask for Privilege: Anti-Semitism in America* (Boston: Little, Brown & Co., 1948); H. Aptheker, *The Negro Problem in America* (New York: International Publishers, 1946); and many other books as well.

[10]D. A. Wilkerson, in his Introduction to Aptheker's book, said: "Precisely this same relationship between material interests and Negro oppression exists today... The per capita annual income of southern Negro tenant farmers and day laborers in 1930 was about $71, as compared with $97 for similar white workers. Multiply this difference of $26 by the 1,205,000 Negro tenants and day laborers on southern farms in 1930, and it is seen that planters 'saved' approximately $31,000,000 by the simple device of paying Negro workers less than they paid white workers" (Aptheker, *op. cit.,* p. 10).

25. The Economics of Racism

Michael Reich

In the late 1950's and early 1960's it seemed to many Americans that the elimination of racism in the United States was finally being achieved, and without requiring a radical restructuring of the society. The civil rights movement was growing in strength, desegregation orders were being issued, and hundreds of thousands of blacks were moving to Northern cities where discrimination was supposedly less severe than in the South. Government reports seemed to validate the optimism: for example, by 1969 the gap between blacks and whites in median years of schooling for males aged 25 to 29 years old was only one fourth the gap that had existed in 1960.[1]

But by 1970 the optimism of earlier decades had vanished. Despite new civil rights laws, elaborate White House conferences, special ghetto manpower programs, the War on Poverty, and stepped-up tokenist hiring, racism and the economic exploitation of blacks has not lessened. During the past twenty-five years the absolute male black-white income gap has more than doubled, while there has been virtually no

permanent improvement in the relative economic position of blacks in America. Median black incomes have been fluctuating at a level between 47 percent and 62 percent of median white incomes, the ratio rising during economic expansions and falling to previous low levels during recessions.[2] Segregation in schools and neighborhoods has been steadily increasing in almost all cities, and the atmosphere of distrust between blacks and whites has intensified.

The author wishes to acknowledge the help of Samuel Bowles, who encouraged him to work on this problem and has provided critical guidance at every stage.

[1] "The Social and Economic Status of Negroes in the United States, 1969," Bureau of Labor Statistics Report No. 375 (October, 1967), p. 50.

[2] The data refer to male incomes, and are published annually by the U.S. Census Bureau in its P-60 Series, "Income of Families and Persons. . . ." Using data for the years 1948 to 1964, Rasmussen found that, after controlling the effects of the business cycle, the average increase in the racial ratio of median incomes was only .3 percent per year, or 5 percent over the 16 years. See David Rasmussen, "A Note on the Relative Income of Nonwhite Men, 1948-64," *Quarterly Journal of Economics* (February, 1970). Thurow, using a slightly different technique, estimated that no relative increase in black incomes would occur after unemployment was reduced to 3 percent. See L. Thurow, *Poverty and Discrimination* (Washington, D.C.: Brookings Institution, 1969), pp. 58-61. And Batchelder found that stability in the ratio over time despite migration of blacks from the South to the North; within regions in the North the ratio declined. Alan Batchelder, "Decline in the Relative Income of Negro Men," *Quarterly Journal of Economics* (November, 1964).

Racism, instead of disappearing, seems to be on the increase.

Racism has been as persistent in the United States in the twentieth century as it was in previous centuries. The industrialization of the economy led to the transformation of the black worker's economic role from one of agricultural sharecropper and household servant to one of urban industrial operative and service worker, but it did not result in substantial relative improvement for blacks. Quantitative comparisons using Census data of occupational distributions by race show that the occupational status of black males is virtually the same today as it was in 1910 (the earliest year for which racial data are available).[3]

This paper presents a radical analysis of racism and its historical persistence in America, focusing on the effects of racism on whites. The paper contrasts the conventional approach of neoclassical economic analysis—with its optimistic conclusions concerning the possibility of eliminating racism—with a radical approach—which argues that racism is deeply rooted in the current economic institutions of America, and is likely to survive as long as they do. A statistical model and empirical evidence are presented which support the radical approach and cast doubt on the conventional approach. The specific mechanisms by which racism operates among whites are also discussed briefly.

THE PERVASIVENESS OF RACISM

When conventional economists attempt to analyze racism, they usually begin by trying to separate various forms of racial discrimination. For example, they define "pure wage discrimination" as the racial difference in wages paid to equivalent workers, i.e., those with similar years and quality of schooling, skill training, previous employment experience and seniority, age, health, job attitudes, and a host

of other factors. They presume that they can analyze the sources of "pure wage discrimination" without simultaneously analyzing the extent to which discrimination also affects the factors they hold constant.

But such a technique distorts reality. The various forms of discrimination are not separable in real life. Employers' hiring and promotion practices, resource allocation in city schools, the structure of transportation systems, residential segregation and housing quality, availability of decent health care, behavior of policemen and judges, foremen's prejudices, images of blacks presented in the media and the schools, price gouging in ghetto stores—these and other forms of social and economic discrimination interact strongly with each other in determining the occupational status and annual income, and welfare, of black people. The processes are not simply additive, but are mutually reinforcing. Often, a decrease in one narrow form of discrimination is accompanied by an increase in another form. Since all aspects of racism interact, an analysis of racism should incorporate all of its aspects in a unified manner.

No single quantitative index could adequately measure racism in all its social, cultural, psychological, and economic dimensions. But, while racism is far more than a narrow economic phenomenon, it does have very definite economic consequences: blacks have far lower incomes than whites. The ratio of median black to median white incomes thus provides a rough, but useful, quantitative index of the economic consequences of racism for blacks as it reflects the operation of racism in the schools, in residential location, in health care—as well as in the labor market itself. We shall use this index statistically to analyze the causes of racism's persistence in the United States. While this approach overemphasizes the economic aspects of racism, it is nevertheless an improvement over the narrower approach taken by conventional economists.

COMPETING EXPLANATIONS OF RACISM

How is the historical persistence of racism in the United States to be explained? The most prominent analysis of discrimination among economists was formulated in 1957 by Gary Becker in his book *The Economics of Dis-*

---

[3]Since income data by race are not available before 1940, a relative index must be based on racial occupational data. Hiestand has computed such an index: he finds at most a 5 percent increase in blacks' status between 1910 and 1960; most of this improvement occurred during the labor shortages of the 1940's. See D. Hiestand, *Economic Growth and Employment Opportunities for Minorities* (New York: Columbia University Press, 1964), p. 53.

crimination.[4] Racism, according to Becker, is fundamentally a problem of tastes and attitudes. Whites are defined to have a "taste for discrimination" if they are willing to forfeit income in order to be associated with other whites instead of blacks. Since white employers and employees prefer not to associate with blacks, they require a monetary compensation for the psychic cost of such association. In Becker's principal model white employers have a taste for discrimination; marginal productivity analysis is invoked to show that white employers hire fewer black workers than efficiency criteria would dictate—as a result, white employers lose (in monetary terms) while white workers gain from discrimination against blacks.

Becker does not try to explain the source of white tastes for discrimination. For him, these attitudes are determined outside of the economic system. (Racism could presumably be ended simply by changing these attitudes, perhaps by appeal to whites on moral grounds.) According to Becker's analysis, employers would find the ending of racism to be in their economic self-interest, but white workers would not. The persistence of racism is thus implicitly laid at the door of white workers. Becker suggests that long-run market forces will lead to the end of discrimination anyway—less discriminatory employers, with no "psychic costs" to enter in their accounts, will be able to operate at lower costs by hiring equivalent black workers at lower wages, thus driving the more discriminatory employers out of business.[5]

The radical approach to racism argued in this paper is entirely different. Racism is viewed as rooted in the economic system and not in "exogenously determined" attitudes. Historically, the American Empire was founded on the racist extermination of American Indians, was financed in large part by profits from slavery, and was extended by a string of interventions,

[4]University of Chicago Press.

[5]Some economists writing on discrimination reject Becker's "tastes" approach, but accept the marginal productivity method of analysis. See, for example, L. Thurow, *op. cit.* The main substantive difference in their conclusions is that for Thurow, the entire white "community" gains from racism; therefore, racism will be a little harder to uproot. See also A. Krueger, "The Economics of Discrimination," *Journal of Political Economy* (October, 1963).

beginning with the Mexican War of the 1840's, which have been at least partly justified by white supremacist ideology.

Today, transferring the locus of whites' perceptions of the source of many of their problems from capitalism and toward blacks, racism continues to serve the needs of the capitalist system. Although an individual employer might gain by refusing to discriminate and agreeing to hire blacks at above the going black wage rate, it is not true that the capitalist class as a whole would profit if racism were eliminated and labor were more efficiently allocated without regard to skin color. I will show below that the divisiveness of racism weakens workers' strength when bargaining with employers; the economic consequences of racism are not only lower incomes for blacks, but also higher incomes for the capitalist class coupled with lower incomes for white workers. Although capitalists may not have conspired consciously to create racism, and although capitalists may not be its principal perpetuators, nevertheless racism does support the continued well-being of the American capitalist system.

Capitalist society in turn encourages the persistence of racism. Whatever the origins of racism, it is likely to take root firmly in a society which breeds an individualistic and competitive ethos, status fears among marginal groups, and the need for visible scapegoats on which to blame the alienating quality of life in America—such a society is unlikely magnanimously to eliminate racism even though historically racism may not have been created by capitalism.

Racism cannot be eliminated just by moral suasion; nor will it gradually disappear because of market forces. Racism has become institutionalized and will persist under capitalism. Its elimination will require more than a change of attitudes; a change in institutions is necessary.

We have, then, two alternative approaches to the analysis of racism. The first suggests that capitalists lose and white workers gain from racism. The second predicts the opposite—that capitalists gain while workers lose. The first says that racist "tastes for discrimination" are formed independently of the economic system; the second argues that racism is symbiotic with capitalistic economic institutions.

The two approaches reflect the theoretical paradigms of society from which each was developed. Becker follows the paradigm of neoclassical economics in taking "tastes" as exogenously determined and fixed, and then letting the market mechanism determine outcomes. The radical approach follows the Marxian paradigm in arguing that racial attitudes and racist institutions must be seen as part of a larger social system, in placing emphasis on conflict between classes and the use of power to determine the outcomes of such conflicts. The test as to which explanation of racism is superior is, in some ways, an illustrative test of the relative explanatory power of these competing social paradigms.

The very persistence of racism in the United States lends support to the radical approach. So do repeated instances of employers using blacks as strikebreakers, as in the massive steel strike of 1919, and employer-instigated exacerbation of racial antagonisms during that strike and many others.[6] However, the particular virulence of racism among many blue- and white-collar workers and their families seems to refute the radical approach and support Becker.

THE EMPIRICAL EVIDENCE

Which of the two models better explains reality? We have already mentioned that the radical approach predicts that capitalists gain and workers lose from racism, while the conventional Beckerian approach predicts precisely the opposite. In the latter approach racism has an equalizing effect on the white income distribution, while in the former racism has an unequalizing effect. The statistical relationship between the extent of racism and the degree of inequality among whites provides a simple, yet clear test of the two approaches. This section describes that test and its results.

First we shall need a measure of racism. The index we use, for reasons already mentioned, is the ratio of black median family income to white median family income (B/W). A low numerical value for this ratio indicates a high degree of racism. We have calculated values of this racism index, using data from the 1960 Census, for each of the largest 48 standard

metropolitan statistical areas (SMSA's). It turns out there is a great deal of variation from SMSA to SMSA in the B/W index of racism, even within the North; Southern SMSA's generally demonstrated a greater degree of racism. The statistical technique we shall use exploits this variation.

We shall also need measures of inequality among whites. Two convenient measures are (1) S_1, the percentage share of all white income which is received by the top 1 percent of white families, and (2) G_w, the Gini coefficient of white incomes, a measure that captures inequality within as well as between social classes.[7]

Both of these inequality measures vary considerably among the SMSA's; there is also a substantial amount of variation in these variables within the subsample of Northern SMSA's. Therefore, it is interesting to examine whether the pattern of variation of the inequality and racism variables can be explained by causal hypotheses. This is our first statistical test.

A systematic relationship across SMSA's between racism and white inequality does exist and is highly significant: the correlation coefficient is -.47.[8] The negative sign of the correlation coefficient indicates that where racism is greater, income inequality among whites is also greater. This result is consistent with the radical model and is inconsistent with the predictions of Becker's model.

This evidence, however, should not be accepted too quickly. The correlations reported may not reflect actual causality, since other independent forces may be simultaneously influencing both variables in the same way. As is the case with many other statistical analyses, the model must be expanded to control for such other factors. We know from previous in-

---

[6]See, for example, David Brody, *Steelworkers in America: The Nonunion Era* (Cambridge: Harvard University Press, 1960); Herbert Gutman, "The Negro and the United Mineworkers," in J. Jacobson, ed., *The Negro and the American Labor Movement* (New York: Anchor, 1968); S. Spero and A. Harris, *The Black Worker* (New York: Atheneum, 1968), *passim.*

[7]The Gini coefficient varies between 0 and 1, with 0 indicating perfect equality, and 1 indicating perfect inequality. For a more complete exposition, see H. Miller, *Income Distribution in the United States* (Washington, D.C.: Government Printing Office, 1966). Data for the computation of G_w and S_1 for 48 SMSA's were taken from the 1960 Census. A full description of the computational techniques used is available in my dissertation.

[8]The correlation coefficient reported in the text is between G_w and B/W. The equivalent correlation between S_1 and B/W is r = -.55. A similar calculation by S. Bowles, across states instead of SMSA's, resulted in an r = -.58.

ter-SMSA income distribution studies that the most important additional factors that should be introduced into our model are (1) the industrial and occupational structure of the SMSA's; (2) the region in which the SMSA's are located; (3) the average income of the SMSA's; and (4) the proportion of the SMSA population which is black. These factors were introduced into the model by the technique of multiple regression analysis. Separate equations were estimated with G_w and S_1 as measures of white inequality.

In all the equations the statistical results were strikingly uniform: racism was a significantly unequalizing force on the white income distribution, even when other factors were held constant. A 1 percent increase in the ratio of black to white median incomes (i.e., a 1 percent decrease in racism) was associated with a .2 percent decrease in white inequality, as measured by the Gini coefficient. The corresponding effect on S_1 was two-and-a-half times as large, indicating that most of the inequality among whites generated by racism was associated with increased income for the richest 1 percent of white families. Further statistical investigation revealed that increases in racism had an insignificant effect on the share received by the poorest whites, and resulted in a small decrease in the income share of whites in the middle-income brackets.[9]

THE MECHANISMS OF THE RADICAL MODEL

Within the radical model, we can specify a number of mechanisms which further explain the statistical finding that racism increases inequality among whites. We shall consider two mechanisms here: (1) total wages of white labor are reduced by racial antagonisms, in part because union growth and labor militancy are inhibited, and (2) the supply of public services, especially in education, available to low- and middle-income whites is reduced as a result of racial antagonisms.

Wages of white labor are lessened by racism because the fear of a cheaper and under-employed black labor supply in the area is invoked by employers when labor presents its wage demands. Racial antagonisms on the shop

floor deflect attention from labor grievances related to working conditions, permitting employers to cut costs. Racial divisions among labor prevent the development of united worker organizations both within the workplace and in the labor movement as a whole. As a result, union strength and union militancy will be less, the greater the extent of racism. A historical example of this process is the already mentioned use of racial and ethnic divisions to destroy the solidarity of the 1919 steel strikers. By contrast, during the 1890's, black-white class solidarity greatly aided mine-workers in building militant unions among workers in Alabama, West Virginia, Illinois, and other coal-field areas.[10]

The above argument and examples contradict the common belief that an exclusionary racial policy will strengthen rather than weaken the bargaining power of unions. But racial exclusion increases bargaining power only when entry into an occupation or industry can be effectively limited. Industrial-type unions are much less able to restrict entry than craft unions or organizations such as the American Medical Association. This is not to deny that much of organized labor is egregiously racist.[11] But it is important to distinguish actual discrimination practice from the objective economic self-interest of union members.

The second mechanism we shall consider concerns the allocation of expenditures for public services. The most important of these services is education. Racial antagonisms dilute both the desire and the ability of poor white parents to improve educational opportunities for their children. Antagonism between blacks and poor whites drives wedges between the two groups and reduces their ability to join in a united political movement pressing for improved and more equal education. Moreover, many poor whites recognize that however inferior their own schools, black schools are even worse. This provides some degree of satisfaction and identification with the status quo, reducing the desire of poor whites to press politically for better schools in their neighborhoods. Ghettos tend to be located near poor white neighborhoods more often than near rich white neigh-

---

[9] A more rigorous presentation of these variables and the statistical results is available in my dissertation.

[10] See footnote 6.

[11] See Herbert Hill, "The Racial Practices of Organized Labor," in J. Jacobson, ed., *The Negro and the American Labor Movement* (N.Y.: Anchor paperback, 1968).

borhoods; racism thus reduces the potential tax base of school districts containing poor whites. Also, pressure by teachers' groups to improve all poor schools is reduced by racial antagonisms between predominately white teaching staffs and black children and parents.[12]

However, a full assessment of the importance of racism for capitalism would probably conclude that the primary significance of racism is not strictly economic. The simple economics of racism does not explain why many workers seem to be so vehemently racist, when racism is not in their economic self-interest. In extra-economic ways, racism helps to legitimize inequality, alienation, and powerlessness—legitimization which is necessary for the stability of the capitalist system as a whole. For example, many whites believe that welfare payments to blacks are a far more important factor in their high taxes than is military spending. Through racism, poor whites come to believe that their poverty is caused by blacks

---

[12]In a similar fashion, racial antagonisms reduce the political pressure on governmental agencies to provide other public services which would have a pro-poor distributional impact. The two principal items in this category are public health services and welfare payments in the Aid to Families with Dependent Children program.

who are willing to take away their jobs, and at lower wages, thus concealing the fact that a substantial amount of income inequality is inevitable in a capitalist society.

Racism also provides some psychological benefits to poor and working-class whites. For example, the opportunity to participate in another's oppression may compensate for one's own misery. The parallel here is to the subjugation of women in the family: after a day of alienating labor, the tired husband can compensate by oppressing his wife. Furthermore, not being at the bottom of the heap is some solace for an unsatisfying life; this argument was successfully used by the Southern oligarchy against poor whites allied with blacks in the inter-racial Populist movement of the late nineteenth century.

In general, blacks as a group provide a convenient and visible scapegoat for problems that actually derive from the institutions of capitalism. As long as building a real alternative to capitalism does not seem feasible to most whites, we can expect that identifiable and vulnerable scapegoats will always prove functional to the status quo. These extra-economic factors thus neatly dovetail with the economic aspects of racism discussed in the main body of this paper in their mutual service to the perpetuation of capitalism.

26. "Women's Place" in the Labor Market

Francine D. Blau

The resurgence of the women's movement in the late 1960's has stimulated increasing interest in the economic status of women. In this paper, I have drawn on existing research to summarize the trends in women's involvement in market work and in their employment status. I have attempted to demonstrate that the persistence of occupational segregation by sex in the labor market is the major obstacle to the attainment of economic equality for women.

I. WOMEN AND MARKET WORK

Women have traditionally engaged in three types of economically productive work. First, they have produced goods and services for the family's own consumption; second, they have engaged in household production for sale and exchange on the market; third, they have worked for pay outside the home. The process of industrialization has brought about a reallocation in the relative importance of these three types of economic roles. We should not, however, thereby conclude that women are newcomers to the paid labor force in the United States.

The participation of a sector of the female population in market work is as old as the original settlement of the North American continent. Spurred by the Protestant ethic that condemned idleness as a sin and by the continual labor shortages of a sparsely populated frontier society, colonial women found the opportunity to engage in a wide range of frequently unconventional market activities.

With the development of the factory system in the textile mills of New England during the late eighteenth and early nineteenth centuries, women and children entered the manufacturing establishments to comprise the overwhelming majority of the country's first industrial work force. It might even be said that they were a crucial element in the early industrial development of the United States, since, in a predominantly agrarian economy with an extremely favorable land to labor ratio, they were virtually the only readily available source of labor for the construction of the infant manufacturing industry.

Toward the end of the nineteenth century, the growing concentration of industry and the increased scale of business organization created a need for workers engaged in coordinating and integrating the activities of the expanded business network. Here again, women moved into the shops and offices to constitute an important share of the needed supply.

Thus we may view the growth of the female labor force in the present century as a continuation of the long-term process of the incorporation of increasing numbers of women into the

Table 1

Women in the Civilian Labor Force, Selected
Years, 1900-1970 (sixteen years of age and
over[1])

Year	Number (in thousands)	As Percent of All Workers	As Percent of Female Population
1900	4,999	18.1	20.0
1920	8,229	20.4	22.7
1930	10,396	21.9	23.6
1940	13,783	25.4	28.6
1945	19,290	36.1	38.1
1947	16,664	27.9	30.8
1950	18,389	29.6	33.9
1955	20,548	31.6	35.7
1960	23,240	33.4	37.7
1965	26,200	35.2	39.2
1970	31,520	38.1	43.3

Sources: U.S. Department of Labor, Women's Bureau, *1969 Handbook on Women Workers* (Washington, 1969), p. 10. U.S. Department of Labor, Manpower Administration, *Manpower Report of the President* (Washington, April 1971), pp. 203, 205.
[1] Pre-1940 figures include all those 14 years of age and over.

paid work force. As the figures in Table 1 indicate, this expansion has become particularly rapid in the years since 1940. It should be noted, however, that this growth has not been smooth and continuous. Under the impetus of the emergency conditions of World War II, enormous numbers of women entered the labor force, but considerable ground was lost in the immediate postwar period.

The long-term shifts in female labor force status that have occurred since 1940 were accomplished primarily by bringing new groups of women into the paid labor force. Before 1940, the typical female worker was young and single. Between 1940 and 1960, older, married women entered or re-entered the labor force in increasing numbers, while the labor force participation rates of women in the twenty to thirty-four year age group remained relatively constant. The years since 1960 have witnessed a sizable increase in the participation rates of all women under sixty-five. The fastest growing group, however, has been young married women, many with preschool age children. Thus, market work has come to encompass significant numbers of women from all sectors of the female population.

II. CHANGES IN EMPLOYMENT STATUS SINCE 1900

The available data indicate that the terms on which women are able to obtain employment remain a pressing social problem, one that gains in importance and urgency as the female work force continues to expand. Two dimensions of the employment distribution of the female labor force are particularly relevant as indices of women's progress towards economic equality in the labor market. First is the degree to which women workers are concentrated in a relatively small number of occupational categories, and second is the extent of occupational segregation by sex, that is, the division of the labor market into predominantly female and predominately male occupations.

Occupational Concentration

While this problem remains acute, there appears to have been some increase in the diffusion of the female labor force over a broader range of occupational categories. In 1900, nearly 30 percent of employed women were concentrated in just one occupational category, that of private household worker, while four of the detailed occupations in the census of that year accounted for 46 percent of the female work force. By 1969, half of the female work force was distributed among twenty-one of the detailed census listings, although five occupations accounted for one-quarter of all employed women. These are, however, merely illustrative comparisons of the relative magnitude of the problem in these two years, since the increasing fineness of the census classifications would tend to impart a downward bias to the measure of concentration. Furthermore, the degree of female concentration still compares unfavorably to that of male workers who are much more widely distributed throughout the occupational structure, with half in sixty-five occupations.

Occupational Segregation

Occupational segregation by sex appears to be as pervasive now as it was at the turn of the century. Well over half of all working women in both 1900 and 1960 were employed in jobs in which 70 percent or more of the workers were female. Moreover, the census data upon which this estimate is based underestimate the extent to which women work in sexually segregated work situations. Sources of bias arise from various kinds of aggregation problems. If we were to define occupations narrowly enough and to take the establishment as our unit of analysis, the estimate of the extent of occupational segregation would be greatly increased.

Regardless of their limitations, these estimates of occupational segregation do provide a rough indicator of the stability of this fundamental characteristic of female employment over a sixty-year period. Thus it appears that the enormous postwar expansion of the female labor force has not altered the segregated nature of female employment. The increasing numbers of women have been absorbed into the labor force not through an across-the-board expansion of employment opportunities, but rather through a growth in traditionally female jobs, particularly in the clerical and service category, through the emergence of new occupations that rapidly became female, and, in some cases, through a shift in the sexual composition of an occupation from male to female.

In this last case, in which a substitution of female for male labor does occur, there appears to be a strong tendency for the occupation to "go female," thus providing some expansion in job opportunities, but still within a segregated context. This phenomenon bears a strong resemblance to the frequently rapid changes in the racial composition of urban neighborhoods.

III. CAUSES OF OCCUPATIONAL SEGREGATION

The persistence of occupational segregation in the face of the enormous changes in the importance of female labor and in the structure of the American economy would appear to require some explanation. I would like therefore to discuss briefly some of the factors that might tend to produce this result.

Institutional Factors

The division of labor on the basis of sex appears to be a universal characteristic of every society of which we have knowledge, from the most technologically primitive through the advanced industrial economies, although there is considerable variation in the allocation of tasks between the sexes. Moreover, occupational segregation by sex within the labor market mirrors the traditional relations of women and men within the family unit. Within the family, the work of women and men is generally viewed as complementary rather than competitive. Sexual segregation of the labor market and the resultant division of female and male workers into two non-competing groups preserves this basic characteristic that governs the relations of women and men in the family.

The basic notion that work should be allocated on the basis of sex and therefore that some tasks are particularly suitable for women and others for men is thus deeply embedded in our tradition and custom. The force of these institutional factors operates on both the supply and demand side to restrict the employment opportunities of women.

On the supply side, girls are socialized to aspire to and train for what are considered to be appropriate female occupations. The educational system frequently further intensifies this problem by channeling women into traditionally feminine pursuits and maintaining quotas on women students in graduate and professional schools in male dominated fields.

On the demand side, there is no reason to assume that employers as a group should be free from socially prevalent attitudes as to what constitutes appropriate female tasks and, indeed, the available studies seem to support this contention. Moreover, the resistance of coworkers and customers to women in certain "nonfeminine" occupational categories may well impose a cost on the employer for violating the accepted social norms.

The Labor Cost Argument

The widely held belief among employers that women have higher average rates of absenteeism and voluntary labor turnover than male workers might also tend to produce occupational segregation by sex. These differences in average labor costs would imply different pay rates for the same job. Insofar as it is frequently not optimal for legal, administrative, and industrial relations reasons to have different pay scales for the same occupation, this consideration might lead to occupational segregation within the establishment. This factor would also tend to make employers unwilling to invest in firm specific training for women for fear of losing their investment. Indeed, it does appear that many predominantly female jobs are those in which general and transferable skills rather than firm specific training are required.

One point should be emphasized at the outset. Even if employer views regarding the average probability of loss of employing women were correct, their actions would still constitute a form of discrimination.[1] Discrimination is the process of forming stereotyped views that all members of a particular group are assumed to possess the characteristics of the group. Thus, the case of an individual female applicant is not considered on the basis of her particular job history or aspirations. Such treatment of women may reduce the cost of screening applicants, but it cannot be considered equitable.

But is the employer view correct? First, employer views formed at a time when most women workers were young and single and apt to leave the labor force permanently upon marriage have not responded to the changing composition of the female labor force discussed in the first section. The increase in the average age of women workers has had the effect of increasing the job stability of the female work

force. Moreover, the rise in the labor force participation rates of young married women in the childbearing ages suggests that new work patterns are in the process of being forged.

Second, women are frequently denied the incentives given to male workers to remain on the job. Substantial investments in firm specific training, good prospects for promotion, and high pay levels decrease the probability of loss of an employee, regardless of sex. Employer practices that restrict women to low paying, dead-end jobs and deny them access to training serve to raise their turnover and absenteeism rates. Thus, a vicious circle may exist whereby employer views are constantly reaffirmed without giving women an opportunity to respond to a different structure of incentives.

IV. THE IMPORTANCE OF OCCUPATIONAL SEGREGATION

Occupational segregation by sex has important implications for other aspects of women's economic status. I would like to discuss two of these linkages: first, the relationship between occupational segregation and female labor force participation, and second, the connection between occupational segregation and pay and status differentials of male and female workers.

Occupational Segregation and Female Labor Force Participation

Occupational segregation may be the limiting factor on the growth of the female labor force. A study by Valerie Kincade Oppenheimer (1970) cited the increase in the *sex-specific demand* for women workers as the crucial factor in explaining the growth of the female labor force and its changing composition between 1940 and 1960. Oppenheimer points out that the expansion in the demand for women workers greatly exceeded the potential supply of the young, single women who were the backbone of the female labor force in the pre-1940 period. Under the pressure of an insufficiency in their preferred source of supply, employers were forced to abandon their prejudices against employing older, married women. Thus, Oppenheimer sees the great influx of these women into the labor force primarily as a *response* to increased job opportunities.

[1] Piore has labeled this "statistical discrimination."

Further research may show that a similar process was in operation in the years since 1960. In order to meet their needs for female labor, some employers may have found it necessary to discard their reservations about hiring mothers of young children, thus making possible the rapid increase in the labor force participation of women in this group that has occurred in recent years.

This analysis which focuses primarily on *demand* factors in explaining changes in female labor force participation at least raises the possibility that had employment opportunities not been restricted to predominantly female jobs, even larger numbers of women might have entered the labor force. The extreme responsiveness of women to the demands exerted by the emergency conditions of World War II and the evidence that the female labor force tends to grow more quickly during the upswing in the business cycle and contract or grow more slowly during recessions would also support this view.[2]

Occupational Segregation and Pay and Status Differentials

The concentration of women in predominantly female jobs and the likelihood that even within relatively integrated occupations women and men tend to work in different industries or establishments results in a virtual "dual labor market" for female and male labor. The dual labor market analysis enables us to explain the pay differentials between female and male workers in terms of supply and demand analysis. Demand is greatly restricted by the sex-typing of jobs. At the same time, the supply of women available for work is highly responsive to changes in the wage rate and employment opportunities in general. The abundance of supply relative to demand, or what has been termed the "overcrowding" of female occupations, would tend to result in a lower deter-

mination of earnings for "women's jobs."[3] Thus, we may replace the familiar statement that women earn less because they are in low paying occupations with the statement that they earn less because they are in *women's jobs*.

Similarly, the common complaint that women are restricted to low status occupations could also be restated in terms of the concentration of the female labor force in *women's jobs*. As long as the labor market is divided on the basis of sex, it is likely that the tasks allocated to women will be ranked as less prestigious or important, reflecting women's lower social status in the society at large.

V. CONCLUSION

I would conclude that the elimination of occupational segregation by sex is essential to the attainment of economic equality for women. This is hardly surprising in that there is no reason to assume that the doctrine of "separate but equal" should be any more valid for women than it is for other groups. Yet, defining the problem in these terms is extremely useful in that it points to policies that would affect the whole female work force and not just those at the upper levels. It means, for example, that we must have more women sales-workers in wholesale trade, more electricians and chefs as well as more female doctors, lawyers, and economists. It also means that more men must move into predominantly female jobs.

Since women presently comprise nearly two-fifths of the civilian labor force and are so heavily concentrated in predominantly female jobs, the attainment of integration is a task of enormous proportions. However, if the preceding dual labor market analysis is correct, a substantial movement of women into the male sector should have the effect of raising incomes of women in predominantly female occupations as well. This should also ease the task of attracting men into presently female pursuits. Thus, the payoff to sizable movements *toward* increased integration could be quite high.

---

[2]I am referring to studies of the cyclical behavior of the labor force which generally indicate that the labor force participation rate, particularly of married women, is very elastic with respect to employment opportunities. Studies of female labor force participation using cross-section data also point to the importance of such indicators of demand as the female wage rate and the level of unemployment. See McNally for a summary of this extensive literature. Of particular interest is the employment of the "femininity index" by Bowen and Finegan as an explanatory variable.

[3]See Bergmann (Mar.-Apr. 1971) for a rigorous development of the overcrowding thesis. The argument presented here is very general but could be extended to take into account differences in quality both within and between the female and male work force. Some of the quality differences between the two groups could be considered as deriving from the dual labor market itself.

27. Sex in the Marketplace

Juanita Kreps

DIFFERENCES IN EARNINGS

The literature contains many references to the fact that women earn less than men. Although sex differences in earnings will be detailed [later], some illustrative figures can be cited in this introductory statement. Male year-round, full-time workers had median earnings of $7,664 in 1968; the median for women who worked full-time for the whole year was $4,457, or 58 per cent of the male's rate. By occupational group, the differences are also impressive (see Table 1). Even in the case of clerical workers, a group dominated by women, the median earnings of females is less than two-thirds that of males. The explanation frequently given for the male's higher wage is his greater experience on the job. Yet a study revealed that 206 companies expected to offer substantially different starting salaries to 1,970

Table 1

Median Earnings of Full-time Year-round Workers, by Sex and Occupational Group, 1968

Major Occupation Group	Median Wage or Salary Income		Women's Median Wage or Salary Income as Percent of Men's
	Women	Men	
Professional and technical workers	$6,691	$10,151	65.9
Nonfarm managers, officials, and proprietors	5,635	10,340	54.5
Clerical workers	4,789	7,351	65.1
Sales workers	3,461	8,549	40.5
Operatives	3,991	6,738	59.2
Service workers (except private household)	3,332	6,058	55.0

Source: U.S. Department of Commerce, Bureau of the Census, *Current Population Reports,* P-60, No. 66.

Table 2

Expected Salaries for June 1970 College
Graduates, by Sex and Selected Field

Field	Average Monthly Salary	
	Women	Men
Accounting	$746	$832
Chemistry	765	806
Economics, finance	700	718
Engineering	844	872
Liberal arts	631	688
Mathematics, statistics	746	773

Source: Frank S. Endicott, "Trends in Employment
of College and University Graduates in Business and
Industry," U.S. Department of Labor, Women's Bureau,
February, 1970.

men and women college graduates with the
same undergraduate majors (Table 2).

One of the factors holding down women's
wages is their tendency to concentrate in low-
paying jobs. One-fourth of all employed women
now work in five occupations: secretary-
stenographer, household worker, bookkeeper,
elementary school teacher, or waitress. Entry
into "men's jobs" is difficult, and access to the
top levels of the better business and professional careers is often blocked by failure to consider women in making promotions to these
jobs. Having been socialized to expect a certain
niche in the occupational hierarchy, women
continue to look for jobs where they know
they can find them, and not to look toward
areas traditionally closed to them.

Attempts to interpret the earnings gap have
not been satisfactory, since there are so many
variables involved. One author summarized the
problem recently by noting that

analysts try to control for the difference in
length of work activity during the year by
comparing the earnings of women and men who
worked the entire year at full-time jobs, but it
is also necessary to allow for the fact that married women have restricted freedom of occupational choice. They may have to put convenience of location or flexibility of hours above
earnings. Married women may not be in a position to accept jobs with overtime pay or to
accept a promotion to a job with heavier

responsibilities. This may lead a wife to take a
job which may not require her primary skill, or
one in which she may not command the best
salary.[1]

MALE-FEMALE DIFFERENCES IN EARNINGS

Balkanization of the labor force into male
and female jobs helps to explain the significant
differences in median earnings of men and
women. Yet large differences persist, even when
job classification, years of school completed,
and other variables are held constant; in short,
male earnings exceed those of females when
there is occupational overlap, and both sexes
are doing the same work.

Women's Earnings: How Low are They?

As figures cited earlier indicate, the median
incomes for the two sexes differ significantly.
For year-round, full-time workers, the female
median is 58 percent of the male's; $4,457 as
compared with $7,664. The sex-related differ-
ence in earnings of full-time workers has been
increasing, moreover; in 1956, the female
median was 63 percent of the male's.

Insofar as the level of formal education warrants a bonus in pay, women again fall short of
the mark. Many of the occupational groups in
which women are heavily concentrated pay low
wages while requiring higher-than-average educational achievement. Oppenheimer illustrates
this phenomenon for several occupational
groups in which women make up more than
half the work force (Table 3). The median number of years of school completed by males and
females in these occupations is higher than the
median for the total male labor force: yet the
median income (for males or females) in these
female-dominated occupations does not compare favorably with the median for all male
workers. She concludes that higher levels of
education do not pay off for either men or
women in these "female" occupations, which
employ 71 percent of all women in professional

[1]Elizabeth Waldman, "Changes in the Labor Force
Activity of Women," *Monthly Labor Review,* Vol. 93
(June, 1970), p. 15.

Table 3

**Relative Income and Educational Standing of
Selected Occupations, 1960[a]**

Occupation	*Ratio of Median Number of School Years Completed in Occupation to Median for Total Male Labor Force[b]*		*Ratio of Median Income in Occupation to Median for Total Male Labor Force[c]*	
	Male	*Female*	*Male*	*Female*
Total	1.00	1.09	1.00	0.59
Professional Workers				
Dancers and dancing teachers	1.12	1.12	0.83	0.61
Dietitians and nutritionists	1.14	1.19	0.76	0.68
Librarians	1.50	1.46	1.01	0.77
Musicians and music teachers	1.34	1.33	1.03	0.29
Nurses	1.17	1.19	0.84	0.71
Recreation and group workers	1.36	1.32	1.00	0.78
Social and welfare workers	1.49	1.48	1.04	0.87
Religious workers	1.47	1.21	0.77	0.49
Elementary teachers	1.53	1.48	1.03	0.85
Teachers, n.e.c.	1.48	1.45	1.10	0.74
Therapists and healers	1.48	1.45	0.97	0.83
Clerical Workers				
Library attendants & assistants	1.23	1.18	0.55	0.54
Physicians' and dentists' office attendants	1.12	1.12	0.68	0.53
Bank tellers	1.14	1.12	0.84	0.63
Bookkeepers	1.14	1.12	0.89	0.64
File clerks	1.12	1.10	0.75	0.59
Office-machine operators	1.13	1.12	0.96	0.68
Payroll & timekeeping clerks	1.13	1.12	1.00	0.73
Receptionists	1.13	1.13	0.77	0.57
Secretaries	1.15	1.14	1.05	0.71
Stenographers	1.14	1.14	1.02	0.70
Typists	1.13	1.13	0.80	0.64
Telephone operators	1.11	1.10	1.07	0.67
Cashiers	1.08	1.08	0.78	0.53
Clerical workers, n.e.c.	1.12	1.12	0.99	0.66
Sales Workers				
Demonstrators	1.08	1.09	__d	0.50
Hucksters and peddlers	0.92	1.09	0.82	0.16

Source: Valerie K. Oppenheimer, *The Female Labor Force*, pp. 100-101.

[a]Includes occupations in which at least 51 percent of the workers were female and where the median school years completed was greater than 11.1—the median for the total male experienced civilian labor force.

[b]Experienced civilian labor force.

[c]Wage and salary workers in the experienced civilian labor force who worked 50-52 weeks in 1959.

[d]Base not large enough to compute a median.

and technical work, 98 percent of all women in clerical jobs, and 42 percent of all female workers.

Data cited earlier reveal differences in earnings by occupational group. In 1968, the annual median for full-time, year-round male professional and technical workers was $10,151; for females, it was $6,691. Figures for other occupations included $7,351 for male clerical workers, $4,789 for female; $6,738 for male operatives (mostly factory workers), $3,991 for women; $6,058 for male service workers, $3,332 for females; $8,549 for men salesworkers, $3,461 for female (Table 1).

Since length of service on the job surely affects wage and salary, and since most married women leave their jobs for a domestic tour of duty, it follows that some portion of the male-female difference in pay for a particular job classification could be attributed to the greater continuity of the male's worklife. For comparison, one needs wage and salary data for members of both sexes, by job classification, educational level, and length of time on the job. Thus, a comparison of the earnings of male and female high school graduates who have been retail sales clerks for five years, in similar types of establishments in a particular locality, would permit generalization. Although data of such detail are not generally available, researchers have drawn some tentative conclusions from the data on male and female earnings in the academic profession—one of the few areas in which several of the variables can be controlled. . . .

Women's Aspirations: How High are They?

Further documentation of sex-related differences in earnings is perhaps not necessary; the data indicate that being male pays some wage premium within many of the occupations which utilize workers of both sexes. But a more important source of bias, perhaps, lies in the woman's selection of her occupation. If women persist in going into those jobs which have traditionally paid low wages, improvements in pay scales can occur only if the demand for these services far outstrips the plentiful supply of workers. The reasons why women select these jobs invite further study. Are there non-monetary rewards in certain careers that more than offset the low pay? Is elementary school teaching appealing to women because they like the work itself, or because it is viewed as an extension of their feminine roles, or because it can be timed to enable women to perform their regular household duties? How much are women willing to pay (in foregone earnings) for time free of market work at the time of day and year that nonmarket work is heaviest?

Clarence Long emphasized the importance of the short work-day to a woman with a reference to her need to be able "to type till five o'clock, and still have time to shop for a cheap roast or a rich husband."[2] His quip raises an important question: Are the market-work—nonmarket-work—leisure choices for women not quite different from those of men? Mincer and Cain have stressed this difference in explaining the larger substitution effect in wives' labor supply; it is nonmarket work (not leisure) that is the substitute for their market work: "In the face of rising incomes and rising wages market work declines for males and single women and their leisure increases, while home-work declines for wives and their leisure and their market work both increase."[3]

But it is not merely that their nonmarket work influences their decision as to whether to enter the labor force; the demands of home and family also influence *which* market jobs women are willing to take. Moreover, the period of heaviest domestic responsibility occurs fairly early in a woman's worklife, when she is likely to be forced to make some quite long-range decisions: whether to acquire further job training, or additional formal education; how many children she will have; whether to continue working, at least part-time, during the child-bearing period. In the face of the demands on her time the young wife is likely to find that the scheduling of her job is the most important single consideration. Her immediate job choice is dictated in large measure by the time constraint imposed in the short run, and this choice in turn directs her subsequent career development.

Laments for wasted womanpower have now reached the popular press. Privately, women have mourned their underutilized and under-

[2]Clarence Long, *The Labor Force Under Changing Income and Employment* (Princeton: Princeton University Press, 1958).

[3]Cain, *Married Women*, p. 7. There may be some dispute (on the part of working wives) as to whether their leisure has increased as they have taken jobs outside the home.

paid talents and education for decades. Although the implied understatement of the present worth of women's work in the non-market sphere calls for reexamination, a recognition of the constraints on women's career choices is a first step in unravelling the complex problem of the low wages accorded to women's jobs, and the tendency for women to remain in those jobs.

Why do women not opt more often for occupations that are dominated by males, yet include some women in their ranks? The movement of both men and women into computer programming is a case in point, albeit an unusual one, since the job itself was new and lacking in traditional taboos. Yet most white-collar jobs are changing in content, giving some scope for integration of the sexes. Is it inevitable that in insurance companies men sell insurance and women do the typing? That in banks men make mortgage loans while women are tellers? Where does the resistance to women entering men's jobs actually lie? And when women are admitted, how is a wage differential justified?

Employers may reason that men merit higher salaries (and additional investments in training), or preference in hiring regardless of pay because they will not withdraw for marriage and childbearing; that men can give more time and effort to the job because they have no domestic responsibilities; that they are more useful because of their greater mobility; that they need more money to support their families. The threat of discontinuity in a woman's worklife is perhaps the greatest single barrier to higher wages for young women. For the older woman, whose children have demanded her attention in earlier years, the lack of job experience is equally damaging to her earnings potential.

The woman who is considering the occupational options may be discouraged from trying to enter a male's field because she accurately perceives employers' reluctance to hire women for these jobs, or because the investment required of her may exceed her estimate of the return, given her expectation of withdrawal from work for a time, and the uncertainty surrounding her subsequent worklife. She may discount too heavily the future stream of earnings accruing from say, two years of education or training, and thus invest too little in human capital. But perhaps not. For the stream of earnings may not be very high for a woman, and she is well aware of this hazard.

Study might reveal that women have been quite realistic in appraising their potential earnings under different assumptions as to the investment in education, or in many cases that they have erred in the direction of over-investing in education, given the career opportunities that are compatible with their usual lifestyle. It is significant that many women are now challenging that traditional lifestyle by posing some fundamental questions: Why should women assume the obligation for child care? Is it not possible (through day care centers and sharing domestic responsibilities with husbands) for women to have uninterrupted worklives?

Such challenges are the first concerted attempts to remove these major constraints imposed on the market activities of women. To the extent that the efforts bear fruit, and women opt for worklife patterns more nearly like those of men (and those of women in certain other countries, notably Sweden), the career aspirations of women will surely rise, particularly among college-educated women. The impact will likely be felt less on the participation rate of college graduates, which is already high, than on the types of careers women choose. Additional investments of resources in education and job training for women, under these circumstances, would seem to bear high rates of return.

The employment circumstances of college-educated women are far from ideal, however. And these women, being more articulate than women with less education, have repeatedly lodged the complaint of sex discrimination. If these women are the wave of the future, employment patterns may be altered substantially. Salary differentials related to sex will be constantly under scrutiny, and hiring policy even more rigorously policed. Restrictions on entry to higher-level jobs will continue to be attacked. Most of all, those women who not only earn an A.B. but also gain an advanced degree, will continue to argue for improved opportunities in the top professions.

28. Combatting Discrimination in Employment

Stanley H. Masters

Collette Moser

In recent years this country has become increasingly concerned with the issue of racial and sexual inequality.[1] Although this problem has many dimensions, economic inequality has received increasing attention. Statistically, relative income differentials are probably the most important measure of economic inequality. For example, the median income of black males was 60.5 percent of white males in 1970, compared with 52.5 percent in 1960.[2] Although this represents some improvement, we are still far from achieving complete racial equality. In contrast, among full-time full-year workers, the median income of females declined from 60.8 percent of the median male income in 1960 to 59.5 percent in 1970.

Although differences in amount and kind of education and in labor force continuity account for part of these income differentials, the most important factor appears to be labor market discrimination.[3] In this article we will discuss efforts to combat such discrimination under Title VII of the Civil Rights Act of 1964 and under federal executive orders requiring affirmative action programs of government contractors. As we shall see, labor market discrimination need not be deliberate; it often occurs despite the conscious intentions of employers. As a result, combatting discrimination requires considerable sophistication.

In discussing legal efforts to fight discriminatory employment activities, we shall look briefly at the issue of enforcement procedures and then turn to substantive issues regarding the legislation. With regard to procedures, the first question is the scale of federal enforce-

The authors are indebted to Jacqueline Brophy, School of Labor and Industrial Relations at Michigan State University for her helpful comments on this paper.

[1] Throughout this paper victims of racial and sexual discrimination will be referred to as "minorities," although it is understood that women are not a numeric minority.

[2] Calculated from data in U.S. Bureau of the Census, *Current Population Report,* Series P-60, Nos. 36 and 80.

[3] Labor market discrimination is defined as the lower earnings occurring in some group after standardizing for differences in productivity that are not caused by such discrimination. Although it is not easy to estimate how much of the lower educational attainment of blacks or the discontinuous labor force participation of many women is due to labor market discrimination, such discrimination appears to be significant even if one standardizes for the entire differential in education or labor force continuity. For blacks, see Stanley H. Masters, "The Effect of Educational Differences and Labor Market Discrimination on the Relative Earnings of Black Males," *Journal of Human Resources,* Vol. 9, No. 2 (Spring, 1974). For women, our conclusion is more speculative.

ment effort. As of fiscal year 1972, total appropriations for "private sector equal employment opportunities" were only forty-seven million dollars, with administration requests up to eighty-one million for 1974.[4] Although the projected increase is encouraging, this figure is very small in relation to many other government activities.[5] For example, government expenditures on manpower programs totaled over four billion dollars in fiscal 1972.[6]

Not only are current enforcement procedures weakened by limited financial resources, but the Equal Employment Opportunity Commission (EEOC), set up under the Civil Rights Act of 1964, had virtually no legal power with regard to employers and was limited to the role of conciliation and negotiation. Until recently suits could be brought only by private individuals or by the Justice Department. Such suits are expensive for private parties, and the activities of the Justice Department in this area have been limited by a small staff and lack of coordination with the EEOC.[7]

In 1972 Congress amended the Civil Rights Act of 1964 to enable the EEOC to sue in the courts whenever it believes a violation of Title VII has occurred. Although this legislation represents a significant improvement, stronger procedures would have been possible and were seriously considered in the Senate. Under this alternative proposal, the EEOC would have been given the power to issue cease and desist orders. Thus, once the EEOC judged that discrimination had occurred, the firm would not have been allowed to continue that discrimination pending trial. This defeated proposal would have been more equitable since it would give minorities the benefit of the doubt *once* the EEOC ruled that discrimination did exist. Even if enforcement procedures were greatly strengthened, however, important substantive issues would still remain.

SUBSTANTIVE ISSUES IN ENFORCING EQUAL OPPORTUNITY LEGISLATION

Title VII of the Civil Rights Act of 1964 states:

It shall be an unlawful employment practice for an employer to fail or refuse to hire or to discharge any individual or otherwise to discriminate against any individual with respect to his compensation, terms, conditions, or privileges of employment because of such individual's race, color, religion, sex, or national origin.[8]

Even though this legislation was designed to improve the economic position of minority groups, it explicitly disavows a number of actions that might be taken to improve the labor market status of blacks, women, and other disadvantaged groups. These restrictions are concisely summarized in a recent article in the *Harvard Law Review,* dealing with the effect of Title VII on racial discrimination.

The Act's effectiveness in promoting minority employment was limited by the principle of color-blindness. Just as the employer was not to discriminate against minority groups, he was also proscribed from showing preference to them. Employers could continue to set rigorous qualifications for their job openings and test for worker productivity, as long as they did so fairly. The Act thus includes an antipreferential provision (e.g., no quotas are to be necessary), affirms the legality of professionally developed ability tests, and protects bona fide seniority systems. Help was to come to the black community, Congress reasoned, by a newfound opportunity to be judged by objective standards.[9]

Restrictions on preferential treatment might be a small price for minority groups to pay in exchange for objective standards that prohibit discrimination against minority group members; but it is not easy to establish such standards.

Let us start with the issue of discrimination in hiring. Let us define such discrimination in the following way: Assume that two identical jobs are available in a given company and that there are two equally qualified applicants. If

---

[4]*Special Analysis of the United States Government, Fiscal Year 1973* (a part of *The Budget of the United States Government,* 1974), p. 180.

[5]Note that the actual increase may be much smaller due to Congressional action.

[6]*Special Analysis, op. cit.* p. 120.

[7]See the discussion in *Federal Civil Rights Enforcement Effort,* a Report of the United States Commission on Civil Rights, 1970, especially Chapter 2, Sections V and VI.

[8]Civil Rights Act of 1964, Section 703.

[9]Employment Discrimination and Title VII of the Civil Rights Act of 1964, an unsigned note in the *Harvard Law Review,* Vol. 84, No. 5 (March, 1971), p. 1114.

one applicant is a black female and the other a white male, then discrimination would occur if the firm hired the white man but not the black woman.[10]

Now let us examine some of the problems that occur when we try to apply this definition to specific cases. Initially we shall concentrate on questions relating primarily to racial discrimination. The first difficulty is in determining when two applicants are equally qualified. In this area, the most controversial issue has been the role of educational requirements, either amount of schooling (e.g., a high school diploma) or scores on various kinds of tests. Recent studies have indicated that schooling is a very crude measure of one's productivity.[11] Even though tests might provide a better measure, it is probably impossible to develop tests that are perfect measures of job performance. Moreover, it is expensive to develop tests that are even moderately accurate; the net costs are likely to be high even after taking account of resulting improvements in worker performances. On the other hand, it may also be costly for the firm to ignore potential differences in productivity among its applicants.

The Supreme Court has ruled that requiring completion of high school or passage of a general intelligence test can be illegal if these requirements operate to disqualify blacks at a substantially higher rate than white applicants and if the requirements are not shown to be significantly related to successful job performance.[12] Although it is not yet clear what standards of proof the courts will require in order for a firm to demonstrate that its requirements are job related, it appears that the courts will have to become involved in some very difficult issues involving trade-offs between efficiency and equity. As we shall argue later, there may be ways to avoid some of those difficulties by judging equity in terms of results as well as procedures.

Even if we can clearly determine when two applicants are equally qualified, there are other difficulties in determining whether or not an employer is discriminating in the overall hiring process. Specifically, an employer's recruitment policies must be considered along with his hiring requirements. For example, many firms recruit primarily through current employees. Such recruitment procedures have significant benefits for both the employer and those considering employment with the firm.[13] If the present work force is virtually all white male, however, important issues of discrimination occur.

The courts have generally ruled that such recruitment procedures are illegal if they result in a work force whose racial composition is significantly different from that of the community.[14] The natural remedy is for the employer to begin advertising his job vacancies in media which serve the black community and/or with civil rights organizations. Similar problems arise with the recruitment of women who frequently have limited access to information on job openings. In recent years, women's caucuses in professional organizations are frequently contacted by employers seeking women trained in particular disciplines. However, the question arises: How much new recruitment activity must be undertaken, especially since quotas in employment are specifically disavowed under Title VII?

Women are subjected to additional discrimination in the hiring process through the concept of men's and women's jobs and the concomitant separate job listings in help-wanted ads. Although such separate listings violate Title VII guidelines, BEOC has had difficulty convincing the courts that "a newspaper which maintains classified advertising columns violates Title VII when it segregates such columns on the basis of sex."[15] However,

[10]If there were only one job available and the white male were hired, it would be impossible to know whether this represented discrimination or a random event—unless we had some additional knowledge of the employer's intentions (e.g., qualified applicants were usually hired on a first-come basis and the black woman had applied first).

[11]For example, see Ivar Berg, *The Great Training Robbery* (New York: Praeger Publishers, 1970).

[12]See *Willie S. Griggs* v. *Duke Power Company* (U.S. Supreme Court, No. 124, March 9, 1971).

[13]For example, see the selection "Information Networks in Labor Markets," by Albert Rees in this book of readings.

[14]See *Harvard Law Review, op. cit.,* pp. 1153-55. As that discussion indicates, however, if an employer's recruitment policies appear to be discriminatory on this basis, it seems reasonable to give the employer a chance to demonstrate that blacks have less interest or skill than whites in his line of work.

[15]Sonia Pressman Fuentes, "The Law Against Sex Discrimination in Employment" (paper presented at the MDK Associates Seminar on Affirmative Action, Dallas, Texas, May 16, 1972). pp. 12-13. The

"due to the Commission's position, and similar positions taken by city and state fair employment practice commissions, newspapers across the country, including the New York City newspapers and the three major newspapers in the District of Columbia, have discontinued the maintenance of sex-segregated columns."[16]

A discrimination issue that affects both women's hiring and work assignment is that of sex segregation of jobs. Under Title VII, the EEOC has ruled that only in exceptional jobs in which sex is a bona fide occupational qualification (bfoq) can jobs be restricted to either sex. The burden of proof of the exception is on the employers. Recent court decisions have viewed bfoq as follows: "A determination that sex is a bfoq for a job cannot be made on the basis of general assumptions regarding the physical capabilities of men or women. In order for sex to be a bfoq for a job, it must be established that the sexual characteristics of the employee are crucial to the successful performance of the job, as they would be for the position of wet-nurse; or that there is a need for authenticity or genuineness, as is the case for the position of actor or actress. In other words, discrimination based on sex is valid only when the *essence* of the business enterprise would be undermined by not hiring members of one sex exclusively."[17] Even some state laws that prohibit the employment of women in certain occupations have been held invalid by Title VII.[18]

Next let us turn from the issue of discrimination in hiring to other issues of discrimination in employment. Perhaps the most important of these issues are promotions, layoffs, and discharges. Promotions and discharges are based

partly on ability (or lack thereof) and thus qualification standards in these areas are subject to many of the same issues as hiring standards.[19] However, seniority also plays an important role in most promotions and almost all layoffs. If there is no history of discrimination in hiring, then seniority rules pose little difficulty since seniority is easier to measure objectively than most other potential criteria. However, if there has been past discrimination, then seniority rules may help perpetuate this discrimination far into the future.

Let us assume that, prior to the Civil Rights Act of 1964, a firm employed blacks and women only in certain unskilled, low-paying positions, and that, for white males, there was a well-defined ladder for advancement with promotions going to the person with the most seniority among those in the next lowest job who are considered qualified.[20] Let us consider how blacks are to be integrated into this seniority system after passage of the Civil Rights Act. Three main possibilities which have been advanced are:

a) "freedom now," requiring displacement of white incumbents by blacks who, without discrimination in the past, would have had their places; b) "rightful place," allowing a black to compete for a position on the basis of his total company service (without having to advance through each step of the ladder); and c) "status quo," preserving intact the rights of white incumbents (blacks must start at the bottom of the white ladder and advance through each step on the same basis as newly entering whites).[21]

BEOC position was not sustained by the District Court in the case of *Brush* v. *San Francisco Newspaper Company*. The case was pending on appeal as of 1972.

[16]*Ibid.*, pp. 5-6, 13. For example, in 1971, courts ruled sex-segregated columns held in violation of the state fair employment practices laws in Pennsylvania and New Jersey.

[17]Fuentes, *op. cit.*, p. 5. A few of the significant court cases on bfoq are as follows: *Diaz* v. *Pan American World Airways, Inc.*, 3EPD para 8166 (5 Cir. 1971); *Weeks* v. *Southern Bell Telephone Co.*, 408 F 2d 228 (C.A. 5, 1969); *Cheatwood* v. *South Central Bell Telephone and Telegraph Co.*, 303 F. Supp. 754 (M.D. Ala., 1969).

[18]See Sec. 1604.2, EEOC Rules and Regulations, 37 Fed. Reg. 6835 (April 5, 1972); *Rosenfield* v. *Southern Pacific Co.*, 3 EPD para 8247 (C.A. 9, 1971).

[19]Although differences in pay based on sex or race are a critical discrimination issue, such distinctions are usually engineered through the job title or seniority system. Where pay differences for same job status have been proven, they have been ruled illegal.

[20]If the firm (or union) is all white, a more extreme possibility is to apply the following analysis based on blacks in the community rather than on blacks in low-paying jobs within the company. See *United States* v. *Sheetmetal Workers Local 36,* 416 F. 2d 123 (8th Cir., 1969).

[21]*Harvard Law Review, op. cit.*, p. 1159. Separate seniority lists based on sex differences have also been ruled in violation of Title VII. A classic case of such separate seniority lines for men and women is that of Libbey-Owens Ford. In 1970 case, the Justice Department suit against the company was terminated by a consent degree in which the company was required to give the women two opportunities to bid into another department and to provide extensive education and

Congress clearly indicated that it was not requiring the freedom-now approach when it protected bona fide seniority systems.[22] Of the two alternatives, the rightful place test generally has been accepted by the courts.[23] Of course, there may be little practical difference between the "rightful place" and "status quo" approach if skills must be learned during each job on the ladder. Consequently, even if all discrimination in hiring and recruiting should cease, it could still take a long time to eliminate all the effects of past labor market discrimination.

Discrimination charges have been levied against a number of firms because of their employment policies toward pregnant employees. The major issues involve the requiring of leaves of absence or the termination of employment contrary to the wishes of the employee. In general, the decisions of the courts and the EEOC hold that it constitutes sex discrimination for an employer:

(1) To fail to accord a pregnant employee the right to work as long as she was not physically disabled;

(2) To cause a female employee to lose seniority because of absence for pregnancy, miscarriage, or childbirth;

(3) To fail to provide female employees the same hospitalization and medical benefits as are provided for wives of male employees;

(4) To fail to provide the same sickness and disability benefits for absence when disabled because of pregnancy, miscarriage, or childbirth as provided when an employee is absent on account of other non-occupational disability.[24]

So far we have argued that it is going to be very difficult to eliminate all discrimination in employment simply by trying to apply the "color-blind" and "sex-neutral" standards of Title VII. Moreover, even if such discrimination could be eliminated, the effects of past discrimination would persist far into the future. Thus we need to consider alternative approaches to combatting discrimination.

Affirmative Action Requirements

The major alternative to the present legal concept of color-sex blindness is the imposition of some kind of quota system. At least two variations of the quota approach are available. The first, which might be called inflexible quotas, means that firms must employ at least a certain percentage of minorities and that no exceptions will be allowed. The second, which might be called target quotas, means that the burden of proof is on the employer to show that he has not discriminated (or has fulfilled his contract commitment to take "affirmative action") if he does not employ as many minorities as stipulated by the quota. To avoid confusing inflexible and target quotas, the latter are usually referred to as goals rather than quotas. Although Congress clearly indicated that Title VII was not to be interpreted as requiring any quota system, the Executive branch has established a system of "goals" with regard to government contractors.[25] Moreover, this system has been upheld in the courts and has been tacitly accepted by Congress.

The government began its present affirmative action program with the Philadelphia Plan, instituted in 1967. Under this plan, contractors for government construction projects in the Philadelphia area must make "good faith" efforts to meet certain goals with regard to the hiring of minority workers. These goals are determined by the Office of Federal Contract Compliance (OFCC) on the basis of such factors as the new hiring predicted for the contractors, the number of minority-group mem-

---

training in advance of transfer. *Local 9 of Glass and Ceramic Workers* v. *Libbey-Owens Ford* (U.S. District Court in Ohio).

[22]However, this approach may be an appropriate remedy for a discriminatory system in effect after the Civil Rights Act of 1964 became effective. See Alfred W. Blumrosen, *Black Employment and the Law* (New Brunswick, New Jersey: Rutgers University Press, 1971), pp. 202-5.

[23]*Harvard Law Review, op. cit.,* p. 1159.

[24]"Keeping Up With the Law," *Summary,* Legal Department, International Union of Electrical, Radio, and Machine Workers, 1972. A large portion of the cases have concerned teachers where leaves of absence have been required after the fifth month of pregnancy. In most but not all of the cases, courts have ruled that the requirement is arbitrary and violates the equal protection clause of the 14th Amendment since it treats pregnancy different from other medical dis-

abilities and without regard to differences in individual abilities. See, for example, 1972 cases of *Bravo* v. *Board of Education, City of Chicago* (Northern District of Illinois); *Le Fleur* v. *Cleveland Board of Education* (6th Circuit, Cincinnati).

[25]See James E. Jones, Jr., "The Bugaboo of Employment Quotas," *Wisconsin Law Review,* Vol. 70, No. 2, for a discussion of the legal aspects of the quota issue.

bers having the necessary skills, and, if this number is limited, the length of time necessary for training. Then these goals indicating the number of minority employees to be hired in specified trades by specified times, are included as part of the job specifications on which the contractor bids. Although the Philadelphia Plan does set up very specific goals, these goals originally applied only to the actual government contracts and did not apply to the contractor's employment on other projects. Since firms could meet these requirements by switching black workers from their private projects rather than by hiring more black workers, the program has recently been changed to cover a contractor's total employment.

Failure to meet the specified goals does not necessarily imply that the contractor has failed to comply with the terms of the contract. In the words of the *Harvard Law Review:*

> A contractor can escape sanctions by proving that he made "every good faith effort" to meet the requirements. Signs of a good faith effort are: (1) communications of employment needs to certain minority community organizations; (2) maintenance of records showing disposition of minority job applications; (3) participation in community minority training programs; and (4) notification of the OFCC area coordinator whenever the employer's efforts to meet his goal have been impeded by union referral practices. It is specifically noted that failure of a union with which the contractor has a collective bargaining agreement to send minority applicants is not a sufficient excuse for noncompliance. Though the precise procedural consequences of failure to meet goals are not outlined in the Philadelphia Plan, it has been assumed that failure to meet specific goals forces the contractor to assume the burden of producing evidence of his good faith effort to meet his goals while the government has the ultimate burden of persuasion on the issue of noncompliance with the Executive Order program.[26]

Originally the Philadelphia Plan was developed as a model to apply to other cities. However, the government's current approach is to encourage the development of "hometown plans," agreements negotiated among unions, contractors, and minority-group representatives to increase the employment of the minority-group on all construction projects in the area. If no satisfactory hometown agreement is nego-

tiated, then the government can fall back on the Philadelphia Plan approach.

The government began its affirmative action program on construction, possibly because

> Urban renewal and government building tend to take place in areas of high minority concentration. In many kinds of work, discrimination can be concealed behind closed doors. But the presence of an all-white construction crew working outdoors in plain sight in a black community is a "blatant insult."[27]

Although union jobs in the skilled construction trades pay very well, they are only a very small percentage of total jobs in this country. Consequently, it was important for the OFCC to develop an affirmative action program for federal contractors in areas outside of construction. Such a program has been developed and is currently expressed in Revised Order No. 4. This order, which was formulated in December 1971, requires nonconstruction contractors with 50 or more employees or contracts of at least $50,000 to have affirmative action programs that include:

(1) A self-analysis to determine whether women and minorities are being underutilized in one or more job classifications.

(2) Corrective action, including goals and timetables, to remedy any deficiencies.

(3) Development or reaffirmation of an equal opportunity policy and dissemination of this policy both internally and externally.

(4) Establishment of a director or manager of Equal Opportunity Programs with many detailed responsibilities in identifying problem areas and developing appropriate programs.

(5) Implementation of internal reporting systems to measure the effectiveness of the affirmative action program.

(6) Support for community and national programs that are designed to improve the educational opportunities available to women and minorities.

One of the most controversial uses of Revised Order No. 4 has been the application of affirmative action requirements to universities, requirements applying to the employment of women as well as blacks. Although educational institutions had been exempt from Title VII until the 1972 amendments to the Equal Employment Opportunity Act, application of

---

[26]*Harvard Law Review, op. cit.,* p. 1298.

[27]*Ibid.,* p. 1294.

Executive Orders 11246 and 11375 had placed the Federal government in the position of overseeing the internal operations of the universities. Backed by Revised Order No. 4, the Department of Health, Education, and Welfare and the Office of Civil Rights have heard charges of sex discrimination levied against hundreds of universities. In some cases, HEW has threatened to withhold funding because charges of discrimination have been intense (e.g., at the University of Michigan, where federal funding amounts to about $60 million). Just as visibility in the black community had made construction work a target for combatting discrimination in the employment of black males, the visibility in the employment and production of educated women gives the university the responsibility for changing patterns of sex-stereotyping and discrimination.

Revised Order No. 4 applies to women as well as blacks. Nash summarizes the other main differences between this program and the Philadelphia Plan:

> The primary difference between the two programs is that the OFCC or an appropriate regional organization analyzes the factors leading to appropriate goal formulation in the construction program, while under Order No. 4 each nonconstruction contractor must make his own analysis. This difference is dictated by the need for a uniform affirmative action approach by each employing entity. Most nonconstruction contractors maintain a relatively constant work force and can establish their own consistent program. But since the construction work force in any locality is in reality employed by all of the construction contractors in the area, goals and timetables for the latter, in order to have a meaningful application to employment, must be developed for the single-employer entity (all contractors) and their employees (all construction employees who move from job to job). The essential requirement of coordinated goal setting is obtained under both programs.[28]

Although the goals and timetables are initially set by the nonconstruction contractor, these goals and timetables can be revised by the OFCC under Revised Order No. 4. For these programs, as for those in construction, goals and timetables are to be based on objective

factors, such as the availability of minority workers at different skill levels, the existence of training opportunities, the expected turnover of present employees, and expected changes in the size of the work force. Even though contracts can be terminated under Revised Order No. 4, this process is often too time-consuming to be very effective. However, the threat of losing future government contracts as a result of inadequate affirmative action programs can be very effective under this order.[29]

THE ADVANTAGES AND DISADVANTAGES OF AFFIRMATIVE ACTION REQUIREMENT

Now that we have summarized the current status of affirmative action requirements, let us discuss more carefully the advantages and disadvantages of this approach. The advantages of the affirmative action requirements compared with the color-blind sex-neutral standards of Title VII are that such requirements are more oriented toward positive actions to help minorities and place a clearer burden of proof on employers with few minority workers.

Despite these advantages, the present affirmative action programs have been fairly controversial. On the one hand, the programs have been criticized for not being tough enough. Proponents of a tougher approach sometimes advocate a system of inflexible quotas. However, this approach does not appear feasible politically and might reinforce racist and sexist stereotypes if minority group members were placed in jobs for which they were not qualified. If inflexible quotas are rejected in favor of

---

28Peter G. Nash, "Affirmative Action Under Executive Order 11246," *New York Law Review* (April, 1971), p. 235.

29*Ibid.*, p. 255. Ashenfelter and Heckman find some evidence that affirmative action requirements have been effective in increasing black employment. More specifically they conclude (p. 11), "First we find that the relative employment of black male workers increased by 3.3 percent more over the period 1966 to 1970 in firms with government contracts than in firms without government contracts, and that this difference is statistically significant. Second, we find that the relative occupational position of black male workers increased by .2 percent more in firms with government contracts than in firms without contracts, but that this difference is not statistically significant." See an unpublished report by Orley Ashenfelter and James Heckman entitled, "Changes in Minority Employment Patterns, 1966 to 1970."

the present emphasis on goals, timetables, and good faith efforts, then the crucial issues are: (1) how ambitious the goals and timetables should be, and (2) how vigorous the government will be in going after firms that make only a minimal effort to meet their goals.

Although many feel that present governmental enforcement efforts are too weak, others feel that the whole affirmative action approach is too stringent an anti-discrimination strategy. Advocates of this view have generally focused on three objections to the affirmative action requirements—an efficiency argument, an equity argument, and a political argument. The efficiency argument maintains that any affirmative action program will increase a firm's costs, since it would be under pressure to hire blacks and women when it would otherwise have been free to hire more highly-skilled white males. Although this argument might have some validity for a system of inflexible quotas, the present affirmative action programs only require an employer to make a good faith effort to meet his target for minority employment. If he has made every reasonable effort to recruit (and/or train) qualified minority workers, then he would not be subject to any sanctions. Even though an employer might be required to undergo some extra expenses for recruiting and training minority workers, it is not clear that such costs will necessarily exceed the costs that a firm might incur by ignoring the potential availability of such workers. (Cf., Becker's view of discrimination.)

The equity argument maintains that, if the individual worker or employer has not discriminated against blacks or women, then he should not have to bear the major burden of any costs involved in improving their economic position. Instead the cost should be borne by society as a whole (e.g., through general taxation). Of course, this argument assumes affirmative action programs do involve important costs to firms and to white male workers. As we have just seen, this argument is somewhat questionable in the case of firms. On the other hand, some white males certainly are hurt by affirmative action programs. The greatest costs in this regard would occur if present employees were laid off so that additional blacks and women could be hired. Such an extreme proposal has been ruled out on equity (and political) grounds. However, white males seeking new jobs will be hurt by affirmative action programs. Two points need to be raised in this regard. First, the cost to such white workers

can be minimized if the government pursues fiscal, monetary, and manpower policies to ensure full employment. Second, since the government affirmative action requirement demands only a good faith effort by government contractors and since discrimination does still exist in the labor market, any harm suffered by white males as a result of affirmative action programs should be viewed primarily as a cost of reducing discrimination against minority groups rather than as an example of discrimination against white males. Although we believe that these arguments make it difficult to attack the present affirmative action programs on equity grounds, these equity considerations do suggest that such programs are likely to face political difficulties.

Numerous political arguments have been advanced against affirmative action programs. First, such programs have been criticized for dividing the working class politically and thereby hurting the economic position of all workers.[30] This argument may have some validity, but the lack of any significant action against discrimination may also lead to tension between workers of different race or sex. A closely related argument maintains that minority workers may be helped more (and at less political cost)[31] if political efforts are concentrated on establishing and *maintaining* tight labor markets. But this is simply an argument for putting top priority on tight labor markets and not an argument for abandoning affirmative action requirements.

Next, some argue[32] affirmative action programs may reinforce racist and sexist stereotypes, since giving some preferential treatment to minorities suggests they are unable to compete successfully on the basis of their own ability. Although this argument might have merit if employers were forced to hire unqualified applicants, there is no such requirement in

[30]For example, see Bayard Rustin, "The Blacks and the Unions," *Harper's Magazine* (May, 1971). This line of reasoning is also consistent with the radical analysis. See the selection by Michael Reich in this book of readings.

[31]Such costs would include: (1) the possibility of not having any positive impact on government policy, (2) possible trade-offs between present and future gains for minority groups, and (3) labor market gains versus gains in other areas such as educational opportunities.

[32]For example, see *Harvard Law Review, op. cit.*, p. 1166.

the present affirmative action programs. By putting employers under more pressure to hire qualified minority workers,[33] the present programs may actually help break down present stereotypes by providing more examples of successful performance by minority workers.

Another criticism that has been raised by the affirmative action "backlash" is one of excessive government intervention, particularly with regard to the educational process. For example, in a speech reprinted in *U.S. News and World Report,* Dr. George Roche, President of Hillsdale College in Michigan, maintains present affirmative action programs put "at stake the institutional integrity of higher education":

> The present situation can be summarized as an assault upon the standards and integrity of the institutions involved.... Already numerous individual injustices, assaults upon the dignity and integrity of our educational institutions and bureaucratic interferences with the educational process have accumulated so rapidly that it will take book-length treatment to examine all the practical and philosophic implications raised by affirmative action.[34]

Such a criticism combines our earlier economic-efficiency argument with a political argument concerning government intervention. With regard to the efficiency argument we need only emphasize that affirmative action programs no more require the hiring of unqualified Ph.Ds than they do the hiring of unqualified plumbers. The government-intervention aspect of the argument is also unpersuasive. Affirmative action programs are not placing controls on what is to be taught or what is to be researched—issues that are truly at the heart of academic freedom. Moreover, these programs do not require that individual A be hired rather than individual B. The Federal government is simply saying that as a *quid pro quo* for using Federal contract funds, the university must subscribe to a program of affirmative action toward minority employees and students.

In summary, we believe that the present affirmative action programs are an important policy device for reducing discrimination in the labor market. Although they have been attacked on several grounds, we do not find these attacks very convincing. In fact, we believe that these programs should be strengthened—especially with regard to their enforcement procedures since the mere existence of an affirmative action plan does not assure implementation and results. As in labor relations generally, distinguishing between "good and bad faith" efforts is difficult.[35]

On the other hand, affirmative action is not the sole answer to the discrimination problem. Changing people's attitudes, improving the marketable skill of minority group members, and maintaining tight labor markets are also important. Rather than viewing such alternative policies as potential substitutes, it appears best to view them as complements, since each is likely to be more effective if the others are being pursued with some success.

---

[33]In addition, employers are under pressure to see that minority members get better training.

[34]*U.S. News and World Report,* January 1, 1973, p. 52.

[35]Some have accused employers of engaging in "bad faith search" efforts, particularly at the university level. Employers obtain names of women, blacks, and other minorities, and make only vague attempts at recruitment. They then use these names to "pad" their affirmative action "good faith" effort recruitment list.

Poverty

In the early 1960s, Americans rediscovered poverty in this country. One of the most important books leading to this rediscovery was *The Other America* by Michael Harrington, who discussed why the poor had become invisible and argues that many are caught in a "vicious circle of poverty."

The antipoverty objective is closely related to the objective of reducing discrimination. These interrelationships are analyzed by Robert A. Levine in his book, *The Poor Ye Need Not Have With You: Lessons from the War on Poverty*. He suggests that we can end low-income poverty through improved income maintenance programs and that "antipoverty programs" in areas such as education should be concerned primarily with reducing inequality of opportunity.

While traditional antipoverty programs to improve education, health, and housing are important, Tobin argues that a prosperous national economy is crucial in dealing with the economic problems of poverty. A tight labor market will be particularly helpful for black men and their families. In addition, he suggests two other top-priority needs in combatting poverty: 1) education and manpower programs to increase the earning capacities of the poor and their children, and 2) a major reform of our present public assistance programs, as illustrated by his proposal for a negative income tax.

Economists have made many proposals for reforming our public assistance (or welfare) programs. One of the most far-reaching plans is that developed by Earl Rolph. He suggests a system of fixed payments to all residents of the United States (e.g., giving everyone 500-1,000 dollars per year) to be combined with a major revision of the income tax. This proposal might reduce the stigma of welfare and also alleviate many of the problems that currently exist in both our welfare and tax systems. At one point presidential candidate George McGovern adopted Rolph's proposal, but he was notably unsuccessful in persuading the public of its merits.

In the past several years, there has been much concern about welfare reform in Congress as well as academia. While almost everyone is in favor of "reform," the term has different meanings for different people. Irwin Garfinkel and Stanley Masters

211

discuss this problem and argue that a crucial issue in evaluating any program to extend benefits to families headed by a working male is the expected effect on work incentives. Recently economists have devoted much attention to estimating the labor supply effects of alternative income-maintenance proposals. In addition to standard empirical analyses, there also have been very costly experiments designed to generate better estimates. Although the results require considerable qualification, there is no evidence that income maintenance programs will induce large numbers of able-bodied male family heads to permanently quit work.

Although welfare reform has held center stage recently in the political debate on poverty, other policies also deserve attention. In the mid-sixties many economists (including Tobin) had high hopes for raising the income of the poor by improving their educational opportunities. As part of the war on poverty the Johnson administration did initiate many educational programs to help the disadvantaged, but economic evaluations, such as the one by Thomas Ribich, have not judged such programs to be very successful. After summarizing his empirical results, Ribich discusses alternative explanations and possible policy implications.

Although economists have generally been critical of raising the legal minimum wage as an antipoverty device on the grounds that low-skilled people would find less jobs available, this approach has much support—especially among trade unionists. Proponents argue that the direct wage effects can be significant, but that employment effects will be small or nonexistent. The theoretical and empirical evidence on these issues are examined in the selection by Kaufman and Foran, who conclude that "minimum wages may very well have the effect of redistributing income in favor of labor."

29. The Other America

Michael Harrington

The millions who are poor in the United States tend to become increasingly invisible. Here is a great mass of people, yet it takes an effort of the intellect and will even to see them.

I discovered this personally in a curious way. After I wrote my first article on poverty in America, I had all the statistics down on paper. I had proved to my satisfaction that there were around 50,000,000 poor in this country. Yet, I realized I did not believe my own figures. The poor existed in the Government reports; they were percentages and numbers in long, close columns, but they were not part of my experience. I could prove that the other America existed, but I had never been there.

My response was not accidental. It was typical of what is happening to an entire society, and it reflects profound social changes in this nation. The other America, the America of poverty, is hidden today in a way that it never was before. Its millions are socially invisible to the rest of us. No wonder that so many misinterpreted Galbraith's title and assumed that "the affluent society" meant that everyone had a decent standard of life. The misinterpretation was true as far as the actual day-to-day lives of two-thirds of the nation were concerned. Thus, one must begin a description of the other America by understanding why we do not see it.

There are perennial reasons that make the other America an invisible land.

Poverty is often off the beaten track. It always has been. The ordinary tourist never left the main highway, and today he rides interstate turnpikes. He does not go into the valleys of Pennsylvania where the towns look like movie sets of Wales in the thirties. He does not see the company houses in rows, the rutted roads (the poor always have bad roads whether they live in the city, in towns, or on farms), and everything is black and dirty. And even if he were to pass through such a place by accident, the tourist would not meet the unemployed men in the bar or the women coming home from a runaway sweatshop.

Then, too, beauty and myths are perennial masks of poverty. The traveler comes to the Appalachians in the lovely season. He sees the hills, the streams, the foliage—but not the poor. Or perhaps he looks at a run-down mountain house and, remembering Rousseau. rather than seeing with his eyes, decides that "those people" are truly fortunate to be living the way they are and that they are lucky to be exempt from the strains and tensions of the middle class. The only problem is that "those people," the quaint inhabitants of those hills, are under-educated, underprivileged, lack medical care, and are in the process of being forced from the land into a life in the cities, where they are misfits.

These are normal and obvious causes of the invisibility of the poor. They operated a generation ago; they will be functioning a generation hence. It is more important to understand that the very development of American society is creating a new kind of blindness about poverty. The poor are increasingly slipping out of the very experience and consciousness of the nation.

If the middle class never did like ugliness and poverty, it was at least aware of them. "Across the tracks" was not a very long way to go. There were forays into the slums at Christmas time; there were charitable organizations that brought contact with the poor. Occasionally, almost everyone passed through the Negro ghetto or the blocks of tenements, if only to get downtown to work or to entertainment.

Now the American city has been transformed. The poor still inhabit the miserable housing in the central area, but they are increasingly isolated from contact with, or sight of, anybody else. Middle-class women coming in from Suburbia on a rare trip may catch the merest glimpse of the other America on the way to an evening at the theater, but their children are segregated in suburban schools. The business or professional man may drive along the fringes of slums in a car or bus, but it is not an important experience to him. The failures, the unskilled, the disabled, the aged, and the minorities are right there, across the tracks, where they have always been. But hardly anyone else is.

In short, the very development of the American city has removed poverty from the living, emotional experience of millions upon millions of middle-class Americans. Living out in the suburbs, it is easy to assume that ours is, indeed, an affluent society.

This new segregation of poverty is compounded by a well-meaning ignorance. A good many concerned and sympathetic Americans are aware that there is much discussion of urban renewal. Suddenly, driving through the city, they notice that a familiar slum has been torn down and that there are towering, modern buildings where once there had been tenements or hovels. There is a warm feeling of satisfaction, of pride in the way things are working out: the poor, it is obvious, are being taken care of.

The irony in this . . . is that the truth is nearly the exact opposite to the impression. The total impact of the various housing programs in postwar America has been to squeeze more and more people into existing slums. More often than not, the modern apartment in a towering building rents at $40 a room or more. For, during the past decade and a half, there has been more subsidization of middle- and upper-income housing than there has been of housing for the poor.

Clothes make the poor invisible too: America has the best-dressed poverty the world has ever known. For a variety of reasons, the benefits of mass production have been spread much more evenly in this area than in many others. It is much easier in the United States to be decently dressed than it is to be decently housed, fed, or doctored. Even people with terribly depressed incomes can look prosperous.

This is an extremely important factor in defining our emotional and existential ignorance of poverty. In Detroit the existence of social classes became much more difficult to discern the day the companies put lockers in the plants. From that moment on, one did not see men in work clothes on the way to the factory, but citizens in slacks and white shirts. This process has been magnified with the poor throughout the country. There are tens of thousands of Americans in the big cities who are wearing shoes, perhaps even a stylishly cut suit or dress, and yet are hungry. It is not a matter of planning, though it almost seems as if the affluent society had given out costumes to the poor so that they would not offend the rest of society with the sight of rags.

Then, many of the poor are the wrong age to be seen. A good number of them (over 8,000,000) are sixty-five years of age or better; an even larger number are under eighteen. The aged members of the other America are often sick, and they cannot move. Another group of them live out their lives in loneliness and frustration: they sit in rented rooms, or else they stay close to a house in a neighborhood that has completely changed from the old days. Indeed, one of the worst aspects of poverty among the aged is that these people are out of sight and out of mind, and alone.

The young are somewhat more visible, yet they too stay close to their neighborhoods. Sometimes they advertise their poverty through a lurid tabloid story about a gang killing. But generally they do not disturb the quiet streets of the middle class.

And finally, the poor are politically invisible. It is one of the cruelest ironies of social life in advanced countries that the dispossessed at the bottom of society are unable to speak for themselves. The people of the other America do not, by far and large, belong to unions, to fraternal organizations, or to political parties. They are without lobbies of their own; they put forward no legislative program. As a group, they are atomized. They have no face; they have no voice.

Thus, there is not even a cynical political motive for caring about the poor, as in the old days. Because the slums are no longer centers of powerful political organizations, the politicians need not really care about their inhabitants. The slums are no longer visible to the middle class, so much of the idealistic urge to fight for those who need help is gone. Only the social agencies have a really direct involvement with the other America, and they are without any great political power.

To the extent that the poor have a spokesman in American life, that role is played by the labor movement. The unions have their own particular idealism, an ideology of concern. More than that, they realize that the existence of a reservoir of cheap, unorganized labor is a menace to wages and working conditions throughout the entire economy. Thus, many union legislative proposals—to extend the coverage of minimum wage and social security, to organize migrant farm laborers—articulate the needs of the poor.

That the poor are invisible is one of the most important things about them. They are not simply neglected and forgotten as in the old rhetoric of reform; what is much worse, they are not seen. . . .*

II

There are mighty historical and economic forces that keep the poor down; and there are human beings who help out in this grim business, many of them unwittingly. There are sociological and political reasons why poverty is not seen; and there are misconceptions and prejudices that literally blind the eyes. The latter must be understood if anyone is to make the necessary act of intellect and will so that the poor can be noticed.

Here is the most familiar version of social blindness: "The poor are that way because they are afraid of work. And anyway they all have big cars. If they were like me (or my father or my grandfather), they could pay their own way. But they prefer to live on the dole and cheat the taxpayers."

This theory, usually thought of as a virtuous and moral statement, is one of the means of making it impossible for the poor ever to pay their way. There are, one must assume, citizens of the other America who choose impoverishment out of fear of work (though, writing it down, I really do not believe it). But the real explanation of why the poor are where they are is that they made the mistake of being born to the wrong parents, in the wrong section of the country, in the wrong industry, or in the wrong racial or ethnic group. Once that mistake has been made, they could have been paragons of will and morality, but most of them would never even have had a chance to get out of the other America.

There are two important ways of saying this: The poor are caught in a vicious circle; or, The poor live in a culture of poverty.

In a sense, one might define the contemporary poor in the United States as those who, for reasons beyond their control, cannot help themselves. All the most decisive factors making for opportunity and advance are against them. They are born going downward, and most of them stay down. They are victims whose lives are endlessly blown round and round the other America.

Here is one of the most familiar forms of the vicious circle of poverty. The poor get sick more than anyone else in the society. That is because they live in slums, jammed together under unhygienic conditions; they have inadequate diets, and cannot get decent medical care. When they become sick, they are sick longer than any other group in the society. Because they are sick more often and longer than anyone else, they lose wages and work, and find it difficult to hold a steady job. And because of this, they cannot pay for good housing, for a nutritious diet, for doctors. At any given point in the circle, particularly when there is a major illness, their prospect is to move to an even lower level and to begin the cycle, round and round, toward even more suffering.

Editor's note: Since Harrington wrote this paragraph in 1962, the poor have become much more visible, especially if they are urban blacks. This increased visibility has come primarily from the press and television, however, rather than from direct experience. Since the media emphasizes the dramatic and the violent, such visibility may have increased the average American's fears rather than his understanding.

This is only one example of the vicious circle. Each group in the other America has its own particular version of the experience, and these will be detailed throughout this book. But the pattern, whatever its variations, is basic to the other America.

The individual cannot usually break out of this vicious circle. Neither can the group, for it lacks the social energy and political strength to turn its misery into a cause.* Only the larger society, with its help and resources, can really make it possible for these people to help themselves. Yet those who could make the difference too often refuse to act because of their ignorant, smug moralisms. They view the effects of poverty—above all, the warping of the will and spirit that is a consequence of being poor—as choices. Understanding the vicious circle is an important step in breaking down this prejudice.

There is an even richer way of describing this same, general idea: Poverty in the United States is a culture, an institution, a way of life.

There is a famous anecdote about Ernest Hemingway and F. Scott Fitzgerald. Fitzgerald is reported to have remarked to Hemingway, "The rich are different." And Hemingway replied, "Yes, they have money." Fitzgerald had much the better of the exchange. He understood that being rich was not a simple fact, like a large bank account, but a way of looking at reality, a series of attitudes, a special type of life. If this is true of the rich, it is ten times truer of the poor. Everything about them, from the condition of their teeth to the way in which they love, is suffused and permeated by the fact of their poverty. And this is sometimes a hard idea for a Hemingway-like middle-class America to comprehend.

The family structure of the poor, for instance, is different from that of the rest of the society. There are more homes without a father, there are less marriage, more early pregnancy and, if Kinsey's statistical findings can be used, markedly different attitudes toward sex. As a result of this, to take but one consequence

of the fact, hundreds of thousands, and perhaps millions, of children in the other America never know stability and "normal" affection.

Or perhaps the policeman is an even better example. For the middle class, the police protect property, give directions, and help old ladies. For the urban poor, the police are those who arrest you. In almost any slum there is a vast conspiracy against the forces of law and order. If someone approaches asking for a person, no one there will have heard of him, even if he lives next door. The outsider is "cop," bill collector, investigator (and, in the Negro ghetto, most dramatically, he is "the Man").

While writing this book, I was arrested for participation in a civil-rights demonstration. A brief experience of a night in a cell made an abstraction personal and immediate: the city jail is one of the basic institutions of the other America. Almost everyone whom I encountered in the "tank" was poor: skid-row whites, Negroes, Puerto Ricans. Their poverty was an incitement to arrest in the first place. (A policeman will be much more careful with a well-dressed, obviously educated man who might have political connections than he will with someone who is poor.) They did not have money for bail or for lawyers. And, perhaps most important, they waited their arraignment with stolidity, in a mood of passive acceptance. They expected the worst, and they probably got it.

There is, in short, a language of the poor, a psychology of the poor, a world view of the poor. To be impoverished is to be an internal alien, to grow up in a culture that is radically different from the one that dominates the society. The poor can be described statistically; they can be analyzed as a group. But they need a novelist as well as a sociologist if we are to see them. They need an American Dickens to record the smell and texture and quality of their lives. The cycles and trends, the massive forces, must be seen as affecting persons who talk and think differently.*

Editor's note: This statement appears to be less true today for blacks, Indians, and some minority groups. However, it still applies with full force for other groups, such as the rural or elderly poor.

Editor's note: For an excellent first-hand account of poverty among urban blacks, see Elliot Liebow, *Tally's Corner* (Little, Brown & Company, 1967).

30. The Poor Ye Need Not Have with You: Lessons from the War on Poverty

Robert A. Levine

The relative stress on the two objectives—antipoverty and equal opportunity—is not a sterile intellectual question, it is crucial for future program direction, for the United States is gripped by both these closely related social problems. The problems of poverty are those of low incomes at the bottom end of the income distribution, those families and individuals whose income is so low that they cannot live a minimally decent life by American standards. The problems range from literal starvation, as has been adequately demonstrated a number of times, up through the misery of trying to exist on the welfare minimum. The programs to attack these problems are those programs designed to establish a floor under the American standard of living.

The problems of unequal opportunity are problems of the ceiling rather than the floor, and ceilings exist on the opportunities of those members of minority groups who are above the poverty line as well as on those below. With the possible exceptions of American Indians and migrant farm laborers, no identifiable group of Americans has a majority or anywhere near a majority of its members in the kind of income poverty defined by the Orshansky line.* Yet, for

Editor's note: The poverty definition developed by Orshansky was the one adopted by the U.S. government. It is discussed in some detail earlier in Levine's book.

several groups, of which Negroes are by far the largest and most obvious, a disproportionately large number of people are in poverty and a disproportionately small, even tiny, number have reached a level where their opportunities are close to equal with those open to the majority group.

The problems of poverty and unequal opportunity overlap. They are so closely related that it is difficult to see either how the floor can be raised without considerable upward movement for the ceiling or how the ceiling can be raised without also raising the floor. The factors that restrict opportunity for the low-income poor (largely present discrimination and the legacy of past discrimination) restrict it all along the line, for the near-poor as well and even for the better-off. It is difficult to see how discriminatory patterns can be broken or programs to compensate for the results of previous discrimination can be instituted for the poor alone. Indeed, attempts to do this have hurt OEO programs.

But even if it were possible to set up compensatory programs restricted to the poor, it seems very likely that antipoverty and equal opportunity programs will be more successful if each is backed up by the other. On the one hand, "inferiority" (both the *feeling* of group failure and the real lack of anybody on the top to give a helping hand) means that the poor individual has a double burden if he is a member of the poor group. Typically, the less capable members of more successful groups, be they WASPs, Jews, or Japanese Americans, have been helped by those at the top. But for blacks, Indians, and other less successful groups, there are few at the top to help. On the other hand, the welfare population at the bottom end of the poor group exerts an inevitable drag on those in the middle and at the top who might as individuals be on their way up. It does not help a black businessmen if the bank looks at him as a member of a bad-risk "welfare class."

Since its start, the ambivalence between the antipoverty and equal opportunity objectives has affected the programs of the War on Poverty. The low-income-raising objective has been dominant, but it has been substantially modified by the other. . . .

In deciding which of the dual objectives the existing programs are best designed for, it is useful to look at four kinds of programs, based on the program-budgeting categories used by OEO. . . . The four categories are Manpower programs, Education, Community Action, and Income Maintenance.

Among the Manpower programs, it is quite clear that the implicit opportunity objective has been central and that even though the programs have for the most part been limited to individuals and families below the Orshansky poverty line, the program benefits have been of a type needed by individuals in low-opportunity groups whether or not they came from families below the Orshansky line. The primary function of the Job Corps, for example, is the education and training of youth so that they may be capable of living an economic life above that of casual labor, to which so many untrained Negroes, Mexican Americans, Puerto Ricans, and rural Southern whites have been doomed. Although low income has been one criterion for youth entering Job Corps, it was one among a set that was designed to distinguish those most liable to a casual low-opportunity, low-income future: poor school performance, broken homes, and so forth. Similarly, the JOBS Program for on-the-job training of adults by private industry has aimed at placing these adults in entry level jobs from which they could progress toward opportunities calling for more and more skill. Most adults, certainly most men, are capable without training of earning incomes above the poverty line in casual or dead-end jobs (unless the poverty line

for the particular family is quite high because the family is large). But future opportunities for janitors and dishwashers are limited, and the objective of the JOBS Program is to bring adults into the blue- and white-collar mainstream of American industry with all the opportunity for advancement implied. This is an objective for the Orshansky poor, but it is an objective shared by many members of low-opportunity groups who are nonetheless above the Orshansky line. . . .

The difficulties with attempting to associate Manpower programs too closely with low-income antipoverty goals are indicated by the fate of the Work Experience Program designed under the original Economic Opportunity Act as a work and training program for adults in categories eligible for Public Assistance. The intended beneficiaries of this program, those eligible for Public Assistance, were among the poorest of the poor and thus the neediest from the low-income standpoint. But need and ability to benefit from training and job opportunities are measured on different scales; some very low-income people are trainable, some not. Being on Public Assistance did not make Work Experience enrollees trainable, and, in fact, the program failed rather miserably because it tried to use the technique of training for job opportunity on individuals whose sole common characteristic was low income rather than ability to succeed in training.

What is true of Manpower programs is also true of Education. The objective of antipoverty education programs is obviously not any immediate change in the income of children in the programs. It is to get them enough education so that they will be able to extend their future education and training to the point where they can hold down decent jobs when they reach working age. This is an opportunity objective par excellence, and it is thus not easy to justify providing Head Start and similar education programs only to children whose family incomes are below the poverty line. The liability to failure in education extends to most of the children in slum areas, and with this liability goes unequal opportunity and disproportionate likelihood of future poverty. Although it seems likely that those at the upper end of the income distribution in the ghetto areas are more likely to make it through the education system, the existing poverty line is too low a cutoff to distinguish those with greatest likelihood of failure. Unlike the OEO programs such as Head Start, Title I of the Elementary and Secondary Education Act recognizes this distinction between poverty and opportunity by providing aid to *schools* with large numbers of low-income children rather than providing the aid to the children themselves. There are many other problems with Title I, but at least it does seem to make the proper distinctions among the objectives of educational programs and their recipients.

Community Action programs are for the most part group-oriented, and as such they tend to conform fairly closely to the group opportunity objectives rather than the low-income poverty objectives. Community Action brings services and organizational help to the geographical and ethnic groups among whom the programs are located. And the help is typically help not for the poor alone but for the black, the Spanish-speaking, the mountain people, and so on.

Some of the services delivered by Community Action, however, are directly related to income, and for these services income lines have a reasonable rationale. That is, health services and legal services are to a great extent the equivalent of income transfer payments except that they are transfers in kind rather than in cash. For this reason, it makes a good deal of sense to deliver them only to those who need the transfer because their incomes are too low to purchase the services directly on the open market. It should be noted that in practice the guidelines for eligibility under OEO health programs in particular are not the Orshansky lines but are locally determined guidelines for medical indigence.

Leaving Income Maintenance aside for the moment, it would thus seem that the bulk of the programs in the other three categories of the War on Poverty are of a type that can aid those with low opportunity for the future whether or not their current incomes are low. Given this situation, it becomes an easy step to say that income eligibility standards ought to be lifted completely from opportunity programs in OEO and in other government agencies. Yet that would still be premature. The lessons of the farm programs of the 1930s and the housing programs of the 1950s must still be heeded. If the new programs cease being programs exclusively for the poor and become instead programs for Negroes, Mexican Americans, and various groups of whites, it seems very likely that the chief beneficiaries may not

be those somewhat above the poverty line who lack opportunity but those a good deal above it who need help far less than their more deprived brethren. . . .

What we end up with is not a simple situation. Many of the existing OEO programs and the opportunity programs of allied agencies such as the Departments of Labor and Health, Education and Welfare are more effective in opening up opportunity for those above and below the poverty line who suffer from unequal opportunity than they are in concentrating solely on the income inequities suffered by those at the bottom of the income distribution. Yet were these programs not aimed at the low-income poor, they would be likely to miss even the near-poor targets most able to benefit from opportunity. Furthermore, were the programs not aimed at the low-income poor, it is difficult to see what help would be available to these truly poor people under current programs, and considerations of equity do argue that these are still the priority people in need. Indeed, the political pressures have been strong all along to put members of groups like the aged poor into programs that are quite inappropriate—simply because these are the only programs around.

Add to these difficulties the fact that the designers of the War on Poverty were not at all clear, either implicitly or explicitly, in distinguishing between the opportunity and antipoverty objectives of the programs and add further into this witches' brew the difficulty of solving either problem, poverty or unequal opportunity, without solving the other first; and the question of what our immediate objective should be becomes a very difficult one indeed. Some quick solutions are possible. It would seem a reasonable idea, for instance, to charge those above the poverty line a fee for high-cost services, with the fee being higher for those with incomes further above the line. This solution meliorates some situations while still leaving the basic question unanswered.

The question of what our immediate objective should be cannot be answered on the basis of "what is right" because both objectives are noble ones. It is not a question that can be answered on the basis of the intentions of the framers because they did not sort out their own intentions. Perhaps there is a key, however, in the fact that although we really do not yet know how finally to solve the unequal opportunity problem, we do know how to end low-income poverty.

Try as we may, we cannot quickly end unequal opportunity because we cannot abolish discrimination overnight, and discrimination, racial and otherwise, underlies most of the inequality under discussion. Even if we could abolish existing discrimination, it would take a generation to abolish the effects of past discrimination—starting with unequal education and going through all the other restrictions that make people today what they are today with the past irretrievable. Creating a situation in which every child born in the United States really has an equal chance at life, liberty, and the pursuit of happiness (or at least where unequal chances are randomized racially) is still not within reach of our action possibilities or even our knowledge.

A solution to low-income poverty, however, is. Separating low-income poverty from the opportunity objectives, we could quite easily end poverty at any time simply by providing those who are poor with enough money so that they are no longer poor, whatever the current poverty line is. Income maintenance is not conceptually difficult, and although which particular program is best is still subject to considerable debate, the feasibility of providing enough income to the poor to end low-income poverty is beyond debate. The aggregate amount of money that would have to be given to the now poor in order to bring them above the poverty line is less than $10 billion. If the income maintenance device adopted were a Negative Income Tax that, in order to fill entirely the poverty income gap, would have to provide substantial income to the near-poor (which is not a bad idea anyhow), the total cost would be on the order of $20 billion a year.[1] Adding in the cost to national production consequent upon the disincentive effects of such a large program, the total cost might be $30 billion a year. I am not proposing such a large program immediately, and if done gradually it would never need to reach these levels. But it should be noted that even $30 billion is about 3 percent of Gross National Product, it is less than a year's growth of GNP, and it is only about two years' growth of federal income taxes at present rates.

For this price, we could take care of the more than 50 percent of the poor who have

virtually no earnings opportunities anyhow—those in families with aged, disabled, and female heads—and we could solve the low-income problem in the United States. And we could make the opportunity programs in manpower, education, and Community Action fields far more effective because we could direct them at those most likely to benefit, both poor and nonpoor, having satisfied the equity requirements of the antipoverty objective through income maintenance. It seems to me that this is the only way to solve the problem of priority between the antipoverty and equal opportunity objectives. Talmudic arguments about which "ought" to go first are very sterile indeed.

There is one more set of considerations. Once we have admitted another program objective aside from ending low-income poverty, we may have opened the door for a whole host of more or less related objectives; the temptation to use the antipoverty rubric to cover *all* the social ills of the United States has never been completely absent. For example, both the antipoverty and the equal opportunity objectives concern the inequities imposed on *people*, but some tendency exists to confuse poor people with poor areas. That is, the confusion is frequently made between antipoverty programs and the set of economic development programs, primarily rural, that attempt to distribute the economic growth of the United States a little more equally geographically than it would otherwise be. These are not primarily programs to end poverty among people as it is meant here. Nor are they necessarily very closely related. . . . Typically, the major effect of such programs has been to prevent middle-class high school graduates from moving out in search of jobs, and frequently even to bring into the area trained and educated people not at all poor.

Similarly, some other programs with objectives sometimes thought to be similar to the antipoverty objectives really turn out in practice not to be very closely related. Programs that attempt to raise the incomes of all members of a particular group frequently fall into this category. They follow this syllogism:

A lot of old folk (children) are poor.

We want to help the poor.

Therefore we ought to give money to old folk (children).

The logic here is less than rigorous. It has been demonstrated time and time again, for example,

[1]If it were a Family Allowance, with equal sums going to the poor, near-poor, middle class, and well-off, the cost would be more than $70 billion.

that raising overall levels of Social Security is a very ineffective way of helping the aged poor; 80 percent of Social Security increases now go to the nonpoor.[2] Indeed even programs that raise the *minimum* payment levels under Social Security are inefficient in helping the income of the poor because many of those at the mini-

mum payment level would be poor if Social Security were the only pension they received, but in fact they receive other pensions such as Civil Service. . . .

Nonetheless, unlike poor areas, nonpoor old folks, and well-off kids, the problem of unequal opportunity is inextricably intertwined with the problem of low-income poverty in the United States. It is intertwined in concept, it is intertwined in current practice, it is intertwined in political and intellectual history. It is only by understanding this connection that the anti-poverty efforts of the last few years can be understood. I believe that it is only by breaking the connection and solving the poverty problem once and for all through income maintenance that the other equally deep problem can begin to be solved.

---

[2]The more you give to Social Security, the less would go to the poor. A 50 percent across-the-board increase in Social Security would net the poor about 12 cents on the dollar. A small increase now would benefit the poor about 20 percent. The larger the increase, the less the poor will benefit. See *Income and Benefit Programs,* Report of the Program Analysis Group on Income and Benefit Programs (U.S. Department of Health, Education and Welfare 1966-2), Table III-4, p. 25.

31. On Improving the Economic Status of the Negro

James Tobin

The economic plight of individuals, Negroes and whites alike, can always be attributed to specific handicaps and circumstances: discrimination, immobility, lack of education and experience, ill health, weak motivation, poor neighborhood, large family size, burdensome family responsibilities. Such diagnoses suggest a host of specific remedies, some in the domain of civil rights, others in the war on poverty. Important as these remedies are, there is a danger that the diagnoses are myopic. They explain why certain individuals rather than others suffer from the economic maladies of the time. They do not explain why the over-all incidence of the maladies varies dramatically from time to time—for example, why personal attributes which seemed to doom a man to unemployment in 1932 or even in 1954 or 1961 did not so handicap him in 1944 or 1951 or 1956.

Public health measures to improve the environment are often more productive in conquering disease than a succession of individual treatments. Malaria was conquered by oiling and draining swamps, not by quinine. The analogy holds for economic maladies. Unless the global incidence of these misfortunes can be diminished, every individual problem successfully solved will be replaced by a similar problem somewhere else. That is why an economist is led to emphasize the importance of the over-all economic climate. . . .

National prosperity and economic growth are still powerful engines for improving the economic status of Negroes. They are not doing enough and they are not doing it fast enough. There is ample room for a focused attack on the specific sources of Negro poverty. But a favorable over-all economic climate is a necessary condition for the global success—as distinguished from success in individual cases—of specific efforts to remedy the handicaps associated with Negro poverty.

THE IMPORTANCE OF A TIGHT LABOR MARKET

. . . The most important dimension of the over-all economic climate is the tightness of the labor market. In a tight labor market unemployment is low and short in duration, and job vacancies are plentiful. People who stand at the end of the hiring line and the top of the layoff list have the most to gain from a tight labor market. It is not surprising that the position of Negroes relative to that of whites improves in a tight labor market and declines in a slack market. Unemployment itself is only one way in which a slack labor market hurts Negroes and other disadvantaged groups, and the gains from reduction in unemployment are by no means confined to the employment of persons counted as unemployed.[1] A tight labor market means not just jobs, but better jobs, longer hours, higher wages. Because of the heavy demands for labor during the second world war and its economic aftermath, Negroes made dramatic relative gains between 1940 and 1950. Unfortunately this momentum has not been maintained, and the blame falls largely on the weakness of labor markets since 1957.[2]

[1]Galloway shows that postwar experience suggests that, other things equal, every point by which unemployment is diminished lowers the national incidence of poverty by .5 per cent of itself. And this does not include the effects of the accompanying increase in median family income, which would be of the order of 3 per cent and reduce the poverty fraction another 1.8 per cent.

[2]For lack of comparable nationwide income data, the only way to gauge the progress of Negroes relative to whites over long periods of time is to compare their distributions among occupations. A measure of the occupational position of a group can be constructed from decennial Census data by weighting the proportions of the group in each occupation by the average income of the occupation. The ratio of this measure for Negroes to the same measure for whites is an index of the relative occupational position of Negroes. Such calculations were originally made by Gary Becker, *The Economics of Discrimination* (Chicago, 1957). They have recently been refined and brought up to date by Dale Hiestand, *Economic Growth and Employment Opportunities for Minorities,* (New York, 1964), p. 53. Hiestand's results are as follows:

Occupational position of Negroes relative to whites:

	1910	1920	1930	1940	1950	1960
Male	78.0	78.1	78.2	77.5	81.4	82.1
Female	78.0	71.3	74.8	76.8	81.6	84.3

The figures show that Negro men lost ground in the Great Depression, that they gained sharply in the nineteen forties, and that their progress almost ceased in the nineteen fifties. Negro women show a rising secular trend since the nineteen twenties, but their gains too were greater in the tight labor markets of the nineteen forties than in the nineteen thirties or nineteen fifties.

Several cautions should be borne in mind in interpreting these figures: (1) Much of the relative occupational

The shortage of jobs has hit Negro men particularly hard and thus has contributed mightily to the ordeal of the Negro family, which is in turn the cumulative source of so many other social disorders.[3] The unemployment rate of Negro men is more sensitive than that of Negro women to the national rate. Since 1949 Negro women have gained in median income relative to white women, but Negro men have lost ground to white males.[4] In a society which stresses breadwinning as the expected role of the mature male and occupational achievement as his proper goal, failure to find and to keep work is devastating to the man's self-respect and family status. Matriarchy is in any case a strong tradition in Negro society, and the man's role is further downgraded when the family must and can depend on the woman for its livelihood. It is very important to increase the proportion of Negro children who grow up in stable families with two parents. Without a strong labor market it will be extremely difficult to do so.

Unemployment. It is well known that Negro unemployment rates are multiples of the general unemployment rate. This fact reflects

progress of Negroes is due to massive migration from agriculture to occupations of much higher average income. When the over-all relative index nevertheless does not move, as in the nineteen fifties, the position of Negroes in non-agricultural occupations has declined. (2) Since the figures include unemployed as well as employed persons and Negroes are more sensitive to unemployment, the occupational index understates their progress when unemployment declined (1940-50) and overstates it when unemployment rose (1930-40 and 1950-60). (3) Within any Census occupational category, Negroes earn less than whites. So the absolute level of the index overstates the Negro's relative position. Moreover, this overstatement is probably greater in Census years of relatively slack labor markets, like 1940 and 1960, than in other years.

The finding that labor market conditions arrested the progress of Negro men is confirmed by income and unemployment data analyzed by Alan B. Batchelder, "Decline in the Relative Income of Negro Men," *Quarterly Journal of Economics,* Vol. 78 (November, 1964), pp. 525-548.

[3]This is emphasized by Daniel Patrick Moynihan in his contribution to this volume.

[4]Differences between Negro men and women with respect to unemployment and income progress are reported and analyzed by Alan Batchelder, *op. cit.*

both the lesser skills, seniority, and experience of Negroes and employers' discrimination against Negroes. These conditions are a deplorable reflection on American society, but as long as they exist Negroes suffer much more than others from a general increase in unemployment and gain much more from a general reduction. A rule of thumb is that changes in the nonwhite unemployment rate are twice those in the white rate. The rule works both ways. Nonwhite unemployment went from 4.1 per cent in 1953, a tight labor market year, to 12.5 per cent in 1961, while the white rate rose from 2.3 per cent to 6 per cent. Since then, the Negro rate has declined by 2.4 per cent, the white rate by 1.2.

Even the Negro teenage unemployment rate shows some sensitivity to general economic conditions. Recession increased it from 15 per cent in 1955-56 to 25 per cent in 1958. It decreased to 22 per cent in 1960 but rose to 23 per cent in 1963; since then it has declined somewhat. Teenage unemployment is abnormally high now, relative to that of other age groups, because the wave of postwar babies is coming into the labor market. Most of them, especially the Negroes, are crowding the end of the hiring line. But their prospects for getting jobs are no less dependent on general labor market conditions.

Part-time work. Persons who are involuntarily forced to work part time instead of full time are not counted as unemployed, but their number goes up and down with the unemployment rate. Just as Negroes bear a disproportionate share of unemployment, they bear more than their share of involuntary part-time unemployment.[5] A tight labor market will not only employ more Negroes; it will also give more of those who are employed full-time jobs. In both respects, it will reduce disparities between whites and Negroes.

Labor-force participation. In a tight market, of which a low unemployment rate is a barometer, the labor force itself is larger. Job opportunities draw into the labor force individuals who, simply because the prospects were dim, did not previously regard themselves as seeking work and were therefore not enumerated as unemployed. For the economy as a whole, it appears that an expansion of job opportunities enough to reduce unemployment by one worker will bring another worker into the labor force.

This phenomenon is important for many Negro families. Statistically, their poverty now appears to be due more often to the lack of a breadwinner in the labor force than to unemployment.[6] But in a tight labor market many members of these families, including families now on public assistance, would be drawn into employment. Labor-force participation rates are roughly 2 per cent lower for nonwhite men than for white men, and the disparity increases in years of slack labor markets.[7] The story is different for women. Negro women have always been in the labor force to a much greater extent than white women. A real improvement in the economic status of Negro men and in the stability of Negro families would probably lead to a reduction in labor-force participation by Negro women. But for teenagers, participation rates for Negroes are not so high as for whites; and for women twenty to twenty-four they are about the same. These relatively low rates are undoubtedly due less to voluntary choice than to the same lack of job opportunities that produces phenomenally high unemployment rates for young Negro women.

Duration of unemployment. In a tight labor market, such unemployment as does exist is likely to be of short duration. Short-term unemployment is less damaging to the economic welfare of the unemployed. More will have earned and fewer will have exhausted private and public unemployment benefits. In 1953 when the over-all unemployment rate was 2.9 per cent, only 4 per cent of the unemployed were out of work for longer than twenty-six weeks and only 11 per cent for longer than fifteen weeks. In contrast, the unemployment rate in 1961 was 6.7 per cent; and of the unemployed in that year, 17 per cent were out of work for longer than twenty-six weeks and 32 per cent for longer than fifteen weeks. Between the first quarter of 1964 and the first quarter of 1965, overall unemploy-

[5]Figures are given in other papers in this volume: see, for example, the articles by Rashi Fein and Daniel Patrick Moynihan.

[6]In 34 per cent of poor Negro families, the head is not in the labor force; in 6 per cent, the head is unemployed. These figures relate to the Social Security Administration's "economy-level" poverty index.

[7]See *Manpower Report of the President* (March, 1964), Table A-3, p. 197.

ment fell 11 percent, while unemployment extending beyond half a year was lowered by 22 per cent.

. . . One more dimension of society's inequity to the Negro is that an unemployed Negro is more likely to stay unemployed than an unemployed white. But his figures also show that Negroes share in the reduction of long-term unemployment accompanying economic expansion.

Migration from agriculture. A tight labor market draws the surplus rural population to higher paying non-agricultural jobs. Southern Negroes are a large part of this surplus rural population. Migration is the only hope for improving their lot, or their children's. In spite of the vast migration of past decades, there are still about 775,000 Negroes, 11 per cent of the Negro labor force of the country, who depend on the land for their living and that of their families.[8] Almost a half million live in the South, and almost all of them are poor.

Migration from agriculture and from the South is the Negroes' historic path toward economic improvement and equality. It is a smooth path for Negroes and for the urban communities to which they move only if there is a strong demand for labor in towns and cities North and South. In the 1940's the number of Negro farmers and farm laborers in the nation fell by 450,000 and one and a half million Negroes (net) left the South. This was the great decade of Negro economic advance. In the 1950's the same occupational and geographical migration continued undiminished. The movement to higher-income occupations and locations should have raised the relative economic status of Negroes. But in the 1950's Negroes were moving into increasingly weak job markets. Too often disguised unemployment in the countryside was simply transformed into enumerated unemployment, and rural poverty into urban poverty.[9]

Quality of jobs. In a slack labor market, employers can pick and choose, both in recruit-

[8]Hiestand, *op. cit.,* Table I, pp. 7-9.

[9]Batchelder, *op. cit.,* shows that the incomes of Negro men declined relative to those of white men in every region of the country. For the country as a whole, nevertheless, the median income of Negro men stayed close to half that of white men. The reason is that migration from the South, where the Negro-white income ratio is particularly low, just offset the declines in the regional ratios.

ing and in promoting. They exaggerate the skill, education, and experience requirements of their jobs. They use diplomas, or color, or personal histories as convenient screening devices. In a tight market, they are forced to be realistic, to tailor job specifications to the available supply, and to give on-the-job training. They recruit and train applicants whom they would otherwise screen out, and they upgrade employees whom they would in slack times consign to low-wage, low-skill, and part-time jobs.

Wartime and other experience shows that job requirements are adjustable and that men and women are trainable. It is only in slack times that people worry about a mismatch between supposedly rigid occupational requirements and supposedly unchangeable qualifications of the labor force. As already noted, the relative status of Negroes improves in a tight labor market not only in respect to unemployment, but also in respect to wages and occupations.

Cyclical fluctuation. Sustaining a high demand for labor is important. The in-and-out status of the Negro in the business cycle damages his long-term position because periodic unemployment robs him of experience and seniority.

Restrictive practices. A slack labor market probably accentuates the discriminatory and protectionist proclivities of certain crafts and unions. When jobs are scarce, opening the door to Negroes is a real threat. Of course prosperity will not automatically dissolve the barriers, but it will make it more difficult to oppose efforts to do so.

I conclude that the single most important step the nation could take to improve the economic position of the Negro is to operate the economy steadily at a low rate of unemployment. We cannot expect to restore the labor market conditions of the second world war, and we do not need to. In the years 1951-1953, unemployment was roughly 3 per cent, teenage unemployment around 7 per cent, Negro unemployment about 4.5 per cent, long-term unemployment negligible. In the years 1955-57, general unemployment was roughly 4 per cent, and the other measures correspondingly higher. Four per cent is the official target of the Kennedy-Johnson administration. It has not been achieved since 1957. Reaching and maintaining 4 per cent would be a tremendous improvement over the performance of the last eight years.

But we should not stop there; the society and the Negro can benefit immensely from tightening the labor market still further, to 3.5 or 3 per cent unemployment. The administration itself has never defined 4 per cent as anything other than an "interim" target. . . .

INCREASING THE EARNING CAPACITY OF NEGROES

Given the proper over-all economic climate, in particular a steadily tight labor market, the Negro's economic condition can be expected to improve, indeed to improve dramatically. But not fast enough. Not as fast as his aspirations or as the aspirations he has taught the rest of us to have for him. What else can be done? This question is being answered in detail by experts elsewhere in this volume. I shall confine myself to a few comments and suggestions that occur to a general economist.

Even in a tight labor market, the Negro's relative status will suffer both from current discrimination and from his lower earning capacity, the result of inferior acquired skill. In a real sense both factors reflect discrimination, since the Negro's handicaps in earning capacity are the residue of decades of discrimination in education and employment. Nevertheless for both analysis and policy it is useful to distinguish the two.

Discrimination means that the Negro is denied access to certain markets where he might sell his labor, and to certain markets where he might purchase goods and services. Elementary application of "supply and demand" makes it clear that these restrictions are bound to result in his selling his labor for less and buying his livelihood for more than if these barriers did not exist. If Negro women can be clerks only in certain stores, whose storekeepers will not need to pay them so much as they pay whites. If Negroes can live only in certain houses, the prices and rents they have to pay will be high for the quality of accommodation provided.

Successful elimination of discrimination is not only important in itself but will also have substantial economic benefits. Since residential segregation is the key to so much else and so difficult to eliminate by legal fiat alone, the power of the purse should be unstintingly used. I see no reason that the expenditure of funds for this purpose should be confined to new construction. Why not establish private or semi-public revolving funds to purchase, for resale or rental on a desegregated basis, strategically located existing structures as they become available?

The effects of past discrimination will take much longer to eradicate. The sins against the fathers are visited on the children. They are deprived of the intellectual and social capital which in our society is supposed to be transmitted in the family and the home. We have only begun to realize how difficult it is to make up for this deprivation by formal schooling, even when we try. And we have only begun to try, after accepting all too long the notion that schools should acquiesce in, even re-enforce, inequalities in home backgrounds rather than overcome them.

Upgrading the earning capacity of Negroes will be difficult, but the economic effects are easy to analyze. Economists have long held that the way to reduce disparities in earned incomes is to eliminate disparities in earning capacities. If college-trained people earn more money than those who left school after eight years, the remedy is to send a larger proportion of young people to college. If machine operators earn more than ditchdiggers, the remedy is to give more people the capacity and opportunity to be machine operators. These changes in relative supplies reduce the disparity both by competing down the pay in the favored line of work and by raising the pay in the less remunerative line. When there are only a few people left in the population whose capacities are confined to garbage-collecting, it will be a high-paid calling. The same is true of domestic service and all kinds of menial work.

This classical economic strategy will be hampered if discrimination, union barriers, and the like stand in the way. It will not help to increase the supply of Negro plumbers if the local unions and contractors will not let them join. But experience also shows that barriers give way more easily when the pressures of unsatisfied demand and supply pile up.

It should therefore be the task of educational and manpower policy to engineer over the next two decades a massive change in the relative supplies of people of different educational and professional attainments and degrees of skill and training. It must be a more rapid change than has occurred in the past two decades, because that has not been fast enough to alter income differentials. We should try particularly to increase supplies in those fields where salaries and wages are already high and rising. In this process we should be very skeptical of self-serving arguments and calculations—that an increase in supply in this or that profession would be bound to reduce quality, or that there are some mechanical relations of "need" to population or to Gross National Product that cannot be exceeded.

Such a policy would be appropriate to the "war on poverty" even if there were no racial problem. Indeed, our objective is to raise the earning capacities of low-income whites as well as of Negroes. But Negroes have the most to gain, and even those who because of age or irreversible environmental handicaps must inevitably be left behind will benefit by reduction in the number of whites and other Negroes who are competing with them.

ASSURING LIVING STANDARDS IN THE ABSENCE OF EARNING CAPACITY

The reduction of inequality in earning capacity is the fundamental solution, and in a sense anything else is stopgap. Some stopgaps are useless and even counter-productive. People who lack the capacity to earn a decent living need to be helped, but they will not be helped by minimum wage laws, trade union wage pressures, or other devices which seek to compel employers to pay them more than their work is worth. The more likely outcome of such regulations is that the intended beneficiaries are not employed at all.

A far better approach is to supplement earnings from the public fisc. But assistance can and should be given in a way that does not force the recipients out of the labor force or give them incentive to withdraw. Our present system of welfare payments does just that, causing needless waste and demoralization. This application of the means test is bad economics as well as bad sociology. It is almost as if our present programs of public assistance had been consciously contrived to perpetuate the conditions they are supposed to alleviate.

These programs apply a strict means test. The amount of assistance is an estimate of minimal needs, less the resources of the family from earnings. The purpose of the means test seems innocuous enough. It is to avoid wasting taxpayers' money on people who do not really need help. But another way to describe the means test is to note that it taxes earnings at a rate of 100 percent.* A person on public assistance cannot add to his family's standard of living by working. Of course, the means test provides a certain incentive to work in order to get off public assistance altogether. But in many cases, especially where there is only one adult to provide for and take care of several children, the adult simply does not have enough time and earning opportunities to get by without financial help. He, or more likely she, is essentially forced to be both idle and on a dole. The means test also involves limitations on property holdings which deprive anyone who is or expects to be on public assistance of incentive to save.

In a society which prizes incentives for work and thrift, these are surprising regulations. They deny the country useful productive services, but that economic loss is minor in the present context. They deprive individuals and families both of work experience which could teach them skills, habits, and self-discipline of future value and of the self-respect and satisfaction which comes from improving their own lot by their own efforts.

Public assistance encourages the disintegration of the family, the key to so many of the economic and social problems of the American Negro. The main assistance program, Aid for Dependent Children, is not available if there is an able-bodied employed male in the house. In most states it is not available if there is an able-bodied man in the house, even if he is not working. All too often it is necessary for the father to leave his children so that they can eat. It is bad enough to provide incentives for idleness but even worse to legislate incentives for desertion.[10]

The bureaucratic surveillance and guidance to which recipients of public assistance are sub-

---

*Editor's note: A marginal tax of 2/3 was established in 1967.

[10]The official Advisory Council on Public Assistance recommended in 1960 that children be aided even if there are two parents or relatives in loco parentis in their household, but Congress has ignored this proposal. Public Assistance: A Report of the Findings and Recommendations of the Advisory Council on Public Assistance, Department of Health, Education, and Welfare, January 1960. The Advisory Council also wrestled somewhat inconclusively with the problem of the means test and suggested that states be allowed to experiment with dropping or modifying it for five years. This suggestion too has been ignored.

ject undermine both their self-respect and their capacity to manage their own affairs. In the administration of assistance there is much concern to detect "cheating" against the means tests and to ensure approved prudent use of the public's money. Case loads are frequently too great and administrative regulations too confining to permit the talents of social workers to treat the roots rather than the symptoms of the social maladies of their clients. The time of the clients is considered a free good, and much of it must be spent in seeking or awaiting the attention of the officials on whom their livelihood depends.

The defects of present categorical assistance programs could be, in my opinion, greatly reduced by adopting a system of basic income allowances, integrated with and administered in conjunction with the federal income tax. In a sense the proposal is to make the income tax symmetrical. At present the federal government takes a share of family income in excess of a certain amount (for example, a married couple with three children pays no tax unless their income exceeds $3700). The proposal is that the Treasury pay any family who falls below a certain income a fraction of the shortfall. The idea has sometimes been called a negative income tax.

The payment would be a matter of right, like an income tax refund. Individuals expecting to be entitled to payments from the government during the year could receive them in periodic installments by making a declaration of expected income and expected tax withholdings. But there would be a final settlement between the individual and the government based on a "tax" return after the year was over, just as there is now for taxpayers on April 15.

A family with no other income at all would receive a basic allowance scaled to the number of persons in the family. For a concrete example, take the basic allowance to be $400 per year per person. It might be desirable and equitable, however, to reduce the additional basic allowance for children after, say, the fourth. Once sufficient effort is being made to disseminate birth control knowledge and technique, the scale of allowances by family size certainly should provide some disincentive to the creation of large families.

A family's allowance would be reduced by a certain fraction of every dollar of other income it received. For a concrete example, take this fraction to be one-third. This means that the

family has considerable incentive to earn income, because its total income including allowances will be increased by two-thirds of whatever it earns. In contrast, the means test connected with present public assistance is a 100 per cent "tax" on earnings. With a one-third "tax" a family will be on the receiving end of the allowance and income tax system until its regular income equals three times its basic allowance.[11]

Families above this "break-even" point would be taxpayers. But the less well-off among them would pay less taxes than they do now. The first dollars of income in excess of this break-even point would be taxed at the same rate as below, one-third in the example. At some income level, the tax liability so computed would be the same as the tax under the present income tax law. From that point up, the present law would take over; taxpayers with incomes above this point would not be affected by the plan.

The best way to summarize the proposal is to give a concrete graphical illustration. On the horizontal axis of Figure 1 is measured family income from wages and salaries, interest, dividends, rents, and so forth—"adjusted gross income" for the Internal Revenue Service. On the vertical axis is measured the corresponding "disposable income," that is, income after federal taxes and allowances. If the family neither paid taxes nor received allowance, disposable income would be equal to family income; in the diagram this equality would be shown by the $45°$ line from the origin. Disposable income above this $45°$ line means the family receives allowances; disposable income below this line means the family pays taxes. The broken line OAB describes the present income tax law for a married couple with three children, allowing the standard deductions. The line CD is the revision which the proposed allowance system would make for incomes below $7963. For incomes above $7963, the old tax schedule applies.

Beneficiaries under Federal Old Age Survivors and Disability Insurance would not be

[11]Adjusting the size of a government benefit to the amount of other income is not without precedent. Recipients of Old Age Survivors and Disability Insurance benefits under the age of seventy-two lose one dollar of benefits and only one dollar for every two dollars of earned income above $1200 but below $1700 a year.

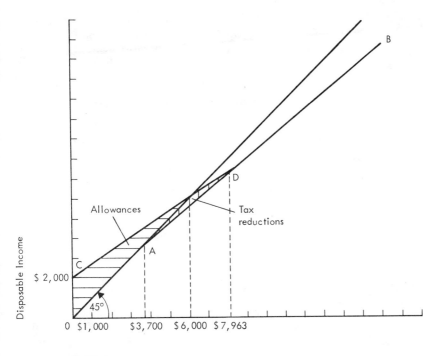

Figure 1

**Illustration of Proposed Income Allowance Plan
(Married Couple with Three Children)**

eligible for the new allowances. Congress should make sure that minimum benefits under OASDI are at least as high as the allowances. Some government payments, especially those for categorical public assistance, would eventually be replaced by basic allowances. Others, like unemployment insurance and veterans' pensions, are intended to be rights earned by past services regardless of current need. It would therefore be wrong to withhold allowances from the beneficiaries of these payments, but it would be reasonable to count them as income in determining the size of allowances, even though they are not subject to tax.

Although the numbers used above are illustrative, they are indicative of what is needed for an effective program. It would be expensive for the federal budget, involving an expenditure of perhaps fifteen billion dollars a year. Partially offsetting this budgetary cost are the savings in public assistance, on which governments now spend five and six-tenths billion dollars a year, of which three and two-tenths billion are federal funds. In addition, savings are possible in a host of other income maintenance programs, notably in agriculture.

The program is expensive, but it need not be introduced all at once. The size of allowances can be gradually increased as room in the budget becomes available. . . .

I referred to programs which make up for lack of earning capacity as stopgaps, but that is not entirely fair. Poverty itself saps earning capacity. The welfare way of life, on the edge of subsistence, does not provide motivation or useful work experience either to parents or to children. A better system, one which enables people to retain their self-respect and initiative, would in itself help to break the vicious circle. . . .

CONCLUSION

By far the most powerful factor determining the economic status of Negroes is the over-all state of the U.S. economy. A vigorously expanding economy with a steadily tight labor market will rapidly raise the position of the Negro, both absolutely and relatively. Favored by such a climate, the host of specific measures to eliminate discrimination, improve education and training, provide housing, and strengthen the family can yield substantial additional results. In a less beneficent economic climate, where jobs are short rather than men, the wars against racial inequality and poverty will be uphill battles, and some highly touted weapons may turn out to be dangerously futile.

The forces of the market place, the incentives of private self-interest, and pressures of supply and demand—these can be powerful allies or stubborn opponents. Properly harnessed, they quietly and impersonally accomplish objectives which may elude detailed legislation and administration. To harness them to the cause of the American Negro is entirely possible. It requires simply that the federal government dedicate its fiscal and monetary policies more wholeheartedly and singlemindedly to achieving and maintaining genuinely full employment. The obstacles are not technical or economic. One obstacle is a general lack of understanding that unemployment and related evils are remediable by national fiscal and monetary measures. The other is the high priority now given to competing financial objectives.

. . . Negro rights movements have so far taken no interest in national fiscal and monetary policy. No doubt gold, the federal budget, and the actions of the Federal Reserve System seem remote from the day-to-day firing line of the movements. Direct local actions to redress specific grievances and to battle visible enemies are absorbing and dramatic. They have concrete observable results. But the use of national political influence on behalf of the goals of the Employment Act of 1946 is equally important. It would fill a political vacuum, and its potential long-run pay-off is very high.

The goal of racial equality suggests that the federal government should provide more stimulus to the economy. Fortunately, it also suggests constructive ways to give the stimulus. We can kill two birds with one stone. The economy needs additional spending in general; the wars on poverty and racial inequality need additional spending of particular kinds. The needed spending falls into two categories: government programs to diminish economic inequalities by building up the earning capacities of the poor and their children, and humane public assistance to citizens who temporarily or permanently lack the capacity to earn a decent living for themselves and their families. In both categories the nation, its conscience aroused by the plight of the Negro, has the chance to make reforms which will benefit the whole society.

32. The Case for a Negative Income Tax Device

Earl R. Rolph

A welfare system aimed at alleviating poverty should adopt the premise that income dispersion, including negative income and small positive income, is normal and will not disappear next year or the year after. Since human productivity varies widely, as do other abilities, there are always some groups whose productivity will be low judged by some standard appropriate for "normal" people. If people of low productivity are to be employed in the absence of special subsidies, employers, to have an incentive to hire them, must be permitted to pay low wage rates. People's incomes from work will leave some of them and their dependents in poverty. To the extent they are denied the choice of working, by the establishment of minimum wages, their incomes will be even lower.

The income distribution as it naturally arises does not guarantee affluence for everyone in an affluent society. Government policy must be consistent with the fact that there are some able-bodied males who are not capable of earning as much as $3,000 a year or even $2,000 a year. Present welfare programs, geared as they are to various presumed causes of personal financial distress, presuppose that people not subject to special difficulties, such as ill health, old age, unemployment, etc., can earn adequate incomes and can bring up children who will develop into effective members of society. The presupposition is scarcely consistent with the facts. Mollie Orshansky found, for example, that 22.3 million people out of 27.9 million defined as poor were in families headed by a male. In addition: "Of the 15 million children counted poor in March 5.7 million were in the family of a worker who had a regular job in 1963 and was not out of work any time during the year.[1] There are poor people who are unemployed or unemployable, but there are others who work and do so regularly. A wage structure that eliminates unemployment and underemployment of people with modest skills cannot be expected to end poverty levels of income, although such a pricing arrangement would result in a vast improvement for many presently disadvantaged groups. There is nothing in economic theory nor in the inherent characteristics of human beings that precludes equilibrium wage rates of one dollar an hour or less for some types of labor services.

If, then, the premise is adopted that the dispersion of income, including low income, is a normal feature of economic affairs, what social measures are appropriate to obtain a socially

[1] Mollie Orshansky, "Who's Who Among the Poor: A Demographic View of Poverty," *Social Security Bulletin*, Vol. 28 (July, 1965), 21, 24.

acceptable level of income for everyone? Negative income tax devices are techniques to solve this problem.

POVERTY GAP APPROACH
TO A NEGATIVE INCOME TAX

One approach to the problem is to define poverty as an amount of income less than some standard taken to be reasonably adequate, treat the difference between a person's actual income and the standard as the "poverty gap," calculate the number of dollars required to close the gap, and give each person the difference between his actual income and the standard.* Poverty is then "cured" since by definition no one is left below the standard. Only few proponents embrace this position as stated in this bald manner. It is, however, a widely embraced basic premise both in and out of official circles.

Implementation would require legislation to define the standard, to provide for a definition of income as close to a person's total gain as is feasible, and to tax income obtained by the person from his own efforts at a rate of 100 per cent up to the poverty standard. Beyond this point, but not necessarily at it, the federal individual income tax may come into operation. We would then have two individual income taxes, possibly administered by different agencies—one for people with incomes below the standard and another for those above it. . . .

The 100 per cent tax rate feature of the poverty gap approach is, of course, unworkable. Apart from other considerations, a 100 per cent tax rate means that people must work for nothing or else conceal their incomes. To enforce such a rate would probably require a return to the relief approach. Then a person who refuses a job may be disciplined by cutting him and his family off the rolls. Recognizing the unworkability of 100 per cent rates, poverty gap advocates have suggested lower rates, such as 80 per cent; few seem willing to go below 50 per cent.

This compromise of principle with practicality requires that the goal of closing the poverty gap be abandoned in favor of a more modest goal and that the non-poor be subsidized. If an income of $3,000 a year for a family of four is taken as the poverty line, and if

Editor's note: At the time Rolph wrote, the philosophy of public assistance was similar to the poverty gap approach. Since 1967 the implicit tax rate has been reduced to 66.7%.

for reasons of enforceability the tax rate is placed at 50 per cent, the goal of ending poverty would require an allowance of $3,000 a year to ensure that a family with a zero income would achieve a disposable income of $3,000. This technique would mean, however, that a family with an income of $5,000 would get an allowance of $3,000, pay $2,500 in gross tax, and receive a net sum of $500 a year from the Treasury. Thus, people who are defined as nonpoor would obtain a net subsidy if the allowance is placed at the poverty line with any tax rate below 100 per cent. To poverty gap thinkers, payments to those above the poverty line are viewed as inefficient or wasteful of public funds.

If, on the other hand, the allowance is placed below the poverty line, the goal of eliminating poverty is partially sacrificed. Instead of a disposable income of $3,000 for a family of four, a smaller allowance must be established. Obviously, the lower the credit, the greater will be the poverty gap remaining. The possible combinations of allowance size and tax rate are indefinitely large, but all would leave the poverty gap more or less unfilled.

There are numerous objections to the establishment of two federal income taxes, one for the poor and one for the non-poor. With two laws, means would have to be found to prevent some members of a family from successfully classifying themselves as poor by splitting off from the family for tax purposes. A large financial incentive would exist to divide the family into zero income units, leaving perhaps only the father to report positive income. The precise gain to a family would depend on the size of the allowance, the tax rate for low incomes, the tax rate for high incomes, and the definition of income. Rules might be devised to minimize family splitting for tax purposes. Effective rules have not, however, been devised for the present federal income tax law for families with property income. It remains feasible to give children assets, the income from which is taxed at lower rates than it would be if left in the names of the parents. The incentive to split income within the family arises from rate graduation under the present law.

A further difficulty in a poverty gap design of a negative income tax is the treatment of people who, in a particular year, have a low income but are not poor. A person with assets of, say, $1,000,000, may in a particular year have an income of a negative amount or a small positive amount. He would, however, be classified as poor under a poverty gap system. A young engineer just completing his Ph.D. degree may have an income of $2,000 in one year, and hence be eligible for negative tax treatment, and have an income of $15,000 the following year. Given the fact that the income of some people fluctuates, there are certain to be people who are highly affluent, judged either by their net worth or by their average income over several years, but who have low incomes in particular years.

According to the usually accepted principles of income taxation, there is no objection to paying money to people who normally pay tax, but who, in a given year, happen to have low incomes. Under present law, for example, there are some modest averaging provisions, and persons in business who report negative incomes in a given year may be entitled to take advantage of loss carry-back and carry-forward provisions. In the case of loss carry-backs, people who so qualify are paid by the treasury for the year in which they suffer losses. In this aspect, the present law is a negative income tax. Provisions would be necessary to ascertain a person's negative or positive tax liability in the event he attains less than the poverty level income in a given year. To avoid hopeless confusion, the two income tax laws would have to be made consistent in their treatment of people with fluctuating incomes.

The above difficulties are a small sample of the actual difficulties likely to arise from having two federal individual income taxes. Until and unless the details of the laws are actually drafted, it is impossible to know all the problems that would emerge and what rules would be needed to prevent abuses. The one sure result is even greater complexity than now exists in income taxation in the United States.

CREDIT TAX APPROACH

There are many ways of designing a single federal individual income tax and a system of allowances. I shall set forth here a plan described as a credit income tax. The goals of this plan are: (1) to redistribute income systematically in the direction of reducing the present inequality, (2) to minimize incentive problems associated with high marginal rates, and (3) to reduce radically the complexity of the present federal income tax law.

The plan would reduce, and reduce substantially, the incidence of genuine poverty in the United States. However, the complete elimination of poverty would be at best a long-run target. As in other areas of economics, the critical issues are in the nature of more-or-less, rather than all-or-none. Poverty can never be totally eliminated unless society places those who are hopelessly incompetent in managing their own affairs in institutions and denies them their freedom.

The credit income tax suggested here has two main features: a system of flat-sum credits to which all residents of the United States would be entitled, and a general proportional income tax with zero exemptions. A person's or a family's net tax liability, plus or minus, is given by the formula, $T = Yr - Cu$, where T is the net tax liability, Y is taxable income, r is the tax rate, C is the size of the credit (assuming uniform per capita credits), and u is the number of credits for the unit (normally the family).

Table 1

The Credit Income Tax[a]

Income	Net Tax	Disposable Income
0	− 2,000	2,000
1,000	− 1,700	2,700
2,000	− 1,400	3,400
4,000	− 800	4,800
6,000	− 200	6,200
8,000	+ 400	7,600
10,000	+ 1,000	9,000
20,000	+ 4,000	16,000
50,000	+ 13,000	37,000
100,000	+ 28,000	72,000
1,000,000	+298,000	702,000

[a]Assumes a tax rate of 30 per cent and credits of $500 a person for a family of four.

To illustrate, suppose the credit is $500 a person a year, and the tax rate is 30 per cent. Table 1 shows the tax liability for a family of four. This combination of tax rate and credit would provide a net payment by the Treasury ranging from $2,000 for a person or family with an income of zero (ignoring truly negative income) to zero at a level slightly in excess of $6,000 of income.

The higher the credit, given the tax rate, the larger will be the net payments made to people with low incomes. On the other hand, the tax rate depends on the size of the credit. The rate also depends on the desired yield of the tax to the Treasury and the size of the tax base. To calculate the tax rate for the country as a whole, the following formula may be used: $r = \Sigma C + R/Y$, where ΣC is the sum of the credits, R is the desired yield, and Y is total taxable income. Taking the population in round figures to be 200 million, the credit to be $400 per capita, the desired yield to be $50 billion, and total taxable income to be $500 billion, we get:

$$r = \frac{\$80 \text{ billion} + 50 \text{ billion}}{500 \text{ billion}} = 26 \text{ per cent.}$$

In recent years, the yield of the federal individual income tax has been in the neighborhood of 9 to 10 per cent of personal income. If personal income were the tax base, a credit of $400 per capita would "cost" about 16 percentage points in the rate. This result does not mean that the average rate of tax would rise from 10 to 26 per cent of personal income. The effective or average rate would remain at 10 per cent. The extra percentage points become the "price" paid for redistribution, including redistribution to one's self.

To implement the credit income tax plan it would be necessary to redraft large parts of the present federal income tax law. It might seem rather drastic to suggest that the federal income tax should be radically changed in order to increase the incomes of people who presently have low incomes. In fact, however, a great part of this task would consist of simplifying the present law. Many of the complexities of the law as it now exists are a direct consequence of graduated rates. As Blum and Calvin have emphasized in this connection, much of the work of lawyers in the tax field arises from the simple fact that the tax rates vary, depending on how much income is reported for tax purposes in a given year.[2] Among other things, all the complexities arising because of incentives that now exist to split income within the family would disappear. In addition, the inequities and the rules designed to deal with these inequities arising from the definition of the tax-paying unit would also disappear. Under a proportional

tax, the problem of averaging, a very serious problem under the present law, is solved automatically.

There are, from the point of view of tax design, large advantages to be gained by eliminating progressive rates. We ordinarily have thought in the past that it was necessary to have increasing rates of tax in order to have progressive taxation. This view turns out to be incorrect. It is possible to have proportional rates and progression by the device of a general credit, as illustrated by Table 1.

There would be social costs associated with the installation of a general credit income tax. For example, people who presently are not required to file would have to file to be eligible for the credit. This is about 10 per cent of the population. Although the group is relatively small, the compliance task would not be simple. Many of the nonfilers have rather complicated problems. Some are small-scale farmers who are not accustomed to keeping books, some are occasional workers at odd jobs. Hence, an educational task of some magnitude would be in order.

From an economic point of view, however, the social costs of the credit income tax would be negative and would be negative by a large amount. Under the present system, many children are growing up without the advantages of proper food, shelter, clothing, medical care, and education. By increasing the financial means of parents, we would give offspring, on the average, higher levels of living. Society would gain in real terms in the form of greater productivity of the current generation of poor children when they become adults and of greater productivity of contemporary poor adults. Financial means are instrumental in obtaining work, when finding a job requires relocation away from depressed areas, proper dress to impress employers, and meeting living expenses while training. A credit income tax would not, to be sure, provide jobs for people with little skill; as already indicated, the legal and institutional restrictions on realistic wage rates for such people must be moderated as a necessary condition for achieving substantial progress in this area.

Closely related, and of much greater importance than an increase in the output of goods and services, is the effect of a credit income tax on the problems arising from concentrated pockets of city poverty. Although city poverty has been a feature of American life since the

---

[2] Walter J. Blum and Harry Calvin, *The Uneasy Case for Progressive Taxation* (Chicago: University of Chicago Press, 1953), p. 15.

latter part of the nineteenth century, the current-day ghettos differ in two important respects from ethnic ghettos of the past: the hope of significant economic improvement within a generation has all but disappeared, and the city poor are no longer content to be poor.

Systematic redistribution in favor of lower income groups by a technique that carries no stigma would immediately end the despair of many of the city poor. This change would be a large improvement. It would also improve the finances of cities by removing a substantial portion of the costs of relief from city budgets, permitting cities to finance measures to assist low income groups. Systematic redistribution would also tend to reduce the migration of the rural poor to the cities. These groups, as beneficiaries of a credit income tax, would find their position improved in their own communities and would, presumably, have little or no incentive to migrate. A city slum, however dismal, has held the only hope of improvement for many of the rural poor in the deep South. This is in part due to capricious methods of distributing relief (not limited to the South), including the practice of granting or withholding relief to "discipline" those whose behavior offends the politically dominant group. A credit income tax by contrast would afford no such power to local officials and would automatically give poor rural people greater economic and political security than they now enjoy.

Socially, the process of preparing people for working and living in metropolitan areas can be achieved at a lower cost in the hamlets of Alabama than in the ghettos of New York or Chicago. The large cities must be given the opportunity to take measures to improve the lot of the city poor without being handicapped by large numbers of newcomers out of the rural South.

CONCLUDING OBSERVATIONS

A credit income tax may appear to some to be a radical measure out of keeping with the American political tradition. Those who are inclined to take this view should weigh against it the large and expensive but inefficient programs that transfer goods and money to some groups at the expense of others. More of the same can be expected in the future in the absence of a program of systematic redistribution. With a credit income tax, any possible excuse for continuing agricultural price sup-

ports, for example, is removed. Subsidized public housing can be opposed without seeming to be ungenerous; low income groups, bolstered by the credit, may buy their own housing services in the market. From the point of view of high income groups, a credit income tax, if the credit is made modest in size, may be the less expensive alternative.

Those who like big government may find a credit income tax objectionable. No measure, to my knowledge, is a greater threat to the growth of nonmilitary government programs; the credit income tax undermines the most telling argument for many of these programs, namely, financial or real assistance to some group or groups.

A credit income tax can be installed in the near future without waiting for the end of the Viet Nam war. The Treasury and the Congress would need to redraft the Internal Revenue Code to include within the definition of Adjusted Gross Income many of the large classes of income presently fully or partially exempt from taxation, to reduce those deductions presently allowed for purposes other than to provide a more accurate definition of taxable income, and to simplify the code as a consequence of the adoption of a one-rate system. I do not wish to imply that such a change would be easy to achieve.

In the initial phase, the determination of the size of the credit may be accomplished by an estimation of the size of the tax base and the fixing of a rate deemed to be politically acceptable, perhaps 25 per cent, and then fixing the credit at the amount that would exhaust the difference between the potential yield and the desired yield of the income tax at that rate. If such a calculation permitted a credit of only $200 per capita a year in the first year, the automatic increase in the potential yield as income increased would permit the credit to be raised.

Once a credit income tax is established, the size of the credit and of the tax rate can be expected to become a political issue of some importance, with many people with persistent low incomes favoring a larger credit and many people with high incomes favoring a lower rate of tax. The political question of what the income distribution ought to be would then be clearly posed. Whatever the outcome over the years, at least a fundamental feature of economic life would become an explicit political question.

33.   Welfare Reform and Work Incentives

Irwin Garfinkel

Stanley H. Masters

The welfare system in the United States has been "reformed" on numerous occasions over the last three centuries.[1] In the last few years, most of the concern has focused on the Aid to Families with Dependent Children (AFDC) Program. There are several conflicting criticisms of this program, some of which are based primarily on equity grounds although others focus on undesirable economic incentives. In the introductory section, we shall discuss these criticisms and indicate some of the reasons why it has been so difficult for the Congress to develop an acceptable set of reforms.

A primary focus of many reform proposals, including President Nixon's Family Assistance Plan (FAP), has been to extend coverage to families headed by an employed male. These proposals have generated great controversy, centering around the effect on labor supply

that might occur if such a proposal were adopted. Because of the importance of this issue, we present in Sections II and III a theoretical and empirical analysis of the labor supply effects that might be expected if a program like FAP were enacted into law.

I. RECENT EFFORTS TO REFORM WELFARE

On the one hand the AFDC program has been criticized for inadequate coverage, inadequate benefits, and excessive variations in benefits. The AFDC program provides aid almost solely to female-headed families. Yet a very large percentage of the poor live in intact, male-headed families. As the national commitment to reduce poverty grew in the 1960s, the AFDC program's failure to provide aid to the working poor came under increasing attack. A related criticism of the program was that because intact families were ineligible for aid, the program encouraged family dissolution.[2] In response to this criticism, Congress amended the Social Security Act in 1961 to provide federal support to states that aided dependent

---

[1]Prior to the passage of the Social Security Act in 1935, welfare was almost solely a state and local responsibility. But there were periodic efforts at reform which characterized most states. For a historical analysis of the evolution of the American welfare system and its forbearer, the British Poor Law, see Samuel Mencher, *Poor Law to Poverty Program: Economic Security Policy in Britain and the United States* (Pittsburgh: University of Pittsburgh Press, 1967) and Karl de Schweinitz, *England's Road to Social Security* (Philadelphia: University of Pennsylvania Press, 1943).

[2]As yet, there is no good empirical evidence to either support or refute this hypothesis.

families with an unemployed male head. As of 1974, however, only about half the states were providing aid to such families. Moreover, no federal assistance is currently given to families headed by an employed male.

The average levels of benefits and the large variation in state benefit levels have also been a source of dissatisfaction to numerous critics of the AFDC program. Liberals have argued that benefits are generally inadequate; some liberals and conservatives have argued that the large disparity in benefit levels has led to undesirable migration, primarily from the rural South to large urban ghettos in the North.[3]

On the other hand, the AFDC program has been criticized because of the recent large increases in the number of beneficiaries and the continuing low employment rates of AFDC mothers. In response to the criticism that the 100 percent marginal tax rates that characterized most state programs prior to 1967 eliminated any economic incentive for AFDC mothers to work, Congress amended the Social Security Act in 1967 to prohibit states from imposing marginal tax rates in excess of 66-2/3 percent (i.e., benefits cannot be reduced by more than two dollars for every three additional dollars earned by the family).[4] In addition, training programs for AFDC mothers were expanded. But employment rates of AFDC mothers did not increase substantially in response to the program and, more important, the rate of increase in the number of AFDC beneficiaries actually accelerated in the late 1960s. Although the reasons for this increase in the number of beneficiaries are not well understood, there are several possible explanations. First, more families are eligible for AFDC as a result of benefit schedules that allow those with higher earnings to supplement their earnings with AFDC payments[5] and court decisions that have eliminated some of the nonfinancial eligibility requirements for AFDC.[6] Finally, perhaps as a result of the publicity and political pressures generated by the Poverty Program and the National Welfare Rights Organization, potential beneficiaries may be more aware of the benefits available to them. Whatever the reason(s) for the increase, the "swelling of the welfare rolls," despite the creation of work incentive and training provisions in the program,[7] has provided an important impetus to "reform" the AFDC program.

Reforming the AFDC program, however, is difficult because of the conflicting objectives of the reformers. For example, most reform proposals involve either reducing or eliminating interstate differentials—partly on equity grounds and partly to reduce incentives for the poor to migrate to high income areas. However, there is also political pressure not to reduce benefits for present AFDC beneficiaries and to keep marginal tax rates reasonably low. Unfortunately if benefits are to be made equal across states, if no one is to be made worse off, and if marginal tax rates are to be kept reasonably low, then the welfare reform is likely to be expensive. But reducing costs is a prime goal for many of those interested in welfare reform.[8] The conflicting objectives of

---

[3] It is not clear whether or not such migration has been induced by differences in AFDC benefit levels. Even if it has, such migration is not necessarily undesirable. A related issue in welfare reform has been an effort to relieve the fiscal plight of states and cities, especially those areas which have received the largest portion of the migrants. Partly for this reason, a complete federal takeover of the welfare system has often been proposed.

[4] Prior to 1962, marginal tax rates were actually greater than 100 percent since no allowance was made for work expenses. Since work expenses can be defined differently by different people, it is possible to vary "actual" marginal tax rates by varying allowances for work expenses as well as by changing statutory marginal taxes. At the present time, the treatment of work expenses varies from locality to locality and even from caseworker to caseworker.

[5] State legislatures have increased the guarantee, G (the amount families would receive if they had no earnings), at the same time that the 1967 amendments reduced the marginal tax rate, r. Therefore, there has been an increase in the breakeven level, G/r, the earnings level below which a family can receive some AFDC benefits.

[6] The 1969 Supreme Court decision, for example, declared that state residency requirements for eligibility were unconstitutional.

[7] The relative ineffectiveness of such programs is not surprising given the low skills of many beneficiaries and their need (at least in the absence of massive day care subsidies) to stay home and look after their children. See Leonard J. Hausman, "The Welfare System as a Manpower and Rehabilitation System," in *Public-Private Manpower Policies,* Arnold R. Weber, Frank H. Cassell, and Woodrow L. Ginsberg, eds. (Madison: Industrial Relations Research Association, 1969).

[8] Integrating in-kind transfer and cash transfer programs poses a similar kind of problem. On the one hand, the large intra- and interstate disparities in bene-

reformers are most apparent on the issue of whether to extend aid to families headed by a working male. Although extending such aid could substantially reduce poverty and also reduce the incentives for family dissolution in the current system, there would clearly be a large increase in the cost of the program.

The cost of any specific proposal to extend aid to the "working poor" is difficult to estimate, however, since it depends on the labor supply effect of the program. If beneficiaries work less as a result of the program, their earnings will fall and their income support payments will rise. Therefore, the greater the labor supply reduction, the greater the cost of the program and, ceteris paribus, the higher the taxes of nonbeneficiaries. This is one reason why there is such great concern about the labor supply effects of such welfare reform proposals. Apart from such economic considerations, however, it also appears that the Puritan work ethic leads many citizens to oppose programs that they believe will encourage male family heads to quit work.

Since the potential labor supply effects are such an important issue in considering the desirability of making all families eligible for income maintenance support, the rest of this article is devoted to an analysis of this issue.[9]

fits received by poor people from income-tested food, housing, and medical care programs has prompted some reform advocates to propose that the benefits be divided more equally among all poor individuals. On the other hand, since all of these income-tested in-kind transfer programs have implicit marginal tax rates, AFDC beneficiaries who also receive benefits from one or more of these programs are faced with marginal tax rates in excess of 66-2/3 percent. To extent the benefits of these programs to all poor individuals, while keeping cumulative marginal tax rates from cash and in-kind programs reasonably low, would again be very expensive. An alternative is to substitute cash transfers for some in-kind programs. But this alternative is also costly. Moreover, even a relatively generous cash transfer program will leave some families who are currently benefiting a great deal from one of the in-kind programs worse off.

[9]An alternative approach to assisting families headed by a working male is to institute a wage or earnings subsidy program. The main advantage of such subsidies, relative to the standard income maintenance approach, is that, since the family receives a subsidy only to the extent that family members work, the incentive to reduce work is likely to be diminished and the incentive to quit work is entirely eliminated.

On the other hand, there are a number of disadvantages to subsidies based on wage rates or earnings

II. ECONOMIC THEORY AND ITS LIMITATIONS

Economic theory assumes that an individual's choice between work and leisure (or other non-work activities) depends on his net wage rate and his non-wage income. Since, other things being equal, the individual is assumed to prefer leisure to work, an increase in his non-wage income will lead him to work less and "consume" more leisure. In other words, there is a negative income effect on labor supply.

A change in the net wage will have a similar income effect on labor supply. However, there will also be a positive substitution effect in this case since an increase in the net wage means that each hour of leisure is now more expensive. Thus an increase in the wage may lead to either an increase or a decrease in the supply of labor depending on whether the substitution or income effect dominates.

All income maintenance programs involve a guarantee, G, the amount of income a given individual or family will receive if they have no other income and a marginal tax rate, r, the rate at which the income support decreases as the family's earnings and other sources of income increase.[10] Income maintenance programs not only increase the beneficiary family's non-wage income, but, as a result of the marginal tax rate, also reduce the net wage of each family member. Thus both the total income effect and the substitution effect will act to reduce the family's work effort. The theory, however, makes no prediction concerning the magnitude of the reduction in labor supply.

Since the adoption of a universal negative income tax (NIT) program like the ones proposed by Tobin or Rolph would make a rela-

(wages times hours worker). For example, some families presumably should be eligible for support even if no one works (i.e., female-headed families where the mother has very young children or families where the parents are disabled). If a separate program is established for such families, however, then husbands will still have an economic incentive to desert or to appear disabled. Another difficulty is that a wage subsidy (and perhaps also an earnings subsidy) provides the poor with less incentive to invest in human capital, primarily because such a subsidy increases rather than decreases the opportunity cost of foregone earnings.

[10]Of course, G and r may be different for different kinds of families. In addition, r may depend on the amount or source of income.

tively large group of families headed by a prime-aged able-bodied male (i.e., the working poor) eligible for aid for the first time, the magnitude of the potential reduction in labor supply is an important question.

III. CROSS-SECTIONAL STUDIES

Since an NIT program would simultaneously increase the amount of non-employment income available to beneficiaries and decrease their net wage rate, one way of estimating the potential labor supply effects of NIT programs is to examine the differences in labor supply of individuals with differing wage rates and differing amounts of non-employment income. For example, in order to estimate the effect of an NIT program with a guarantee of $3,000 and a tax rate of 50 percent on the labor supply of a worker with a $3.00 per hour wage rate and no non-employment income, one would compare the labor supply of individuals with $3.00 per hour wage rates and no non-employment income to the labor supply of individuals of the same sex, age, race, years of schooling but with a wage rate of only $1.50 per hour and non-employment income of $3,000. Several researchers have devoted a great deal of time and ingenuity in order to use sample-survey data for this purpose.[11] Although all of these studies indicate that an NIT program would lead to fairly substantial reductions in the labor supply of wives in beneficiary families, for several reasons these sample-survey studies do not enable us to make very accurate predictions of the magnitude of the labor supply reductions of able-bodied male heads that would be induced by an NIT program. First, especially for the poverty population, there is little non-employment income that does not depend directly on a person's labor force status (as in the case of unemployment compensation or most welfare payments). Second, due to methodological differences in the studies, the range of estimated reductions in labor supply is quite large. Third, and perhaps most important, individuals

[11] See *Income Maintenance and Labor Supply: Econometric Studies,* Glen G. Cain and Harold W. Watts, eds., Institute for Research on Poverty Monograph Series (Chicago, Ill.: Markham Publishing Co., 1973), and William G. Bowen and T. Aldrich Finegan, *The Economics of Labor Force Participation* (Princeton, N.J.: Princeton University Press, 1969).

with different wage rates and different amounts of non-employment income are likely to differ in other important ways, which have not been measured in the survey but which may affect work effort independently of wage rates and non-employment income. For example, workers earning $3.00 per hour are likely to have more secure and less onerous jobs than those earning only $1.50 per hour. They may also be more economically ambitious. Similarly, the more economically ambitious an individual is, the more likely he is both to work long hours and to try to accumulate assets that give him non-employment income from rents, dividends, or interest. In the absence of independent measures of ambition and of the non-pecuniary desirability of jobs, we cannot be sure that the differences in labor supply associated with differences in wage rates and non-employment income are not really attributable at least in part to differences in the unmeasured variables. Thus, even if all the estimates derived from sample-survey data were consistent, these estimates would still be open to question.

IV. THE NEW JERSEY INCOME MAINTENANCE EXPERIMENT

An alternative method of estimating the magnitude of labor supply reductions that could be induced by a negative income tax is to conduct a controlled experiment. Although experimentation is common and uncontroversial in the physical sciences, in the social sciences it is uncommon and highly controversial. The reasons for the differences are apparent. When human beings are the subject of investigation, it is difficult to control all the forces that affect behavior. Moreover, there are ethical limits to the amount of control that can be exerted. Consequently, social science experimentation is relatively rare, and what little there is has been done on a very small scale.

In the last few years, however, several large-scale income maintenance experiments have been initiated. The first, a five-million dollar undertaking popularly known as the New Jersey Income Maintenance Experiment, began in August 1968 and lasted three years. The experiment was conducted in four New Jersey cities: Trenton, Paterson, Passaic, Jersey City; and in Scranton, Pennsylvania. Only families whose normal income was below 1-1/2 times the Social Security Administration's poverty level were selected to participate in the experiment. Finally, in order to focus on intact families, the sample was further limited to families that included at least one working-age male (aged 18-58, and neither disabled nor a full-time student) plus at least one other family member.[12]

Families were assigned on a stratified random basis to either one of eight experimental groups or to a control group. The eight experimental groups correspond to eight different NIT plans. The guarantees in the plans ranged from one-half to one and one-quarter times the poverty level. For a family of four in 1973 these guarantees vary from about $2,000 to approximately $5,000 Marginal tax rates range from 30 to 70 percent.

As expected, experimental family members during the 3 years of the experiment worked less than control family members—about 9 percent less.[13] Experimental husbands worked about six percent fewer hours than control husbands, and experimental wives worked about 14 percent less than control wives. The first two differences are statistically at the 95 percent level (i.e., the probability of finding such a

large difference by chance is less than 5 percent). Perhaps an even more important finding is the lack of any significant difference between the percent of experimental and control husbands who did not work at any time during the experiment. Thus the experimental results appear to refute the claim that NIT programs will induce large numbers of poor, able-bodied, male family heads to permanently quit work. Moreover, unlike the President's Family Assistance Program, there was no work requirement in the experimental NIT plans.

A very interesting, if not well understood, finding is that experimental families earned only 4 percent less than control families and experimental husbands actually earned slightly more than control husbands. Thus although experimental family members worked less than control family members, they earned more while they worked. Although these results may reflect peculiarities of the experimental situation,[14] it is also possible that the NIT payments enable experimental family members to be choosy about the jobs they take. That is, either they may take longer to search for a high-paying job when they become unemployed or they may be more willing to quit their current job to look for a better one.

Although the results reported above confirm or are at least consistent with economic theory, some results were inconsistent with theory. According to theory, labor supply reductions should be greater the larger the guarantee and,

[12]For a more detailed discussion of the experimental design see Harold W. Watts, "Graduated Work Incentives: An Experiment in Negative Taxation," *The American Economic Review*, Vol. 59, No. 2 (May, 1969).

[13]The differentials reported in the text represent the average differentials between experimental and control participants for all incomes. (These differentials are adjusted via regression analysis for differences among experimental participants in health status, educational attainment, and age of the husband, family size, ethnicity, location, and welfare status.) Since there are a priori reasons for believing that the labor reduction induced by a given NIT plan will on average be larger the lower a family's income or earnings capacity is, the average differentials would have been smaller if families with incomes greater than 1 1/2 times the poverty level had been included in the experiment. Conversely, the average differentials would have been larger if the analysis had been restricted to the poorest families who participated in the experiment. The results reported in the text are taken from Irwin Garfinkel, "The Effect of Welfare on the Labor Supply Response in the Urban Work Incentives Experiment" in *The Final Report of the Graduated Work Incentive Experiment in New Jersey and Pennsylvania* (Report to the Office of Economic Opportunity, August, 1973). The results may differ slightly from those reported in other papers due to differences in sample selection and model specification.

[14]Because experimentals had to file income report forms every two weeks in addition to responding to the quarterly questionnaire, it is possible that they learned more rapidly to report gross rather than net wages. To the extent that this learning phenomenon was responsible for the higher reported wage rates of experimentals, the differential should narrow over time. For white husbands in the sample, this is precisely what happened, but for blacks the wage rate differentials actually grew over time.

Another possible explanation is that average experimental earnings would not decline as much as hours if experimental participants with low wage rates reduced their labor supply more than those with higher wage rates. An examination of the data, however, revealed that this compositional effect was not a major factor in accounting for the wage rate increase. For a more detailed analysis of the alternative explanations for the wage rate increase see Harold Watts and John Mamer "Wage Rate Responses," in *The Final Report of the Graduated Work Incentive Experiment in New Jersey and Pennsylvania* (Report to the Office of Economic Opportunity, August, 1973).

holding income constant, the larger the tax rate in the NIT plan. The actual relationships were not so neat. The most disturbing finding was that in many cases while holding income constant, labor supply increased rather than decreased as tax rates increased.

These perverse relationships among plans may well be due to sample size problems. Although 1,353 families were originally enrolled in the experiment, due to family splits and sample attrition only 741 both were intact and had filled out over half the quarterly questionnaires. Of these, 292 were assigned to the control group leaving 29, 35, 63, 70, 51, 46, 54, and 101 respectively for each of the eight plans. Given the number of families in each plan, unusual or eccentric behavior on the part of a few individuals in the plans with smaller sample sizes could easily dominate the average labor supply values in those plans and thereby lead to relative distortions among the plans. Since the experimental group as a whole is so much larger than the group in any particular plan it is more likely that cases of unusually low labor supply will be cancelled out by cases of unusually high labor supply. Consequently, the possibility of the differential between controls and all experimentals being dominated by a few unusual cases is reduced. For this reason, we believe the differential between controls and all experimentals is more reliable than the differentials between controls and experimentals in any particular experimental NIT plan.

In addition to sample size, the experimental results were affected by two other serious experimental problems. The first is that the experiment lasted only three years. On the one hand, a temporary income guarantee increases lifetime incomes by a smaller amount than would a permanent guarantee, which suggests that the labor supply reductions that would be induced by a permanent guarantee are underestimated by the experiment. On the other hand, although a permanent program would reduce the price of leisure permanently, the experiment reduces it temporarily. That is, for experimental families leisure is on sale. This suggests that the experimental tax rate effects overestimate the labor supply reductions that would be induced by a permanent NIT program. The second problem is that during this period New Jersey and Pennsylvania had relatively generous welfare programs, for which families with an able-bodied male head were eligible for aid. Since control families were already potentially eligible for a welfare program, the experimental control labor supply differentials for all eight plans would have been larger had the experiment been conducted in a state with a less generous program. Although on the whole the quantitative magnitude of the biases arising from these two problems appears to be rather small, the analyses upon which this conclusion is based are rather crude.[15]

Despite the shortcomings of the New Jersey Experiment, it has provided us with some useful information. It appears to confirm evidence from cross-section data that the labor supply of wives will be highly responsive to NIT plans. On the other hand it suggests that the labor supply of able-bodied, prime age husbands will be relatively insensitive to NIT plans. These results are not surprising, since the social pressure for husbands to work full time is so strong that, in most cases, it probably precludes choice, although there are no such social pressures for wives to work. It is worth emphasizing, however, that wives make up a very small proportion of the labor supply of poor families,[16] so that even a relatively large percentage reduction in the labor supply of these workers will result in only small increases in the cost of NIT programs. Recall that in spite of the .14 percent reduction in the labor supply of wives, the reduction for the family as a whole was only 9 percent.

Perhaps the most important finding is that the experiment provides no evidence that NIT programs will induce large numbers of able-bodied male family heads to permanently quit work. Even a guarantee as high as $5,000 for a family of four, which is more than twice as high as the guarantee proposed by President Nixon in his Family Assistance Plan, does not appear to have induced a significant number of able-bodied male family heads to quit their jobs.

[15]See Garfinkel, *op. cit.*, and Charles E. Metcalf "Predicting the Effects of Permanent Programs from a Limited Duration Experiment," also in *The Final Report of the Graduated Work Incentive Experiment in New Jersey and Pennsylvania.*

[16]Many families, however, are not poor according to the Social Security Administration's definition of poverty only because the wife works.

34. Education and Poverty

Thomas I. Ribich

PAYOFFS OF THE VARIOUS EDUCATION PROGRAMS

Our main task . . . was to arrive at a judgment about what types of educational change yield the most favorable payoff rates. The paucity of observations and the conceptual and measurement difficulties encountered, and only partially resolved, during the course of calculating benefit-cost ratios make it clear that for the present this judgment can only be very tentative. Nevertheless, three conclusions seem worthy of stress.

1. Vocationally oriented training, at least in the form of recent manpower training programs, exhibits a higher rate of payoff than does general education. The rates are sufficiently in excess of those computed for improvements in general education that it is difficult to dismiss this result as an accident due entirely to the particular estimating techniques used. It should be noted also that job training would likely appear an even more favorable option if a weighted benefit-cost estimate were performed. . . . This is so because, in the case of job training, there is not as much guesswork involved in concentrating the educational effort on those who will likely have low incomes in the future. Of the poor children who are still in the public schools, many will do well as adults independently of an extra educational thrust at

this time. For those who are in (or about to enter) the labor market, the signs of future income difficulties are more clear-cut. It is also likely that the dispersion in income gains associated with improved general education is likely to be greater than in the case of job retraining. Thus, even if the average payoff rates were identical for general education and job training, we could anticipate that a larger proportion of the individual gains from job retraining would take place in the income ranges that are of greatest concern in a war on poverty.

It should come as no great surprise that an extension of vocational training brings about a higher average amount of economic success, per dollar spent, than does general education. That, after all, is its nearly exclusive aim. General education, on the other hand, is normally expected to yield a rich assortment of direct and indirect benefits in addition to that of simply raising incomes. These anticipated benefits should be kept in mind when it comes to final policy decisions; that is, the apparent superiority of vocational training as an antipoverty weapon must surely be tempered by the consideration that general education may be preferable on other counts.

2. The payoff-rate evidence gives no strong indications that special emphasis should be placed on the very early school years or on the preschool years. Contrary to most current

opinion, "the younger the better" is not an unassailable maxim. In the two compensatory education programs that recorded outcomes at different grade levels, children in the upper levels appeared to have gained at least as much, dollar for dollar, as did children in the lower grade levels. And the preschool programs observed did not clearly indicate that payoff rates here are any higher than they are for educational improvements in the school years. Thinking again in terms of a weighted benefit-cost estimate (which counts as more important the gains received by poorer individuals) this conclusion also would apply a fortiori. Waiting until the later school years to try to identify those in serious danger of earning poverty level incomes is surely easier than attempting this guess when the child is very young.

3. The very last point made in regard to increased per pupil expenditures deserves reiteration. That is, rates of payoff appear to be higher from adding expenditures in those school districts that are now spending relatively little. As with the first two conclusions, a weighted benefit-cost estimate would reinforce this result. The children in the lowest cost school districts have accumulated the least knowledge, and it can be inferred that they will experience the highest rates of adult poverty if educational improvements are not made.

A secondary, but also important, task . . . was to observe whether payoff rates were high enough to justify a heavy education emphasis in the war on poverty. The answers to this question depends on many issues neglected in these chapters. And even for the narrow type of measurement employed, the only relevant and defensible statement possible is an impressionistic one: with the exception of job retraining, the ratio of financial benefits to costs for educational improvements is found to be generally less than unity. Those ratios, it should be noted, did not include graduated weights according to relevant income ranges. And, . . . unweighted benefit-cost ratios would have to be something in excess of unity before education could be regarded as clearly superior to transfers or other forms of direct help. The case for education as an antipoverty device—measuring poverty solely as a shortage of income—is thus not as secure as it first seemed to be.

This is hardly the end of the story. Much work remains to be done in improving the sorts of estimates attempted here and in gaining more observations. Issues not dealt with in our earlier analysis must also be considered. We now turn our attention to this latter concern in an attempt to provide an overall reconsideration of the case for education in antipoverty efforts. . . .

SUMMARY OF ADDITIONAL BENEFITS

These additional considerations do not add a great deal to the "case for education" as it applies to the goal of poverty reduction. Intergenerational benefits turn out to be a small fraction of first generation benefits. And the implication of supermarginal change can, at present, be expressed in only a qualitative fashion: the extension of education may be justified somewhat beyond the point where simple benefit-cost ratios have a value of unity.

The other anticipated advantages of education are another matter. If one feels strongly enough about the psychic benefits of education, the corrupting influence of transfer payments, the goal of equal opportunity, or the need for economic growth, education might be a preferred course of action even if its measurable contribution to poverty reduction is small per dollar of cost. For most of these goals, additional measurements can be of assistance, but they cannot dictate what the trade off should be between reducing poverty and furthering other social aims.

An earlier caution deserves repeating: alternatives to education may do nearly as much (and in some cases, more) to achieve some of the "side" benefits frequently anticipated from education. It is not enough to say that improved education has a second generation effect, promotes more equal opportunity, and reduces antisocial behavior. Simple income transfers should, to some extent, do the same. And more specific forms of direct help (for example, improved housing) may give rise to secondary effects every bit as great as those accruing from an equal dollar amount of improved education. Future measurements and policy judgments should not ignore this possibility. . . .

WARNINGS TO THE POLICY MAKER

Is it possible to arrive at any clear-cut policy conclusions out of this study? In particular, what does the analysis imply for the role of education in an antipoverty effort? Before trying to answer this question, let us address ourselves briefly to the question of whether the low rates of financial return calculated in this study make any sense. It should be emphasized once more that these calculations relied upon very unsure assumptions. Still, they seem to be the most reasonable assumptions available, and they are generally consistent with what other students of the economics of education have judged to be appropriate. But is the outcome reasonable? Can it really be that improved general education results in average financial gains that are less than costs, therefore implying a fortiori that education is a relatively expensive and inefficient means of bringing people out of poverty?

One possible explanation for our empirical results is that the "culture of poverty" militates strongly againstly educational progress for the children of this culture. On the other hand, it is yet to be established with any certainty that educational improvements affecting more affluent individuals give rise to payoff rates that are significantly better than the ones calculated for individuals in poverty. From the available evidence, it is not clear that relatively high status students profit a great deal more from improvements in educational quality.[1]

An alternative and more convincing explanation stems from the earlier discussion in this [article] of education's numerous potential by-products. Many of these by-products have a social and non-pecuniary nature. And if social decisions have, in the past, been influenced by the hope of receiving these by-products, it could be argued that education already has been expanded and intensified to the point where it can no longer be justified in terms of direct financial profitability. If greater equality of opportunity, improvement in citizenship, and the perpetuation of a cultural heritage were considerations entering into past educational decisions (can this be doubted?), it is not surprising that a still greater intensification of our

[1]The calculations performed with low status pupils in the Project Talent sample were duplicated for pupils in the next-to-highest socioeconomic quintile. Though the spread of scores between the lowest and the highest expenditure categories was greater than the spread among low status pupils, the weighted-average (yearly equivalent) gain in test scores associated with a $100 increase in expenditures was practically the same for both groups.

educational efforts may result in private financial gains that fall short of costs.

Thus, it is possible to provide a very traditional economic rationale for the low rates of return on improved education. Economists have long recognized that differential rates of return, for similar factors of production, can often be explained on the basis of compensating nonfinancial advantages. And, to the degree that society perceives large nonpecuniary advantages in education and has reacted rationally to this perception, a similar explanation is available for the low rate of financial payoff for the programs examined in this study. These low rates of return do not belie the existence of capital market imperfections. One can simply conclude that these are more than counterbalanced by the influence of governmental support of education.

What then should be said about the high rates of return . . . associated with undertaking additional levels of schooling? These payoff rates suggest that an individual who chooses (voluntarily) to undertake continued study, at any educational level, tends to earn a high rate of return on his own investment and a high before-tax rate of return on total resource costs. The answer to this apparent contradiction with the findings of the present study is that inducing heavier flows of students through additional increments of education may require an expensive program of counseling and persuasion. It follows, then, that these previously calculated rates of high return for voluntary school continuance are not necessarily inconsistent with the conclusion that available policy alternatives yield low payoff rates. The students involved—and their motivation—are, after all, quite different.

Thus, while it cannot be stated with certainty that improved education (of the kind and scope examined) results in income gains to the poor that are less than costs, it is useful to discuss policy implications that might follow under the assumption that a heavy emphasis on general education is not the most efficient way to approach poverty alleviation. Even this presumption does not lead to hard and fast rules about the direction of policy. Any one of several alternative policy attitudes can be adopted. Depending on temperament and value premises, a policy maker might reasonably choose any one of the following positions.

First, a policy maker could feel that the

alleviation of poverty is only one of many benefits. The intangible benefits of education (social and private) may be considered much more important than the goal of generating income gains. Thus, a heavy emphasis on the improved education of the poor could be justified even if only a relatively small amount of poverty is alleviated as a result.

Second, he may feel that large amounts of transfers and other direct help are simply out of the question. The handout connotation of such approaches may result in a near-absolute constraint. Therefore, even though the alleviation of poverty is paramount in the mind of a policy maker, he may feel compelled to choose an apparently less efficient approach to this goal.

Third, he may feel that poverty is more than a matter of income and that while income is changed by transfers, the changes he seeks—in attitude, motivation, etc.—are only the result of education and other nontransfer programs.

Fourth, it might be argued that the evidence of low payoff rates to relatively modest educational improvements suggests that revolutionary changes in the school system are called for. It might be argued that slum schools should be saturated with vast amounts of new personnel and equipment, thus bringing matters to a new threshold where low status students would end up gaining economic competence worth much more than the costs of the saturation. However, the cross-section analysis with Project Talent schools, which dealt with reasonably large dollar differences in expenditures per student, did not establish that large changes are any more efficient than small ones. It may be that the real need lies in a revolution of attitudes, organization, and approach of public school systems. While it is unclear where one turns for evidence on the efficacy or permanence of such a revolution, it is not unreasonable for the policy maker to prefer the gamble in this direction. Additionally, he may feel that social attitudes have changed and with them the returns to increased expenditure and effort.

Fifth, the evidence of low payoff rates might be used to justify a major reorientation of the war on poverty, in the direction of a heavier emphasis on transfers and other forms of direct help. A strong devotion to the goal of poverty alleviation, an absence of serious constraints on policy choice, and a distrust of revolutions could prompt such a reorientation.

Finally, one could argue that education and direct help expenditures should be designed to work in close tandem. A somewhat heavier emphasis, than now exists, on direct help programs could be justified, but with the proviso that they be tied closely to education programs. If there is a (formal or informal) budget constraint, of some sort, this implies that less of the new spending on antipoverty programs should be channeled into education. This, however, might result in little, if any, loss in terms of foregone improvements in educational performance. Indeed, additional marginal expenditures aimed directly at improving the economic well-being of poor families may do more for educational performance than marginal expenditures in the schools. Our results provide many clues that socioeconomic class is a powerful determinant of educational outcomes; and a relatively small improvement along this dimension, as a result of government programs, may lead to substantial improvements along the dimension of educational performance.

This possibility makes doubly difficult the search for an optimum mix between education and direct help. But to ignore possible complementarities between the two would be a clear mistake. The importance of such effects remains to be measured, and this sort of measurement surely has a high priority in future research.

35. The Minimum Wage and Poverty

Jacob J. Kaufman

Terry G. Foran

INTRODUCTION

This paper examines the relationship between legislated wage minima and poverty. This is certainly not a novel context in which to view minimum wages since the Fair Labor Standards Act of 1938 stated that:

"It is hereby declared to be the policy of this Act, ... to correct and as rapidly as practicable to eliminate ... labor conditions detrimental to the maintenance of the minimum standard of living necessary for health, efficiency, and general well-being of workers."[1]

. . . From its inception up to the present the federal legislation in this field has been concerned primarily with the elimination of poverty. If raising the minimum wage would eliminate poverty, then the only argument remaining would be that of values. It is interesting to note that, according to one survey, 61 percent of university economists opposed the amendments to the minimum wage law even though 88 percent favored the so-called "War on Poverty."[2] Apparently, the majority thinks

[1] Sections 2(a) and 2(b) Fair Labor Standards Act.

[2] *Business in Brief,* No. 68, June 1966, issued by the Chase Manhattan Bank. 79 percent of Business Economists opposed the legislation.

that minimum wage legislation is an inadequate tool for the elimination of poverty.

The primary concern of this paper is the investigation of the role of a minimum wage law as a vehicle for the elimination of poverty. No attempt is made to compare the efficacy of such legislation with other measures which are, or might be, employed to fight poverty. Such an undertaking is beyond the scope of the present paper. . . .

THE OBJECTIVES
AND THEORETICAL CONSIDERATIONS
OF MINIMUM WAGE LEGISLATION

Federal Legislation

Minimum wage legislation has a long history, both foreign and domestic. Although the Fair Labor Standards Act of 1938 (FLSA) contained statutory minima; the administrator was allowed some discretion, reflecting, in part, a concern over the adverse employment effects of such legislation and an interest in spreading available work. The latter objective is revealed in the overtime provisions of the law.

It is important to point out that the coverage of the Act, even with its most recent amendments, is not universal and excludes certain industries engaged in interstate commerce and all industries engaged in intrastate commerce. There are about 41.4 million workers presently covered by the FLSA. Those covered are primarily nonsupervisory employees. The excluded nonsupervisory employees fall into the following categories: outside salesmen, domestics, agriculture, retail trade and services. Others not covered by the Act are: self-employed; governmental workers; unpaid family workers; and executive, administrative, and professional employees.

The minimum wage was originally set at 25 ¢ an hour in 1938. It was increased to 75 ¢ in 1949. The 1956 amendment raised it to $1.00. The 1961 amendments raised the wage of previously covered workers to $1.15 in 1961 and to $1.25 in 1963. The timing of the increases for newly covered employees was more gradual. The same is true of the timing provided for by the 1966 amendments. For the previously covered workers the legislated floor was raised to $1.40 in 1967 and will be increased to $1.60 by February of 1968.

The purpose of including this brief wage chronology is twofold. First, it provides a benchmark for later discussion, and, second, it demonstrates the concern on the part of advocates of the minimum wage over the possible unemployment effects of raising wages. The planned gradual wage increases attest to the fairly well grounded belief that too large an increase in the minimum wage might have serious unemployment repercussions.

State Legislation

Complementing the federal minimum wage legislation—in fact antedating it—is the minimum wage legislation in the individual states. Today, 38 states, the District of Columbia, and Puerto Rico have such laws. . . .

Theoretical Considerations

The standard argument of minimum wage proponents is that it raises the wages of the poorly paid and, therefore, boosts their incomes. Opponents retort that "It's better to receive a low wage than no wage at all," suggesting that a legislated minimum wage eliminates jobs. Although the arguments as stated in this fashion appear rather simple, they do,

however, succinctly summarize the major area of conflict. This has been the primary issue in the literature to date. But it is not the only pertinent question. One question which does not appear to have received adequate attention is: What is the combined effect of the wage change and the employment change? That is, what is the effect on labor's share? This question is probably most relevant to the poverty problem.

Under competitive conditions each worker is paid the value of his marginal product. Therefore, given a normally downward sloping demand curve for labor, a minimum wage will cause the least efficient workers to be laid off, unless certain conditions held. Although these conditions will be discussed below, at present, assume the competitive state.

Minimum wage regulation is not universal. Its coverage applies to specific industries within the economy, although it is likely that part of its effect is similar to that which would be generated from a general regulatory wage. The effect of the minimum wage as a specific regulatory device is the same as that which occurs from a decline in demand for labor in particular sectors.

> In this case, it is not the unemployment which is economically speaking, the most significant effect of regulation (in an extreme case, where the affected firms are abnormally prosperous, and the rise in wages is only just sufficient to prevent their expanding employment or to diminish their expansion, there may be no net unemployment due to the regulation); the important effect is the redistribution of labor— the fact that some men are prevented from securing employment in a trade where they would be better off than they are otherwise condemned to be.[3]

However, if there are no industries available or suitable to absorb the unemployed, then the unemployment created will not be of a temporary nature. This unemployment "must go on until the artificial wages are relaxed, or until competitive wages have risen to the artificial level."[4] Realistically, the former alternative may be discounted.

It is probably more realistic to assume, in light of the type of regulation provided for in

---

[3]Hicks, *The Theory of Wages,* 2nd ed. (London: MacMillan & Co., 1964), p. 180.

[4]*Ibid.,* p. 181.

the Fair Labor Standards Act and its evolution, that, if competitive conditions hold, there will be some redistribution of labor; but more predominantly there will be unemployment which will be eliminated only with the restoration of preexisting wage differentials. This is due to the imperfect mobility of labor, and the trend toward greater coverage under the federal minimum wage law.

Given the present assumptions, then, one can expect a certain amount of lengthy unemployment as a result of an increase in the minimum wage. The question thus becomes "how much unemployment?" This question really breaks down into two questions: (1) What percentage of workers lose their jobs? and (2) How does the increased unemployment compare to the increase in wages? The first is the traditional query; the second is relevant to the total wage bill, or labor's share.[5]

In short-run, both answers are given by the elasticities of the relevant demand curves for labor. The relevant demand curves are the industry demand curves, because of the assumption of competitive conditions and, more realistically, because of the manner of coverage stipulated in the Fair Labor Standards Act and its amendments. The elasticity of the short-run demand curve for labor will depend on the technique of production, the demand for the product, and the supply curves of other (nonfixed) factors. The two pertinent factors for discussion are output market elasticity and percentage of labor cost to total cost, because they are the only factors amenable to empirical investigation. The more elastic the demand curve for labor the greater the unemployment which will result from any given wage increase. The demand curve for labor will be more elastic the greater the percentage of labor cost to total cost and the more elastic the demand for the product sold by the industry.

The evidence seems to indicate that those industries primarily affected by minimum wages have both a relatively high percentage of labor cost to total cost and have relatively elastic product demand curves. Four out of the

five industries surveyed by the U.S. Department of Labor after the increase in the minimum wage in 1950 possessed a degree of monopoly power well below the average for manufacturing. As a general rule, the lesser the degree of monopoly the more elastic the product demand curve. A comparison of the lowest paying industries in 1954 showed that five out of the six had below average degrees of monopoly, and above average relative labor costs.

In general, the labor demand curves in those industries affected by minimum wage legislation will be more elastic than in other industries. This statement is made on the basis of the only observable parameters affecting these curves. The implications for employment changes and labor's share in the short-run are clear. Adverse employment changes will be relatively large and labor's absolute share will decline. These changes will be accentuated, the higher the minimum is above the old wage in any particular industry. If these assumptions are valid, the long-run results are the same. First, the increased ability to substitute factors increases the elasticity of the demand for labor. Thus, machinery may be used to replace labor. Second, certain types of product lines may be dropped because they are no longer profitable. Third, the least efficient firms in the industry may find their demise hastened by the added burden imposed by the minimum wage rate.

To what extent are these conclusions modified by relaxing the implicit assumptions of the above analysis? If the relevant laborers were not operating at peak efficiency before the establishment of the minimum wage, it is possible that they may subsequently do so, thus increasing their productivity and preventing unemployment. The only plausible reason for this occurrence is the spur of threatening unemployment. This particular influence, however, will probably not be great enough to save many jobs.

The second assumption to be dropped is that of the maximizing firm. This calls for the introduction of the standard textbook "shock effect." The basic premise underlying the shock effect is that management is too lazy and content to bother maximizing. The minimum wage thus "shocks" management out of its lethargy with the higher costs. It begins to alter its technique of production in an effort to cut costs, thus increasing worker productivity and preventing unemployment. However, as pointed

[5]This discussion has ignored the question of a minimum wage setting a barrier to the expansion of further employment. This is, of course, an important aspect of the impact of a minimum wage. To the degree that a minimum wage causes workers to lose jobs, it must *a fortiori* be a barrier to further employment.

out by Stigler,[6] and as argued above, the industries primarily affected by minimum wage legislation are, by and large, competitive and have a higher percentage of labor cost to total cost. Thus, it is unlikely that the managements in these industries have overlooked opportunities to minimize labor costs.[7]

In this same context, it might be noted that if one accepts Hicks' theory, then any sort of "shock" received by management as the result of a wage increase will result in "induced" innovation, as the result of the change in relative factor prices. "Its effect on the marginal productivity of capital is bound to be much more favorable than its effect on the marginal productivity of labour.[8] In other words, the types of inventions adopted because of higher minimum wages can be expected to be of a labor-saving type and, as such, they will have the least effect upon mitigating unemployment. The impact of this type of innovation would be to reduce labor's share.

A second factor which might mitigate against the unemployment effects of higher minima is the existence of monopsony in the labor market. When an employer has monopsony power he finds it necessary to increase wages to hire additional workers. If he cannot discriminate among his employees he must not only pay the new higher wage to the worker just hired, but also raise the wage of his other workers. Because of this, his additional labor cost of hiring one more worker is greater than the wage paid to that new worker. This will constrain the employer from hiring further workers. The effect of a minimum wage set above the old wage will, within a certain range, eliminate this constraint because now the cost of a new worker is simply the wage rate he gets paid. The result of this may be that a minimum wage will cause no unemployment and may even cause more workers to be hired.

However, it is unlikely that the monopsony element exists to any great degree in the low-wage areas covered under the Wage-Hour Act,

and if it does, it is unlikely that a nationally set minimum will fall within the relevant range in many cases. . . .

IMPACT STUDIES ON MINIMUM WAGES

There is no question that the immediate impact of raising minimum wages is to increase the wage of covered workers. There is also little question that given a once-and-for-all increase, preexisting differentials eventually will be reestablished. There may also be an almost immediate increase of the wages of non-covered workers due to personnel policies and a worker efficiency rationale. From the preceding discussion it has been shown that there will be some unemployment under a static situation. This unemployment will be greater, if entire firms are forced out of business, to the extent that they themselves are not dissolved by merger, and to the extent to which their shares of the market are lost to the industry. Further, this unemployment may either be accentuated or alleviated by technological changes introduced by the affected firms. The questions with regard to unemployment, therefore, are how much and for how long.

Naturally, the economy is not as static as is the theory. The difficulty of isolating the effects of minimum wages in a dynamic economy is obvious. Nonetheless, scholars, after stating this, proceed to do the best that is possible under existing conditions. It is to this research that we now turn.[9]

---

[6] G. Stigler, "The Economics of Minimum-Wage Legislation," *American Economic Review,* June 1946, pp. 358-363. Reprinted in W. Bowen, *Labor and the National Economy* (New York: Norton & Co., 1965), p. 43.

[7] For a point of view different from this see the argument of R. Lester, *Economics of Labor,* 2nd ed. (New York: Macmillan, 1964), pp. 516-518.

[8] J. Hicks, *op. cit.,* p. 204.

[9] At the outset of this discussion, it should be stated that much of the writing on the impact of minimum wages is in the nature of summarizing the studies that have been done. This discussion is in part a summary of summaries. For the sake of expediency the following borrows heavily from the summaries printed in:

(1) Peck, *Economic Factors in Statutory Minimum Wages* (Washington: The Logis. Ref. Ser., L. of C. 1948).

(2) J. F. Maloney, "Some Effects of the Federal Fair Labor Standards and upon Southern Industry," *Southern Economic Journal* (July, 1942), pp. 15-21.

(3) H. Weiss, "Economic Effects of a Nationwide Minimum Wage," *Industrial Relations Research Association, Proceedings* (1956), pp. 154-166.

(4) H. M. Douty, "Some Effects of the $1.00 Minimum Wage in the United States," *Economica* (May, 1960), pp. 137-147.

The first minima were the 25¢ and the 30¢ hourly rates, and finally the 40¢ hourly rate. In this early period there were not many special studies conducted to determine the impact of the legislation. "Of the 690,000 workers estimated to be receiving less than 30¢ an hour in the spring of 1939, 54 percent were in the South."[10] At the time, in the southern fertilizer industry, 17 percent of common labor was receiving less than the minimum. About 55 percent of the common labor in the cottonseed crushing industry was also below the minimum. The increase in average hourly earnings in this industry between 1937-38 and 1939-40 was 30 percent. The wages of the unskilled workers rose more than the skilled. Despite a period of rising prosperity, employment decreased 19 percent. The indications were that, after the imposition of the minimum wage, labor-saving machinery was adopted in the industry.

The seamless hosiery industry was also rather severely affected by the initial minimum. Comparing employment in the industry for the first 9 months of 1938 with employment for the first 9 months of 1939, it was found that employment was 10.1 percent higher in the later years for the industry as a whole but 7.4 percent less for those establishments which were paying an average hourly wage below 25¢ before the minimum was set. Most of the plants which suffered the greatest declines were in the South. "Over the two-year period (1938-1940) employment in northern plants increased by 4.9 percent but decreased 5.5 percent in Southern plants."[11]

The firms in the industry made the predictable adjustments, following the legislation, of introducing labor-saving machinery and altering existing equipment to produce new lines of products. . . .

Another set of studies undertaken by the Department of Labor was designed to determine the impact of the $1.00 minimum wage. The major part of the survey program was directed toward 12 manufacturing industries which were known to come under the impact of the new increase.

In all of the industries studied there was an increase in the average hourly earnings immediately following the wage increase. These increases ranged from 5.3 percent to 21.7 percent. The wage structures in the industries were compressed, and the immediate indirect impact on the wages of non-affected workers was small. The re-establishment of preexisting differentials was not particularly in evidence in the short-run. The evidence indicates that employers began to re-establish the differentials in the second payroll period following the increase in the statutory wage; this was continued into the third payroll period. In other words, the restoration of an equilibrium wage differential following the impact of a legislated disequilibrium is a slow process.

There did not appear to be any effect on workers in non-covered industries as a result of the wage increase in other industries.

The employment effects were adverse in all but one of the twelve industries, with employment declines ranging from 3.2 percent to 15 percent in the year following the increase in the minimum. A very small percentage of plants interviewed stated that the discharges were the result of the higher minimum wage, nonetheless the evidence is fairly convincing that this was the case. Certainly declining demand, inefficiency, substitution of machinery, or whatever reasons might have been offered by those interviewed, would not negate this conclusion. . . .

Utilizing traditional data sources, such as the census of manufacturers, Kaun has conducted a study covering the post-war period from 1947 to 1958, which included the increases to 75¢ and $1.00.[12] On the assumption that the low-wage industries would be most significantly affected by the statutory increases, Kaun found that there were greater increases in the capital-labor ratio over the period in those industries assumed to be primarily affected by minimum wages. Minimum wages cause a decline in labor intensity as a result of the substitution of capital for labor. Kaun also found that there were definite adverse effects on the number of establishments in five low-wage paying manufacturing industries. . . .

It appears that the experience of states with minimum wage laws has been essentially the same as it has been for the country under the F.L.S.A. Further, the experiences of both are essentially consistent with the conclusions drawn from traditional economic theory.

Given downward sloping demand curves for

[10]Maloney, op. cit., p. 17.

[11]See H. M. Douty, "Minimum Wage Regulation in the Seamless Hosiery Industry," Southern Economic Journal (Oct., 1941), p. 184.

[12]D. Kaun, "Minimum Wages, Factor Substitution and the Marginal Producer," Quarterly Journal of Economics (1965), pp. 478-486.

labor, when this labor is being hired under non-union, non-monopsony conditions, static economic theory postulates a fall in employment as the result of an increase in the wage. This unemployment will be greater in the more competitive firms which are affected. The unemployment which is thus created will be eliminated with the re-establishment of an equilibrium wage differential.

Further basic conclusions of economic theory are that factor substitution may occur following a wage increase, and that certain inefficient firms will be forced out of business. It should be noted that this theory and its conclusions are not restricted to the perfectly competitive state but hold equally well for an economy populated by various degrees of monopoly in the product market.

The overwhelming bulk of the evidence on the impact of minimum wages supports these conclusions. The fact that, in certain instances, adverse employment changes were noted as being rather minor in no way vitiates the theory. The theory assumes no changes in the variables, whereas in reality product demand may be expanding to such an extent that the impact of the minimum wage is the curtailment of the expansion of employment, rather than a rise in unemployment. . . .

MINIMUM WAGE LEGISLATION AND ITS IMPACT UPON DISADVANTAGED GROUPS

Existing evidence indicates that younger and older workers, women, workers with little education, and non-white workers are "disadvantaged" in today's labor market. These people carry the burden of unemployment and poverty. The concern over poverty in recent years has drawn attention to these particular groups. Since minimum wage legislation is considered a tool to combat poverty, it is not unusual that attention has been drawn to its possible impact on the disadvantaged.

If minimum wage legislation causes adverse employment effects, then it seems to follow intuitively that these disadvantaged groups of workers will be most harmed by legislated wage floors. A number of economists [including Milton Friedman and Yale Brozen] have attempted to bolster their intuition with evidence.[13] . . .

. . . There appears to be nothing in the data to substantiate the claims of Friedman and Brozen. . . .

THE MINIMUM WAGE AND INCOME DISTRIBUTION

It has been asserted that "The manipulation of individual prices is neither an efficient nor an equitable device for changing the distribution of personal income."[14] It is of course true that a higher wage rate does not necessarily yield an adequate income. Nevertheless, it is one of the primary ingredients. In fact, wage income is the primary source of income of low-wage families. In 1955, 63.4 percent of the income of non-farm multi-person families with incomes under $4,000 was derived from wages and salaries. In 1964, of the 47.5 million families with incomes under $3,000, about 50 percent had one family member employed and 20 percent had 2 family members employed. In other words, a good deal of the poverty which exists today is wage related.

Therefore, if minimum wage legislation is a factor in redistributing factor shares in favor of labor, one possible inference might be that it is effective in redistributing the personal distribution of income toward the low income classes. A redistribution of income in favor of the low income classes is usually defined as alleviating poverty. If it can be shown that minimum wages do alter the personal distribution of income through its influence on factor shares in the manner suggested then it must be considered an effective weapon to combat poverty.

One major difficulty with this simple proposition is that the necessary data are not available to test it empirically. The least aggregative data available on labor's share are on the S.I.C. 2 digit classification level. The Labor's Share data utilized below are from Schultz and Tryon.[15] One caveat with respect to the data is that the

[13]Yale Brozen and Milton Friedman, *The Minimum Wage Rate*, (Washington: The Free Society Association, Inc., April 1966), pp. 46-47.

[14]G. Stigler, *op. cit.*, p. 44.

[15]U.S. Congress Joint Economic Committee, *Prices and Costs in Manufacturing Industries*, Study Paper No. 17 (Washington: GPO, 1960).

employee compensation figures used to derive the estimates include both wages and salaries, so that a change in "labor's share" can be attributed to an increase in the salary component. The earnings and employment statistics are those presented in the B.L.S. series.

The basic assumption made for purposes of this analysis is that those industries which in 1947 had the lowest average hourly earnings would be the industries most affected by minimum wage increases. In other words, it is assumed that the dispersion of wages about the average is the same in all industries. . . .

Rank correlations were used because of the smallness of sample and the historical nature of the data. The value for the correlation of levels of earnings in 1947 (lowest to highest) against changes in labor's share for the period cited (highest to lowest) was +.691 which is significant at the 1 percent level. The relative increases in wages for the period correlated against wage levels was not significant (+.196). If anything the sign of the coefficient would indicate that the higher paying industries experienced greater relative wage increases. Despite this, however, the low paying industries seemed to experience the smallest increases in employment: the rank correlation between wage levels and employment changes was +.327 (significant at the 5 percent level), indicating that the higher paying industries had the greatest increases in employment, or that the low wage industries experienced the least amount of increased employment over the period.

The conclusion must be then that the increase in labor's share in the low wage industries was not the result of increased labor productivity or product demand pulling up wages. The evidence of small employment changes indicates, to the contrary, that the relative wage increases, although not necessarily the highest in manufacturing, were the result of a cost-push factor.

The villain most commonly sought in the case of a wage-push mechanism is unionism. Correlating wage levels in 1947 with degrees of unionism yields a coefficient of +.503, which is significant at the 1 percent level, and indicates that the higher paying industries have the greatest degree of unionism; or, conversely, that the low paying industries had the least amount of unionism. Such a correlation detracts considerably from unionism being the explanation of the cost-push factor in the low wage industries. Another possible, and traditional, explanation is the contagious nature of union increases; i.e., the "sympathetic pressure" which transmits wage increases in the organized sector to the unorganized sector. This factor, however, is to be doubted as an explanatory variable in the present case. If union wage increases in the high paying firms were transmitted to the low paying firms, then the percentage increases in the latters' wages would be greater. The evidence indicates that this is not the case for the period under study in which the low wage industries did not have greater relative wage increases.

A third possibility is that minimum wage legislation was a causal factor in the wage-push in the low wage industries in the post-war period, and that the result of this wage-push was a greater increase in labor's share than occurred in other, less affected industries. . . .

The connection between [the] increased labor's share in the low wage industries of the economy and the personal distribution of income is at best tenuous. In fact from 1947 to 1961 the percentage of total family income accruing to the bottom 2/5 of consumer units fell from 16 percent to 15.6 percent, a slight movement toward greater inequality. If minimum wages have been effective in the manner postulated a movement toward greater equality in the distribution of income would be expected.

One explanation offered for the relative stability of the postwar personal distribution of income is that an increase in the wage and salary component tending to create more equality was offset by an increased share of wages and salaries going to the top 10 percent of consumer units. This latter development being primarily due to the increased number of high income salaried managers and professionals.[16]

Thus, the possibility presents itself that the increased labor share evidenced in low wage industries may be due primarily to an increase in the salary component. However, it is equally possible that this increased labor share is at the lower end of the distribution, but is not reflected in the personal distribution because it has been outweighed by the factors creating inequality.

This brief study of labor's share is far from

---

[16]W. Avril, *The Size Distribution of Income in the U.S.: 1947 to 1961* (unpublished master's thesis at The Pennsylvania State University, 1965).

adequate. In large part this is due to the paucity of appropriate data. The correlations above do not unequivocally demonstrate that minimum wage legislation has increased labor's share. However, they do hold out a fairly strong possibility that this may have been the case, and further that, even though this may not have created an increased equality in the distribution of income, it may have helped prevent a movement toward greater inequality.

CONCLUSION

The nexus between minimum wages and the problem of poverty is not easily demonstrated. The connection runs from increased wages through changes in employment to the aggregate effect of both on labor's share, and the effect of this on the personal distribution of income. Also important is the consideration of who the individuals are and who are most affected by these changes.

The conclusions of this paper—which, it must be stressed, are not all conclusive—are:

(1) minimum wages raise the wages of workers;
(2) minimum wages create adverse employment effects, but there is no strong evidence that this unem-

ployment is unequally distributed toward the "disadvantaged" groups in society;

(3) minimum wages may very well have the effect of redistributing income in favor of labor, thus creating a tendency toward less inequality in the personal distribution of income.

Many argue that the number of "poverty" families affected by minimum wage hikes is a small proportion of the total "poverty" category. This, however, is not a relevant argument. Granted, there are more efficacious means to eliminate poverty, but no comprehensive program is available. Social security goes *part* of the way; unemployment compensation goes *part* of the way; all welfare measures go *part* of the way; and minimum wage legislation goes *part* of the way.

Of all these means of eliminating poverty, the minimum wage is the only one which does not impair worker incentives. In fact, it will increase the incentive to work in most instances in a way that a negative income tax cannot be expected to do.

As with any other measure designed to reduce poverty, the benefits to society which result from a rise in the minimum wage must be weighed against the costs to society. This paper has attempted to point out these benefits and costs.

INDUSTRIAL
RELATIONS

V

THE LABOR MOVEMENT

The Labor Movement

The preceding selections have been concerned primarily with the operations of labor markets. In addition to individual workers, many institutions, including firms, employers' associations, federal, state, and local governments, and trade unions, play an important role in labor markets. Trade unions and other worker organizations have arisen for many reasons and have taken a wide variety of forms. The selection by Philip Taft discusses some of the many theories that have arisen to explain the origin and behavior of the labor movement. Among the theories discussed are those developed by the Webbs, Marx and Lenin, Hoxie, and Commons.

One of the most influential theories is the one developed by Selig Perlman in *A Theory of the Labor Movement,* written in 1928. In his view workers generally have had their economic attitudes "determined by consciousness of scarcity of opportunity" and thus have tended to band together to control and ration job opportunities. In attempting to achieve their objectives, workers have had to combat not only the capitalist employers but also the anti-capitalist intelligentsia, which has tried to channel worker protest into a more fundamental revolution against capitalism. Although the intelligentsia has been a very important force in the historical development of the European labor movement, it has been much less influential in America. In this country the major protagonist of the labor movement has been the capitalist class, a class whose position has been strengthened by many of our pioneer traditions.

The differences between the labor movement in the United States and in Europe are also discussed in the more recent selection by Everett Kassolow. European workers generally have been more concerned with transforming society and advancing the entire working class. Thus they have put much greater emphasis than their American counterparts on political activities. In recent years, however, the differences between the American and European labor movements appear to be diminishing.

As the preceding selections indicate, the American labor movement has been more oriented toward collective bargaining and less interested in radical political programs than the European movement. Nevertheless, there have been numerous attempts to radicalize American labor. The selection by Walter Galenson discusses these attempts and indicates some of the reasons why such attempts have had little success.

36. Theories of the Labor Movement

Philip Taft

Generalizations to explain the origin and nature of the trade union movement have been developed by a variety of writers. Even a superficial observation of the labor movement reveals a multitude of facts, some of them isolated and some contradictory. A theory is an attempt to give an ordered explanation, to account for the origin and behavior of labor unionism. It may also serve as a basis for predicting the conduct and policies that may be followed by the labor movement in the future. Policies in this connection must be regarded in a broad sense rather than the operations on a day-to-day basis. The first part of the discussion examines the theories which seek to explain the origin of the labor movement. It is followed by an analysis of theories dealing with the behavior of the labor movement, and a section which attempts to discuss the various views in the light of contemporary developments.

THE ORIGIN OF THE LABOR MOVEMENT

Brentano

One of the earliest attempts by a non-socialist writer to deal with this question was made by the German economist and historian,

I am greatly indebted to Professors Milton Derber and David McCabe and to my colleague, Professor Caleb Smith, for a number of helpful suggestions.

Lujo Brentano. Writing in the third quarter of the 19th century, Brentano was convinced that "Trade-Unions are the successors of the old Gilds."[1] Brentano, unlike the contemporary critics who see trade unions as a "gild type" of monopoly, was not opposed to organizations of workers. On the contrary, he believed they were both necessary and desirable as offsets to the power of the employer. Unions, in Brentano's opinion, arose under "the breaking up of an old system, and among the men suffering from this disorganization, in order that they may maintain independence and order."[2] ...

Brentano emphasized that the objectives of the trade unions as of the craft gilds "was the maintenance of an entire system of order," or of a standard of life which was being undermined by the growing factory owners. Instead of being a revolutionary mass bent on destroying the system of private property, Brentano emphasized the conservative aspects of trade unionism in its desire to return to an earlier time. In this view, the trade union arose as a result of the breakdown of the customary rights enjoyed by the worker, and it was an attempt to create a new equilibrium by elaborating a

[1] Lujo Brentano, "On the History and Development of Gilds," *English Gilds*. Edited by Toulmin Smith (London: Early English Text Society, 1870), p. clxv.

[2] *Ibid.*, p. xlvi.

system of rules to govern industry. The view that the trade unions were descended from the gilds has been challenged by the Webbs. Nevertheless, the notion that the trade unions arose because of the disturbance of an established custom shows that Brentano well understood one of the essential causes for the origin of trade unionism. An attempt to change a rule or a rate has frequently led to organization. Considering that his essay was written in the 1860's, when most of the English unions were groupings of skilled men, the insistence upon their resemblance to craft gilds is perhaps better understood.

Moreover, the scarcity consciousness which is a characteristic of the skilled unions, in the United States as well as elsewhere, shown in the restrictive rules and the limitation upon admission, is certainly an attitude found in the gilds. Even where no direct connection exists, the spirit is not different. However, Brentano neglected the difference between the "mercantile" attitude of a gildsman and the wage consciousness of a worker. Yet, his emphasis upon the conservative traditional nature of unions, their insistence upon protecting their job territory by restrictions upon free entry and technological change, caught a significant aspect of early trade unionism.

The Webbs

The Webbs, who followed Brentano chronologically, refused to accept the latter's interpretation of the origin of the labor movement, although they admired many of his insights. To the Webbs, the origin of trade unionism depended upon the separation of classes. The Webbs defined a trade union as "a continuous association of wage earners for the purpose of maintaining or improving the conditions of their working lives."[3] They, therefore, dated the beginning of English trade unionism in the latter part of the 17th century with the appearance of a property-less wage earner. The journeymen's revolts of earlier times were interpreted largely as movements against the authority of the gild, and the "bachelors' companies" they find to have been a subordinate branch of the masters' gild. It was only when the skilled

journeyman found his prospect for advancement into the ranks of the masters greatly diminished that stable combinations among the handicraftsmen arose. It was only when "the changing conditions of industry had reduced to an infinitesimal chance the journeyman's prospect of himself becoming a master, that we find the passage of ephemeral combinations into permanent trade societies."[4]

The basic cause for the origin of trade unions, according to the Webbs, was "in the separation of classes, or in the separation of the worker from the means of production. This is itself due to an economic revolution which took place in certain industries." Unions arose as soon as "the great bulk of the workers had ceased to be independent producers, themselves controlling the processes and owning the materials and product of their labour, and had passed into the conditions of lifelong wage-earners, possessing neither the instruments of production nor the commodity in its finished state."[5] This separation of classes or the separation of the worker from the means of production preceded, to some extent, the development of the factory system. The reduction of the worker to a mere wage-earner, dependent upon others for employment, may have come about as a result of one or many of several causes. In the tailoring trade, the masters came from a small segment—the journeymen who had acquired the highest level of skills. The great majority of the workers were poor, employed as sewers who prepared the material for their more skilled brethren. Increasing capital requirements accentuated the class divisions within the trade. It was possible

> to start a business in a back street as an independent master tailor with no more capital or skill than the average journeyman could command, yet the making of fine clothes worn by the Court and the gentry demanded then, as now, a capital and a skill which put the extensive and lucrative trade altogether out of the reach of the thousands of journeymen whom it employed.[6]

In the woolen industry, class differentiation with its mass of permanent wage-earners followed the rise of the "rich clothiers," who

---

[3]Sidney and Beatrice Webb, *The History of Trade Unionism* (London: Printed by the Authors for the Students of the Workers Educational Association, 1919), p. 1.

[4]*Ibid.*, p. 6.

[5]*Ibid.*, p. 26.

[6]*Ibid.*, p. 31.

provided the raw materials, and encouraged the division of labor so that a different set of workers would be employed at each stage of manufacturing. The merchant capitalists or clothiers purchased the wool, had it carded and spun into yarn by one group of workers, had it changed into cloth by another group, the weavers, and finally turned the product over to a new set of workers to be dressed. While the workers still retained the tools of their trade, they could acquire, as a rule, neither the capital nor the knowledge to enter business. Consequently, a class of permanent wage-earners who had scant hopes of ever becoming capitalists arose, with the result that permanent organizations of labor were devised to protect the standard of life.

The universal cause which accounts for the origin of trade unionism is the separation of the worker from the means of production with the consequent rise of a permanent class of workers dependent upon an employer. While other conditions may tend to create a permanent class of wage-earners, the rise of the factory system was the most pervasive cause of the separation of the worker from the means of production. For the Webbs, it had

> become a commonplace of modern Trade Unionism that only in those industries in which the worker has ceased to be concerned in the profits of buying and selling—that inseparable characteristic of the ownership and management of the means of production—can effective and stable trade organization be established.[7]

Yet, this explanation raises a problem, for there had always existed in English industry a large class of unskilled and low-paid workers virtually debarred from rising to independent craftsmen. The ill-paid farm laborer, and others of low skill, however, had not been the pioneers of trade unionism. On the contrary, it was the highly skilled journeyman who for years had been the object of government protection who was the first to form labor unions. It was not the worker who had the lowest bargaining power but the one with the greatest sense of independence who pioneered the trade union movement. This was inevitable, for only the worker with a great sense of independence was willing to challenge the authority of the employer in the early days of organization, and it required some threat to existing customs and

standards to initiate organization. Therefore, it was not the property-less proletariat of Marx but the labor aristocrat who was the pioneer of trade unionism. The Webbs and Brentano agreed that a threat to established relations is likely to stimulate organization of labor in defense of the old conditions or in an effort to establish a new equilibrium. The Webbs, however, placed emphasis upon the class nature of a union; that it arose when the possibilities of class mobility had been reduced and when the worker felt that he had nothing but his labor to sell. The Webbs' view underlines the special character of the trade union which, despite many attitudes of the old gild, was a new type of organization. . . .

Marxism

Marxist ideas on trade unions are intimately and inextricably related to the general Marxist assumptions and conclusions on social institutions and the directions of their development. In common with the Webbs, Marx and his followers explained the origin of trade unions by the rise of a working class bereft of control over the instruments of production. While the Webbs regarded labor unions as a means used by workers to maintain or improve their traditional standards of life, Marx regarded them as only one—and by no means the most important—weapon in labor's armory for waging the class war. . . .

At best, trade unions could only deal with short-run, day-to-day problems. They were a response to the need of labor to protect its day-to-day interests. They were spontaneous efforts by workers to restrict the effects of competition in the labor market.[8] Unions were class organizations, which came into existence to protect the worker against the employer. It was the pressure of the employer which drove the worker to revolt. Soon, however, labor established

> permanent associations in order to make provision beforehand for these occasional revolts. . . . Now and then the workers are victorious but only for a time. The real fruit of their battle lies not in the immediate result but in the expanding union of workers. The union is helped on by the improved means of communication that are created by modern industry and

[7]*Ibid.*, p. 41.

[8]A. Lozovsky, *Marx and the Trade Unions* (New York: International Publishers, 1942), p. 16.

that place the workers of different localities in contact with one another. It was just this contact that was needed to centralize the numerous local struggles, all of the same character, into one national struggle between classes. But every class struggle is a political struggle.[9]

This statement, although it was written in 1847, expressed the essentials of the Marxist view of trade unionism, even though Marx continued to write for 35 years and Engels for almost 50 years after these words appeared. Union organizations were an attempt to support the revolts made inevitable by the exploitation by the capitalist. Labor might have been able to gain temporary concessions but not permanent relief. Therefore, the isolated revolts had to be continually enlarged until they became the living embodiment of the struggle between classes. In line with his views on the origin and nature of trade unionism, Marx inspired a resolution at the first congress of the International Workingmen's Association (First International) which advised the trade unions to seek actively the abolition of the wage system. The trade unions[10] were more than institutions for the daily struggle with employers. They were a means of mobilizing the strength of labor against the capitalist class. "While, however, the trade unions are absolutely indispensable in the daily struggle between labour and capital, still more important is their other aspect, as instruments *for transforming the system of wage labour and for overthrowing the dictatorship of capital.*"[11]

Selected Catholic Writers on Trade Unionism

The attitude of Catholic clergymen and writers on trade unionism was extremely important in the United States because members of the faith were heavily represented among industrial workers. The question before Catholic students was whether the unions arose to defend the worker against superior economic

force or were a section of a movement challenging religion and existing governments. . . .

Catholic laymen and theologians had been watching the evolution of modern industrialism, with its accompanying evils, with growing concern. Not only was modern industry threatening to undermine established institutions, but the excesses of some businessmen and their inordinate lust for gain were encouraging the spread of radical social doctrines. The Bishop of Mainz, Wilhelm Emanual von Ketteler, insisted that the church take the lead in eradicating the industrial evils of his time. . . .

The writings and works of these reformers culminated in Pope Leo XIII's *Rerum Novarum,* a document which addressed itself to the social problems of the time. At the outset, the Pope attacked the doctrines of materialistic socialism then making considerable headway on the continent. He, however, fully endorsed the trade unions seeking the protection of the worker in industry. Trade unions arose, according to Pope Leo, to redress the advantages held by the employer and to form voluntary associations as was the natural right of man.

Robert Hoxie

Robert Hoxie was impressed by the diversity in the structural arrangements and in the functioning of unions. He found "that unionism has not a single genesis, but that it has made its appearance time after time, independently, wherever in the modern industrial era a group of workers, large or small, developed a strong internal consciousness of common interests."[12] He was convinced, moreover, that unions, over time, responded to changes in conditions, needs and attitudes. He found that unionists "are prone to act and to formulate theories afterward,"[13] and that they attempted to meet whatever problems events had placed before them. Unions arose out of group needs and as they were not uniform, a single theory will not suffice. The

union program, taking with it all its mutations and contradictions, comprehends nothing

[9]Karl Marx and Frederick Engels, *Manifesto of the Communist Party* (Chicago: Charles H. Kerr and Company, no date), p. 26.

[10]Oscar Testut, *L'Internationale* (Paris: E. Lachaud, 1871), p. 126. Lozovsky, *op. cit.,* p. 16.

[11]G. M. Stekloff, *History of the First International* (London: Martin Lawrence, Ltd. 1928), p. 84. Italics in source.

[12]Robert Hoxie, *Trade Unionism in the United States* (New York: D. Appleton and Co., 1928), p. 34. The first edition was published by D. Appleton & Co., 1919.

[13]*Ibid.*

less than all the various economic, political, ethical and social viewpoints and modes of action of a vast and heterogeneous complex of working class groups, molded by diverse environments and actuated by diverse motives; it expresses nothing less than ideals, aspirations, hopes and fears, modes of thinking and action of all these working groups. In short, if we can think of unionism as such, it must be as one of the most complex, heterogeneous and protean of modern social phenomena.[14] ...

Hoxie was a shrewd and careful observer, but he overstressed the importance of the differences he noticed between unions. Significant differences in the structure and function of unions existed, but these differences may have reflected the differences in the industrial environment or in the make-up of the membership. If unions are a response to differing group psychology, it is difficult to explain why, despite differences, unions always perform certain basic functions for their members. While one may find Hoxie's explanation of the origin of unions incomplete, his stress on diverse causes did highlight the differences in the structure and the functioning of unions, both with respect to their internal affairs and with respect to collective bargaining. These differences have always existed within American trade unionism, and the attitudes of the workers composing the union have undoubtedly played some role in determining the quality of a particular labor organization. It is difficult to give weight to specific factors, but the make-up of the membership and its response to the problems of industry obviously contribute to determining a union's form and attitudes. Hoxie's emphasis upon variety of origin called attention to a facet in the origin of labor organizations unstressed by other writers.

John R. Commons

John R. Commons was one of the pioneer investigators of labor. In explaining the origin of labor unions, Commons, similarly to the Webbs, in England, based his conclusions upon an examination of records rather than upon an *a priori* theory. Commons attributed the rise of labor organizations to the differentiation of classes, which was in turn due to the expansion of the market. The artisan who embodied

within himself the mercantile, manufacturing, and labor functions is, over a period of time, metamorphosed on one side into a capitalist merchant; on the other, into a manufacturer buying labor, and a wage-earner selling his labor power. The differentiation in function was accompanied by increasing competition—both due to the widening of the market. Facing increasingly severe competition, the merchant capitalist attempted to impose the burdens upon labor by depressing wages. Labor responded by forming labor unions, which sought "the practical remedy ... the elimination of the competitive menace through a protective organization or protective legislation."[15]

Commons maintained that unions arose to overcome the workers' inferior bargaining position. Moreover, he saw in labor organizations the culmination of an age-long process of extending freedom.

> The restraints which laborers place on free competition, in the interests of fair competition, begin to be taken over by employers and administered by their own labor managers. Even organized labor achieves participation with management in the protection of the job, just as the barons and the capitalists achieved participation with the King in the protection of property and business. A common law of labor is constructed by selecting the reasonable practices and rejecting the bad practices of labor, and by depriving both unions and management of arbitrary power over the job.[16] ...

THE BEHAVIOR OF THE LABOR MOVEMENT

The Webbs

The Webbs' theory or theories of union behavior were based upon an exhaustive examination of the practices of labor organization, and they concluded: "For the improvement of the conditions of employment, whether in respect to wages, hours, health, safety, or comfort, the Trade Unionists have, with all their multiplicity of Regulations, really

[14]*Ibid.*, p. 35.

[15]John R. Commons, *Labor and Administration* (New York: The Macmillan Co., 1913), p. 261.

[16]John R. Commons, *Legal Foundations of Capitalism* (New York: The Macmillan Co., 1924), pp. 311-12.

only two expedients, which we term, respectively, *The Device of the Common Rule* and the *Device of the Restrictions of Numbers.*"[17] The principle of the common rule included all terms of employment which uniformly apply to entire groups of workers. Having observed the operation of the principle of the common rule, the Webbs attempted to explain its pervasiveness throughout the trade union movement. The alternative to standardized wage rates and working conditions is free competitive bargaining, by individuals of unequal bargaining power, over the terms of employment. "Such a settlement, it is asserted, inevitably tends, for the mass of workers, towards the worst possible conditions of labor."[18] Consequently, the "Device of the Common Rule is a universal feature of Trade Unionism, and the Assumption on which it is based is held from one end of the Trade Union world to the other."[19] The common rule was a universal principle of trade union policy, which had been devised to equalize the bargaining power of the parties. The enforcement of this policy depended upon conditions in the industry and trade, and the standardizing of wages and hours; the enforcement of sanitary and safety rules and the multitude of other regulations governing the conditions of work were all manifestations of the principle of the common rule. The other principle, restriction of numbers, expressed itself usually through limitation on apprenticeship and entrance into the union. Through these devices the supply of labor in the trade was restricted and the bargaining position of the particular group enhanced.

The Device of the Common Rule, first stated by the Webbs, summarized union policy and practice in the United States as well as in other democratic countries. From the beginning of their existence, the unions in the United States aimed at standardizing wages and working conditions, and the principle enunciated by the Webbs was useful in that it drew attention to a universal policy of trade unionism. On the other hand, the policy of restricting numbers, practiced by both British and American unions of skilled craftsmen, was not as universally practiced as the Device of the Common Rule.

[17]Sidney and Beatrice Webb, *Industrial Democracy* (London: Longmans Green & Co., 1911), p. 560. Italics supplied.

[18]*Ibid.,* p. 561.

[19]*Ibid.,* p. 561.

Yet they called attention to a policy which the American unions have enforced through apprentice regulations, high initiation fees, and closed books.

While the Webbs believed that unions arose as a result of the separation of classes, they did not emphasize class struggle concepts in the formation of policies by trade unions. Unions in working out their attitudes towards wages and other conditions of employment have been guided by one of several assumptions, described by the Webbs as the "Doctrine of Vested Interests, the Doctrine of Supply and Demand, the Doctrine of the Living Wage."[20] The first principle was used to justify opposition to technological change or other innovations which affected adversely the position of a craft. In addition, the Webbs showed that this principle explained the attitude of unions that established conditions must never be lowered. American unions have often resisted technological changes which diminish jobs of the group, and the difficulty of reducing standards in organized plants is widely recognized. The Webbs' observation that the Doctrine of Vested Interests had been weakened among English trade unionists is also true in the United States. It is only in the older artisan-type of union that resistance to technological change is very great. Yet, the doctrine still explains much about the attitude of the older craft union and of some present ones.

The Doctrine of Supply and Demand was, for the Webbs, a summation of the policies practiced by the English unions to place themselves in a strategic position in their dealings with their employers. Rules that regulated the ratio of helpers to journeymen were examples of the application of this principle. Emphasis upon this principle led unions to follow a more aggressive wage policy in periods when business was brisk. "Middle-class public opinion, which had accepted as inevitable the starvation wages caused by Supply and Demand in the lean years, was shocked . . . at the nerve of coal miners and ironworkers . . . demanding ten shillings or even a pound a day."[21] But the policy of governing the union's demand for concessions by conditions in the labor market was widespread in the United States as well as England. This principle explains the conduct of the building trades and coal miners' unions in

[20]*Ibid.,* p. 562.

[21]*Ibid.,* p. 575.

the United States which insist upon wages as high as possible at the moment. The Webbs showed that the pursuit of the supply and demand principle might at times lead to strong organization at both sides of the bargaining table, and eventually to collusive arrangements whereby the public pays a higher price for the product or service than it otherwise would. The collusive bargains in the building trades in American cities whereby the primary interest is in stable prices of labor, as long as the higher costs can be shifted to the consumer, is a good example of the principle.

Supply and demand has not adequately served the unions in all circumstances. Sometimes the unions fell back upon the doctrine of the living wage which manifested itself in the view that the conditions of the labor market should never be allowed to push the standards of living below a given level. In contrast to the supply and demand view, the doctrine of the living wage stressed the rights of the individual to a "civilized" even if indefinite standard. This view was developed later in time both in England and in the United States. It has been especially attractive in both countries to those organized workers who lacked the monopoly position due to special skill and years of training. . . .

Marxism

The view on trade unions initially propounded by Marx has been accepted by his followers. While they must be promoted and encouraged, it was because of the power of the unions to rally and to discipline large masses of workers, and not because of their capacity to win permanent improvements in the position of labor. The unions could resist the oppression of labor by industry, but they could not permanently solve the problem facing the worker in a capitalistic society. . . .

Lenin

Lenin's views on trade unions did not differ essentially from those of other Marxists. More explicitly than others, he tried to define the relation of the union to the political labor movement. He distinguished, first of all, between two types of consciousness, *social democratic consciousness* and *trade union consciousness*. The latter arose spontaneously among workers and its origin was due to the burdens and oppression faced by the worker in

a system of capitalism. In contrast, *social democratic consciousness* arose from without, "quite independently of the spontaneous growth of the labor movement; it arose as a natural and inevitable outcome of the development of ideas among the revolutionary Socialist intelligentsia."[22] Trade unionism came into being as a result of spontaneous action by labor to build a defense against the employer. There was nothing particularly novel in this view, except that Lenin was only incidentally concerned with the origin of unionism. Instead, he sought to define the position of the trade unions in relation to the revolutionary party. . . .

. . . Trade unionism was simply a method of gaining minor concessions, one which was subordinate to the struggle for socialism. Consequently, he warned against the tendency to exaggerate the importance of strikes.

> When strikes spread widely among the workers, then some workers (and some socialists) begin to think that the working class can limit itself solely to strikes and strike funds or societies, and by means of strikes alone the working class can win a significant improvement in its conditions or even win freedom. . . . *But this is a mistaken notion.* Strikes are *one* of the means of struggle of the working class for its freedom, but not the only means.[23]

Strikes were important as they revealed openly the existence of the class struggle. Lenin was not very favorably impressed with trade unions which limit themselves to gaining concessions for their members. For him, this was a manifestation of a state which divided the workers, encouraged "opportunism among them" and caused "temporary decay in the working class movement." Moreover, the

> receipt of high monopoly profits by the capitalists in one of the numerous branches of industry, in one of the numerous countries, etc., makes it economically possible for them to corrupt certain sections of the working class, and for a time a considerable minority, and win

[22]Lenin, *What is to be Done* (New York: International Publishers, 1929), p. 33.

[23]Quoted from Lenin, *Socimenija* (3 ed., Moscow, 1932-1937) II, 597 in Thomas T. Hammond, "Lenin on Russian Trade Unions Under Capitalism, 1894-1904," *The American Slavonic and East European Review* (Dec., 1949), p. 277.

them to the side of the bourgeois of a given industry or nation against all others.[24]

The compromises and gains of the trade unions were due at least in part to the capitalist, grown rich from exploiting the economically backward colonies, bringing part of his gain to the organized working class with higher wages.

Lenin's views were in fact the views held by Marx and his followers on this question. All agreed that unions were a spontaneous result of the worker's desire to defend himself against the oppression and exploitation of the employer, but as they did not regard favorably the possibilities of permanent improvement in the conditions of labor under capitalism, they believed that the chief function of the unions was to organize and discipline the masses and to train them to act together. In Western European countries and the United States where organization of labor was permitted, the unions soon achieved a position where they were able to refuse to subordinate their views to those of the Marxists. In Russia where the trade unions were weak, they were unable to develop an independent life or policy before or after the Revolution. The consequence has been that the unions have become subordinate to the Marxist political party, the Communist Party. Unions have been, in the Soviet Union since 1920, transmission belts between the Party and the working masses. The relationship between the unions and the political party delineated in Marxist theory has come to fruition in the Soviet Union. . . .

Robert Hoxie

It was noted above that Hoxie rejected a monistic interpretation of unionism. For him, it was a variegated protean phenomenon. Maintaining that workers exposed to the same industrial conditions are likely to develop similar attitudes, he sought to show that differences in structure and function of unions reflect differences in the psychology of their members. Hoxie's structural distinctions were similar to those of other writers. His functional types represented something original, and showed a high level of ingenuity. They were widely accepted and influenced the thinking of many students of the subject. Hoxie divided labor organizations into four principle types— business unionism, uplift unionism, revolutionary unionism and predatory unionism. The last was divided into two sub-classes, hold-up unionism and guerilla unionism.

Each of these groups had differentiating characteristics. Business unionism concentrated upon immediate goals, it concerned itself with the interests of its members rather than with labor as a whole, and its thinking was directed towards higher wages and improved working conditions. The capitalist system was accepted and no concern was shown for distant goals. A business union was likely to emphasize discipline in the organization and frequently develops strong leadership.

Uplift unionism was a trade conscious or even class conscious union which tried to raise the cultural and moral level of its members. Stress was placed upon mutual insurance and this type was likely to be democratic in its internal management. It also "drifts easily into political action and the advocacy of cooperative enterprises, profit sharing, and other idealistic plans for social regeneration."[25]

Revolutionary unionism manifested itself in two forms, socialist unions and revolutionary unions. The former aspired to replace capitalism and depended upon political action to achieve its larger aim. This type of union was likely to be critical of present day institutions, and democratic in its internal affairs. The revolutionary union was described as syndicalistic. It emphasized direct action, repudiated political activity, and looked forward to a society of free industrial (producer) cooperatives.

"Predatory unionism is distinguished by a ruthless pursuit of the thing in hand by whatever means seem most appropriate at the time, regardless of ethical and legal codes or effect upon those outside its own membership."[26] This unionism might have been conservative or radical in philosophy, and its distinguishing mark was its ruthless tactics. Predatory unionism was divided: the sub-type, hold-up unionism, might have appeared outwardly as a bargaining type of business unionism, but it was monopolistic, boss-ridden, violent, and corrupt, and frequently combined with the employer to achieve its aims; guerilla unionism had all the attributes of hold-up unionism, except that it

[24]Lenin, *Imperialism* (New York: International Publishers, 1939), p. 106.

[25]Hoxie, *op. cit.*, p. 47

[26]*Ibid.*, p. 50.

would not enter into deals with the employer.

Hoxie's analysis of union types concentrated upon some special characteristic which was then interpreted as the essence of the particular group. Such a method helped to bring out the diversity in the attitudes and policies of unions, but it obscured the even more basic similarities. Moreover, there is a question whether certain of the types described by Hoxie are unions at all. All unions are business unions, in the sense that they bargain with employers. Their other characteristics are likely to be accidental in the sense that they are not essential for the carrying out of the union's main functions. Nevertheless, Hoxie was a keen observer of unionism who underlined the variety of forms in which unionism expressed itself. His work is a warning against both glib generalizations and the making of hurried distinctions. . . .

Selig Perlman

Professor Perlman's theory is related to the views developed by Commons. Professor Perlman attempts to devise a general theory of the labor movement, one which will apply to all areas and times, although he notes the specific and peculiar characteristics of the labor movements of different countries. Professor Perlman attempts to deduce a philosophy of labor from the conduct of the worker and from the nature of the institutions labor has created. He contrasts this approach with the one developed by the intellectuals—"the main characteristic of the intellectual" is to regard "labor as an 'abstract' mass in the grip of an abstract 'force.' By the intellectual is meant, of course, the educated non-manualist, who has established a contact with the labor movement, either through influence acquired over trade union bodies, or else as a leader of labor in his own right."[27] . . .

. . . What is attempted is a distinction between two approaches to the labor movement. Does labor concern itself through its organizations with the day-to-day problems in a pragmatic experimental manner or does it devote itself primarily to building a new type of economy. . . .

CONCLUSION

As one surveys the theories of trade unionism, it is obvious that even when incomplete they usually deal with some significant aspect of labor activity. . . .

Theories of labor usually are formulated by students rather than by participants in the labor movement. One writer, who is both, has always felt that the lack of philosophy of American labor was one of its fatal defects. According to him, "the philosophy of no generalizations [is] intended to keep the movement free from doctrinaire shackles. It has achieved little in this direction. It was responsible for a half a century of needless wanderings in the intellectual void, and only now it begins to dawn on some of the leaders of the second generation that the American labor movement is badly in need of an orientation."[28]

Twenty-five years after those lines were written, and after the American labor movement has grown in size and power, it still is without that philosophy. The solace that one can take from these events is that American labor has done quite well, both absolutely and comparatively. It has hedged millions of workers with a diversified system of protection and raised standards at every level. It need not hang its head in shame when it compares its achievements with the labor movements of other countries—those who know their destinations and travel in well-charted seas. Let those who are concerned about American labor's lack of philosophy engage in a bit of comparative analysis. Is there any labor movement anywhere which so zealously defends the interests of its members, which hedges its members with so much protection, which seeks to squeeze as many concessions out of the employer as the unions of the United States? What mysterious effect would a philosophy have upon the conduct of the unions? When the CIO was organized, some thought the millennium had arrived, and that labor would be fully caparisoned with a modern up-to-date philosophy. Instead, the CIO unions have gone the way of all trade union flesh—the way of no philosophy. Some

---

[27]Selig Perlman, *A Theory of the Labor Movement* (New York: Augustus Kelley, 1949) pp. 280-283. The first edition was published by Macmillan in 1928.

[28]J. B. S. Hardman, "The Mind of Labor, Ideas and Leadership," *American Labor Dynamics,* edited by J. B. S. Hardman (New York: Harcourt, Brace & Co., 1928), p. 284.

unions in the past—the garment workers, machinists, brewery workers, and others—had, at one time, a philosophy: socialism. Without making invidious comparisons, it is only fair to say that those unions were not superior, in most respects, to others which did not have a philosophy. . . .

The American labor movement focuses its main attention on the shop and upon the interests of its members. It is capable of sacrifice and solidarity in behalf of other groups and issues, but, as the power of each union is derived from the gains it wins for its members, it can never neglect this primary purpose without the risk of undermining its influence. . . . The trade union thinks essentially in terms of individuals and the power exercised over them on the job. To limit that power, or "to constitutionalize" it, is the job of the union, and as long as men are ambitious to advance or have a love of power the union's task will remain unfinished.

Unions, in the main, are concerned with day-to-day problems. Their attitudes are influenced by the economic, political and social conditions in which they operate. Writers who have developed theories of labor have sometimes seized upon certain aspects of union organizations and have tended to over-stress particular characteristics. Unions cannot remain permanently anchored in their views or activities. Their survival depends upon their ability to adjust to changing circumstances. Were economic activity reduced to a level so that more than 10 per cent of the labor force were chronically unemployed, much of the basis for a strong trade union movement would be undermined. The search for relief from such disastrous conditions might lead labor to embrace new doctrines and develop different tactics. Should they fail to protect the economic position of their members, their outlook and policies would inevitably undergo overhauling—not because their orientation is wrong but because it may not be suitable under all circumstances. American unionism has a philosophy of simple pragmatism. Such a philosophy is not as ostentatious and lacks the architectonic grandeur of philosophical systems such as Marxism. This perhaps makes American trade unionism less attractive to those who enjoy the aesthetic experience of beholding a beautiful intellectual system. However, the absence of these qualities helps to make the American movement more democratic, tolerant, and flexible. Trade unionism in the United States is a means of protecting the individual against arbitrary rule and raising his standard of living. While it may not rank high for philosophy, it deserves high score on the latter count.

37. A Theory of the Labor Movement

Selig Perlman

This article does not claim to give a full history of the several national labor movements, which the author has chosen as the most significant—the British, the German, the Russian, and the American. Rather it gives a survey of the historical development of these movements in order to show the grounds upon which the author, in the course of more than fifteen years of study and research, has arrived at his theory of the labor movement. . . .

Three dominant factors are emerging from the seeming medley of contradictory turns and events in recent labor history. The first factor is the demonstrated capacity, as in Germany, Austria, and Hungary, or else incapacity, as in Russia, of the capitalist group to survive as a ruling group and to withstand revolutionary attack when the protective hand of government has been withdrawn. In this sense "capitalism" is not only, nor even primarily, a material or governmental arrangement whereby one class, the capitalist class, owns the means of production, exchange, and distribution, while the other class, labor, is employed for wages. Capitalism is rather a social organization presided over by a class with an "effective will to power," implying the ability to defend its power against all comers—to defend it, not necessarily by physical force, since such force, however important at a crisis, might crumble after all—but to defend it, as it has done in

Germany, through having convinced the other classes that they alone, the capitalists, know how to operate the complex economic apparatus of modern society upon which the material welfare of all depends.

The second factor which stands out clearly in the world-wide social situation is the role of the so-called "intellectual," the "intelligentsia," in the labor movement and in society at large. It was from the intellectual that the anti-capitalist influences in modern society emanated. It was he who impressed upon the labor movement tenets characteristic of his own mentality; the "nationalization" or "socialization" of industry, and political action, whether "constitutional" or "unconstitutional," on behalf of the "new social order." He, too, has been busily indoctrinating the middle classes with the same views, thus helping to undermine an important prop of capitalism and to some extent even the spirit of resistance of the capitalists themselves.

The third and the most vital factor in the labor situation is the trade union movement. Trade unionism, which is essentially pragmatic, struggles constantly, not only against the employers for an enlarged opportunity measured in income, security, and liberty in the shop and industry, but struggles also, whether consciously or unconsciously, actively or merely passively, against the intellectual who would frame its programs and shape its policies. In this struggle by "organic" labor[1] against dominance by the intellectuals, we perceive a clash of an ideology which holds the concrete workingmen in the center of its vision with a rival ideology which envisages labor merely as an "abstract mass in the grip of an abstract force."[2]

Labor's own "home grown" ideology is disclosed only through a study of the "working rules" of labor's own "institutions." The trade unions are the institutions of labor today, but much can be learned also from labor's institutions in the past, notably the gilds.

It is the author's contention that manual groups, whether peasants in Russia, modern wage earners, or medieval master workmen, have had their economic attitudes basically determined by a consciousness of scarcity of opportunity, which is characteristic of these groups, and stands out in contrast with the business men's "abundance consciousness," or consciousness of unlimited opportunity. Starting with this consciousness of scarcity, the "manualist" groups have been led to practising solidarity, to an insistence upon an "ownership" by the group as a whole of the totality of economic opportunity extant, to a "rationing" by the group of such opportunity among the individuals constituting it, to a control by the group over its members in relation to the conditions upon which they as individuals are permitted to occupy a portion of that opportunity—in brief, to a "communism of opportunity." This differs fundamentally from socialism or communism, which would "communize" not only "opportunity," but also production and distribution—just as it is far removed from "capitalism." Capitalism started from the prem-

ise of unlimited opportunity, and arrived, in its classical formulation, at "laissez faire" for the individual all along the line—in regard to the "quantity" of opportunity he may appropriate, the price or wage he may charge, and in regard to the ownership of the means of production. "Communism of opportunity" in the sense here employed existed in the medieval gilds before the merchant capitalists had subverted them to the purposes of a protected business men's oligarchy; in Russian peasant land communities with their periodic redivisions, among the several families, of the collectively owned land, the embodiment of the economic opportunity of a peasant group; and exists today in trade unions enforcing a "job control" through union "working rules."

But, in this country, due to the fact that here the "manualist" had found at hand an abundance of opportunity, in unoccupied land and in a pioneer social condition, his economic thinking had therefore issued, not from the scarcity premise but from the premise of abundance. It thus resulted in a social philosophy which was more akin to the business men's than to the trade unionists' or gildsmen's. Accordingly, the American labor movement, which long remained unaware of any distinction between itself and the "producing classes" in general,—which included also farmers, small manufacturers, and small business men,—continued for many decades to worship the shrine of individualistic "anti-monopoly." "Anti-monopoly" was a program of reform, through politics and legislation, whereby the "producing classes" would apply a corrective to the American social order so that economic individualism might become "safe" for the producers rather than for land speculators, merchant capitalists, and bankers. Unionism, on the contrary, first became a stabilized movement in America only when the abundance consciousness of the pioneer days had been replaced in the mind of labor by a scarcity consciousness—the consciousness of job scarcity. Only then did the American wage earner become willing to envisage a future in which his union would go on indefinitely controlling his relation to his job rather than endeavoring to afford him, as during the anti-monopoly stage of the labor movement, an escape into free and unregulated self-employment, by willing for him a competitive equality with the "monopolist."

In America, the historical struggle waged by

---

[1] Trade unionists and intellectuals alike use the term "labor," which has an abstract connotation. But, to the trade unionists, "labor" means nothing more abstract or mystical than the millions of concrete human beings with their concrete wants and aspirations.

[2] I use frequently the term "ideology" in imitation of the usage of socialist intellectuals taken over from Napoleon's term applied by him in contempt to the idealists of his day. I find, however, that the term has quite the same meaning as that which scientists call "ideas" and "theory," philosophers call "idealism" or "ethics," and business men and working men call "philosophy." Unionists speak of "the philosophy of trade unionism." If they were "intellectuals," they would call it "theory," "ideology," "ideas," or "idealism," or "ethics," all of which I sometimes include in the term "mentality."

labor for an undivided expression of its own mentality in its own movement was directed against the ideology of "anti-monopoly." But in Europe the antithesis to the labor mentality has been the mentality of the intellectual.

Twenty-five years ago, Nicolai Lenin[3] clearly recognized the divergence which exists between the intellectual and the trade unionist, · although not in terms of an inevitable mutual antagonism, when he hurled his unusual polemical powers against those in the Social-Democratic Party, his own party at the time, who would confine their own and the party's agitational activities to playing upon labor's economic grievances. He then said that if it had not been for the "bourgeois intellectuals," Marx and Engels, labor would never have got beyond mere "trifling,"—going after an increase in wage here and after a labor law there. Lenin, of course, saw labor and the trade union movement, not as an aggregation of concrete individuals sharing among themselves their collective job opportunity, as well as trying to enlarge it and improve it by joint effort and step by step, but rather as an abstract mass which history had predetermined to hurl itself against the capitalist social order and demolish it. Lenin therefore could never have seen in a nonrevolutionary unionism anything more than a blind groping after a purpose only vaguely grasped, rather than a completely self-conscious movement with a full-blown ideology of its own. But to see "labor" solely as an abstract mass and the concrete individual reduced to a mere mathematical point, as against the trade unionists' striving for job security for the individual and concrete freedom on the job, has not been solely the prerogative of "determinist-revolutionaries" like Lenin and the Communists. The other types of intellectuals in and close to the labor movement, the "ethical" type, the heirs of Owen and the Christian Socialists, and the "social efficiency" type, best represented by the Fabians—to mention but English examples,—have equally with the orthodox Marxians reduced labor to a mere abstraction, although each has done so in his own way and has pictured "labor" as an abstract mass in the grip of an abstract force, existing, however, only in his own intellectual imagination, and not in the emotional imagination of the manual worker himself.

LABOR AND CAPITALISM IN AMERICA[4]

The most distinctive characteristic of the development of the labor movement in America has not been, as in Germany, a slow but certain shedding of the philosophy originally imparted by an intellectual leadership. No intellectuals, in the true sense of the word, presided at its birth. The main feature of its development has been rather a perpetual struggle to keep the organization from going to pieces for want of inner cohesiveness. For, it has had to cope with two disruptive tendencies: First,—American labor has always been prone,—though far more in the past than now,—to identify itself in outlook, interest, and action, with the great lower middle class, the farmers, the small manufacturers and business men,—in a word, with the "producing classes" and their periodic "anti-monopoly" campaigns. Second,—and here is a tendency of a rising rather than diminishing potency,—the American employer has, in general, been able to keep his employees contented with the conditions, determined by himself, on which they individually accepted employment. Both these tendencies have seriously hindered the efforts of trade unionism towards stability and solidarity. The first tendency proved inimical because the organized wage earners would periodically be drawn into the whirlpool of politics under the banner of the "anti-monopoly" parties,—so, under the American system of party politics, invariably suffering discussion, and ultimately disintegration. The second of the tendencies mentioned has balked unionism because the employer, wielding the initiative, has been able successfully to carry his own individualistic competitive spirit into the ranks of his employees. Moreover, both factors making for disintegration go back to a common cause. For whether the labor organiza-

[3] "The history of all countries attests to the fact that, left to its own forces, the working class can only attain to trade union consciousness,—that is, the conviction that it is necessary to unite in unions, wage the struggle against the bosses, obtain from the government such or such labor reforms, etc. As to the socialist doctrines, they came from philosophic, historic and economic theories elaborated by certain educated representatives of the possessing classes, the Intellectuals. In their social situation, the founders of contemporary scientific socialism, Marx and Engels, were bourgeois intellectuals." Lenin in *What Is To Be Done?*

[4] See my *History of Trade Unionism in the United States* (The Macmillan Co., 1922).

tion has succumbed to the lure of a political reform movement aiming to shield the "small man" and the "man on the make," and has broken up in political dissension; or whether it has failed to get started because the individual laborer has accepted the incentive of a bonus wage and of a better opportunity for advancement within the framework of a non-union bargain,—the ultimate explanation, at all events, lies in the basic conditions of life in the American community—economic, political, ethnic, mental, and spiritual. Some of these are a heritage from the past, others of more recent origin, but all are closely interwoven with the present and the future of American labor.

The Basic Characteristics of the American Community

1. The strength of the institution of private property. A labor movement must, from its very nature, be an organized campaign against the rights of private property, even where it stops short of embracing a radical program seeking the elimination, gradual or abrupt, "constitutional" or violent, of the private entrepreneur. When this campaign takes the political and legislative route, it leads to the denial of the employer's right to absolute control of his productive property. It demands and secures regulatory restrictions which, under American constitutional practice, are within the province of the "police power" vested in the states and granted by specific authority to Congress; only they must, in every case, square with "public purpose," as that term is interpreted in the last analysis by the United States Supreme Court. When the same campaign follows the economic route,—the route of unionism, strikes, boycotts, and union "working rules"—the restrictions on the rights of property are usually even more thoroughgoing and far-reaching, since unions are less amenable to judicial control than are legislatures and Congress. A third form of the labor movement seeks to promote cooperative production and distribution,—neither of which is practiced appreciably in this country. This cooperative movement sets out to beat private capitalism by the methods of private business: greater efficiency and superior competitive power. To the advocates of the rights of private property, this third mode of the labor movement is the least offensive.

Because the labor movement in any form is a campaign against the absolute rights of private property, the extent to which the institution of private property is intrenched in the community in which a labor movement operates is of overwhelming importance to it. . . .

The enormous strength of private property in America, at once obvious to any observer,[5] goes back to the all-important fact that, by and large, this country was occupied and settled by laboring pioneers, creating property for themselves as they went along and holding it in small parcels. This was the way not only of agriculture but also of the mechanical trades and of the larger scale industries. Thus the harmony between the self-interest of the individual pursuing his private economic aim and the general public interest proved a real and lasting harmony in the American colonies and states. This Adam Smith saw in 1776, his eye on the frugal and industrious class of masters of workshops still on the threshold of their elevation by the industrial revolution yet to come. Every addition to the total of the privately held wealth was at the same time an addition to the productive equipment in the community, which meant a fuller satisfaction of its wants and a higher level of the general welfare. Moreover, being held in small parcels, wealth was generally accessible to whomever would pay the price in industry, frugality, and ingenuity. Furthermore, this condition had not been destroyed even with the coming in of modern "big business," combinations, mergers, and "trusts." For, too often does the grandeur of business on its modern gigantic scale, the magnitude of billion dollar corporations completely hide from one's view those other millions of small businesses. These, here and now, may be forced to struggle hard for existence, perhaps only to fail in the end. But failing, still others will take their place and continue to form a social layer firm enough to safeguard against even a possible revolutionary explosion from below. The earnestness with which judges will rush to stand between legislatures and menaced property rights; the rigor of their application of the injunction to keep unionists and strikers from interfering with those rights in their own way; the case with which a typically American middle class

[5]The utter disregard of the property rights of distillers, brewers, and others engaged in the drink traffic resulted from the intensity of the moral passion evoked—the historical heritage of puritanism. Had private property been less entrenched than it is, the property owning groups would have been more hesitant to remove even one stone of the arch.

community may work itself up, or be worked up, into an anti-radical hysteria, when Soviet missionaries or syndicalist agitators are rumored to be abroad in the land; and the flocking to the election polls of millions to vote for the "safe" candidate—all are of one piece, and are to be explained by the way in which the American community originated and grew. . . .

2. The lack of a class consciousness in American labor. The overshadowing problem of the American labor movement has always been the problem of staying organized. No other labor movement has ever had to contend with the fragility so characteristic of American labor organizations. In the main, this fragility of the organization has come from the lack of class cohesiveness in American labor. . . .

The cause of this lack of psychological cohesiveness in American labor is the absence, by and large, of a completely "settled" wage earning class. Sons of wage earners will automatically follow their fathers' occupations in the mining districts, which, because of their isolation, are little worlds in themselves. The Negroes in industry are, of course, a hereditary wage earning group. And apparently such a class has developed also in the textile centers. To be sure, the great mass of the wage earners in American industry today, unless they have come from the farm intending to return there with a part of their wages saved, will die wage earners. However, many of these do not stay in a given industry for life, but keep moving from industry to industry and from locality to locality, in search for better working conditions. Moreover, the bright son of a mechanic and factory hand, whether of native or immigrant parentage, need not despair, with the training which the public schools give him free of charge and with whatever else he may pick up, of finding his way to this or that one of the thousand and one selling "lines" which pay on the commission basis; or, if his ambition and his luck go hand in hand, of attaining to some one of the equally numerous kinds of small businesses, or, finally, of the many minor supervisory positions in the large manufacturing establishments, which are constantly on the lookout for persons in the ranks suitable for promotion. It is, therefore, a mistake to assume that, with the exhaustion of the supply of free public land, the wage earner who is above the average in ambition and ability, or at least his children, if they are equally endowed (and the children's opportunities color the parents' attitude no less

than do their own), have become cooped up for good in the class of factory operatives. For today, the alternative opportunities to being a lowly factory hand are certainly more varied and entail less hardship than the old opportunity of "homesteading" in the West and "growing up with the country." . . .

Another cause of the lack of "class-consciousness" in American labor was the free gift of the ballot which came to labor at an early date as a by-product of the Jeffersonian democratic movement. In other countries, where the labor movement started while the workingmen were still denied the franchise, there was in the last analysis no need of a theory of "surplus value" to convince them that they were a class apart and should therefore be "class conscious." There ran a line like a red thread between the laboring class and the other classes. Not so, where that line is only an economic one. Such a line becomes blurred by the constant process of "osmosis" between one economic class and another, by fluctuations in relative bargaining power of employer and employee with changes in the business cycle, and by other changing conditions.

Next to the abundant economic opportunities available to wage earners in this country, and to their children, immigration has been the factor most guilty of the incohesiveness of American labor. To workers employed in a given industry, a new wave of immigrants, generally of a new nationality, meant a competitive menace to be fought off and to be kept out of that industry. For, by the worker's job consciousness, the strongest animosity was felt not for the employer who had initiated or stimulated the new immigrant wave, but for the immigrants who came and took the jobs away. When immigrants of a particular nationality acquired higher standards and began rebuilding the unions which they destroyed at their coming, then a new nationality would arrive to do unto the former what these had done unto the original membership. The restriction of immigration by the quota system has at last done away with this phenomenon, which formerly used to occur and recur with an inevitable regularity.

American labor remains the most heterogeneous laboring class in existence—ethnically, linguistically, religiously, and culturally. With a working class of such a composition, to make socialism or communism the official "ism" of the movement, would mean, even if the other conditions permitted it, deliberately driving the Catholics, who are perhaps in the majority in the American Federation of Labor, out of the labor movement, since with them an irreconcilable opposition to socialism is a matter of religious principle. Consequently the only acceptable "consciousness" for American labor as a whole is a "job consciousness," with a "limited" objective of "wage and job control"; which not at all hinders American unionism from being the most "hard hitting" unionism in any country. Individual unions may, however, adopt whatever "consciousness" they wish. Also the solidarity of American labor is a solidarity with a quickly diminishing potency as one passes from the craft group,—which looks upon the jobs in the craft as its common property for which it is ready to fight long and bitterly,—to the widening concentric circles of the related crafts, the industry, the American Federation of Labor, and the world labor movement.

38. The Development of Western Labor Movements: Some Comparative Considerations

Everett M. Kassalow

As a means of making analysis of labor movements abroad more dramatic and vivid, let us first examine the special nature and character of the American labor movement. Needless to say, any brief survey of Western labor movements must necessarily be oversimplified at practically every stage.

SPECIAL INFLUENCES IN U. S. LABOR MOVEMENT DEVELOPMENT

A number of special forces shaped the development of the American labor movement. In the United States the capitalist enterprise system did not have to contend with a previously existing feudalism and a rigid set of class attitudes and practices. There were some traces of a feudal land system in America, but these were relatively unimportant. Indeed, the free frontier tended to encourage the emergence of new landholders.

The absence of feudalism meant, of course, that the triumph of capitalism for this and other reasons was ultimately more widespread and more successful in the United States than anywhere else. There were none of the usual aristocratic inhibitions on willingness to work, nor any excessive preoccupation with leisure pursuits that characterized the ruling classes of Europe.

The lack of a feudal tradition also served to blur class lines from an early period in American history. When an explosive, dynamic capitalism was combined with this, social mobility—though perhaps exaggerated in some of our literature—was certainly greater in American life than in that anywhere in Europe. Again, as a consequence of these factors, there was less tendency for class lines and attitudes to develop in the lifelong pattern that they had in Europe. The special form of American capitalism with its great emphasis on internal markets early resulted in a relatively high standard of living for the great mass of people, further weakening the possibility of the emergence of persistent class attitudes. The heavy flow of immigration into America also made any "unity" of the working classes more unlikely.

Full citizenship and voting rights for the male, white, urban working class existed at a relatively early date in American history. This too made the workers feel they were full partners in the growing society.

The establishment of free public education for all citizens long before the Civil War helped complete the integration of American workers into their society. Illiteracy among the masses persisted in most of Western Europe well into the latter half of the nineteenth century and was certainly a factor in alienating workers from the newly developing social orders.

The possibility of a higher standard of living

and the possibility of social mobility into managerial and entrepreneurial positions tended at a relatively early point to make the American labor movement a highly economically oriented institution. By the latter part of the nineteenth century its feet were rather firmly set on the road of wages, hours, and working conditions, all of which were to become institutionally contained within the framework of collective bargaining and written agreements. (Of course, there were syndicalist and socialist exceptions, but in retrospect they were just that—exceptions to the main pattern of development.)

All these factors tended to give what Bruce Millen has called an "exclusionist" character to the American trade union movement. Its concentration was upon benefits to members rather than any great interest in the economic fate of the working class as a whole. Finally, for a great part of its history the American movement largely confined its activities to a limited number of trades and industries. Since the rise of the mass unionism of the thirties, the horizon of American labor has broadened considerably; but even today it is a relatively narrower movement than those in other Western countries.

On the other hand, the lack of class feeling as well as powerful opposition from employers (and often from public authorities) made both the existence and the continuity of unionism difficult in the American environment. This in turn led the unions to lay great emphasis upon exclusive bargaining rights, closed and union shops, and other forms of union security. Since the limitations of space do not permit a return to this point, suffice it to note that European unions have almost never resorted to these forms. This is largely true because the cement of class attitude made this additional bond unnecessary for the permanent existence of unionism. Since, as we shall see below, the typical European union was ideologically committed, it also would have been somewhat contradictory to compel "non-believers" to join the union and pay dues to it.

EUROPEAN LABOR: A CLASS MOVEMENT

Let us now examine some broad contrasts with the labor movements which developed in Western Europe. In the first place the social and political background was considerably different in Europe. To an extent (though this is still argued among historians) some of the early unions were influenced by the medieval guild tradition. Feudalism was firmly intrenched, leaving rigid class lines and social and economic distinctions many of which still persist. By the same token, European capitalism was less successful in shattering older attitudes and practices, which also reinforced the tendency to develop or continue class distinctions and class attitudes. The idea of the "naturalness" of group activity and group recognition has deep and lasting roots in Europe.

Against this background the European labor movement emerged as part of the attempt of the European working classes to achieve broad social, economic, and political objectives. In keeping with other European class movements, it created or inherited a total ideology and *Weltanschauung*. The European working class, developed within a more rigid type of society than that of the United States, committed itself to the advancement of the entire working class. It bent to this task by radically transforming the entire society. Political democracy developed later in Western Europe than in the United States, and this too tended to consolidate a class attitude of opposition on the part of European workers toward their societies and governments. The working-class movements in most countries, in these earlier years, came to embrace Marxism and the doctrine of revolutionary change—though not necessarily by violent means. More generally, it was committed to replacing the system of capitalism and private property and production with socialism and production for use.

It is worth noting that the ideological aspects of the British Socialist Party and trade-union movement, however, differed from those of the continent. British socialism was colored by Britain's nonconformist religious tradition in much the same way that Marxism colored the continental movements. British socialist feeling was, however, no less intense because of its religious—as opposed to the continent's Marxist—background.

It should be clear immediately that all these movements were less exclusionist than the American labor movement. Basically they embarked upon a course of advancing the entire working class by transforming the total society, in contrast to the emphasis of the American movement on the immediate specifics of wages, hours, and working conditions for its members only.

The discussion that follows presents the main forms and programs the European working class movements took. However, what is described is not entirely true of any one movement, since generalizations are necessary. Even what is described as the general model is certainly more true of the United Kingdom, Scandinavia, Holland, Switzerland—and to an important extent Germany, Austria, and probably Belguim—than it is of France and Italy.

Typically, the European labor movement developed country by country as a two- or three-pronged affair. There were first of all the trade unions; second, the labor, political, or socialist movements; and third, workers' cooperative movements—both of the consumer and producer variety. Each of these parts of the over-all working-class movement was intended to play an important role in the transformation of the society, but we shall focus upon the trade unions and the political parties. The cooperative movements have tended to become a bit less important in Europe in the post-World War II decades as central state planning and the elaboration of social welfare programs have come to be the pivot of socialist economics. The cooperatives may therefore be less important than the trade unions or the political parties in today's socialist complex, but they should be kept in mind, since they do indicate the broad front behind which the work of European labor has operated to engage its members' lives, in contrast to the almost exclusively trade union form of the American movement. . . .

PARTY-UNION RELATIONSHIPS

It is sometimes difficult for Americans, especially American trade unionists, to understand the great emphasis European workers place upon political movements and workers' political parties. In the eyes of European workers, however, the party and the trade-union movement are of equal importance in the advancement of the working class.

Since this development of parallel movements, party and union, is of critical importance in the study of labor movements anywhere in the world—especially outside the United States—this aspect should be stressed. There is no simple formula which determines which will emerge first, the political or the industrial (or union) arm of the working class. . . .

In general, it can be said that where the trade unions developed before the socialist party, they generally had a hand in organizing the party and tended to exercise great influence in it. The lack of universal suffrage in a number of countries gave the unions a priority in development.

The unions, as opposed to the parties, tended to be more pragmatic and less dogmatic or doctrinal than the parties. Inevitably, working in the day-to-day industrial sphere, the unions concentrated on more immediate gains, while the party was concentrating on a global program. This was particularly true before World War I, when the parties were remote from any day-to-day responsibilities in most countries and continued to expound a "purer" brand of socialism. However, membership and leadership in the unions and party were often intermixed, especially in the early days, and both subscribed broadly and equally to the general goal of a socialist society.

During the period from World War I to World War II a pattern tended to appear in which the union continued to be to the right and the socialist parties to the left of the combined labor movement. However, as the socialist parties began to approach and share governmental power to a modest extent in the twenties and the thirties almost everywhere in post-World War II Europe, the situation began to change. Confronted with the difficult problems of actually governing and the necessity to conciliate other forces, such as the farmers and the new white-collar groups, if they were to remain in power, the partie moved away from the old dogmas. Since World War II this tendency has been accelerated as socialist parties have, on occasion, governed either alone or in coalition in almost every European country. Today it is often the union wing of the labor movement which is out on the left expressing irritation with the excessive "statesmanship" and conciliatory tactics of the party leadership.

These are broad generalizations; no attempt has been made to set up any rigid rules for judging union-party relations. Moreover, it might be fairer to say that the parties and the unions are arms which perform different functions for the working class. As these functions and needs vary in the course of social evolution, each arm receives changing emphasis.

Returning to historical development, the important advances of the unions, the rise in living standards, the establishment of social security systems, the obviously effective and influential roles which most of the socialist parties have come to play within existing parliamentary systems—all of these factors have tended to cool the revolutionary ardor of most of the Western labor movements with the passage of time. Their very achievements and growing power helped to integrate these labor movements into their societies.

Most of the socialist parties, as already noted, started out under strong Marxist influence.[1] Today in Scandinavia, Austria, and the Netherlands (to choose some examples), Marxism has long since been overtaken by reformism, and there is only moderate interest in the nationalization of industry. The emphasis today tends to be more and more upon planning for full-employment and welfare programs.

The rather recent *formal* conversion of the German Social Democratic Party from Marxism to something like welfare-statism is a good case in point (I emphasize the word formal here, for most European socialist parties long ago abandoned Marxism as a matter of practical operations). At its 1959 Congress the German SPD made its "final break . . . with the fundamental tenets of Marxism. . . . The name of Karl Marx and the concept of Marxism are missing from the declaration of principles, . . . words like 'class' and 'class struggle' are also carefully avoided. . . . The notion that the working class . . . is destined, by overthrowing capitalist class-society, to bring about the classless society, . . . has now been thrown by the German Social Democrats on the scrap heap of social utopias. . . . The transfer of the means of production to common ownership, which has hitherto represented the essence of every socialist program, has been stripped of its overriding importance. . . . The SPD has dropped the idea that socialism requires the nationalisation of the whole of industry, not only 'for the time being' but as a matter of principle."[2]

The same kind of transition, for practical purposes, has been accomplished by nearly all the socialist parties of Europe. Occasionally, however, some diehard traditionalists, as in Great Britain, have resisted formal changes in the official party program, and the theoretical

commitment to extensive nationalization of industry lives on as a doctrine, if not a reality.

STRAINS OF ECONOMIC PLANNING ON PARTY-UNION RELATIONSHIPS

While each has its separate province, party and union sometimes encounter severe strains and some conflict of interest in their relationships. Particularly is this the case today in the face of the central economic planning for full employment that is being undertaken by some socialist governments. The reconciliation of such economic planning with the traditional freedom of unions to bargain freely for wage increases can present some severe problems for the labor movement. . . .

An almost classic example of the tension which can develop between the twin poles of party and union can be found in a description of the activities of Ernest Bevin in Alan Bullock's brilliant biography of that great British union leader. The first Labour government in Great Britain took office at the end of 1923. This period coincided with an economic upswing, and Bevin, on behalf of the dock and tramway workers, was anxious to make an effort to restore some wage cuts suffered in earlier years. He moved swiftly, and after a successful strike these unions won an impressive economic victory. Bevin was highly satisfied with the results. Bullock notes, however:

> This satisfaction was not shared by the Labour Government, MacDonald, in particular, out of sympathy with down-to-earth trade-union demands and increasingly inclined to take a high line about national responsibilities, was greatly angered by the strikes and never forgave Bevin for the embarrassment he caused the Government. This did not worry Bevin. But there were others in the Labour Party besides MacDonald who felt that Bevin had behaved irresponsibly and shown less than the loyalty the unions owed to the first Labour Government ever to take office. This impression was strengthened by the aggressive manner in which Bevin asserted his independence and expressed his contempt for politicians as a race.

A controversy broke out in the Socialist press in which the economist J. A. Hobson accused the unions of following a "separatist"

[1] The British Labour Party is an important exception. Differences in class relationships, civil rights traditions, and the influence of non-conformist religion helped produce a non-Marxian socialism in England.

[2] F. R. Allemann, "German SPD Party Abandons Marxism," *Forum-Service* (December 26, 1959).

policy. Bevin had to deal with the question of whether or not it was incumbent upon the unions to wait for the government to set up some new machinery to settle the workers' wage claims or whether the unions' strike action was correct. He commented:

> We are all too aware of the Government's difficulties and desire as much as anyone to assist in the success of Britain's first Labour Government. A policy of industrial truce would, in our view, even if it were possible, not be to the best interests of the Government. There is work to do on the industrial field as well as in the political arena. While it is true that the two are to some extent part of the same effort, we must not lose sight of the fact that governments may come and governments may go, but the workers' fight for betterment of conditions must go on all the time.

Bullock further notes:

> Nor did the rank-and-file members of the Union disagree with Bevin. They had waited a long time to recover the wage cuts they had suffered and to see some practical benefit from the Union they supported. They saw no reason why, the first time they gained the advantage in a dispute, they should not press it home simply because a Labour Government was in office. If that fact made the employers more reluctant to fight it out, so much the better: what did they pay the political levy and support the Labour Party for, if not to secure such advantages? No one could say the employers were reluctant to take advantage of the Tories being in office to force wages down and use the power of the State to defeat the miners. It was too high a price to pay for office if the only way the Labour Government could retain the Parliamentary support of the Liberal Party was to take sides against the unions in the legitimate defence of their members' industrial interests.

There is, however, a postscript to this interesting interlude. When Labour came to power in 1945, it had gained a clear majority in Parliament, unlike the 1923 Labour government, which was a minority government dependent upon the votes of other groups if it was to stay in power. Then Bevin was willing to face the issue of the national responsibility of the labor movement, as opposed to the immediate sectional interests of the trade unions. During this period he came, as a member of the government, to recommend to the unions a policy of "wage restraint which placed a heavy strain on the loyalty and forbearance of the trade unions."[3]

In a sense we have here an illustration of the pressures in today's world which often tend to put the socialist party to the right of its trade union ally. From what has already been said, it is scarcely necessary to add at this point that although these movements are two- and three-pronged, the trade unions jealously guard their own independence. Americans sometimes have the feeling that these union and political movements are one and the same thing. This is simply not the case. The unions, for example, have their own independent financing, policy conventions, and officers. In terms of structure and finances, the unions are in some ways more clearly independent of the parties than are the parties from the unions. The parties frequently, as we have seen, are highly dependent upon the unions for financial support. Furthermore, it is quite common for a socialist party specifically to reserve a few seats on the party's executive committee for representatives of the trade union movement. The same is not true in the reverse.

Some American experts have tended to see this process as one in which the unions gradually "emancipate" themselves from the parties. This is also inaccurate. Rather, as one writer describes the situation in Sweden, the relationship is essentially "one of interdependence."[4] Functions and responsibilities vary as economic and political conditions change, but both arms continue to perform vital functions.

COLLECTIVE BARGAINING: SOME KEY DIFFERENCES

The unions then are independent and have as *their* main sphere *industrial action* and *representation* on behalf of the working class. In this sense, of course, they resemble American

[3]Alan Bullock, *The Life and Times of Ernest Bevin, Trade Union Leader, 1881-1940*, Vol. 1 (London: William Heinemann, Ltd., 1960), pp. 242-45.

[4]Donald J. Blake, "Swedish Trade Unions and the Social Democratic Party: The Formative Years," *The Scandinavian Economic History Review*, Vol. 8, No. 1 (1960), p. 43.

unions. Furthermore, in the broad structural sense, there are many similarities, such as the existence of national unions along industrial or craft lines or both, a central federation, and some form of local organization.[5]

It is fair to say, however, that in their bargaining and industrial activities they do have a different attitude toward government action and political action than do American unions. Typically, for example, in many of these countries the unions accept government legislation as the regulator of such items as paid vacations and paid holidays. They also look to the government almost exclusively for social security items such as pensions, health, and welfare in contrast to American unions which also bargain "privately" on many of these items. In some European countries such as France, Belgium, Austria, the system of shop stewards owes its existence not to union agreements but to a state-sponsored series of plant elections. The rights and functions of these stewards are generally defined by legislation and only occasionally supplemented by union agreements.

NEW TRENDS IN UNION BARGAINING STRUCTURES AND POLICIES

With respect to wages and hours, bargaining in Western Europe is usually done by industry on a regional or even a national basis. Unlike the industrial-relations pattern in the United States, there is much less emphasis upon bargaining with particular employers and enterprises. Union devotion to ideals of class solidarity and class equality coupled with employers' traditions of operating through strong associations tend to deter bargaining at the plant or firm level. One of the concomitants of this has been that, in comparison with American unions, European unions are less influential and less active at the plant level.

The enormous industrial changes and the

great growth of the European economies in the past decade are causing some changes in traditional European union bargaining attitudes and structure. Confronted with complex problems of automation, as well as with the opportunity for economic advances on a scale hitherto unknown, some European unions have found that nation-wide, industry-wide, or region-wide bargaining is not entirely adequate. Bargains struck this way tend to be set in terms of what the marginal or relatively less efficient producer in a given industry can afford to pay.

Actually, in a number of European countries, especially in the highly prosperous large metal companies, the wage rates and earnings of workers today are often far above the rates negotiated in industry-wide agreements on a national or regional basis. As a consequence, rate setting in many major firms in a few countries has passed largely into the hands of the employers.

The so-called shop stewards' revolt in Great Britain in the past decade stems in part from certain structural weaknesses in the British trade union movement and the need to exercise greater worker control over wages and working conditions at the plant level.

Some of the European unions are responding to these challenges by placing new emphasis upon bargaining at the plant and firm level. The old union notion of working-class solidarity is being distorted in the context of the European "economic miracle." These unions may, however, run up against the problem of reconciling more energetic wage bargaining with price stability in the face of the strong and sustained full employment, which most European countries have successfully achieved in the past decade.

EUROPEAN LABOR AND THE ISSUE OF WORKERS' CONTROL OF INDUSTRY

Most European unions have not been content to limit their plant objectives to wages, hours, and working conditions. Socialist influence and tradition have led most of the labor movements to inscribe high on their platforms the doctrine of workers' control over industry, in the sense of industrial decisions on production, investment, and marketing. On the other hand, the doctrine that workers must have a

[5]In the matter of local organization in some countries there are patterns considerably different from ours, but space limitations preclude further discussion of this. Similarly, in Europe the central labor federations, or confederations as they are called (the equivalents of our own AFL-CIO), often exercise greater power and influence over the labor movement as a whole than does the AFL-CIO.

share and *co-responsibility* in the management of enterprise has also had firm standing in European Catholic social doctrine since the latter part of the nineteenth century.[6]

These two different streams of social doctrine, as Frederic Meyers has commented, led to the establishment by legislation of systems of worker "representation," or at least worker consultation in the management of enterprise in a number of European nations.[7] There has been considerable American interest in the operation of the German co-determination laws; but forms of worker participation in, or consultation with management also exist in some other countries in Europe.

To date these "experiments" have not had a serious impact. The real business of running the enterprise remains in management's hands. In some countries, however, these devices have helped to increase the workers' power to influence many of the working conditions that we normally take for granted as within the province of collective bargaining in the United States, as opposed to managing the enterprise in the broader sense of that term.

This tradition of workers' control and participation in management is, however, a deep one.

EVALUATING UNITED STATES AND EUROPEAN MOVEMENTS

. . .

Sharp and direct comparisons between American unionism and the European labor movements are obviously impossible. Different conditions produce different movements. It can be said, however, that in some respects European movements have been more effective than our own. They have succeeded in building a greater degree of security on the part of European workers. This is reflected in more comprehensive social security and medical care systems, greater protection against layoff, longer paid vacations, and union cooperative travel and recreation programs which have tended to enlarge the lives of European workers. Workers' housing is commonly a product of union cooperatives. This whole range of activities tends to create unity and a sense of allegiance between workers and their movements which is much stronger than in the United States.

In contrast, however, the European movements are considerably weaker than the American at the factory floor or the enterprise level, and they have given workers much less control over their day-to-day working conditions. Again, while it is hard to generalize in terms of sheer economic achievement, the advantage must be given to the greater bargaining power of the American labor movement.

It cannot be denied, however, that a number of European labor movements (encompassing labor parties and unions) are a broader and more powerful social force in their own countries than the American labor movement. In some of these societies (for example, in the United Kingdom, Austria, the Low Countries, or Scandinavia) the European labor movement has even assumed a full or a large measure of national governmental power.

Some of the evolutionary forces at play in the United States and in Western Europe seem to be bending the respective lines of union development closer together. Note, for example, that whereas some European unions have had to take more action at the plant level, American labor finds itself drawn into a new government-sponsored national labor-management committee. Again, United States labor has also increased its political activities sharply in the past decade, as it has become painfully clear that the attainment of full employment and a more just society are to a considerable extent beyond the competence of collective bargaining, important as the latter is.

[6]Syndicalist and guild socialist influences, which have since largely disappeared from Western Europe, also helped develop workers' interest in the issue of participating directly in management, around World War I.

[7]Frederic Meyers, "Workers' Control of Industry in Europe," *Southwestern Social Science Quarterly* (September 1958).

39. Why the American Labor Movement Is Not Socialist

Walter Galenson

ATTEMPTS TO RADICALIZE AMERICAN LABOR

Many radical ideologies of Europe, as well as some that were native to the United States, have been urged upon the American labor movement at various times in its history. There were many who believed that one or another had taken permanent root. Martin Tranmael, the founder of Norwegian socialism, once told me that he came to the United States in 1900 in order to study a successful Socialist movement. Daniel De Leon, a prominent American Socialist of the turn of the centrury, was regarded by Lenin as an outstanding Marxist theorist and practitioner. European Socialists still make pilgrimages to the California ranch of Jack London, although his own countrymen have long forgotten his political views.

The first American labor movement of any importance was the Knights of Labor, established in 1869 as a secret society, but converted a decade later into an open trade union federation. Like many of the early European trade unions, the Knights advocated producers' co-operatives as a means of eliminating the exploitation of labor, and the eventual failure of the co-operatives which it sponsored was a major cause of its decline. However, the Knights of Labor was in no sense a revolutionary organization. It was prepared to work within the framework of capitalism provided that the worst abuses were mitigated through collective bargaining and social legislation. One must keep in mind that in the heyday of the Knights, the American worker already enjoyed the right to vote and free public education. These demands of early European socialism did not have to be won by revolutionary activity.

The American Federation of Labor, formed in 1886, supplanted the Knights of Labor as the most representative organization of American workers, and it has occupied that status right down to the present day. It was challenged from the left on numerous occasions, but always emerged unscathed. The AFL was led for many years by Samuel Gompers, a cigar maker by trade, who helped establish the pragmatic approach to political and economic problems which has been its hallmark. Gompers, an immigrant from England, had been a student of Socialist doctrine and was not altogether unsympathetic to the Socialist point of view, but his experience as a labor leader convinced him that it had little chance of success under American conditions. He eventually became a staunch foe of socialism, and its major antagonist within the trade unions.

In 1892, the Socialist Labor party, which had been established two decades earlier, fell under the control of Daniel De Leon, a university teacher and a Marxist fundamentalist.

Despairing of making headway within the AFL, he gathered together the remnants of the Knights of Labor and some Socialist-inclined local unions in New York to form the Socialist Trade and Labor Alliance. The Alliance never achieved any real organizational success, though its career was attended by a great deal of furor.

A more serious threat to the Gompers leadership came from Socialist-oriented groups within the AFL. At the AFL conventions of 1893 and 1894, they tried to secure endorsement of collective ownership of the means of production as well as other Socialist demands. Although they were unable to gain a majority for their program, the Socialists teamed up with some personal enemies of Gompers to defeat him for the AFL presidency in 1894, the only time in his long career that Gompers suffered this fate. The moderate Socialists within the AFL continued their efforts to gain control of the organization, and for several decades they were a force to be reckoned with. In 1902, a resolution that would have committed the AFL "to advise the working people to organize their economic and political power to secure for labor the full equivalent of its toil and the overthrowal of the wage system and the establishment of an industrial co-operative democracy" was defeated only by the narrow margin of 4897 to 4171 votes. The Socialists ran their own candidate against Gompers at the 1912 convention, and gained about one-third of the total vote, being supported, among others, by the delegates of the United Mine Workers, the Brewery Workers, the Machinists, and the Typographical Union. However, Socialist party opposition to American participation in the First World War greatly reduced Socialist strength within the AFL.

Another in the series of efforts to build a radical labor movement independent of the AFL came with the formation of the Industrial Workers of the World in 1905. At its inception, it embraced most of the existing left wing groups, including Daniel De Leon's Socialist Labor Alliance and the followers of Eugene V. Debs, perhaps the most popular Socialist leader in American history. (Debs was imprisoned in 1918 for his opposition to the war, ran for the Presidency of the United States from prison in 1920, and polled close to a million votes for the Socialist party.) But the dominant elements in the IWW came from the western part of the United States, which was then in the process of transformation from a frontier to a settled industrial area. The Western Federation of Miners, an organization of metal miners representing workers in Idaho, Colorado, and Utah, provided the IWW with leadership.

The preamble to the IWW constitution began categorically: "The working class and the employing class have nothing in common"; on this much, the disparate constituency could agree. But differences of opinion soon developed on many issues, including the desirability of political activity within the framework of the capitalist state. Within a few years, Debs, De Leon, and the Western Federation of Miners all withdrew, leaving the IWW in the hands of an uncompromising, direct action group headed by William D. Haywood and Vincent St. John.

The IWW became the spokesman *par excellence* of the migratory workers who at the time constituted a substantial proportion of the labor force in the West. Working in isolated mining camps, in lumbering operations, on large farms, and on the docks of Pacific Coast ports, these men were homeless and rootless, without families, hounded as "hoboes" and "bums" when they were unable to secure work, which was largely seasonal in character at best. Their ideology was a native American syndicalism; its main ingredients were a rejection of capitalism and all its works, and belief in the efficacy of the strike as a means of securing economic gain, and of the general strike in bringing about the eventual overthrow of capitalism. Collective bargaining and the collective agreement were not for them; they were not in one job long enough to make this a feasible procedure, and it was too slow a means of alleviating the poor condition of labor which they faced. The IWW was never very clear about the nature of the Socialist commonwealth which would take over on the great day when all the nation's workers folded their arms and brought capitalism tumbling down. Its job was to prepare for that day by strikes (revolutionary gymnastics), sabotage, and any other means of weakening capitalism.

The formal structure of the IWW was extremely loose. Combined offices and "flop houses," where penniless members could secure a night's lodging and food, were maintained in a number of cities. Dues payments were sporadic, although the members were intensely loyal to the organization and paid when they could. The IWW led some major strikes of metal and lumber workers during the war, and suffered severe repression both by the government and by vigilante action. Hundreds of its leaders were imprisoned, some were lynched by mobs. William D. Haywood fled the country while out on bail awaiting trial, escaped to Russia, and died an unhappy man after having learned that communism had as little use for syndicalism as did capitalism.

While the action of the government undoubtedly hastened the demise of the IWW, its days were numbered in any event by changes in the economic conditions which had led to its creation. The West was settling down; miners, loggers, and longshoremen were acquiring steady employment and families. Their trade unions began to adopt collective bargaining. Nevertheless, the IWW tradition has not entirely disappeared; the Mine, Mill and Smelter Workers' Union, successor to the Western Federation of Miners, and the West Coast Longshoremen's Union are among the few American labor unions still controlled by Communists, while in the organizations of West Coast seamen and lumber workers, one can still detect some trace of IWW psychology.

With the eclipse of the Socialists within the AFL and the IWW outside it, the mantle of opposition fell to the Communist party, which had been formed as a breakaway from the Socialist party soon after the Russian revolution. For some years it followed a policy of "boring from within" the AFL under the guidance of William Z. Foster, an able trade union organizer. However, in 1928 it was directed by the Red International of Labor Unions to establish an independent trade union center, and the outcome was the Trade Union Unity League. While the League was never very large, it served an important function as a training ground for Communist organizers.

But a much more serious challenge to the AFL came from within its own ranks. The AFL had declined steadily in membership and vitality after 1920, and the economic depression that hit the country in 1929 weakened it still further. A group of AFL union leaders blamed the AFL difficulties on too strict adherence to craft union structure, and advocated industrial unionism as the only way in which workers in the mass production industries could be organized.

The Committee for Industrial Organization (which later became the Congress of Industrial Organizations) was a revolt of the unskilled and semi-skilled workers against the craftsmen who controlled the AFL. Like the "new unionism" of Great Britain in the 1890's, or the transformation of Scandinavian unionism a decade later, it reflected the aspirations of the less privileged labor groups to a greater voice in determining labor conditions and their resentment against exclusion from the union movement. The men who led the CIO were not radicals: John L. Lewis, head of the coal miners' union, was a lifelong Republican, while Sidney Hillman and David Dubinsky, who were presidents respectively, of the men's and ladies' garment workers' unions, had some early connection with socialism but had long since lost any sympathy for Marxism. The CIO was not established to remake the social order. Its only goal was to organize the workers in the steel, automobile, electrical equipment, rubber, textile, and other mass production industries.

It is fair to say that the CIO was somewhat to the left politically of the AFL, but it was never under the domination of anti-capitalistic elements. Philip Murray, who succeeded John L. Lewis as president in 1940, was a cautious Scotch ex-coal miner, who had been Lewis' chief lieutenant for many years. Walter Reuther, who became president on the death of Murray, had once been a member of the Socialist party, but turned later to staunch support of the Democratic party.

However, the CIO did have an internal Communist problem of no mean dimensions. With the advent of the United Front policy in 1934, the Communist party dissolved the Trade Union Unity League and turned its attention once more to the AFL. The organization of the CIO afforded it a tremendous opportunity, for there was a great need of trained organizers, and the Communists were only too willing to oblige. Working for little pay and performing arduous and often dangerous jobs, well disciplined Communist groups established themselves in leadership positions. At the height of their power, they controlled half a dozen major CIO unions and had powerful factions in a number of others.

From the outbreak of war in Europe in September, 1939, to the Nazi attack upon the Soviet Union, the Communist-dominated unions were in the forefront of the struggle against American assistance to the democratic nations, and this brought them into sharp conflict with the CIO leadership. But when Russia entered the war, their policy changed over night, and an internal crisis was averted. After the war, tensions once more arose with the growing coolness between the United States and the Soviet Union. When in 1948 the Communist unions supported former Vice President Henry Wallace on a third party ticket in an effort to defeat the Democratic candidate, Harry S. Truman, Philip Murray decided that the Communists would have to go, whatever the cost in CIO strength. A number of Communist unions were expelled from the CIO in 1949 and 1950, and in some cases the CIO set up new unions in an effort to hold the members. Communist power in the labor movement declined precipitously thereafter, and today there are not more than 150,000 workers in the few independent unions under Communist control. Even this does not tell the whole story, for few of the rank and file members are Communists, and many of the leaders have only a tenuous relationship with the Communist party.

By 1955, the issues that had divided the AFL and CIO were gone. The mass production workers were organized into powerful trade unions, and many of the AFL craft unions had expanded their jurisdictions until they were almost indistinguishable from the CIO unions. Both federations supported the Democratic party on the political front. As a result, the AFL-CIO merger was consummated. . . .

Until 1950, there was scarcely a period in which socialism, in one of its many forms, did not play a significant role on the American labor scene. But during the past decade, Communist strength has dwindled into insignificance, and no ideology of the left has arisen to take its place. Nor is there any immediate prospect that one will emerge. Not a single responsible trade union leader advocates an independent labor party, and there are no proponents of government ownership of industry. Prediction of events to come is a hazardous undertaking, but few would quarrel with the observation that the future of American socialism does not seem bright.

THE DETERMINANTS
OF AMERICAN LABOR IDEOLOGY

European socialists have been prone to attribute the pragmatism of American labor to the "backwardness" of the American worker. The late Harold Laski predicted that eventually the American working class would throw off the blinders that prevented it from seeing the truth about class conflict and catch up with the British. In the light of what is happening in Britain, these views are not as popular as they once were, but there is still enough economic determinism in the European Left to make the thesis seem tenable.

The fact of the matter is that these visions of the future have as little to do with reality as the utopia of Edward Bellamy or the gehenna of George Orwell. The American worker had the alternative of taking the paths pointed out to him by persuasive prophets—Daniel De Leon, Morris Hillquit, Eugene V. Debs, William Z. Foster, William D. Haywood, or Norman Thomas, to name a few. Yet in the final analysis, he chose to follow such proponents of business unionism as Samuel Gompers, William Green, and George Meany, who promised only a little more of the goods of this world each year. This result flowed from the conjuncture of certain fundamental conditions in the American environment

The standard of living. It should be observed first that there is no necessary one-to-one relationship between living standards and radicalism. In many countries it is among the better paid workers in the metal trades, on the railroads, in the mines, and on the docks, that foci of discontent exist, while the poorer paid textile, service, and farm laborers are quiescent. Yet there does seem to be a general tendency for economic well being and political conservatism to go hand in hand, as European Socialists are beginning to discover. . . .

The relatively high American standard of living is not difficult to understand. A vast continent, richly endowed with natural resources, was settled by some of the most energetic and ambitious people of Europe. The productivity of labor, both in the factory and on the farm, was high because of its relative scarcity in relation to capital and land. Unemployment was mainly of a frictional or cyclical character, and not the permanent structural unemployment found in many countries. If employment opportunities in an area dried up, the American worker simply moved where jobs were more abundant. He had no ancestral village to tie him down. The phenomenal growth of California in the last two decades attests to continuing high labor mobility. It is as though Western Europe were a single nation and the underemployed peasants of southern Italy could move freely to Great Britain and Sweden.

It has often been remarked that it is inequality, rather than absolute living standards, which gives rise to discontent. Karl Marx once observed: "A house may be large or small; as long as the surrounding houses are equally small it satisfies all social demands for a dwelling. But if a palace arises beside the little house, the little house shrinks into a hut." There has always been, and there still is great inequality of income and wealth in the United States. Whether the degree of inequality is greater or less than in Europe is still a matter of statistical debate. But the political consequences of inequality can be quite different, depending upon the absolute base. A small difference in income may be less tolerable to the worker living on the margin of existence than a large difference to the man who is well off. Statistical comparisons cannot convey anything of the resentments felt, respectively, by a worker who, together with his family, occupies a single room and spends his entire income for inadequate food and clothing, and by a worker with a comfortable house, an adequate diet, and money left over for recreation, when each views a millionaire driving by in his limousine.

The rate of economic growth. The rate of growth of the American economy has been very impressive, even by modern, forced-draught standards. . . .

One of the greatest sources of tension in the modern world is the disparity between the material aspirations of people in underdeveloped nations and the capabilities of their economies. Economic stagnation is not necessarily inconsistent with political stability until the onset of industrialization creates a large class of people who become dissatisfied with their standard of life, and who are able to develop organizational means of protest. We have not yet established the rate of economic advance necessary to prevent undermining of confidence in a prevailing social order. But it is perfectly clear that for the United States, at least, this rate was achieved. It might be objected that European nations developed, too, but that their workers turned to socialism. I would urge in reply that their rates of growth were probably lower during the critical years in which labor's ideology was taking shape; that progress was not nearly as obvious to the working man; and that there was not the optimistic view of the future that prevailed in America. E. H. Phelps Brown, in *The Growth of British Industrial Relations* (London, 1959), has pointed out that "the industrial development of the twenty-five years before the First World

War brought no conspicuous or concentrated changes in the working life of the British people." This can certainly not be said of the United States, when new industries and new factories were everywhere springing up, and old ones were growing.

Not all American workers shared the fruits of industrial growth. The IWW episode was illustrative of the alienation of a substantial group with poor conditions of labor and low expectations for future improvement. But the great majority maintained their faith in capitalism because within their experience, this system delivered the goods.

The absence of class consciousness. A hundred and twenty-five years ago, Alexis de Tocqueville wrote: "America, then, exhibits in her social state an extraordinary phenomenon. Men are there seen on a greater equality in point of fortune and intellect, or, in other words, more equal in their strength than in any other country of the world, or in any other age of which history has preserved the remembrance.". . . .

The ideal of equality carries over strongly into industrial life. The great deference shown to European managers is absent in the American plant. There is in its place a certain camaraderie, reinforced by the fact that if manager and worker should chance to meet outside the factory, they are likely to be indistinguishable in dress and speech. As soon as the British worker opens his mouth, it is clear to which class he belongs. But one can sit around a table with American labor and management personnel and not be at all conscious of any class differences.

It might have been anticipated that the myth of equality would be dissipated by the hard facts of reality. It is neither easy nor usual for an ordinary worker to attain high position in a large corporation. Most American workers have no illusions on this score. Nevertheless, there is no indication that a working class in the European sense is developing. Even the worker solidarity that appeared during the union organizing drives of the 1930's is vanishing under the impact of full employment prosperity.

Differences in national origin, cutting vertically through every stratum of the population, are an important cause of weak class consciousness. Italian, Irish, German, Polish, and French-Canadian workers, to name but a few of the major groups found in the American labor force, are just as likely to feel a community of interest with non-workers of the same nationality as with workers of different nationality. . . .

National and racial divisions among workers have had a particularly deleterious effect upon the growth of American socialism. The immigrants who brought Marxism to the United States often remained cut off from the native American, and confined their activities to fellow workers from the "old country." In 1917, 33,000 out of 80,000 Socialist party members belonged to fourteen semi-autonomous foreign language federations, each with its own newspapers, benefit societies, etc. This situation has been well summarized in the following words: "The immigrants played a dual role in the development of American socialism. They were largely responsible for its birth. They were also largely responsible for stunting its growth. They could transplant the theory of socialism but they could not naturalize it. In the formative years, therefore, an unequal and uneasy relationship existed between foreign-born and native Socialists. The former enjoyed the prestige of intellectual superiority but could not effectively spread the gospel. The latter suffered from a sense of theoretical inferiority but were indispensable in presenting the face of the party to the general public. It was not unusual for the top leadership of local Socialist groups to be native-born while a majority of the rank and file were foreign-born." (Theodore Draper, *The Roots of American Communism,* New York, 1957)

The Socialist party was never able to shake off its foreign flavor. Once the stream of immigrants from Europe was cut off, it lost its main source of recruits. The children of immigrants, anxious to demonstrate their Americanism, turned their backs on socialism. There was lacking the European tradition of handing down a political creed from father to son. Many working class children moved into the ranks of professionals, thus depriving the workers of good leadership material.

A final factor militating against the formation of a cohesive working class in the United States was the character and structure of the AFL. At its formation, the AFL represented a revolt of the skilled trades against the heterogeneous Knights of Labor, which, it was felt, tended to subordinate the interests of the craftsman to those of the general worker. Craft structure continued for many years to be the AFL shibboleth. The theory was developed that because of the fragility of American working class loyalties, only the mutual bond of a common craft could prevent unions from splintering, thus providing an ideological basis for craft selfishness.

The exclusiveness of the crafts was strengthened by the very substantial occupation wage differentials that prevailed. In 1907, the American skilled wage level stood at 205 per cent of the unskilled, compared to about 150 per cent for Great Britain. Occupational differentials have narrowed everywhere since then, but the tendency toward equalization has been weaker in the United States than in Europe. The American "aristocracy of labor" was less than anxious to embrace industrial unionism when craft structure had paid off so well. There were a few industrial unions in the AFL before the New Deal, notably the United Mine Workers and the International Ladies' Garment Workers, but the locus of power was the skilled building trades unions, relatively stable in membership and possessing substantial financial resources. . . .

Political barriers to socialism. It is almost a cliche that the tradition of the American two-party system provided an insurmountable obstacle to the establishment of a labor party. But putting the matter this way is merely to beg the question. In Britain, one of the great parties of the nineteenth century, the Liberals, yielded to a newly organized Labour party. In many other countries, the same process occurred as the labor movement asserted its independence. The right question to ask is this: Why did not the Democratic party in the United States yield its paramountcy to a labor party with the rise of the industrial worker? . . .

Samuel Gompers, who more than any other man made explicit the non-partisanship of American labor, wrote in 1920: "The effect of a separate political labor party can only be disastrous to the wage earners of our country and to the interests of all forward looking people. The votes that would go to a labor party candidate would, in the absence of such candidate, go to the best man in the field. In no case would he be an enemy of labor. There can be no hope of success of labor party candidates. The effect, therefore, of a political labor party will be to defeat our friends and to elect our enemies. Labor can look upon the formation of a political labor party only as an act detrimental to the interests of labor and exactly in line with that which is most ardently desired by those who seek to oppress labor."

This statement makes clear the basic reason for the opposition of the leaders of American unionism to independent labor action: the firm conviction that there would be no success. American labor leaders are certainly not averse to winning political power; they would like to sit in the Cabinet, and John L. Lewis once envisioned himself as a Vice-Presidential candidate running alongside Franklin D. Roosevelt. When Lewis broached the subject to Roosevelt, the latter is reported to have replied: "Which place were you thinking of, John?" But they have been realistic enough to realize that such honors, which many European working class leaders have obtained, were unlikely of attainment via the third party route.

Why was this true? For one thing, industrial workers in the United States, the land *par excellence* of industrialization, have never constituted a majority of the population. In 1950, 46 per cent of all those employed were classified as professional, technical, managerial, and clerical workers, while another 15 per cent were in categories not prone to unionization: private household workers, service workers, and farm laborers. By 1958, the non-worker group percentage had risen to 48 per cent, while industrial workers had shrunk to about 37 per cent of the labor force. Thus, even if wage earners were a solid bloc, they would still fall far short of a majority unless they could count on substantial support from white-collar employees, who have shown little inclination to vote labor anywhere. In the past it was the farmers who blocked labor's road to political power. Today it is the growing middle class—white-collar workers, professionals, the self-employed—which stands in the way.

Secondly, American workers have never voted in the same automatic fashion as European workers. European Socialist parties first gained working class allegiance by elementary democratic demands for universal suffrage and free public education, which American workers have enjoyed for a century, and which therefore could not be utilized as issues by aspiring labor politicians.

Since 1928, most trade unions have supported the Democratic party on the national level, and have urged their members to vote, in turn, for Alfred E. Smith, Franklin D. Roosevelt, Harry S. Truman, Adlai Stevenson, and John F. Kennedy. But even during the Roosevelt era, when American workers were united as never before behind a man whom they felt had rescued them from economic disaster, a minority of trade union leaders and workers supported the Republican party. Among the prominent Republican laborites have been Hutcheson pere and fils, presidents of the large Carpenters' Union; John L. Lewis; and Dave Beck and James Hoffa of the Teamsters' Union. . . .

The political tactics of American labor have not worked badly. The Democratic party is a loose coalition of various interest groups, rather than the representative of a particular economic sector of the population. It includes some of the most anti-labor elements in the country, from the South; the political machines of the large Northern cities, which at best are neutral on issues of labor interest; and staunch labor supporters from areas in which the trade union movement is strong. By operating within the Democratic party structure, the unions are able to secure for themselves, on a *quid pro quo* basis, much broader influence than they could hope for as minority independents.

This method is not without its dangers. If public opinion turns against the unions, as it did after the 1945-1947 strike wave, and the 1958-1959 corruption exposures, they are left defenseless, since non-labor politicians cannot be expected to brave the wrath of the electorate in support of an unpopular cause. In normal times, however, the unions are able to achieve constant legislative gains, and in periods of economic crisis, the Democratic party has even been transformed into a powerful instrument for major social reform.

The triumph of collective bargaining. The method of collective bargaining, as opposed to the method of legal enactment, to use the terminology of the Webbs, has proven eminently successful in the United States, contributing in no small measure to a reluctance on the part of workers to rely upon the state. A great many objectives which are essentially social in character have been achieved by private bargaining. One need only cite the proliferation of pension plans, health and welfare schemes, and the guaranteed annual wage. . . .

The basic instrument of trade union control is the grievance machinery which is found in virtually every collective agreement. Almost any aspect of work can be raised as a grievance, discussed with management, and finally carried to compulsory arbitration by an impartial outsider. There has grown up a comprehensive body of industrial common law which management disregards only at its peril.

It is now very difficult for an American business concern to promote or discharge an employee except on the basis of strict seniority. The speed of the assembly line, the size of the working crew on a machine or process, the work load, are all subject to union challenge. Unions may negotiate with management on the quality of meals to be provided employees; on recreational and sanitary facilities; on protection against injuries; in short, on virtually the entire range of subject matter which is within the purview of European labor-management committees. Normally, they still do not have any right to participate in the formulation of production or financial plans, but they are moving in this direction, and it will probably not be too long before this stronghold of management is invaded. . . .

THE FUTURE

One need not be rash in making the prediction that traditonal socialism has little future in the United States. There are still a few advocates around, but their voices are no longer heard. The Communist party and the various splinter Socialist groups have no influence whatever on political events. The trade unions are committed more firmly than ever to working within the existing two-party system. . . .

The forces that in the past shaped the unique character of the American labor movement continue unabated, for the most part. Material living standards remain the highest in the world, and they are improving at a fairly rapid rate. Of class consciousness, one can only say that everything is tending to diminish the possibility of developing a closely-knit, cohesive working class. The number of industrial workers is shrinking in relation to other groups, and the unions are fully aware of the fact that even to hold their own, they must somehow attract white-collar employees and professionals. Paradoxically, the only development that may foster manual worker cohesiveness is the tendency of manual wages to rise faster than those of white-collar employees, for the manualists may become concerned about protecting their differentials.

VI

COLLECTIVE
BARGAINING

Introduction

Collective bargaining is a continuing relationship between one or more unions and one or more employers, for the purpose of reaching joint decisions on employee compensation, job tenure, and other conditions of employment. Harry Shulman and Neil Chamberlain point out that, although the content of collective agreements differs widely from industry to industry, the basic aims are largely the same. They emphasize the quasi-compulsory nature of the relationship, in which neither party is free to break off relations and contract with somebody else; the benefits that the parties can expect to gain from the agreement; and the continuity of bargaining. The day-to-day adjustment of differences through the grievance procedure may be as important as the more dramatic contract negotiations.

What a union can gain through collective bargaining depends partly on its ability to inflict economic damage on the employer in the event of disagreement. Albert Rees emphasizes the primacy of the strike as a source of union power, and analyzes union policy in using the strike weapon. Other sources of union power, such as consumer boycotts and control of labor supply, are—in practice—of secondary importance.

295

40. The Process of Bargaining

Harry Shulman

Neil W. Chamberlain

Collective bargaining is a concept, like law or government, which denotes some fundamental characteristics, but permits great variety in adaptation to specific needs and situations. Wage negotiations in the bituminous coal industry, with their incident parliamentary organization and procedures, hardly resemble the wage negotiations with a single shirt manufacturer in New Haven. The representation of employees and the nature and the process of adjustment of "grievances" on a building construction site present different problems requiring different methods from those in an automobile assembly plant. The detailed provisions of a collective agreement in a manufacturing plant are hardly transferable to an agreement covering hotel waiters, newspaper or magazine writers or university stenographers. But the basic conditions and aims are largely the same. And the primary approach—the effort to consider and understand each other's needs, desires, fears and to inquire, negotiate and adjust jointly—that is also largely the same.

Theoretically, collective bargaining does not require a comprehensive collective agreement for a stated period of time. It requires only the recognition of the bargaining agency and of the principle of action that mutual problems be jointly considered and jointly decided. But while each party, if it were in full control, might wish to retain its freedom to deal with problems as it deems best when confronted by them, the fact of joint participation makes commitment for the future almost inevitable. The desire of each party to be assured about the other's future conduct—that is, the desire for stability and security—makes the comprehensive collective agreement for a term the normal concomitant of collective bargaining. This reduces the possibility of solving problems on the basis of spot judgments without formulated policies. It requires each party to think into the future, to anticipate situations and to determine solutions before the situations arise. It requires the making of policy—which, when agreed upon, becomes the collective agreement.

Typically, then, collective bargaining involves first, the negotiation of a general agreement as to terms and conditions of employment, and second, the maintenance of the parties' relations for the period of the agreement. The first process is the dramatic one which catches the public eye and which is sometimes mistaken to be the entire function of collective bargaining. But in fact, it is to labor relations approximately what the wedding is to domestic relations. It launches the parties on their joint enterprise with good wishes and good intentions. The life of the enterprise then depends on continuous, daily cooperation and adjustment. . . .

From this point of view, the heart of the

collective agreement—indeed, of collective bargaining—is the process for continuous joint consideration and adjustment of plant problems. And it is this feature which indicates the great difference between the collective labor agreement and commercial contracts generally. The latter are concerned primarily with "end results"; the former, with continuous process.

The legal status of collective labor agreements has been the subject of much discussion in the legal literature and of considerable development in the courts. The early notion, still dominant in England, is that the collective labor agreement is not a legally enforceable transaction, that it is a statement of principles and purposes which must depend on good faith and self help and does not of itself create legal rights and obligations. In American courts this notion has given way to the conception of the collective labor agreement as a legally enforceable contract. But the practical significance of this newer conception has been only slightly illustrated. Employers have maintained that, in fact, only they, and not the unions, have been responsible in law for breach of contract. The provision of the Taft-Hartley Act subjecting both unions and employers to suit in the federal courts for breach of collective agreement does not define the scope of the liability which the courts are authorized to enforce, but it has caused widespread concern among unions and has led to extensive efforts on their part to secure exculpatory or non-liability clauses.

Whatever the legal status of the collective labor agreement may be, however, it is entirely clear that court enforcement can play only a relatively minor role in labor relations under such an agreement, just as in domestic relations. The nature of the agreement and of the parties' relations makes resort to the courts a theoretical and unsuitable remedy—except only in extreme cases and in those in which disruption has already taken place. For it must always be remembered that performance of the agreement is not the entire aim or object of the parties' relation. Their object is the operation of the enterprise in which each has indispensable tasks. And the agreement is a means of aiding them in their performance of those tasks and in the operation of the enterprise for their joint benefit.

The labor agreement is not made between parties who seek each other out for the purpose of entering into a business transaction and who can shop around among competitors for the most favorable connection. It is made, rather, between parties who find themselves already in a joint enterprise and who have little or no choice in selecting each other for the relationship. The union hardly chooses the employer; and the employer does not choose the union. Both are dependent on the same enterprise; and, as a practical matter, neither can pull out without destroying it. Even when a dispute between them results in suspension of operations (a strike or lockout), they must strive so to adjust the dispute as to resume their relationship.

Of necessity and quite independently of the agreement, the parties must live and work together daily and continuously. Their differences and frictions require adjustment not merely in terms of redress for past wrongs but more importantly in terms of facilitating today's and tomorrow's cooperation. While conformance with the collective agreement is intended as a means to that end, it is not the only means and is not a guaranteed cure-all.

The collective agreement applies to the relationships of a large number of people with various personalities, temperaments, ambitions, fears and tensions. While we speak of "the employer" and "the union" as entities, the agreement deals not merely with the relationships between numerous people—machine hands, laborers, craftsmen, rate checkers, plant policemen, several ranks of foremen, labor relations men, superintendents and so on. To think merely in terms of "employer" and "employees" or "management" and "union" is to miss a very important fact in labor relations—the fact that the relationships involve numerous people whose interests, needs, jobs and performances cannot be compressed, without distortion, into two general rubrics.

This means that what is sought is the satisfaction or adjustment of the needs, desires, or expectations of numerous people, rather than of certain officials on each side. And the adjustment is needed in numerous situations and under dynamic conditions. Even in the most stable enterprise there may be almost daily changes in details of operation and perhaps also in personnel. Each change may be of trifling significance to the enterprise as a whole; but to the individuals immediately affected it may appear of major importance.

The collective agreement cannot prescribe an indisputable rule of thumb for every dispute, difference, dissatisfaction or situation that may arise during its term. This is true for a number of reasons. First, it is humanly impossible to anticipate all the situations with all their variations and all the pressures that attend them when they do arise. But even if it were possible thus to anticipate, it would be undesirable to lay down absolute, advance prescriptions in detail. For, by common paradox, while the parties want and need security, they also want and need freedom to act as occasion requires. Moreover, attempts at such advance prescription in detail would tend to prevent adoption of an agreement—first, because the negotiations would be endlessly protracted, and second, because agreement on the application of a principle in numerous hypothetical cases is infinitely more difficult than agreement on the principle itself. Again, the collective agreement must be susceptible of comprehension and administration by ordinary workers and supervisors; and it normally requires ratification by the union membership. Abundance of detail and minutiae may discover independent, individual objections of minor importance which may be aggregated (intentionally or otherwise) into a quite unwarranted total hostility. Like a political platform, a collective agreement may need to avoid "red flags."

For a number of reasons, then, the collective labor agreement must leave much to silence, to inference or to general statement. Like modern legislation in complex affairs, it must rely on administration to fill in the details and provide the needed adjustments. This requires continuous joint consideration of problems with the collective agreement as one aid to their solution.

But paradoxically again, the collective agreement also looses forces tending toward rigidity and unreasonableness. These are the temptations to refer all questions to the agreement; to argue about what the agreement provides and not about what the problem is and how it can best be met; to insist upon literal compliance without proper consideration of need, purpose and spirit; to couch requests and answers in terms of the agreement even when doing so conceals the parties' real concerns; in short, to think in terms of the agreement alone and not in terms of the problems or needs of the enterprise and of those engaged in it.

Remembering that the purpose of the parties' relationship is mutual benefit from the operation of their enterprise, the test of their success and maturity is not the rigidity of their compliance with the agreement, but rather the extent of their readiness sympathetically to understand and consider each other's needs and cooperate in efforts at adjustment—even by modification of prior agreement. The mechanism is normally the grievance procedure—either alone or in combination with other practices of joint meetings for discussion of general problems.

Like the rest of the collective agreement, the grievance procedure may be tailored to meet the requirements of the particular enterprise. In a small plant a single provision for a conference between the union representative and the "boss" may suffice. In larger plants, a series of steps or appeals may be required, each calling upon a different or higher level of authority. This assures participation by top authority when really necessary, but saves it from being swamped by minor grievances. It also affords opportunity to subordinate authorities to participate and effect adjustments within their special competence and concern. Various details may or may not be made parts of the procedure: time limits for the filing of grievances, appeals, or answers, requirements as to writing and employee signatures, limitations on the subject matter, and so on. Limitations and formalities have undoubted values; but their adoption or enforcement requires an appraisal of their values in relation to the cost of leaving frictions and dissatisfactions to fester without remedy. In any event, the adequacy of the grievance procedure for the maintenance of good relations depends less upon its structure than upon the spirit with which the individuals involved use it. If they are impatient, resentful, petty, arrogant, misanthropic, legalistic, non-understanding or unwilling to understand, the best procedure will fail.

Even under ideal conditions, however, agreement in all instances can hardly be expected. In the past, unadjusted grievances and claims of contract violation were left to the parties' own power and to self-help. Resort to the courts was, and is, hardly a practical remedy. This is due only in minor part to the uncertain status in law of suits for enforcement of collective labor agreements. The major reason is that court litigation is an inappropriate method of securing harmonious cooperation in an enterprise involving continuous, daily, joint performance. The expense is too great for most of the disputes; the inevitable delay in securing final adjudication prolongs conflict; the spirit of litigation bolsters antagonism; the proceedings require professional representation and technicality beyond the competence of the clients; the emphasis is upon winning a case rather than restoring or maintaining a desired relationship; and the simple alternative of judgment for the plaintiff or defendant excludes the possibilities of intermediate adjustments which might be more appropriate and more helpful.

Accordingly, in recent years arbitration has been increasingly resorted to as the terminal step in grievance procedures. In some cases, separate consent to arbitrate is required for each dispute; in others, there is general advance agreement to arbitrate future disputes not satisfactorily resolved by the parties themselves. In some, the tribunal consists of several individuals; in others it consists of one. In some the composition of the tribunal is tri-partite either in the sense that, in addition to the impartial chairman, each party designates a member or in the further sense that the member designated is actually a representative of the party; in others, the tribunal is wholly non-partisan. In some cases, a separate tribunal must be constituted for each dispute; in others a standing tribunal is constituted to serve for a stated term or so long as it continues to be satisfactory to both parties. And in some cases the arbitrator is appointed by the parties upon their own nomination and investigation; in others, the parties delegate to a third body the nomination or appointment of the arbitrator.

Arbitration, in other words, like collective bargaining, is a flexible procedure which can be suited to different needs or desires. In some circumstances, it tends to become quite formal, rigid and legalistic. It then serves only the function of final adjudication—even as court litigation. But court litigants normally do not have to live together; their disputes generally relate to past events; the welfare of neither is dependent on that of the other; and a victory in the litigation is just as sweet whether it is the product of wisdom and understanding, or of confusion, misapprehension, or seduction by a witness or counsel. A labor dispute is wholly different. Though the dispute may formally relate to past events, the parties' major concern is with the present and the future; the parties must continue their relationship and work together during the dispute and after its determination; while the parties are in adversary positions, neither can disclaim interest in the other and neither can afford unduly to embitter the other; and a determination which is not wisely addressed to the problem and which does not contribute to greater harmony and understanding for the parties may be only a temporary victory which a little time may uncover as a serious loss. Arbitration employed with these differences in mind may be a powerful factor in promoting investigation, diagnosis and education for cooperation by the parties in their joint venture.

41. The Sources of Union Power

Albert Rees

§1. THE STRIKE

The strike is by far the most important source of union power, and the union is now virtually the sole organizer of strikes. This last was not always true; at one time spontaneous strikes among unorganized workers were frequent. In 1958, however, strikes that did not involve any union were less than 1 per cent of recorded strikes, and accounted for less than 0.05 per cent of man-days lost from strikes.[1] Some unauthorized strikes of union members are still immediate expressions of worker discontent, but collective bargaining provides other channels for handling most grievances.

The strike is a planned withholding of labor designed to impose union demands on the employer or to prevent the employer from imposing his demands on the union. It is traditional to divide work stoppages into strikes and lockouts, the former occurring where the workers walk off the job, the latter where the employer withholds employment from them. But the employer almost never needs to do this. At the expiration of an agreement he can always announce his terms unilaterally and allow the union the choices of striking, reaching an agreement, or working without an agreement during further negotiations. Almost the only occasion for a true lockout arises when a union calls a strike against one member of an employers' association; the other employers may then close down to make common cause with the struck employer. In this [article], I shall use the word "strike" to cover all work stoppages, including the few that fit the traditional definition of the lockout.

The strike is the most conspicuous and dramatic aspect of labor relations and provides the labor movement with its heroes, martyrs, and folklore. To the general public, the prevention of strikes seems to be the chief problem in industrial relations and industrial peace is considered the chief goal. The economist is likely to be somewhat less concerned with the direct losses from strikes, and more concerned with the consequences as expressed in the terms of settlement. The strike keeps resources idle for days or months, but the settlement can determine the way in which resources are used for many years.

In recent years there have been roughly 3,000 to 5,000 recorded strikes a year in the United States (see Table 1). In 1958, a relatively peaceful year, there were 3, 694 recorded

[1]U. S. Bureau of Labor Statistics, Bulletin No. 1258. This is also the principal source of the other statistics in this section.

Table 1

Number of Strikes, Workers Involved, and Man-Days Idle, 1946-60

Year	Number of Strikes Beginning in Year	Workers Involved (1,000)	Man-Days Idle	
			Number (1,000)	Per cent of Estimated Working Time
1946	4,985	4,600	116,000	1.43
1947	3,693	2,170	34,600	0.41
1948	3,419	1,960	34,100	0.37
1949	3,606	3,030	50,500	0.59
1950	4,843	2,410	38,800	0.44
1951	4,737	2,220	22,900	0.23
1952	5,117	3,540	59,100	0.57
1953	5,091	2,400	28,300	0.26
1954	3,468	1,530	22,600	0.21
1955	4,320	2,650	28,200	0.26
1956	3,825	1,900	33,100	0.29
1957	3,673	1,390	16,500	0.14
1958	3,694	2,060	23,900	0.22
1959	3,708	1,880	69,000	0.61
1960	3,250	1,375	19,250	0.17

Source: *Historical Statistics of the United States,* 1960, p. 99, and Bulletins of the Bureau of Labor Statistics.

strikes involving over 2 million workers and almost 24 million man-days of idleness. But this idleness was only 0.22 per cent of the estimated working time of all workers. The range of such estimates for 1947-60 is 0.14 to 0.61, and 1946 is the only year in which the estimated loss exceeded 1 per cent.

The available statistics are of limited value in assessing the cost of strikes. On the one hand, strikes also cause secondary idleness not included in the statistics. For example, a steel strike can cause railroad workers to be laid off for lack of traffic or automobile workers to be laid off for lack of materials. On the other hand, there are very important offsets to strike losses. Most strikes cause production to be displaced in time or location rather than to be lost altogether. A strike against one producer in a large industry may be completely offset by the increased output of his competitors. When an entire industry faces a threat of strike, it will often increase its output in anticipation; if the strike occurs, it may again produce at higher than normal levels for some time after the strike is over. If the industry struck is a supplier of materials to other industries, these industries can draw on inventories during the strike and replenish them afterward, so that there may be little effect on the output of final products.[2]

The possibility of offsets in time depends, of course, on the durability of the product. They are not possible for highly perishable goods or for services, and for many services offsets in location are also impossible. Since America has a large stock of automobiles and abundant facilities for keeping them in repair, a strike against automobile manufacturers could go on for months with little inconvenience to consumers. In contrast, a strike against a local bus line has an immediate impact. Moreover, if a bus strike prevents people from getting to work today, they will not be compensated by the possibility of going back and forth twice tomorrow. However, unions and management go to great lengths to avoid strikes that would cause severe hardships to the public, and strikes that create real emergencies are fortunately rare.

[2]For an excellent analysis of the costs of steel strikes in terms of production of final products, see E. Robert Livernash, *Collective Bargaining in the Basic Steel Industry* (Washington, D.C.: U.S. Department of Labor, 1961), Chapter III.

In considering the costs of strikes, some non-economic factors should also be taken into account. A strike can have a cathartic effect, cleansing away accumulated tensions and making possible new approaches to stubborn problems. It can provide a release from the monotony of routine work and a sense of excitement not present in a mere vacation. Frequently such factors improve productivity when the strike is over. Of course, the costs of a prolonged strike can more than offset gains of this kind.

It is a favorite calculation of newspapers to compute the wage increases won in a strike and compare them with the wages lost during it, a calculation which often shows that workers have lost more wages than they will regain during the life of the agreement. Such calculations misjudge what is at stake. The strike is part of a long-range strategy for both parties. Union gains won without a strike are usually won through the threat of a strike, stated or implied. Such threats cannot retain much force if they are never carried out. Then too, in attempting to push gains just to the point at which a strike is averted, a union will sometimes misjudge its opponent. Once a strike is begun, whether through design or miscalculation, its settlement is not wholly a rational matter, but one that involves subtle questions of organizational and personal prestige. Union members can easily come to believe that the continued existence of their union is at stake, and they will then no longer reckon the outcome in cents per hour. It is no more possible to understand the causes or consequences of a strike by setting up a balance sheet than it would be for a dispute between nations.

Until about 1940, it was common for employers to attempt to operate struck plants, using non-striking employees or new employees recruited for the purpose. Unions engaged in mass picketing to prevent the strikebreakers or "scabs" from entering the plant. . . . [V]iolence often occurred in such circumstances—fighting on the picket line, cars overturned, windows broken, and even shooting and dynamiting. The unions tended to be blamed for violence, though there were undoubtedly cases in which strikebreakers or employers were at fault. The outcome of such a strike depended critically on the position of the police and the courts. Injunctions against picketing and ample police protection for non-strikers could break the strike, and usually did. In a few more recent cases, police have prevented violence by forbidding strikebreakers to cross picket lines, an action that forces the employer to discontinue operations. Often the police or the courts now take a more lenient attitude toward strike violence than toward violence under most other circumstances.

Since World War II it has been unusual for employers to attempt to operate during a strike. The old pattern occurs largely in small communities and in the South. The effects of a strike where operations continue are particularly bitter in a small community. Friendships, social organizations, even families shatter as the community divides into strikers and strikebreakers, and the wounds may take years to heal.

Where the employer does not try to operate, the strike becomes a war of attrition. Around the silent factory, a few token pickets may chat with a lone policeman while their neatly painted signs lean against a fence. Maintenance crews may enter by prearrangement to keep equipment in good shape; sometimes the employer furnishes coffee and doughnuts to the pickets.

An effective strike imposes on both parties losses whose nature depends in large part on the scope of the strike. The employer must continue to meet fixed charges while receiving no revenues. If only one employer is struck in an industry, he may lose both customers and workers to competitors and he is not assured of getting all of them back when the strike ends. Customers often turn to more dependable suppliers or decide to produce their own requirements. At the same time, those strikers who cannot find other work are losing their wages. In some cases the union provides regular strike benefits, but these are possible chiefly in small strikes conducted by large unions.

The union strategy of striking one employer at a time, thus putting the struck employer at a competitive disadvantage, can be met by the formation of a united front among employers. This will usually force the union to strike a whole industry at once. If any competitive forces pressing employers toward settlement remain, they arise from other industries or from imports, and these pressures are usually weak. The dues of working union members cannot, in an industry-wide strike, provide benefits for the strikers. Benefits taken from accumulated strike funds or contributions from other unions will usually be reserved for cases of severe hardship. The ability of strikers to find work elsewhere will be sharply restricted. However, a strike against a whole industry can cause secondary unemployment on a large scale, or halt the flow of final products to consumers. The pressure of public opinion or the intervention of government may then force a settlement.

The ability of a union to win a strike depends on a number of factors. These are related to but not identical with the factors determining its ability to raise wages. . . . A union can be said to win a strike when it gains concessions that the employers were unwilling to make before the strike, and when these meet, in whole or in large part, the union's true demands (as distinguished from demands made for tactical purposes).

A strike hurts an employer most if the demand for his product is strong and profits are high. If demand is weak, he may lose little by shutting down, and can more easily regain lost production when the strike is over. Perhaps in part for this reason, chronically depressed industries like apparel have had low strike rates. Similar forces produced a high correlation between the number of strikes and the level of business activity for the period 1915-1938.

Another major determinant of the union's ability to win is the degree of skill and specialization of the members. The more skilled and specialized they are, the more difficult it is for management to carry on production by using strikebreakers or non-striking supervisory employees.

The ability of unions to win strikes does not necessarily govern the frequency with which they strike. If their power is great, mere threat of a strike may be all that is necessary. The propensity of a union to strike also depends in part on the philosophy and attitudes of its leaders and members. A high propensity to strike by unions of miners, seamen, and longshoremen has been noted for several countries. A well-known study of this phenomenon suggests that the isolation of miners and maritime workers from the larger society contributes to this high propensity,[3] though this interpretation has been disputed by other scholars.

[3]See Clark Kerr and Abraham Siegel, "The Interindustry Propensity To Strike," in A. Kornhauser, R. Dubin, and A. Ross, eds., *Industrial Conflict* (New York: McGraw-Hill Book Co., 1954).

§2. GOVERNMENT INTERVENTION IN STRIKES.

When a strike inflicts serious damage on neutral parties or on the general public, government is sooner or later forced to intervene. The party to the strike that considers itself least likely to win in the absence of intervention will encourage intervention by its statements or its behavior, while the other party will of course discourage it. The outcome of the strike will almost always be influenced by any forceful government intervention; only by the sheerest accident could strong intervention produce the result that would have occurred without it.

The intervention of government in many major strikes is an important reason why unions seek to develop political power even where they have little or no political program. The power to influence elections is a valuable adjunct to the power to strike. The role of government in strikes may also help to explain why American unions have largely avoided formal alliances with political parties. The more an elected official can be certain of the support of one party to an industrial dispute come what may, the more he may lean toward the other in an attempt to gain added political strength. Thus we observe, ironically, conspicuous instances of intervention favorable to unions by conservative elected officials, and of adverse intervention by officials with labor support. . . .

§3. WILDCAT STRIKES AND SLOWDOWNS

A wildcat strike is one conducted in violation of an agreement or without proper authorization from higher union bodies—by a department or unit without authorization from the local union or by a local union without authorization from the national union. (In most unions such authorization is required.) Many wildcat strikes, especially spontaneous ones, arise from dissatisfaction with union policies and thus cannot be considered a source of union strength. At other times, however, a union may tacitly condone or encourage strikes that it officially disowns. Wildcat strikes sometimes occur during negotiations for a new agreement, when they may exert pressure for a quicker settlement.

It may seem odd that although spontaneous strikes of nonunion workers are now rare, wildcat strikes by unionists are fairly common. One explanation is that the penalty for striking is less severe in the latter case. Unions will usually agree to employer discipline of workers who strike in violation of an agreement, but they will oppose penalties they regard as excessive. Some wildcat strikes occur when workers feel there is an emmediate threat to their health or safety. If they cannot convince their supervisors of the danger, a wildcat strike is their only recourse. Union opposition to severe or automatic penalties for wildcat strikers is based in part on cases of this kind.

Some observers of industrial relations report a decreasing frequency of wildcat strikes in recent years. In part this may result from the maturing of union organizations and greater control of union members by their leaders. In part, it is reported to result from more severe and consistent use of discipline by management, since management often found that to settle a wildcat strike by making concessions invited the use of similar tactics in the future.[4]

We can regard the authorized strike as the heavy artillery of the trade union, and the wildcat strike and the slowdown as its small arms—weapons suited for limited engagements and local objectives. The slowdown is a temporary slackening of the normal pace of work designed to put pressure on management to gain some objective. The workers remain on the job and appear to be engaged in their usual activities.[5] "Slowdown" is a narrower term than restriction of output, which may be permanent. The ability to restrict output permanently is a consequence of having power to begin with, and not a source of additonal power. For the slowdown to be effective as a pressure tactic, management must be aware of it. In contrast, restriction of output undertaken to prolong a job may be most successful if management is unaware of it.

The most frequent source of slowdowns is dissatisfaction with incentive wage rates, and grievances of this kind give rise to slowdowns in non-union as well as union plants. A slowdown is almost never formally authorized by a union

but may be conducted with tacit union consent. Its advantage over the wildcat strike is the protection from discipline afforded the participants. In a well-run slowdown, management observes the reduction in output but cannot detect the subtle changes in work behavior that cause it and therefore cannot identify the individual participants.

§4. CONSUMER BOYCOTTS AND UNION LABELS

The consumer boycott and the union label are opposite sides of the same coin. A boycott urges consumers not to buy products made by nonunion labor, whereas a union label on consumer goods encourages sympathetic shoppers to choose products made under union conditions. In general, these are weak weapons. However, the consumer boycott is sometimes effective against retail establishments in localities where union membership is concentrated, and the union label has helped to organize industries such as work clothing whose products are heavily consumed by manual workers. Where union strength rests largely on the power to strike, the label can be of more value to the customer than to the union. Thus in most union print shops, the label or "bug" is used only at the request of the customer, yet little political campaign literature appears without it.

The proper public attitude toward the union label would be an important and difficult question if the weapon were more powerful. The principle that workers should be free to join or not to join unions of their own choosing would seem to require that they be free from consumer pressures as well as from management pressures. On the other hand, it can be argued that consumer freedom extends to knowledge about the working conditions under which products are made. On this view, the union label on a loaf of bread stands on the same footing as the label that it contains artificial preservatives—each may be of intense interest to some buyers and be totally ignored by others.

§5. SECONDARY BOYCOTTS

The secondary boycott is a strike or threat of strike in which the union's complaint is not against the employer struck but against someone with whom he does business. For example,

---

[4]See Sumner H. Slichter, James J. Healy, and E. Robert Livernash, *The Impact of Collective Bargaining on Management* (Washington, D.C.: Brookings Institution, 1960), pp. 663-91.

[5]See R. S. Hammett, Joel Seidman, and Jack London, "The Slowdown as a Union Tactic," *Journal of Political Economy,* Vol. 65 (April, 1957).

the workers in a retail store may refuse to handle the products of a struck manufacturer. If their employer directs them to do so, they may walk out altogether in an effort to force him to buy from another supplier.

The use of the secondary boycott is now severely restricted by law. Some of the restrictions are part of the Landrum-Griffin Act of 1959, which at this writing is still too recent to permit any confident evaluation of their exact meaning or effects. . . .

§6. CONTROL OF THE LABOR SUPPLY

The control of the labor supply is often considered to be a source of union power. The term can have several meanings. Most of those that apply to true unions, as distinguished from union-like organizations, have already been covered under other headings.

The most effective type of control of the labor supply is control over the number of people who can be trained for an occupation or profession. By limiting the number trained, the organization can protect or raise the earnings of its members. There is strong evidence that the American Medical Association has had such power,[6] but it is doubtful whether any organi-

[6] See Milton Friedman and Simon Kuznets, *Income from Independent Professional Practice* (New York: National Bureau of Economic Research, 1945), pp. 8-21 and 118-37.

zation ordinarily considered a union possesses similar power. Craft unions often operate apprenticeship programs in co-operation with employers and require employers under most circumstances to give preference in employment to those who complete such programs. However, union apprenticeship programs do not by any means train all of the journeymen in the skilled trades. Many workers pick up their skill on the job in non-union employment, especially in smaller communities. They may later move into union employment, for few unions will deny membership to all those not trained in union apprenticeship programs. While such a source of supply exists, the union cannot effectively limit entry to the trade by limiting the number of apprentices of union employers or unduly lengthening the period of apprenticeship.

The closed shop, which requires employers to hire only union members, is sometimes considered to be a control of the labor supply, but this view seems forced where qualified non-union members are available. It would be better to say that the union, by its power to strike, denies the employer access to part of the supply so that he is forced to choose between operating solely with union labor and solely with non-union labor. Of course, the union's power to strike is increased if there are few non-union workers in a trade and if these are reluctant to work for struck employers. . . .

The Legal Environment

For more than a century, ground rules for union and employer behavior in collective bargaining were laid down by court decisions. Beginning with the National Labor Relations Act of 1935, however, Congress and state legislatures have regulated in increasing detail the internal operation of trade unions, bargaining units and procedures, the content of collective agreements, and the use of strikes and other economic weapons. A major administrative agency, the National Labor Relations Board, has been created to monitor the new ground rules. Charles Gregory outlines the long evolution of legal controls that has brought us to the present stage.

Clark Kerr argues that the central problem in an industrial society is to achieve an acceptable division of power among individuals, organized groups, and the state. In the area of industrial relations, this comes down to the relative rights and responsibilities of workers, unions, business organizations, and citizens as represented by government. The United States, he believes, has gone too far in detailed regulation of industrial relations. He outlines four simple laws that he thinks would adequately protect the interests of all parties and would be superior to the present complicated legal structure.

During the 1950s there was much discussion of possible malfeasance and abuse of power by trade union leaders. This led eventually to the Landrum-Griffin Act of 1959, which imposed controls on internal union government. The second reading from Kerr, written before the passage of the Landrum-Griffin Act, explores the meaning and feasibility of "union democracy," and then asks what contribution legislation can make to this objective. Compare Kerr's proposals with what Congress actually did, and evaluate their relative merits.

42. Government Regulation or Control of Union Activities

Charles Gregory

EARLY JUDICIAL CONTROL OF LABOR UNIONS

Before 1910, the regulation and control of American labor unions was chiefly by judge-made law. Workers who used economic pressure to spread union organization in the early 1800's were held guilty of common-law criminal conspiracy. But this device for controlling unions was abandoned around 1850. Courts soon began to allow peaceful strikes for immediate benefits. But most judges thought that campaigns to extend union organization were unlawful. Actions for damages had become the only recourse in these cases. Then around 1880, state courts developed a far more effective device—the labor injunction. This remedy protected only against the tortious invasion of property rights. But our state courts soon invented theories making most peaceful union self-help pressures unlawful.

The courts had always allowed business combinations to eliminate trade rivals and control markets. No legal wrong was done if they were pursuing self-interest and gain. But if *unions* sought to protect *their* standards by eliminating nonunion employers and workers, the courts held this to be wrongful for the spread of unionization led to monopoly. And though monopoly was not tortious according to common law, the courts declared it to be an illegal purpose for union self-help. This was enough to support the labor injunction. Moreover, peaceful secondary boycotts and organizational picketing were made torts in themselves. Thus the courts applied a double standard by denying to unions what they let business groups do.

THE LABOR INJUNCTION

The labor injunction was the most ruthless anti-union weapon ever devised. It was used to protect business only when unions threatened employers with organizing pressures. This remedy was far more effective than other legal sanctions. Criminal prosecutions and damage suits required extensive pleadings, months of waiting, and jury trials. But a judge could issue an injunction without a jury trial. And he could issue a temporary injunction without any trial at all. Thus strikes, picket lines, and boycotts could be smothered before they really got started. Anyone disobeying an injunction was summarily thrown into jail for contempt of court, again without jury trial.

SHERMAN ANTI-TRUST ACT—1890

As industry grew larger, employers began to produce for markets in other states and buy materials from outside. Then the Sherman Anti-Trust Act was passed in 1890. It was believed to be designed to apply only to business organizations as an anti-trust measure. This act was enforced by indictments, triple damage suits, and injunctions. Under its terms, federal courts soon began to apply it to labor unions and to regard most union interferences with the movement of goods in interstate commerce as unlawful restraints of trade. Unions exerted organizational pressures on nonunion employers by peaceful secondary boycotts. Because they disrupted the interstate movements of goods, the Supreme Court ruled that these boycotts violated the Sherman Act. But clearly they were not restraints of trade at all. The unions were simply trying to improve their conditions of work—not to monopolize the market for goods. They obstructed the transit of goods; but so did train robbers. And nobody would think of suing *them* under the Sherman Act.

But the Supreme Court refused to declare simple strikes unlawful under the Sherman Act merely because they disrupted the flow of goods in commerce. To show a violation in this area required proof that the strike was intended to unionize the employer—and for the purpose of eliminating competition between union-made and nonunion-made goods in interstate markets. Thus bargaining strikes which also obstructed the flow of goods in commerce would never be violations. Clearly the Supreme Court was using the Sherman Act merely as a device to stop the spread of union organization. And its concern over the movement of goods in commerce was only *incidental.*

ANTI-INJUNCTION MEASURES: THE CLAYTON ACT OF 1914 AND THE NORRIS-LA GUARDIA ACT OF 1932

At the same time, the labor injunction flourished in common law in federal and state courts. In 1914, Congress passed the Clayton Act to limit use of the injunction against union self-help pressures in labor disputes. Section 6 of the Act declared that the labor of a human being was not a commodity. Section 20 seemed to offer some relief from the court's injunctive process. But this measure was so narrowly construed that injunctions against union organiza-

tional drives continued. All that the Clayton Act *actually* did was to allow further injunctive relief against unions under the Sherman Act. In the 1920's, Professor Felix Frankfurter headed an attempt to promulgate a *really* effective anti-injunction law. The result was the Norris-La Guardia Act of 1932. This act defined permissible labor disputes broadly enough to include organizational drives against nonunion employers. It required only that the union have an economic interest in employment conditions at the nonunion plant. Then it described the permissible union self-help techniques—the strike, the secondary boycott, and picketing. Such devices when used in a labor dispute as defined were nonenjoinable in federal courts.

CHANGING FEDERAL POLICY—NATIONAL LABOR RELATIONS ACT OF 1935

While this act did not legalize organizational pressures, it removed the injunction, employers' only effective defense against unions. Certainly it meant congressional approval of union expansion throughout entire industries by economic self-help. But it left employers free to fight back with economic weapons by discriminating against employees who supported unionism. The National Industrial Recovery Act of 1933 and the amended Railway Labor Act of 1934 had introduced the principle that employees could join unions without employer interference. But in 1935, Congress passed the National Labor Relations Act, or Wagner Act, to replace the NIRA which was ruled unconstitutional. That statute prohibited anti-union conduct by most employers. If an employer interfered with his employees' attempts to organize unions or tried to dominate such unions, if he discriminated against employees for their union interest or refused to bargain with newly formed unions, he was committing unfair labor practices. The National Labor Relations Board, set up under the terms of the Wagner Act, ordered these unfair practices stopped and granted remedies such as reinstatement of employees with back pay. And the federal courts enforced these orders. Thus, Congress proclaimed the national policy of strong affiliated labor unions organized throughout entire industries. In upholding this statute, the Supreme Court greatly expanded the commerce power of Congress to cover virtually all important units of industry and production. Thereafter unions began to form and grow rapidly.

REPRESENTATIONAL FUNCTIONS OF THE NATIONAL LABOR RELATIONS BOARD

The Labor Relations Board administers an elaborate procedure enabling workers to select or reject unions. Many employers voluntarily recognize unions formed or chosen by their employees. The Board conducts elections when necessary, especially where two or more unions are competing for representational rights. The Board has strict rules governing attempts by outside unions to displace already recognized unions. It will protect an established employer–union contract relationship for three years. Then an outside union may call for an election. To avoid needless conflict, the AFL-CIO has developed no-raiding pacts, administered by an impartial arbitrator. The Board's enormously complicated task of handling these representational matters is a most important aspect of regulating and controlling unions today.

UNION IMMUNITY FROM ANTI-TRUST LAWS

The anti-injunction and Wagner acts clearly made the expansion of union strength the prevailing national policy. At the same time, the interpretations of the Sherman Act remained unchanged. Under them, union self-help pressures to extend unionism and eliminate nonunionism were still legal. The Supreme Court should have recognized this contradiction and have overruled its earlier decisions, making organizational strikes and boycotts illegal under the Sherman Act. But what it did in the 1941 Hutcheson Case was to indulge in some judicial sleight of hand. It said that since peaceful union self-help conduct in a broad labor dispute context is no longer enjoinable, it is lawful for all purposes—even under the Sherman Act. It based this incredible inference on Section 20 of the Clayton Act which was rejuvenated by the later Norris-La Guardia Act. In effect, the Hutcheson doctrine removed labor unions from the jurisdiction of the Sherman Anti-Trust Act. However, it could still be applied if the unions' conduct was violent or if they connived with employers to restrain trade. . . .

RAILWAY LABOR ACTS–1926 AND 1934

After decades of bitter strikes, the railroad brotherhoods were firmly established. In the 1926 Railway Labor Act, Congress provided mediation and voluntary arbitration of bargaining disputes, with emergency powers vested in the President. This was unsatisfactory since the carriers still interfered with the union organization of their employees. The amended Railway Labor Act of 1934 created boards of adjustment to dispose of grievances and the National Mediation Board to handle all unsettled bargaining and representational disputes. It clarified and enforced the rights of employees and unions to organize and bargain collectively, introducing the principle of majority rule. Moreover, in 1951, Congress permitted the carriers and brotherhoods to contract for the union shop.

Changes in labor relations laws and policies were constant from 1935 to around 1950. But World War II dominated this period. Thus, although there were many strong unions by 1941—unions maintaining a tremendous pressure for higher wages and other concessions—in industries that had never been organized before, and this continued during the war, a war economy could not afford to have strikes. The War Labor Board was created to handle the constantly recurring disputes between unions and employers. Although strikes never were prohibited, the unions made voluntary no-strike pledges that were honored almost 100 per cent.

War Labor Board tripartite panels held hearings on bargaining demands. Sometimes they persuaded the parties to settle. Usually they made recommendations on issues that remained unsettled. The War Labor Board affirmed or modified these, in the end promulgating final contracts. The War Labor Board kept wages at a reasonably stable level, made a sensible compromise on the issue of union security, and refused to include novel items in collective agreements. But most important for the future of labor relations, it added grievance arbitration to thousands of contracts.

POST-WORLD WAR II CHANGES

After the war, the big unions sought wage increases, union security, stronger seniority provisions, vacations, and paid holidays, as well as pensions and insurances of all kinds. With wartime restrictions off, they conducted industry-shaking strikes. Simultaneously, the National Labor Relations Board expanded the employer's duty to bargain, including many new items. These great strikes provoked widespread demands for compulsory arbitration. Australia and New Zealand have long arbitrated their bargaining disputes; but early experiments in the United States were declared unconstitutional by the Supreme Court. At present, industry and organized labor would both rather continue free collective bargaining with strikes than share the dismal experience of countries having compulsory arbitration. . . .

TAFT-HARTLEY ACT–1947

The intensive strikes for money items and the closed union shop immediately after World War II contributed to Congress' passage of the Taft-Hartley Act in 1947. Title I of this statute is the amended National Labor Relations Act. The original National Labor Relations Act designated only unfair labor practices of employers. Unions were free to exercise any organizational and bargaining pressures. Unions were guaranteed the right to strike, and employees the right to engage in concerted activities. The National Labor Relations Board protected most of this conduct from employers' reprisals. When labor organizations had become very strong, extreme union self-help tactics were regarded as intolerable. This conduct included pressures against employers to force their employees to organize, pressures directly against employees themselves, secondary picketing and boycotting which implicated neutral employers and their employees, and even pressures against employers to ignore National Labor Relations Board certifications of other unions. Most unions sought the closed or union shop.

UNIONS' UNFAIR LABOR PRACTICES

Congress amended the National Labor Relations Act by defining six unfair labor practices of unions. The first made it unfair for unions to restrain or coerce employees. The second prohibited unions from trying to make employers discriminate against nonunion employees. The third was a union's refusal to bargain in good faith with the appropriate employer. But the fourth was the most elaborate: Subsection A outlawed union secondary labor boycotts; whereas, Subsection B allowed secondary tactics if the union was certified to the employer against whom the pressure was aimed. Subsection C outlawed union attempts to make an employer deal with a union when another union had been certified to him by the National Labor Relations Board. Subsection D made it an unfair practice for unions to engage in work-jurisdiction disputes, where two unions claim the right to do certain work, and each strikes if the employer gives the work to members of the other union.

The fifth unfair labor practice was to prevent excessively large initiation fees under a valid union-shop agreement. In a union shop, an employer is free to hire anyone he pleases, but he must agree to discharge an employee who refuses to join the union or who does not pay his dues. Under the Wagner Act, federal policy accepted the closed union shop if the employer agreed to hire only union members. This is forbidden by the 1947 statute. But employers, now free to hire anybody they please, may make and enforce agreements requiring both new and old employees to join the union. However, Congress deferred to the states in 1947 by specifying that any state was free to forbid agreements making employment conditional on union membership. Now there are about twenty of these so-called right-to-work statutes. A corporation with plants in forty states may have a master contract with one union covering all these plants; but half of these plants might be union shops and half of them not because of local right-to-work laws.

Whether to have union security or right-to-work statutes is a contentious issue. Supporters of right-to-work laws say that they allow employment without paying tribute to unions. Opponents of these acts say they are meant to keep unions weak by denying them financial support from workers who profit by union bargaining gains. They call such nonunion workers free riders. A compromise is the so-called agency shop where an employee pays the equivalent of union dues without actually joining the union. The National Labor Relations Board finds this compromise acceptable; but right-to-work states are in disagreement about the agency shop. Unions want Congress to permit union shops throughout industry as it did on the railroads in 1951. . . .

NATIONAL EMERGENCY STRIKES

In the Taft-Hartley Act, Congress provided a method of controlling national emergency strikes, except those handled under the Railway Labor Act. Whenever the President thinks an industry-wide strike imperils the national health or safety, he sets up an emergency board to investigate and report to him. The President may then direct the Attorney General to have the strike or lockout enjoined. Federal mediators undertake to secure agreement between the parties. If the dispute is not settled in sixty days, the National Labor Relations Board files a supplemental report containing the employer's last offer to the union. The National Labor Relations Board then conducts a secret ballot among the employees to see if they wish to accept the offer. The injunction is then dissolved. If settlement has not been reached, the strike may be resumed. By that time, the President has made a complete report to Congress.

This device has been invoked twenty-four times, and the Supreme Court upheld this procedure in the steel strike of 1959. It declared that by "national health" Congress meant that of the economy as a whole and the general well-being of the country. Another technique used during the war was seizure and public operation of strike-bound plants. The Supreme Court declared that the President has no such power of seizure, however, in the absence of specific legislation granting him such authority. The President has appointed groups to handle disputes between unions and employers under contract with the Atomic Energy Commission or engaged in missile construction. When mediation fails, the appropriate panel takes jurisdiction, requesting the parties to appear and submit their claims. After hearings, the panel makes recommendations disposing of the various demands presented. The parties' submission to this procedure is entirely voluntary, but it has been effective in avoiding disruptive strikes.

ENFORCEMENT OF COLLECTIVE BARGAINING

Since 1935, a kind of self-government, far more effective than any imposed control or regulation, has evolved in collective bargaining. This is chiefly a result of increased union responsibility. A generation ago, labor unions generally could not sue or be sued. The Wagner Act greatly increased the number of unions and resulting collective agreements, but provided no means for their enforcement. Finally in 1947, Congress provided that the parties might sue each other in the federal courts if the employer operated in interstate commerce. Under this vague provision, the Supreme Court would not let unions directly sue to enforce promises dealing with the terms and conditions of individual employment. Federal courts could enforce promises to unions, however, including commitments to arbitrate unsettled grievances arising under contracts.

GRIEVANCE ARBITRATION

Since World War II, thousands of collective agreements provided for such arbitration. Now that unions could compel employers to comply with promises to arbitrate, it became possible to enforce provisions dealing with individual terms and conditions of employment. This whole development of grievance arbitration has become one of the most stabilizing controls in modern labor relations. Strikes seldom occur now, except when new agreements are bargained. With longer and longer contract terms, arbitration of unsettled matters arising under them will greatly minimize wasteful disputes.

The largest single issue in grievance arbitration is the discipline and discharge of employees for just cause. To justify a discharge, an employer must show that the penalized employee was guilty of something like theft, insubordination, or fighting, or was in violation of a plant rule meriting this extreme penalty. This power of the employer to impose discipline in proper cases is an effective method of controlling employees and even unions themselves. The privilege of employers to hire permanent replacements in bargaining strikes affords another control over unions. Moreover, unions may not terminate collective agreements and call bargaining strikes without a sixty-day notice to mediation officials. The Taft-Hartley Act also lets employers recover damages from unions for harm caused by specified unfair labor practices. In such cases, Congress requires the National Labor Relations Board to seek injunctions. Unions violating no-strike pledges still remain free from injunctions; but they are subject to damage suits, and employers may discharge employees who participate in such strikes. . . .

REGULATION
OF INTERNAL UNION AFFAIRS

Traditionally, courts refused to interfere with the internal affairs of labor unions, treating them like clubs and lodges. They would protect vested property rights of members, but only when remedies within the organization were exhausted. Many unions would not admit Negroes or would only let them join auxiliaries, with no voting rights. But some courts now regard this as a denial of equal protection under the Constitution. The National Labor Relations Board recently revoked the certification of a union that refused to admit or represent Negroes. Unions are under fire where they prevent Negroes from obtaining employment by denying them membership. Since 1959, in the Landrum-Griffin Act, Congress has required unions to file elaborate reports with the government concerning their internal affairs. This statute also grants redress to employees against union officials who deny them the right to participate in union meetings and elections. But its chief concern is to prevent union officials from misappropriating funds. As unions have become more powerful, a greater measure of control has been necessary to insure their fiduciary responsibilities. Furthermore, unions are now sufficiently public in nature so that disclosure of their internal affairs is essential.

FUTURE POLICY CONSIDERATIONS
IN CONTROLLING LABOR UNIONS

There is now much concern over the size and power of our nationally affiliated unions. Many believe that unions should now be brought within the reach of the anti-trust laws to prevent them from abusive practices. This is anathema to labor unionists who recall how the Sherman Act was used to render them powerless a generation ago. A better proposal may be to exempt unions from the anti-trust laws and to outlaw their abusive practices under the National Labor Relations Act.

At present, labor unions continue to enjoy almost complete immunity from the anti-trust laws. Their great power must always present a temptation to abuse it. And our free labor unions may some day become so strong and large that Congress may be forced to curtail their power by measures similar to anti-trust controls. There is even talk that widespread and crippling strikes should be outlawed. Whether this does happen depends largely on how our labor unions shoulder their increasing responsibilities. With the growing maturity of bargaining relationships between employers and unions, it need never occur.

43. Industrial Relations and the Liberal Pluralist

Clark Kerr

One eternal problem of an industrial society—of any society but it need not necessarily arise in so acute a fashion elsewhere[1] —is the distribution of power. An industrial society not only permits or encourages a vast increase in population but it throws people closely together in enormous clusters. And the more productive such a society, the more dependent the welfare of each person becomes, through the process of the division of labor, on the reasonably continuous and efficient performance of each other person. Quite literally, each of us becomes our brother's keeper; and he becomes ours.

This forces, as the greatest imperative of an industrialized economy, the imposition of a veritable "Iron Maiden" of laws and customs and rules preferably to encourage but also perforce to command a disciplined discharge of duty. The burden of these rules may lie lightly on the person grown accustomed to the industrial way of life and knowing no other, but heavy it is indeed for the workers just out of the Kentucky hills, or just off a tribal preserve in South Africa, or fresh from the Arabian desert. The detail of the rules necessary to make an industrialized and urbanized civilization operate effectively is most intricate and precise.

This is not to suggest that there are not other grave problems of an industrial society such as the provision of security within a dynamic economic setting, or the achievement of some degree of distributive justice. But these others are usually subject to simpler solutions than is the issue of the distribution of power. Nor is this to suggest that the only consequence of industrialization is submission to a yoke of social control. If it were, the populace of the world would not be so hungry for industrialization. Particularly as consumers of all sorts of goods and services, members of industrialized societies gain great new freedoms; but in their roles as producers, they must fit into a highly disciplined system. Industrialization may well be worth the price almost no matter how high; but it is nevertheless an urgent social concern that that price be no higher than absolutely necessary; that the essential discipline necessary for the proper working of the industrial order not have compounded on top of it pressures for conformity which draw their inspiration not from the requirements of the industrial technology but from the desires of institutions and their leaders to exercise power for other reasons than productive efficiency.

If the individual must surrender a large measure of personal autonomy in his conduct as the price for more leisure and a higher standard of life and the other benefits of industrialization, it becomes important what these rules may be

---

[1]Except perhaps in an economy based on a complicated irrigation system, as in ancient Egypt.

which set his performance for him and who shall determine them. Centers of power there will be. In the extreme case, only one. This conjures up visions of *1984* and the *Brave New World*.

But one need not turn to literature to find such a condition. The essence of the Russian experiment in industrialization is the concentration of rationality, in the sense of full knowledge and known purpose, and of essential decision-making authority in a single center of power. Many argue—some liking the burden of their argument and others detesting it—that this is the eventual result of industrialization regardless of how it is first undertaken. Only thus, they say, can there be that rational planning and that preservation of social order in the face of conflicting economic interests which can maximize the material products of an industrial system; and, additionally, this maximization may be a necessity for external survival as well as internal welfare.

However, other systems, such as our own, have survived and vastly prospered with a diffusion of power into substantial, or even large, numbers of centers; and these systems have made the greater contribution to human freedom and to variety of endeavor.

The central problem of these systems is a very complex one. By the very nature of the industrial system, power cannot be truly atomized; and social justice needs more of a definition than the one credited to Socrates of "Minding your own business." Power, in such a pluralistic system, must be distributed in some acceptable fashion among individuals, organized groups and the state. Thus the problem is more complicated than the classic one of the relationship of man and the state, elusive as the solution to that one may be. The role of the organized group must be defined as well as that of both the individual and the state. This is, for example, the central problem of our federal labor legislation. . . .

THE ROLE OF LABOR LEGISLATION

I do not think it necessary or wise to have such comprehensive governmental labor legislation as the Taft-Hartley Act.[2] We have in the

United States today more government interference in labor relations than in any of the other democratic and developed nations of the world with the possible exception of Australia. Great Britain and the Scandinavian countries, for example, have far less legislation. In Britain, government interest is mainly along four lines: to provide (1) for mediation services, (2) against forced political contributions, (3) against political strikes, and (4) against the use of violence in labor disputes.

The Wagner Act and the Taft-Hartley Act in the United States were passed largely in response to temporary needs which no longer fully exist. The first act was designed to encourage union organization to balance worker power against employer power. This has now been largely accomplished. The second act was in response to the many strikes which occurred in the decade 1936 to 1946 and the violence in connection with some of them. Today there are many fewer strikes and very little violence.

Such intensive governmental interference has several disadvantages. It gives more authority to the government, it appears to me, than is necessary and less autonomy to private groups than is desirable. Too great reliance is placed on government law rather than on the responsibility of the parties.[3] This takes such conflict as there is unduly into the political arena where it becomes more difficult to settle. It is questionable whether there should be any general law on labor legislation, since a general law particularly invites an attempt to cover all possible abuses by the antagonists and encourages a large-scale political battle. It might be better to have specific laws, subject to specific changes, to cover specific problems where a clear case has been made for government intervention.

Turning to the three problem areas of a pluralist system [accommodation, progress, and liberty], I should like to suggest reliance, aside from the applicable provisions of non-labor laws, on four specific laws. In the area of accommodation, we need a law establishing a mediation service, but only mediation. Provisions for special handling of emergency disputes (wartime aside) seem to have created more emergencies than they have settled, as Harbison and others have noted. Also, we probably still need, although not necessarily permanently, a law on representation elections. Union security

---

[2]It should not be understood that the suggestion for less federal control is made so that more opportunity may be opened for control by the several states.

[3]As Leiserson once pointed out, you cannot by merely passing a law make the parties "live happily ever after."

issues, however, can probably best be left to the parties themselves. As to rules of the game, these are generally quite well set out in non-labor laws and court rulings affecting the use of violence, the sanctity of contract, and so forth, with the exception of the propriety of pressuring third parties to get at second parties and here a third specific labor relations law may be advisable. On the question of Communist unionism, this is being handled as effectively as possible by the two major union federations, although requirements for greater democracy in unions would no doubt help eliminate this problem as they did in Australia.

When we turn to the criterion of progress, it would seem that our present anti-trust laws, including the *Apex* interpretation which bans union-employer collusion, are sufficient to the task.

Application of the third standard of liberty probably involves the greatest controversy. Cole railed at the Osborne decision which, in Britain, limited trade union compulsory collections of political contributions. Here is where the pluralist and the liberal pluralist may come to the parting of the ways; the former arguing for the autonomy of the private association from the absolutism of the state and the latter also for the independence of the individual from the absolutism of the group—even if this means some state interference in the internal affairs of the group. My own view is that the right of access, the right of participation (partly covered by the right to representation of one's own choosing in dealing with employers), and the right of judicial review should be provided by the state if not supplied by the private groups

themselves. As to the appropriate span of influence of unions and corporations, this is hardly subject to state control, except in the case of forced political contributions and perhaps also the vesting provisions of pension plans. These several questions of worker freedom might properly be the subject of a fourth specific law.

These four laws, taken together, would somewhat reduce the total burden of law and, as separate laws, be more politically manageable than one omnibus law. Any legislation in this area should, of course, be based to the extent possible on the consent of the parties themselves.

CONCLUSION

There can be no single and fully agreed upon structure for a pluralistic system. It would be pleasing to all who have philosophical leanings toward the Jeffersonian system if no private association or the state itself had any claim on an individual's behavior, except as the conscience of the individual rendered acquescence. But many laws must be passed and rules adopted in an industrial society. The best that can be expected is that they will emanate from a whole series of majorities, in the many public and private states of a pluralistic system, rather than from a single majority in the governing group of a monolithic state. The essence of pluralism is the offering to the individual of these many majorities instead of one—and one from which there is no escape.

44. Unions and Union Leaders of Their Own Choosing

Clark Kerr

NEEDS FOR LABOR SELF-SCRUTINY

American government has been under critical scrutiny almost since the founding of the nation. American industry was subjected to an intensive national review, particularly in the 1930's. It had become big and powerful and sometimes corrupt. The great depression was laid at its doorstep, since it was the most prominent doorstep around at the time. American unions are today undergoing similar scrutiny. They, in turn, have become big and powerful and sometimes corrupt.

Now it is said by some that only the unions can scrutinize themselves; that it is not the proper business of anybody else. They are private, voluntary associations. The corporations said this once also and they were scrutinized; and the unions will be too. Unions are private associations but their actions are clothed with the public interest, for they affect the levels of wages and prices, the access of individuals to jobs, the volume and continuity of production, and many other important aspects of society. Also, they are seldom really voluntary. Even in the absence of the closed or union shop, social pressure often assures membership.

From Center for the Study of Democratic Institutions of the Fund for the Republic (1958).

At the same time, along with external efforts, the unions should scrutinize themselves, and the more effectively they undertake this scrutiny (and they are doing surprisingly well) the less need there is for external scrutiny and external reform. Our pluralistic system has three main organized elements, state, corporation, and union. It is essential that each element function effectively and consequently that each element be subject to both internal and external criticism.

Several issues involving labor are abroad in the land. Three of them are inherently simple issues confined to specific segments of the labor movement and, beyond that, issues which run also into American life generally. These are corruption, collusion, and violence.

Corruption exists, and it is bad; but right and wrong are quite evident and hardly open to debate. Few unions are involved, and other institutions in society have known and do know it also. Some remedies, including proper accounting procedures, are relatively easy to identify although not always so easy to apply effectively.

Collusion also exists, and it also is bad; but again the nature of virtue is not hard to define, although the line where it ends may be hard to draw in particular cases. (Virtue and this problem of the drawing of lines have met before on other stages.) Relatively few unions are affected and then nearly always jointly with their employers; and collusion, too, accompanies human nature almost throughout the span of social relationships.

Violence also is to be condemned. It has decreased greatly as a union tactic, however, and is subject to control by the many devices civilized man has created to insure law and order.

These are issues, and they will be for a long time; they deserve attention, but they are peripheral to the main contemporary controversy.

CENTRAL ISSUE: UNIONS AND WORKER FREEDOM

The great issue is the impact of the union on the freedom of the worker. This issue is not simple; it is most complex. It is an issue which runs through all or nearly all of the union movement and is central to its very existence. While not unknown as an issue in the spheres of government and the corporation, it is less intensely manifested there at the present time. Our nation has had a long and most successful experience in creating a democratic framework for our government and protecting the liberties of individual citizens. Our corporations are not expected to be run on a democratic basis. They are founded on the model of the individual entrepreneur making his own decisions; seldom do corporations have either a captive labor force or captive consumers, and when they have captive consumers they are usually subject to state control.

The unions are different. They have not had, like our government, a long and successful experience in developing a system of checks and balances, in limiting their sphere of endeavor, in defining and protecting the internal rights of their members. Unlike the corporation, they are founded on the assumption of internal democracy. They are associations of individuals, not collections of capital funds. Moreover, increasingly they have a captive membership. It is usually not possible just to withdraw in protest without penalty, if the member does not like the organization, its leaders, or its policy. We have here most frequently a more or less compulsory organization with substantial impact on the lives of its members.

American unions do make a major overall contribution to a democratic industrial society, and this is the first and also the most important observation to be made about their impact on worker freedom. They usually create a two-party legislative system governing the life of the work place. In their absence, the rules would be set exclusively by the employer. Through the unions, the workers can have a direct impact on the nature of the rules under which they work. Without a union they can also have an impact, by their choice of employers, but this is much less direct. Also, unions usually insist on a grievance mechanism and this brings a judicial process into industrial life which is more impartial than when the employer sits as both prosecutor and judge. Beyond that, they create a new power center which can, if it wishes, stand against the power centers of the state and the corporation, and these latter power centers have gained in their absolute strength in recent years. A rough balance between private and public power centers is the essence of a pluralistic society, and a pluralistic society is the only firm foundation for democracy in an economy based on industrial production.

Thus the unions have generally brought a better legislative and judicial process into industrial life and a better balance among the power groups of society. They have done this without the feared consequences that gave rise to such apprehensions in times just past. It was feared that industrial conflict would tear society apart. In fact, industrial peace is now the commonplace; and, except for the few unions still under Communist domination, American unions most certainly contribute to the social stability and security of our whole system. It was feared that unions would hamper productive efficiency and stifle progress. Undoubtedly many union rules do retard production, but there is no evidence that the overall effect has been anything but relatively minor; and some new methods have been better received because of union consultation than they otherwise would have been in the light of the inherent conservatism of the work place. It was feared that unions might distort inter-industry wage structures and also that their actions would assure wild inflation. In fact, it is one of the wonders of the economic world that unions have had so little effect on wage structures. Their impact on price levels, while open to dispute, has certainly been no more than moderate. Exaggerated fears of costly social conflict, strangled production, and rampant inflation due to unions have proved largely without substance.

But a fear does remain that unions may take too much freedom from the worker; and this fear may not prove so groundless. If they do, they will not be the only institutions in our mass society which have conduced toward conformity. Big unions, big corporations, big government, and small individuals seem to be the order of the day.

Unions almost of necessity reduce the freedom of the worker in some respects. If freedom is defined as the absence of external restraint, then unions reduce freedom, for they restrain the worker in many ways. They help to establish formal wage structures, seniority rosters, work schedules, pace of output, and the pattern of occupational opportunities, all of which limit his freedom of choice. They decide when he shall strike and not strike. They are—and this is one of the essentials to an understanding of unionism—disciplinary agents within society. They add to the total network of discipline already surrounding the workers through the practices and rules of the employer. They too insist upon order and obedience—inherent in their very existence. Two bosses now grow where only one grew before.[1]

Some loss of freedom, however, is inevitable in an effective industrial system. It will occur, more or less, whether the system is run by the employers alone, by the state alone, or even by the unions alone. Industrial society requires many rules and reasonable conformity to these rules. There must be a wage structure, a work schedule, and so forth, no matter who operates the system. This loss of freedom is one of the prices paid by man for the many benefits in income and leisure that can flow from industrial society. The challenge is that this price not be any higher than necessary.

The issue lies in the "more or less." The loss of freedom of the industrial worker will be

substantial, as compared with the self-employed farmer or craftsman, but it may be less rather than more; and unions can make it both less or more.

UNION DEMOCRACY: DIFFICULTIES, DETRIMENTS, AND VIRTUES

Before turning to how the reduction of freedom may be less rather than more, three introductory observations will be made.

1. Democracy in unions is inherently difficult to achieve. A union is variously expected to be at one and the same time, as Muste[2] so well pointed out long ago, an army, a business, and a town meeting. Unions have usually ended up by being a business, serving the members but sometimes with little more influence over the conduct of the business by the members than stockholders have over a corporation. They have sometimes ended up as an army and have justified it, as Lloyd Fisher once remarked, just as the Communists have tried to justify their "people's democracy," by reference to "capitalist encirclement." They have almost never ended up as a town meeting. The pull is most insistently toward being a "business."

2. A good deal more democracy exists in unions than these comments and most external observations would indicate. The national unions are the most visible entities and they are usually the least subject to democratic pressures. But at the local level, in many unions, there are contested elections, substantial turnover of officers, and face-to-face relations between members and leaders, and there is the least entrenched bureaucracy. Particularly at the shop level, between shop stewards and workers, is there a responsive relationship. To the workers, the local level is usually the most important. That is where he lives and where his grievances are handled.

3. It is sometimes argued that unions need not or even should not be democratic. Different reasons are given for this conclusion. One line of argument is that unions have become largely functionless organizations, and nobody really cares whether they are democratic or not. The state guarantees full employment and social security, and the employer has been seduced by human relations. Consequently, the worker has a job—often paid above the contract rate—a pension, and also a friend, perhaps even a psychiatrist; and

---

[1]This is not to suggest that it is not often and perhaps almost universally better to have two bosses than one, for the union boss may help liberate the worker from the unilateral rule of the employer boss; but the worker is still subject to a web of rules, and this web tends to be more thickly woven as a result of the presence of the union.

[2]A. J. Muste, "Factional Fights in Trade Unions," in *American Labor Dynamics* (New York: Harcourt Brace, 1928).

there is nothing for the union to do. Or, it is sometimes said, unions have become quasi-governmental bureaus. They help set minimum wages and schedules of hours and process grievances, as government bureaus sometimes do both here and abroad. Their work is largely routine and best handled in good bureaucratic fashion; and so again why worry about democracy? Occasionally, it is also noted that unions function best if they are removed from the pressures of democratic life. They must respond to many pressures, not those of the membership alone but also the needs of the industry, the welfare of society, the concerns of other unions. They should take a longer view of events than the current membership is likely to take, for they are organizations with a continuing life. They will be more widely responsible to society and more businesslike in their operations if they are not subject to the uncertainties of active democratic participation. It is concluded that democracy causes internal and external strife and irresponsibility.

Each of these reasons has some point to it. Unions perform less of a function than two decades ago; their work has become more routine with pattern-following and grievance precedents; and internal democracy can cause external trouble, particularly for employers.

But the case for democracy can still be persuasive. If democracy is a superior form of government, as most of us would insist, it would be preferred in practice wherever it is possible. Also, the workers can have a more effective voice in industry if they have an effective voice in their unions; and they are more likely to be satisfied with society if they have a sense of participation. Additionally, if the unions lose responsiveness to worker interests, an opportunity is created for other organized elements more politically motivated to move in to represent these interests, as has happened in certain European countries.

ONE-PARTY GOVERNMENT—
THE UNION CASE

The overwhelming majority of all the organizations of man throughout history have been ruled by one-party governments. Most of the time in most parts of the world all organizations have been under one-party rule. In certain parts of the world at certain times in history there have been a few two-party (or multiparty) organizations; but one-party rule is the standard and well nigh universal case. The trade union is no exception. The International Typographical Union in the United States is the single deviant specimen on a national level.

Even in the democratic United States the corporation, the political party, the fraternal order, the religious denomination, the farm organization, the welfare group, the student government are all one-party organizations. Only in the public area, where it is by all odds the most essential, do we have two-party government.

The neglect of the one-party model of government, in the light of its great significance, is most astounding. The rare instances of two-party and multi-party government have attracted most of the study. Certain it is that two-party government, as Lipset[3] has so persuasively argued, does have much to recommend it. It provides criticism of the existing government, makes ready an alternative government if the members want it, reduces apathy, and does much else of value. But most men all of the time—and all men some of the time—function in one-party social organizations, as do union members.

Why are unions one-party governments? The answers are several. Partly, it is the requirement of unity in the face of external conflict. Partly, it is the control exercised by the leaders over the mechanism of the organization. But the root of the problem is much deeper. It goes beyond the fear of the enemy and the desire of the leaders. It is that there are no continuing conflicts except over ideology, and ideological conflicts tend to split unions rather than to create two-party systems within them. Witness the separate unions in several European countries and the split-off of Communist unions in the United States. Ideology aside, issues over wage increases, the handling of grievances, and so forth may lead to factions and leadership rivalry but not to two-party systems on a continuing basis.

So unions are one-party governments. Does this mean that they are inevitably "undemocratic"? If only two-party systems are really democratic, then the answer is obviously in the affirmative. But if organizations where the supreme power is retained by the members and

[3]S. M. Lipset, M. Trow, and J. Coleman, *Union Democracy* (Glencoe, Ill.: Free Press, 1956).

which are reasonably responsive[4] to membership desires may be called "democratic," even in the absence of a two-party system, then unions may be and many are "democratic."

HISTORICAL PRESSURES ON UNION GOVERNMENT

There are dangers in any one-party government,[5] but the one-party government may serve its members well. It is most likely to do so in the long run, however, if it is under the proper pressure. Traditionally, this pressure on trade union government in the United States has come from four sources; all of them, unfortunately, now largely of historical importance only. In the passing of these four sources of pressure lies much of our current problem.

[4]There are those, of course, who would argue that the proper test of an organization is not the degree of responsiveness to the needs of those involved but rather the degree to which the persons involved actually and directly participate in the decision-making process. For them, only town meeting democracy is fully satisfactory; and, given the nature of industrial society, their test can be met by very few consequential organizations. It should be noted that "responsiveness" is not only a different test from "participation" but is also different from the test of "performance." "Performance," in the sense of "bringing home the bacon," may be quite exceptional without, at the same time, having any or at least much connection with "responsiveness." "Performance" refers to results; "responsiveness" to the processes which connect leadership behavior with membership desires. Performance, however, will usually be superior in the long run where responsiveness exists; and this is one of the basic tenets of democratic thought. And perhaps it should also be noted that active participation, where it is possible, is often an effective means of assuring responsiveness but is by no means a guarantee of such responsiveness—in fact, it can serve as a technique of control. The view taken here is that performance alone is not enough and that participation, as through a two-party system, is more than can be expected under the circumstances, and, consequently, that the appropriate test is responsiveness. Responsiveness rests on a minimum degree of participation and will yield, usually, a reasonable measure of performance.

[5]This is true particularly if there is no judicial protection against the use of arbitrary power, as is often the case. Due process can be as important as democratic assent to the leadership.

1. When union membership was more voluntary, leaders had to be responsive to the workers to find and retain members, and this was an effective check on authority. As noted earlier, union membership is now—one way or another—often compulsory, the law notwithstanding; and it is likely to become more so. Union security—with all its other advantages—and leadership responsiveness tend to move in somewhat opposite directions. The voluntary sale and the forced sale lead to different behavior in any walk of life. This is not to support voluntary membership through the compulsion of the state, for it seems neither possible in many situations nor, on balance, wise.

2. When dual unionism, now largely a relic of the past, was an active force, it had somewhat the same impact as voluntary membership. Not individuals but groups of people could and did shift allegiance and this acted as a check and balance. The idea of one union in one jurisdiction, however, is so firmly bedded in American union philosophy that dual unionism can exist only sporadically and temporarily.

3. The more or less permanent faction, stopping short of a second party but hovering in the wings ready to rush out on any inappropriate occasion, was a check on the leadership in many unions. The old-line Socialists served this function for many, many years, but the New Deal and time brought their demise. The Catholic faction continues in a few unions but usually only in those under left-wing control; otherwise there is little basis for a Catholic faction. There are few permanent factions today and fewer still in prospect.

4. The employer, particularly the recalcitrant employer, has historically been a check and balance on the union leadership. We have here two organizations—the company and the union—appealing to the same constituency. If they are in conflict, each will criticize the other and may even stand ready to attempt to destroy the other. But the day of fighting the unions is largely past, at least under conditions of full employment. The separation of interests between the leaders of the two organizations is decaying. Industrial peace pays. Consequently, company pressure on most unions has been greatly reduced or has even totally disappeared.

NEW ELEMENTS IN UNION DEMOCRACY

With union membership increasingly compulsory, dual unionism declining, the permanent faction disappearing, and company opposition more rare, is there any hope for "democracy" or leadership responsiveness to membership interests in trade unions? There still is, for there are substitutes for these historical pressures. Six such possibilities will be suggested, with particular emphasis on the sixth.

1. Membership interest. Union memberships are traditionally apathetic except in some crisis; and very little can be done about it. Compulsory strike votes proved a farce in World War II, and most bargaining issues cannot properly be put to membership vote. But some experiments might be undertaken with polling of membership opinion and with advisory referenda, and even the use of television as a means for leaders to reach members (since members seldom will come to meetings) might be profitable.

2. "Professional" leaders. Much is written currently about management as a profession. Perhaps union leaders might also become professional in the sense that they might be specifically trained for their jobs and might develop an "ethic" to guide their conduct—an ethic which sets boundaries to their behavior.[6]

3. A new faith for the union movement. In unions where the last vestiges of active democracy disappeared long ago, certain leaders today still serve their members well because of their adherence to the "old faith" of the union movement. But the "old faith" attracts few new adherents. It was a fighting faith growing out of evil conditions for the workers and union-busting by the employers. The conditions which gave rise to it no longer exist in the United States. They do continue to a degree even today in England and Germany, and there the "old faith" still sets standards for union leaders. The social reformer holds himself and is held by his environment to a higher code of conduct than the business leader of the business union who quickly takes on the coloration of the industry with which he deals. If its ethics are high, his will be also; if they are low, so are his. The business union is a segment of the business.

What might this new faith be? It cannot be either "more, more, more, and now" or a vision of class conflict. It might be, as suggested later, the development of the unions as a liberating force in industrial society; and there might be a consequent integration of the union leader more into the intellectual and less into the business community.

4. Local autonomy. Local unions, by their inherent nature, clearly can provide more opportunities than can national unions for democratic participation by the members. Consequently, the more autonomy there is at the local level, the greater the democratic life of the union movement is likely to be. The big drop in democratic participation comes in the move from the one plant to the multi-plant local or the district union. In the one plant, rival leaders can become known and be effective, issues can be discussed on a face-to-face basis, and democracy can be effective.[7] The multi-plant unit serves the interests of the entrenched leadership in a most emphatic way. The one-plant local with real authority is the most democratic entity in the trade union movement. Considerable constitutional reform in most unions would be prerequisite to effective single-plant locals. Among other things, the institution of the "receivership" by regional and national officials would need to be curtailed.

5. Union decertification. It is certainly desirable to continue some mechanism through which members can exercise an option in favor of another or no union at all. Such an option will rarely be employed, but it should be available. If it is available and is used occasionally, it can act as a minor check and balance on union leadership.

6. Discharge through rebellion. The two-party system within unions, as we have seen, is an historical oddity. The regularly contested election is a rarity. Yet union officials do get changed other than as a result of death or retirement. Union officials are, in effect, "hired" by the membership for the duration of their good behavior as tested imprecisely by the membership. The trouble comes when they need to be "fired." The mechanism then is a contested election in which the old leader is voted out of office. For such a contested election to take place two prerequisites are necessary: It must be possible for a faction to form and for its members to be reasonably free from retaliation through the operation of an impartial judicial process; and there must be secret elections at appropriate intervals. Other actors must be allowed to stand in the wings and be permitted to move on stage when the audience

---

[6]They might, like city managers, for example, be specifically trained for their jobs and responsible to an elected governing board.

[7]In several European countries it is the local works council, with substantial powers, which arouses worker interest and participation.

calls them. The dissatisfied individual and the antagonistic faction must be given an opportunity.

The term "competitive discharge" might be used in the sense that the leader is subject to constant evaluation by the members and is also subject to discharge through the process of electing a competitor who is free to appear when the conditions warrant.[8] In the two-party system, the question is as to the better person; in the "competitive discharge" case, it is whether the incumbent should be fired or not.[9] Deposed union leaders usually feel—and they are correct in their feeling—that they have been fired, not that they have been defeated. Among other things, they almost never seek election again, once having been discharged. They are like the old bull in the buffalo herd brought to his knees by the young challenger.

If trade union democracy is defined as a system of government where the supreme power is largely retained by the members and can be exercised by them in an emergency at any and all levels, then the effective right of competitive discharge, by itself, is a sufficient basis for trade union democracy. The essential feature of a trade union constitution is whether it guarantees this right of competitive discharge.

[8]In one major Icelandic union, for example, this principle is explicitly recognized, rather than being camouflaged. The incumbent officers are automatically reelected at each "contract reopening period" (if the stated election time may be so designated) unless a certain number of members petition for an opposition slate on the ballot, in which event a contested election is conducted. More common practice in the United States is to go through the formality of an election each time, but usually there is opposition only if the incumbent is in an unfavorable position.

[9]Such question is most likely to be raised in an urgent fashion at the time of a "crisis" (a strike, an attack by a rival union, an unsuccessful wage negotiation, the disclosure of misuse of funds, etc.). Such crises hold within themselves the possibilities of constructive democratic action, if a minimum of democratic machinery is available; otherwise an open revolt, usually taking the form of the organization of a rival union, is the only alternative and a very difficult one. Unfortunately, under the "competitive discharge" system an ineffective leader can retain his position much longer (*i.e.*, until a crisis creates the condition for his downfall) than he could under the competitive election system. The machinery which is used to handle the "competitive discharge" can, of course, also be employed to handle the problem of replacement after the death of a leader.

This is the most we can reasonably expect, and it is also probably enough.

THE NEW INDUSTRIAL FREEDOM?

The central issue presented earlier was the impact of unionism on worker freedom. This issue goes beyond the internal relationship of leader to member which we have just been discussing, to the rules the union makes or helps to make affecting the life of the worker as worker and to the span of activity of the union.

Industrial society, as we have noted, requires a great web of rules to bind people together and to secure their cooperative performance within an extraordinarily complex and interrelated productive mechanism. And the burden of these rules on the individual can vary quite substantially. It can be comparatively heavy or comparatively light.

For it to be comparatively light, two principles are basic. First, the rules should provide the maximum power of individual choice consistent with efficient production; the greatest possible provision to move freely within limits set by the imperatives of industrial society itself.

Second, each institution should be narrowly oriented toward its primary function whether production of goods, representation of economic interest, or salvation of souls. The individual will have greater freedom if the span of control of each institution with which he is associated is relatively narrow. The institution which encompasses the totality of the life of the individual can subject him to its power and control in a way no limited-function institution can.

The power to do as one pleases, which is the essence of freedom, rests on rules with broad limits and institutions with narrow limits. One of the great and continuing—and even eternal—challenges of industrial society is how to structure it to maximize not only the wealth of the world but also the freedom of man.

These general principles apply also to unions. The rules they make or join in making can channel a great deal of the occupational life of an individual. To begin with, all unions should be open unions—open to everyone without discrimination except on the grounds of ability to perform the work. In addition, the rules governing a man's working life should give him maximum freedom of choice inside the union. Illustrations from three important areas will indicate the possibilities.

1. Seniority rights are important in almost all areas of human relationships. They are the basis for settling many problems; but they can be a prison too. Some unions allow the transfer of seniority rights from one place of employment to another, or permit some percentage of positions, in one case every fourth position, to be filled outside of local seniority lists. Such arrangements increase the mobility opportunities of workers.

2. Private pension plans often have no vesting provisions, and this tends to tie the worker for life to a single place of employment. His status becomes not unlike that of the serf on the manor tied to his lord, who in our case may be plural—the company and the union. Reasonable vesting rights aid the mobility and thus the freedom of workers.

3. Hours of work must be scheduled, but these schedules can provide for local option by individual groups of workers instead of a uniform national schedule. (A local group may prefer one holiday to another or longer vacations and as a consequence longer hours per week.)

They can provide some part-time jobs for the aged or for women or for men who want a second job. Developing an appropriate balance between the time spent on earning income and time spent on leisure is an important aspect of welfare in any society, and it can best be done on an individual basis. The opportunities for experiment in this area are great.

A union, like many another institution, often seeks to extend its sphere of activity until it covers more and more of the life of its members, not only as workers but also as consumers and citizens. If the limited-function corporation and the limited-function state and the limited-function church are desirable, so also is the limited-function union. Union paternalism (housing projects, vacation resorts, recreation facilities) has little more to recommend it than employer paternalism. Union political activity, while inevitable and often desirable, should not infringe on the rights of the member as citizen.[10] He should not be required to support,

financially or otherwise, a political party or candidate not of his own choice. The union should find its primary function in relating to the worker as worker, not also as consumer and as citizen.

Trade unions have historically been fighting organizations. They have emphasized unity within their own circles and the "standard rate" in the labor market. But now they are established, secure, and accepted. Full employment in the economy and grievance machinery in the plant give the individual worker a status largely unknown twenty-five years ago. The union attitude of limited class warfare directed at the surrounding society and of discipline directed at the individual member no longer is required by the new situation.

Might the unions turn their attention from the old slogans and the old dogmas, to undertake a new orientation toward their role in industrial society? This new role might well be that of a liberating force in industrial society, of a force helping to structure industrialization to meet the desires of the single individual as well as the organized group. This would be an historic mission and a mission which employers might well join for they too have pressed for conformity and against individuality among the workers.

THE WORKER, THE UNION, AND THE STATE

The title of this paper suggests that national policy might move from the "unions of their own choosing" of the 1930's to "union leaders of their own choosing" and even, to a degree, to "union rules of their own choosing." But how is this to be accomplished? Action by the unions themselves would be most desirable, and there has been a surprising amount of it during the past year. Experience here and abroad, however, suggests it will not be sufficient and that behind the good intentions of most union leaders will need to stand the power of the law, as in the case of corporations in the past.

This is a troublesome issue. The pluralist will defend the private association from the control of the state. The individual, however, also needs defense against the control of the private government of the trade union, and ultimately this can be guaranteed only by the state. If the state is to interfere in the internal life of trade unions—and it does so quite significantly al-

[10]The traditional union political activities in the United States, lobbying in regard to legislation affecting unions and workers as workers and distributing informational data on the records of candidates in the same areas, do not interfere with the rights of the union member as a citizen. Compulsory political levies and political strikes do interfere with these rights and also with the proper functioning of a democratic society.

ready—then it is important that this interference be wisely conceived, for the power to control is the power to destroy. Unions should in no way be destroyed as independent power centers. Clyde Summers has recently suggested[11] four guide lines for such interference, and each one seems worthy of consideration: It should be minimal; it should be segregated from laws on other matters; it should encourage responsible self-regulation by the unions; and it should be enforceable.

In this discussion of the impact of unions on the freedom of workers, six aspects of the problem were particularly emphasized: local union autonomy, a new faith for the union movement, secret elections of officers, independent judicial processes, permissive rules on entry to the union and on movement within industry, and narrow limits to union functions.

Four of these areas may lend themselves properly to legislation:

1. In Australia,[12] union members can, under certain circumstances, ask the state for the conduct of secret elections of officers.

2. Again in Australia and to an increasing extent in the United States, union members can appeal to the courts for protection against retaliation for internal political dissent. In this connection the private external review boards of the Upholsterer's Union and the United Automobile Workers are a most interesting

[11]"Legislating Union Democracy," paper presented to annual meeting of the Industrial Relations Research Association, September 1957 (to be published in the *Proceedings*).

[12]See L. S. Merrifield, "Regulation of Union Elections in Australia," *Industrial and Labor Relations Review* (January, 1957).

device, paralleling private arbitration of grievances against companies.[13]

3. Protection from discrimination in getting into a union, as well as in getting a job, is already provided in some states. Such provisions call for the open union instead of the open shop.

4. Prohibition of compulsory political contributions is now provided in both the United States and Great Britain.

Adequate legislation in these four areas would assure a reasonable degree of democracy and of individual freedom. Beyond what the law might require, many unions have provided and may provide considerably more democratic life and individual liberty. The Ethical Practices Committee of the AFL-CIO has made a substantial contribution in these directions.

The trade unions, as noted at the start, are going through a period of crisis. This crisis originates as much from self-examination by labor leaders as from the more obvious external criticisms. Out of this crisis may well come more representative government within unions and more rights for the individual worker. Since they are an important element in our pluralistic society, the effective functioning of the trade unions is contributive to the national welfare. As an element of a democratic society, they should be responsive to their members. As an element of a society founded on the significance of the individual, they should contribute to his freedom. "More, more, more, and now" is no longer enough.

[13]The encouragement of such private judicial processes better fits a pluralistic society with its independent power centers than the institution of a public labor court approach, as in Germany.

Bargaining Objectives,
Bargaining Power,
and Industrial Conflict

What are the parties to collective bargaining really after? What are the central objectives of the union? What areas of responsibility and initiative does management wish to retain? Frederick Harbison and John Coleman explain the main objectives on each side of the table, which they argue are similar in all collective bargaining relationships. They then ask why in some cases labor and management are able to reconcile conflicting objectives and to live in relative harmony, whereas in other cases they live in an armed truce with continuing tension.

"Bargaining power" is a familiar concept; but to say precisely what is meant by this is not easy. The definition developed by Neil Chamberlain and James Kuhn is one of the most widely discussed and used. The definition is in terms of the cost of agreeing on the terms offered by the other party *versus* the cost of disagreement. If a union can reduce the employer's cost of agreeing to the union's terms, or if it can increase the cost to the employer of disagreement, its bargaining power is enhanced. Chamberlain and Kuhn then analyze the tactics commonly used by union and management bargainers to increase their respective bargaining power.

Collective bargaining can lead either to an agreement or to a strike, which is costly to the parties and sometimes to the public. The United States and many other countries maintain a staff of government mediators, whose function is to intervene as neutral third parties in deadlocked negotiations, in an effort to break the deadlock and achieve a voluntary settlement. What does a mediator actually do, and what determines whether his efforts will prove successful? Clark Kerr analyzes this question, drawing an interesting distinction between *tactical mediation*, involving intervention in a conflict that has already occurred, and *strategic mediation*, involving restructuring the bargaining situation so that conflicts are less likely to occur in the future.

45. Goals and Strategy in Collective Bargaining

Frederick A. Harbison

John R. Coleman

OBJECTIVES OF COMPANY AND UNION LEADERS

We begin by asking: What are management and union leaders striving for in collective relations? This question deserves some careful thought because it is confusing to talk in generalities about "conflict of interests" or "harmony of interests" without a precise understanding of what such interests are. Although neither company executives nor labor leaders make a practice of sitting down and spelling out their objectives, it is possible for the observer to get a rough outline of these goals by analyzing their statements and actions over a period of time.

In this study we have not made use of the psychiatrist's couch or the poll-taker's multiple choices. We have simply talked with a great many persons in both companies and unions and tried to extract the more cogent implications of what they were saying. Then we "played back" our analysis to many of the persons interviewed. When they said, "Yes, of course, that's what I meant to say," we felt we were on the right track.[1]

---

[1] We have assumed throughout that men have objectives, for themselves, and for the institutions with which they identify themselves. As long as one looks at this or that man, the personal objectives may take

1. Management's Objectives

What does management try to achieve in its bargaining relationships with a union? An analysis of the cases we studied suggests that management's objectives in collective relations may fall into five broad categories: *first*, the preservation and strengthening of the business enterprise; *second*, the retention of effective control over the enterprise; *third*, the establishment of stable and "businesslike" relationships with the bargaining agents; *fourth*, promotion of certain broad social and economic goals; and *fifth*, advancement of personal goals and ambitions. In combinations of various kinds and with varying emphasis from case to case, these objectives become in essence the driving forces behind managerial policy and actions. Taken as a whole, they help to explain what management is striving for in collective relations.

a. Preservation and strengthening of the business enterprise. Management is first of all concerned with the institutional well-being of

---

precedence. But when one looks at the actions of a group of men, he is confronted with something more than the sum of the objectives of the group's members. There are institutional objectives which may at any time be just as important as the goals of the individuals in determining what sort of adjustment will be made between groups.

326

the business it is running. In order to survive and grow, a business must in the long run produce and sell goods or services at a profit. It must be able to compete successfully with other enterprises in the same line of activity. In more specific terms, management is concerned with the *financial* and *organizational* well-being of the enterprise. From the financial point of view, management strives to produce earnings which are sufficient to finance necessary expansion of the enterprise, to provide the owners with a "fair return," to attract additional capital funds if necessary, and to provide some reserves for contingencies. Thus, a healthy business must provide at least a modest return to its owners and plough back into the enterprise money to insure its long-run strength.

Closely associated with a firm's financial well-being is the organizational health of the enterprise. As a going concern, a business is primarily an organization of men whose activities must be coordinated for a common purpose. This calls for teamwork and the development of morale in the working force. The importance of this aspect of the firm's health is well indicated by the fact that, when executives talk with each other, questions besides that of the profit record come into the discussion in evaluating the success of a particular business. The development of a "good organization" in which there is high morale among all employees frequently becomes, in the minds of the managers, an end in itself as well as a means for achieving the firm's financial objectives.

The union may threaten the survival and growth of the enterprise in several ways. It may press demands which impair the financial health of the business or it may undermine management's efforts to build a loyal organization. Management, for its part, may react in different ways. It may try to erect defenses against the union and to hold it at arm's length; or it may try to use the union as a means of helping to build a better organization and even try to enlist its support in improving the financial condition of the firm. In short, though the institutional objective of management is fairly constant, the *means* of achieving that objective in relations with organized labor can be quite varied.

b. Retention of effective control over the enterprise. In order to achieve the institutional objective set forth above, management is constantly striving to retain its control over the enterprise and its freedom to exercise its central managerial functions. If management is held responsible for the success of the business, then it must have the authority to direct its activities and to make fundamental decisions in the operations of the enterprise. In specific terms, management seeks to retain control in such areas as the financing of the business, the sale of its product, the setting of production standards, the lay-out of the plant, the selection, promotion, transfer, and discipline of employees, and the general direction of the working forces. At almost every turn, however, the union usually challenges unilateral managerial exercise of such functions; it seeks to limit management's discretion and to police management's actions. To most executives, consequently, the union constitutes an actual or potential interference with the proper exercise of managerial responsibilities. A major objective of management in collective relations, therefore, is the minimization of union interference with managerial functions.

Here again, a company may employ different means to achieve the same ends. It may try to stake out areas of exclusive managerial prerogatives, to draw lines between matters subject to unilateral determination and matters subject to joint management-union determination, or to erect defenses to keep the union out of the areas of vital control over the enterprise. On the other hand, it may look upon the union as an instrument to aid in implementing managerial policies and actions, and thus will share decision-making with the union. The first of these approaches is essentially a negative, defensive action. The second seeks to minimize the union's interference by accenting the positive contribution which the union can make in certain areas.

c. Stable and businesslike relations. Another objective of management is the establishment of "businesslike" relations with the union with which it deals. It usually attempts to develop an orderly process of settlement of grievances and complaints. It wants the union leaders to live up to the contract and to take some responsibility for making the union members abide by it as well. Management signs a labor agreement to eliminate uncertainties in its labor relations, to buy industrial peace at least during the life of the agreement, and thus to bring about a measure of stability in its formal relationships with employees. Though there is sometimes a great deal of talk about the need for membership participation in union affairs, management is primarily interested in dealing with "responsible" union officers who can exercise some measure of control over the unruly members in the organization. Management also wants to deal with "responsible" union leaders who recognize the problems faced by the company and who thus refrain from making "unreasonable" or "irresponsible" demands which might seriously jeopardize the enterprise.

Management may try to build up stable and businesslike relations in several ways. It may demand a "management security clause" in the contract; it may insist on prompt disciplining of all union officers or members who violate the terms of the contract; it may seek in many different ways to build up the prestige of "responsible" union leaders; it may agree to the union shop; or it may resort to undercover deals with labor officials to achieve its ends. In the course of appraising and re-appraising its position *vis-a-vis* the union, it will choose that course of action which holds the best promise of making relationships stable, predictable, and "businesslike."

d. Broad social and economic goals. In many cases management is deeply concerned with goals broader than the preservation and strengthening of a particular business. It seeks to defend the system of private enterprise as the very basis of general economic progress and individual liberty. It fears and deplores whatever it interprets as encroachments upon individual initiative, freedom to venture, and the theory of the competitive market. In many cases the union is looked upon as a threat to the free enterprise idea, particularly when allied politically with a greater potential threat to the system—government. To other leaders in management a responsible union is a potential bulwark of free enterprise. But whatever their view, men in management's ranks like to feel that their own approach to the union helps to promote the kind of collective bargaining which is most consistent with the goals of an economy of free enterprise.

e. Advancement of personal goals and ambitions. The objectives of management, however, do not stop with building the business or preserving the free enterprise system. As human beings, the members of management have purely personal goals and ambitions as well. In collective relations as in other phases of business management, executives like to establish a reputation. They may strive to be "firm, but

fair," to "command the respect of the employees," to be "sympathetic but at the same time practical," or simply to be known as "good, sound businessmen with reasonable and practical judgment."[2]

In relations with unions, reputations can be built in many ways. One employer may pride himself on refusing to "appease power-hungry labor leaders," while another may get a real sense of achievement by finding ways of "working in harmony with organized labor." Regardless of the means employed, however, individual managers are anxious to harmonize their policies and actions in collective relations with their personal goals, ambitions, and their own concepts of the behavior appropriate for an enlightened, successful, and socially conscious business leader.

2. Objectives of the Union

What does the union leadership try to achieve in collective bargaining with the employer and what are the principal driving forces which explain the policies and actions of union leaders? We can abstract from our interviews and contacts with labor leaders a set of objectives parallel to those pursued by management. The objectives of the union leadership fall into five broad categories: *first,* the preservation and strengthening of the union as an institution; *second,* the carrying out of the formal purpose of the union to get "more" for the membership; *third,* the acquisition of a greater measure of control over jobs to implement the first two objectives; *fourth,* the pursuit of certain broad social and economic goals; and *fifth,* fulfillment of personal goals and ambitions of the leadership.

a. Preservation and strengthening of the union as an institution. The first concern of the union leadership is, of necessity, the building of the union as an institution and the pro-

[2]From a somewhat different approach Professor E. Wight Bakke puts the personal goals of managers in these categories: (1) the society and respect of their fellows; (2) economic well-being comparable with that of their customary associates; (3) independence in and control over their own affairs; (4) an understanding of the forces which affect them; and (5) integrity within themselves and with respect to their relationship with the world and the peoples about them. "The Goals of Management," (pp. 141-42) in *Unions, Management, and the Public,* edited by Bakke and Clark Kerr (New York: Harcourt, Brace & Co., 1948).

motion of its security and stability as an organization. To most union leaders this is an end in itself, just as to management the preservation and strengthening of the enterprise is an end in itself. Professor Arthur Ross has observed that the "formal rationale of the union is to augment the economic welfare of its members; but a more vital institutional objective—survival and growth of the organization—will take precedence whenever it comes into conflict with the formal purpose.[3] This perhaps overstates the case. But few first-hand observers of the unions included in this study would deny that labor leaders do place very heavy emphasis upon the well-being of the organization as such and may occasionally give that well-being preference over the immediate economic advantages for the membership. The union leadership is continuously concerned with the institutional survival and growth of the organization in the face of management opposition, the apathy of much of the membership, the potential inroads of rival unions, the possible weakness of the union treasury, and the potential threats of adverse government legislation and community sentiment.

The union leadership may achieve this end in different ways. It may try to build the members' allegiance by attacking management; in other cases, it may be forced to cooperate with management to keep the business prosperous as the only means of insuring the institutional survival of the union. It may build support in one case by creating issues and calling strikes, whereas in another case it may feel the necessity of avoiding conflict. One factor which will have an important bearing upon the course of action pursued by the union will be the internal political situation and hence the relative security of the incumbent leadership. In every situation, however, the union leaders must weigh the effects of their contemplated actions in terms of the effects they will have on the organization.

b. Promotion of the economic welfare of the members. The stated reason for the existence of a union is to protect and advance the general well-being of the workers it represents. Its mission is, in times of prosperity, to get "more" for the members in terms of wages, better working conditions, and "fringe benefits" of all kinds. In times of recession, it must protect

what the workers have already secured. It must also seek under all circumstances to protect the individual job interests of the workers. A union which fails to "deliver" in these respects may not be able to survive as an organization in the long run no matter how lofty its aims may be.

Some union leaders are in a position to force concessions from an employer by brute force; others may reason that they can get more by the conciliatory approach. Some may proceed in their bargaining tactics without particular attention to management's needs; others must pare down their settling terms to conform to the company's "ability to pay"; still others may be forced to induce the members to give more production in order to get more pay.

c. The acquisition of control over jobs. In order to implement the twin objectives of building the organization and promoting the economic well-being of the members, union leaders are constantly driven to acquire more and more control over jobs, and are thus impelled to encroach upon what company executives conceive to be the areas of vital managerial functions. In order to keep their organization together and to protect the workers' interests, union leaders feel that they either have to protest company actions, police them, or actually participate with management in making important decisions which will affect individual jobs and employment opportunities as a whole.

The means of acquiring job control are diverse. To mention only a few which are utilized in these industries, they range from making seniority rules more rigid to outright limitations on the employer's freedom to hire; from informal discussions about the introduction of new machinery and processes to outright opposition to technological improvements; or from policing management's disciplining of hourly workers to telling the company whom to select as foremen.

d. Promotion of broad social and economic goals. Most labor leaders are concerned to some extent with goals which are much broader than building their particular unions and getting more for the workers. By and large, they hold to the philosophy of the primacy of human needs—that human welfare must be placed before profits, that men are more important than machines, and that the preservation of the dignity of the individual workingman is more important than the preservation of any particular economic system. Most of them believe in

[3]Arthur M. Ross, *Trade Union Wage Policy* (Berkeley; University of California Press, 1948), p. 43.

"more equal distribution of wealth" as a general principle, and they are also in favor of curbing the economic power of employers. In nearly all cases, they look upon collective bargaining as one of the means for the achievement of those ends. As a matter of practical expediency, this almost always means a here-and-now acceptance of the existing enterprise system even by union leaders who seek to modify it by making it "more responsive to human needs" or to supplant it entirely at some future date by a different economic system.

The position of most labor leaders on the matter of social goals might be summarized as follows: first, get what you can within the sphere of collective bargaining as one means of advancing the welfare of labor, and second, turn to political action as a way of supplementing what you get through negotiating with private employers.

e. Pursuit of personal goals and ambitions. The actions and policies of union leaders are also explained in part by their personal goals and ambitions. Union leaders are usually interested in their own personal position within the union as well as in the development of the organization as an institution. They strive to acquire personal status and power and to build reputations as "good fighters for labor," "respected citizens in the community," and "competent bargainers." In collective relations with management, there are many ways of building prestige and satisfying such personal goals, ranging all the way from baiting the employer to playing the role of a "labor statesman."

In comparing management's objectives in collective relations with those of union leaders, however, an important distinction must be made. Relationships with unions are only one of the many problems which face the employer. Most of the energies of management are directed to the other activities of operating a business, such as procurement of materials, engineering, production planning, financing, and sales promotion. Management-union relations in most companies is not the central problem in operating the business. In the case of the union, however, collective bargaining is the central problem; it is the area in which most of the energies of union officers must be concentrated. To be sure, there is an increasing tendency for union leaders to devote more attention to community relations and political action, but these matters seldom overshadow the core function of collective bargaining.

3. Determinants of Conflict and Cooperation

Simply placing management's objectives alongside those of the union gives us a partial explanation of why modern labor-management relations in the mass production industries often involve a struggle for power. The union's quest for "more" appears to be in conflict with management's desire to protect the financial well-being of the firm. Management's concern for retaining its prerogatives must often be in basic conflict with the union's objectives of acquiring control over jobs. In building its institutional structure, the union may compete for the allegiance of workers with a management which is trying to build loyalty within the business organization. The labor leader's notions of human welfare often conflict with management's picture of "the economic facts of life." And finally, the concern of both labor leaders and company executives over their own personal goals and ambitions may lead to a bitter struggle for personal prestige. To a large extent, management and union leaders are simply after different things when they face each other at the bargaining table. Theoretically, at least, they have little in common and a great deal to quarrel about. There is no doubt that this is the pattern in many collective bargaining situations today.

Yet in many other cases employers and labor leaders appear to get along very well together. In some cases, moreover, they work hand-in-hand to increase output and improve efficiency. What then is the explanation of the existence of such relatively harmonious or cooperative relationships? Where harmony prevails, do labor and management have a different set of objectives from those situations where conflict is the rule? We think not. Our examination of many different labor-management relationships leads us to believe that management and labor leaders have roughly the same objectives in all kinds of relationships. We hold that the explanation of relative compatibility in each case is to be found in the different ways the parties view their objectives and in the different policies followed in pursuing them. *In other words, the different types of labor-management relationships are explained not so much by the ends sought by the parties as by the means employed to achieve these ends.*

46. Bargaining Power

Neil W. Chamberlain

James W. Kuhn

THE COSTS OF AGREEING
AND DISAGREEING

. . . We may define bargaining power as the ability to secure another's agreement on one's own terms. A union's bargaining power at any point of time *is*, for example, management's willingness to agree to the union's terms. Management's willingness in turn depends upon the cost of disagreeing with the union terms, relative to the cost of agreeing to them.

If the cost to management of disagreeing with the union is high relative to the cost of agreeing, the union's bargaining power is enhanced. (If a strike is very costly to management and the union's terms are quite inexpensive, the union's chances of getting its demands are improved.) If the cost to management of disagreeing with the union is low relative to the cost of agreeing to the union's terms, the union's bargaining power is diminished. (If sales are off and production is being cut back anyway, a strike may be relatively inexpensive compared with the cost of the union's demand. In such a case, the union's chance of getting its demands are not good.) These statements in themselves reveal nothing of the strength or weakness of the union relative to management, since management might possess a strong or weak bargaining power to press its own terms. Only if the cost to management of disagreeing with the union's terms is greater than the cost of agreeing to them and if the cost to the union of disagreeing with management's terms is less than the cost of agreeing to them is the union's bargaining power greater than management's. More generally, only if the difference to management between the cost of disagreement and agreement on labor's terms is proportionately greater than the difference to labor between the costs of disagreement and agreement on management's terms can one say that labor's bargaining power is greater than management's.

Bargaining power defined as we have done here is not an inherent attribute of the parties or some absolute "amount" of power available for any and all bargaining situations. The parties may change it as they use .different tactics to influence each other.[1] The passage of time also may bring changes of bargaining power for unions and management as economic conditions shift or as public opinion and govern-

[1] Prof. Carl Stevens suggests that shifts and changes of tactics should be viewed as the use of existing bargaining power to gain objectives rather than as ways of changing the magnitude of bargaining power. "On the Theory of Negotiations," *Quarterly Journal of Economics*, vol. 72 (1958), p. 93, footnote 2.

mental influence mobilize for or against one of the bargainers.[2] Bargaining power changes too with the nature of the demands made, the costs of agreement and disagreement being relative to the demands. In general the greater the demand, the greater the resistance to it and therefore the less the bargaining power.

The word "cost" is here being used in a broad sense, as disadvantage, thus including pecuniary and nonpecuniary costs. Not all costs can be reduced to a common denominator, of course, but in making decisions some sort of balance *must* be struck, even with respect to incommensurate matters, if decision is to be made and action undertaken. The very incommensurability of certain issues makes possible the changing of minds that might be unpersuaded if all significant issues could be reduced by an economic calculus to a numerical balance or imbalance. . . .

Several points are to be noted about this definition of bargaining power: (1) It takes into account the total situation, not only the striking or resistance capacities of the parties, but the economic, political, and social circumstances insofar as these bear upon the cost of agreement or disagreement. In fact, there appears to be no meaningful way in which a union's striking power, for example, can be separated from surrounding economic and political forces. (2) It allows for the real possibility that bargaining power may shift over time. It is not static, but dynamic. Even within brief periods of time, relative positions may change considerably as the parties maneuver for advantage in the bargaining process. (3) The concept of bargaining power, which is here oriented toward a group decision-making process, is not exclusively tied to two-party negotiations. Although in this analysis we shall primarily be interested in the union-management relationship, the concept is equally applicable to situations involving joint decisions of more than two parties. (4) If agreement is reached, it must be on terms which for all the parties concerned represent a cost of agreement equal to, or less than, a cost of disagreement.

(5) If disagreement persists, it must be because of terms which for at least one of the parties concerned represent a cost of disagreement equal to, or less than, a cost of agreement.[3] (6) Bargaining power for any party may be increased by anything which lowers the relative cost of agreement to the other party or raises the relative cost of disagreement.

In elaborating this concept of bargaining power, let us first turn our attention to the factors which influence the cost of disagreement, following which we shall consider the determinants of the costs of agreement.

In terms of an agreement process, the most meaningful view of the costs of someone's disagreeing with you on your terms is that person's conception of the costs. His prediction or estimate of the cost to him of disagreeing with you is conclusive with him. He may be either right or wrong, of course, as he may discover during negotiations or as you may be able to convince him. Consequently, bargaining power becomes in part a matter of influencing the psychological reactions of the negotiators; one may use the tactic of sheer bluff, but it is also possible to influence another's estimate of the cost of disagreeing on your terms by a straight factual approach if you believe he is operating on an unwarrantably optimistic estimate.

UNION TACTICS AND THE COSTS OF DISAGREEING

The most widely recognized tactics are those by which one party seeks to make the cost of disagreement on its terms high to the other. The union uses the strike, withholding labor until its terms are met; the employer uses the lockout, withholding employment until his terms are met. Regardless of who initiates either action, *both* parties are subjected to

---

[2]Prof. A. Carter adds a "time term" to his bargaining model, adapted from J. Pen's model in "A General Theory of Bargaining," *American Economic Review,* vol. 42 (1952), pp. 24-42. He believes that "time automatically tends to bring about a settlement, for the passage of time gradually increases the [cost of disagreement] . . . for both parties." *Theory of Wages and Employment* (Homewood, Ill.: Richard D. Irwin, Inc., 1959), pp. 123-26.

[3]Professor Stevens points out that two parties may fail to reach a settlement and continue bargaining even though one may enjoy a greater coefficient of bargaining power than the other. The reason is, he explains, that there is not only a necessary condition for settlement, the *existence* of an "acceptable" settlement, but also a sufficient condition; i.e., the parties must be informed and aware of the possible settlement. Disagreement could thus persist because the parties are unaware of their available route to settlement. See *Strategy and Collective Bargaining Negotiation* (New York: McGraw-Hill Book Company, 1963), pp. 21-22, 169.

costs, of course. When a union conducts a strike aimed at closing an employer's business operations, the employees must also bear a cost—their loss of wages. The employer's estimate of how long his employees will submit to their loss of wages will partly determine his estimate of the duration of the strike and consequently the cost to him of rejecting the union's terms. Similarly, in the event of a lockout the employer, while initiating action, is himself equally subjected to some loss from cessation of operations. The losses may be those of present profits, for example, or perhaps even of future profits through loss of customers. The union's estimate of how long the employer will or can stand such a drain will affect, in part, its estimate of the cost of refusing to agree on his terms.

As a result, each party has made efforts to increase the effectiveness of these tactics and to render itself immune to the tactics of the other. The efforts have centered primarily around the union's seeking to strengthen the strike weapon and management's seeking to weaken it. In some of the earliest recorded turnouts of journeymen, we find evidence of the use of strike benefits to lengthen the staying power of the workers and thus increase the cost to the masters of disagreeing with them. Strike benefits were used at least as early as 1805, in the strike of the Philadelphia shoemakers, and in the 1827 conspiracy trial of the Philadelphia journeymen tailors, there was even an attempt made to buy off strikebreakers with strike benefits. On the other hand, employers throughout the years have generally sought to limit the union's interference with members who sought to return to work or nonunion workers who sought to replace the strikers.

The tactical aspects of conducting strikes have been carefully and thoroughly explored by both unions and management. Each attempts to conduct itself so that maximum costs fall upon the other party while only minimum costs are imposed upon itself. The timing of a strike, for example, can be a matter of considerable importance. A strike against an automobile firm just after it has invested in retooling for a model change and when it is ready to begin its competitive sales campaign for the new model would probably be more effective than at any other time of the year. The printing unions in New York for many years timed the expiration of their agreements with newspaper publishers to coincide with the beginning of the period of heaviest advertising, between Thanksgiving and Christmas. A strike at that time would cause the greatest loss of advertising revenues to the papers. Also, a strike by the Hatters in the first part of the year, before Easter, would cause a more serious loss to hat manufacturers than a strike in the summer.

Under some conditions striking workers may find that the costs of a strike decrease over time rather than increase. For example, in the state of New York, unemployment insurance becomes available to strikers after eight weeks. Two months after the beginning of the long New York City newspaper strike of 1962-1963, the average striker was receiving enough strike benefits and unemployment pay to total $120 weekly, a payment comparable to his regular take-home pay. In the long steel strike of 1959, federal, state, and local government benefits and relief provided the striking steelworkers with at least $22,750,000 worth of aid. Full records might well have disclosed the total government assistance to have been in excess of $45 million, according to the union's secretary-treasurer.[4] Or, if other related jobs are plentiful, strikers may find work elsewhere and feel little pressure to agree with management's terms.

The very structure of unions is in part determined by strike effectiveness. One advantage of the craft union structure is the key position which skilled workers frequently play in an enterprise, coupled with the relatively low wage bill which they entail. A strike of a handful of powerhouse employees may close down an entire plant, involving the employer in a substantial cost of disagreeing on their terms, whereas because of their small number the cost of agreement may be negligible in comparison, even if they demand an "outrageous" pay increase. The cost of disagreement to the employer can be materially reduced, however, if striking craftsmen can be replaced, and here enters one powerful incentive for craft unions to exercise control over *all* workers with given skills and training who might provide replacements for the striking craftsmen.

In the case of unskilled or semiskilled workers, there is little possibility of gathering under one union all those who could substitute for striking employees. The very lack of skill increases the opportunity for substitution. At the same time that it becomes easier for the employer to find substitutes for any given semiskilled worker, growth in the size of industrial establishments makes it more difficult to re-

[4] *The New York Times,* September 19, 1960.

place an entire body of employees. Here an industrial union shows greater strike effectiveness by being able to take away from the employer virtually his whole working force in event of disagreement. Unsurprisingly, therefore, the industrial union has its greatest strength in large plants rather than small shops, since in the latter the possibility of the employer's replacing the whole staff of employees in event of strike still remains.

In addition to the strike as a bargaining weapon, the device of picketing has been developed to a high degree of usefulness by the unions. This generally serves to support a strike, though it may be used independently. A picket line advertises a strike and strengthens it insofar as members of other unions refuse to cross it, whether they are engaged in their personal or their employer's business. The picket line has acquired an almost religious significance to many union members, so that its violation takes on aspects of sacrilege and taints the offender. In the presence of such dogma, it becomes possible for even a small group of employees to isolate the company from the economy, inflicting a cost of disagreement upon the company out of all proportion to their significance to its operations. As a single instance, the refusal of 371 photoengravers to accept a settlement similar to that won by the nearly three thousand typographers after a 3½-month strike in New York in 1962-1963 continued the strike for nearly an additional week. The picket line of the photoengravers, like that of the typographers earlier, kept some seventeen thousand newspaper unionists idle at a time when they were ready to work and kept newspapers from approximately thirteen thousand newsdealers anxious to stock the main item of their sales.[5]

The cost to the employer of disagreement with the union is thus in some instance dependent upon the union's ability to provoke sympathetic action by unionists in other establishments or other trades. Striking workers frequently seek the support of the powerful Teamster brotherhood, which by reason of its strategic function of delivering supplies and removing finished products can sometimes bring enormous pressure upon an employer.

In addition to the picket line, a means by which unions in the past (less frequently today) sought to increase the cost to the employer of disagreeing with them by arousing outside

support was the secondary boycott. This has now been outlawed by the Taft-Hartley and Landrum-Griffin Acts, though unions occasionally still covertly resort to it. . . .

Such overt labor actions as strikes, picketing, and secondary boycotts may be accompanied by violence. The literature of industrial relations has been filled with recitals of bloody conflict and even death, as employers and unionists have sought grimly to make good their efforts to keep the price of disagreement high for each other. Strikers have sought to stop back-to-work movements, and employers have sought to use strikebreakers.[6] More significant than the possibility of violence is the fact that the reliance on overt tactics for increasing bargaining power has had its repercussions on the very governmental form of the unions. Effective and efficient use of these tactics often necessitates a tightly held leadership operating on authoritarian and military principles. Democracy within unions can be afforded only between contests with the employer. From the time the agreement is reached on the demands to be made upon the company until those demands are surely won or lost, union leaders argue that the actions of members must be firmly controlled to restrain the weakest of the individual strikers from capitulating or providing leverage for the employer to split the striking organization.

If the above tactics are the more dramatic methods by which a union attempts to impose upon management a high cost of disagreeing with it, more subtle ways of imposing costs have been discovered. One primary cost of disagreement may simply be the refusal of the other party to cooperate in the daily tasks of production. Such lack of cooperation has sometimes taken on organized aspects, in the form of slowdowns.[7] One industrial relations manager described how on-the-job pressure may create a cost of disagreement that brings results.

[6]A peculiarity of American labor law is the requirement that employers recognize and bargain collectively with a union certified by the NLRB only as long as there is no strike. Once the union strikes, the employer is free to bargain individually with any worker he can get to accept employment. Back-to-work movements thus threaten the strike, strikers' jobs, and even collective bargaining itself.

[7]See Richard S. Hammett, Joel Seidman, and Jack London, "The Slowdown as a Union Tactic," *The Journal of Political Economy,* vol. 65 (1957), pp. 126-34.

[5]April 1, 1963.

He relates the experience he and his New York electrical company had in trying to get workers to accept new work methods and new wage rates:

> We needed the changes if our control panels were going to be competitive. In recent years other firms had caught up with our sales and it was a question whether we could stay in this part of the business. No serious opposition to the new standards developed until we got to the panel-wiring department. As soon as we put in the new standards the production from all fifty men dropped from a third to a half. Now they knew the old standards were too loose and they knew we had to raise them. . . .

> We'd raised them 25 units and we might have been off 5 units either way, maybe. But they accused us of making it too tight and wanted us to cut back 10 or 12 units. On the average the wirers had been making from $2.61 to $2.80 an hour and a few of the fast ones made as much as $3.20. Now they were making only $1.60 to $1.80. For five months they refused to work overtime too. That was allowable under the contract unfortunately. Well, I can tell you, our production schedules were really being hurt. They finally gave up the overtime ban but kept on with the slowdown for another four months. We couldn't fire them because they're too skilled and replacements are hard to get. Besides we needed that production. Finally we gave in and dropped 12 points to get out of our tight production corner.

Noncooperation as a cost of disagreement need not always assume an organized form, however. Resentment over management failure to concede some point which employees deem of little moment to management but of considerable significance to themselves may result in unpremeditated holding back. Even such a little matter as refusal of the right of employees to smoke on the job, where no safety or efficiency reason for refusal appears to exist, may create a resentment which finds its expression in early quitting, lingering in the washroom for an illicit cigarette, or any of a number of outlets for private aggression. The failure of agreement between unions and management, both across the bargaining table and down in the shop, developing simply from incentive to noncooperation probably engenders an attitude of latent hostility that makes future agreement more difficult and more costly.

The threat to management of a loss of cooperation in production loses much of its potency as a cost of disagreement if management believes that its employees have already developed an antagonism leading to loss of on-the-job cooperation. The loss becomes a "sunk" cost, so to speak, something which having already been lost cannot be lost again. Only if the employer is made to believe that cooperation can effectively be reestablished by conceding his terms does its loss add to the employees' bargaining power. Loss of cooperation may be a strong bargaining card for the union before it is played, but once played it has much less effect because further disaffection will add only marginal future costs of disagreement to the employer.

MANAGEMENT TACTICS AND THE COSTS OF DISAGREEING

The discussion, so far, has run in terms of the union's power to make disagreement with its terms costly to the employer. It is here that the dramatic actions of industrial relations are encountered. But managements and employers, too, are able to make costly the workers' disagreement with their terms. In the past, their methods of achieving this often bore a more precise resemblance to those of the union than at present. The so-called "La Follette hearings" in the United States Senate in the period from 1937 to 1939 on the violation of free speech and the rights of labor by companies and employers' associations resulted in thousands of pages of printed testimony on the use of violence and intimidation in opposing employee organization for collective bargaining. The boycott was matched by a blacklist and sabotage by the *agent provocateur*. These forms of pressure have now been rendered illegal by various legislative acts, but the decisions of the National Labor Relations Board continue to reveal intimidatory actions by some managements designed to render the unions' disagreement with them costly, such as discharge for union activity, encouragement of rival unions, or even closing of plants!

By far the most common method by which management can increase the cost to the union of disagreeing is by withholding the employment of the latter's members except on terms agreeable to management. The unionists' alternative to agreement becomes the lockout and thus a loss of jobs and income. If sales are low and customers' inventories high, as was the situation for steel in June, 1959, employers may decide that the cost of a work stoppage would be considerably lessened. The steel industry that year was able to produce nearly 3½ million tons more steel, even with its plants closed down for 116 days, than it produced the year before, and only 6½ million tons less than the year after. Employers do not have to wait for market conditions to lessen the cost of a work stoppage; in a number of industries—air transportation, railroads, newspaper publishing, and Hawaiian sugar growing—employers have developed strike insurance. In 1960, for example, the Long Island Railroad sustained a twenty-six-day strike and was greatly aided by insurance benefits received amounting to about $50,000 a day.[8] Two years earlier, six major airlines agreed to a mutual assistance pact under which they would pay a struck airline any increased revenues received as a result of the diversion of passengers or freight. In the first eight months of the pact, the airlines paid out over $9,500,000, a large portion of that sum going to Capital Airline.[9] From strike insurance, several of the New York newspapers that ceased operation in the prolonged 1962-1963 work stoppage, either because they were struck or because they locked out their employees, received a total of $2,250,000.[10] In the New York work stoppage the ITU called a strike against only four of the newspapers, but the managers of the four other papers in the city also suspended operations, locking out their employees. They thus imposed a greater burden upon the striking union, requiring it to provide strike benefits for a larger number of members, and they also denied work to many other members of other printing trades unions.

The lockout, as presently practiced, is not a distinct action from the union's strike but, rather, constitutes a way of looking at the same action from another point of view. At contract renewal time, the employer insists on a reduction in wages. The union rejects this decision, and the employer withholds agreement on any other basis. The union calls out its members rather than accept it or, alternatively, seeks a wage increase. The employer refuses it and insists that wages be kept at existing levels. The union strikes to secure its objective, and the

[8]*Business Week,* September 17, 1960, p. 144.

[9]*The New York Times,* September 9, 1960.

[10]April 1, 1963.

employer refuses to reinstate the strikers except on the old wage scales. Thus the initiative in setting off the action rests with one or the other, but the resulting action involves simultaneously a withholding of labor and a withholding of employment. The relative cost to each of disagreeing with the other will depend upon a variety of conditions, including the economic and political circumstances in which the parties find themselves. But the costs are relative—the dollar loss of income to the workers cannot be laid alongside the dollar loss of income to the company because a dollar of income has a different value in each case.

Moreover, the cost to the employees may be more than simply temporary loss of income. It may involve an actual loss of job, through replacement either by other workers or by machines. And the cost to the union as an organization may be loss of members and even of bargaining rights.

Finally, each party may resort to public opinion and political pressure to add to the other's discomfiture. By picketing, newspaper advertising, press releases, or radio speeches each may try to arouse the public to express disapproval of the other's course of conduct, in the hope that the pressure of governmental officials, social disapproval, and loss of public favor will constitute a further disadvantage which the other will be unwilling to incur. The uncertainty and diffuseness of public response and the difficulty of making social pressure articulate render such tactics of questionable value, however, except under unusual circumstances, such as when the public's own welfare or convenience is involved or when a particular controversy is converted into a question of general principle (whether "one man is more powerful than the United States government," for example). . . .

BARGAINING POWER AND THE COSTS OF AGREEING

Our discussion is by no means intended to be an exhaustive analysis of the costs to one of the bargaining parties of disagreeing with the other, on which relative bargaining powers partly rest. It does indicate, however, the way in which the strength of one party is in part dependent upon the other party's cost of disagreeing on its terms. The further determinant of one's bargaining strength is the cost to the other of *agreeing* with it on its own terms. As we have seen, it is the relative cost to the bargaining opponent of agreement and disagreement on one's own terms which establishes one's bargaining power. Let us turn next, then, to a brief consideration of some of the costs of agreement. This is a matter which is no less complex than the costs of disagreement. For convenience we shall dissect it into three subcategories: (1) direct costs of concessions, (2) secondary costs of concessions, and (3) nonmarket costs of concessions.

From the definition of bargaining power used here, it is evident that the higher the monetary demands, the higher the costs of agreement to the party on whom the demands are made, and the weaker the bargaining power of the demanding party (with some modification that will be shortly noted). The definition thus stresses that bargaining power is *relative* to what is being bargained for. A group's bargaining power may be weak relative to one set of demands, whereas the *same group's* bargaining power may be strong relative to a different set of demands. Since the different demands affect the costs of disagreement and agreement to the other party differently, bargaining power varies with the demands.

The direct costs of agreement will generally be tied up with specific money costs. How much will a wage demand increase the wage bill, or how much will be added by a more liberal vacation plan or group insurance program? Here the amount which is directly added to the year's budget will be the most pertinent consideration. In addition to the amount of the direct costs, the duration of the increases and additions will also be pertinent. If a company believed that a wage increase once granted would extend for only one year or if a union believed that a wage cut once instituted would be withdrawn at the end of the year, there would be less resistance than one usually finds to wage changes. Experience has convinced managements that once a pay increase is granted or a union's demand gets written into the collective agreement, it is there to stay. At any rate, it will not easily be removed. Similarly, unions have acquired the belief that a "backward step" can be retraced only by repeating the struggles they have once gone through.[11] For either bargainer, then, the cost

of agreement may not be the monetary loss simply for the period for which the agreement is reached, but for some indefinite period beyond. If the wage cost of agreement is limited to a definite time, it will be because one of the bargainers is willing to accept the costs at a later date of forcing a readjustment. These future costs, properly discounted, must be added in as part of the cost of the present agreement. . . .

Direct costs may not be easy of computation. In some instances nothing but guesswork is possible. What will be the cost in relaxed incentive or foremen's morale and authority if greater control over discipline is granted the union or if straight seniority is recognized in layoffs and promotions? What will be the cost in reduced output if union stewards are given the right to challenge time studies? What will be the cost of a severance-pay plan? The number of jobs regularly available depends upon the state of technology and the level of general business activity. The former cannot be accurately forecast for more than short periods, and the government's changeable willingness to push and maintain full-employment measures determines the latter. The acceptance of such costs *may* be nothing more than an exercise in optimism, and their rejection a reflection of pessimism. One needs to examine the terms of agreement realistically; they may promise gain as well as cost, and both ought to be evaluated. Disciplinary systems in which unions participate can improve morale. Employee representa-

---

[11] An effective statement and examination of the rationale of this position are to be found in Prof. Henry C. Emery's article of years ago, "Hard Times and the Standard Wage," *Yale Review*, vol. 17 (1908), pp. 251-67. Speaking of the unionists, Emery concluded (pp. 266-67):

> What they dread most of all is a reduction of wages, not so much because they unreasonably refuse to make any sacrifices when the whole community is suffering, but because they believe, and they think they know from experience, that a reduction of wages once made is very difficult to restore. . . . When the manufacturer cannot pay standard wages and run full time at a profit, let him curtail his production, let some men be discharged, but let the level of wages continue intact. Then, when the readjustment comes, there will be no need of a fight, but, automatically, as the demand for products increases, the capitalist's self-interest will send him again in search of more labor.

The primary difference in this respect between the time when Emery was writing and today is that unions now are less inclined to await the "readjustment" but, rather, tend to compel it.

tion in time studies sometimes facilitates their acceptance. To the extent that such results are possible, the cost of agreement may be restrained and even reduced.

The secondary costs [to] one party of agreeing on the other's terms present problems of a somewhat different nature. In the first place, if more than one union exists in the company, the concessions won by one of them are likely to provide precedents which the others will insist on following.[12] A wage increase is not likely to be awarded to one union and denied to others in the same plant. Similarly, where a union is negotiating with a number of competing firms, it is often obligated to grant to all firms whatever concessions it may grant to any individual firm. This is the so-called "most-favored nations" arrangement, to borrow a term from international tariff agreements, under which the most favorable terms conceded to one buyer must be generalized to all. The direct cost to the union of agreeing with an employer on a 10-cent wage reduction may thus carry with it a secondary cost of an equal reduction in all other plants in the same trade or industry in the competitive area.

A secondary cost to the employer is likely to be the impact of improved terms for those in the bargaining unit on those who are outside the bargaining unit. If the pay or vacation plan or pension system of rank-and-file production workers is improved, such conditions must also be improved for foremen and higher levels of management, entailing further costs.[13]

Some companies make a practice of retaining percentage pay differentials between levels of authority, with foremen receiving a specified differential over their highest-paid workers, with second-line management receiving a stated differential over the foremen, and so on up the ladder. In such situations it has sometimes become a standing joke that the union wins pay increases for management. Thus secondary costs of agreeing with the union must be added to the direct costs of such agreement.

The change in production costs as a result of wage adjustments and the change in prices and the resulting changes in product demand constitute what is unquestionably the most important secondary cost. These changes should perhaps be considered direct costs, since their calculation is necessary before one can even determine changes in the total wage bill. The degree of slack in the employer's cost structure and the degree of competition in his product market will be highly relevant considerations to both parties in determining the cost of agreement on the other's terms. If added costs can be absorbed without affecting price or if reduced labor costs are simply compensatory and do not lower price, secondary effects on demand for the product can be ignored. If, however, price changes result from labor-cost changes, the more competitive the product market, the more significant will be the secondary results. The greater the elasticity of demand facing the individual seller, the more marked will be the response to his price changes, either up or down.[14]

Lastly, there are nonmarket costs of agreeing to the other's proposals. These are factors which are not associated with the cost-price relationship but which generally involve "matters of principle." One example concerns the union's status. On the one hand, if managements entertain some objection to the very presence of a union in their plant and conceive of them as being inimical and undesirable from either a personal-interest or a social point of view, the cost of agreement with the union will be to establish that which they would prefer to eliminate. Such recognition of the union has in point of history (until perhaps the late 1930s) been one of the costs of agreement which American employers generally have been most

---

[12]After the ITU, Local 6, and the New York newspaper publishers' association reached an agreement in 1963 on a benefit package of $12.63, the other printing unions demanded and got the same-sized package. "The stereotypers, the mailers, the deliverers and all the other crafts evaluated every offer with slide-rule care to make sure that it added up to exactly the $12.63 in total benefits the printers had received." *The New York Times,* April 1, 1963.

[13]In late 1962 Kaiser Steel and the United Steelworkers concluded an agreement on a unique monthly productivity-sharing plan which promised considerable benefits to the workers. Two months later Kaiser found it desirable to extend the plan so that supervisors and other nonunion employees might also share in the benefits.

[14]Those interested in pursuing this aspect of bargaining power with some theoretical elaborateness, though according to a different definition of bargaining power, are referred to Dunlop, *Wage Determination under Trade Unions,* chap. 5.

reluctant to assume. On the other hand, to a union which is fighting to gain the support and adherence of employees in a given plant, the cost of agreeing on management's terms may be to brand it as ineffectual and even venal. "Selling out" to management is a phrase of opprobrium sometimes applied literally as well as figuratively; the result may be that hard-won members or employees on the verge of signing up with the union will fall away, and the organization will collapse. . . .

There is also a tactical cost of agreement, associated with the principle of the opening wedge. A union or management may object less to the direct or secondary costs of some particular proposal than to the possibility of its being used as a springboard for some future demand which they are totally unwilling to consider. Unions have been antagonistic to any grievance or arbitration review of expulsions from the union which automatically entail discharge from employment under a union security agreement. They oppose such reviews, not because of a fear of having a few employees reinstated to their jobs against the wishes of the union, but because of a much deeper fear that this will establish a precedent for outside intervention in union affairs, thereby threatening the union's bargaining power.

In some instances, managements have been hesitant about agreeing to the participation of unions in the description and classification of jobs, contemplating the danger that this might lead to the union's insistence on discussion and agreement prior to any reassignment of duties among employees and open the possibility of establishing "job jurisdictions" as binding as craft jurisdictions. Such examples might be multiplied. Here the cost of agreement includes an admission of interest by the other party in an area which is sought to be retained with exclusive discretion.

There are indeed certain principles which unions and managements may adhere to so firmly that they constitute creeds with deep ethical or moral roots, the compromise of which will scarcely be considered. In some such instances the cost of agreement may be viewed as infinite. Some managements have closed down their plants rather than give in to the union, and some unions have allowed their organizations to disintegrate during a protracted strike rather than agree on manage-

ment's terms. In these situations the cost of agreement on the other's conditions is set so high that presumably the cost of disagreement on those same conditons could not be raised to top it. The cost to management of agreeing on the union's terms, for example, would be regarded as so great that the union would be unable to make the cost of disagreement any greater. In such a situation the union's bargaining power would be weak relative to its demands.

CONCLUSION

When bargaining power is viewed in this manner, it follows that it may be altered in one of two ways: (1) by changing the cost to the other party of agreement on one's terms or (2) by changing the cost of disagreement. Generally speaking, the union may increase its bargaining power either by *increasing* the cost to management of *disagreeing* on the union's terms or by *reducing* the cost to management of *agreeing* on the union's terms. This conclusion is subject to an important modification, however. A union or management may not always be able to alter one of these determinants of its bargaining power independently of any effect on the other determinant. One cannot always assume that a union will automatically increase its bargaining power by reducing the cost to management of agreeing on the union's conditions. Bargaining power and its two components are relative to particular proposals. If a union were to reduce its wage demands from 10 cents to 2 cents, for instance, such action would *tend* to lessen the cost to management of agreeing with the union; hence it would seem to increase the union's bargaining power relative to the new demand. But before one could arrive at such a conclusion, it would be necessary to observe the effect of this action upon the union's membership. By reducing the prize to be gained, the union may have weakened the desire of its members to fight for it. Whereas the employees might have been willing to strike for a 10-cent-an-hour increase, they may decide that 2 cents an hour is not worth fighting for. In any event, if management believed such to be the effect, it would conclude that the cost of disagreeing with the union even on the latter's reduced demands would have been substantially lessened. The union's bargaining power relative to the revised terms it was seeking would depend upon management's revised estimates of the costs of both agreement and disagreement. The result might as well be weaker bargaining power for the union as stronger.[15]

[15]At the same time, even should management conclude that the workers would be unwilling to strike for the 2-cent increase, its careful appraisal of the situation might lead it to believe that its refusal to grant even this "measly" pay raise (as the workers might regard it) would involve intangible costs of disagreement in the form of distrust, hatred, or noncooperation, rendering disagreement more expensive than agreement. An astute union leadership would point out such a possibility, but regardless of whether or not it did, as long as management recognized this element it would enter into a calculation of the union's bargaining power. Of course, if neither group considered this possibility, it would not enter at all into determination of the union's bargaining power. *Bargaining power is a subjective concept*—and a complex one.

47. Industrial Conflict and Its Mediation

Clark Kerr

TACTICAL MEDIATION

Guidance by a third party to an acceptable accommodation is the essence of mediation, which thus stands midway between conciliation, that is, adjustment of a dispute by the parties themselves, and arbitration, that is, decision by a third party. Mediation, in its traditional sense, involves the intervention of a third party into a particular dispute, and this participation of a third party in a situation which is already given will be called "tactical" mediation. "Strategical" mediation consists, instead, of the structuring of the situation itself, of the creation of a favorable environment within which the parties interact. The purpose of tactical mediation is to bring existing nonviolent conflict between the parties to a mutually acceptable result so that there will be no need for it to become violent or to end violent conflict by agreement or by transfer to nonviolent means. Strategical mediation aims instead at reducing the incidence of conflict and channeling it along nondestructive lines of development.

Tactical mediation is a particularly appealing method of reducing industrial conflict. It is simple to apply. It relies on persuasion rather than on force. It is almost universally supported, at least at the verbal level. But what contribution, in fact, can a tactical mediator make to the resolution of a conflict which the parties cannot provide for themselves? The parties will usually be more familiar with the situation and will have the greater incentive. Viewed analytically, the following are the major potential contributions.[1]

1. Reduction of irrationality. The mediator can bring the parties toward a more rational mood by giving the individuals involved an

---

[1] This discussion will deal with an analysis of the mediation process. It will not describe legal mechanisms or actual techniques. A particularly helpful recent discussion of mechanisms and techniques is found in Elmore Jackson, *The Meeting of Minds* (New York: Harper & Bros., 1952). For a discussion of techniques see also Rose, *op. cit.;* E. L. Warren and I. Bernstein, "The Mediation Process," *Southern Economic Journal,* XV, No. 4 (April, 1949), 441-57; F.H. Bullen, "The Mediation Process," *Proceedings of the New York University Annual Conference on Labor,* 1948, pp. 105-43; and John T. Dunlop and James J. Healy, *Collective Bargaining,* rev. ed. (Homewood, Ill.: Richard D. Irwin, 1953), chap. iv.

For a study relating the mediator's personality and background to the mediation process see Irving R. Weschler, "The Personal Factor in Labor Mediation," *Personnel Psychology* (Summer, 1950).

opportunity to vent their feelings to him, by keeping personal recriminations out of joint discussions, and by drawing the attention of the parties to the objective issues in dispute and to the consequences of aggressive conflict.[2]

2. Removal of nonrationality. The mediator can aid the parties in reaching a full appreciation of reality by clarifying the intentions of the parties toward each other, the issues in controversy, and the pertinent facts and by leading each party to accurate calculations of the cost of aggressive conflict and of the prospective results of such conflict. Quite commonly, each party, particularly when collective bargaining is new to it, underestimates these costs and overestimates the potential gain. The mediator can often bring a truer estimate of the strength of the opposite party and a truer expectation of the outcome than is available initially.[3] While it is not normally too difficult to assist the leaders in these realizations, the task of reaching the constituencies on both sides is often an impossible one. The constituencies may come to recognize reality only through the fire of combat, for the endurance of a strike often serves an educational purpose. It is one of the functions of a strike to raise the calculation of cost and reduce the prospect of gain. The intervention of a mediator is sometimes timed to correspond with the growing recognition of true costs and realistic prospects.

3. Exploration of solutions. Not only can a skilled mediator help the parties explore solutions which have occurred to them independently, but he can create new solutions around which positions have not yet become fixed.[4] In collective bargaining, as elsewhere,

there are several means to the same end, and some of these means will be less abhorrent than others to the opposite party. The mediator can assist in finding those solutions in which, for a given cost to one party, the advantage of the other is maximized or, phrased reversely, in which a certain gain for one party can be secured at the minimum cost to the other. The exploration of solutions is generally most effective before the positions of the parties have become strongly solidified. It is particularly difficult to mediate disputes when the parties have rationalized or theorized their positions or have tied them in with a general ideological orientation. They are then not practical problems but matters of principle.

4. Assistance in the graceful retreat. All, or almost all, collective bargaining involves some retreat by both parties from their original positions. The union normally asks for more than it expects ultimately to receive, and the employer offers less than he expects ultimately to concede. There are at least two major reasons for this. First, neither party is likely to know exactly what the best offer of the other party will be. Thus it is only prudent to make one's own original demand well below or well above the most likely level of concession of the opponent to avoid any chance of having foregone a possible gain. Second, to insist to the end on the original proposal is almost an unfair labor practice, under the rules of the game, for it denies the other party the opportunity of forcing some concession and thus claiming a victory of sorts.

Normally both parties must retreat from their original positions, and much of the fascination of collective bargaining is in the tactics of retreat. Each party seeks to discover and profit from the best offer of the other without disclosing and having to concede his own. The mediator can assist the retreat in at least three ways. First, he can call the parties together. Particularly when a strike is in process, neither side may wish to request negotiations for fear it will betray a sense of weakness. The mediator

---

[2]Sometimes, however, the mediator may encourage settlement by inducing an irrational desire on the part of the representatives for agreement through the use of all-night sessions or of liquor, for example.

[3]The mediator, however, is unlikely to be interested in removing nonrationality in those cases in which one or both parties has overestimated the strength of the opponent or has underestimated the potential result. Furthermore, he normally wishes to encourage an exaggerated estimate of costs and a minimal estimate of gains. In other words, his goal is a peaceful settlement, not the removal of a nonrationality in the parties, although the latter, in the standard situation, conduces to the former.

[4]George W. Taylor has emphasized the "art of proposing the alternate solution" as the crucial part of the mediation process. The skillful application of this art

also involves assistance in the "graceful retreat" (see below), which Taylor has termed bringing about a "consent to lose." (See "The Role of Mediation in Labor-Management Relations" [address at a conference of regional directors of the Federal Mediation and Conciliation Service, Washington, D.C., June 23, 1952], pp. 15 ff., and "Instead of Strike-bargaining," *New York Times Magazine,* July 6, 1947, p. 27.)

can help avoid such embarrassment by issuing the call.

Second, the mediator can act as a go-between on the making of offers. Not only is it unwise to retreat a step without getting the other party to retreat a step also, but any open retreat at all may be unwise if it appears that no agreement may be reached, for then the parties may wish to resume their original positions unemcumbered by face-to-face concessions. The mediator can help control the pace of retreat, for, if one party initially retreats too rapidly, the other may miscalculate the ultimate stopping point, and, in trying to push too far, cause aggressive conflict. Moreover, the mediator can speed up the retreat for both sides by making it more revocable, since he, rather than the parties themselves, seems to be making the suggestions. The more revocable a concession, the easier it is to make. The mediator makes it possible for the parties to yield without seeming to yield and thus to disclose their true positions to each other without being eternally committed to them. Each offer, after all, is presented as the "last offer," not as the "next to last" offer, and there is no point in prematurely becoming committed to the truly last offer unless it is necessary and will settle the controversy.

Third, he can help "save face." The mere entrance of a mediator is a face-saving device. In collective bargaining there are no really objective tests of the performance of the representatives of each side, yet their constituencies seek to test them, and they seek to justify their stewardship. Appearances thus are important. One proof of capable stewardship in negotiations is that the results are as good as or better than those achieved in similar situations elsewhere; another is that concessions were wrung from the opposite party; another is that an elected negotiating committee participated in the negotiations; and another is that the controversy was so hard fought that a mediator had to be brought in.

But a mediator may do more than put in an appearance: he may make recommendations, perhaps even public recommendations (as in the case of a so-called "fact-finding board").[5] A party can sometimes accept such recommendations, particularly if they come from a person

of prestige, when it could not make a similar offer itself or accept such an offer from the other party.[6] The mediator shoulders some responsibility for the result, and the responsibility of the representatives is consequently lightened. The bargaining positions and arguments of the parties are preserved more intact for the next conflict. The public normally lends its support to third-party recommendations, and this makes their acceptance also more accountable. Such recommendations may even be privately handed to the mediator by one or both parties, with the comment that they will be acceptable if the mediator will take public responsibility for their suggestion. Defeat or partial defeat at the hands of a third party is more palatable than a similar surrender to the second party.

5. *Raising the cost of conflict.* A mediator may also raise the cost of conflict to one or both parties as an inducement to settle by bringing or threatening to bring public wrath down on their heads, by persuading their allies to withdraw their support, by threatening retribution (or reward) from government or customers or some other source, by going behind the backs of the representatives to reach and influence the principals in favor of a settlement. But these tactics are not normally pursued and are usually reserved for only the most crucial cases of great public concern. The mediator masquerades as a friend of the parties, and particularly of their representatives, with whom he has face-to-face dealings, and these are the acts of an enemy. Moreover, no mediator who employs such tactics is long acceptable as a mediator.

Some disputes are not subject to a mediation settlement short of aggressive conflict, regardless of the skill of the mediator. There are situations where aggressive conflict has positive values in itself—where there is some institutional gain from such conflict, such as a larger or more devoted membership; where the leaders need an external war to improve their internal positions; where one or both parties want to "burnish the sword"; where, as Pigou notes,[7]

---

[5] Advanced forms of mediation approximate arbitration, just as arbitration of disputes over new contractual arrangements (as contrasted with grievance disputes) often takes on many of the aspects of mediation.

[6] "Agreement" requires that both parties reach the same point in their concessions to each other. "Acceptability" only means that they are close enough to a point set by a third party so that they will not revolt against it. The range of "acceptability" may, of course, be wide or narrow.

[7] Pigou, *op. cit.,* p. 454.

an employer may wish to use a strike to get rid of excess stocks or may encourage a strike during slack period so that one during a peak period will be less likely; where an employer uses a strike as an excuse for raising prices or for withholding production until a more favorable tax period arrives; where one or the other party seeks to further some end external to the relationship—it might be political, or it might be the union leader's need for an occasional strike to encourage the sale of "strike insurance"; or where a strike is desired as a relief from tension. A strike for strike's sake must run its course.

A particularly difficult controversy to mediate, strangely enough, is one in which the costs of aggressive conflict to each party are enormous.[8] Then any one of many solutions is better than a strike, and the process of narrowing these possible solutions to a single one is an arduous task.

While several important types of dispute are not susceptible to effective mediation at all, short of aggressive conflict, mediation does undoubtedly settle some controversies peacefully.

THE CONTRIBUTION
OF TACTICAL MEDIATION

Mediation, undoubtedly, does make a substantial net contribution to the reduction of aggressive industrial conflict, but this does not mean that it does so in every case: indeed, it may even increase the propensity to strike. It may encourage a strike, of course, where an unskilled mediator serves only to turn the parties more against each other or to obscure solutions; but it may do so also when the mediator is skilled, for he may aid the parties to fight, as well as to retreat, gracefully. (The sophisticated negotiator is more likely to need help to fight gracefully under certain circumstances than to retreat gracefully under the same circumstances.) If the public is opposed to strikes and may take action against them, the participation of a mediator in a dispute may convince it of the good faith of the parties' attempts to reach a settlement, making the

public more tolerant of a strike and thus making it easier for the parties to strike; or, if a strike is in process, the entrance of a mediator may forestall more drastic public intervention and thus make it possible to strike for a longer period.

Likewise, if a strike serves a leadership but not a membership purpose,[9] the use of a mediator may help convince the membership that the leaders made a determined effort to reach a settlement, when in fact they did not, and thus ease membership acceptance of strike costs. This ruse will not be successful if the membership is sufficiently sophisticated, but this is very seldom the case.

The mediator has been employed in both these situations as a device to make the situation appear different from what it really is, to camouflage true intentions, to mislead the public or the members. This is "for-the-record" mediation. (See cases 1 and 2 below.)

The mediator may be an unwitting party, in the hands of skilled practitioners, to this deception, but he may also participate willingly, for basically he works for the representatives of both sides, not for the principals or for the public. It is the representatives with whom he associates and from whom he expects acceptance. But in some cases, particularly those of vital public concern, the mediator may go behind the backs of the representatives to reach the principals (or, in the case of the union, also to higher levels of the union organization) and encourage them to press their representatives for a peaceful settlement; or he may go over their heads to the public to exert pressure for settlement, by, for example, attacking the stubbornness of the representatives of one or both parties. (See cases 5 and 6 below.) The former is particularly difficult, however, for it involves a partial or complete repudiation of the repre-

---

[8]*Ibid.*, pp. 460-61.

[9]This assumes, of course, that there is a "membership purpose," but the membership may be and sometimes is so divided in its desires or interests that no single membership purpose can be said to exist.

[10]Mediation occurs at four levels of intensity: (1) where the mediator convenes the parties and transmits their offers back and forth (often called "conciliation"); (2) where the mediator makes suggestions and raises considerations on his own; (3) where the mediator makes public recommendations; and (4) where the mediator tries to manipulate the situation against the wishes of the representatives.

sentatives. The latter is especially effective in a culture, such as that of Germany, which places great stress on law and order and great reliance on public authority, and, conversely, it is less effective in the United States.[10] Where the public is unconcerned about a strike or is concerned but is unable to take effective action or where the membership has no control over its representatives, the mediator, of course, has no recourse beyond the representatives themselves. (See cases 3 and 4 below.)

More common are the situations in which the mediator can aid the leaders or members or both toward a more rational position or can bring skill beyond that available to the parties in making proposals or in aiding the retreat. (See cases 7, 8, and 9 below.)

Table 1 sets forth analytically these various situations.[11] It does not exhaust all the possible combinations, for reality is immensely complex, although other combinations not specifically set forth may be suggested. Particularly, the table abstracts from reality in giving only two alternatives ("Yes" and "No") to such questions as membership control of leaders, when, in fact, there is an infinite number of degrees of control.

Case 1 is the "pure" situation of full rationality, representativeness, and skill all around. Here the mediator can help the parties reach a settlement, if they want to agree, but he is not really necessary. If the parties do not wish to agree, however, his presence can only serve to fool the public about intent to settle and thus increase the propensity to strike. The public, of course, may not care whether a strike occurs or not, and then the mediator's influence is neutral (case 3); or, if the public does care enough, the mediator may turn against the parties and bring public pressure to bear on them (case 5).

Case 2 is one of misrepresentation in a context of leader-membership responsiveness. The representatives of one or both parties want a strike which will not benefit the members. Here the mediator serves only to hoodwink the members, unless he is willing to go behind the backs of the representatives (case 6). The membership may not be able to control the representatives, however, and here the mediator serves no or little purpose, one way or the other, if the representatives desire a strike (case 4).

Cases 7, 8, and 9 show, respectively, where the mediator adds to the rationality of the leaders and the members, to the rationality of the members where the leaders are already rational, and to the skill available to the leaders on one or both sides.

The nine cases may be described in order, as follows:

1. The case of the hoodwinked public. The servant-of-the-parties mediator helps the parties to fool an agitated public into thinking that all is being done which can be done to encourage a peaceful solution, even though the parties are intent on warfare.

2. The case of the hoodwinked membership. The servant-of-the-parties mediator helps the leaders to fool the ignorant members into thinking that the maximum effort toward settlement is being made, when, in fact, the leaders want a strike for their own purposes.

3. The case of the indifferent public. The public does not care one way or another whether there is a strike or not, and so there is no point in trying to fool it through introducing a mediator into the situation.

4. The case of the impotent members. The members have no control over their leaders, and so nothing is to be gained by a pretense of a bona fide effort at settlement through mediation.

[11]This table assumes, as does the general discussion, that irrationality and nonrationality, misrepresentation of membership interests by leaders, and lack of skill conduce toward aggressive conflict, and this is normally true. But there are contrary situations—the leaders or members or both may overestimate the cost of a strike; the leaders may be too lazy and bureaucratic to want to manage an otherwise desirable strike, or they may "sell out" to the other party; or, through lack of skill, representatives may stumble into an agreement they never wanted. Generally, nevertheless, there is less peace, rather than more, because of lack of rationality, skill, and representativeness.

When the leadership misrepresents the membership in favor of peace, unauthorized or "wildcat" strikes may occur, and they are particularly difficult to mediate because the conflict is a three-way affair—membership versus leadership versus employer. Generally, cessation of the membership versus leadership controversy is a prerequisite to effective mediation of the leadership versus employer conflict.

Table 1

**Tactical Mediation—The Structure of Individual
Case Situations**

Situational Factors	Increase		Neutral		Decrease				
	1	*2*	*3*	*4*	*5*	*6*	*7*	*8*	*9*

Certain Type Situations and the Effect of Mediation on Propensity Toward Aggressive Conflict

Situational Factors	1	2	3	4	5	6	7	8	9
Leaders (on both sides):									
Are they rational?	Yes	Yes	Yes	Yes	Yes	Yes	No*	Yes	Yes
Are they skilled?	Yes	Yes	Yes	Yes	Yes	Yes	Yes	Yes	No*
Do they represent their members?	Yes	No*	Yes	No	Yes	No*	Yes	Yes	Yes
Members (on both sides):									
Are they rational?	Yes	No*	Yes	Yes	Yes	No*	No*	No*	Yes
Do they control their leaders?	Yes	Yes	Yes	No*	Yes	Yes	Yes	Yes	Yes
Public:									
Does it dislike a strike, and is it able to penalize the parties?	Yes*	Yes	No*	Yes	Yes*	Yes	Yes	Yes	Yes
Mediator:									
Is he responsive to the wishes of the leaders rather than to those of the members and the public?	Yes	Yes*	Yes	Yes	No*	No*	Yes	Yes	Yes

Definitions: (1) "Propensity toward aggressive conflict" includes both the proneness to strike and the duration of the strike. (2) "Rational" means full and accurate knowledge of costs and results of aggressive conflict. (3) "Skilled" means ability to retreat gracefully, if so desired, without third-party assistance or gracefully to avoid a retreat, if so desired, with third-party assistance. (4) Leaders may "represent their members" either by working solely for membership goals (such as "burnishing sword") or by working for leadership goals (impeding the rise of a rival) where the latter calls for the same action as the former. (The representative of the single employer may be the employer himself, although on the employer side, as well as on the union side, the principals do not usually directly represent themselves.) (5) "The members control the leaders" when the members are able to prevent leadership action contrary to membership desires.

Basic assumptions: (1) There is a rational basis for some aggressive conflict in that conflict pays one or both parties, and the parties do not wish to avoid it. (2) Nonrationality, irrationality, and lack of skill of leaders or members and action flowing from leadership, as contrasted with membership interests, all increase the propensity toward aggressive conflict. (3) The membership, or at least a majority of it, is relatively homogeneous in its interests. (4) The mediator is skilled.

*Asterisks denote the particularly significant factors in each case.

5. *The For-God-and-Country case.* The public servant mediator takes the side of an agitated public and puts pressure on the parties against their will toward a peaceful settlement.

6. *The For-God-and-the-Common-Man case.* The public servant mediator turns against the leaders in order to achieve a settlement where he believes the leaders are, for their own selfish reasons, choosing a strike against the interests of an ignorant membership.

7. *The case of general lack of appreciation of the situation.* The mediator introduces rationality to both leaders and members.

8. *The case of selective lack of appreciation of the situation.* The mediator helps leaders bring rationality into the views of the members.

9. *The case of awkwardness.* The mediator supplies negotiating skills which the leaders lack.

Cases 7, 8, and 9 are certainly the most common of all, and they occur most frequently where small employers and local unions are involved and the members and the leaders are inexperienced; cases 3 and 4 are probably the next most common and arise chiefly when there is sophisticated leadership of well-established organizations in industries of no special concern to the public; cases 1 and 2, which come next in order of probable importance, develop when the leadership is highly sophisticated but must be careful of the sensitivities of the public and the members; and cases 5 and 6 are the least common and take place only where the conflict is of enough concern for the mediator to sacrifice his standing by taking action contrary to leadership interests. Historically, as collective bargaining moves, albeit quite slowly, from cases 7, 8, and 9 to cases 1, 2, 3, and 4, with the growth in size of organizations and the gain in sophistication of leaders, mediation can serve less and less of a positive purpose, except as it undertakes the disagreeable tactics implicit in cases 5 and 6. Compulsory mediation, as practiced in some countries, is no more effective than voluntary mediation unless such tactics are employed.

When a member joins an organization, he does so, in part, to purchase rationality and skill not otherwise available to him. If this purchase were always a successful one, mediation would be largely unnecessary. It finds its justification basically in the failings in this act of purchase—leaders are not skilled or are not rational or are not representative, or the members do not believe them if they are. [12]

There is no convincing evidence that tactical mediation has had much of an effect in reducing the totality of aggressive industrial conflict. Strikes seem to go their own way, responsive to other, more persuasive forces. To understand the role of tactical mediation, we must thus examine not only the internal characteristics of situations but also the external environments within which they arise. [13]

[12]This leadership-membership relationship is a difficult one, at best, for, if the members are not themselves rational, they can hardly know whether they did, in fact, purchase rationality, and, if they are rational, the purchase may be unnecessary. The former is the more common case and helps explain the usual skepticism and cynicism of the members vis-à-vis their representatives.

[13]Proposals for strengthening the effectiveness of the mediation process have generally been concerned with recommendations which are confined within the tactical-mediation orbit. Establishing orderly organized-procedure arrangements or fixing a definite time period as appropriate for mediation ("after collective bargaining has ended in disagreements and before a

STRATEGICAL MEDIATION

A strike is not an isolated event, a solitary episode. It occurs within a given social context, a surrounding economic and political environment. The major variations in the incidence of such conflict relate not to the efficacy of the direct ministrations to the conflict, such as tactical mediation, but to the total milieu within which it arises. Fewer strikes are experienced in Sweden than in the United States, and fewer in the garment industry than in coal-mining, not because tactical mediation is more skilled in Sweden than it is in the United States or is more skilled in one industry than in another, but rather because of the differing surrounding environments. Aggressive industrial conflict varies greatly from nation to nation, industry to industry, firm to firm, and time to time. Which situations are most conducive to nonviolent, and which to violent, conflict?

Strategical mediation is concerned with the manipulation of these situations and thus with factors quite external to the parties themselves. [14] From one point of view, society is a huge mediation mechanism, a means for settling disagreements between rival claimants—tax-

work stoppage has begun"), as Leiserson, for example, has suggested, could at best reflect in the efficacy of tactical mediation but could not circumvent the inherent limitation of tactical mediatory practice per se. (See William M. Leiserson, "The Role of Government in Industrial Relations," in *Industrial Disputes and the Public Interest* [Berkeley and Los Angeles: Institute of Industrial Relations, University of California, 1947], and his presidential address before the Industrial Relations Research Association, "The Function of Mediation in Labor Relations" in L. Reed Tripp [ed.], *Proceedings of the Fourth Annual Meeting of the Industrial Relations Research Association* [1951]).

[14]Intermediate between tactical mediation and strategical mediation lies "preventative tactical mediation." It takes for its province more than the individual dispute but less than the total relevant environment. It deals with the relationships of the parties in general. It may be concerned with a long-run change in the attitudes of the parties toward each other or toward their mutual problems, with the nature of the leadership on one side or another, with the pressures to which the parties may be subject, with the timing of contract expiration dates, or with the alliances of the parties. It seeks to manipulate the parties and their relationships in advance in favor of nonviolent conflict.

payers and recipients of benefits, buyers and sellers, proponents of opposing political ideologies—so that people may live together in some state of mutual tolerance. Some societies mediate their disagreements, through their markets, their courts, their political processes, more effectively than do others. Society in the large is the mediation machinery for industrial as well as other forms of conflict.

Two recent studies demonstrate the crucial relationship of the environment to the industrial conflict. The first[15] investigated the strike proneness of industries in eleven nations and found that some industries (like mining and longshoring) universally evidenced a high propensity to strike and others (like clothing and trade) a low propensity. The second study[16] summarized the environmental characteristics of a series of industrial plants in the United States noted for their industrial peace and concluded that these plants all fell within a definable environmental setting. Drawing on these two studies and, among others, on recent ones by Ross and Irwin[17] and by Knowles,[18] the social arrangements which seem in the long run generally most favorable to nonviolent industrial conflict, within the cultural context with which we are here concerned, may be set forth as follows:

[15]Clark Kerr and Abraham Siegel, "The Interindustry Propensity To Strike—An International Comparison" (to be published by the Society for the Psychological Study of Social Issues, in a volume on *Industrial Conflict*, edited by Robert Dubin, Arthur Kornhauser, and Arthur Ross).

[16]Clark Kerr, "Industrial Peace and the Collective Bargaining Environment," published by the National Planning Association as part of its final report in its series on "Causes of Industrial Peace."

[17]Arthur M. Ross and Donald Irwin, "Strike Experience in Five Countries, 1927-1947: An Interpretation," *Industrial and Labor Relations Review* (April, 1951), pp. 323-42. See also comment by Adolf Sturmthal (pp. 391-94) and rejoinder by Ross (pp. 395-98) in the April, 1953, issue of the same journal.

[18]*Op. cit.* See also his paper presented to the Second Congress of the International Sociological Association, Liege, Belgium, August, 1953, "Strike-Proneness and Its Determinants." Another paper presented to the same congress by Harold L. Sheppard, "Approaches to Conflict in American Industrial Sociology," suggests that only those studies of industrial conflict which take account of the broader environmental milieu can be productive of fruitful generalization.

1. Integration of workers and employers into society. To the extent that workers and employers consider themselves primarily citizens with roughly equal status, privileges, and opportunity, the sting is taken out of their relationship. The greater the social mobility, the more mixed in membership the various social associations, the more heterogeneous the community's occupational composition, the more accepted the institutions of workers and the greater their participation in general community life, the more secure the worker in his job and the higher his skill—the less violent will be the industrial conflict in the long run.

2. Stability of the society. The incidence of strikes is directly related to major changes in the operation of the society—particularly to the business cycle and to wars.[19] Each major economic or political change creates a new situation for the parties, and they must adjust their relationship to it, often in a trial of strength. Similarly, unusually rapid growth or decline of an industry or technological change in it is likely to raise problems in a form which invites a violent solution. The parties normally can adjust more peacefully to gradual than to precipitous change.[20]

3. Ideological compatibility. The attitudes of people and groups toward each other and their over-all orientation toward society affect industrial relationships. Where people believe in brotherly love or the equality of man, for example, their disagreements will be fewer, less sharp, and more amenable to easy compromise. Where, however, they believe in the inevitable opposition of classes, in the rapacity of other men, then violent industrial conflict is more likely. The perspectives of men, it should be noted, are not unrelated to their actual experi-

[19]See Sheila V. Hopkins, "Industrial Stoppages and Their Economic Significance," *Oxford Economic Papers* (new ser.) (June, 1953), pp. 209-20, for one of the more recent of the many studies which note the tendency of fluctuations in business activity to affect the frequency and duration of industrial unrest.

[20]See Robin M. Williams, Jr., *The Reduction of Intergroup Tensions* (Social Science Research Council Bulletin No. 57), pp. 56-58, where the propositions that "intergroup conflict is the more likely the more rapid and far-reaching the social changes to which individuals have to adjust" and that "conflict is especially likely in periods of rapid change in levels of living" are singled out as significant factors in the incidence of hostility and conflict.

ences in their social environments. The close co-operation of leaders of industry and labor in the Netherlands during the German occupation in World War II, for example, has been a source of their intimate relations since then.

4. Secure and responsive relationship of leaders to members. For the minimization of violent industrial conflict, it is desirable that leaders be (a) relatively secure in their positions and (b) responsive to their constituencies. Security of position, on the union side, for example, means lack of intense rivalry for leadership and solidarity of the organization against defection of its members or attack by a rival group. When the leaders are under pressure directly or indirectly, they may respond by encouraging an external war. Vested interests in conflict may be particularly damaging when the leaders make the decisions but the members pay the costs. Under these conditions the leaders will seek to assure the irrationality or non-rationality of the members.

At the same time, leaders should be responsive to their constituencies; otherwise, they may make aggressive use of the organization as a means to an end external to the life of the organization, or by their neglect they may encourage internal revolt with its repercussions. It is relatively easy in many mass organizations for the leadership to exploit the membership in one fashion or another. The proper combination of security and responsiveness of leadership is not always readily attainable, for these two requirements point in somewhat contrary directions.

5. The dispersion of grievances. The mass grievance, one which is held by many people in the same place at the same time against the same antagonist, grows and feeds on itself. Society can more readily accommodate and adjust the small grievance.[21] Thus it is helpful if discontent can find several outlets—individual

[21]A society riven by many minor cleavages is in less danger of open mass conflict than a society with only one or a few cleavages. . . . In the most extreme case of mass violence: An essential step in the development of revolution is the gradual concentration of public dissatisfaction upon some one institution and the persons representing it" (quoted from L. P. Edwards, *The Natural History of Revolution* [Chicago: University of Chicago Press, 1927], p. 46, in Robin M. Williams, Jr., *op. cit.,* p. 59). Williams points out further that "the reduction of intergroup conflict depends upon . . . proper canalization of existing

quitting of jobs and political expression, for example, as well as organized economic action; if it is directed against several individuals and groups—the merchant, the landlord, the state, for example—rather than against an employer who also provides housing, retail facilities, and law enforcement; if it coagulates into small lumps by craft, by firm, by industry, rather than over the whole society; if it finds expression a little at a time, rather than in a single explosion; if it can be blunted by the imposition of relatively impersonal laws and rules standing between the parties on the basis of which decisions can be made which flow not alone from the parties in controversy but from less volatile sources; if it finds expression in several stages through appeal or through periodic reopening of questions and if it seldom encounters a final barrier to its voicing; if freedom to act and react is constantly preserved. At the opposite extreme is the mass grievance against a single source of power, subject to a single personal decision.

6. Structuring the game. As we have seen above, rules which reduce the risks of the parties and limit the means they may employ, without unduly stifling the conflict, can make a substantial contribution to non-violent resolution of controversy or can mitigate the destructive consequences of violent conflict. Rules which guarantee the independent sovereignty of each party, which raise the cost of fighting (as does multiemployer bargaining),[22] which set some fairly precise norms for the settlement (as does the "pattern bargain"), which prohibit use of certain provocative means of combat, which limit conflict to intermittent periods, which confine the subjects for disagreement to some reasonable area at any one time—all aid the nonviolent settlement of industrial disputes. The rules of the game aid rationality—knowledge of costs and consequences—and thus diplomatic resolution of controversies. Fortunately, in industrial relations, contrary to international relations, these rules are enforcible by society if not accepted by the parties voluntarily.

These are not easy prescriptions, although all

hostilities, through sanctions, diversions, redefinition of situations, etc." (p. 62).

[22]A high degree of horizontal and vertical integration of worker and employer interests does not, however, prevent strikes. Witness, for example, the largest strike in Swedish history—the metal-workers' strike of 1945.

of them are potentially subject to some utilization—not, however, in totality by any single "third party" or even by a single institution. Strategical mediation relates to an over-all community approach to its organization and to the handling of its problems, and to a general philosophical orientation toward the management of the affairs of men.

CONCLUSION

Industrial conflict, then, may be affected in three crucial ways: (1) by reducing the sources of mutual discontent; (2) by affecting the process by which decisions to act are made, either (a) by reducing the power to make such decisions (through control of one party by the other or of both by the state) or (b) by facilitating the making and implementing of decisions to act nonviolently; and (3) by channeling the conflict along the least destructive lines. Tactical mediation is concerned with 2b; strategical mediation, with 1 and 3. It is suggested that the latter, by the advance creation of favorable situations, can make the greater contribution to the minimization of aggressive industrial conflict and particularly of its most socially harmful aspects.

Substantive Issues in Bargaining

An ancient issue in collective bargaining is the demand for a union shop or some other provision for "union security." Unlike a wage demand, this issue is not readily compromised. It has aroused employer resistance, public controversy, and both federal and state legislation. Paul Sultan explores the pros and cons, emphasizing that this is essentially a power issue and pointing out that a union security clause can sometimes be advantageous to the employer.

The subject matter of collective bargaining is not static. The content of collective agreements reflects what union members consider most important at a particular time. Unions today bargain about issues that did not exist in 1930; other new issues will certainly have arisen by the year 2000. Derek Bok and John Dunlop outline areas which they believe will become increasingly important in the future. These include employee education and training; greater scope for individual preference in such matters as work schedules and fringe benefits; restructuring of jobs; and other steps to reduce alienation and increase the inherent interest of work.

351

48. The Union Security Issue

Paul E. Sultan

The union security issue was created at the very inception of labor organization in America, and the cycles of conflict it has since engendered have followed (with a time lag) the waves of union growth. Today, even if one accepts the permanence of union organization and the maturity of bargaining relations, those contract terms making explicit union security are continuing sources of controversy. What elements contribute to the enduring quality of this problem?

The persistence of the conflict can in part be explained by the complexity of the issues involved. For example in orthodox economic theory, competition was presumed to dominate market structures. Unfortunately the nineteenth-century blueprint of the competitive society provides a poor description of twentieth-century reality. But we have not yet fully fashioned the devices for balance and control where the discretionary exercise of power shapes, rather than is shaped by, impersonal market forces. In this setting, the union security issue represents the clash between those inspired by the historic ideals of the competitive society and those awed by the size—and resigned to the permanence—of large scale industrial organization.

Superimposed on this field of controversy is the dispute over the relevance of political de-

mocracy to union-management power relations. The notion seems well established that the mechanism of democracy is as relevant to economics as it is to politics. Perhaps we have been drawn to this conviction because of the hope that somehow democracy *within* the organization can provide that degree of restraint and control no longer assured by external market pressure. But those concerned with political freedom in a market setting often fail to grasp the inextricable relationship of such freedom to power; too often these are regarded as opposite rather than complementary elements in the bargaining relationship. As a case in point, in the three-way interdependence of the worker, union and management, the union-management economic (power) relationship can be and is affected by the union-membership political (democratic) relationship. We have not yet fully explored the manner in which the extension of the latter democratic relationship may disrupt the former power relationship, but obviously the individual worker's freedom cannot be analyzed in any context that ignores the reality of market power. If this relationship be acknowledged, how does one measure and then establish that balance between individual rights and group discipline that would offer workers the optimum of political influence and economic gain? And would that optimum be consistent with alternative maximizing goals, such as the maintenance of price level stability or increased economic growth?

Finally, we have an aversion to issues in which merit can be found on both sides, blinded as we are with the notion that virtue is undivided and that the task of analysis is to identify the villain in the piece. Unable to conceive, then, of the conflict of good against good, a kind of Gresham's law has operated, with the bad arguments driving out the good, with emotionalism swamping rationalism. Indeed, one weary student of the subject decided to determine the weight of evidence by placing the mass of material received from partisans on his bathroom scale.[1]

In this [article] we shall focus on only a few aspects of this intricate problem. We shall make a statistical survey of the form and extent of such security agreements, . . . [and] we shall weight the advantages of union security agreements, both in terms of the power balance between unions and management and the political relations of union membership to union leadership.

THE FORM AND SCOPE
OF UNION SECURITY

Since 1954, the proportion of contracts containing union security clauses has levelled off at 81 per cent. But this stability should not obscure significant shifts in the form these have taken in the last fifteen years. For example, the 1947 Taft-Hartley ban on the closed shop caused a rapid growth in the union-shop agreement (17 per cent in 1946 to 49 per cent in 1949-1950). And since 1950, union-shop coverage has increased steadily by displacing maintenance-of-membership agreements. By 1958-1959,[2] the union shop represented over 90 per cent of all security arrangements. How-

ever, a fifth of these did exempt certain groups from membership requirements—in some cases those who were not members at the effective date of the agreement, or those whose religious convictions prevented such membership. . . .

The 19 per cent of agreements not containing a union security clause represent, implicitly or explicitly, a "sole bargaining" relationship, for the exclusive bargaining principle is embodied in federal law. And some contracts, while making no provision for union security, do contain a clause to encourage membership. Such a harmony clause might read:

> The employer states to the union that it has no objection to and it believes that it is in the best interests of the employees, the union, and the employer, that all employees within the unit become and remain members of the union.

Union check-off arrangements have increased in coverage from 20 per cent of collective bargaining agreements in 1942 to 77 per cent of agreements in 1958-1959. Seventy-six per cent of sole bargaining contracts contained check-off provisions, while 70 per cent of the union-shop and membership-maintenance contracts contained this provision. Thus, the less secure the union, the greater the impulse to negotiate such an agreement. It is not surprising, therefore, that 85 per cent of workers under major agreements in right-to-work states were covered by such provisions, as against 68 per cent under agreement in states without such laws[3]. . .

SOME POWER IMPLICATIONS
OF THE CONTROVERSY

To those familiar with the long history of those contracts negotiated by employers in which *non*-membership was a condition of employment, the role of the employer as the champion of employee freedom of choice on the matter of union membership may seem somewhat incongruous. The lustre on the shield of others in the right-to-work crusade seems somewhat tarnished because of the evident anxiety of these organizations to avoid identifi-

[1]When the author complained to a Teamster official about the implausible economic analysis employed by unions in the 1958 California right-to-work campaign, the unionist explained: "Right-to-work laws are being sold like a bar of soap and we're going to unsell them like a bar of soap."

[2]Rose Theodore, "Union Security and Checkoff Provisions in Major Union Contracts, 1958-59," *Monthly Labor Review*, Vol. 82, No. 12 (December, 1959), p. 1351.

[3]Rose Theodore, "Union Checkoff Provisions," *Monthly Labor Review*, Vol. 83, No. 1 (January, 1960), pp. 26, 28. . . .

cation with other agencies concerned with those broader forms of employment discrimination based on race, creed, or color. Thus, if the inspiration for the right-to-work movement is the evil of discrimination, it is puzzling that the attack should be given such a narrow focus. It is not surprising, therefore, that some should suspect that the target is not discrimination itself, but union power that allows such union discretion to arise in the first place. It is not irrelevant to speculate, therefore, on the way in which the extension of minority interests within the labor force might affect the power balance between unions and management.

If one accepts the cynical view that employer interest in right-to-work often reveals a circuitous device to weaken union power, how is this accomplished? A union certified by a narrow majority of employees is nevertheless legally obligated to represent all employees in the bargaining unit. The limited financial base for representation and bargaining activities may frustrate union success. Much union staff time is taken up in "selling" union membership to potential members. Such activity may divert energies from more constructive duties. Union leadership may become increasingly harassed, for not only does dissension exist within the union over the burden of carrying the "free rider," but officers and business agents feel it is politically expedient to push every grievance, regardless of its merit. With a loss of a security clause, the cost of administration for the union may increase at the very time that the financial base to support such activity is reduced.

More important than this is the possibility of an open challenge to union control during an impasse in bargaining or during a prolonged strike. Non-members may be more willing to contemplate returning to the job, and the smaller the proportion of employees falling within the orbit of union discipline and the union's communication media, the greater is the risk that a strike may fail. This consideration is particularly crucial if the number of non-members within the plant, combined with non-members wanting work in the plant, is greater than the number of employed union members that go out on strike. . . .

Finally, the existence of a right-to-work statute may give the employer a psychological edge in a contest for employee support. During an organizing campaign, the employer may stress the incapacity of the union to retaliate against anti-unionists, regardless of the outcome

of the election. Paraphrasing the Lewis strategy of the thirties, the employer may advertise: "Our state laws proclaim your freedom not to join a union."

Beyond the strategy of gaining recognition, day-to-day relations with the union may prove more disruptive. The necessity of being sensitive to individual grievances, responsive to every faction in the local can lead to a situation one writer described as minority rule. In preparing for bargaining sessions, union representatives will accumulate the aggregate of demands made by all factions rather than screen these in terms of what is economically feasible. Management will be assigned the total blame for modest concessions at the conference table. Such spirited bargaining may result not only in sharper conflicts, but greater instability in the cost-price structure. Right-to-work legislation is not likely, therefore, to lead to either tranquility in union-management relations, or stability in cost-price relations.

But if belligerence creates problems for the employer and the public, its opposite may create problems for the membership. Given the new look in bargaining negotiations—sometimes called hard bargaining—union officers may be tempted with some variant of the theme: If you can't beat them, join them. Such an accommodation may take the form of a union security clause. The subtle transformation of union policy from militancy to maturity, from conflict to cooperation, may enjoy the sanction of all who have not fully contemplated its impact on individual employee interests.

Put in more general terms, once the union conceives of its stability in terms of the stability of management, both may cooperate with each informally to satisfy the organizational imperatives they both face. The accommodation process can very easily involve policies that antagonize portions of the labor force. In such a case both management and the union may be the target for employee criticisms. It should be appreciated that there is no legal prohibition against a union recommending that an individual be fired so long as that request is not related to unionism. For example, a union can request the discharge of members expelled for Communistic activities, of employees drinking on the job, for activities that endanger the safety of other employees, or for general incompetence. In traditional analysis of union-management relations, there has been no lack of evidence of the subterfuge management may employ to "get" an employee who has been the spearhead of union organizational activities. The problem of establishing that the discharge of such employees was inspired by incompetence rather than union activity has been a thorny one indeed. But if both the union and management agree informally that certain troublemakers should be discharged, the chances of those so discriminated against may be limited. Management and the union may be joint depositors in the bank of evidence against the individual. Such a person may not only lack a forum in which to give expression to his difficulties, but lack the personal resources to continue single-handedly a struggle against the legal talent of two organizations. Such a situation is certainly isolated today, but the picture of small individuals caught between the common interests of two power mechanisms is one that bears consideration for the future. The adjustment of the union to the economic necessities or rhythms of corporate life may be labeled "maturity" or "responsibility" in the bargaining relationship, but it is an adjustment that may deny the individual with divided or dual disloyalities a sanctuary and—in extreme cases—his employment.

The seriousness of this possibility has yet to be established. But it does suggest that the union is going to have to make greater efforts to satisfy not only the majority of the workforce, but the peculiar interests of dissident minorities. An effort will have to be made, if not to institutionalize, at least to legitimatize, dissent. Our analysis suggests that while nonmembership may not be the best control device over union policy, some control mechanism beyond the resistance power of management may yet be necessary. In our concern with the possibility that union-management harmony may be secured at the public expense, we have neglected the possibility that it may also be secured at the individual worker's expense.

49. Frontiers of Substantive Bargaining

Derek C. Bok

John T. Dunlop

The earliest collective-bargaining agreements encompassed little more than a scale of wage rates and the standard hours of the work day. Over the years, the range of subjects in written agreements has greatly expanded. During World War II, unions made great strides in bargaining for grievance arbitration and other safeguards to protect their members against unfair decisions on the part of management. In the past twenty years, the most significant growth in the scope of bargaining has probably been in the areas of pensions, health and welfare, and insurance. More recently, there has been renewed activity in the development of programs to cushion the shock of unemployment and technological change. The question naturally arises whether substantive issues that are emerging today will carry collective bargaining into new fields. . . .

New needs develop for a variety of reasons. With rising wage levels, more and more workers can more readily satisfy their basic wants. As a result, union members may set less store on getting new pay increases and acquire a keener interest in greater economic security, longer vacations, better working conditions, better education and training, and the like. This tendency is mirrored in a long accumulation of survey data, suggesting that income matters relatively less to employees now than it did decades ago when the economy was closer to subsistence levels.[1]

Changes in technology are an even more fertile source of new needs. The rise of the factory spawned a whole host of new concerns growing out of noise, monotony, machine hazards, pace of work, and discipline. In recent years, automation and technological change have created their own special problems. In some plants and industries, more expensive equipment has reduced traditional skill requirements, leaving the worker with more free time and making him more dependent upon the social aspects of the job. In other instances, modern technology has demanded new and more complicated forms of training in order to equip employees for fresh responsibilities.

Today, one of the most intriguing tendencies of many employees is their desire for greater individuality, autonomy, and freedom of choice once they have achieved higher levels of education, income, and economic security. . . .

To many critics, unions (along with other large organizations) cannot satisfy the worker's desire for greater individuality and autonomy; they inevitably swallow up their members and press them into a common mold. Other writers

[1] See Victor H. Vroom, *Work and Motivation* (New York: John Wiley and Sons, 1964).

observe how little unions have appreciated the psychological needs of their members. As Arthur Kornhauser puts it: "American unionism concentrates its efforts on restricted economic gains for the members. The findings of our study, as well as a great deal of other evidence, show how shallowly these usual activities of the organization enter into the life patterns of workers and how very slightly they engender active involvement."[2] Perhaps these arguments are valid. Yet there are various ways by which unions can increase the opportunities for freedom and self-realization in work, and it is in these endeavors that some of the most interesting and important frontiers of bargaining can be found.

TRAINING AND EDUCATION

Programs of training and education can increase freedom by widening the types of work that the employee can perform. Such programs are likely to be the next sector of major expansion in the scope of bargaining....

. . . To some degree, the rising interest in education and training can be linked to the rediscovery by economists of the significance of "human capital.". . .

A period of prolonged high and expanding employment, such as the nation has experienced in recent years, provides further incentives for training programs. Skilled employees become harder to find, while the needs for these skills continue to grow. Through hard experience, many employers find that systematic training programs offer a more effective or less expensive method of meeting their needs than wage increases, advertising, raiding, or extensive use of overtime. In this setting, federal manpower programs and equal-opportunity regulations have provided an example, an opportunity, and a spur to fill employment needs from the ranks of disadvantaged groups. Labor unions or managements alone, or both through collective bargaining, have begun to make provision for the recruitment and training of new personnel from the disadvantaged and for the upgrading of the least-qualified and least-skilled among present employees.

The factors just mentioned do not exhaust the list. The widespread concern over technological displacement, particularly in the early 1960's, was another influence promoting joint labor-management interest in retraining programs; . . .whatever the mix of factors at work, training and education programs are being provided for in an increasing number of collective-bargaining relationships. . . .

The expansion of collective bargaining into formal training, beyond apprenticeship, may raise eyebrows on the grounds that these functions are more appropriately the province of the public-school system. But this conventional view fails to recognize the extent to which other institutions are already in the training business. Large-scale business enterprises are very much educational institutions; training of a labor force is a joint output with production and services. In enterprises with sophisticated technology this is particularly significant. IBM has a larger annual expenditure for training and education in various forms than the budget of Harvard University. The military has also become a significant training institution. Many proprietary schools have been established to train workers for such jobs as airplane mechanics, programmers, hairdressers, and clerical occupations. Moreover, new relationships between the formal educational system and both labor and management are required if educational preparation for work and programs of periodic retraining are to become more successful.[3] Managements and unions are likely henceforth to carry a larger share of responsibility for long-term employee development[4]. . . .

TOWARD GREATER SELF-DETERMINATION FOR THE EMPLOYEE

Most agreements specify differing benefits and levels of compensation for different groups of workers according to their job classification,

[2]Arthur W. Kornhauser, *Mental Health of the Industrial Worker, A Detroit Study* (New York: John Wiley and Sons, 1965), p. 291.

[3]Garth L. Mangum, *Reorientating Vocational Education* (Washington, D.C.: National Manpower Policy Task Force, May 1968).

[4]For a discussion see Neil W. Chamberlain, "Manpower Planning," in *Frontiers of Collective Bargaining*, John T. Dunlop and Neil W. Chamberlain, eds. (New York: Harper and Row, 1967), pp. 211-32.

department, length of service, method of wage payment, marital status, or other categories. But variations of this kind do not necessarily give much freedom of choice to the individual employee. Within the group to which the individual belongs, the terms of employment may be identical, with few if any options being left to the discretion of each worker. One wonders, therefore, whether ways can be found within collective bargaining to enlarge the area of free choice available to individuals in the same job classification or with the same length of service.

To put the issue in proper perspective, it is necessary to recognize the considerable extent to which collective-bargaining agreements already offer scope for the varying preferences of employees. Piecework and incentive-pay systems allow a worker to make a limited choice between income and effort, a choice that cannot be made under the standard wage rate. Most promotion procedures also allow the individual to choose whether to bid for the higher job, and provide that the junior will be preferred if he has displayed ability which is plainly superior to others with greater seniority. Vacation provisions ordinarily allow employees to make a limited choice of dates for their vacation subject to the operating needs of management; in some cases, there is the further choice of whether to take the paid vacation or work instead and draw vacation pay on top of regular compensation. The allocation of overtime may involve further opportunities for choice, subject to the imperative of equitable distribution of overtime among employees interested in such work (and income) and the right of the management to require enough overtime from the types of workers required to produce the added output desired. The assignment of employees among shifts also provides an occasion for some recognition of individual preference. At times, in plants with continuous operations, all employees in a department may vote to decide between working on a fixed shift or rotating periodically among shifts. The principle of seniority ordinarily is used to allow individual employees a choice among fixed shifts. Retirement plans increasingly contain individual vesting provisions, which reduce the costs of moving from one job to another and allow workers to retire at an earlier age if they wish to do so. . . .

Another way to expand the area of individual choice is to alter the requirements of the job. For example, management may provide for two individuals to work part time to cover a single position. For many sales positions in tight labor markets, this arrangement has already proved successful in appealing to the large number of persons who prefer to work part time on a regular basis. In the usual case, the two employees can make their own schedules, provided that they keep the job filled at the specified hours. They may divide the work as between mornings and afternoons, between weeks, or may exchange hourly flexibility to suit personal necessities. While the arrangement may involve higher costs by virtue of fringe benefits and administrative costs (unless part-time wage rates or salaries are set correspondingly lower), the flexibility to management in tight labor markets and to employees seeking regular part-time work is appealing, especially in sectors employing female workers. In the future, such use of part-time work may become increasingly widespread as employers seek to attract women to fill the growing number of tasks requiring persons with high levels of intelligence and education.

While the opportunities for individual choice and the exercise of options can no doubt be enlarged, there are limits to such expansion. Full individual bargaining is virtually a negation of collective negotiation; it can also eliminate bargaining's market-stabilizing function, which enables unions to protect their members by "taking wages out of competition." Nevertheless, to the extent that individual employees can exercise choices that do not harm other employees or the union, or impose higher costs on management, the effort is worth making and a clear social gain will have been achieved.

An obvious way to expand individual choice still further is to group certain fringe benefits—such as vacations, holidays, supplementary unemployment compensation, health and welfare, and pension contributions and sick leave—into a lump-sum account for each individual and permit employees to distribute the compensation involved among the various programs in accordance with their own individual preferences. Such an arrangement may permit workers and their families to adjust their contributions to their age and style of life. At certain periods, particularly in the child-rearing years, employees may be especially concerned with health and insurance; at later stages, pensions and vacations may have a higher priority. The allocation of a fixed percentage of compensation to medical insurance, vacation and pensions throughout a working life is insensitive to these shifting interests and unresponsive to changing needs of employees and union members. For added flexibility, compensation arrangements might also recognize that emergencies, prolonged illness, family problems, and the like, create periods of particular stringency, so that provision could be made for contingency reserves to be available in case of special need.

At one time these notions would have been dismissed as impractical. Today, the computer makes it feasible to administer the maze of individual choices involved. Nevertheless, the proposal has its limits. There is a legitimate concern that individuals may not make adequate provision for pensions, medical care, or some other benefit and may later become a serious charge on the community or the parties, as well as bitterly critical of both labor and management for not providing sufficient compensation. It is not a sufficient reply to extol consumer sovereignty or stress the moral responsibility of the individual employee. Experience abundantly demonstrates that individuals can repeatedly fail to make adequate provision for remote contingencies, to their eventual misfortune. As a practical matter, therefore, any plan for expanding individual choice in allocating benefits would need to specify certain minimum allocations, particularly for health and welfare insurance, disability and pensions. Another limitation concerns the extent to which risks are spread within a group of employees. If individuals who are seldom ill make no expenditures on health and welfare plans, the adverse selection will result in very much higher charges for those with illnesses. The provision of at least some minimum level of benefits again seems indispensable. Even with these limitations, however, the scope for increasing individual choice seems large indeed. And now that so many collective-bargaining relationships have matured, there should be much less reason for unions to fear that individual options will be used to divide the members and undermine the collective-bargaining relationship.

THE NATURE OF WORK

Fresh challenges for collective bargaining arise not only from new interests of workers but from the discovery of needs that have existed all along. Over the past few decades, many of the most subtle and interesting forms of satisfaction and discontent have come to light in precisely this way. In many cases, the discovery of these needs has been the work of industrial psychologists in reaction against the mechanistic theories of scientific management developed by Frederick Winslow Taylor at the turn of the century.

To Taylor, an engineer by training, maximum productivity could be achieved by designing jobs with sufficient exactness to take advantage of the most efficient sequence of motions on the part of the individual worker. Under this system, the employee was left little freedom and spontaneity. What was required was "... not to produce more by his own initiative but to execute punctually the orders given extending into the smallest details."[5] Various rationalizations were developed to make this system seem more palatable from the employee's standpoint. To Taylor himself, scientific management could only improve the morale of the workers since it increased output and thereby raised wages as well. To Henry Ford the new concepts would be welcomed because "... the average worker ... wants a job in which he does not have to put forth much physical effort. Above all, he wants a job in which he does not have to think."

As time went on, it grew increasingly clear that Taylor's principles often went awry because they failed to take adequate account of the psychological and group reactions of employees. In silent protest against the system, workers set informal production norms far below their real potential. If only to relieve the tedium of work, they invented all manner of artful dodges to befuddle the company engineer into setting easier quotas on their jobs. They were absent too often from work; they quit too frequently for other jobs; they were involved in too many accidents and unwittingly broke too many tools. In the face of these difficulties, research teams were called in by many of the more progressive companies. As these investigators got more deeply into the problem, they began to discover a whole battery of desires and discontents that colored the attitude of workers toward their jobs.

Some of these dissatisfactions had to do

[5]The quotations in this paragraph are from Georges Friedmann in *Industrial Society, The Emergence of the Human Problems of Automation*, Harold L. Sheppard, ed. (Glencoe: The Free Press, 1955), pp. 153, 365.

with the physical environment—the design of the machine, the color of the walls, the temperature of the room. Others involved the pace of work and led to much research to trace the effects of rest periods, assembly-line speeds, and the rhythm of the job on monotony and fatigue. An entire school of thought sprang up on the subject of human relations in the workplace; studies accumulated on the techniques of supervision and the impact of informal work groups and their norms on the behavior of employees.

Still other researchers grappled with the problem of alienation in work. The specialization of tasks recommended by Taylor had narrowed many jobs to the point where they had lost meaning; the worker could not perceive the purpose of his work and how it contributed to the entire production process. At the same time, specialization also multiplied the number of interdependent jobs, and thus gave rise to more onerous forms of coordination and supervision. Out of the research directed at these problems came a series of experiments on the design of jobs.[6] These inquiries have centered on three aspects of the job: the variety of tasks to be performed; the amount of discretion given to the men in deciding how to perform the work; and the respective roles of employees and supervisors in establishing the norms and sanctions for the job. Some of the most interesting experiments have involved the creation of teams of workers. These groups are given a wide range of functions to perform—preferably all the functions that make up a natural unit or process of production. The members of the team have broad responsibility for deciding upon the organization of work, the methods to be used, the standards to be observed. Conversely, foremen and supervisors lose much of their coercive authority and assume a supportive role, giving advice and technical aid and marshaling help as needed from other parts of the company. Under such conditions, Taylor would have predicted little but anarchy and confusion. Yet many of the experiments have resulted in large improvements in quality and productivity, with marked reductions in turnover and accident rates. The very magnitude of these gains suggests a deep need on the part of many workers for many

autonomy, variety, and creativity in their work. . . .

These . . . lines of research suggest a significant challenge for collective bargaining. To be sure, the problems to be solved are not of crisis proportions. Many workers find considerable . . . satisfactions in their job. Others do not seem to mind repetitive, uninteresting work. Indeed, a survey of 3,000 factory workers in 1947 revealed that a full 79 percent found their jobs to be "mostly" or "nearly always" interesting. At the same time, the 20 percent of factory workers who reported their work to be dull "all or most of the time" represent many millions of human beings. In addition, a full 59 percent of the entire sample asserted that they would choose a different trade or occupation if they were free to start over again. A number of pilot projects in motivation and job design have also had a strong enough impact on productivity and turnover to suggest great scope for enlarging the interest and attractiveness of work. Indeed, large majorities of the workers involved in these projects have much preferred the new jobs to the old. In sum, there appear to be important needs that remain unfulfilled for large numbers of workers.

Employers and unions have responded quite differently to this challenge. On the part of management, the reaction is spotty, but a number of companies have shown real interest in the subject. They have experimented in new techniques, sponsored research, and have sometimes made extensive changes in their methods of job design and supervision, ordinarily because these changes have been more profitable. Unions, on the other hand, have shown little or no interest in the psychological dimensions of work. If boredom has been a problem to their members, unions have responded by providing escapes from work; they have bargained for shorter hours, longer vacations, more frequent rest periods. But very seldom have they interested themselves in work enrichment, job design, and other ways to make the content of work more meaningful and interesting. Even the Auto Workers Union, for all the talent in its staff, has hardly scratched the surface of these problems, although many of its members have assembly-line jobs that are so repetitive and rapidly paced as to be among the most dispiriting occupations to be found in American industry.

These responses, of course, are not entirely unexpected. Although unions and man-

---

[6]See Louis E. Davis, "The Design of Jobs," *Industrial Relations, A Journal of Economy and Society* (October, 1966) pp. 21-45.

agements may share a common concern over the welfare of the worker, their motivations and capabilities are critically different. Management's interest in the feelings of their employees is buttressed by the lure of achieving greater levels of efficiency. Since qualified experts report that most factory workers perform well below their capability, the alert executive can hardly fail to consider the realm of industrial psychology as a possible means for improving productivity, and perhaps lowering rates of turnover and accidents as well, in order to lower costs. And when he learns that disgruntled employees have joined a union in his competitor's factory, he is bound to examine the morale of his work force with quickened interest. Thus motivated, he finds it natural to call upon the professional, the researcher, the specialist, and set them to work upon the problem. This is the procedure he has learned in business school and the response he has relied upon in attacking questions of marketing, production, forecasting, and other problems that have arisen within his organization.

Yet one can hardly say that the businessman has done all there is to do to improve morale and satisfaction within his plant. Far from it. If morale conflicts with efficiency—as it sometimes does—the employer cannot make substantial compromises to benefit his employees without running serious competitive risks. Assembly-line jobs may be a crashing bore, but no auto company is going to manufacture cars by hand. Moreover, many of the newer concepts of job design are extremely difficult to implement, even though they are said to promise substantial productivity gains. To create autonomous work crews setting their own standards and disciplinary rules will require management's giving up part of its authority. Such innovations contradict deep-seated managerial instincts and threaten to downgrade the supervisory personnel. As a result, though many managers keep abreast of research on job design, comparatively few have tried to put the new concepts into practice. Instead, the tendency has been to search for milder—and probably less effective—palliatives ranging from bowling teams and better company newspapers to the simple grouping of petty, routine tasks in what is euphemistically referred to as "job enlargement." In view of the record thus far, one recent study has concluded that ". . . the most formidable obstacle which the creation of meaningful work encounters is management

and supervisor resistance."[7] There is little reason for this situation to alter on a broad scale unless the potential gains in productivity make such changes irresistible.

These inhibitions create opportunities for the enterprising labor leader. He can insist upon bargaining over the quality of work, or at least ask that study committees be established to pursue the matter further. In highly fragmented industries, labor organizations might even be able to carry out the needed research in job design that none of the small employers could afford to undertake by themselves. Yet these opportunities are not easily seized in the union environment. Even if a union official reads an article on the discontents of work, he is unlikely to find time to pursue the subject unless it is forced upon him by pressures welling up within his organization. Such pressures did arise to move unions beyond wage bargaining to job security, fringe benefits, seniority, and other equitable safeguards. But members are much less likely to exert pressure for job enrichment, autonomous work groups, and other changes catering to subtler psychological needs. Most workers do not readily articulate these needs nor do they know much about the possible cures. In addition, employers do not seem to conceive of the union as an instrument for securing changes of this kind. The union, for its part, lacks management's familiarity with research. As a result, the labor leader does not put specialists to work on these problems or familiarize himself enough with existing literature to articulate these needs to the rank and file. Even if he did, implementation of new job designs would require local leaders of exceptional talent. Not only must they work well with management and elicit genuine cooperation from the men, they must also have a considerable grasp of the business and technological details involved in restructuring patterns of work and authority.

For these reasons, it is unlikely that unions will begin suddenly to play a major role in improving the quality of work. The task requires precisely the resources that unions find in such short supply: a capacity for research at headquarters and a corps of able local leaders to put new ideas to work in the shop and factory.

[7]Fred K. Foulkes, "Meaningful Work: A Study of Company Programs" (unpublished Ph.D. thesis, Graduate School of Business Administration, Harvard University, 1967).

In addition, real progress along these lines would require a special type of relation between labor, management and workers—one that employers as well as union leaders might find hard to accept. Most of the research on basic changes in job design suggests that the company must embrace the new concepts wholeheartedly, and make thorough efforts to insure that every echelon of management understands and supports the innovations being tried. Without these attitudes and preparations, different parts of the company work at cross-purposes, and the employees do not have enough confidence in management's intentions to cooperate fully. As a result, it seems doubtful that much progress can be made if unions have to force their employers to introduce changes in the content and design of work. Grudging compliance is simply not enough; there must be an atmosphere of mutual trust, and this is a climate that currently exists in only a minority of labor-management relations. The fault is not all on the side of management. In union ranks, there are many leaders who prefer to operate in an atmosphere of discontent and opposition. Without discontent, members may cease to believe that unions are necessary. Without an opponent, union officials may lack a symbol to use in whipping up militancy and determination among the rank and file. To these leaders, the newer concepts of work may be distasteful because they blur the lines between workers and management and weaken the adversary spirit.

In short, the prospects for union initiative are not bright. But they are not hopeless. Many unions do work in harmony with a number of employers. And practical experience, as well as research, testify to the fact that loyalty to the union can be strong however friendly the relations with management. On the other side of the table, employers are bound to be skeptical and suspicious of union proposals to alter the methods of work. Yet many of these changes do promise to improve productivity, and considerable experience has accumulated in some firms to demonstrate these results empirically. As a result, for all the difficulties, there are also opportunities that do not exist in other areas of bargaining, where the union's gain is inevitably management's loss.

Unions could conceivably reap enormous advantages if they should begin to interest themselves in the enrichment of work. To millions of members, particularly workers of a younger generation, there is the chance of being able to have a more meaningful, enjoyable experience during the working day. To organizers, there is the opportunity to learn much more about the needs and motivations of those who will be asked to join the union. To the labor movement itself, there is the possibility of gaining the interest and recognition that comes to organizations at work on the growing edge of important social problems. In the last analysis, it is only these possibilities that create any real hope for union action along these lines. For the obstacles are large enough—and the political incentives sufficiently slight—that no union leader can be expected to make much of a commitment without a vision of great reward, to himself, to his organization, or to his membership.

VII

SPECIAL TOPICS

Emergency Disputes

As the previous readings have indicated, collective bargaining is central to our present industrial relations system. Although the broad outline of our present system is widely accepted, many controversial issues still exist. In addition to substantive bargaining issues, there are also important questions involving the bargaining process. Our next two selections deal with one of the most frequently debated public policy issues in industrial relations—what the government should do when a collective bargaining dispute threatens to create a national emergency.

Willard Wirtz discusses the case for prohibiting such strikes by judicial injunction, government seizure of plants, or by compulsory arbitration. He maintains that the government role in emergency disputes should not be just to stop a fight or impose new terms on the parties, but should encourage the settlement of disputes by the parties themselves through the collective bargaining process. Given this objective, he argues for a "choice-of-procedures" approach whereby government mediators could recommend any one of a variety of government actions—including injuctions, seizure, and compulsory arbitration—if mediation fails. Not only would this approach take cognizance of the differences among labor disputes, but it would also encourage the parties to reach their own agreement by introducing greater uncertainty with regard to each party's costs and benefits if the government does intervene.

Some of the advantages of the choice-of-procedures approach can be obtained simply through compulsory arbitration, as the selection by Carl Stevens indicates. Compulsory arbitration has often been considered incompatible with collective bargaining because arbitrators frequently split the differences between the positions of the two parties, thus giving each party an incentive to take extreme positions rather than to make any concessions. As Stevens emphasizes, however, other approaches to compulsory arbitration are also possible. For example, it is possible to limit the arbitrator to accepting the position of one of the two parties. If this "one-or-the-other" criterion were accepted, then each party would have an incentive to make concessions in an effort to increase the chances that the arbitrator would choose its position as the more reasonable of the two alternatives. Moreover, the parties would also have an incentive to reach their own agreement rather than risk the possibility of an adverse decision by the arbitrator.

50. The "Choice-of-Procedures" Approach to National Emergency Disputes

W. Willard Wirtz

One possible conclusion from the debate about whether "emergency labor disputes" should be handled by injunction, seizure, compulsory arbitration, fact finding, or mediation is that the answer to this riddle lies perhaps less in any one of these devices than it does in all of them. Increasing emphasis is being placed upon "flexibility" as the essential quality in any satisfactory governmental approach to national crisis resulting from a collective bargaining stalemate. The key feature of a number of recent proposals is that the executive agency charged with responsibility in this area should be authorized to invoke, in a particular case, not a single preordained procedure but rather any one of several procedures.

This line of thinking starts from the simple fact that the elements in labor disputes, their causes and consequences, are invariably different. "Emergency" and "dispute" and "public interest" are being recognized as imprecise words, and "emergency dispute" as a term which is meaningless because it can mean so many different things. Experience with the procedure established in Title II of the Taft-Hartley Act has revealed its basic defect as being the prescription of a single form of compulsion for all "emergency disputes," regardless of circumstance or broader equities. There is a growing sense that there has been committed here the old mistake of assuming that since the

language offers a single phrase to label a set of troubles, there must be a single remedy available to cure them.

COLLECTIVE BARGAINING AND EMERGENCY DISPUTES

These proposals for flexible procedures depend, too, upon a more subtle and refined logic. If the function of government in the area of industrial dispute were simply to stop strikes when the public interest becomes sufficiently affected, there would appear neither need nor justification for consideration of a variety of procedures. The labor injunction does that job, usually with great dispatch. If, at the other extreme, government's function here were to fix the terms upon which arguments will be settled, then some form of compulsory arbitration would be the only thing worth talking about. The "choice of procedures" theory develops from the reasoning that the function of government in this area is neither just to stop a fight nor to settle an argument, but is rather to implement and possibly even to force the settlement of serious disputes *by the collective bargaining process*. It is realization of the protean nature of collective bargaining and of the desirability of making this process work even in crisis which gives the argument of government "flexibility" whatever strength it has. . . .

The essential quality of collective bargaining theory is that the "right" answers are those which are produced by the pressure of grouped ("collective") economic forces upon each other, dollars grouped in the corporate employer on the one hand, employees grouped in the union on the other. The rightness of the answers is defined, at least tentatively, in terms of the process which is relied upon to produce them. And it is recognized that, for better or for worse, the components of economic force which press against each other will vary widely with the various industries in which the bargaining process is used. There are basic differences in the character, financial structure, business prospects, organization, immediacy of public dependency, and degree of regulation in the coal, steel, transportation, and atomic energy industries. The forces which will exert pressure toward settlement in collective bargaining conferences in one industry will be ineffective or even nonexistent in another. Coal can be easily stored, and the industry is plagued by overproduction. Yet in transportation the situation is different, for there the nation's economic lifeblood flows through these arteries every minute and hour of the year. So "collective bargaining" too emerges as a single phrase covering an infinite variety of relationships—and basically dependent for its acceptance upon full realization that it is a form of letting free enterprise pursue freedom's essentially unscheduled course.

The "emergency dispute" issue becomes, in one way of stating it, whether the government will, when crisis results from private collective bargaining, turn to a form of compulsion or decision making lying entirely outside the collective bargaining scheme, or will, in the alternative, seek by special devices to make the bargaining process work despite the difficulties which have arisen. The case for the choice-of-procedures approach rests on the propositions that collective bargaining can and should be made to work even in these crises, but that this can be accomplished only if whatever governmental participation becomes necessary is geared to the essentially variable quality in the collective bargaining process. The corollary of this is, as has been stated, that the proper function of government in these cases is not just to stop an argument, nor to fix the terms for resolving it, but to implement its settlement by the parties themselves through the collective bargaining process.

THE 1949-1950 COAL CASE

Whatever substance there may be in these generalizations will better emerge by consideration, necessarily brief, of a specific case. The 1949-1950 coal case commends itself for this purpose not only for its illustration of the deadening effect upon collective bargaining of the single-compulsion form of governmental interposition in the dispute, but also because attempts were made in that case to introduce a kind of administrative "flexibility."[1]

The 1949-1950 coal strike went on, in one form or another, for about a year. Before it was over, the coal supply situation had become sufficiently acute that the Interstate Commerce Commission ordered reductions in train service, "coal emergencies" were declared in several states and by a number of cities, and scattered schools and institutions closed for lack of heat. Private collective bargaining had operated with notable ineffectiveness. Months of glaring across various tables had yielded what the presidential board of inquiry was subsequently to describe as "only a 'fantastic' assortment of vague demands"; the real issues had seemingly been buried deeper and deeper, while "the parties stood alternately in ceremonious insistence upon what would invariably be described subsequently as 'conditions precedent.' " The miners had kept insisting that agreement upon a wage increase was the "condition precedent" to any discussion of nonwage issues. The operators had been equally adamantine in demanding settlement of union security and other nonwage issues before they would discuss wages.

Special significance attaches to what happened at a collective bargaining session between the northern operators and the United Mine Workers Union on February 2, 1950. There, after these long months of sparring, union representatives made the following motion:

The mine workers move that we proceed to

---

[1] The author of this article was a member of the presidential board of inquiry in this 1949-1950 coal case. Comments made about it here are restricted to those for which there is basis in the published reports of the proceedings of that board.

negotiate a contract and that in the negotiations all matters before the conference are subjects for consideration and negotiation and are not to be considered as conditions precedent to agreement.[2]

Upon the introduction of this resolution, the operators withdrew from the conference.

Relatively close attention to the development of the 1949-1950 coal controversy warrants the conclusion that the union resolution at the February 2 session reflected a serious intention and desire to proceed finally with bargaining, which had been all form and no substance for the preceding ten or twelve months. There is similar basis for the conclusion that the operators' withdrawal from this conference reflected a decision that their bargaining position would be stronger if they waited the additional few days which were bound to bring presidential intervention under the Taft-Hartley Act and a consequent injunction against the strike in effect at that time.

A casting of moral judgments would permit the conclusion that the "fault" basic to the crucial February 2 development was that the union had waited to make its move until it was sure of rejection, that the government should have invoked the Taft-Hartley Act earlier, or that the operators' withdrawal was wholly unwarranted. But no moral judgment is either warranted or intended here. The point is simply this: Just when the 1949-1950 coal negotiations had reached a promising stage, bargaining broke down because one party recognized that its own inaction would result in the issuance of an injunction against the other party. The result, at least in part a product of the statutory inflexibility, was that there was no further bargaining in the ordinary sense.

The presidential board of inquiry was set up four days later. It resorted, in connection with the discharge of its fact-finding function, to what could probably be considered a minor experiment in flexible execution of the statutory obligation. Dispensing with the usual routine public hearings of statements by the parties, the board directed them instead to sit down and bargain—with the board members as observers. This was done. The "observed bargaining" session went on for eight hours.

[2]*The Labor Dispute in the Bituminous Coal Industry*, Report to the President, submitted by the Board of Inquiry under Executive Order 10106 (February 11, 1950), pp. 4-5.

This administrative tactic was reasonably successful so far as uncovering the basic issues (mainly money) and assessing responsibility (mutual) for the bargaining difficulties were concerned. This was at least partly, it may be guessed, because the parties couldn't quite make out what the board was up to, and accordingly cooperated fully because of a vague fear of the unknown price of any other course of action. But if there was expectation that this observed bargaining might also conceivably bring about a break in the negotiation stalemate, that hope was frustrated. No agreement was reached. The board filed its sterile report on February 11, and an injunction was issued against the strike immediately thereafter.

There can be no way of *proving* that the failure of collective bargaining efforts in the four weeks following the February 2 meeting in the 1950 coal case was a consequence of the statutory procedures. It is a subjective judgment that it was, although there is the obvious fact, too, that this stalemate did not set in with the institution of the statutory proceedings but had been going on for many months before. Throughout this crucial four-week period, the parties' attention was occupied by a whole series of legal developments which had nothing to do with the merits of the bargaining controversy: the issuance of a preliminary injunction, later of a more permanent order, the contempt hearing when the miners refused to go back to work, and then the court's ruling acquitting the union. There can be only conjecture as to whether these goings-on slowed up what would otherwise have been the pace of collective bargaining. To one thing, however, the record bears ample witness: Nothing done in the carrying out of the Taft-Hartley Act procedures hastened the settlement of the 1950 coal case by so much as an hour.

The circumstances of the final settlement of that case offer one additional element of possible relevance to the consideration of the efficacy of more flexible governmental procedures. Perhaps that settlement came as the result solely of economic forces or of the working out of the well-laid plans of shrewd bargainers, unaffected by anything the government did or didn't do. Yet it seems more than coincidence that the settlement which was reached finally on March 3 coincided almost to the hour with the President's transmission to Congress of a recommendation that the mines be seized. There had been leaks and rumors and some direct reports of the plans for such seizure for several days before. The parties to the dispute had obtained relatively clear pictures of what the terms of seizure would be. The chairman of the board of inquiry had been kept in close touch, as a specially designated White House representative, with the progress or lack of progress in the bargaining between the operators and the union. The general assumption was that the terms of the anticipated seizure would be geared in one way or another to the parties' bargaining positions. It seems a reasonable conclusion, although again a subjective one, that the prospect of governmental seizure was an important factor in affecting the timing and perhaps even something of the terms of the eventual 1950 coal dispute settlement.

This history has dual relevance to the present discussion. It illustrates the either neutral or negative effect of the Taft-Hartley Act emergency dispute provisions on the bargaining to which they are applied. It offers, beyond that, what is perhaps the closest approximation in federal government experience to the use of a choice-of-procedures approach. There was fact finding here, mediation, an injunction, and finally threatened seizure.

The possible significance of the record of governmental participation in the 1950 coal case lies in its suggestion that a procedure only slightly different from the one improvised by the board of inquiry and the President's office would have offered promise of substantial effectiveness. The difficulty was that from the time the board met, and even before, everyone knew exactly what the government representatives had to do and what they could not do—regardless of what the circumstances might seem to warrant. These predetermined procedures were in no way instruments for implementing or forcing collective bargaining. Because they were predetermined, they had lost their effectiveness.

It is reasonable to believe that if the 1950 board of inquiry had had, as it met with the parties, power to make a report recommending that any of a *variety* of dispute-settling procedures be followed, the union and the operators would have settled that case in early February (when the board met with them) instead of a month later. It may be seriously doubted whether, going back a step in the proceedings, the operators would have withdrawn from that February 2 bargaining conference if they had known that the consequent governmental inter-

vention might take the form of *either* an injunction against the union *or* seizure of the properties. It seems a conservative judgment that the intransigence of both parties in that case could have been substantially broken by responsible mediatory approaches by governmental representatives clothed with the authority to recommend publicly the institution of whatever procedures—injunction, seizure, fact finding with recommendations, compulsory arbitration—would have been considered best fitted to the circumstances if the intransigence persisted. The likelihood is that no actual resort to any of those courses would have proved necessary. The area of agreement which the parties found in a brief, ninety-minute session on March 3 was equally existent a month earlier, and there is fair reason to believe it would have been found then if the alternative had been the risking of uncertain procedural consequences.

ALTERNATIVES TO THE TAFT-HARTLEY APPROACH

... Judgment regarding any governmental disputes-settling procedure can be meaningful only in terms of alternatives. If the alternatives are (1) a statutory prescription that an injunction be obtained in all cases, or (2) a legislative authorization to the executive to use whichever of several procedures appears most appropriate in a particular case, the reasoning which supports the choice-of-procedures approach seems to find much firmer ground.

THE INJUNCTION

Support for the exclusive use of the injunction is based primarily (where something more is reflected than an uncomplicated feeling that unions are evil) on the feeling that the government's only appropriate function in an emergency of this kind is to stop its *immediate* cause (the strike) and that this is properly accomplished in the most direct manner available and without reference to fault, equity, or other consequence. It is questionable whether the injunction will in fact always work more quickly to restore production than would other procedures. But even if it did, there would remain the question of whether this gain of a few hours would warrant doing this much violence to the institution of collective bargaining and to the established traditions of freedom of enterprise from governmental interference. A cataloguing of the experience of democratic capitalism reveals that we have in the main accepted painful kicks in our economic shins as the price of letting private economic units settle their arguments in rough and tumble style, and further that where we have felt compelled to deny to one or another such unit the power to use its economic force, we have almost always set up an alternative procedure (as in the rate-setting procedures for utilities) for determining the issue which would otherwise have been determined by the use of that force.

Collective bargaining is the only process we recognize for settling industrial disputes. Where its functioning seems to break down, the appropriate government obligation would appear to be not just to order the argument stopped—on one party's terms—but rather to take whatever steps are available to make the parties themselves reach in timely fashion that solution to their dispute which experience shows has always been the eventual product of bargaining. And if the collective bargaining process is to be pliant, the government's hand must be free to act with discretion in aiding the parties to reach agreement.

FLEXIBILITY AND UNLIMITED EXECUTIVE POWER

Account must be taken of the protest that the choice-of-procedures type of law would create in the executive department that kind of discretion in the exercise of power which permits of its corruption. There can be no complete answer to this criticism. Yet it must be kept clear that the only practicable measure of the misuse of power is in terms of its effect upon the subjects of that use. When, under the present law, a strike is stopped by an injunction, the exercise of governmental power is no less real for its having been authorized by a statute passed years earlier by Congress. If that injunction is either unfair or ineffective as applied to the particular case, the evil of the exercise of centralized power is no less than if it resulted from either the inadvertent or malicious error of an executive or judicial officer armed with discretionary authority to apply the injunction. There is as much power exercised in the one case as in the other, and the auto-

maticity regulating the form of its exercise in the one instance is as great a potential source of injustice as is the possible abuse of discretion in the other. It has not been shown, and is probably not true, that the exercise of executive discretion in these situations would result in greater unfairness than does automatic application of a single legislative prescription. It does not appeal to reason to argue that recourse in all household emergencies to a particular bottle of patent medicine avoids the possibility of human error which arises if the doctor is called in.

The danger of abuse of executive power under "flexible" procedures is nonetheless real, however, for having its parallels. There has accordingly been a good deal of attention to various devices for counteracting or at least limiting this danger. These involve, in general, proposals for distribution of various parts of the function among different offices of government and for conducting the various procedures as openly as possible, probably with the participation of "public" representatives.

COMPULSORY ARBITRATION AND SEIZURE

Another criticism of the choice-of-procedures proposals is that the choice includes not only the injunction, which defeats collective bargaining in one way, but the alternatives of compulsory arbitration and seizure, which would defeat it in another. Here again there can be, in the absence of actual experiment, no completely confident answer to this reaction. It is essential that it be recognized, however, that the theory behind these proposals is that the availability of a variety of stern governmental devices will reduce the likelihood of any of them, or at least the worst of them, actually being used. There is in a sense a parallel here to the history of recent thinking about that other field of force. The nation grew up on the theory that building armaments was playing with matches, yet is moving now into adulthood on the perhaps desperate premise that armed power offers the only assurance that the arms will not have to be used.

MEDIATION AND MEDIATION PLUS

Mediation is accepted by the choice-of-procedures proponents as the form of governmental activity most compatible with collective bargaining. Their argument is that mediation will be more effective where the much less palatable alternatives of injunction *or* seizure *or* compulsory arbitration loom in the background. It was not seizure, but the *threat* of seizure, which seemed to break the deadlock in the 1949-1950 coal case. There is a good deal of reasonableness in the argument that a mediator would be better equipped to persuade, and the parties more inclined to accept persuasion or to make their own peace on their own terms, if that persuasion were backed up by power to institute alternative procedures if it failed. And it takes a strangely strong feeling about such a measure as compulsory arbitration wholly to understand the objection to it where every conceivable opportunity for reaching agreement in a national emergency has failed.

Recognizing the emphasis in the choice-of-procedures proposals on the central importance of the mediation process requires taking account of the possibility that the "best" answer in this troubled area may be a law providing only for mediation itself. Some of the most thoughtful students of the emergency disputes problem who have also had the fullest actual experience with it urge that there should be no law in this area except one recognizing the government's responsibility to bring the parties together and to reason with them—with no provision for added trimmings which might conceivably be helpful to the mediator in certain cases but which might also complicate his problem seriously in others.

Those who take this position of reliance solely on mediation oppose as strongly as do the choice-of-procedures advocates such arrangements as that embodied in the present statutory requirement for automatic imposition in all cases of an injunction. They subscribe equally to the idea that flexibility is a basically essential element in any governmental disputes-settling policy, and to the notion that the government's function even in these emergency cases is not just to stop a strike but to implement the settlement of the dispute by the parties themselves. The line between the two points of view is actually a thin one. This becomes clear in the light of the suggestion by those who would like to see the law provide only for mediation that if there is ever a "real" emergency which mediation cannot temper, the Congress will undoubtedly step in with some special legislative order, and if it doesn't, the President will. So in a sense the difference is

only between two approaches both primarily and basically dependent on mediation, both equally insistent upon creating broad governmental discretion, but one of which would provide in advance for certain last-resort procedures while the other would leave this matter entirely open until an emergency actually materializes.

In one important respect, however, the choice-of-procedures type of proposal meets an element of need which the exclusive reliance on mediation fails to recognize. There is a prevailing attitude on the part of people generally today—a "public" view—that the law should include some kind of firm insurance against work stoppages in essential industries. The attraction of the injunction is that it satisfies this general feeling, regardless of how unfair and ineffective it may actually prove in practice. And "mediation," especially when its nature as a form only of persuasion—without compulsion—is explained, falls far short of filling the prevailing public conception of the need which is involved here. It is part of the recommendation of the choice-of-procedures approach that it may both satisfy the public idea of the kind of thing that is needed to meet the emergency disputes problem and at the same time provide what is essentially a mediation process.

THE ROLE OF PUBLIC OPINION

It seems worth insisting that the popular reactions to a matter of this kind cannot properly be ignored, even though they may conceivably be the products of what experts in the field consider regrettable lack of complete understanding. . . .

PROBLEMS OF FLEXIBILITY

It is by no means clear that the choice-of-procedures kind of proposal offers the ultimate promise in this connection. . . .The laws [it calls] for would necessarily provide for what will appear to be complex procedures, not easily described or understood. This makes them susceptible to editorial or political attack in which a single feature, lifted from its context, can be used effectively to discredit the whole proposal. The adoption and retention of the automatic injunction procedure in the present law attests the fact that as the economy and society become more complex, and as the right answers become increasingly complicated, the wrong but simple answers enjoy a growing advantage in the political arena. There is, similarly, enough substance to the point about the danger of abuse of the discretionary authority contemplated by these plans to increase their vulnerability to political opposition....This was too rich fare for a political campaign, for there was no opportunity to go into details which would have been necessary to answer the broadside of criticism. Although legislative councils would permit of fuller exploration of such details, there would remain a considerable degree of danger on this score.

Such a statute would not, furthermore, wholly satisfy people's expectations for certainty from the law. If the answer to the question "What happens if there is a nationwide strike?" must start out "Well, that depends," a good many minds will not even entertain the rest of the explanation. People think of the law too much as something that ought to offer definite answers, recognizing it too little as an instrument for living with some problems to which there can be no clear or certain answers. Here again the nation's acceptance of the Taft-Hartley injunction formula illustrates the prospect that even a law offering bad answers will be accepted, if those answers are specific, in preference to a law which simply lays out an approach to seeking the right answers in the particular facts of a situation when it arises.

CONCLUSION

There is no justification here, however, for the cynicism of a conclusion that there just isn't any good answer to this problem. Recognition of the political difficulties which must be anticipated in seeking the adoption of a better type of legislation does not mean that any of them are insuperable....The increasing acceptance throughout the American body politic not only of the fact of powerful trade unions but also of their infinite potential for good is laying the basis for more objective consideration of what to do about such matters as "emergency disputes."

51. Is Compulsory Arbitration Compatible with Bargaining?

Carl M. Stevens

Although informed industrial relations opinion in the United States has traditionally opposed compulsory arbitration, there have been some recent indications of a change in this attitude.

Several factors may account for the development. Among them seems to be a growing conviction that in our interdependent, defense-oriented economy there are many situations in which, for one reason or another, a strike is not acceptable and therefore, for lack of an alternative, compulsory arbitration is inevitable.[1] The enactment by Congress in August 1963 of a compulsory arbitration statute to terminate a railroad dispute which threatened a nationwide railroad stoppage perhaps tended to confirm the view that, in certain circumstances, compulsory arbitration may indeed be "inevitable."

In addition, attention has been drawn to the fact that there are a growing number of situa-tions in which the right to collective bargaining is predicated upon giving up the right to strike. In these cases, at least, compulsory arbitration warrants consideration as a substitute. For example, President Kennedy's Executive Order 10988 extended collective bargaining rights to employees of the federal civil service, but precluded recognition of any labor organization which asserts the right to strike against the government. With reference to federal civil service bargaining, a union executive has been quoted: "... we feel that there should be some form of compulsory arbitration machinery in lieu of the right to strike."[2] ...

This paper is primarily concerned with one important issue, namely: Is compulsory arbitration of new contract disputes compatible with "genuine" collective bargaining? More particularly, an attempt will be made to delineate those properties of compulsory arbitration systems which are especially relevant to the issue.

A central point in the case against compulsory arbitration has long been that it is not compatible with collective bargaining, i.e., that resort to compulsory arbitration will attenuate and subvert collective bargaining. The availability of the strike strategy, it is argued, is such an essential part of collective bargaining that to

This paper, except for a few additions, was written during the author's 1962-1963 tenure of a Social Science Research Council Faculty Research Fellowship. The author wishes to express his thanks to Neil W. Chamberlain, John T. Dunlop, Stephan Michelson, Melvin W. Reder, and Jesse Simons for helpful comments on an earlier draft.

[1]For a recent expression of this view, see T. E. Lane, "Special Government Disputes Panel," *Proceedings of the Industrial Relations Research Association Spring Meeting* (Madison, Wis., 1964), p. 419.

[2]Quoted by Max S. Wortman, Jr., in "Collective Bargaining Strategy and Tactics in the Federal Civil Service," *ibid.*, p. 490.

preclude it, as by compulsory arbitration, is virtually to eliminate collective bargaining itself.[3] This proposition may not be as self-evident as most of its proponents seem to think. In what follows, an attempt is made to examine the functional role of the strike. The question is then raised whether some types of compulsory arbitration might not fulfill the more crucial functions of the strike and, in consequence, be compatible with collective bargaining.

FUNCTIONS OF THE STRIKE

Generally, the strike is a technique by means of which each party may impose a cost of disagreement on the other.[4] The central role usually assigned to the strike in analysis of collective bargaining is predicated upon the notion that a technique for imposing a cost of disagree-

[3]Similar evaluations have been made of the role of the strike in other industrial relations systems. For example, O. Kahn-Freund, in a discussion of British institutions, remarks: "Collective bargaining as we understand it is unthinkable without social sanctions. . . . Collective bargaining cannot work without the ultimate sanction of the strike and the lockout, no more than the law of, say, the sale of goods could work without the law of bankruptcy." See "Legal Framework," in Allen Flanders and H. A. Clegg, eds., *The System of Industrial Relations in Great Britain* (Oxford: Blackwell, 1954), p. 101.

[4]Strikes are of various kinds—for example, political strikes, economic strikes, demonstration strikes, bargaining strikes, etc. In this inquiry we will be concerned with strikes generally thought to be characteristic of the American industrial relations system, i.e., economic strikes to secure alterations in terms and conditions of employment in particular workplaces. My enumeration of strike functions is highly selective. Hopefully, those most important for the analysis have been included, but some omissions may be significant, e.g., that strikes may serve a valuable "catharsis" function.
The lockout is neglected at this stage of the discussion. This is, perhaps, warranted on the ground that ordinarily (with decentralized bargaining) the employer has no strategic need to lockout. He pays the wages. The employees either agree to work for these wages or not. If not, they may strike. If the employer resists their demands, he may "take" a strike. Thus, under ordinary circumstances, striking and taking a strike are the two sides of the direct action coin—rather than strike and lockout. The lockout may be strategically significant in the event that there is a bargaining alliance on the employers' side, e.g., the lockout may be used in an effort to forestall divide-and-conquer tactics by the union.

ment is necessary to invoke the processes of concession and compromise which are an essential part of normal collective bargaining negotiations.

In principle, a cost of disagreement might be imposed in other ways. However, the strike is more than just one way of discharging this function. Like the boycott, the strike reflects the symbiotic nature of the economic relationship involved. Thus the strike provides a kind of benchmark which may be helpful in arriving at a particular solution in negotiations. If the parties do strike, the outcome of the strike negotiations will be the solution, and in some instances this may be the only way in which a solution is available. Usually, however, the actual occurrence of a strike will not be necessary in order that the "particular solution" function be served. The expected cost of a strike will serve as a standard against which each party may weigh the expected cost of any given concession and hence determine the least favorable terms which will be acceptable to him.

Any institution possessing the above properties could be regarded as a "strike-like" institution in its functional relationship to the working of collective bargaining negotiations. Our central question then is: To what extent may compulsory arbitration exhibit these properties?

ARBITRATION AS A "STRIKE-LIKE" INSTITUTION

There is a tendency to use the term "compulsory arbitration" as if it referred unambiguously to a single kind of institutional arrangement. This is, of course, not the case. Compulsory arbitration arrangements may differ in a number of ways.[5] Thus, it is necessary at the outset to identify the type of compulsory arbitration with which we shall be concerned—at least in terms of those properties which are crucial for the analysis. Actually, it will be convenient to do this in two stages. Initially, we shall merely attempt a general characterization of the arbitration system contemplated. Later, more details can be added.

[5]For a discussion of this, see Orme W. Phelps, "Compulsory Arbitration: Some Perspectives," *Industrial and Labor Relations Review*, Vol. 18 (October, 1964), p. 91.

Compulsory arbitration institutions can and have combined compulsion and voluntarism in various ways.[6] For example, the Australian compulsory arbitration system includes a special kind of voluntary element in that individual parties may, so to speak, contract out of it.[7]...

A compulsory arbitration system which includes such a voluntary element involves a problem of choices very different from that of a compulsory system which does not contain such an element. The kind of compulsory arbitration with which we shall be concerned does not include this type of voluntary element. That is, our model assumes that the strike and lockout are precluded—the strike strategy is not available to the parties.[8]

[6]There is usually a voluntary "background" element in compulsory arbitration in democratic societies which may be viewed as a particular instance of the general proposition that in a democratic society it is not feasible to maintain political institutions which do not have the consent of the governed. British experience provides a nice illustration of this element. In 1951, the Conditions of Employment and National Arbitration Order 1305, which had been adopted during World War II, was replaced by Industrial Disputes Order 1376. In a discussion of these orders, O. Kahn-Freund emphasizes their cooperative nature, noting that Order 1376 was "...founded, like its predecessor, on an agreement between the T.U.C. and the B.E.C." *Op. cit.,* p. 92. Industrial Disputes Order 1376 ceased to have effect on March 1, 1959, and the organ of compulsory arbitration, the Industrial Disputes Tribunal, came to an end with it. In announcing this change, the Minister of Labour noted that the success of the compulsory arbitration system had very largely depended upon the willingness of employers and the unions to make it work during a critical period. He noted the Government's conclusion that in more normal times compulsory arbitration was not in keeping with British institutions. He also pointed out that it had become clear that the system no longer carried the assent of employers. See *Ministry of Labour Gazette,* November 1958 and January 1959.

[7]See Kenneth F. Walker, *Industrial Relations In Australia* (Cambridge, Mass.: Harvard University Press, 1956). For an account of more recent developments, particularly regarding penalties for illegal strikes, see J. E. Isaac, *Trends in Australian Industrial Relations* (Melbourne: Melbourne University Press, 1962).

[8]Generally speaking, compulsory arbitration and strikes are by no means necessarily mutually exclusive institutions either in practice or prescription. Again with reference to British experience, although a modified version of the compulsory arbitration system was retained under Industrial Disputes Order 1376, the right to strike was restored.

Another characteristic important for analysis is the question of who may invoke the arbitration authority. We begin with a model in which either party may request reference to arbitration. Thus, one or the other side may be coerced to participate in the arbitration process, and both are bound by the award. Since this is an arbitration system in which the strike and lockout are not available strategies, the parties must choose between agreement and arbitration. An additional characteristic of this model is that it is applied selectively to certain negotiations, i.e., it is not an economy-wide institution such as the Australian system.

Compulsory arbitration of this type provides an instrument through which each party may impose a cost of disagreement upon his opposite number. Generally speaking, it seems quite possible that a threat to arbitrate, much like a threat to strike, might invoke the negotiatory processes of concession and compromise which are characteristic of normal collective bargaining. Consider, for example, a party who is informed that if he adheres to his currently announced position at the deadline, his opponent will take him to arbitration. If, in the first party's view, there is a position that is less favorable to himself than his announced position, but more favorable than the probable arbitration award, he may be induced to retreat toward this position....

The parties' hypotheses about the *relationship* between the arbitration award and their prearbitration negotiation and positions may be a crucial determinant of their expectations about the award, as well as an important influence in other ways on their prearbitration negotiation. In the following section we examine the implications of several such hypotheses.

ARBITRATION CRITERIA AND NEGOTIATION

The parties' expectations about the relationship between an arbitration award and their own prearbitration negotiations depend on the criteria employed, and/or expected to be employed, by the arbitration authorities. For purposes of this section we may distinguish three categories of arbitration criteria: compromise, one-or-the-other, and principles. Much that may be said about these criteria will apply to their use in a variety of arbitration systems. More particularly, however, we will be concerned with the implications of resorting to them in the context of the arbitration model discussed above.

Compromise. There is a long history of opinion that arbitration "normally amounts to little more than an attempt to split the difference. . . ."[9]

The compromise criterion may be operative in an arbitration system whether the arbitration authority avows it or not. For example, the Australian system has apparently leaned quite heavily on various social and economic principles, such as a living wage, fair wages, ability to pay, and a number of macro-economic criteria. However, as Walker points out, although the tribunals have never openly adopted a compromise policy, their awards have often seemed to indicate that they were not unmindful of the advantages of compromise.[10]

The impact of the compromise criterion will depend somewhat on what difference is to be split. But whatever the precise nature of the compromise formula, it is hard to avoid the conclusion that its use under a system of strong compulsory arbitration will not be consonant with genuine prearbitration negotiation. In the type of system under consideration, either party may invoke compulsory arbitration. Hence, each party must be concerned with what is passed on to arbitration from prearbitration negotiation. Each party may feel that if he makes large demands and no concessions, this will tend to influence the arbitration award favorably. Walker says of the Australian system, "The parties often exaggerate their claims before tribunals in order to offset the result of a compromise decision."[11]

Clearly these attitudes will be likely if the arbitration authority is supposed to operate in terms of a naive compromise formula. Even if the compromise formula is more subtle, however, it may be hard to contrive a compromise-based compulsory arbitration system in which the parties view their prearbitration concessions as nonprejudicial to the arbitration outcome.

In general, then, with a strong compulsory arbitration system operating under the compromise criterion, we would expect prearbitration negotiation to generate a very different record from that generated by nonarbitrated negotiation. This type of compulsory arbitration is unlikely to serve simply as an adjunct to something resembling "normal" collective bargaining. Rather, it constitutes a different kind of negotiation system—one in which the parties view themselves (from the outset) as in an adversary relationship before a tribunal.

One-or-the-other. Under the one-or-the-other criterion, the parties know that the arbitrator will present as its award the final prearbitration position of one party or the other.[12] Precisely what is meant by the "final prearbitration position" depends on the types of procedures followed in the prearbitration and arbitration phases. It will be helpful to distinguish two types.

Type I. Phase 1: direct negotiation between the parties with no third-party participation. Phase 2: the arbitration authority makes its decision with no further hearing, i.e., on the basis of the record generated by the parties during Phase 1.

Type II. Phase 1: as above. Phase 2: the arbitration authority makes its award after a hearing, i.e., the parties present their cases during the arbitration phase, and the arbitration authority is tripartite, composed of representatives of the parties as well as (a minority) of impartial third-party members.

Under Type I, the final prearbitration positions are those occupied by the parties just before the arbitration phase begins. Under Type II, because of the provision for a hearing and because of the tripartite nature of the arbitration authority, the arbitration phase itself is very apt to involve negotiations. Hence, the final prearbitration positions to which the one-or-the-other criterion refers may be positions

---

[9]See, for example, "The Conciliation and Arbitration of Industrial Disputes—II: The Machinery of Conciliation and Arbitration: An Analysis," *International Labour Review*, XIV (December, 1926), 852.

[10]Walker, *op. cit.,* p. 307.

[11]*Ibid.,* p. 307. In this connection, it is an interesting feature of the federal machinery in Australia that the law provides that the awards must keep within the range of claims of the parties.

[12]Professor Reder has pointed out to the writer that this criterion really represents one particular case of a class of criteria, i.e., one could generate a large number of cases by permitting the arbitrator to choose among functions of the final offers rather than the final offers themselves. He has also commented that it is not intuitively obvious that the particular case selected for attention here is the optimal one.

occupied during the arbitration phase, but before the authority has rendered its decision.

Under Type I, the one-or-the-other criterion is well designed to encourage genuine prearbitration negotiation. Generally speaking, this criterion generates just the kind of uncertainty about the location of the arbitration award that is well calculated to recommend maximin notions of prudence to the parties and, hence, compel them to seek security in agreement. Moreover, under this criterion—and unlike the case under the compromise criterion—there is no reason to suppose that big claims may be rewarded and concessions penalized. Indeed, expectations may tend to be the other way around, as each party may assume that the arbitrator will reject an "exaggerated" position in favor of an opponent's more moderate claim.

The writer knows of no examples of Type I compulsory arbitration of new contract disputes operated under the one-or-the-other criterion. In principle, such a system would run the danger of generating unworkable awards and, hence, of breaking down. This would be likely if for some reason the system failed to evoke genuine prearbitration negotiation. In this case, the arbitration authority might be forced to choose between two extreme positions, each of which was unworkable to one (or even both) of the parties. Although this danger exists in principle, there is no prima facie reason why it would be likely to eventuate in practice. Indeed, assuming that the parties are not deliberately attempting to subvert the system, this very danger might provide them with additional incentive to seek security in agreement.

Under Type II, the one-or-the-other criterion is also well designed to encourage genuine negotiation, and what has been said about Type I applies here as well. Two major differences may be noted. The arbitration hearing phase under Type II is very apt to involve mediation; this may be an advantage. Also, under Type II, the independent members have considerable control over the outcome. They will vote with one side or the other to establish the award, and this provides them with potentially usable power. Thus, for example, the independent members may convey to party A that his position seems unreasonable, and therefore they see no real choice but to vote with party B. Across the hall, so to speak, the same point (in reverse) may be made to party B, i.e., that the neutral members see no real choice but to vote with party A. Working both sides of the street in this

fashion, the neutral members may be able to induce the parties to converge on an outcome deemed by them to be appropriate. From one point of view, this may be an advantage in that it helps to preclude the situation in which the arbitration authority is forced to choose one of two unworkable or undesirable positions. (Neutral member power of this kind may not, however, be an unmixed blessing, as the discussion in the next section will suggest.)

British Wages Councils (a statutory minimum wage-fixing device) provide an institutional analogue to our Type II.[13] The boards of the Wages Councils are composed of equal numbers of employers' and workers' representatives and an odd number of independent members. In describing council procedure, Bayliss says, "The independent members of a council can vote with one side or the other and so break a deadlock, but they have no power of initiative. The work of a council depends on both sides being willing either to come to agreement or to put forward motions for which the independent members are prepared to vote."[14] The jurisdictional scope (terms and conditions of employment) of the councils is broad. This consideration, Bayliss notes, combined with the rights of employers and trade unions to request the establishment or abolition of councils, has made the distinction between voluntary collective bargaining and statutory wage-fixing as narrow as it could be and still be compatible with Parliament's ultimate responsibility under the system.

Principles. Under the principles system, the parties believe that the arbitration authority will establish its award on the basis of one or more social and/or economic principles, e.g., ability to pay, cost of living, various macroeconomic criteria, etc. As previously noted, the Australian system exhibits this posture.

[13]For an illuminating account, see F. J. Bayliss, *British Wages Councils* (Oxford: Blackwell, 1962). The councils were not established as arbitration authorities (in any direct and simple sense), but to provide for the legal enforcement of minimum terms and conditions of employment in certain trades and industries. They exhibit a number of features which are not attributed to our Type II, e.g., council awards apply to whole trades or industries, such awards are referred to the Minister who may approve them or refer them back, etc. The point is not that the councils are identical with Type II, but rather that some of their properties are analogous to crucial properties of Type II.

[14]*Ibid.,* p. 80.

The consequences of this system for negotiation between the parties depend very much upon the particular principles supposed to be employed by the arbitration authority. One may think of a number of principles which might be employed, but no attempt will be made to enumerate and analyze them all here.[15] Rather, we shall simply mention certain characteristics of principles which will be significant in the light of the foregoing analysis. If compulsory arbitration of this kind is to be consonant with and is to encourage collective bargaining, the principles upon which the awards are based must be such that the parties have appropriately divergent expectations about the award and/or appropriate uncertainty with respect to it. A simple principle (e.g., that awards shall follow a cost-of-living index, or that awards shall follow other settlements which are identified) will tend to lead the parties to the same expectations about the outcome. Hence, however meritorious such principles might be on some grounds, they would not be well contrived from the point of view of compatibility with collective bargaining. Uncertainty which might encourage collective bargaining could be introduced by the use of a rather complicated set of principles (e.g., various criteria adduced in wage negotiations). However, unless the arbitration authority could devise a technique for actually basing awards on a combination of principles, it might find itself using the principles to rationalize awards which basically were simply compromises.

Moreover, an arbitration institution incorporating the principles criterion confronts a basic difficulty. From one point of view, the job of compulsory arbitration is to manage industrial disputes without resort to direct action by the parties. In this view, one solution achieved without strike or lockout is as good as any other solution—insofar as discharge of the task assigned to arbitration is concerned. Whether, in a particular instance, the parties like compulsory arbitration or not, its dispute-precluding function may seem to have a certain legitimacy—even to them.

If arbitration awards are to be based on principles, however, it is no longer true that one settlement is as good as any other. The principle employed selects the "right" settlement, e.g., one which is consistent with a national wages policy aimed at holding the line on inflationary money wage increases, It is frequently pointed out that society may well have as important and as legitimate an interest in "correct" outcomes of collective bargaining negotiations as it has in the achievement of an outcome without a work stoppage. Nevertheless, in the context of an industrial relations system such as our own, an arbitration institution designed to serve, say, a national wages policy (rather than merely to preclude stoppages) may well appear to the parties to represent a perversion of the proper function of arbitration. And consequently, such an arbitration institution may be basically unacceptable in a way that another is not. . . .

CONCLUSION

The argument of this paper leads to the conclusion that a strong compulsory arbitration system may be compatible with collective bargaining. By a "strong" system is meant one in which (1) resort to a strike or lockout is really precluded, (2) either party can invoke arbitration (in which event it is never refused), and (3) a tripartite arbitration authority (or a one-party authority operating without a hearing) bases its awards on the one-or-the-other principle. The availability to the parties of an arbitration strategy under this type of system would seem to serve some of the functions usually associated with a strike strategy. For example, the arbitration stategy affords a technique for imposing a cost of disagreement and thus for evoking the negotiatory responses of concession and compromise.

---

[15]There is a long history of search for arbitration principles. For an interesting earlier discussion, see A. C. Pigou, *Principles and Methods of Industrial Peace* (London: MacMillan, 1905). On the basis of considerations relating to diminishing marginal utility, Pigou was led to conclude (p. 43), "There is, in short, *prima facie* ground for believing that arbitrators, in framing their awards, ought to take account of the relative wealth of the different parties concerned." A potential source of arbitration principles is to be found in the criteria frequently adduced by the parties themselves in wage negotiations. See Sumner H. Slichter, *Basic Criterion Used in Wage Negotiations* (Chicago: Chicago Association of Commerce and Industry, 1947).

Public Employee Bargaining

In the past few years, collective bargaining has become important in the public as well as in the private sector. To many, this development has been a source of much satisfaction; others, however, view the increase in union power among state and local government employees with considerable alarm. Everett Kassalow discusses some of the reasons for the increase in unionism among public employees and suggests several ways of improving collective bargaining procedures in the public sector.

Harry Wellington and Ralph Winter analyze the relative merits of collective bargaining in the public and private sectors. They argue that the social cost of collective bargaining is small in the private sector because firms are generally under considerable economic pressure to resist wage demands by unions that would lead to large cost increases. On the other hand, local government officials are said to be under much less economic pressure to resist union demands. Moreover, Wellington and Winter argue that voters (and thus public officials) are concerned primarily with the inconveniences resulting from a strike. Thus the strike is a particularly potent weapon for government employee unions and gives them an unfair advantage over other interest groups with competing claims on municipal government.

This analysis by Wellington and Winter is disputed in the selection by John Burton and Charles Krider, who argue that it may often be more equitable for public employee organizations to pursue their objectives through collective bargaining rather than by lobbying in the political arena. Thus Burton and Krider would allow strikes by most government employees. However, they would still prohibit strikes by policemen and other public employees who provide essential services. For such workers, they agree with Wellington and Winter that disputes must be settled by some nonstrike procedure, such as compulsory arbitration.

52. Trade Unionism Goes Public

Everett M. Kassalow

Strikes of public employees, once a novelty, are no longer unusual. During one three-month period, not so long ago, a casual check showed social workers' strikes in Chicago, Sacramento, and White Plains; slowdowns of firefighters in Buffalo and of policemen in Detroit; strikes among university maintenance employees at Ohio State, Indiana, and the University of Kansas Medical Center; a three-day "heal-in" by the interns and residents of the Boston City Hospital; "informational" picketing, with a strike threat, by the Philadelphia School Nurses' Association; teachers' strikes in a dozen communities, ranging from West Mifflin, Pennsylvania, and Gibraltor, Ohio, to South Bend, Indiana, and Baltimore, Maryland. Such strikes and slowdowns among teachers, policemen, firemen, etc., have become daily occurrences. Because there had been a growing feeling that industrial relations were becoming more "mature," strikes of this sort in sectors hitherto unidentified with unionism have led to confusion. Large-scale unionization of government workers is a relatively new phenomenon in this country, although it has been common in almost all other democratic industrial countries of the world. That large-scale public-employee unionism was also inevitable in the United States at some time is clear. But why now? What new forces account for the current upsurge of public unionism?

I. THE RESPECTABILITY OF UNIONS

The first of these forces has been the institutionalization of trade unionism in American life. Unions date back more than 150 years in the United States. But large-scale unionism dates only from the late 1930's, and it has only been in the past decade or so that collective bargaining has become widely accepted as the appropriate way to settle wages and working issues. During this decade unionists have become respectable. Union leaders have been named to innumerable presidential commissions dealing with every conceivable problem area of the country's foreign and domestic business.

It is not surprising thus that, despite the revelations in the senate investigations of the malfeasance of Jimmy Hoffa and a few other union leaders, public opinion surveys show that union officers have registered a significant gain in occupational prestige between 1947 and 1963. This gain is clearly attributable to the widespread acceptance of the basic value of unionism in society, and this legitimacy is being transferred to public employees as well. For this reason, unionism among government workers has begun to advance rapidly, and there is every prospect it will continue to grow.

There is a second, more specific reason for the recent growth of government unionism, and

380

this is Executive Order 10988 issued by President John F. Kennedy in January 1962, which encouraged unionism in the federal service. In its support of public unionism, this order was as clear and unequivocal as the Wagner Act of 1936 had been in its support for unions and collective bargaining in the private sector. It declared that "the efficient administration of the government and the well-being of employees require that orderly and constructive relationships be maintained between employee organizations and management."

In New York City, earlier orders issued by Mayor Robert Wagner resulted in the "breakthrough" of unionism in 1961 among 44,000 teachers. Kennedy's order has a spillover effect in legitimating unionism in states and local public service. Further, the reapportionment of state legislatures seems to have had a generally liberalizing effect, and a flow of new legislation in a dozen states has expedited public employee bargaining.

The enormous growth in public employment has also acted to transform the status of the government worker. Between 1947 and 1967, the number of public employees increased over 110 per cent (see Table 1). (During the same

A New Kind of Worker

The spread of unionism among government civil servants and teachers is a partial answer to the old question of whether substantial numbers of white-collar employees can be unionized. It is true that much of the growth of public unionism, principally the American Federation of State, County and Municipal Employees and the American Federation of Government Employees (which operates at the federal level) has been among blue-collar employees. (Over two-thirds of the AFL-CIO's State, County and Municipal Employees union, for example, are blue-collar workers.) But some important footholds have been gained among white-collar workers and (because teachers are the largest number unionized) among professionals.

Between 20 and 25 per cent of all local and state employees are teachers, and it is among them that the significant contest in unionization has been taking place. For the organization of teachers has had its impact not only in traditional union circles, but also among other associations of public service employees that formerly limited themselves to fraternal and professional questions. Prominent among these is

Table 1

Public Employment Trends *

	1947	*1967*
All Public Employment	5,474,000	11,616,000
Federal employment	1,892,000	2,719,000
State and local employment	3,582,000	8,897,000

*The public employment increase since 1947 has been primarily in the state and local sector. According to U.S. Labor Department projections, between 1965 and 1975 this same sector will increase by an additional 48 per cent, whereas total private employment will only grow some 24 per cent.

period, private nonagricultural employment increased only 42 per cent.) Clearly, the day has passed when being a civil servant is a prestigious matter. At a time when unions and bargaining have become increasingly accepted elsewhere in the society, this expansion of public employment, with its consequent bureaucratization and depersonalization of relationships, has undoubtedly encouraged unionization in the public sector.

the National Education Association (NEA). Under competition from the AFL-CIO American Federation of Teachers (AFT), the NEA has radically altered its views on bargaining in recent years. From a reluctant acceptance of only "professional negotiations," combined with opposition to strikes, the NEA now is at the point where some of its affiliates sign fullscale collective agreements. At its convention in 1967, the NEA even came to accept strikes, where circumstances render them necessary. In the fall of 1967, the Governor of Florida was led to denounce NEA activities in that state for seeking "blackboard power."

In the large cities, such as New York, Chicago, Detroit, Boston, and Philadelphia, the AFT has won bargaining rights. In smaller cities the NEA has led the way and has won sole bargaining rights in Denver, Milwaukee, Niagara Falls, and a few other fairly middle-sized cities. Some NEA officials argue that the turn of teachers to AFL-CIO unionism in the large cities reflects administrative breakdown in those areas where educational systems are contracting, equipment is aged, and population is fleeing to the suburbs. The NEA points out that in far western cities such as Seattle, San Diego, Portland, and Los Angeles, where educational systems are still expanding and plant is still relatively new, the AFT has not made serious inroads. These cities as well as some others in the Middle West that are still unorganized (such as, for example, Minneapolis and St. Paul) are the likely battlegrounds in the next few years of teacher unionism. The likelihood is that the AFT will become dominant in the large, urban areas, whereas the NEA will hold its strength in smaller towns and possibly generally in the South. Some top AFT leaders have begun to talk about greater cooperation and even a possible merger with the NEA. The NEA with a membership close to a million will, in any case, be of continuing national influence on educational policy.

Like the NEA, other independent state and local public employee associations whose activities until recently have largely been limited to welfare and fraternal programs, are now turning their attention to collective bargaining. These associations, strong among white-collar employees, include, at the state level alone, over 400,000 members who, in turn are loosely grouped into a national joint body. These associations have the additional advantage, in some states, of being favored by public managers.

As is clear from the many strikes reported, a great many different groups in the public sector are on the move. To the extent that one can judge, the new unrest seems to be greatest among those who have very clearly identifiable professions and/or strategic occupations. Teachers, for example, have clearly been in the forefront of public employee labor agitation in the past few years. Nurses have begun to make demands in the large cities. Social workers, a group with old traditions in public employee bargaining, are extending their organization significantly. Firemen and policemen have been revealing a new militancy. In their summer 1968 conventions the AFL-CIO's fireman's union and the independent American Nurses Association both removed clauses prohibiting strikes from their respective constitutions. In contrast, such professional groups as engineers and architects (admittedly employed on a much smaller scale in the public sector than either teachers or nurses) are much less affected. These occupations continue to enjoy a generally more favorable labor market than the other professionals, and this would seem to be a clue to the difference.

Because it is likely that legislation encouraging collective bargaining in the near future will be enacted in more states, unionism at this level will clearly grow. The Department of Labor has projected that local and state employment will exceed 10 million by 1970, and unionism in this sector must almost inevitably grow in importance on the American labor scene.

Unions in Public Employment

The sharp increase in collective bargaining in the public service has served to offset the decline in traditional unionism (see Tables 2 and 3).[1] Whereas union membership in the private sector actually fell from 17.189 million to 16.467 between 1956 and 1964, union membership among government workers increased from .915 million to 1.453 million during the same period. The economic boom since 1964 has led to a broad increase in national union membership, but union membership continues

[1] Note that Tables 2 and 3 are based on different sources. The second is taken from AFL-CIO reports, and reflects that body's affiliated unions' per-capita membership payments to the Federations, of an average annual basis, during the biennial period indicated. The first table is based on U.S. Department of Labor data, and it includes some independent unions as well as the AFL-CIO affiliates. For a number of reasons, the reports of the latter to the Department of Labor are often somewhat higher than their payments to the AFL-CIO. Finally, it should be noted that the Department of Labor reports do not include, in their over-all union count, such bodies as the National Education Association or the American Nurses Association, important segments of which have begun to bargain and sign collective agreements in recent years.

Table 2

Trade Union Membership, U.S. Based Unions (000's), 1956-1966

	1956	1964	1966
Nongovernment	17,189	16,467	17,409
Government	915	1,483	1,717

Table 3

Membership Changes AFL-CIO and Selected Unions 1956-1967 to 1966-1967 (000's)

	1956-1957	1960-1961	1966-1967	Per cent Change 1956-1957 to 1966-1967
AFL-CIO	12,883	12,482	13,781	7
American Federation of Government Employees	56	68	196	250
American Federation of State, County and Municipal Employees	147	188	297	102
American Federation of Teachers	48	57	125	160

to grow more rapidly in government than in the private economy.

Three public unions have been in the forefront of this general advance: As a percentage of total union membership, government unions rose from approximately 5 per cent in 1956 to 8 per cent in 1964, and 9 per cent in 1966.

Thus between 1956-1957 and 1966-1967 the AFL-CIO as a whole (including its rapidly growing government unions) made a modest recovery from its decline to the early 1960's and managed to increase its membership by 7 per cent. But during this same ten-year period public employee unions have doubled and tripled their membership. Even these figures, based as they are on biennial averages, understate the current membership *for public employee unions.* By the end of 1968 the American Federation of Government Employees (AFGE), which organized federal workers, had jumped to 300,000. Some of AFGE's victories in bargaining rights elections such as a 21,000 employee air base unit in September 1968 have

been reminiscent of the CIO's organization of mass production industries of the late 1930's. The progress of the State, County, and Municipal Employees (AFSCME) has been made in smaller units, but it had reached 400,000 late in 1968.

The rapid expansion of membership among the federal unions, state, county, and municipal and teachers' unions has been accompanied by the sort of internal turmoil that usually goes with growth. Major conflicts for top union leadership positions have erupted in all three of these public employee unions during the past half dozen years. As membership rolls and treasuries expanded, moreover, and full-time elected and appointive posts opened up, struggles also occurred at the regional and local levels. With the prospect for continuing, substantial membership growth, we can expect relatively high instability and at least a fair amount of election conflict to continue among the officials of these unions.

We can also expect the leaders of the rapidly

expanding public employee unions to move into larger roles in the top councils of the AFL-CIO itself. One reason why this has not been true up to now is the persistence of a long-standing conflict between the AFGE and some of the older, craft unions who want the AFGE to limit itself to white-collar, classified employees, and leave blue-collar unionizing in air bases, shipyards, ordinance depots, and the like to craft unions, notably the Metal Trades Council, which has long been active among these government employees. This the AFGE has refused to do. Early in 1967 it publicly opposed the official stand taken by the AFL-CIO (and the Metal Trades Council) before a congressional committee considering new legislation to reorganize those government wage boards which have the power to set wage rates for federal blue-collar employees.

Still it cannot be long before some of the leaders of the leading public employee unions will be accorded seats on the AFL-CIO top executive council. Union size has always been one significant factor in the choice of the twenty-nine member council. The State, County, and Municipal Workers Union is already among the ten larger unions in terms of membership size. Its leader, the pugnacious Jerry Wurf, will probably receive a council seat. The American Federation of Government Employees may also be close to that level by the 1970 convention. Aside from size, the AFL-CIO will also stand to benefit from a more representative public image when teachers and other government employee representatives help to make up its executive council.

II. PUBLIC MANAGEMENT AND COLLECTIVE BARGAINING

The growth of unionism in the public sector has been so rapid that public management has found it difficult to assimilate it in recent years. Even with the best intentions, the process would pose problems to public managers who until recently have had complete authority in personnel matters, within civil service laws and regulations. In many cases the older practices of benevolent paternalism persist, and new ideas about bargaining come slowly. Even though unionism has become accepted in every major industry, the personnel officers in government often have little notion of how to deal with a

union, and episodes quaintly reminiscent of labor history thirty years ago frequently occur. One federal union organizer describes his experience in dealing for the first time with an old line air-base personnel director. The union had only recently won its exclusive bargaining rights, and the organizer led his committee into a small personnel office. The director sat behind a small table and told the union committee to remain standing in the crowded office as it prepared to present its demands. The organizer refused to negotiate under these circumstances and eventually a larger office and a large table and sufficient chairs were found. Eventually, too, the old personnel director was eased out of his position. At various levels, this experience has been and will be repeated countless times before the new bargaining process takes hold.

The civil service commissions present the most fundamental problem. In the federal government, as well as in many states, these bodies have been the unilateral source of rules and regulations for government employees. In the first stages of the new unionism, these commissions have become the principal management authority. But these commissions often serve both as employer and arbiter, and determine what groups of employees can or should be grouped together for bargaining purposes, or what the proper scope or area of this bargaining should be. In private unionism, the NLRB has been the arbiter of such questions, and it is unlikely that the government unions will allow the "employer" both to make such crucial determinations and also to bargain.

It is sometimes difficult to remember that one of the original reasons for the creation of civil service commissions was to protect the employees from political attack and insecurity of tenure. To trade unions, seeking to assert their rights and to modify old rules and regulations, the commissions now appear primarily as retrograde authority. Thus, efforts by the federal government to continue the Civil Service Commission as executor of the various federal laws regulating employment, while trying to graft on to it new rights and duties of administration in the new collective bargaining process, have drawn much criticism. The "depression psychology" and its memories of insecurity has come to an end in the minds of most government workers today, and similarly the old "concept of Civil Service," as President Jerry Wurf of the American Federation of State,

County and Municipal Employees has argued, "falls by the wayside." Wurf notes that his "own union's early history was concerned with the bettering of the Civil Service. But, if you look at Civil Service today, it is really a management tool, which is unilaterally established, and the workers have no say in how it functions."

Several states have already acted to empower a separate new agency to certify unions, help select mediators and arbitrators, define union rights and protections, etc., and the federal government is seriously considering similar action. Clearly, what most public employee unions want is their own version of the Wagner Act's National Labor Relations Board to do for collective bargaining in the public sector what the NLRB did for the private sector in the 1930's. Civil Service Commissions just don't fit that picture, and many are likely to be phased out of this new area of public administration.

Strikes in the Public Service

No subject in recent years has provoked as much heat as the matter of strikes among public employees. It is probably the most difficult problem in the public employee field. Even expert arbitrators and mediators, men of hard-headed, pragmatic experience, have taken surprisingly rigid, ideological positions on this matter.

Curiously, this issue is being debated as though the American experience was unique. But the fact is that many other countries have faced this same problem, and a wide range of solutions have been tried. Some countries have substituted compulsory arbitration for the right to strike, thereby presumably offering the unions a fair alternative to break "impasse" situations. Other countries have widely conceded public employees the right to strike, though a few groups such as policemen, firemen, or the military may be excepted by law or voluntary agreement.

Although the United States has its own history, it is difficult in the light of experience both here and in other nations, to swallow the categorical judgment of a distinguished American labor arbitrator that: "Neither compulsory arbitration nor strikes are appropriate in public employment relations." His argument rests on the traditional citizen-taxpayer's absolute right "to establish priorities of competing executive agencies." But this does not take into account the countless ways in which this absolute fiscal right has been transferred to independent boards of education, transport authorities, public utility agencies and the like, over the years.

Before taking hard and arbitrary positions, it is well to put strikes in a proper perspective. Over the past two decades or so, strikes in the United States have generally been declining. Occasional upsurges occur, particularly during periods of war or defense—induced inflation, but generally the number of strikes have declined as union-management relations have matured. There is good reason to believe that, once the organizing phase is over, public employee unions will prove even less strike prone than those in private industry. For one thing, working conditions are generally more secure and often more pleasant and less onerous than in private industry. For this reason it is important to note that as unionism and the bargaining process is extended for the first time to millions of new employees and new institutions (public agencies) considerable friction and tension will occur. The very inexperience of the new union leaders and the public managers guarantees this. But neither should the historic trajectory of unionism be ignored either.

Because there are inherent difficulties in the adjustment to new bargaining public officials need to approach these difficulties with caution, rather than be obsessed with strikes and punishment for strikes. Admittedly, in today's transition period, most cities or states are not likely to concede the right to strike to public employees. However, rather than setting forth elaborate punishment systems for strikes which may occur, officials should take positive steps, wherever possible to improve relations.

The Need for Procedures

New unions are generally very much concerned about their own security and legitimacy. Public authorities, by law and by practice, ought to expedite ways and means of extending recognition, and exclusive recognition where the union demonstrates its majority status. Attempts to provide for clumsy proportional representation of employee groups by competing unions or associations should be avoided. The principle of granting a union that represents a majority sole and exclusive bargaining rights has been found to work best, by far, in the United States, and becomes the eventual guarantee of mature relationships.

But even with the best of intentions there will be some impasses and some seemingly irreconcilable conflicts. To deal with these, state and/or local legislation has to spell out, in advance, the kinds of procedures open to parties to resolve these difficulties. If the procedures are known before, there will be fewer "crises," for it is when procedures must be improvised at the last moment that one side or the other feels "put upon." Some states have had success with provisions that stipulate that, in the event of an impasse, the parties accept a fact-finding inquiry. Such recommendations often carry great weight in inducing the parties to accept a settlement. Arbitration may be a possible solution for public employee-management disputes in critical areas. Even though this would involve a break with the tradition of bargaining in the private sector, such history cannot be a direct guide for public bargaining. The almost accidental way in which New York City's sanitation strike, early in 1968 ended in a *joint* submission to arbitration is an indication that new pressures can lead to the acceptance of hitherto rejected solutions.

The operation of the so-called Taylor Law in New York State illustrates the problem with punitive legislation. Despite provisions banning public employee strikes, with penalties such as dismissal or the withdrawal of recognition or check-off rights from the unions, etc., the law did not head off the New York City teachers' strike or the sanitation strike. If anything the withdrawal of the teachers' union check-off of dues and the eventual imprisonment of the local union's president Albert Shanker for fifteen days, in the wake of the 1967 New York City strike, seems to have kept union militancy at a high pitch long after the strike was over.

Theodore Kheel, an experienced mediator of New York City public employee disputes, has attacked the Taylor Law on the ground that "by prohibiting strikes of public employees, the law eliminates collective bargaining. . . ." It also creates a bad atmosphere for bargaining, Kheel contends, by compelling unions to exert pressure through threats to violate the law. Kheel's critique of the Taylor Law and its pat formula is quite cogent. But in his refusal to make any distinction between public and private collective bargaining, so far as the right to strike is concerned (though he does not rule out strikes by policemen and firemen as "unthinkable") he

does go too far. One should not anticipate that in all states, or in the federal government, collective bargaining must necessarily take on all the features of private bargaining including the right to strike for most employees.

It does not seem that the strike issue will be important in *federal* labor-management relationships. A liberal managerial policy, including important wage and benefit improvements in the past decade, has set a good framework. In his recent appearance before a special government committee reviewing experience to date under Federal Executive Order 10988, AFL-CIO President George Meany concluded that the order "has brought significant improvements in labor relations within the federal government." Although Meany recommended a number of changes in the workings of the new system, he did not question the legislative ban on strikes in the federal service. Nor did the AFL-CIO December 1967 convention resolution on federal employee bargaining say anything about the existing legal prohibition on strikes by federal government employees. Most of the unions which deal with federal employees have a voluntary strike ban provision in their constitutions.

At the state and local level, where organizing has met with more resistance, the strike issue remains more troublesome. Even here, in the words of AFSCME President Wurf, whose own union jealously defends the right to strike, at least

The debate [now] seems to center around the right to strike, rather than the right to organize and bargain. . . . It seems only yesterday . . . that the right to bargain was at stake. . . . Now the right to strike is what is being discussed. . . . As painful as the situation is at times, it is an important step forward.

From what has already been suggested, bargaining in the public sector has to be viewed as an evolving process. What might seem to be best today, is likely to be obsolete tomorrow. The first written agreement between General Motors Corporation and the United Automobile Workers Union signed some thirty years ago was a one-page memorandum. Twenty-five years later it was a printed contract running over 200 printed pages.

At present, general wage and hour conditions are not subject to negotiations in most public employee bargaining relationships. Both in the case of classified federal civil servants and a large proportion of state and local employees, these matters are reserved to the legislators. It seems difficult to believe that public employees, once their unions are established, will be content with a situation in which bargaining over the most basic issues is outside their purview. The general management attitude that, "We can talk about individual workers' problems, or the lights or noise in this room, but general wages and hours are out—left solely to the legislature," won't go down well. Here again the United States can look to the experience of other countries. The typical European nation entered the modern era with civil servants regarded as part of "His Majesty's Service." The private, let alone the public lives of these servants was subject to close and highly arbitrary scrutiny by the government. Personal oaths to king or emperor were given as a condition of employment. The Europeans have passed from these quaint and paternalistic times to a situation where full bargaining rights are now accorded to public employee unions. Their activities and rights now run to bargaining power over general wage and hour changes, holidays, vacations, and most of the economic benefits that one associates with a private sector collective agreement in the United States.

53. The Limits of Collective Bargaining in Public Employment

Harry H. Wellington

Ralph K. Winter, Jr.

I. THE CLAIMS
FOR COLLECTIVE BARGAINING
IN THE PRIVATE SECTOR

Those who deny the validity of the claims for collective bargaining in the private sector will surely not find those claims to have merit in the public. We do not intend to debate the merits of these claims. We must, however, if we are fully to test our thesis that a full transplant of collective bargaining to the public sector is inappropriate, presume a minimal validity of the claims that are made for it in the private.

Four claims then, are made for a private-sector collective bargaining. First, it is a way to achieve industrial peace. The point was put as early as 1902 by the Industrial Commission:

> The chief advantage which comes from the practice of periodically determining the conditions of labor by collective bargaining directly between employers and employees is that thereby each side obtains a better understanding of the actual state of the industry, of the conditions which confront the other side, and of the motives which influence it. Most strikes and lockouts would not occur if each party understood exactly the position of the other.[1]

Second, collective bargaining is a way of achieving industrial democracy—that is, participation by workers in their own governance. It is the industrial counterpart of the contemporary demand for community participation.[2]

Third, unions that bargain collectively with employers represent workers in the political arena as well. And political representation through interest groups is one of the most important types of political representation that the individual can have. Government at all levels acts in large part in response to the demands made upon it by the groups to which its citizens belong.[3]

Fourth, and most important, as a result of a belief in the unequal bargaining power of employers and employees, collective bargaining is claimed to be a needed substitute for individual bargaining.[4] Monopsony—a buyer's monop-

[1]*Final Report of the Industrial Commission* (1902), p. 844.

[2]See, e.g., testimony of Louis D. Brandeis before the Commission on Industrial Relations, Jan. 23, 1915, S. Doc. No. 415, 64th Cong., 1st Sess. 8, 7657-81 (1916).

[3]See generally H. Wellington, *Labor and the Legal Process* (1968), pp. 215-38.

[4]See, e.g., *Final Report of the Industrial Commission* (1902), p. 800.
It is quite generally recognized that the growth of great aggregations of capital under the control of single groups of men, which is so prominent a feature

oly,[5] in this case a buyer of labor—is alleged to exist in many situations and to create unfair contracts of labor as a result of individual bargaining. While this, in turn, may not mean that workers as a class and over time get significantly less than they should—because monopsony is surely not a general condition but is alleged to exist only in a number of particular circumstances[6]—it may mean that the terms and conditions of employment for an individual or group of workers at a given period of time and in given circumstances may be unfair. What tends to insure fairness in the aggregate and over the long run is the discipline of the market.[7] But monopsony, if it exists, can work

substantial injustice to individuals. Governmental support of collective bargaining represents the nation's response to a belief that such injustice occurs. Fairness between employee and employer in wages, hours, and terms and conditions of employment is thought more likely to be ensured where private ordering takes the collective form.[8]

There are, however, generally recognized social costs resulting from this resort to collectivism.[9] In the private sector these costs are primarily economic, and the question is, given the benefits of collective bargaining as an institution, what is the nature of the economic costs? Economists who have turned their attention to this question are legion, and disagreement among them monumental.[10] The principal concerns are of two intertwined sorts. One is summarized by Professor Albert Rees of Princeton:

> If the union is viewed solely in terms of its effect on the economy, it must in my opinion be considered an obstacle to the optimum performance of our economic system. It alters the wage structure in a way that impedes the growth of employment in sectors of the economy where productivity and income are naturally high and that leaves too much labor in low-income sectors of the economy like southern agriculture and the least skilled trades. It benefits most those workers who would in any case be relatively well off, and while some of

---

of the economic development of recent years, necessitates a corresponding aggregation of workingmen into unions, which may be able also to act as units. It is readily perceived that the position of the single workman, face to face with one of our great modern combinations, such as the United States Steel Corporation, is a position of very great weakness. The workman has one thing to sell—his labor. He has perhaps devoted years to the acquirement of a skill which gives his labor power a relatively high value, so long as he is able to put it to use in combination with certain materials and machinery. A single legal person has, to a very great extent, the control of such machinery, and in particular of such materials. Under such conditions there is little competition for the workman's labor. Control of the means of production gives power to dictate to the workingman upon what terms he shall make use of them.

[5]Our use of the term monopsony is not intended to suggest a labor market with a single employer. Rather we mean any market condition in which the terms and conditions of employment are generally below that which would have existed if the employers behaved competitively.

[6]There is by no means agreement that monopsony is a significant factor. For a theoretical discussion, see F. Machlup, *The Political Economy of Monopoly* (1952), pp. 333-79; for an empirical study, see R. Bunting, *Employer Concentration in Local Labor Markets* (1962).

[7]See, e.g., L. Reynolds, *Labor Economics and Labor Relations,* 3rd ed. (1961), pp. 18-19.

To the extent that monopsonistic conditions exist at any particular time one would expect them to be transitory. For even if we assume a high degree of labor immobility, a low wage level in a labor market will attract outside employers. Over time, therefore, the benefits of monopsony seem to carry with them the seeds of its destruction. But the time may seem a very long time in the life of any individual worker.

[8]See, e.g., Labor-Management Relations Act §I, 29 U.S.C. §151 (1964).

[9]The monopsony justification views collective bargaining as a system of countervailing power—that is, the collective power of the workers countervails the bargaining power of employers. See J. K. Galbraith, *American Capitalism* (1952), p. 121 *et seq.* Accepting the entire line of argument up to this point, however, collective bargaining nevertheless seems a crude device for meeting the monopsony problem, since there is no particular reason to think that collective bargaining will be instituted where there is monopsony (or that it is more likely to be instituted there). In some circumstances collective bargaining may even raise wages above a "competitive" level. On the other hand, the collective bargaining approach is no cruder than the law's general response to perceived unfairness in the application of the freedom of contract doctrine. See H. Wellington, *supra* note 3, at 26-38.

[10]Compare, e.g., Simons, "Some Reflections on Syndicalism." 52 *J. of Pol. Econ.* 1 (1944), with, e.g., Lester, "Reflections on the 'Labor Monopoly' Issue," 55 *J. of Pol. Econ.* 513 (1947).

this gain may be at the expense of the owners of capital, most of it must be at the expense of consumers and the lower-paid workers. Unions interfere blatantly with the use of the most productive techniques in some industries, and this effect is probably not offset by the stimulus to higher productivity furnished by some other unions. [11]

The other concern is stated in the 1967 Report of the Council of Economic Advisors:

> Vigorous competition is essential to price stability in a high employment economy. But competitive forces do not and cannot operate with equal strength in every sector of the economy. In industries where the number of competitors is limited, business firms have a substantial measure of discretion in setting prices. In many sectors of the labor market, unions and managements together have a substantial measure of discretion in setting wages. The responsible exercise of discretionary power over wages and prices can help to maintain general price stability. Its irresponsible use can make full employment and price stability incompatible. [12]

And the claim is that this "discretionary power" too often is exercised "irresponsibly." [13]

Disagreement among economists extends to the quantity as well as to the fact of economic malfunctioning that properly is attributable to collective bargaining. [14] But there is no disagreement that at some point the market disciplines or delimits union power. As we shall see in more detail below, union power is frequently constrained by the fact that consumers react to a relative increase in the price of a product by purchasing less of it. As a result any significant real financial benefit, beyond that justified by an increase in productivity, which accrues to workers through collective bargaining, may well cause significant unemployment among union members. Because of this employment-benefit relationship, the economic costs

imposed by collective bargaining as it presently exists in the private sector seem inherently limited. [15]

II. THE CLAIMS FOR COLLECTIVE BARGAINING IN THE PUBLIC SECTOR

In the area of public employment the claims upon public policy made by the need for industrial peace, industrial democracy and effective political representation point toward collective bargaining. This is to say that three of the four arguments that support bargaining in the private sector—to some extent, at least—press for similar arrangements in the public sector.

Government is a growth industry, particularly state and municipal government. While federal employment between 1963 and 1968 has increased from 2.36 million to 2.73 million, state and local employment has risen from 6.87 to 9.42 million, [16] and the increase continues apace. With size comes bureaucracy, and with bureaucracy comes the isolation and alienation of the individual worker. His manhood, like that of his industrial counterpart, is threatened. Lengthening chains of command necessarily depersonalize the employment relationship and contribute to a sense of powerlessness on the part of the worker. If he is to share in the governance of his employment relationship as he does in the private sector, it must be through the device of representation, which means unionization. [17] Accordingly, just as the increase in the size of economic units in private industry fostered unionism, so the enlarging of governmental bureaucracy has encouraged public employees to look to collective action for a sense of control over their employment destiny. The number of government employees, moreover, makes it plain that those employees are members of an interest group which can organ-

[11] A. Rees, *The Economics of Trade Unions* (1962), pp. 194-95.

[12] Council of Econ. Advisors, *1967 Annual Report* (1967), p. 119.

[13] See ibid. at 119-34. See generally J. Sheahan, *The Wage-Price Guideposts* (1967).

[14] See, e.g., H. G. Lewis, *Unionism and Relative Wages in the United States* (1963), and earlier studies discussed therein.

[15] See generally J. Dunlop, *Wage Determination under Trade Unions* (1944), pp. 28-44; M. Friedman, "Some Comments on the Significance of Labor Unions for Economic Policy," in *The Impact of the Union*, D. Wright, ed. (1951), p. 204.

[16] *Labor Relations Yearbook—1968*, (1969), p. 451.

[17] See *Final Report of the Industrial Commission* (1902), p. 805; Summers, "American Legislation for Union Democracy" 25, *Mod. L. Rev.* 273, 275 (1962).

ize for political representation as well as for job participation.[18]

The pressures thus generated by size and bureaucracy lead inescapably to disruption—to labor unrest—unless these pressures are recognized and unless existing decision-making procedures are accommodated to them. Peace in government employment too, the argument runs, can best be established by making union recognition and collective bargaining accepted public policy.[19]

Much less clearly analogous to the private model, however, is the unequal bargaining power argument. In the private sector that argument really has two aspects. The first, which we have just adumbrated, is affirmative in nature. Monopsony is believed sometimes to result in unfair individual contracts of employment. The unfairness may be reflected in wages, which are less than they would be if the market were more nearly perfect, or in working arrangements which may lodge arbitrary power in a foreman, i.e., power to hire, fire, promote, assign or discipline without respect to substantive or procedural rules. A persistent assertion, generating much heat, relates to the arbitrary exercise of managerial power in individual cases. This assertion goes far to explain the insistence of unions on the establishment in the labor contract of rules, with an accompanying adjudicatory procedure, to govern industrial life.[20]

Judgments about the fairness of the financial terms of the public employee's individual contract of employment are even harder to make than for private sector workers. The case for the existence of private employer monopsony, disputed as it is, asserts only that some private sector employers in some circumstances have too much bargaining power. In the public sector, the case to be proven is that the governmental employer ever has such power. But even if this case could be proven, market norms are at best attenuated guides to questions of fairness. In employment as in all other areas, governmental decisions are properly political

decisions, and economic considerations are but one criterion among many. Questions of fairness do not centrally relate to how much imperfection one sees in the market, but more to how much imperfection one sees in the political process. "Low" pay for teachers may be merely a decision—right or wrong, resulting from the pressure of special interests or from a desire to promote the general welfare—to exchange a reduction in the quality or quantity of teachers for higher welfare payments, a domed stadium, etc. And we are limited in our ability to make informed judgments about such political decisions because of the understandable but unfortunate fact that the science of politics has failed to supply us with either as elegant or as reliable a theoretical model as has its sister discipline.

Nevertheless, employment benefits in the public sector may have improved relatively more slowly than in the private sector during the last three decades. An economy with a persistent inflationary bias probably works to the disadvantage of those who must rely on legislation for wage adjustments.[21] Moreover, while public employment was once attractive for the greater job security and retirement benefits it provided, quite similar protection is now available in many areas of the private sector.[22] On the other hand, to the extent that civil service, or merit, systems exist in public employment and these laws are obeyed, the arbitrary exercise of managerial power is substantially reduced. Where it is reduced, a labor policy that relies on the individual employment contract must seem less unacceptable.

The second, or negative aspect of the unequal bargaining power argument, relates to the social costs of collective bargaining. As we have seen, the social costs of collective bargaining in the private sector are principally economic, and seem inherently limited by market forces. In the public sector, however, the costs seem to us economic only in a very narrow sense and are on the whole political. It further seems to us

[18]For the "early" history, see S. Spero, *Government as Employer* (1948).

[19]See, e.g., *Governor's Committee on Public Employee Relations, Final Report* (State of N.Y., 1966), p. 9.

[20]See, e.g., N. Chamberlain, *The Union Challenge to Management Control* (1948), p. 94.

[21]This is surely on reason which might explain the widely assumed fact that public employees have fallen behind their private sector counterparts. See Stieber, "Collective Bargaining in the Public Sector," in *Challenges to Collective Bargaining,* L. Ulman, ed. (1967), pp. 65, 69.

[22]See Taylor, "Public Employment: Strike or Procedures," 20 *Ind. & Lab. Rel. Rev.* (1967) 617, 623-25.

that, to the extent union power is delimited by market or other forces in the public sector, these constraints do not come into play nearly as quickly as in the private. An understanding of why this is so requires further comparison between collective bargaining in the two sectors.

III. THE PRIVATE SECTOR MODEL

While the private sector is, of course, extraordinarily diverse, the paradigm case is an industry which produces a product that is not particularly essential to those who buy it and for which dissimilar products can be substituted. Within the market or markets for this product, most—but not all—of the producers must bargain with a union representing their employees, and this union is generally the same through the industry. A price rise of this product relative to others will result in a decrease in the number of units of the product sold. This in turn will result in a cutback in employment. And an increase in price would be dictated by an increase in labor cost relative to output, at least in most situations.[23] Thus, the union is faced with some sort of rough trade-off between, on the one hand, larger benefits for some employees and unemployment for others, and on the other hand, smaller benefits and more employment. Because unions are political organizations, with a legal duty to represent *all* employees fairly,[24] and with a treasury that comes from per capita dues, there is pressure on the union to avoid the road that leads to unemployment.[25]

This picture of the restraints that the market imposes on collective bargaining settlements undergoes change as the variables change. On the one hand, to the extent that there are non-union firms within a product market, the impact of union pressure will be diminished by

the ability of consumers to purchase identical products from non-union and, presumably, less expensive sources. On the other hand, to the extent that union organization of competitors within the product market is complete, there will be no such restraint and the principal barriers to union bargaining goals will be the ability of a number of consumers to react to a price change by turning to dissimilar but nevertheless substitutable products.

Two additional variables must be noted. First, where the demand for an industry's product is rather insensitive to price—i.e., relatively inelastic—and where all the firms in a product market are organized, the union need fear less the employment-benefit trade-off, for the employer is less concerned about raising prices in response to increased costs. By hypothesis, a price rise affects unit sales of such an employer only minimally. Second, in an expanding industry, wage settlements which exceed increases in productivity may not reduce union employment. They will reduce expansion, hence the employment effect will be experienced only by workers who do not belong to the union. This means that in the short run the politics of the employment-benefit trade-off do not restrain the union in its bargaining demands.

In both of these cases, however, there are at least two restraints on the union. One is the employer's increased incentive to substitute machines for labor, a factor present in the paradigm case and all other cases as well. The other restraint stems from the fact that large sections of the nation are unorganized and highly resistant to unionization.[26] Accordingly, capital will seek non-union labor, and in this way the market will discipline the organized sector.

The employer, in the paradigm case and in all variations of it, is motivated primarily by the necessity to maximize profits (and this is so no matter how political a corporation may seem to be). He therefore is not inclined (absent an increase in demand for his product) to raise prices and thereby suffer a loss in profits, and he is organized to transmit and represent the market pressures described above. Generally he will resist, and resist hard, union demands that exceed increases in productivity, for if he accepts such demands he may be forced to raise prices.

---

[23]The cost increase may, of course, take some time to work through and appear as a price increase. See A. Rees, *The Economics of Trade Unions* (1962), pp. 107-9. In some oligopolistic situations the firm may be able to raise prices after a wage increase without suffering a significant decrease in sales.

[24]*Steele* v. *Louisville & N.R.R.,* 323 U.S. 192 (1944).

[25]The pressure is sometimes resisted. Indeed, the United Mine Workers has chosen more benefits for less employment. See generally M. Baratz, *The Union and the Coal Industry* (1955).

[26]See "Trends and Changes in Union Membership," 89 *Monthly Lab. Rev.* 510-13 (1966); Bernstein, "The Growth of American Unions 1945-1960," 2 *Lab. Hist.* 131 (1961).

Should he be unsuccessful in his resistance too often, and should it cost him too much, he can be expected to put his money and energy elsewhere.[27]

What all this means is that the social costs imposed by collective bargaining are economic costs; that usually they are limited by powerful market restraints; and that these restraints are visible to anyone who is able to see the forest for the trees.[28]

IV. THE PUBLIC SECTOR MODEL

The paradigm case in the public sector is a municipality with an elected board of aldermen, and an elected mayor who bargains (through others) with unions representing the employees of the city. He bargains also, of course, with other permanent and *ad hoc* interest groups making claims upon government (business groups, save-the-park committees, neighborhood groups, etc.). Indeed, the decisions that are made may be thought of roughly as a result of interactions and accommodations among these interest groups, as influenced by perceptions about the attitudes of the electorate, and by the goals and programs of the mayor and his aldermanic board.[29]

Decisions that cost the city money are generally paid for from taxes and, less often, by borrowing. Not only are there many types of taxes, but also there are several layers of government which may make tax revenue available to the city; federal and state as well as local funds may be employed for some purposes. Formal allocation of money for particular uses is made through the city's budget, which may

have within it considerable room for adjustments.[30] Thus, a union will bargain hard for as large a share of the budget as it thinks it possibly can obtain, and beyond this to force a tax increase if it deems that possible.

In the public sector too, the market operates. In the long run, the supply of labor is a function of the price paid for labor by the public employer relative to what workers earn elsewhere.[31] This is some assurance that public employees in the aggregate—with or without collective bargaining—are not paid too little. The case for employer monopsony, moreover may be much weaker in the public sector than it is in the private. First, to the extent that most public employees work in urban areas, as they probably do, there may often be a number of substitutable and competing private and public employers in the labor market. When that is the case, there can be little monopsony power.[32] Second, even if public employers occasionally have monopsony power, governmental policy is determined only in part by economic criteria, and there is no assurance, as there is in the private sector where the profit motive prevails, that the power will be exploited.

As we have seen, market-imposed unemployment is an important restraint on unions in the private sector. In the public sector, the trade-off between benefits and employment seems much less important. Government does not generally sell a product the demand for which is closely related to price. There usually are not close substitutes for the products and services provided by government and the demand for them is inelastic. Such market conditions are, as we have seen, favorable to unions in the private sector because they permit the acquisition of benefits without the penalty of

[27]And the law would protect him in this. Indeed, it would protect him if he were moved by an anti-union animus as well as by valid economic considerations. See *Textile Workers Union* v. *Darlington Mfg. Co.,* 380 U.S. 263 (1965).

Of course, where fixed costs are large relative to variable costs, it may be difficult for an employer to extricate himself.

[28]This does not mean, of course, that collective bargaining in the private sector is free of social costs. It means only that the costs are necessarily limited by the discipline of the market.

[29]See generally R. Dahl, *Who Governs? Democracy and Power in an American City* (1961). On interest theory generally, see D. Truman, *The Governmental Process* (1955).

[30]See, e.g., W. Sayre and H. Kaufman, *Governing New York City* (1960), pp. 366-72.

[31]*Cf.,*M. Moskow, *Teachers and Unions* (1966), pp. 79-86.

[32]This is based on the reasonable but not unchallengeable assumption that the number of significant employers in a labor market is related to the existence of monopsony. See R. Bunting, *Employer Concentration in Local Labor Markets* (1962), pp. 3-14. The greater the number of such employers in a labor market, the greater the departure from the classic case of the monopsony of the single employer. The number of employers would clearly seem to affect their ability to make and enforce a collusive wage agreement.

unemployment, subject to the restraint of non-union competitors, actual or potential. But no such restraint limits the demands of public employee unions. Because much government activity is, and must be, a monopoly, product competition, non-union or otherwise, does not exert a downward pressure on prices and wages. Nor will the existence of a pool of labor ready to work for a wage below union scale attract new capital and create a new, and competitively less expensive, governmental enterprise. The fear of unemployment, however, can serve as something of a restraining force in two situations. First, if the cost of labor increases, the city may reduce the quality of the service it furnishes by reducing employment. For example, if teachers' salaries are increased, it may decrease the number of teachers and increase class size. However, the ability of city government to accomplish such a change is limited not only by union pressure, but also by the pressure of other affected interest groups in the community.[33] Political considerations, therefore, may cause either no reduction in employment or services, or a reduction in an area other than that in which the union members work. Both the political power exerted by the beneficiaries of the services, who are also voters, and the power of the public employee union as a labor organization, then, combine to create great pressure on political leaders either to seek new funds or to reduce municipal services of another kind. Second, if labor costs increase, the city may, even as a private employer would, seek to replace labor with machines. The absence of a profit motive, and a political concern for unemployment, however, may be a deterrent in addition to the deterrent of union resistance. The public employer which decides it must limit employment because of unit labor costs will likely find that the politically easiest decision is to restrict new hires, rather than to lay off current employees.

Even if we are right that a close relationship between increased economic benefits and unemployment does not exist as a significant deterrent to unions in the public sector, might not the argument be made that in some sense the taxpayer is the public sector's functional equivalent of the consumer? If taxes become too high, the taxpayer can move to another community. While it is generally much easier for a

consumer to substitute products than for a taxpayer to substitute communities, is it not fair to say that, at the point at which a tax increase will cause so many taxpayers to move that it will produce less total revenue, the market disciplines or restrains union and public employer in the same way and for the same reasons that the market disciplines parties in the private sector? Moreover, does not the analogy to the private sector suggest that it is legitimate in an economic sense for unions to push government to the point of substitutability?

Several factors suggest that the answer to this latter question is at best indeterminate, and that the question of legitimacy must be judged not by economic, but by political criteria.

In the first place, there is no theoretical reason—economic or political—to suppose that it is desirable for a governmental entity to liquidate its taxing power, to tax up to the point where another tax increase will produce less revenue because of the number of people it drives to different communities. In the private area, profit maximization is a complex concept, but its approximation generally is both a legal requirement and socially useful as a means of allocating resources.[34] The liquidation of taxing power seems neither imperative nor useful.

Second, consider the complexity of the tax structure and the way in which different kinds of taxes (property, sales, income) fall differently upon a given population. Consider, moreover, that the taxing authority of a particular governmental entity may be limited (a municipality may not have the power to impose an income tax). What is necessarily involved, then, is principally the redistribution of income by government rather than resource allocation,[35] and questions of income redistribution surely are essentially political questions.[36]

[33]Organized parent groups, for example.

[34]See generally R. Dorfman, *Prices and Markets* (1967).

[35]In the private sector what is involved is principally resource allocation rather than income redistribution. Income redistribution occurs to the extent that unions are able to increase wages at the expense of profits, but the extent to which this actually happens would seem to be limited. It also occurs to the extent that unions, by limiting employment in the union sector through maintenance of wages above a competitive level, increase the supply of labor in the non-union sector and thereby depress wages there.

[36]In the private sector the political question was answered when the National Labor Relations Act was

For his part, the mayor in our paradigm case will be disciplined not by a desire to maximize profits, but by a desire—in some cases at least—to do a good job (to effectuate his programs), and in virtually all cases either to be reelected or to move to a better elective office. What he gives to the union must be taken from some other interest group or from taxpayers. His is the job of coordinating these competing claims while remaining politically viable. And that coordination will be governed by the relative power of the competing interest groups. Our inquiry, therefore, must turn to the question of how much power public employee unions will exercise if the full private model of collective bargaining is adopted in the public sector.

V. PUBLIC EMPLOYEE STRIKES AND THE POLITICAL PROCESS

Although the market does not discipline the union in the public sector to the extent that it does in the private, the paradigm case, nevertheless, would seem to be consistent with what Robert A. Dahl has called the " 'normal' American political process," which is "one in which there is a high probability that an active and legitimate group in the population can make itself heard effectively at some crucial stage in the process of decision,"[37] for the union may be seen as little more than an "active and legitimate group in the population." With elections in the background to perform, as Mr. Dahl tells us, "the critical role . . . in maximizing political equality and popular sovereignty,"[38] all seems well, at least theoretically, with collective bargaining and public employment.

But there is trouble even in the house of theory if collective bargaining in the public sector means what it does in the private. The trouble is that if unions are able to withhold labor—to strike—as well as to employ the usual methods of political pressure, they may possess a disproportionate share of effective power in the process of decision. Collective bargaining

would then be so effective a pressure as to skew the results of the " 'normal' American political process."

One should straightway make plain that the strike issue is not *simply* the essentiality of public services as contrasted with services or products produced in the private sector. This is only half of the issue, and in the past the half truth has beclouded analysis.[39] The services performed by a private transit authority are neither less nor more essential to the public than those that would be performed if the transit authority were owned by a municipality. A railroad or a dock strike may be much more damaging to a community than "job action" by teachers. This is not to say that governmental services are not essential. They are, both because the demand for them is inelastic and because their disruption may seriously injure a city's economy and occasionally the physical welfare of its citizens. Nevertheless, essentiality of governmental services is only a necessary part of, rather than a complete answer to, the question: What is wrong with strikes in public employment?

What is wrong with strikes in public employment is that because they disrupt essential services, a large part of a mayor's political constituency will press for a quick end to the strike with little concern for the cost of settlement. The problem is that because market restraints are attenuated and because public employee strikes cause inconvenience to voters, such strikes too often succeed. Since other interest groups with conflicting claims on municipal government do not, as a general proposition, have anything approaching the effectiveness of this union technique—or at least cannot maintain this relative degree of power over the long run—they are put at a significant competitive disadvantage in the political process. Where this is the case, it must be said that the political process has been radically altered. And because of the deceptive simplicity of the analogy to collective bargaining in the private sector, the alteration may take place without anyone realizing what has happened.

Therefore, while the purpose and effect of strikes by public employees may seem in the beginning merely designed to establish collective bargaining or to "catch up" with wages and

---

passed: the benefits of collective bargaining (with the strike) outweigh the social costs.

[37]R. Dahl, *A Preface to Democratic Theory* (1956), p. 145.

[38]*Ibid.*

[39]See, e.g., S. Spero, *Government as Employer* (1948), pp. 1-15.

fringe benefits in the private sector, in the long run strikes must be seen as a means to redistribute income, or, put another way, to gain a subsidy for union members,[40] not through the employment of the usual types of political pressure, but through the employment of what might appropriately be called political force. . . .

While there is increasing advocacy for expanding the scope of bargaining in public employment and in favor of giving public employees the right to strike—advocacy not just by unionists but by disinterested experts as

well[41]—the law generally limits the scope of bargaining and forbids strikes. This is often done with little attention to supporting reasons. Ours has been an attempt to supply these reasons. . . .

. . . In the future, if strikes are to be barred, sophisticated impasse procedures must be established. If, on the other hand, some strikes are to be tolerated, changes in the political structure which will make the municipal employer less vulnerable to work stoppages must be developed. . . .

---

[40]Strikes in some areas of the private sector may have this effect, too. See note 29 *supra*. The difference in the impact of collective bargaining in the two sectors should be seen as a continuum. Thus, for example, it may be that market restraints do not sufficiently discipline strike settlements in some regulated industries, or in industries that rely mainly on government con-

tracts. If this is so—and we do not know that it is—perhaps there should be tighter restraints on the use of the strike in those areas.

[41]See, e.g., Wollett, "The Taylor Law and the Strike Ban," in *Public Employee Organization and Bargaining*, H. Anderson, ed. (1968), p. 29.

54. The Role and Consequences of Strikes by Public Employees

John F. Burton, Jr.

Charles Krider

Reason is the life of the law.

Sir Edward Coke

The life of the law has not been logic: it has been experience.

Oliver Wendell Holmes

The vexing problem of strikes by public employees has generated a number of assertions based largely on logical analysis. One common theme is that strikes fulfill a useful function in the private sector, but are inappropriate in the public sector, because they distort the political decision-making process. Another is that strikes in nonessential government services should not be permitted because it is administratively infeasible to distinguish among the various government services on the basis of their essentiality. The present article attempts to evaluate these assertions in terms of labor relations experience at the local level of government. . . .

This paper was prepared as part of a *Study of Unionism and Collective Bargaining in the Public Sector* which is being conducted by the Brookings Institution with financial support from the Ford Foundation. The views are the authors' and are not presented as those of the officers, trustees, or staff members of the Brookings Institution or of the Ford Foundation.

Helpful comments on an earlier draft of this paper were received from Paul F. Gerhart, Robert B. McKersie, Arnold R. Weber, and Harry H. Wellington.

I. THE ROLE OF STRIKES IN THE PRIVATE SECTOR

Wellington and Winter have catalogued four claims which are made to justify collective bargaining in the private sector.[1] First, collective bargaining is a way to achieve industrial peace. Second, it is a way of achieving industrial democracy. Third, unions that bargain collectively with employers also represent workers in the political arena. Fourth, and in their view the most important reason, collective bargaining compensates for the unequal bargaining power which is believed to result from individual bargaining. Wellington and Winter recognize that the gains to employees from collective bargaining, such as protection from monopsony power, are to be balanced against the social costs resulting from the resort to collectivism, such as distortion of the wage structure. While noting that considerably disagreement exists among economists concerning the extent of the benefits and costs, they stress the fact that costs are limited by economic constraints. Unions can displace their members from jobs by ignoring the discipline of the market. These four justifications for private sector collective bargaining are presumably relevant to some

[1] Wellington and Winter, "The Limits of Collective Bargaining in Public Employment," 78 *Yale L.J.*, 1112-13 (1969). Hereinafter cited as Wellington and Winter.

degree whether or not strikes are permitted. Nonetheless, one can conceptualize two models of collective bargaining—the Strike Model, which would normally treat strikes as legal, and the No-Strike Model, which would make all strikes illegal—and evaluate whether, in terms of the above justifications, society benefits from permitting strikes. . . .

Use of the Strike Model instead of the No-Strike Model appears to enhance all but the third of the four claims for private sector collective bargaining offered by Wellington and Winter.[2] While they do not provide a claim by claim analysis of the consequences of permitting strikes, their endorsement of strikes in the private sector must indicate that they believe the Strike Model preferable to the No-Strike Model. . . .

II. CONSEQUENCES OF STRIKES IN THE PUBLIC SECTOR

The best procedure for evaluating public sector strikes would be to investigate the respective impacts of the Strike Model and the No-Strike Model on each of the claims made for collective bargaining. Such an analysis should consider the economic, political, and social effects produced. An inquiry into these effects is particularly important since several authors who have implicitly endorsed the Strike Model in the private sector have done so more on the basis of noneconomic reasons than economic reasons.[3] Nonetheless, the attack on the Strike Model in the *public* sector has been based largely on the evaluation of the fourth claim for

[2]The first reason offered—it is a way to achieve industrial peace—appears to be inconsistent with the notion of permitting strikes as a method of increasing the employees' bargaining power. One possible resolution of this apparent contradiction is that the enhanced bargaining power of the employees will enable them to work out mutually satisfactory terms with their employer without having to resort to the strike, while workers with limited bargaining power will often engage in strikes as an expression of their futility. This explanation is not totally compelling, however, and one may therefore have to justify collective bargaining among parties with equal power on grounds other than the diminution of strikes. The favorable consequences of the last three claims offered by Wellington and Winter for private sector collective bargaining presumably offset any possible increase in strikes.

[3]A. Rees, *The Economics of Trade Unions* (1962), pp. 194-97.

collective bargaining, that relating to unequal bargaining power. We will attempt to meet this attack by confining our discussion to the economic consequences of collective bargaining with and without strikes.

Even an examination confined to economic consequences is difficult. The most desirable economic data, which would measure the impact of unions on wages and other benefits, are unavailable. Our approach will be to review carefully the various steps in the analytical model developed by Wellington and Winter by which they arrive at the notion of sovereignty. If we find that the evidence available on public sector strikes contradicts this model, we shall conclude that the differential assessment they provide for public and private strikes is unwarranted.

A. Benefits of Collective Bargaining

Wellington and Winter believe the benefits of collective action, including strikes, are less in the public sector than in the private sector since (1) the problem of employer monopsony is less serious, and (2) any use of monopsony power in the public sector which results in certain groups, such as teachers, receiving low pay may reflect, not a misallocation of resources, but rather a political determination of the desired use of resources.

Wellington and Winter assert that employer monopsony is less likely to exist or be used in the public than in the private sector.[4] But as they concede,[5] referring to Bunting, monopsony is not widespread in the private sector and, except in a few instances, cannot be used as a rationale for trade unions. They provide no evidence that monopsony is less prevalent in the public than in the private sector. Moreover, other labor market inefficiencies, common to the public and private sectors, are probably more important than monopsony in providing an economic justification for unions. For example, the deficiencies of labor market information are to some extent overcome by union activities,[6] and there is no reason to assume that this benefit differs between the public and private sectors.

[4]Wellington and Winter, *supra* note 1, at 1120.

[5]*Ibid.* at 1113.

[6]"Under purely competitive conditions, it is assumed that perfect knowledge of existing wage rates in other firms, regions, and occupations, and mobility of both

Assuming there is monopsony power, Wellington and Winter believe that collective bargaining in the private sector can eliminate unfair wages "which are less than they would be if the market were more nearly perfect."[7] They assert, however, that low pay for an occupation in the public sector may reflect a political judgment which ought not to be countered by pressures resulting from a strike. To say, however, that the pay for an occupation would be higher if the employees had the right to strike than if they did not is not independent proof that strikes are inappropriate. The same criticism could be made of any activity by a public employee group which affects its pay. An independent rationale must be provided to explain why some means which are effective in raising wages (strikes) are inappropriate while other means which are also effective (lobbying) are appropriate. Whether the Wellington and Winter discussion of the politically based decision-making model for the public sector provides this rationale will be discussed in more detail subsequently.

B. Costs of Collective Bargaining

Wellington and Winter's discussion of the cost of substituting collective for individual bargaining in the public sector includes a chain of causation which runs from (1) an allegation that market restraints are weak in the public sector, largely because the services are essential; to (2) an assertion that the public puts pressure on civic officials to arrive at a quick settlement; to (3) a statement that other pressure groups have no weapons comparable to a strike; to (4) a conclusion that the strike thus imposes a high cost since the political process is distorted.

Let us discuss these steps in order:

(1) Market restraint. A key argument in the case for the inappropriateness of public sector strikes is that economic constraints are not present to any meaningful degree in the public sector.[8] This argument is not entirely convincing. First, wages lost due to strikes are as important to public employees as they are to employees in the private sector. Second, the public's concern over increasing tax rates may prevent the decision-making process from being dominated by political instead of economic considerations. The development of multilateral bargaining in the public sector is an example of how the concern over taxes may result in a close substitute for market constraints.[9] In San Francisco, for example, the Chamber of Commerce has participated in negotiations between the city and public employee unions and has had some success in limiting the economic gains of the unions. A third and related economic constraint arises for such services as water, sewage and, in some instances, sanitation, where explicit prices are charged. Even if representatives of groups other than employees and the employer do not enter the bargaining process, both union and local government are aware of the economic implications of bargaining which leads to higher prices which are clearly visible to the public. A fourth economic constraint on employees exists in those services where subcontracting to the private sector is a realistic alternative.[10] Warren, Michigan, resolved a bargaining impasse with an American Federation of State, County and Municipal Employees (AFSCME) local by subcontracting its entire sanitation service; Santa Monica, California, ended a strike of city employees by threatening to subcontract its sanitation opera-

---

labor and capital would tend to eradicate unnecessary wage differentials (i.e., differentials which did not truly reflect the marginal productivity of labor). Both knowledge and mobility, however, are very imperfect in the real market. The existence of trade unions to a large extent compensates for the lack of knowledge and represents a force tending toward wage standardization for similar work." A. Carter and F. Marshall, *Labor Economics: Wages, Employment, and Trade Unionism* (1967), pp. 324-25.

[7]Wellington and Winter, *supra* note 1, at 1116.

[8]"It further seems to us that, to the extent union power is delimited by market or other forces in the public sector, these constraints do not come into play nearly as quickly as in the private." Wellington and Winter, *supra* note 1, at 1117.

[9]McLennan and Moskow, "Multilateral Bargaining in the Public Sector," 21 *Ind. Rel. Res. Assn. Proceedings* 31 (1968).

[10]The subcontracting option is realistic in functions such as sanitation and street or highway repairs, and some white collar occupations. Several other functions, including hospitals and education, may be transferred entirely to the private sector. The ultimate response by government is to terminate the service, at least temporarily. In late 1968, Youngstown, Ohio, closed its schools for five weeks due to a taxpayer's revolt. 281 *Gov. Emp. Rel. Rep.* B-6 (1969). In late 1969, 10 Ohio school districts ran out of money and were closed down. *Wall Street Journal,* Dec. 19, 1969, p. 1, col. 1.

tions. If the subcontracting option is preserved, wages in the public sector need not exceed the rate at which subcontracting becomes a realistic alternative.

An aspect of the lack-of-market-restraints argument is that public services are essential. Even at the analytical level, Wellington and Winter's case for essentiality is not convincing. They argue:

> The Services performed by a private transit authority are neither less nor more essential to the public than those that would be performed if the transit authority were owned by a municipality. A railroad or a dock strike may be much more damaging to a community than "job action" by teachers. This is not to say that government services are not essential. They are both because they may seriously injure a city's economy and occasionally the physical welfare of its citizens.[11]

This is a troublesome passage. It ends with the implicit conclusion that all government services are essential. This conclusion is important in Wellington and Winter's analysis because it is a step in their demonstration that strikes are inappropriate in all governmental services. But the beginning of the passage, with its example of "job action" by teachers, suggests that essentiality is not an *inherent* characteristic of government services but depends on the specific service being evaluated. Furthermore the transit authority example suggests that many services are interchangeable between the public and private sectors. The view that various government services are not of equal essentiality and that there is considerable overlap between the kinds of services provided in the public and private sectors is reinforced by our field work and strike data from the Bureau of Labor Statistics. Examples include:

1. Where sanitation services are provided by a municipality, such as Cleveland, sanitationmen are prohibited from striking. Yet, sanitationmen in Philadelphia, Portland, and San Francisco are presumably free to strike since they are employed by private contractors rather than by the cities.

2. There were 25 local government strikes by the Teamsters in 1965-68, most involving truck drivers and all presumably illegal. Yet the Teamsters' strike involving fuel oil truck drivers in New York City last

winter was legal even though the interruption of fuel oil service was believed to have caused the death of several people.[12]

(2) Public Pressure. The second argument in the Wellington and Winter analysis is that public pressure on city officials forces them to make quick settlements. The validity of this argument depends on whether the service is essential. Using as a criterion whether the service is essential in the short run, we believe a priori that services can be divided into three categories: (1) essential services—police and fire—where strikes immediately endanger public health and safety; (2) intermediate services—sanitation, hospitals, transit, water, and sewage—where strikes of a few days might be tolerated; (3) nonessential services—streets, parks, education, housing, welfare and general administration—where strikes of indefinite duration could be tolerated.[13] These categories are not exact since essentiality depends on the size of the city. Sanitation strikes will be critical in large cities such as New York but will not cause much inconvenience in smaller cities where there are meaningful alternatives to governmental operation of sanitation services.

Statistics on the duration of strikes which occurred in the public sector between 1965 and 1968 provide evidence not only that public services are of unequal essentiality, but also that the a priori categories which we have used have some validity. As can be seen from Table 1, strikes in the essential services (police and fire) had an average duration of 4.7 days, while both the intermediate and the nonessential services had an average duration of approximately 10.5 days. It is true that the duration of strikes in the intermediate and nonessential services is only half the average duration of strikes in the private sector during these years.[14] However, this comparison is somewhat misleading since all of the public sector strikes were illegal, and

[11]Wellington and Winter, *supra* note 1, at 1123.

[12]*N.Y. Times,* Dec. 26, 1968, p. 1, col. 1, and Dec. 27, 1968, p. 1, col. 5.

[13]We consider education a nonessential service. However, because our portion of the Brookings Institution study excludes education, our analysis in this article will also largely exclude education.

[14]U.S. Bureau of Labor Statistics, Dept. of Labor, *Analysis of Work Stoppages 1967, Bull. No. 1611,* p. 4 (1969).

Table 1

Duration of Strikes by Essentiality of Function

	Average Duration in Days	*Standard Deviation** in Days*
Essential	4.7	7.9
Intermediate	10.3	18.5
Nonessential	10.6	20.1
Education	7.2	8.9

*Based on data collected by the Bureau of Labor Statistics on strikes during 1965-68 involving employees of local government.
**Standard deviation is a measure of dispersion around the average or the mean.

many were ended by injunction, while presumably a vast majority of the private sector strikes did not suffer from these constraints. It would appear that with the exception of police and fire protection, public officials are, to some degree, able to accept long strikes. The ability of governments to so choose indicates that political pressures generated by strikes are not so strong as to undesirably distort the entire decision-making process of government. City officials in Kalamazoo, Michigan, were able to accept a forty-eight day strike by sanitationmen and laborers; Sacramento County, California, survived an eighty-seven day strike by welfare workers. A three-month strike of hospital workers has occurred in Cuyahoga County (Cleveland), Ohio.

(3) The strike as a unique weapon. The third objection to the strike is that it provides workers with a weapon unavailable to the employing agency or to other pressure groups. Thus, unions have a superior arsenal. . . . Conceptually, we see no reason why lockouts are less feasible in the public than in the private sector. Legally, public sector lockouts are now forbidden, but so are strikes; presumably both could be legalized. Actually, public sector lockouts have occurred. The Social Service Employees Union (SSEU) of New York City sponsored a "work-in" in 1967 during which all of the caseworkers went to their office but refused to work. Instead, union-sponsored lectures were given by representatives of organizations such as CORE, and symposia were held on the problems of welfare workers and clients. The work-in lasted for one week, after which the City locked out the caseworkers.
. . . Wellington and Winter . . . claim that no

pressure group other than unions has a weapon comparable to the strike. But this argument raises a number of questions. Is the distinctive characteristic of an inappropriate method of influencing decisions by public officials that it is economic as opposed to political? If this is so, then presumably the threat of the New York Stock Exchange to move to New Jersey unless New York City taxes on stock transfers were lowered and similar devices should be outlawed along with the strike.

(4) Distortion of the political process. The ultimate concern of Wellington and Winter is that "a strike of government employees . . . introduces an alien force in the legislative process."[15] It is "alien" because, in the words of the Taylor Committee Report:

> Careful thought about the matter shows conclusively we believe that while the right to strike normally performs a useful function in the private enterprise sector (where relative economic power is the final determinant in the making of private agreements), it is not compatible with the orderly functioning of our democratic form of representative government (in which relative political power is the final determinant).[16]

The essence of this analysis appears to be that certain means used to influence the decision-making process in the public sector—those which are political—are legitimate, while

[15]State of New York, *Governor's Committee on Public Employee Relations, Final Report*, 15 (1966). Hereinafter cited as *Taylor Committee Report*. The committee chairman was George W. Taylor.

[16]*Taylor Committee Report, supra* note 15, pp. 18-19.

other—those which are economic—are not. For several reasons, we believe that such distinctions among means are tenuous.

First, any scheme which differentiates economic power from political power faces a perplexing definitional task. . . .

Second, even assuming it is possible to operationally distinguish economic power and political power, a rationale for utilizing the distinction must be provided. Such a rationale would have to distinguish between the categories either on the basis of characteristics inherent in them as a means of action or on the basis of the ends to which the means are directed. Surely an analysis of ends does not provide a meaningful distinction. The objectives of groups using economic pressure are of the same character as those of groups using political pressure—both seek to influence executive and legislative determinations such as the allocation of funds and the tax rate. If it is impossible effectively to distinguish economic from political pressure groups in terms of their ends, and it is desirable to free the political process from the influence of all pressure groups, then effective lobbying and petitioning should be as illegal as strikes.

If the normative distinction between economic and political power is based, not on the ends desired, but on the nature of the means, our skepticism remains undiminished. Are all forms of political pressure legitimate? Then consider the range of political activity observed in the public sector. Is lobbying by public sector unions to be approved? Presumably it is. What then of participation in partisan political activity? On city time? Should we question the use of campaign contributions or kickbacks from public employees to public officials as a means of influencing public sector decisions? These questions suggest that political pressures, as opposed to economic pressures, cannot *as a class* be considered more desirable.

Our antagonism toward a distinction based on means does not rest solely on a condemnation of political pressures which violate statutory provisions. We believe that perfectly legal forms of political pressure have no automatic superiority over economic pressure. In this regard, the evidence from our field work is particularly enlightening. First, we have found that the availability of political power varies among groups of employees within a given city. Most public administrators have respect for groups which can deliver votes at strategic

times. Because of their links to private sector unions, craft unions are invariably in a better position to play this political role than a union confined to the public sector, such as AFSCME. In Chicago, Cleveland and San Francisco, the public sector craft unions are closely allied with the building trades council and play a key role in labor relations with the city. Prior to the passage of state collective bargaining laws such unions also played the key role in Detroit and New York City. In the No-Strike Model, craft unions clearly have the comparative advantage because of their superior political power.

Second, the range of issues pursued by unions relying on political power tends to be narrow. The unions which prosper by eschewing economic power and exercising political power are often found in cities, such as Chicago, with a flourishing patronage system. These unions gain much of their political power by cooperating with the political administration. This source of political power would vanish if the unions were assiduously to pursue a goal of providing job security for their members since this goal would undermine the patronage system. In Rochester, for example, a union made no effort to protect one of its members who was fired for political reasons. For the union to have opposed the city administration at that time on an issue of job security would substantially have reduced the union's influence on other issues. In Chicago, where public sector strikes are rare (except for education) but political considerations are not, the unions have made little effort to establish a grievance procedure to protect their members from arbitrary treatment.

Third, a labor relations system built on political power tends to be unstable since some groups of employees, often a substantial number, are invariably left out of the system. They receive no representation either through patronage or through the union. In Memphis, the craft unions had for many years enjoyed a "working relationship" with the city which assured the payment of the rates that prevailed in the private sector and some control over jobs. The sanitation laborers, however, were not part of the system and were able to obtain effective representation only after a violent confrontation with the city in 1968. Having been denied representation through the political process, they had no choice but to accept a subordinate position in the city or to initiate a strike to change the system. Racial barriers were an important factor in the isolation of the Memphis sanitation laborers. Similar distinctions in racial balance among functions and occupations appear in most of the cities we visited.

C. Conclusions in Regard to Strikes and the Political Process

Wellington and Winter . . . reject the use of the Strike Model in the public sector. They have endorsed the No-Strike Model in order "to ensure the survival of the 'normal' American political process."[17] Our field work suggests that unions which have actually helped their members either have made the strike threat a viable weapon despite its illegality or have intertwined themselves closely with their nominal employer through patronage-political support arrangements. If this assessment is correct, choice of the No-Strike Model is likely to lead to patterns of decision making which will subvert, if not the "normal" American political process, at least the political process which . . . Wellington and Winter meant to embrace. We would not argue that the misuse of political power will be eliminated by legalizing the strike; on balance, however, we believe that, in regard to most governmental functions, the Strike Model has more virtues than the No-Strike Model. Whether strikes are an appropriate weapon for all groups of public employees is our next topic.

III. DIFFERENTIATION AMONG PUBLIC SECTOR FUNCTIONS

The most important union for local government employees, The American Federation of State, County, and Municipal Employees (AFSCME), issued a policy statement in 1966 claiming the right of public employees to strike:

> AFSCME insists upon the right of public employees . . . to strike. To forestall this right is to handicap free collective bargaining process [sic]. Wherever legal barriers to the exercise of this right exist, it shall be our policy to seek the removal of such barriers. Where one party at the bargaining table possesses all the power and

authority, the bargaining becomes no more than formalized petitioning.[18]

Significantly, AFSCME specifically excluded police and other law enforcement officers from this right. Any local of police officers that engages in a strike or other concerted refusal to perform duties will have its charter revoked.

Can a distinction among functions, such as is envisioned by AFSCME, be justified? In view of the high costs associated with the suppression of strikes, could each stoppage be dealt with, as Theodore Kheel suggests, only when and if it becomes an emergency?

Despite arguments to the contrary, we feel that strikes in some essential services, such as fire and police, would immediately endanger the public health and safety and should be presumed illegal. We have no evidence from our field work to support our fears that any disruption of essential services will quickly result in an emergency. But the events which occurred on September 9, 1919, during a strike by Boston policemen provide strong proof, those which occurred on October 7, 1969, following a strike by Montreal policemen would appear to make the argument conclusive. . . .

In the case of strikes by essential employees, such as policemen, the deterioration of public order occurs almost immediately. During the first few hours of the police walkout in Montreal, robberies occurred at eight banks, one finance company, two groceries, a jewelry store and a private bank.[19] In the case of the Boston police strike of 1919, outbreaks began within four hours after the strike had commenced. Such consequences require that strikes by police and other essential services be outlawed in advance. There is simply no time to seek an injunction.

Even if a distinction in the right to strike can be made among government functions on the basis of essentiality, is such a distinction possible to implement? The Taylor Committee based their argument against prohibiting strikes in essential functions but allowing them elsewhere on this difficulty:

> We come to this conclusion [to prohibit all strikes] after a full consideration of the

[17]Wellington and Winter, *supra* note 1, at 1125-26.

[18]*International Executive Board AFSCME, Policy Statement on Public Employee Unions: Rights and Responsibilities* 2 (July 26, 1966).

[19]*N.Y. Times,* Oct. 8, 1969, p. 3, col. 1.

views ... that public employees in non-essential governmental services, at least, should have the same right to strike as has been accorded to employees in private industry. We realize, moreover, that the work performed in both sectors is sometimes comparable or identical. Why, then, should an interruption of non-essential governmental services be prohibitᵉd?

To begin with, a differentiation between essential and non-essential governmental services would be the subject of such intense and never ending controversy as to be administratively impossible.[20]

Despite the conclusion of the Taylor Committee it appears that in practice a distinction is emerging between strikes in essential services and strikes in other services. Employee organizations and public officials do in fact treat some strikes as critical, while other strikes cause no undue concern.

Our analysis of the Bureau of Labor Statistics strike data pertaining to the last four years suggests that it is possible to devise an operational definition of essential service. First, as we have indicated above, strike duration was considerably shorter in the essential services than in the intermediate or nonessential services (see Table 1). These data suggest that, except in police and fire services, public officials have some discretion in choosing to accept long strikes. Second, the statistics reveal that managers have been able to distinguish between essential and nonessential services in their use of counter sanctions. In strikes involving essential services, injunctions were sought more frequently and employees, because of their short run indispensability, were fired less frequently. Injunctions were granted in 35% of the essential strikes, and in 25% of the intermediate, but only in 19% of the nonessential strikes. Third, partial operation was attempted more frequently in essential services. By using non-strikers, supervisors, replacements or volunteers, local governments were able to continue partial operation during 92% of the essential strikes, but in only 80% of the intermediate, and 77% of the nonessential strikes. Such data suggest that it may be administratively feasible to differentiate among public services so as to permit some, but not all, public employees to strike. Indeed, public administrators already seem to be making such distinctions. ...

[20]Taylor Committee Report, supra note 15, p. 18.

IV. IMPLICATIONS FOR PUBLIC POLICY

We have expressed our views on the market restraints that exist in the public sector, the extent of the public pressure on public officials to reach quick settlements, the likely methods by which decisions would be made in the No-Strike Model, and the desirability and feasibility of differentiating among government services on the basis of essentiality. In this light, what public policy seems appropriate for strikes at the local government level?

In general, we believe that strikes in the public sector should be legalized for the same reasons they are legal in the private sector. For some public sector services, however—namely, police and fire protection—the probability that a strike will result in immediate danger to public health and safety is so substantial that strikes are almost invariable inappropriate. In these essential functions, the strike should be presumed illegal; the state should not be burdened with the requirement of seeking an injunction. We would, however, permit employees in a service considered essential to strike if they could demonstrate to a court that a disruption of service would not endanger the public. Likewise, we would permit the government to obtain an injunction against a strike in a service presumed nonessential if a nontrivial danger to the public could be shown.[21]

The decision to permit some, but not all, public employee strikes cannot, of course, take place in vaccus publicum jus. Mediation, fact finding, or advisory arbitration may be appropriate for those functions where strikes are

[21]The Labor Management Relations Act (Taft-Hartley Act) is a statute which presumes strikes are legal unless an emergency is involved. 29 U.S.C. § § 176-180 (1969). The President may delay or suspend an actual or threatened strike which if permitted to occur or continue will constitute a threat to the national health or safety. The emergency procedures have been invoked 29 times since 1947. This experience should provide some guidance in formulating an operational version of our policy which would permit strikes in nonessential functions unless a nontrivial danger to the public could be shown. We realize that it may be more difficult to formulate an operational version of our policy for essential functions. We are not aware of any experience with a statute which permits the presumption of illegality for strikes to be rebutted under appropriate circumstances.

permitted. Where strikes are illegal because of the essential nature of the service, it may be necessary to institute compulsory arbitration.[22]

[22]Michigan has recently enacted a statute applicable to public police and fire departments which imposes penalties on striking employees and establishes a binding arbitration procedure for negotiating disputes. Arbitration is available upon the request of either party in the dispute. *Mich. Comp. Laws* § § 423.232-247 (1948).

Newly Organized Workers

Although the recent growth in unionization has been most pronounced among government employees, unionization has also made important gains in a number of other areas ranging from college professors to migrant farm workers.

The recent increase in the unionization of professors is discussed in the selection by Myron Lieberman. He discusses why this trend is likely to continue and what the consequences are likely to be. Among the consequences that he foresees and applauds are increased power for college administrators and the development of student organizations to bargain with both faculty unions and administrators. In Lieberman's view, "the paradox of faculty unionization is that although it is a faculty initiative, perhaps its most salutary effects will not be what it does for professors, but what it will do to make administrators more efficient, more alert to innovation, and more responsive to the public interest."

Another group of workers who have recently started to organize into an effective union are migrant farm workers. The selection by Joan London and Henry Anderson traces the development of the United Farm Workers Organizing Committee (UFWOC) under the leadership of Cesar Chavez. Farm workers have traditionally been very difficult to organize, at least partly because of the ease of importing strike breakers. Chavez has attempted to overcome this problem by a variety of means. Initially he developed his organization by concentrating on relatively simple things the farm workers could do to help each other, such as forming a credit union. Strikes were avoided as long as possible. Then when a grape strike was attempted, it was soon supplemented by a consumer boycott that became one of the most successful in union history. Although the UFWOC is not as securely established as most other AFL-CIO unions, it has been much more successful than previous efforts to organize migrant workers.

55. Professors, Unite!

Myron Lieberman

If you think campus unrest is a thing of the past, consider this scenario: It is late summer, sometime in the '70s. For months, union representatives of the 2,000 faculty members of the State University at Muddy Pond (SUMP) have sparred with the administration over a new contract. Now union officials dourly inform the press that a faculty strike is a real possibility unless there is some "give" by the administration on salaries and fringe benefits. Asked where the money is to come from, a union spokesman hints at higher student fees. Then, just as the SUMP administration is about to approve this solution, the executive secretary of the University Union of Students calls a press conference and reads the following statement:

The 40,000 students of SUMP have had enough. They now pay an average of $2,000 each in tuition. This comes to $80 million, or 20 per cent of the university budget. Aside from the fact that higher fees will drive hundreds of needy students off the campus, we are appalled at the faculty union's persistent refusal to accept student participation in faculty evaluation. We have also noted with growing concern the administration's effort to raise dormitory rents and cafeteria prices.

The executive committee of the student union has therefore unanimously voted in favor of a mass refusal to pay any tuition at all if it goes up as a result of the faculty union's intolerable pressure on the administration. We support adequate faculty compensation. But any increase at this time should be contingent upon real faculty accountability and should be fixed only through bargaining in good faith with the University Union of Students.

The student spokesman means business, and the faculty union representatives know it. For one thing, the student union has an imposing war chest: $20 dues are paid each year by about 20,000 students. For another, the student union has lately filed ten lawsuits against various professors, alleging that their arbitrary and capricious grading has caused severe financial hardship and loss of reputation for the student plaintiffs. Even pro-strike professors don't want to see student unionists sifting through their lectures, examinations, and grades for evidence of incompetence or unfairness.

And so, behind the scenes, a compromise is worked out. The strike threat by students and faculty is resolved by agreement on a modest raise with no immediate hike in tuition. The students also get a faculty-administration pledge to disclose certain data on grades. And the student and faculty unions agree to undertake a joint lobbying effort to increase SUMP's legislative appropriations.

FACULTY SOLIDARITY

To many Americans, the most incongruous figures in this scenario would be the faculty. Students are assumed to be activists who dominate weak and confused administrators. But professors supposedly have no business belonging to unions and threatening to strike. It's little wonder the public thinks so, when most professors do also. Or did until the past year or two.

Unseemly or not, the unionization of college and university faculties will be one of the most important developments in higher education in the next decade. To be sure, the trend is still a modest one. At the start of this school year, only about 50,000 (or 6 per cent) of the country's 836,000 faculty members were employed under the terms of a union contract. And the collective bargaining that went into those contracts involved only about 180 campuses out of a U.S. total of 2,700. Only six universities had contracts—Southeastern Massachusetts, Central Michigan, Rutgers, the City University of New York, Long Island University, and the University of Wisconsin (for teaching assistants)—while most of the rest were community colleges or technical institutes.

Even so, professorial collective bargaining is on the rise throughout the country. As the 1971-72 academic year began, the Senate Professorial Association (an affiliate of the National Education Association) was bargaining on a single contract that will cover twenty-seven public institutions of higher education in New York. In Pennsylvania, an election was scheduled for October 6, to determine who would represent the faculties of thirteen state colleges and one university. Election petitions have been submitted in such diverse institutions as the University of Rhode Island, Wayne State University, and the University of Hawaii. In California, which has the nation's biggest public campus system, roughly two-thirds of the faculty in the state colleges now favor unionization and collective bargaining, compared to less than half in 1967.

In assessing the pace of professorial unionization, one must remember that it took only nine years to organize 65 per cent of the nation's schoolteachers for collective bargaining. Two teacher unions, the National Education Association (1,000,000 members) and the American Federation of Teachers (250,000 members) achieved this result in fierce competition with each other for teacher members. Both the NEA and the AFT (including their state and local affiliates) have made impressive gains in salaries, fringe benefits, and working conditions by hard bargaining and willingness to take other militant job actions.

It is virtually certain that college and university faculties will follow this pattern in the 1970s. Faculty members have always been concerned about money and security, but they have sought these things as individuals, negotiating their status and rewards privately with deans and department heads. That they should now be bargaining collectively like auto workers or longshoremen or custodians at their own institutions requires some explanation, but it shouldn't be surprising. One reason is that the legislative situation is vastly more favorable to collective bargaining in higher education, and will be even more so in the future, than it was in the 1960s for public-school teachers. In 1962, only Wisconsin had formally legalized collective bargaining by public-school teachers, whereas by the summer of 1971, about fifteen states had enacted legislation authorizing collective bargaining in higher education. Many others are likely to follow if federal legislation does not resolve the problem soon.

Indeed, federal jurisdiction over labor relations in private institutions of higher education (which employ about one-third of all academic personnel) is a recently accomplished fact. A 1970 ruling of the National Labor Relations Board held that the NLRB would assume jurisdiction over employment disputes in private institutions of higher education, provided that the institutions had a significant impact on interstate commerce. Subsequently, the NLRB ruled that it would assume jurisdiction over labor disputes in private institutions with a gross income of $1,000,000 or more. This ruling placed more than two-thirds of private higher education under NLRB jurisdiction and greatly stimulated unionizing activities in private institutions.

IN SELF-DEFENSE

Anyone familiar with labor-management transactions elsewhere in the economy can readily understand why professors are rapidly seizing their opportunities to bargain collectively. A collective-bargaining contract provides much better protection against capricious or unfair management than a policy statement adopted unilaterally by management. By the same token, policies on academic freedom that are adopted unilaterally by boards of regents can be changed unilaterally. And this is what often happens when a policy comes under severe political or economic attack, precisely when protection is needed most.

Then, too, a professor's grievance may not be with the policy of a governing board, but with the way the policy is being carried out by the administration. Suppose, for example, that a board adopts a policy that guarantees a twelve-hour teaching load "except in emergencies." The faculty might have been agreeable to this policy, but the administration may then start interpreting "emergency" so broadly as to undercut the policy. Without a collective-bargaining contract, the faculty could do very little about this kind of interpretation. With such a contract, faculty members could take their grievances to an impartial third party for binding arbitration. Such procedures are normally used by unions to prevent management from interpreting away rights presumably granted in the collective-bargaining contract.

Many other positive features of collective bargaining are attracting professors into unions. But unionization and collective bargaining are also a defensive reaction to the fact that education is no longer a fair-haired boy in the competition for public and private support. Everywhere, higher education is under unprecedented budgetary pressure threatening basic salaries and tenure, as well as traditional professional perquisites such as sabbaticals and travel allowances. Even cutbacks in the number of faculty, unthinkable in the education boom of the '60s, are a reality on some campuses. In many fields—English and physics, for example—there are many more Ph.D.s looking for jobs than there are openings. This tends to drive down starting and low-echelon salaries, making younger faculty members especially apprehensive—and interested in unionization.

Conditions vary from campus to campus, but virtually all observers expect the next few years to be particularly difficult. A recent study of seventy-six public institutions indicated that ten expected to finish the 1970-71 school year

with a deficit, with the number likely to increase substantially in the near future. The measures these schools are taking to meet the financial squeeze include deferring maintenance, eliminating new programs, and freezing or cutting back on faculty. In private higher education, the financial picture is typically more critical than in public institutions. In both sectors, therefore, faculties sense a coming assault on privileges and perquisites they have enjoyed for years; they are organizing in self-defense.

While the American Association of University Professors (AAUP) seems confused and ambivalent on the issue, the NEA and AFT are more than eager to organize faculties for collective bargaining. This was not always the case. Back in the early '60s, when the drive to organize public-school teachers for collective bargaining got underway, only the AFT was criticizing the presumption (widely held among teachers themselves) that "professionals" simply didn't bargain collectively, no matter what the potential benefits. The NEA was overwhelmingly committed to a legislative instead of a collective-bargaining approach to terms and conditions of employment for teachers. But when the AFT won the right in 1962 to represent teachers in New York City, the NEA, though squeamish about the union label, galvanized itself to union militancy.

To their growing role as passionate suitors of the professorial hand, the NEA and AFT bring imposing assets. NEA already has more than one million members, and its annual budget exceeds $29 million. Although its membership in higher education is less than half the AAUP's 90,000, the NEA is enrolling professors at a much faster rate, and its members typically pay much more than AAUP members in state and local dues. At every government level throughout the country, the NEA and its affiliates have staff and resources available for every aspect of unionization and collective bargaining. It already bargains for more professors, including those in two of the three largest systems of public higher education, than all other faculty organizations combined. If NEA affiliates can win all or even most of this year's major representation elections (e.g., those for all the state colleges in Pennsylvania and all of higher education in Hawaii), the organization will very probably become the dominant professorial union in the country.

In the immediate future at least, the NEA's

main opposition will come from the AFT, now one of the fastest growing unions in the AFL-CIO. AFT prospects will depend largely upon the financial crisis in higher education and the legislative attempts to limit or abolish tenure, to increase teaching loads, and to cut back on other faculty conditions of employment. At the senior college and university level, the federation's best opportunities appear to be in urban institutions. The AFT is also a strong contender in community colleges, especially where faculty often come from an AFT local and tend to look to it for organizational support. Rather surprisingly, private higher education represents another promising area for federation growth. The desperate financial crisis in private institutions is forcing most of them to make an all-out effort for public support. AFT and AFL-CIO policies favor such support; the NEA has been silent. The AFT also stands a good chance this fall of winning representation rights for the regular full-time faculty at the twenty institutions constituting the City University of New York. Such a victory would be an extraordinary boost to AFT affiliates elsewhere, especially at the senior college and university level. Ordinarily, however, AFT growth will be hindered rather than helped by system-wide bargaining. In a number of states, the AFT could probably win a majority at one or more institutions but be unable to gain a majority in the state system as a whole. If each campus is considered a separate bargaining unit, AFT affiliates will gain bargaining rights on those campuses where it has a majority. If bargaining is on a system-wide basis, the AFT's prospects will be less favorable, since it is not so likely to win statewide elections.

The American Association of University Professors is currently running a poor third in the race to represent faculties; its affiliates have bargaining rights on only 6 of the 180 or so campuses where faculties bargain collectively. The reasons for the AAUP's poor showing thus far seem obvious to everyone but leaders of the association itself. The leadership at first opposed the inclusion of professors under state laws granting bargaining rights to public employees. When such opposition proved fruitless, the leadership tried to exorcise the evil at its 1968 convention. For sheer fatuousness, the record of this convention may never be equaled. The convention adopted a policy statement asserting that because of its "special characteristics" the academic community should beware of "dependence on external representative agencies," i.e., faculty unions. The statement did accept a kind of collective bargaining, but proposed that the professors should be represented by so-called faculty councils. Since the weakness of faculty councils is one of the major causes of faculty unionization, the statement served only to make one thing perfectly clear: the AAUP was completely befuddled by the whole business.

The AAUP's statement also asserted that "the Association believes itself, by virtue of its principles, programs, experience, and broad membership, to be well qualified to act as representative of the faculty in institutions of higher education." Actually, the AAUP is badly handicapped by the weakness of its state and local affiliates, which are mostly paper organizations without funds, facilities, or personnel experienced in bargaining. Indeed, many of the grievances processed by AAUP's national office over the years would never have arisen under a collective-bargaining agreement, and most of the others would have been settled much sooner, at less cost, and with more equity to the employee, under binding arbitration. These considerations, coupled with the association's grudging and confused acceptance of collective bargaining, make the AAUP's claim "to be well qualified to act as representative of the faculty" seem pompous nonsense to many faculties.

These comments may seem unduly critical, but they hardly begin to tell it like it is. In absolute terms, AAUP membership was slightly less in 1971 than in 1968. Since the total number of faculty eligible for membership had increased by 89,000 since 1968, the AAUP has actually been enrolling a declining proportion of the professoriate in recent years. Even if its policies change, it may take years before the Association can compete successfully with NEA and AFT. In fact, it may not get that chance.

CONSEQUENCES

The stakes in the rivalry are enormous. By 1980, institutions of higher education will employ approximately one million academicians, excluding administrative personnel. Add them (and their dues of about $100 million) to the three million teachers paying about $300 million in dues by 1980, and you have a powerful lobby for the cause of education in local, state, and federal legislatures. Whether the lobby will also gain better instruction for students is a debatable question. Nevertheless, we can point to certain consequences of faculty unionization that seem inevitable at this point. They will affect all of us, as parents, students, and taxpayers. Let us look at them briefly.

The end of "faculty self-government." The concept of "faculty self-government" translates differently at different institutions. In practice, it may be anything from total institutional or departmental anarchy to the right of an individual faculty member to do as he pleases, regardless of institutional or public needs and interests. The most widely accepted statement on the subject was adopted in 1966 by the AAUP, the American Council on Education, and the Association of Governing Boards of Universities and Colleges. This statement included the following:

> The faculty has primary responsibility for such fundamental areas as curriculum, subject matter and methods of instruction, research, faculty status, and those aspects of student life which relate to the educational process. . . .

> The governing board and president should, on questions of faculty status, as in other matters where the faculty has primary responsibility, concur with the faculty judgment except in rare instances and for compelling reasons which should be stated in detail.

This statement goes far in explaining why higher education is one of this country's most irresponsible institutions. When a faculty controls tenure, promotions, courses, and grades, if only by exercising a veto, to whom is it responsible except itself? What can be done about a tenured faculty that approves the appointment of incompetent professors? About academic departments or individual professors who use their entrenched positions to offer more courses in trivial subjects? Under "faculty self-government," nothing can be done about it. As long as faculties are the sole judges of their own actions, it is hopeless to expect higher education to be responsive to public needs and interests.

The advent of unionization and collective bargaining is bound to inject a measure of management accountability into these matters.

Despite what professors may think, decisions on personnel or programs are not right just because the faculty makes them. If they are right, it is because certain criteria were applied in making them. The crucial question becomes, therefore, not who made the decisions, but who is responsible for the criteria being followed. Under collective bargaining, the faculty has, of course, a major role in establishing the criteria. What they lose under collective bargaining is the operational responsibility for making and carrying out the decisions made according to those criteria. But their loss will be higher education's gain. The role of a faculty should not be to administer an institution but to ensure that administration is fair and equitable. Unfortunately, pathetic confusions about professionalism have misled faculty members into believing that professors at each institution are entitled to make management decisions. The tragedy is that so many administrators, governing boards, and legislatures have been conned into accepting this irresponsible doctrine. Collective bargaining will force professors out of administration, but administrators will be monitored by faculty unions in the performance of their administrative duties. This brings me to a second major consequence of faculty unionization.

College and university administrators will be forced into a management role, while boards of governors and trustees will lose power. Most institutions of higher education, both public and private, are governed by boards of trustees or regents, who are distinguished, rich, politically influential, or perhaps all of these. Such boards usually enjoy broad latitude in conducting their business. If, for example, sabbaticals are on the agenda one month but other items seem more urgent at the time, the board has no difficulty in postponing consideration of the sabbatical question until the next meeting.

Under collective bargaining, this open-ended approach to the terms and conditions of faculty employment will no longer be possible. The very nature of bargaining requires that such matters be considered as a package by a fixed date. If agreement on a package is not reached, the outcome is likely to be a strike or job action of some sort. And in the absence of an agreement, neither the administration, nor the board, nor the faculty will find it easy to go about their business as usual.

More significantly, negotiators for the governing board must have authority to negotiate. A faculty union, like any other union, will not bargain with management representatives who are no more than messengers. Thus the dynamics of bargaining leads to a shift in power from the board to a bargaining team that will be part of the administration.

As administrators confront their management responsibilities, we can expect them to take a growing interest in educational productivity. "Productivity" has an unpleasant ring to most professors. Many contend that you can't measure it at all and shouldn't even try. Nevertheless, a recent study sponsored by the Carnegie Commission on Higher Education concluded that the cost of producing a credit-hour of instruction rose about 3 per cent a year between 1930 and 1967. Even most professors would be slow to claim that quality has kept pace with those increasing costs. Thus an early outcome of collective bargaining will be to force administrators to question the means they use to attain institutional objectives. In the long run, this will lead to a painful but necessary analysis of the objectives themselves. Do we really need this section, this course, this program, this building, this dormitory? Once collective bargaining forces administrators to think hard along these lines, we can expect substantial changes in both the goals and operations of higher education.

Faculty unionization will be accompanied by a tremendous growth in organizational staff and resources. Collective bargaining requires an enormous amount of work. Though professors have more time for these tasks than most people, they recognize that the do-it-yourself approach is not very effective. As faculty unions strive to become bargaining agents, they need personnel to assess the issues, prepare and distribute organizing literature, plan the strategy, and deal with a host of logistical, legal, budgetary, and tactical problems.

This full-time professional staff will present administrators with some serious problems. Administrators who have little or no bargaining experience will increasingly confront union representatives who are veterans at the game. The early bargaining results, therefore, are likely to have unfortunate consequences for students and taxpayers generally. Collective bargaining will be an expensive adult-education course for administrators willing to spend money to get out of trouble, but not willing to spend it to stay out of trouble in the first place.

There will be greater political activity by professorial groups. Right now, professors are highly organized by subject matter or field of interest. There are hundreds of local, state, and national academic societies. As a group, however, academic organizations wield relatively little political influence. A convention of sociologists may denounce Congressman Claghorn, but Claghorn knows that the sociologists have no organization that can turn out the vote in his district. A denunciation by a faculty union with full-time staff at all levels of government would be something else again.

As unionization gains momentum, the political influence of professors will increase correspondingly. The reason will not be their brilliance, a thought that would occur only to those who confuse professors with intellectuals. Rather it will come from their dollars and availability as leg workers. Professors are relatively affluent in our society. Whereas assembly-line workers cannot suddenly take off for New Hampshire or California to work in a primary campaign, professors often can. Sooner or later, however, some political leaders are going to raise embarrassing questions about professors suddenly dropping their duties to push some professorial cause far away from the classroom.

Finally, as suggested in our opening scenario, faculty unions will stimulate the organization of student unions. The student population at many institutions is certainly large enough to support an independent student union to protect and further student interests. These unions will be financed and directly controlled by students. In most cases, they will employ permanent professional staffs who will provide continuity in student representation. The student unions will seek to participate in bargaining between the faculty and the administration, and they will often be the decisive factor in resolving disputes between these groups.

In these disputes, students will usually line up with the administration against the faculty. After all, the students are in the best position to know when professors cancel classes to "consult" in Washington, or when graduate assistants turn back sloppily graded and unannotated term papers. Students also know when professors assign their own textbooks in class, thereby collecting more royalties. If a student union decided to stop this practice, it might easily uncover state laws prohibiting public employees from getting kickbacks. It's just that no one ever thought of applying these laws to professors. In any case, the viability of student unions will depend on their ability to act effectively on campus issues. If they can do this, they could have a beneficial impact on higher education.

Let me conclude on an optimistic note, justified more by collective-bargaining experience elsewhere than by limited experience with it in higher education. Unionization and collective bargaining are conservative processes, especially in public employment. If one believes, as I do, that our society should always be on guard against arbitrary and capricious acts by public agencies, then strong and independent employee organizations are essential. They must be able to demand that politicians and public administrators explain their actions. They must be able to protect their individual members. They must be able to expose and criticize the shortcomings of particular employers. Individuals cannot do these things; neither can faculty organizations controlled by the administration. The paradox of faculty unionization is that although it is a faculty initiative, perhaps its most salutary effects will not be what it does for professors, but what it will do to make administrations more efficient, more alert to innovation, and more responsive to the public interest.

Unionization and collective bargaining are conservative also in the sense that they are well-established institutions in our society. The ultimate paradox is that such a conservative process, by being introduced so late into higher education, will have such revolutionary outcomes.

56. Cesar Chavez

Joan London

Henry Anderson

Leadership of an effective social movement need not necessarily arise from the persons most likely to benefit from it. Primary leadership of the abolition movement did not and could not come from slaves. Leadership of the child labor movement did not and could not come from children.

During most of the history of the farm labor movement in California, primary leadership did not come from the isolated, semicaptive groups which made up the agricultural work force. Leadership came from political groups (such as the IWW), urban unionists . . . intellectuals . . . the clergy . . . and sometimes even from representatives of foreign governments. . . .

There is a fine justice, however, when leadership is assumed by a person who is himself from the aggrieved group and has never really left it. That has now occurred in the farm labor movement in California. It has achieved its greatest successes under the leadership of Cesar Chavez. . . . Chavez is a Chicano (Mexican-American) who worked in the fields as he organized; who looks and talks and acts as farm workers do; who is trusted by farm workers as perhaps no other leader of the movement has ever been.

The Chavez clan, headed by Cesar's grandparents, came to the United States as refugees from the Mexican revolution. Joining other displaced persons, they moved across the Southwest with the crops, but unlike most of the others, they were able to save enough to make a down payment on a farm of their own near the Colorado River in Arizona. There, in 1927, Cesar Estrada Chavez was born. His father's name, Librado, means Freedom.

The Chavez family managed to hold its land through most of the Depression, yielding only in 1938 to the combination of forces arrayed against small landowners. Migrants again, they started west, unprepared for the viciousness which California's farm labor jungle had assumed during the Depression.

For the next several years, they lived in their car, or in tents without heat or light; went without shoes in the winter; ate wild mustard greens to stay alive; were used mercilessly by labor contractors. In time, the family learned the tricks of labor contractors, learned where to find work, how long to stay, when to move on.

Cesar Chavez does not recall these memories bitterly, but matter-of-factly, and often with self-deprecatory humor. This style, and the memories themselves, are significant elements in his leadership of the Spanish-speaking farm workers of the Southwest. . . .

. . . In 1952, a crucial meeting took place . . . between Chavez and Fred Ross of the Community Service Organization.

The CSO was an outgrowth of the Industrial Areas Foundation, itself an outgrowth of Saul

Alinsky's Back of the Yards movement which organized the lower-middle-class area around the Chicago stockyards in the early 1940's. The core of Alinsky's organizing philosophy is the belief that social change is more basic and lasting if the people affected by problems identify those problems for themselves and band together in interest-groups to deal with them. Alinsky enjoyed titillating friends and foes alike with frequent allusions to "radical" and "revolutionary," but his technique was actually a revolution against nothing so much as the paternalistic social-worker mentality. . . .

The organizing assumptions [were]: no decision-making by outside elites; no demagoguery, bombast, or empty threats; rather, a long series of small meetings in private homes, gradually joining in a larger structure. When the time came for a confrontation with existing institutions, the power would be real, not merely theoretical, and could be channeled overnight into picketing, boycotting, sitting-in, voting the rascals out, or other appropriate forms of action.

It is not true, as has often been alleged, that Chavez was "trained by Alinsky." He got all his training in San Jose, while working as a laborer during the day, and in the evenings going to house meetings with Fred Ross. After Chavez proved his competence and perseverance, Ross offered him a job, at $35 a week, organizing on his own. Chavez accepted, although he felt very "awkward" talking to strangers, and sometimes drove around the block several times before he "got up enough nerve" to preside at a house meeting in a new neighborhood. He retains this natural modesty to the present day. . . .

Chavez's organizing skills were so evident that, in 1960, he was appointed General Director of the national CSO. With the help, among others, of Dolores Huerta, who became his principal assistant, he built the CSO to a strength of twenty-two active chapters in California and Arizona.

As a direct result of CSO efforts, two major pieces of legislation were enacted. Old Age Security benefits were extended to first-generation Mexicans even if they had not become naturalized citizens; and the state disability insurance program was extended to agricultural workers. The latter was an important advance even though workers themselves had to pay the premiums through a 1 percent payroll deduction. It was the first social insurance program which required all agricultural employers in the state to report precisely who worked for them, how long, and how much they earned: information basic to the ultimate stabilization of the farm labor market.

Despite such achievements, Chavez began to grow restive in his position. Some CSO leaders felt that the solution to the economic and social problems of Spanish-speaking persons was for them to get out of agricultural employment altogether and turn it over to braceros.* Chavez could not have disagreed more. The only solution, he believed, was to end the bracero system and upgrade farm work until it was no longer a badge of inferiority, and no longer something from which people would want to flee to the cities. Chavez felt that farm labor organizing should receive the overwhelming emphasis in CSO's program.

Chavez let it be known that he would have to reconsider his place within CSO if the 1962 convention turned down a rural-oriented organizing program. . . .

With no outside support of any kind, Chavez began to organize agricultural workers. In order to avoid any suggestion that the organization would function immediately as an orthodox trade union, he called it the Farm Workers Association. . . .

Chavez is not a dogmatic man, but he came close to it on one point: support from outside, he was sure, could do more harm than good in the formative stages of a movement. . . .

Chavez felt that large or even medium-sized financial contributions carry strings which may strangle a young, immature organization, but he did not necessarily extend the same theory to an organization which had firmly charted its own course and proved its own vitality. By the end of 1965, Chavez was accepting substantial financial contributions to FWA and not only were they doing no harm, they were enabling the organization to survive what would otherwise have been fatal circumstances.

Another of Chavez's organizing concepts, which could probably be traced to the influence of Father McDonnell, was the necessity for sacrifice. In much the same spirit, Jack London had said shortly after the 1913 Wheatland Riot, "It is always the things we fight for, bleed for, suffer for, that we care the most for."

*Editor's note: "Braceros" are contract workers from Mexico.

Dues in FWA were deliberately set at a level which represented a substantial sacrifice for most farm workers: +3.50 per month. Furthermore, the privileges of membership were limited strictly to those whose dues were current, unlike [farm workers], and other previous organizations, which had been very lenient about such matters. In an interview, Chavez explained: "When members pay so much, they feel they aren't just hangers-on. They feel they are the important part of the organization—that they have a right to be served. They don't hesitate to write, to call, to ask for things. The idea that they, alone, are paying the salary of the man who is responsible to them is very important."

There were many other mansions in the house of Chavez's organizing philosophy. He scrupulously avoided talk of strikes while the Association was small and had no chance of winning. He avoided mass meetings and other means to quick but evanescent membership increases and enthusiasms. He avoided crisis psychology. He assumed he had time enough, and he used time itself as an organizing tool, to let self-seekers and mere talkers drop away, and to let natural leaders of integrity emerge.

Chavez knew that the stereotype of farm workers' homogeneity was false. He knew that Mexican, Anglo, Filipino, and Negro agricultural laborers were often suspicious of one another. He knew that the concerns of out-of-state migrants were not quite the same as the concerns of in-state migrants, and that neither were the same as the interests of the home guard. He knew that many farm workers were likely, at first, to be apathetic or even antagonistic toward unionization: year-round hands who thought of themselves as part of management; green carders who wanted only to return to Mexico with as much money and little trouble as possible; wetbacks who were subject to deportation if they attracted any attention; wounded, disillusioned veterans of previous organizing drives which had failed; housewives, students, and other casual workers who had no intention of remaining in agriculture.

Chavez knew that farm worker "solidarity" was a dream of old radicals or romantic urban friends of the movement, and that in time of crisis some workers would scab on others. The task of the genuine organizer was not to strive for an impossible unity, but to organize as many as possible of the real farm workers: those who had a serious attachment to agriculture and were most essential to the functioning of the industry.

Every night, fighting his fatigue after working in the fields all day, Chavez went to the homes of this type of worker, explaining the Farm Workers Association, pointing out the short-run kinds of things members could do by working together: they could form a credit union; help one another with workmen's compensation and other quasi-legal problems; get preferential rates on insurance. . . .

By the middle of 1964, the Association was self-supporting. It had perhaps a thousand dues-paying members, in more than fifty local groups, spread over seven counties. Chavez no longer needed to work in the fields. The primary problem now became one of satisfying the members' desire for accomplishment, without entering into precipitate adventures of the type which had led to the demise of so many earlier farm labor organizations.

FWA took a "militant" position for the first time in May, 1965, when it assisted a rent strike against the Tulare County Housing Authority, to protest rent increases of 40 percent at two farm labor camps with very substandard facilities. In the summer of 1965, there were two small strikes, involving FWA members on horticultural farms. Both won their objectives: wage increases, and the rehiring of members who had been discharged.

Something electric was in the air by late August.

No matter how sound its basic plan, how shrewd its day-to-day tactics, and how great the magnetism of its leaders, the career of every social movement is shaped at many crucial points by historical accidents and by unbelievers who know not what they do. The "Delano movement"—which, after September, 1965, the FWA was often called—began fortuitously, and at critical junctures received help from unlikely sources.

When Public Law 78 ended on December 31, 1964, the U.S. Department of Labor continued to admit braceros to California simply by calling them something else and changing the rules slightly. The 1965 rules required payment of $1.40 an hour. Through this requirement, quite unintentionally, the Department of Labor, never renowned as a fearless friend of the farm labor movement, helped set the stage for events in Delano.

The second major impetus came from the

self-organized Filipino workers who had joined AWOC* six years earlier, and were never members of FWA at all. The AWOC representative assigned to this Filipino group was Larry Itliong. In 1929, when he was fifteen, Itliong had left his home in the Philippines to come to the United States. He had worked in the fields for some years, then moved into the Northwest fishing and canning industries where he helped organize his compatriots. When he joined the staff of AWOC, he made his headquarters in Delano, which served as "home base" for a sizable number of Filipino agricultural workers.

Table grapes are among the crops in which Filipinos have long specialized. California grapes ripen first in the Coachella Valley each year. There, in May, 1965, fortuitous links began coming together into the start of a long chain.

Coachella Valley growers were told by the Department of Labor that they would have to pay braceros $1.40 an hour. Filipino grape pickers felt they were entitled to the same rate. When they did not receive it, they turned for help to Larry Itliong and AWOC. There was a brief work stoppage. Largely through the leverage of the growers' desire for braceros, the Filipinos won their wage demand.

By September, many of these same workers had moved north to the Delano area, where the table grape season was just beginning. The growers were offering $1.20 an hour, plus a "bonus" of five cents per man per box. The workers saw no reason why they should get less than they had in the Coachella Valley. Again they turned to AWOC. Registered letters, asking for a meeting, were sent to the ten Delano grower-shippers who employed most Filipino grape workers. The letters were ignored. A majority—some say as many as 90 percent—of the Filipinos walked off their jobs.

From the beginning of the strike on September 8, it was taken for granted that FWA members would not cross the Filipinos' picket lines into the premises of the ten struck grower-shippers. But would they be strikebreaking if they continued picking other grapes in the Delano area? It was a painful dilemma for Chavez and the other FWA leaders. They calculated they were about two years away from being prepared for a major strike. On the other hand, how could they permit themselves to give

the appearance of scabbing on another farm workers' organization? They decided to put the question to a vote of the FWA membership.

An emergency meeting was called for September 16, the 145th anniversary of the independence of Mexico from Spain. The largest hall in Delano overflowed, with many members standing outside. Emotions were overflowing too. When no one voiced any misgivings about extending the strike to all Delano grape growers, Chavez took it upon himself to explain how great the sacrifices would be and how limited were FWA's resources.

Nonetheless, the vote for *la huelga* (the strike) was unanimous. The cries went up: "Viva la huelga!" "Viva la causa!" "Viva Cesar Chavez!"

Grape growers evicted the Filipinos from their camps and imported strikebreakers without informing them that a strike was in progress. The growers doubtless expected the strike would run its course within a few weeks, as had been the case with every strike during AWOC's six-year history. From the day FWA entered the strike, however, there were important differences between this and AWOC-led strikes.

Delano growers found they were dealing, not with traditional labor theories and techniques, but with a "new breed" of farm workers, taking their inspiration from Thoreauvian friends of the movement who refused to be intimidated by laws which they conscientiously considered unjust. The new Thoreauvians included civil rights workers who had gone to jail in defiance of the South's notions of law and order; students who have been challenging the "multiversity"; Reverend Chris Hartmire and other young ministers and priests who believed that true reverence lies in the social gospel.

Growers first tried to crush the new breed by time-tested means. They called on their nearly total control over the Kern County sheriff's department and courts. On October 18, forty-four pickets, including nine clergymen, were arrested for chanting "Huelga" from the side of a public road. Cesar Chavez was arrested for trying to communicate with strikebreakers from a light plane equipped with a loudspeaker. He, Dolores Huerto, and other strike leaders were arrested again and again, and had to devote much of their time and energy to court appearances.

Veteran labor reporters for California's metropolitan newspapers said the strike could

---

*Editor's note: Agricultural Workers Organizing Committee of the AFL-CIO.

not possibly be won. Since collective bargaining laws did not apply to agriculture, it was a naked test of strength, and how could the strength of penniless farm workers compare with that of multimillion-dollar corporations?

Paying no attention to the labor experts, Chavez and the other members of the FWA executive committee invented their own precedents as they went along. They decided to follow the grapes out of the fields and to try to upset the distribution system. FWA representatives traced many grape shipments to terminals in San Francisco, Oakland, Stockton, Los Angeles. Some individual members of the Teamsters respected the FWA picket lines. Members of the International Longshoremen's and Warehousemen's Union refused to load "hot" grapes. . . .

FWA continued probing, searching, upsetting stale formulations. In mid-December, the quest for new directions yielded an inspiration: a boycott against the products of Schenley Industries, one of the two largest Delano firms. The concept of a consumer boycott had been considered many times in the history of the farm labor movement, and had always been rejected as unworkable. FWA went ahead, undeterred. The movement quickly expanded across the country. Trade unionists, students, and other urban sympathizers who had not been able to come to Delano personally could now assist la huelga in useful ways. FWA representatives were dispatched to most of the major cities in the country to organize and coordinate local boycott groups.

On December 18, 1965, a few days after the boycott began, Walter Reuther came to Delano. He pledged $5,000 a month support from his United Automobile Workers union. . . .

In March, 1966, Senator Harrison Williams, Democrat of New Jersey, brought his Subcommittee on Migratory Labor to California for public hearings. The ostensible purpose was to gather testimony on a sheaf of six farm labor bills introduced by Williams, but the practical effect of the hearings was to focus public attention on the Delano grape strike more sharply than ever.

On the final day of the hearings, Senator Robert F. Kennedy lent his full influence to the FWA cause. He told the Kern County sheriff, "I suggest you read the Constitution of the United States before you arrest any more strikers."

And Kennedy stated, "If we can get a man on the moon by the end of the 1960's, it seems we should be able to work out collective bargaining for farm workers after talking about it for thirty years." His words were transmitted nationally.

From this public relations triumph, FWA vaulted immediately to another. It seems to have been Chavez's own idea, originally: a march to the state capitol in Sacramento to petition Governor Pat Brown to do something about collective bargaining rights for farm workers. The idea was explored within the FWA executive group. Why not time the march to arrive on the steps of the capitol on Easter morning, which was about a month away? Someone pointed out that this meant the march would take place during the Lenten season, and ought properly to have an aspect of sacrifice and penitence. Someone else noted that many such processions take place in Mexico during Lent, and are known as *peregrinaciones* or pilgrimages. . . .

The length of the march was more than 230 miles. . . . For twenty-five days, the Delano pilgrims marched. Several dozen farm workers walked every step of the way. For greater or lesser periods of time, these *originales* were joined by many other farm workers, public officials, churchmen, newspapermen, and California citizens of all types. Each night, the march paused in a farm labor community where hospitality was provided in the homes of local farm workers. There was a nightly rally at which the Plan of Delano was read; *corridas* (ballads) about the strike and the march were sung; El Teatro Compesino, the Farm Workers Theater, presented skits lampooning *esquiroles* (scabs) and *patroncitos* (growers); and everyone had a chance to see Cesar Chavez, limping with blisters.

. . . News of the march appeared in the California press for twenty-five consecutive days. It was scarcely possible any longer for a literate person to remain unaware of the Delano movement.

On April 6, just four days before Easter, the line of march was galvanized by news which seemed heaven-sent: Schenley had agreed to recognize FWA and to negotiate a contract covering all Schenley field workers in the Delano area. The boycott had won its objective. On the following day, an even more astounding development was announced. After years of implacable opposition to farm unions, officials of the Di Giorgio Corporation suddenly announced that they were offering representation elections to three groups: FWA, AWOC, and an "Independent Kern-Tulare Farm Workers Association."

At high noon on Easter Sunday, with the banner of the Virgin of Guadalupe extending a benediction over all, more than ten thousand persons stood on the steps and adjacent lawns of the state capitol as the peregrinación reached its triumphant conclusion. Prayers, speeches, songs, pledges of support, cries of *Viva!* filled a three-hour rally.

The uninitiated hailed Di Giorgio's offer of representation elections as the beginning of the end for the open shop in California agriculture, but as a matter of fact it was full of booby traps. For instance, the company proposed to let strikebreakers vote, but not strikers. In several meetings between FWA and company representatives, little progress toward eliminating the booby traps was made. The company accused FWA of bad faith and broke off negotiations. FWA thereupon launched a boycott of Di Giorgio's two most readily identifiable products: Treesweet frozen juices, and S & W canned goods.

The company then played its trump card, announcing that the Teamsters union would make a good representative for its Delano workers, and should be included on the ballot. The Teamsters graciously agreed. On June 22, the company abruptly announced that the election would be held within forty-eight hours, under its own ground rules.

Moving fast, FWA and AWOC obtained a court order prohibiting the unauthorized use of their names on the ballot. Two choices remained: the Teamsters and "no union," with the company urging a vote for the Teamsters. Predictably enough, the Teamsters won, but their victory was something less than overwhelming. Of 732 workers eligible to vote under the company's rules, 9 wrote in the name of FWA, 3 wrote in AWOC, 60 voted for "no union," 281 voted for the Teamsters—but 379 declined to vote at all, which is what FWA and AWOC had urged.

Nevertheless, it was a gloomy hour for Cesar Chavez and his organization. For years, knowledgeable observers of the farm labor movement had said, "If the Teamsters ever decide to get

into it, look out." With the exception of a couple of contracts with Salinas Valley lettuce growers in 1961, the Teamsters had always stayed out of the fields. But now it looked as though the Teamsters were staking a claim to field workers, and it looked as though nothing could save FWA.

Cesar Chavez and his associates were not panicked. First, they mobilized pressure on Governor Brown. Brown appointed Ronald Haughton, a nationally respected arbitrator, to investigate the Di Giorgio election. Haughton recommended a new election, under fair and reasonable rules. The next step was to induce Di Giorgio and the Teamsters to accept this recommendation. Clergymen called on Teamster officials of their faith. Brown probably used his personal influence with Robert Di Giorgio, an old schoolmate and friend. The full story may never be known, but by July 16, all parties concerned had agreed to a new election.

Under the new rules, everyone who had worked for Di Giorgio for fifteen days or more since the beginning of the strike was eligible to vote. All these persons were by definition strikebreakers, and might be expected to follow the company's advice of a vote for Teamsters. Di Giorgio workers who had left their jobs when the strike began were also eligible to vote, but by now they had scattered through the Western states and Mexico, usually without forwarding addresses.

FWA had two practical problems, each of which seemed insuperable: to change the attitudes of company-oriented workers; and to locate former employees dispersed over much of the North American continent. Labor experts predicted, as usual, that FWA could not win and the Teamsters could not lose.

FWA went about its business. Fred Ross, Chavez's mentor from fifteen years before, appeared in Delano and began training dozens of volunteer organizers to go into Di Giorgio camps to talk with strikebreakers. When it came to the former employees, Chavez relied heavily on a method which the experts could not have anticipated, since it was quite outside any orthodox union experience.

Through a many-filamented "grapevine," the message went out, penetrating to truck farms in eastern Washington, cotton empires in Texas, tiny villages on the high plateaus of central Mexico. From mouth to mouth, the message went: "Be in Delano on August 30."

"Why?" "I'm not sure, exactly. But Cesar says it's important." That was enough to bring scores of former grape workers back to Delano on the appointed date.

The Teamster campaign was conducted by professionals who did not scruple to use such tactics as red-baiting and race-baiting. FWA replied with some invective of its own—of which "jailbird" and "Judas" were representative—but it had far more meaningful arguments. The contract just signed with Schenley proved that FWA was of tangible benefit to its members. The contract provided a starting wage of $1.75 an hour, compared to the $1.40 which other growers were paying; there was a union hiring hall which ended the abuses of labor contractors; there were provisions for seniority, stewards, paid vacations, and other forms of security and dignity California farm workers had never known before.

On August 22, FWA and AWOC merged into a new entity, known as the United Farm Workers Organizing Committee (UFWOC), AFL-CIO. Cesar Chavez became director; Larry Itliong, assistant director. A few sectarians thought this move indicated Chavez had "sold out" his ideals to Big Labor. In point of fact, the problem of dual unionism had troubled FWS and AWOC from the beginning; a merger would soon have been necessary under any circumstances. In further point of fact, a merger was necessary at this particular time in order to preserve anything at all of FWA and its ideals. Chavez knew that losing to the Teamsters would mean the end of the Delano movement, and he foresaw a loss if the legitimate farm worker vote were split between FWA and AWOC.

As a final point of fact, the terms of the merger were such that Chavez retained complete autonomy in strategic and tactical decision-making, the right to continue using volunteer organizers, and all the other prerogatives he considered essential.

The election campaign neared its close. Teamster representatives sponsored a final rally, with free beer, and promptly at 5:00 P.M., as was their wont, retired to the Stardust Motel, Delano's finest, where they swam in the pool or relaxed in air-conditioned rooms. UFWOC representatives worked until late at night, talking with workers in their homes or in labor camps.

Early in the morning on August 30, farm workers began arriving at the polling places, for the first bona fide representation election in California agriculture. They continued to arrive throughout the day, making farm labor history. The official results were announced on September 2. UFWOC had received 530 votes, the Teamsters, 331; 12 workers preferred no union. Cesar Chavez and his dedicated band of amateurs had won a contest against the largest, richest union in the world in league with one of the largest agricultural corporations. . . .

In 1967, the union began winning recognition, negotiations, and contracts through "card checks." When union representatives had pledge cards from a clear majority of a company's field workers, they asked for collective bargaining without the delay and acrimony of a contested election which would only result in a union victory in the end. Through card checks, UFWOC has obtained contracts with some of the major wineries in California, including Gallo, Almadén, Christian Brothers, Paul Masson, and Franzia. . . .

Organizers reported that most employees of the Giumarra Vineyard Corporation wanted union representation. Chavez wrote to Joseph Giumarra, asking for a meeting "to work out a method to settle the question of recognition. . . ." There was no reply. Other overtures were spurned. Several hundred Giumarra workers voted unanimously to strike. Giumarra flooded his vineyards with green carders.* Union efforts to staunch this flood were largely unavailing. UFWOC leaders undertook [another] consumer boycott, emboldened by [their previous successes]. In August, 1967, the great grape boycott began.

Unlike [the previously boycotted firms], Giumarra dealt in fresh grapes for the table, with no readily identifiable brand name. Furthermore, he began borrowing labels from other table-grape growers—a tactic of doubtful legality under the 1966 "Truth in Packaging" Act. To meet this tactic, UFWOC leaders decided they would have to boycott all California table grapes. They dispatched their best organizers to the major urban centers of the United States and Canada, and trained new organizers to go to cities which had been untouched in previous boycotts.

Mayors or city councils of Cleveland, De-

---

*Editor's note: Green carders are Mexican citizens with green identification cards required by the U.S. government.

troit, San Francisco, and other cities endorsed the table-grape boycott. . . . New York City was nearly completely "shut down." . . .

All the contenders for the 1968 Democratic presidential nomination supported farm workers' right to collective bargaining, and supported the boycott as a legitimate device to secure that right. Hubert Humphrey, after he won the nomination, met personally with Cesar Chavez. . . .

Thousands of tons of grapes have been diverted from table use to wineries. Others have had to be sold on the fresh market at reduced prices. Some have been quietly dumped. Even opponents of the boycott concede that it had been 20 to 25 percent effective: total income to grape growers has been that much less than it would most probably have been without the boycott. . . .

. . . [Even though the] growers induced the Department of Defense to increase shipments of grapes to Vietnam from 468,000 pounds in 1967 to 2,167,000 pounds in 1969. . . .

. . . [In May, 1970], came the breakthrough the Delano strikers had been pointing toward for over four and a half years. Two of the largest Delano table-grape growers, Bianco Fruit Corporation and Bruno Dispoto, signed contracts. They had been two of the very first firms truck in September, 1965, and two of the most extreme in their opposition to AWOC, FWA, and UFWOC. Their agreement to terms was thus particularly symbolic—but it was also particularly substantial. These were giants of the industry, operating more than 3,200 acres of vineyards and producing 1.2 million boxes of table grapes a year.

These contracts call for wage increases of 25 to 35 cents an hour; employer contributions to UFWOC health and welfare fund; an additional contribution to go into an "economic development fund" to aid workers displaced due to age or mechanization; protections against pesticides; and "successor clauses" which tie the union contract to the land regardless of whether ownership is transferred.

At the time of the signing, Bruno Dispoto said, "We worked hard on this contract. It is one that we can live with, one that should interest other growers in the industry." The last clause is the key. Some 95 percent of California's table-grape production was not covered by union contract at that time.

Can the sales of union-picked grapes be encouraged as effectively as the sales of non-union grapes were discouraged? The boxes in which fresh produce is packed are usually left in the back rooms of markets. Will consumers go to the trouble of finding out whether boxes of grapes bear UFWOC's union label of a black thunderbird on a red and white background? Or can some other means of notification be devised?—for example, bunches individually packaged in plastic bags carrying the union label.

If answers to such questions are forthcoming—if the sales of growers with contracts flourish while others continue to languish—it is difficult to see that any rational agribusinessman would choose to go on committing economic suicide. There is one important new element in the equation: UFWOC is no longer standing entirely alone against the whole table-grape industry. Dispoto, Bianco, and the other companies under contract will be promoting their own product, which will be tantamount to discouraging sales of the nonunion product.

In short, UFWOC has driven a wedge into the table-grape industry, and it will never again constitute a united front against unionization. Henceforth, one portion of the industry will, in effect, be working with the union to persuade the other portion of the industry to move from the labor practices of the late nineteenth century to those of the late twentieth. During most of the history of the farm labor movement, California growers have employed a strategy of "divide and conquer" against nascent unions. A union is now, for the first time, in a position to use the same leverage on the industry. . . .

How "radical" is Cesar Chavez? Tremendously. Not very. Everything depends on one's point of view, and one's terms. . . .

To allege, as some do, that Chavez is "out to destroy California agriculture" is preposterous. He is the least vindictive of men. Of all farm labor leaders, he best understands agriculture and its real problems as distinguished from its fantasies. He well realizes that the interests of the union's members presuppose a healthy agricultural industry. When the growers of grapes or any other major commodity recognize the union, Chavez plans to turn his nationwide apparatus around, and have his community coordinators urge consumers to buy more grapes, or whatever crop is involved. . . .

The desires of farm workers are essentially conservative, in that they include only those things which the American economy has demonstrated it is quite capable of conferring upon other workers: reasonable wages, reasonable safety and other working conditions, reasonable fringe benefits, reasonable job security, and underlying all a reasonable voice in determining what is reasonable. . . .

Despite many disappointments, Chavez, other UFWOC leaders, and the membership retain a basic confidence in the democratic process. True, they are wary of administrative agencies. This attitude hurts the feelings of some persons from within those agencies, who consider themselves friends of the movement. The union's wariness is not directed against individuals; it is directed against bureaucracies in which individuals, however sympathetic, are not free agents. As Chavez once put it, "You can't build an organization around something that can be given or taken away at the whim of some bureau chief. We have to build around programs we can be sure of—and the only programs we can be absolutely sure of are those where we do the policing ourselves."

But for all this caution, Chavez depends in many ways upon the ultimate workability of representative democracy, with an executive branch and an independent judiciary. Although the union has seldom if ever won a case in a municipal or county court, it keeps trying, and often wins on appeal. . . .

Chavez [asked] for legislation which would exempt agricultural workers from those sections of the Taft-Hartley and Landrum-Griffin Acts defining secondary boycotts and recognition picketing as "unfair labor practices."

Some of Chavez's friends were taken aback by this demand, since the movement had for years marched under the slogan of "Equal rights for farm workers." Then Chavez explained: he was asking for the same rights other workers had enjoyed *when they were at a comparable stage in their organization.*

The Wagner Act of 1935 was openly "pro-union," in order more nearly to equalize the bargaining strengths of workers and employers. The Wagner Act permitted secondary boycotts: that is, boycotts against businesses which were not directly involved in a labor dispute but which handled struck goods. The Wagner Act also permitted organizational picketing: that is, picketing before a union had been recognized as collective bargaining agent, in order to pressure a company into holding a representation election. By 1947, most industries had become organized, and many unions had become very powerful. Seeking a new balance of power, the Taft-Hartley Act banned some of the unions' weapons. The Landrum-Griffin Act of 1959 banned others.

Chavez says, "We too need our decent period of time to grow strong under the life-giving sun of a public policy which affirmatively favors the growth of farm unionism." . . .

When the Delano strike began, and Chavez obtained from both AWOC and FWA members a pledge that it would be conducted nonviolently, his beliefs were probably largely pragmatic. Violence would be counterproductive; damaging growers' property would only stiffen their resistance; assaulting strikebreakers would only alienate church and liberal sympathy and support. And, as Congressman Phillip Burton recently said, "Nonviolence is the greatest selling point we have in Washington. I know all about the Watts business, and the squeaking wheel getting the grease, and all of that. But this is different. If the union ever starts using strong-arm tactics, we're dead. . . ."

Unions and Minorities

Throughout its history the union movement has frequently been represented as championing the cause of the disadvantaged worker. Although skilled workers have often been easier to organize than unskilled, the ideology of the labor movement has generally been very egalitarian—especially since the rise of the CIO during the 1930s. In recent years, however, the racial policies of many unions have been under attack. Unions in the construction crafts and in other areas are charged with excluding blacks and with other discriminatory practices. The selection by Herbert Hill focuses on discriminatory practices within unions where blacks constitute a significant proportion of the membership. In addition to discussing the prevalence of such discrimination, Hill discusses how black caucuses within these unions are attempting to change union policies.

In contrast to Hill's political and legal focus, Orley Ashenfelter presents a quantitative economic analysis of the effect of unions on the relative wages of blacks and whites and of females and males. Although he cannot measure the extent of discrimination in union markets, he does investigate whether there is more or less discrimination against black and female workers in the average unionized labor market or in the average nonunion labor market. Ashenfelter concludes that, although the construction unions have had a negative effect on black wages, the overall effect of all unions has been to slightly *increase* black wages relative to white wages—a result that may occur because many unions (especially industrial unions) have raised wages by a greater percentage for unskilled than skilled workers. Although unions appear to have increased the relative wages of blacks, Ashenfelter estimates that they have slightly decreased the relative wages of females.

Although racial discrimination by unions has received the most attention, Ashenfelter's results indicate that sexual discrimination by unions may be at least equally important. The selection by Alice Cook examines four specific issues involving women and trade unions: the attitude of unions toward protective legislation for women; the effect of recent federal legislation such as the Equal Pay Act on union practice and policy; the degree to which collective bargaining agreements have special clauses pertaining to women; and the participation of women in the political life of unions. Cook concludes that there have been few changes in union attitudes or practices on these issues in recent years.

57. Black Protest and the Struggle for Union Democracy

Herbert Hill

"Black Power" has finally come to organized labor. Although the slogan remains ambiguous, implicit in all its uses is a challenge to the traditional system of racial controls by whites over blacks and a demand that the basic condition of Negro life in the United States, that of powerlessness, be ended.

BLACK STEELWORKERS

Delegates to the 1968 Chicago convention of the United Steelworkers of America (AFL-CIO) were made aware of the emergence of the "Black Power" issue as they were handed a series of leaflets each day by members of the Ad Hoc Committee, the nationwide caucus of black steelworkers which had placed picket lines at the entrance to the convention auditorium. The Ad Hoc Committee succeeded in making the question of Negro exclusion from leadership positions within the union a major public issue for the first time.

In a widely distributed leaflet entitled "An Open Letter to President I. W. Abel From A Black Steelworker," the caucus stated:

The time has come for black workers to speak and act for ourselves. We make no apologies for the fact that we as black workers and loyal trade unionists now act on our own behalf. Furthermore we are fully prepared to do so.

Part of the demands involved the lack of black representation in USW leadership positions:

Of more than 1,000 employees of the International, less than 100 are Negroes. Of 14 departments in the International, only 2 have Negro personnel. One of these 2 departments is the Civil Rights Department (obviously). Of more than 30 Districts in the International, there are no Negro directors and only one sub-district director. Blacks were in the forefront during the formation of this Union over 25 years ago. Through the acceptance of crumbs down through the years instead of our just deserts, we now find ourselves hindmost. . . .

An important factor in the development of the black caucus is that the Steelworkers Union is vigorously defending its traditional discriminatory practices in a series of law suits pending in federal district courts in Birmingham, Alabama, and Columbus, Ohio.

Litigation brought by Negro workers involves charges that the union maintains separate racial seniority lines and other discriminatory job provisions in its contracts with the United States Steel Corporation and other steel manufacturers. This issue was brought to the attention of the international union leadership in 1957 by the National Association for the Advancement of Colored People and there has been a decade of protest by Negro steelworkers including the filing of complaints with the NLRB. The union is, however, defending the discriminatory provisions in its collective bargaining agreements, although the federal courts in several recent decisions have declared such contractual agreements to be illegal.

A survey made by the Steelworkers Union in 1964 of the status of Negroes in unionized steel plants in Youngstown, Ohio, revealed the great disparity between the job status of white and Negro workers. The survey concluded that:

> ... given the same seniority and education, the white employee's chances for advancement are substantially greater than are the Negro's and this is true at all levels of seniority, at all levels of education, and at all job levels. Furthermore each of the tables reveals that a white employee with little or no formal education has a better opportunity for advancement than a Negro high school graduate.

A study of Negro employment in the basic steel industry of Pittsburgh made for the Equal Employment Opportunity Commission released during April 1968 observes that:

> Negroes comprise 12.27 percent of the laborers, 12.93 percent of the service workers, and 10.86 percent of the semiskilled operatives, but only 3.21 percent of the craftsmen. They are, therefore, almost twofold over-represented in the lowest classification and equally disproportionately under-represented in the most skilled blue-collar work.

All of the available data sustains the charge made by the black caucus that there is a significant connection between the exclusion of Negroes from leadership positions within the union, that is, their powerlessness, and the depressed status of Negro workers within the steel plants.

AFL-CIO CIVIL RIGHTS DEPARTMENT

The Negro workers also demanded that Steelworkers President I. W. Abel, who is both a Vice-President and Executive Council member of the AFL-CIO and was recently appointed by George Meany to replace Walter Reuther as head of the Industrial Union Department of the Federation, "secure the reorganization of the Civil Rights Department of the AFL-CIO. We insist that a Negro trade unionist be appointed Director of the Civil Rights Department. . . ."

The attack on the AFL-CIO Civil Rights Department is at least of equal importance to the demands for reform within the Steelworkers Union itself:

> The present director of the AFL-CIO Civil Rights Department [Donald Slaiman] has no involvement with Negro workers and their problems. He does not know of our problems. He does not represent us. He does not act in our interests. We believe we speak for many thousands of Negro workers not only in the Steelworkers Union but in other AFL-CIO affiliates with large Negro memberships when we demand the replacement of a white paternalist with a Black trade unionist who can honestly represent Negro workers and act on their behalf. . . . For years Negro workers have stopped filing complaints with the AFL-CIO Civil Rights Department because experience has taught us that the department is unable to function on our behalf. *Most often it represents the discriminators in organized labor rather than the Black workers who are the victims of white racism within the house of labor.* [emphasis added]

Factually, the Ad Hoc Committee is correct in citing the Federation's Civil Rights Department as a major offender, and as black militance has grown within the ranks of organized labor so has the discontent with this department. Immediately after the merger of the AFL and the CIO in 1955, a Civil Rights Committee and its administrative agency, the Civil Rights Department, were established to carry out the constitutional mandate to abolish discrimination in affiliated unions. The constitution stipulated that one of the purposes of the AFL-CIO was "to encourage all workers without regard to race, creed, color or national origin or ancestry to share equally in the benefits of union organization." In establishing the Civil Rights Committee, the constitution provided that it have "the duty and the responsibility to assist the Executive Council to bring about at the earliest possible date the effective implementation of the principle stated in this constitution of nondiscrimination in accordance with the provisions of this constitution."

From the beginning, however, there were

indications that the Federation had little intention of abiding by its own declarations. In December, 1957, James B. Carey, the first chairman of the Civil Rights Committee, resigned. In his resignation he publicly attacked the Federation's reluctance to move against racist elements among its affiliates. According to a *New York Times* dispatch on the resignation, Carey claimed that "he had not been given enough power or freedom to do an effective job of stamping out racial bias in unions. . . . He felt he was being hamstrung." His position was sustained by the repeated findings of federal courts and civil rights agencies in complaints by Negro union members of patterns of discrimination which persisted despite oft-repeated claims to the contrary by George Meany.

Carey was replaced by Charles S. Zimmerman, a vice president of the International Ladies Garment Workers Union. His term of office did not serve to mollify black protests against the Department's inaction, and in 1959, after the AFL-CIO convention at which the continuing racist practices of many labor unions were excoriated by A. Philip Randolph, Zimmerman was replaced by William F. Schnitzler, the secretary-treasurer of the Federation. His tenure has not been marked by any new departure that would have indicated a willingness by the Federation to move against racial discrimination. The failure of the AFL-CIO Civil Rights Department to carry out its constitutional functions is further demonstrated by the fact that, as the Ad Hoc Committee stated, Negroes no longer even try to redress their grievances, but go directly to the courts and the various public agencies—the NLRB, state and municipal FEPC's, and the Equal Employment Opportunity Commission. (See Hill, "No End of Pledges," *Commonweal*, March 15, 1968.)

The standard response of the Federation in the face of repeated proof of racial discrimination within affiliated unions by public and private agencies, is first to deny the existence of such practices and then to mount an intensive public relations campaign to demonstrate labor's devotion to an abstraction called "civil rights." But mostly the defense has moved along the lines articulated by President Meany at a hearing of the National Advisory Committee on Civil Disorders when he was questioned about specific examples of racial discrimination by unions. Meany was asked about several instances of white AFL-CIO members walking off the job at the direction of union officials when Negroes were hired[1] and about Negroes who had passed written qualifying examinations to join craft unions but failed the "orals," while whites who had lower scores were accepted into membership. Carl Rowan's syndicated column (December 29, 1967) accurately depicts Meany's reaction to the questioning: "Meany allowed as how 'powers of persuasion' were all he had and that he was doing his best to use them against 'autonomous unions.' " Black trade unionists have been quick to point out, however, that on matters other than racial discrimination, Meany has frequently acted in disregard of "autonomy" and that in reality the Federation is more centralized and bureaucratically controlled at present than ever before in its history—a fact that led, in part, to the breakaway of the United Automobile Workers earlier this year.

Black caucuses, however, are not only attacking the failure of the Federation's Civil Rights Department to eliminate racist practices by labor unions, 14 years after the merger; but black workers are also increasingly critical of the Department's activities in support of the racial status quo by intervention with state and federal agencies on behalf of AFL-CIO affiliates charged with violating fair employment practice laws. . . .

In several recent landmark federal court decisions involving the Tobacco Workers Union, the Papermakers and Paperworkers Union, the Asbestos Workers and the Brotherhood of Pulp, Sulphite and Paper Mill Workers, among others, the courts have declared that separate racial seniority lines and other contractual provisions in collective bargaining agreements leading to job assignments on the basis of race are violations of the law. Even though the federal courts are now for the first time providing clear legal definitions of what constitutes racial discrimination in employment, administrative remedies still are blocked since many labor unions continue their defiance of the law and attempt to defend their traditional racist practices in complex court challenges. The legal departments of

[1]On May 17, 1968, white workers belonging to Local 89 of the International Brotherhood of Electrical Workers in Philadelphia walked off their jobs at the construction site of the new U.S. Mint Building, when two Negro mechanics, hired at the insistence of the Office of Federal Contract Compliance, appeared. Previous walkouts by building trades unions at public construction sites had occurred in St. Louis, New York, and Memphis among other cities.

many labor unions are now busily engaged in introducing a tangle of procedural legal questions in an attempt to prevent change by conducting a rearguard holding action in the courts. This, too, is a basic measure of the Federation's policy.[2]

BLACK UNIONS AND BLACK CAUCUSES

Black unions and black caucuses within unions are essentially responses by black trade unionists to the adamant resistance of organized labor to Negro demands for fundamental changes in racial policies and practices. The Independent Alliance of Skilled Crafts in Ohio, the Maryland Freedom Labor Union, the United Community Construction Workers of Boston, the United Construction and Trades Union in Detroit, the Allied Workers International Union in Gary, and similar groups in Seattle, Chicago, Oakland, and elsewhere are examples of independent black unions. The growth of these organizations attests to their appeal to two groups of black workers: those Negroes who live and work in ghetto areas where AFL unions make no attempt to organize and those Negroes in the building trades who, having been denied admission to the AFL craft unions, are attracted to black-controlled hiring halls. These are now being used by building contractors seeking public construction contracts as a result of a 1967 federal court decision (*Ethridge* v. *Rhodes*) which requires contractors to demonstrate that they have an integrated labor force in order to bid for public construction contracts. The black unions demonstrate the practical possibilities inherent in this approach and may be increasingly used

[2]Litigation brought by the Department of Justice and private parties is currently pending against many labor unions including: International Brotherhood of Electrical Workers; United Papermakers and Paperworkers; United Steelworkers of America; Brotherhood of Railway Clerks; International Association of Bridge, Structural and Ornamental Iron Workers; Brotherhood of Railway Carmen; Pulp, Sulphite and Paper Mill Workers; International Association of Heat and Frost Insulators and Asbestos Workers; Brotherhood of Railroad Trainmen; the United Association of Journeymen and Apprentices of the Plumbing and Pipefitting Industry; Sheetmetal Workers International Association; Aluminum Workers International Union; International Association of Machinists, among others.

as legal precedents become more widely established for the enforcement of Title VII. . . .

But black caucuses which operate within unions are becoming even more significant and their importance lies in their direct attack upon discriminatory racial practices, together with their threat to established labor union bureaucracies. Some of the more noteworthy examples of such caucus activity have occurred in the American Federation of Teachers, the Amalgamated Transit Workers, the United Automobile Workers, and the International Ladies Garment Workers Union, in addition to the United Steelworkers of America.

Division 241 of the Amalgamated Transit Workers (AFL-CIO) in Chicago has been controlled for years by an all-white group under the leadership of James J. Hill. This group has perpetuated itself in office by repeatedly bringing in three thousand retired white drivers to outvote what has now become a Negro majority of working members. The existence of a large black caucus known as the Concerned Transit Workers came to light during July and August of 1968 when it conducted a series of strikes which crippled Chicago bus operations for several weeks. The strikes, however, were not against the employer, the Chicago Transit Authority, but against the union's leadership. Striking Negro workers placed picket lines around the Transit Authority's garages, defied a court injunction ordering them back to work, and forced the international to place Division 241 in trusteeship.

Nathaniel Howse, attorney for the Concerned Transit Workers, is quoted in the *Chicago Tribune* of August 29th as saying that the members of the black caucus were considering withdrawing from the Amalgamated Transit Workers and forming their own independent union after exhausting all attempts to secure equal representation in the union leadership through reform measures.

Howse stated that if such efforts failed the Negro drivers "would become members of a new union if it were to become the bargaining representative for drivers through some election process."

The United Automobile Workers of America, although more sensitive to "the race question" than most other unions, has had a tradition of active Negro caucuses since the early 1940's. Today there are several such caucuses operating in local unions as well as on a district-wide basis. The emergence of a national Negro caucus in the UAW in the late 1950's which openly challenged the Reuther leadership on the issue of Negro participation in policy-making positions led ultimately to the election in 1962 of Nelson ("Jack") Edwards, the first Negro executive board member of the union.

On the recent death of Joseph McCusker, regional director of the UAW's politically important Region 1-A in Detroit, two Negroes campaigned for the office. Marcellus Ivory was elected and became the first Negro to hold the position of regional director in the UAW, a most influential post in the daily affairs of the union. Because of the dramatic rise in the black membership of the UAW—over 60 percent for example in Local 7 in Detroit—black caucuses within the Union will continue to grow in power and influence.

One black nationalist group, DRUM (Dodge Revolutionary Union Movement), has crippled auto production by a series of "wildcat strikes" by Negro workers at the Chrysler corporation's largest Detroit facility, Hamtramck Assembly plant. At this installation where over half of the 7,000 hourly-rated workers are Negroes, the black caucus not only attacked the Chrysler Corporation for its failure to promote Negroes to supervisory jobs, but also attacked the UAW itself for its failure to exert sufficient pressure on the company to eliminate discriminatory employment practices. (A similar disruption of production occurred during October when the Afro-American Employees Committee staged a "sit-down" strike at the Hotpoint Electrical plant in Chicago.)

The DRUM newsletter suggested that if the UAW does not begin to move decisively against discriminatory practices the black caucus would call on its members to withhold their union dues. (A major problem for Negro workers in the UAW has been the Skilled Trades Department which is frequently referred to by black auto workers as "the deep south of the UAW.") . . .

Another "liberal" union, the American Federation of Teachers (AFL-CIO), has also come under sharp attack from Negroes recently both within and outside its ranks. The major conflict is over the issue of decentralization and local control of schools in black communities. Coupled with this issue are the growing charges, especially from the AFT's nation-wide black caucus, the African-American Teachers Association, of growing conservatism on the part of the union leadership and of its insensitivity to Negro demands and community interests. The national caucus, led by Edward Simpkins, a vice-president of the Detroit Federation of Teachers, has repeatedly attacked the AFT's failure to support Negro communities on educational issues. . . .

During the recent strike of the United Federation of Teachers which closed the New York City school system, the profound differences between Negroes and organized labor on basic community issues sharply emerged. The American Civil Liberties Union was quite correct in concluding in a report issued on October 10th that "the UFT has used 'due process' as a smokescreen to obscure its real goal, which is to discredit decentralization and sabotage community control."

In the course of the New York school strike, the United Federation of Teachers was joined by other labor unions opposed to local control of public schools in black communities. This was especially true of the discriminatory building trades craft unions who feared that black-controlled school boards would insist upon awarding lucrative school construction and maintenance contracts to Negro-owned contractors who employ the majority of black skilled workers still excluded from the major AFL craft unions. . . .

INTERNAL DEMOCRACY

The new black caucuses are not merely confronting racial discrimination, but are also significantly raising the broad question of internal union democracy and, for the first time, resorting to legal action on this front. These challenges may have long-term consequences for the future development of organized labor.

On April 19, 1968, federal Judge Constance Baker Motley handed down a 57-page decision in the federal court for the Southern District of New York which voided the election of officers within the National Maritime Union. Judge Motley's decision was upheld by the United States Court of Appeals in a suit brought by the union leadership. In her opinion Judge Motley noted the rigid restrictions written into the NMU's Constitution and stated that "it now takes a minimum of ten years to become eligible for national office. No other union studied, except possibly the International Ladies Garment Workers Union, required so much time for its members to qualify for national office."

For the Negro members of the ILGWU this decision had a special relevance. The first public announcement of a black caucus within the ILGWU occurred on April 16, 1967, when the New York Congress of Racial Equality (CORE) held a press conference to protest the 1967 agreements signed by the ILGWU and stated that the "ILGWU has for years permitted conditions to exist which keep the vast majority of black workers in the lowest paying jobs and has denied black workers a policymaking voice in the union through restrictive constitutional provisions." . . .

It is important to note that the membership of the ILGWU is denied the same right to internal political activity that is accepted as commonplace in the United Automobile Workers Union and in certain other labor organizations. Members of the ILGWU are not permitted to have clubs, groups, or caucuses within their union except for a designated period of three months before conventions every two years. They are specifically forbidden to do so, as the ILGWU constitution prohibits all membership caucuses, groups, and clubs (page 2, Article 8, Section 16 of the ILGWU Constitution). This denial of workers' democratic rights prevents the organized discussion of matters vital to every union member and prevents the offering of rank-and-file candidates for union office.

The implications of these restrictions on internal political activity are made more significant by the eligibility requirements for union office within the ILGWU. In order to be eligible to run for President or General Secretary-Treasurer, a member must be a delegate to the convention, which immediately reduces the number eligible to approximately 1,000 out of 450,000 members; the worker must have been a union member for ten years and a paid officer for at least five years. This means that no member who is not on the paid staff of the union is eligible for these offices.

In order to run for the General Executive Board of the ILGWU, page 14, Article 3, Section 6 of the ILGWU Constitution reads:

> No member shall be eligible to hold a general office unless he or she has been a member of the ILGWU in continuous good standing with respect to the office of vice president for at least 5 years prior to the convention, during

three years of which he had held a full time, paid elective or appointive office. . . .

Under these conditions no more than four or five non-white persons would be eligible to run for the General Executive Board of the union, and virtually none at all for the top leadership positions. This explains why there is not a single Negro on the twenty-three member General Executive Board, not a single Negro Vice President of the union, and not a single Negro local union manager, the latter usually are handpicked by the administration even in locals with a majority of non-white members. (See Hill, "Sewing Machines & Union Machines," *The Nation*, July 3, 1967; and also *Congressional Record-House*, January 31, 1963, pp. 1496-1499.)

These restrictions on political activity plus the eligibility requirements for major offices are clearly violations of the Bill of Rights for Members of Labor Organizations contained in the Labor-Management Reporting and Disclosure Act of 1959 (Section 101A2 and Section 401-E). . . .

Although the procedures established by the Labor Management Reporting and Disclosure Act of 1959 are time-consuming and cumbersome and litigation against the offending union must be brought by the Secretary of Labor, Negro workers will use this new body of law together with other more direct forms of protest with increasing frequency. Since Judge Motley voided the NMU election (which had placed Joseph Curran into office for his thirteenth consecutive term) other federal court judges have rendered decisions in cases brought by rank-and-file workers against the Brotherhood of Painters, Decorators, and Paperhangers, and against locals of the Hotel and Restaurant Employees and Bartenders Union. The Operating Engineers Union was forced to amend eligibility rules after the Labor Department found them excessively restrictive and in violation of the law. . . .

Growing Negro caucuses will, with increasing frequency, avail themselves of the new protections emerging from court decisions and administrative rulings. As the order of priority on social issues becomes vastly different for whites and Negroes, black union caucuses will also engage in independent political action, even if this course brings them into sharp conflict with the political positions of "liberal" labor organizations. This has already occurred in several instances in Detroit, to take but one example, where the Trade Union Leadership Council, the city-wide organization of black auto worker caucuses, turned to an independent political course; sharply broke with the United Auto Workers over local candidates in several Detroit elections; and won significantly over UAW opposition.

Thus, the issues and conflicts have now become public. Negro caucuses are operating with increasing visibility, no longer satisfied to carry on their struggles within the confines of "acceptable" procedures. The racial intransigence and insensitivity of many labor unions to the interests of the black community and to the increasing radicalization of Negro demands suggest sharp confrontations in the near future. This problem leads to fundamental questions—the inability of the hierarchies of organized labor to become attuned and responsive to their own black memberships and to the needs and aspirations of Negro workers in the United States.

There is now emerging a new black working class concentrated in both heavy industry and the service occupations, especially in the public sector. Negro teachers constitute 37 percent of those teaching in Chicago public schools, there are black majorities in the labor forces employed at several major auto manufacturing plants in and around Detroit, over 90 percent of the garbage collectors in Memphis are Negro. Black workers constitute 25 percent of the membership of Local 1014 of the United Steel-workers of America employed at the huge U.S. Steel works in Gary. In District 8 of the steel-workers union in Baltimore, Negroes constitute 40 percent of membership. A number of the largest ILGWU locals in New York City now have a large majority of non-white members. The presence of black majorities or near-majorities in major industrial plants and labor unions means that Negroes are now strategically concentrated both geographically and occupationally to exercise a new leverage within organized labor.

This development is due in part to the changing occupational pattern of white workers, but is also the result of profound changes in the demographic characteristics of the Negro people. If the rate of growth since 1950 of the black population continues, one in eight Americans will be non-white before 1972. (For additional data see Hill, "Demographic Change and Racial Ghettos: The Crisis of American Cities," *Journal of Urban Law,* University of Detroit, vol. 44, Winter, 1966.) . . .

Black caucuses and independent Negro unions are creating a new sense of community among their members, and they are also forcing on the labor union bureaucracies the task of eliminating the discrepancies between their increasingly high blown rhetoric and their persistently sorry performance. This is being done not only with regard to the urgent issues of racial justice and equality, but also on the basic question of internal union democracy as well.

58. Discrimination and Trade Unions

Orley Ashenfelter

Racial, sexist, and other prejudices are filtered through the institutions of the labor market before they are turned into the differences in wages or earnings that cannot be accounted for by differences in productive ability and that we label as discrimination. Economists typically avoid efforts to analyze the nature and determinants of prejudice itself, and prefer to concentrate on analyses of the effects that various institutions have in exacerbating or mitigating the amount of discrimination that results from a given set and level of prejudices. It is unlikely that this preference stems wholly, or even largely, from any evidence that public policies designed to decrease the extent of discrimination are less likely to be successful in changing the former than the latter, but rather from the fact that the economist's tools are better equipment for convincing analyses of phenomena directly observable in the market place. This paper contains the results of a quantitative investigation into the effects of the presence of one such institution, trade unionism, on the extent of discrimination against black and female workers. The analysis is conventional in the sense that we do not attempt to explain the nature of prejudice or how it varies. Instead, we concentrate on the observable differences in institu-

Presented at Conference on "Discrimination in Labor Market," October 7-8, 1971. Sponsored by Industrial Relations Section, Woodrow Wilson School and Conference Office, Princeton University.

tional settings and what effect they have on the ratio of black to white wages, assuming all the while that prejudices either do not vary or vary independently of institutional settings.

The first section of the paper contains a definition of the effect of unionism on the wages of blacks relative to whites and sketches a procedure for empirical analysis of this question. The second section contains a discussion of the likely determinants of a union's policy regarding race, while the third, fourth, and fifth sections contain the basic empirical results and their interpretation. The last section contains a discussion of the implications of our analysis and empirical results.

1. AN EMPIRICAL FRAMEWORK

In order to make our discussion concrete we require a quantitative definition of what we mean by the effect of the presence of trade unionism on the wages of black workers relative to the wages of white workers. A useful way to approach this problem is to distinguish at a point in time between three separate hypothetically observable average wage rates that might exist in the economy for a given race-sex group. The first of these is the average observed wage rate of all *union* workers in that race-sex group. The second of these is the average observed wage rate of all *nonunion* workers in that race-sex group. The third of these is the average wage in that race-sex group that would be observed in the *absence of all unionism* in the economy. We will assume throughout that all average wage rates have been standardized for differences among groups in average skill levels, regardless of the race, sex, or unionization status of that group. Interest centers primarily on the effect of the presence of unionism on the average wage of all black workers as a proportion of the average wage of all white workers and the average wage of all white female workers as a proportion of the average wage of all white male workers. Although the empirical material below focuses on both of these issues, for expositional purposes it is convenient to frame our discussion here in terms of the former only, with the understanding that other groups are implicitly being discussed by analogy.

With the stage set in this way, we define the effect of the presence of unionism on the average black/white relative wage as the proportionate difference between the current average wage of blacks relative to whites and the average wage of blacks relative to whites that would prevail in the absence of all unionism in the economy.[1] If, for example, the ratio of the average black wage to the average white wage were currently .60 (.62), and if it would be .62 (.60) in the absence of unionism, the effect of the presence of unionism would be to reduce (increase) the black/white wage ratio by .03[=(.60 - .62)/.62], or 3 percent, from what it would be in the absence of unionism. Since we cannot observe the black/white wage ratio in the absence of unionism, however, it is necessary to look more closely at this definition before we can give it operational content.

Now it is a relatively straightforward matter to show that, as we have defined it, the effect of the presence of unionism on the black/white ratio can be decomposed into three separate effects.[2] One of these effects is simply the difference between the fraction of the black work force that belongs to unions and the fraction of the white work force that belongs to unions. Given that black workers who are in unions gain as much relative to black workers who are not in unions as white workers in unions gain relative to white workers who are not in unions, it follows that whether a black worker is more or less likely to get into a union than a white worker is an important determinant of the overall effect of unionism on the black/white relative wage. In other words, if a typical black worker gains just as much from belonging to a union as a white worker, then the crucial question is whether black workers are as likely as white workers to get into unions. A second determinant of the overall effect of unionism on the black/white wage ratio is the difference in the size of the union/nonunion wage advantage for black workers compared to the size of the union/nonunion wage advantage for white workers. If, for example, the likelihood of a black worker being unionized does not differ from that of a white worker, then the crucial question is whether, once black workers are in unions, they gain as much from unionization as do white workers.

Though they may pose difficult measurement problems, each of these components of the effect of the presence of unionism on the black/white wage ratio is observable. A third determinant is not generally observable. This is the difference between blacks and whites in the effect of the presence of unionism in one part of the economy on the wages of the corresponding groups of nonunion workers in the remainder of the economy. Since it will not be possible to *estimate* the size of this component of the effect of unionism on the black/white wage ratio, it is necessary to emphasize the possible importance of this factor. The presence of unionism in one part of the economy will generally change the wages of nonunion work-

---

[1]We may be more precise if we put this in symbols. Letting R_b and R_w represent the current average wages of blacks and whites, respectively, and R_b^c and R_w^c the average wages of blacks and whites that would exist in the absence of unionism, we define the effect of the presence of unionism on the black/white relative wage as $\Delta = [(R_b/R_w) - (R_b^c/R_w^c)] / (R_b^c/R_w^c)$.

[2]In symbols, let B and W represent the fractions of all black and white employees in the economy who belong to unions; let M_b represent the proportionate wage difference between black union and nonunion

workers and M_w the proportionate wage difference between white union and nonunion workers; and let D_b represent the proportionate difference between the wage of nonunion black workers and the wage they would have in the absence of unionism, and similarly for D_w. Then the effect of the presence of unionism on the black/white wage ratio is approximately $\Delta^* = BM_b - WM_w + (D_b - D_w)$. This is discussed more fully in my "Racial Discrimination and Trade Unionism," *The Journal of Political Economy,* May/June, 1972, Pt I.

ers from what they would have been in the absence of unionism. If, as a result of unionism, for example, wages are higher in the union sector than they would be in the absence of unionism, then total employment in that sector may be reduced from what it would have been. At least some of those workers who would have been employed in the union sector will have to be employed in the nonunion sector, and this may result in wages in the nonunion sector being bid below what they would have been in the absence of unionism. Alternatively, the threat of unionism emanating from the unionized sector may induce some nonunion employers to buy off that threat by raising wages above what they would have been in the absence of unionism. In either case the presence of unionism in one part of the economy has affected wages in the other part. Whether these indirect effects of unionism have a larger or smaller effect on the wages of nonunion black workers or nonunion white workers cannot be determined. Of course, if these effects are relatively small, or if they do not differ much in their incidence as between black and white workers, they will not seriously affect our estimates of the effect of unionism on the black/white wage ratio.[3]

Before we turn to a more detailed analysis, it is interesting to ask whether this general framework allows us to put any bounds on the size of the effect of unionism on the black/white wage ratio, given the available knowledge of general union wage effects? It is easy to see that we can define such bounds, and that they imply that the effect of unionism on the black/white wage ratio is not likely to be very large in either direction. Suppose, for example, that the average wage of all union workers is fifteen percent higher than the average wage of nonunion workers and that one-third of white male em-

ployees belong to unions.[4] Suppose also, as is contrary to fact, the extreme case where no black workers are in unions. Since one-third of the white work force would have had their wages raised by fifteen percent, the overall average wage of black workers relative to white workers would have decreased by the proportion .05 (= 1/3 x .15), or five percent. Given an overall ratio of the wage of black males to white males of .60 in the absence of unionism, even in this *extreme case* the black/white wage ratio would decline to only

$$.57 \ [= .60 - .05 \ (.60)]$$

in the presence of unionism.[5]

2. UNION RACE POLICY

Most unions have at least implicit policies regarding race. Moreover, these policies seem heterogeneous to an outside observer, even despite the show of unanimity that is displayed by the leadership of the largest federations. The espoused policies range from the open declarations of nepotism that have been associated with some of the unions in the building trades[6] to the strong attachments to, and support from, civil rights organizations that have been associated with some of the unions in the governmental sector.[7] Assuming that the policies of many of these unions reflect democratic decision-making, it is interesting to inquire as to the reasons for the observed differences in racial policy. One possible explanation, of course, is

---

[3]Even if neither of these conditions is satisfied, our estimates of the effect of unionism on the black/white wage ratio by sector will all be affected by the same proportion so long as labor supply curves are very elastic to each sector, and the incidence of threats of unionism does not differ by sector or race. This is true because highly elastic supply curves imply a fixed relationship among sectoral wage rates in the absence of unionism. Likewise, they imply the *same* fixed relationship among the nonunion wage rates in these sectors, and this implies similar proportionate changes in each sector. Thus, our sectoral estimates would still be good estimates of the effect of unionism on black/white wage ratios in one sector relative to another.

[4]These are approximately the results that H. Gregg Lewis reports in *Unionism and Relative Wages in the United States* (Chicago, 1963).

[5]I hasten to add that knowledge of the effect of unionism on the black/white relative wage provides no information about the effect of unionism on the level of the wage of black or white workers. In the example above the drop in the *ratio* of black to white wages could have resulted from decreases or increases in the absolute wage rates of both groups, so long as these wages did not change proportionately.

[6]See, as an example, the discussion of the United Association of Plumbers in Richard P. Nathan, *Jobs and Civil Rights* (Washington, D. C., 1969), pp. 194-195.

[7]See, as an example, the discussion of the 1968 Memphis strike by the American Federation of State, County, and Municipal Employees in Ray Marshall and Arvil Van Adams, "Racial Negotiations—The Memphis Case," mimeo., 1969.

that the extent of prejudice amongst the (white) rank-and-file workers of these unions varies, and that such differences are the cause of different policies. This is obviously not a very attractive explanation, both because the observed racial policies appear to vary more than one would expect on this basis and because it does not open up much hope for the possibility of falsification by a test involving observable variables. An alternative way to proceed is to hold the extent of prejudice constant and to inquire as to the effect of observable factors upon a union's racial policy. We follow this latter procedure here, with an eye toward any implications we may discover regarding differences in union racial policies and their impact on the black/white wage ratio.

Given the racial preferences of the white rank-and-file workers in the union's jurisdiction, that union's policy regarding race will presumably depend in large measure on the extent to which black workers make up a sizeable fraction of the union's jurisdiction both prior and subsequent to unionization. This is true because effective unionization requires that the union enroll enough of the workers in firms with identical products that the demand for all union labor is not highly elastic.[8] Failure to organize extensively enough will result in the inability of the union to obtain higher wages and better working conditions for its members, which, after all, is its reason for existence. Now if black workers make up a sizeable fraction of the workers in the labor markets that must be organized for a union to be effective, the union leadership (and implicitly, the white rank-and-file) faces a choice. Since black workers are less likely to join or remain with the union unless offered, and accorded, relatively equal treatment, the leadership may choose either to offer such treatment and obtain a higher probability of organizing extensively or to organize without black workers. So long as black workers make up a sizeable fraction of the union's jurisdiction, of course, the latter choice may well be tantamount to the choice of no union at all. Thus, where there is an effective union we should expect a more egalitarian (less discriminatory) race policy the larger the fraction of that union's jurisdiction that was made up of

substitutable black workers prior to unionization.

This single principle seems to go a long way toward explaining the history of union racial policies in the United States. On the one hand, it predicts that where racial animosities run high *and* where black workers are a large substitutable work force it is less likely that effective unions will be formed. The U.S. South fits both of these conditions and it seems likely that this is at least one of the reasons that white workers in the South remain nonunion even today.[9] On the other hand, it also predicts a positive correlation between the extent to which a union's race policy is relatively egalitarian and the extent to which blacks were represented in the union's jurisdiction prior to effective unionization. As it turns out, the empirical coincidence between these two factors is indeed very high. Among the building trade unions, for example, the Bricklayers as well as the Plasterers and Cement Finishers may be contrasted with the Plumbers and Pipefitters as well as the Electrical Workers. The former trades contained significant numbers of skilled black workers prior to unionization whereas the latter trades have been unionized since their inception simply because they are a result of a much later technology. As is well known, the former of these craft unions are also much less discriminatory than the latter.[10] Likewise, the relatively egalitarian policies followed by the Packinghouse Workers, the United Mine Workers and many of the industrial unions that organized the mass production industries in the 1930's were undoubtedly due in large part to the sizeable fractions of these union's jurisdictions that were composed of black workers prior to unionization.[11] . . .

A second important determinant of a union's policy regarding race is presumably the set of methods by which it seeks to affect wages and working conditions. At one *extreme* the

---

[8]By effective unionization I mean unionization that results in higher wages for a union of workers than would otherwise have been the case had these workers remained nonunion.

[9]For a quantitative assessment of the importance of this issue see Ray Marshall, *The Negro and Organized Labor* (John Wiley and Sons, 1965), pp. 196-202.

[10]For a detailed discussion see Herbert Northrup, *Organized Labor and the Negro* (Harper and Brothers, 1944), pp. 43-44.

[11]See Walter A. Fogel, *The Negro in the Meat Industry* (University of Pennsylvania, 1970), pp. 67-73, for a good discussion of the case in meatpacking, for example.

union affects wages and conditions by exercising control of the supply of labor. Organization in this instance has historically followed the lines of a narrow skill grouping, both so as to keep the ratio of labor costs to total costs low in the union's jurisdiction and so as to maintain control of entrance to the skill. A natural *concomitant* of a discriminatory race policy in this situation is exclusion of blacks from the union and thus from employment in the union's jurisdiction. An important *result* of such exclusionary policies is the elimination of promotion possibilities for black workers within an industry organized on the basis of narrow crafts even when black workers make up a substantial fraction of the industry. At the other extreme the union affects wages and conditions solely through the use of a bargained settlement based on a strike-threat. Organization in this instance must normally be all inclusive so as to ensure the efficacy of a possible strike. A discriminatory race policy in this situation typically cannot result in direct union exclusion from employment because the hiring decision remains in the hands of the employer, and once hired it is essential that a worker's support be enlisted. So long as the union bargains over working conditions, however, it may be able to insist upon discriminatory treatment of black workers, particularly with respect to seniority and promotional possibilities.

As the above discussion indicates, it is not clear from the available evidence what aggregate effect the presence of unionism is likely to have had on the wages of blacks relative to whites. Nevertheless, the above discussion does suggest the hypothesis that industrial unions are likely to be less discriminatory (more egalitarian) than craft unions.[12] First, the fraction of blacks in the jurisdictions of industrial unions both prior and subsequent to unionization has typically been much larger than in the case of craft unions. As we have seen, this generally implies a more egalitarian race policy. Second, craft unions tend to have greater control of the supply of labor and the hiring process than do industrial unions, and this also will tend to make them more discriminatory. We will turn

to the evidence below, therefore, with an eye toward testing this hypothesis.

3. THE EXTENT OF UNIONIZATION

As we observed in the first section, one crucial determinant of the effect of the presence of unionism on the black/white or male/female wage ratio is the extent of unionization of black and female workers relative to white male workers. Until very recently detailed information on the distribution of unionization by race or sex was virtually non-existent. Fortunately, this problem has been remedied somewhat in recent years because of the 1967 Survey of Economic Opportunity, an expanded version of the Current Population Survey that both over-sampled in low income areas and included a question on union membership. Table 1 contains estimates from this source of the percentage of the employees in each of four race-sex groups who belonged to unions. These are undoubtedly the best estimates of the racial distribution of the extent of unionization that will be available for some time, unless a question on union membership is someday included in a general population census. The major disadvantage of these data is that union membership was not determined for government employees, so that the data we will discuss refer only to *private* wage and salary workers.[13]

The most striking impression given by Table 1 is the remarkable similarity of the extent of unionization of the black and white work forces. About 31 percent of white male workers belong to unions, which is nearly identical to the 32 percent of black male workers in unions. As can be seen from Table 1, this result is a combination of a slightly lower extent of unionization among black workers than among

[12]As is well known the terms "craft" and "industrial" as applied in this context are not strictly appropriate. A term better than craft union might be "referral" union, so as to appropriately signify that the union typically has some connection with the hiring process.

[13]The only other source of data on the racial composition of union membership of which I am aware is the University of Michigan Survey Research Center's annual Survey of Consumer Finances, which does include a question on union membership. The sample size of the SCF is much smaller than that of the SEO, so that the information from it does not give the detail presented here. I have, however, compared the estimates of extent of unionization by race and occupation from the two sets of data, and they are very similar. I am indebted to Professor George Johnson of the University of Michigan for making the SCF data available for the comparison.

Table 1

**Percentage of Private Wage and Salary Workers
Belonging to Unions, 1967, by Aggregate
Occupation, Race, and Sex**

Occupation Group	Race-Sex Group			
	White Males	Black Males	White Females	Black Females
Blue-Collar Workers	42.7	36.1	22.5	22.3
Sales Workers	7.0	39.0	7.0	16.0
Clerical Workers	23.0	36.0	8.0	21.0
Managerial Workers	9.0	29.0	4.0	0.0
Professional Workers	11.0	16.0	4.0	10.0
All Workers	31.0	32.0	12.0	13.0

Sources: These data are derived from the 1967 Survey of Economic Opportunity. Since this survey is especially supplemented by a relatively unique sampling design, estimates of population proportions such as these must be computed by weighting individuals by estimated probabilities of being sampled. See, for example, the discussion in U.S. Bureau of the Census, *Current Population Reports,* series P-20, No. 216, "Labor Union Membership in 1966." I owe a debt of gratitude to Professor Daniel Saks of Michigan State University for providing me with these calculations during his stay at The Brookings Institution.

white workers in the blue-collar occupations, but a slightly higher extent of unionization for the former in the white-collar occupations. These differences are not, however, very substantial.

The second most striking impression from Table 1 is the very large discrepancy between the extent of unionization of male and female workers. Whereas 31 to 32 percent of male workers are union members, only 12 to 13 percent of female workers are union members. Moreover, the differences between men and women in extent of unionization exist in virtually every occupation group, including the white-collar occupations.

Perhaps to the surprise of some, these data do not paint the overall picture of a labor movement that is strongly exclusionary on the basis of race. To some extent the roughly equal unionization figures for blacks and whites may simply reflect a number of offsetting demographic and geographic characteristics of the two work forces. On the one hand, for example, the extent of unionization tends to be low in the South, which is the home of a disproportionately large number of black workers. On

the other hand, the extent of unionization tends to be high in urban areas, and these are also the home of a disproportionately large number of black workers.

Since male blue-collar workers comprise the bulk of American unionists, Tables 2 and 3 contain a more detailed picture of the extent of unionization of white and black workers in this group. These data should shed some light on the hypothesis that craft unions are likely to be more exclusionary than industrial unions. Of the industries in the tables, only construction is organized solely along craft lines, so that this hypothesis predicts a significantly smaller extent of unionization of black workers relative to white workers in the construction industry than in the other industries in the tables. This clearly turns out to be the case for both craftsmen and operatives. Whereas well over one-half the white craftsmen in the building trades belong to unions, only about one-quarter of the black craftsmen in the building trades belong to unions, and the same discrepancy exists for operatives. Likewise, the extent of unionization of black and white craftsmen and operatives in the remainder of the industry groups in Tables

Table 2

**Percentage of White Male Blue-Collar Private
Wage and Salary Workers Belonging to Unions,
1967, by Occupation and Industry**

Occupation Group	All Industries		Selected Major Industries			
		Construction	Durable Manufacturing	Non-durable Manufacturing	Transportation, Communication, Utilities	Wholesale and Retail Trade
Craftsmen	47.	53.9	53.2	48.3	66.9	16.3
Operatives	48.	53.4	57.6	47.2	65.1	18.6
Laborers	30.	28.2	51.0	48.8	59.7	16.8
Service Workers	19.	N.A.[a]	29.5	41.6	N.A.[a]	12.0

[a]Not available because too few employees in the sample were in this category.

Sources: See Table 1.

Table 3

**Percentage of Black Male Blue-Collar Private
Wage and Salary Workers Belonging to Union,
1967, by Occupation and Industry**

Occupation Group	All Industries		Selected Major Industries			
		Construction	Durable Manufacturing	Non-durable Manufacturing	Transportation, Communication, Utilities	Wholesale and Retail Trade
Craftsmen	40.	26.9	67.6	40.5	62.7	20.3
Operatives	44.	21.5	64.5	39.3	62.1	14.2
Laborers	33.	35.1	49.6	35.3	56.1	14.7
Service Workers	19.	N.A.	47.3	30.3	N.A.	11.3

Sources: See Table 1.

2 and 3 is very similar. For example, 44 percent of white non-construction craftsmen are unionized, while 46 percent of blacks in this group are unionized. For non-construction operatives the comparable figures are: white workers 48 percent, and black workers 45 percent. We conclude, therefore, that the craft-dominated building trades unions show a much smaller extent of unionization of black workers relative to white workers than is true in the industrially organized sector. This is strong evidence in support of the hypothesis that craft unions are more discriminatory than industrial unions.

In sum, we observe a similar extent of unionization of black and white male workers in non-construction industries and among construction laborers. We also observe a significantly smaller extent of unionization of skilled black workers than of skilled white workers in

construction. Finally, taken together with a significantly greater level of unionization among black white-collar workers, we observe that the overall extent of unionization of black and white male workers is virtually identical.

4. UNION/NONUNION WAGE DIFFERENTIALS

As we also pointed out in the first section, a second crucial determinant of the magnitude of the effect of the presence of unionization on black/white and female/male wage ratios is the differential between union and nonunion average wage rates and whether this differential varies between race-sex groups. Holding the likelihood of being in a union constant, for example, how large a wage advantage does a black worker gain from being in a union and is this advantage greater or smaller than would accrue to a similarly placed white worker?

Table 4 contains estimates for male workers of the proportionate difference between the hourly wage rates of union and nonunion workers from the same source as the data in Tables 1-3. Differences between union and nonunion workers in education, experience, and many other characteristics that might be associated with wage rates have been controlled so as to make these comparisons a skill-corrected set. Thus, the union and nonunion workers that we are comparing are statistically as similar as we can make them. The results in Table 4 are collapsed somewhat, in terms of the number of industry groups for which union/nonunion differentials are reported, only because initial calculations showed remarkably similar union/

nonunion wage differentials for all of the nonconstruction industry groups.[14]

The most striking impression given by Table 4 is the very significant difference for both race groups between union/nonunion wage differentials of blue-collar workers in the construction industry as compared to union/nonunion wage differentials of blue-collar workers in all other industries. The average union wage exceeds the average nonunion wage by at least 30 percent in each occupation group in the construction industry for *both* black and white workers, and it is significantly higher than 30 percent in most of these building trades occupations. On the other hand, the average union wage exceeds the average nonunion wage by only about 10 percent for the total of the blue-

[14]For a report of these more detailed results see Orley Ashenfelter, *op. cit.*

Table 4

Estimates of Proportionate (in logs) Union/ Nonunion Wage Differentials by Occupation for Males[a]

Occupation	White Workers		Black Workers	
	Non-Construction	Construction	Non-Construction	Construction
Craftsmen	.027	.333	.118	.416
	(.022)	(.035)	(.035)	(.056)
Operatives	.142	.362	.197	.285
	(.020)	(.086)	(.023)	(.094)
Laborers	.177	.390	.274	.377
	(.044)	(.075)	(.032)	(.049)

	All Industries	All Industries
Professional Workers	.120	.282
	(.046)	(.120)
Managerial Workers	.006	−.116
	(.050)	(.112)
Clerical Workers	.018	.112
	(.041)	(.049)
Sales Workers	−.007	.275
	(.064)	(.093)
Service Workers	.034	.165
	(.050)	(.038)

[a]Estimated standard errors of estimated coefficients are enclosed in parentheses.

Source: See text.

collar workers in other industries. Second, in the building trades occupations there is no strong relationship between skill level and the size of union/nonunion wage differentials, with differentials approximately the same in each of the occupation groups. On the other hand, there is a strong inverse correlation between the size of union/nonunion wage differentials and skill level in all other industries. The average wage of unionized non-construction craftsmen, for example, is 2.7 percent higher than the average wage of comparable nonunion workers; but the average wages of unionized non-construction operatives and laborers are 14.2 percent and 17.7 percent higher than comparable nonunion workers. Third, although union/nonunion wage differentials are very similar for both black and white workers in the construction sector, they are higher for black workers than for white workers in all but one of the other occupation-industry categories listed in Table 4. This, of course, is additional strong evidence for the hypothesis that craft unions are likely to be more discriminatory than industrial unions.

Finally, I have brought together the estimated union/nonunion wage differentials by race and sex in Table 5. As can·be seen from the table, the estimated differentials are higher

white and female/male wage ratios. We therefore turn to these results in the next section.

5. THE OVERALL EFFECTS OF THE PRESENCE OF UNIONISM

Recall that we have defined the effect of the presence of unionism on the black/white wage ratio as the proportionate difference between the current ratio of black to white wages and what we estimate that ratio would be in the absence of unionism. As we have seen, the size of this effect depends on the differences in the extent of unionization between blacks and whites that we reported in Section 3, and the differences in union/nonunion wage differentials reported in Table 4. As it turns out, the fact that the estimated union/nonunion wage differentials in this latter table vary inversely with skill level for both black and white workers implies that the overall effect of unionism on the black/white wage ratio will also depend on the distribution of black and white workers by skill level. For this reason Table 6 contains estimates of the fraction of the total wages and salaries received by black and white male workers in each occupation and industry listed in Table 4. Thus, for example, 18.0 percent of the

Table 5

Overall Estimates of Percentage Union/Nonunion Wage Differentials by Race and Sex, 1967

White Males	Black Males	White Females	Black Females
9.7	20.5	15.0	7.2

for both white females and black males than for white males, while the estimated differential for black females is lower than all of the preceding three. Taken together these results imply that, if they get into unions, both black males and white females gain higher wage advantages than do white males. As we have seen, the larger wage advantage for black males than for white males results solely from higher wage advantages in non-construction industries. These results contain only a part of the story, however, until they have been coupled with the extent of unionization data presented in Section 3 to produce estimates of the overall effect of the presence of unionization on the black/

total wage and salary dollars received by white male workers per hour was received by workers who were craftsmen in the non-construction industries. The compensation distribution in Table 6 is similar to a conventional occupational distribution, except that each occupational category has been weighted by its economic importance, where the latter is measured by its average wage rate.[15]

Combining the results in Section 3 with the

[15]Instead of .180 being the probability that a white male worker is a non-construction craftsman, it is the probability that a dollar from a white male worker was earned by a non-construction craftsman.

Table 6

Estimates of the Proportion of Total Compensation of Private Wage and Salary Workers Received by Occupational Groups for Males

Occupation	White Workers		Black Workers	
	Non-Construction	Construction	Non-Construction	Construction
Craftsmen	.180	.073	.106	.048
Operatives	.208	.010	.325	.013
Laborers	.048	.015	.144	.070

	All Industries	All Industries
Professional Workers	.147	.041
Managerial Workers	.134	.014
Clerical Workers	.065	.062
Sales Workers	.069	.012
Service Workers	.036	.112
Private Household Workers	.001	.001
Farm Workers	.014	.054

Source: These estimates are obtained by weighting employment by mean wage rate for each category and then deflating by the sum of these quantities. Employment estimates and mean wage rates are from the 1967 Survey of Economic Opportunity (see the notes to Table 1).

Table 7

Estimates of the Effect of Unionism on the Average Wage of Black and Female Workers Relative to White Male Workers

Difference between:	
Black Male Workers and White Male Workers in	
(1) Construction: Blue-Collar Occupations	−.050
(2) Non-Construction: Blue-Collar Occupations	.039
(3) White-Collar Occupations	.026
(4) All Workers	.034
White Female Workers and White Male Workers	−.019
Black Female Workers and White Male Workers	−.028
All Black Workers and All White Workers	.017

data in Tables 4 and 5 gives the overall effects of unionization on black/white and female/male wage ratios that are given in Table 7.[16]

[16]These estimates are obtained as $\Delta = \Sigma\, E_{bi}M_{bi}B_i - \Sigma\, E_{wi}M_{wi}W_i$ where the E_{bi} and the E_{wi} are the entries in Table 6, the M_{bi} and M_{wi} are the entries in Table 4, and the B_i and W_i are aggregations from Tables 1, 2, and 3. See Orley Ashenfelter, *op. cit.,* for the more technical details, and comparable estimates from other data sources.

First, as can be seen from the table, the effect of unionism in the building construction trades is to lower the ratio of black to white male wages by about 5 percent in those trades. As we have seen, this does not result from differences in the wage advantage of black workers once they are in one of these unions, but from the fact that the likelihood of a black worker in the building trades gaining access to a union job is less than half the likelihood of a white worker gaining access to such a job. Second, the effect of unionism in the non-construction blue-collar occupations is to raise the ratio of black to white male wages by about 3.9 percent in those occupations. This positive effect does not result from differences in the extent of unionization of black and white workers in these occupations. Rather, it results from the fact that (i) within each of these occupations the union/nonunion wage advantage is greater for black workers than for white workers, *and* (ii) black workers tend to be disproportionately concentrated in those occupations where union/nonunion wage advantages are greatest for both black and white workers. Taken together with the positive effect of unionism on the black/white wage ratio in white-collar occupations, these results imply that the overall effect of the presence of unionism is to raise the black/white wage ratio for male workers by about 3.4 percent.

Finally, the effect of unionism is to reduce the ratio of white female wages to white male wages by 1.9 percent, and to reduce the ratio of black female wages to white male wages by 2.8 percent. As we have seen, the main reason for this negative effect of unionism on the female/male wage ratio is the fact that female workers are only about one-third as likely as male workers to belong to unions. The combined effect of unionism on the wages of males and females implies that the ratio of black to white wages of all workers might have been 1.7 percent higher in 1967 than it would have been in the absence of all unionism.

6. CONCLUSIONS AND IMPLICATIONS

In this paper we have examined the question of whether the presence of trade unionism in the American economy exacerbates or mitigates the extent of labor market discrimination against black and female workers. It is important to stress that none of our findings imply that most, or indeed any, American trade unions do not discriminate against black workers. We simply ask whether there is more or less discrimination against black and female workers in the average unionized labor market or in the average nonunion labor market, but not whether discrimination is entirely absent from either. With this limitation in mind the following concluding remarks seem appropriate:

First, on an empirical level we consistently find a higher ratio of black to white wage in labor markets. We also consistently find the ratio of black to white wages in labor markets organized by craft or "referral" unions differs little from that ratio in unorganized labor markets. At the same time we find that the proportion of black workers who are unionized differs little from the proportion of white workers who are unionized in the industrial union sector, but that the former is about one-half of the latter in the craft union sector. Under certain simplifying assumptions these results taken together imply that in 1967 the ratio of black to white male wages might have been 4 percent higher in the industrial union sector and five percent lower in the craft union sector than they would have been in the absence of all unionism. The average of these two effects is positive, however, so that the ratio of black to white male wages may have been some 3.4 percent higher in 1967 than it would have been in the absence of unionism. Combining the effect of the presence of unionism on the wages of black males relative to white males with its effect on the wages of black females relative to white females suggests that the ratio of the wages of *all* black workers relative to *all* white workers might have been 1.7 percent higher in 1967 than it would have been in the absence of unionism. Finally, comparable estimates for female workers imply that the ratio of white female to white male wages might have been 1.9 percent lower than they would have been in the absence of unionism.

Second, the most important conclusion that I draw from these results does not, in fact, concern their sign, but their magnitude. All in all, they suggest to me that the presence of trade unionism is not a major factor affecting wage differentials between black and white workers or between male and female workers. For example, the hourly wage of black male workers was a little greater than 70 percent of the hourly wage of white male workers in 1967. Thus, the male black/white wage ratio would have to increase by roughly 45 percent to bring black and white wages into equality. According to our results above the presence of unionism may have increased the male black/white wage ratio by as much as 4 percent, which is less than one-tenth of the change that would be required for complete equality. Even if the sign of our effect were somehow incorrect, the basic point would remain. When compared with the size of the overall gap in hourly wages between black and white or male and female workers, the effect of unionism does not appear to be very important.

Finally, these results have a number of implications for some specific areas of public policy. To begin with, they imply that efforts to combat discrimination by unions in the building trades are likely to have a greater pay-off to black workers than are efforts in other sectors. This is true both because the presence of unionism in the building trades reduces the black/white wage ratio there, *and* because this is accomplished primarily by excluding black workers *who are already in the building trades* from access to union membership. Of course, whether greater resources should actually be devoted by private and public agencies to fighting discrimination in this sector than in others also requires an assessment of the relative costs of so doing. This also raises the issue of the general strategy that should be followed by private and public civil rights organizations in dealing with discrimination in the craft sector. One strategy, which is clearly being followed even today by some activists, is to try to get black workers into the building trades unions, using any of a large number of tactics. As we have seen, black workers who get into unions in this sector do gain very significant wage advantages and these are not much different from the wage advantages of white workers who get into these unions. In a sense, the existence of unionism in the building trades results in a pot of gold that may be distributed arbitrarily among workers. Given that this pot of gold exists, it seems only equitable that black workers should receive their share of it, and such a position essentially implies a strategy that calls for efforts to get black workers admitted to these unions. A second and far more radical strategy, of course, would involve an effort to significantly weaken the building trades unions. This could result either in a significant reduction in the extent of unionism of white workers in these trades or in a reduction of the already very large wage differentials that accrue to unionized building trades workers. Efforts to suspend or repeal the Davis-Bacon Act could be one part of such a strategy, for example. If one were interested strictly in efficient resource allocation, the second of these strategies would clearly be preferable. From the point of view of increasing the total income that accrues to the black community, however, I suspect that the first of these strategies may be preferable. The choice between them, therefore, is likely to depend in part on one's judgments regarding the equity versus efficiency issues involved. If it turns out that a strategy based on significantly increasing the extent of unionization of black workers in the building trades is unsuccessful, it would not be surprising to find a new and somewhat unusual conjunction of interest groups that were determined to significantly weaken the strength of many of the craft unions in the U.S.

59.   Women and American Trade Unions

Alice H. Cook

...Conditions descriptive of working women generally in the 1960's apply to trade-union women as well,[1] although only about three and one-half million of the twenty-four million working women are in unions. The median working woman today is forty-one years of age, was married at eighteen, and had her last child at twenty-six. She was out of the work force for about twelve years, and has been working more or less regularly for eight years since she returned to employment, and will continue to work, although somewhat spasmodically, until she retires. When fully employed, she earns only 60 per cent of that earned by her male counterpart.[2] (If she is an operative or service worker—the trades more highly organized than clerical and retail sales where most women

work—she earned only about 55 per cent of the male average.)

Of the three and a half million women in unions almost one-fifth are in the apparel unions, the International Ladies Garment Workers (385,854), the Amalgamated Clothing Workers (282,750), and a half-dozen smaller organizations, where women constitute three-quarters or more of the union membership. Three other unions have high percentages of women: the Hotel and Restaurant Workers (200,061), the International Brotherhood of Electrical Workers (241,800), and the Retail Clerks (213,778). Women are scattered through 142 of the 189 unions recorded in the Bureau of Labor Statistics (BLS) *Labor Union Directory,* but in only twenty-six do they make up anywhere near half of the total membership.

In the recent past, however, two important statutory changes affecting working women have come into effect. These apply, of course, to trade-union women but, depending upon the historic policies and traditions of individual unions, have varying impact. They are the Equal Pay Act of 1963 and the inclusion of sex as a forbidden basis of discrimination in the Equal Opportunity Act of 1965. While these laws by no means replace the many state acts written to protect working women against hazards peculiar to their sex, and, on the whole,

[1] U.S., President (Kennedy), *American Women: Report of the Commission on the Status of Women* (Washington, D.C.: Government Printing Office, 1963); and U.S. Department of Labor, Women's Bureau, *1965 Handbook on Women Workers.*

[2] I am using the crude figures of comparison. For a more sophisticated treatment and a weighting of variables, including degree of education, age, seniority, and the like, cf. Harry Sanborn, "Pay Differences between Men and Women," *Industrial and Labor Relations Review,* vol. 17, No. 4 (July 1964), pp. 534-550. Sanborn finds that the weighted differential in pay is closer to 12 to 13 per cent.

supplement these statutes, nevertheless some interesting problems of overlap of federal and state jurisdictions over the employment of women workers have emerged, and will be considered here.

ISSUES AND METHODS

As a consequence of these trends and events, it seemed to me useful before undertaking to write this article to make inquiries into four areas of union life affected by them. The first has to do with union policy in respect to the traditional protective legislation of the states, affecting as it does such matters as night work, total weekly hours of employment, provision of rest and first-aid facilities, prohibitions of lifting loads above a certain weight, and the like. Do unions still support legislation of this type and see it as needful and helpful in defining working conditions for women? Do their women still accept and want to extend the operation of such legislation? Or do these laws, these days, tend to interfere with the employment of women, and are women asking their unions to work for their repeal?

The second subject of my inquiry was: What effect are the new laws on equality having upon union practice and policy? Are grievances arising, growing out of their implementation, from either men or women? Are union members beginning to formulate new demands based on the norms established by this legislation? Are problems emerging within the unions as a result of the simultaneous enforcement of equal-rights legislation and protective legislation?

Third, I wanted to know in what, if any, ways collective agreements recognize the special problems of women workers.

Finally, I sought information on the present status of the political role of women in unions, particularly in those unions where they make up a substantial proportion of the membership. . . .

I mailed questionnaires on these subjects to some forty national unions and later interviewed national officers and staff members in about twenty of them, as well as talking with women leaders in six national and large local unions. The unions queried were selected because they were known to have substantial numbers of women in their memberships. In addition, they were selected so as to provide a cross section covering the large industrial unions—automobile workers, steelworkers, and electrical workers; some of the old-line craft unions such as the bookbinders and the shoeworkers; unions in the textile and needle trades, office employment, communications, and hotels, where women make up 75 to 90 per cent of the members; and professional unions such as the Newspaper Guild and the Guild of Musical Artists.

While the area covered is too small and varied to provide significant tabulations of the replies, I will, nevertheless, endeavor to summarize the results of my inquiries so as to produce an up-to-date report on problems and trends.

UNIONS AND PROTECTIVE LEGISLATION FOR WOMEN

On the whole, unions continue to pass resolutions reaffirming, as the American Federation of Labor-Congress of Industrial Organizations (AFL-CIO) did at its 1965 convention, "traditional support of programs to protect women against exploitation and substandard conditions of work." It is difficult to find evidence that implementation of such resolutions occupies much of the time and resources of the organizations, except for some concern with raising state wage minima among unions of service workers not covered by federal laws.

However, one important union has broken decidedly with this tradition. The United Auto Workers (UAW), as a result of pressure from its women members in California, has swung in the other direction. That state provides a statutory weekly limitation of work for women to forty-eight hours. [3] a circumstance which has had the effect, so the union alleges, of closing off some employment opportunities to women, as overtime work becomes available in sufficient amount to exceed forty-eight hours a week of total employment. The Women's Department

---

[3]It should be noted that twenty-five states and the District of Columbia have set maximum hours at eight per day, forty-eight or less per week, or both. Eight states have a maximum nine-hour day and a 50- or 54-hour week. Nine states have a maximum of ten hours a day and from fifty to sixty hours a week. *1965 Handbook on Women Workers, op. cit.,* p. 239.

of the UAW strongly supports this action of its California members and has aligned itself with women's organizations associated in NOW, a militant equal-rights organization, which looks upon protective legislation as restrictive of opportunities for women and consequently undesirable.[4]

At the other end of the scale, when Delaware recently repealed all of its protective laws for women, the Communications Workers of America (CWA) sent out a circular calling attention of their members to

> recent action of the Delaware state legislature . . . and warning delegates [to the recently held 1966 convention] that employer organizations all over the country are setting their sights on repealing or weakening to the point of ineffectiveness such laws now on the statute books in the states. . . . Communications Workers of America's legislative department will be on the alert for any proposed state or national legislation aimed at destroying or weakening to any degree the limited protective standards that the workers now enjoy.[5]

It may be that unions' policies are determined not in general terms, but quite specifically by their current experience of where advantage for their members seems to lie. In industries where three-shift operation is common or frequent practice, where men and women work on many of the same jobs, and where women who are primary wage earners share with men the desire to get as much overtime pay as possible, women workers—and their unions—will be restive under restrictive legislation. On the other hand, where the majority of women members are secondary earners, where they are young and have school-age children, where their jobs are insulated to some considerable degree from competition with men, and where night work or overtime work is a rare exception, they will probably feel no burdensome restrictions flowing from the legislation and may, indeed, actually welcome the limits it sets on their employment.

By and large, however, unions seem to be taking the view that traditional protective legislation provides genuine and desirable protection for unorganized women and in doing so sets a useful floor under standards for organized women. Moreover, such legislation, as they see it, has frequently served to improve standards for men as well as women. Thus, while heralding the new equality legislation, they want to be sure "to preserve the long-standing and essential standards won through protective legislation and recommend the strengthening of protective labor standards for women."[6]

EQUAL-RIGHTS LEGISLATION AND UNION PRACTICE

While some new kinds of grievances have inevitably come to the attention of union officers with the publication on every establishment's bulletin board of the 1963 and 1965 legislation, most unions long ago supported equal-pay practices and included appropriate clauses in their contracts. On the whole, however, in union shops, as in nonunion ones, men's and women's jobs exist in accepted differential categories. The result is that men and women rather seldom do the same work.

Where separate male and female classifications exist, it is not uncommon for unions to write separate agreements covering each. One such union shows rates for unskilled men at a minimum straight-time hourly rate of $3.22, while a comparable classification for women shows a $2.74 rate. Working foremen under this contract earn $3.98 an hour while foreladies get a $3.07 rate. Similarly, many companies and unions have agreed to set up male and female seniority lists on the assumption that layoffs should follow these lines of job categories and of type of skill. In a prominent industrial union, agreements covering conditions at a number of well-known firms show no highest rate for women above the lowest rate for men.

Since the equal-opportunity laws have gone on the books, unions are having to deal with grievances in which women are testing their right, and with it their ability to cross the invisible lines to doing "men's work." Some unions that I interviewed were encouraging local unions where these problems arise to

---

[4] In California, however, the Hotel and Restaurant Workers Union is leading the fight to defend the existing hours legislation.

[5] Communication Workers of America (CWA), Letter to all local presidents from the Office of the President, July 22, 1966.

[6] Amalgamated Clothing Workers of America (ACWA), Twenty-fifth Biennial Convention, Resolution No. 25.

handle them radically by rapidly introducing rules and lists which eliminate all formal distinctions within the shop except those which can be applied equally to men and women, as based on ability to perform required work.

In many of the older craft unions, membership has, in effect, traditionally been hierarchical, with "helpers," "specialists," "apprentices," and "journeymen" occupying differential statuses and having differentiated benefits. These unions tend to look upon the occasional application of a woman for a man's job as an aberration, indulged in by a young woman who has not yet been socialized to the trade. They rely on social control by her peers to maintain the *status quo ante*. "Women won't feel so good working on a job that by rights belongs to a man," and will then refrain from entering the reserved occupations. In interviews with unions of this kind, no indication was visible that the traditional lines between men's and women's work had not been drawn with the wisdom of the ages and for eternity.

Widespread enforcement of the new laws will probably result in the rapid and general introduction into industry of such devices as integrated seniority lists, the abolition of "male" and "female" job classifications, and of open opportunity on promotion, or, at least, open bidding on vacant jobs. So far as state protective laws are concerned, the approach will probably be not to abolish them, as Delaware has precipitately done, but to amend them so that their protective features apply generally to the weak—the young, the old, the handicapped—rather than solely or even explicitly to the female. How long it will take unions to rethink their policies will depend upon the pressures arising not only from state and federal enforcement officers, but within the shop from employers, on the one hand, and from women members, on the other. These pressures will gradually converge upon the bargaining table and on the resolutions committee at the convention and will register themselves in new contract provisions, new norms in grievance handling, and a fresh approach to policy on protective legislation.

CONTRACT PROVISIONS FOR WOMEN WORKERS

Aside from provisions for maternity leave—without pay—special provisions for women, as such, are rare in union contracts. In some cases, the distinctions referred to above between men's and women's rates of pay are spelled out. Occasionally, one finds specific clauses for women on hours, shifts, and overtime. Usually, however, the reason for this special consideration is an explicit effort to conform to state legislation on sanitary conditions, rest facilities, and the like, rather than being the result of original negotiation at the insistence of women members or because of special consideration for them.

So far as fringe benefits are concerned, employers occasionally have complained in the course of bargaining for insurance benefits that women are more expensive to insure than men, since, during certain years at any rate, their benefit payments are higher on sickness plans and, in the form of pensions, are paid out longer after retirement. Union officials, queried about this aspect of the problem, noted that these points are rarely hampering, for a variety of reasons. Some married women whose husbands are covered for family benefits by their own employers may be excluded from these plans. Moreover, pension benefits for women are typically paid at a lower rate than is the case for men. No available study of union experience in these matters exists which would measure whether, in reality, women may be receiving not more, but rather less than the sums to which they might be entitled were they looked upon as independent workers rather than spouses or second earners.

In a number of European countries and in Japan, women are granted under law or contract or both what amounts to a menstrual leave of a day a month.[7] In the United States, only one of the unions studied, the American Guild of Musical Artists, has such a provision.

Common usage in union contracts covering maternity leave is to permit it for periods up to eighteen months, although a year is more usual, without loss of seniority or other contractual rights, but also without remuneration of any kind. Countries elsewhere in the world with a history, at least in recent times, of reimbursement for sick leave often provide for full payment for a stated period before and after delivery, usually up to a total of six months' wages at the birth of a child. The common though diminishing practice in the United

[7]In Germany, such leave is usually referred to as a day off for doing the monthly laundry. In Japan, it is one form of the maternity leave available to women.

States of not reimbursing workers for income lost through illness has set a norm for the handling of pregnancy and delivery costs to reimbursement for medical expenses only, and not for income.

In sum, it would appear that unions perceive the realm of special protection for women as that of the government's to regulate and, thus, feel no need for further attention to women's work in the contract.

THE POLITICAL LIFE OF WOMEN IN UNIONS

...General information on the role of women in trade-union life is almost completely lacking. Only a few unions have endeavored to undertake a census and a critical evaluation. The most complete of these which came to my attention is that of the International Union of Electrical, Radio, and Machine workers (IUE). [8] It shows a total in that union, throughout the country, of 562 women holding local union office, ranging in rank from presidents (18), to secretaries (108) and members of executive boards (272), to trustees (108), plus 43 chief stewards and 595 shop stewards. Other unions described a similar kind of spread of participation as indicated in reports reaching them on elected officers.

The picture at the national level is quite different, even among those organizations where women make up more than half of the membership. "Tokenism" is the standard practice in placing one, or at the very most two, women on the national executive boards. [9] National staffs of organizers and of experts show a higher level of representation, but women remain more the exception than the rule even in these appointed offices, rarely rising above the level of assistant to the department chief, although there have been a very few notable exceptions.

The unions of Europe and Asia typically include a Women's Department in their union's structure, a department which functions at each level of the organization from the national to the local and whose titular director is a member of the national executive board. These departments and their staffs serve to politicalize the female membership, who often, by tradition and law, have had little experience in public life. In doing so, they function as an interest group within the political life of the union, formulating special contract demands and policy statements and providing training for women as leaders, while they constantly alert the union to women's representational needs and rights.

Union leaders, however, are more often than not uneasy about the political self-consciousness among women members which such a department generates when it is successful. But to the extent that it can and often does confine women's activities within its limits, there to ventilate and exhaust their grievances, the device is probably a least-cost answer to increasing women's participation in union affairs without risking serious challenge to traditional male hegemony.

In the United States, a few unions, notably the UAW, have established such a Women's Department. [10] For the most part, American unions have not undertaken, either through this device or any other, to discuss, analyze, and treat the special problems of their women members. . . .

. . . The hard fact in the late 1960's is that less attention is being paid by the unions today to the special needs and problems of their women union members than was the case earlier in the century. Women's pages in the union journals are devoted, where they exist, to syndicated columns on consumer problems and to recipes and household hints.

Indeed, the union leaders are rather complacent about a situation in which leadership among their women is relegated to secondary positions at the local level. A number of explanations are offered and have wide acceptance. [11]

---

[8]International Union of Electrical, Radio, and Machine Workers (IUE), Department of Civil Rights and Minority Affairs, "Women in the IUE: A Preliminary Report," February 1966 (Mimeographed).

[9]The IUE has two women members; the UAW has one. The ACWA and the International Ladies' Garment Workers Union (ILGWU) have one woman member each.

[10]The AFL-CIO's Committee on Political Education has a Woman's Division.

[11]For a discussion which covers many of these points, cf. George Strauss and Leonard Sayles, *The Local Union*, rev. ed. (New York: Harcourt, Brace, 1967), pp. 124-27.

One of the most frequent is that a high percentage of women are, in effect, holding two jobs—one in the plant and the other as a housewife—and have no time for activity in the union or elsewhere in the community. Some of these, if they can, work part-time, or even always on the night shift. Others, while their children are young, never become permanent workers and hence do not identify themselves as regular members either of the work force or of the union.

Second, even among women who work most of their adult lives, there is a ten- to fifteen-year intermission which falls in their twenties and early thirties, a time when most men are taking on their first positions of leadership. Because women miss out in the first round of election and selection, they are permanently handicapped in reaching the top positions.

Third, as we have seen, women tend, by comparison with men, to occupy unskilled or semiskilled positions, locations from which relatively few unionwide leaders emerge.[12] While there are a number of exceptions, women generally assume positions of top leadership only when men are in a decided minority in the shop.

Fourth, the "psychological difficulties" for women are considerable. As one local leader put it: "Women are their own worst enemies—they underrate their own political abilities." In other interviews, women saw themselves as "too emotional in tight situations, particularly at the bargaining table." Older women, from among whose ranks leaders might be expected to come, "don't want to rock the boat; prefer to live in a pleasant atmosphere." Because most

[12] A number of studies of local unions show that leaders tend to come from the ranks of the highly skilled workers whose occupations include considerable mobility through the shop. Cf. Strauss and Sayles, *op. cit.*, pp. 80-84.

employers are men, women, as well as men, tend to believe that men are better suited to deal with them.

These views shift radically in the unions of professionals, where, in work life as in union life, women move rapidly, without constraint or restraint, into leadership roles. They do so partly as a result of their better educational preparation, but it is partly as a consequence of their acceptance of middle-class norms of sex-equality. Admittedly, however, even in middle-class life, "men are more equal than women," or as one woman put it to me: "You just have to be a whole lot more competent to get the same jobs and run for the same offices."

If this is so in middle-class professional organizations, how much more applicable it is to working-class life! Not only are examples of equality hard to find in the shops and unions, but both men and women in this stratum generally perceive men to be better fitted temperamentally, as well as by training, for political leadership. A national union president strongly believes that in his organization, where women make up more than half of the membership, "men just don't want women for presidents of mixed locals."

Thus, although women play a not inconsiderable role in the shop and local union, they are rarely found as officers of the intermediate bodies, the joint boards, and district councils, and almost never appear on major negotiating teams or on national executive boards, national staffs, and among the national officers. Moreover, union structure, with rare exceptions, provides no channels for mobilizing women to consider their special problems and to formulate policy on them. Even when they are in a majority, women play the role, and are assigned the status, of a minority—moreover, a minority still in that state of political self-consciousness where "tokenism" suffices to meet its demands.

Unions and National Politics

Although unions generally have concentrated their efforts on collective bargaining, they have also tried to obtain some of their objectives through the political arena. Consequently the political role and power of unions has become a controversial issue.

The selection by Derek Bok and John Dunlop analyzes the political power of organized labor, concluding that this power is much weaker "than one might suppose on taking note of the millions of union members and the size of union treasuries." First, there is often disunity among labor leaders and apathy toward politics on the part of the rank and file. Second, unions are actively opposed in the political arena by a variety of other powerful interest groups. Despite these limitations on union political power, they conclude that unions are an important political force looking out for the interests of workers and low-income groups, people who are not generally represented by the other powerful political lobbies.

In the past the political objectives of unions were often centered on legislation affecting collecting bargaining. Since the New Deal, however, unions have become involved in a much wider range of political issues. The selection by Barbash discusses four interrelated policy areas where the labor movement has been especially active during the past decade: macroeconomic policies for full-employment, wage-price policies, policies for adjusting to technological change, and manpower policies for the disadvantaged.

60. Labor in National and State Politics

Derek C. Bok

John T. Dunlop

[There is] a whole battery of restraints that confine the political power of labor much more than one might suppose on taking note of the millions of union members and the size of union treasuries. Within the ranks of labor, there are three principal limitations: the disunity of the labor organizations, whose leaders often adopt disparate political tactics and work for disparate political objectives; the unwillingness of union members to shift their habitual party allegiances; and, finally, the apathy of the members toward political action, an attitude rooted in a broad distrust of politics and in the traditional primacy of collective bargaining in the American system of industrial relations. Outside the union hall, still further obstacles intrude. Labor's power to demand special concessions from a Democratic administration is often blunted because the Federation has little choice but to support the party. Unions are also hemmed in by opposing interest groups which counter their lobbying efforts, expose their activities to publicity, and work to defeat their favored candidates. Above all, success in politics ultimately requires votes. As a result, in the highly publicized areas in which unions deal, few legislators wish to make concessions to unions that will offend broad segments of the electorate.

The limits on labor's political influence are mirrored in the work of Congress over the past thirty years. After all, the most favorable laws ever received by labor were enacted in the thirties, when unions had no campaign organizations and made no serious effort to lobby, even for such vital laws as the National Labor Relations Act. In subsequent years, as labor's political effort gathered momentum, the Taft-Hartley restrictions were enacted, followed by the Landrum-Griffin Act twelve years later. More recently still, labor has failed to eliminate right-to-work laws and other legal restraints, despite the presence of a friendly administration. In short, the record suggests that organized labor has not been able to achieve important legislative goals unless its objectives have corresponded with the sentiments of the electorate or the prevailing convictions in Congress.

Despite these limitations, it would be wrong to assume that labor's political power has been negligible. Without union efforts, workers and low-income groups would have little organized political support, and their interests would be more vulnerable to the pressure of other powerful groups. Through constant lobbying and political campaigning, unions have doubtless helped to give birth to Medicare and to enlarge social security and unemployment and workmen's compensation benefits. In addition, labor's success in registering voters and persuading them to go to the polls must have contributed something to the success of the Democratic party in maintaining control over Congress in all but two sessions since 1933, and holding the Presidency during all but three terms.

It is extremely difficult to estimate whether labor's influence in national politics will increase or decline. Much will turn on whether unions can identify themselves with political issues that really matter to their constituents. In an era when broad social legislation and collectively bargained fringe benefits are already an established fact, union members are likely to feel less strongly about labor's traditional political objectives, yet it is difficult to imagine other goals that can unite a large majority of union members. With the growing unionization of hospital workers, sanitation men, and farmworkers, on the one hand, and teachers, policemen, and federal employees, on the other, the union movement seems to be growing more heterogeneous, thus complicating the problem of finding a platform that the bulk of the membership can support with enthusiasm. If such goals cannot be found, the result will be increased apathy and greater susceptibility to the lure of other causes and candidates than those endorsed by labor's high command.

At the same time, there are still large numbers of low-income, unregistered voters, and the Federation may succeed in bringing them to the polls as its techniques become more sophisticated and better financed. To be sure, many other forces will have to combine with union efforts before the electorate can be significantly enlarged, and many groups will help determine the demands that eventuate from this new political force. But it is probably unrealistic to expect voting rates to persist indefinitely at their present level among low-income groups or to ignore the fact that a rise in these rates will almost inevitably help labor to realize many of its broad social and economic goals.

In the light of this discussion, what answer can be given to the various groups who have been so critical of labor's political role? To those who fear that unions will corrupt the political process and manipulate Congress, the conclusions should be reassuring. To many other readers, however, the answer will doubtless seem inconclusive. Those who support the "welfare state" objectives of the labor movement will applaud any progress the unions make and castigate them for not doing more.

Those who dislike these objectives will keep on criticizing the unions and even cry out for legislation to curb their campaign activities. So long as labor's efforts are judged by the goals it pursues, no convincing verdict can be reached, for the goals themselves are rooted in value premises on which honest men will inevitably disagree.

There is a deeper sense, however, in which the political activities of unions can be appraised in a less controversial manner. In the last analysis, the major thrust of labor's activities has been to increase the political participation of poorer segments of society and to provide a coordinated and coherent political voice to workers who would otherwise be largely disorganized. Whatever one may think of the political platform that results from this activity, it is hard to deny the value of these endeavors in a democratic society. It is precisely because issues of policy are so often controversial that the nation has based its system of government on the vote of all interested members. Under these circumstances, one can hardly disapprove of the efforts of any organization to broaden the participation of all interested groups in the political process. The society has likewise witnessed the growth of a host of organized interest groups that press whatever influence and arguments they can muster on executive and legislative officials. Under such a system, one can scarcely oppose the effort of labor unions to provide an organization of their own to promote the interests of their members and of other working people.

These arguments are more than theoretical. If one examines the field of labor and protective legislation, one will quickly discover the effects of a lack of organization and participation in the political process. The least organized groups with the lowest levels of voting participation include agricultural workers, domestic servants, and unskilled labor in small shops and marginal industries. In the great majority of states, these employees are systematically excluded from workmen's compensation systems, minimum-wage laws, and unemployment insurance, and they are likewise deprived of any law permitting them to organize and bargain collectively without fear of retaliation. Even those who disapprove of such measures will be hard-pressed to justify the discriminatory treatment that denies the benefits of these laws to those who appear to need them most. Such discrimination, however, is the natural fate of those who remain unorganized in a highly organized political system. To the extent that unions work to correct this imbalance, they bring a greater measure of fairness to the entire governmental process.

61. Trade Unions and National Economic Policy

Jack Barbash

The contemporary economy in the United States is dominated by two immediate problems: "(1) What can be done to curb our present inflationary movements without creating appreciable unemployment? (2) How can this kind of effort be related to a broadening of economic opportunities that would help bring an end to poverty."[1] Earlier in the postwar period, depressed areas, adjustments to technology, and recurring recessions occupied the center of policy concerns. . . .

American trade unionism has been involved in four major policy areas relevant to this inquiry: (1) full employment and general economic policy, (2) wage-price policy, (3) adjustment to technological change, and (4) manpower policy for the disadvantaged. Collective bargaining continues to be the principal means through which the unions have asserted their interests in these policy areas. Law and its administration, although subordinate to collective bargaining, have become, however, increasingly important in union strategy.

I

In a generation, that is since the New Deal, the mainline trade union movement has broadened the scope of its public policy concerns from defensive reactions against anti-union measures, like the injunction and the "yellow-dog contract," to broad economic policy with major emphasis on full employment objectives. For the 1970 Congress, by way of example, the AFL-CIO gave the highest priorities to "rising unemployment, occupational safety, environmental pollution, expanded health education, manpower training and anti-poverty programs, skyrocketing interest rates and monetary policy reform, true bargaining rights for farm workers and situs picketing rights for the building trades."[2] Only the latter two could be considered "pure" trade union issues. The following have been mainly responsible for the enlargement of trade union policy perspectives: (1) the demonstration, which began with the New Deal, that the state could serve as ally and not only as adversary in the advancement of labor interests; (2) the emerging awareness that the condition of the nation's economy has much to do with the effectiveness of the trade union performance; and (3) the ascendancy of the industrial union interest in the American

---

[1] U.S. Department of Labor, Manpower Administration, *Assessing the Economic Scene* (Washington, D.C.: Government Printing Office, 1969), p. 1.

[2] AFL-CIO, *Labor Looks at Congress,* 1969 (Washington, D.C., 1970),p. iii.

454

trade union movement and hence the broadening of the trade union base in the working population. At the present time, the support mustered by the AFL-CIO and assorted national unions may constitute the single most powerful political influence behind the broad range of full employment and welfare legislation. . . .

II

The formulation of collective bargaining approaches to a national wage-price policy in peacetime bears the special imprint of the UAW and Walter Reuther, its president. In 1945 Reuther argued the proposition that to raise wages without increasing prices was indispensable to the maintenance of a full employment economy. "We are not going to operate as a narrow economic pressure group which says 'we are going to get ours and the public be damned.' "[3] In the 1957 negotiations Reuther proposed a price reduction for 1958 car models in return for which "the UAW promised to give full consideration to the effect of such reductions on each company's financial position in drafting our 1958 demands and in the negotiations." The UAW offered to abide by an impartial review of whether "the granting of our demands would necessitate restoration of part or all of the $100 per car price reduction."[4] But automobile management rejected the appropriateness of the union interest in price policy and the UAW proposals were never put to the test.

For several years the UAW has proposed a notification and hearing procedure for price and wage increases which "envisage a Review Board for conducting the necessary hearings and a Consumer Counsel representing the public interest. Advance notice would have to be given of any price increase proposed by the corporation that functions as the 'price leader' in any major industry. . . . The Consumer Counsel would be able to initiate hearings in cases where he believed prices should be reduced. . . . Unions would be required to participate in the hearings and to justify their demands in

cases where the corporation involved claimed that granting those demands would necessitate the proposed price increase or would prevent a decrease."[5]

The wage-price guideposts instituted by the Council of Economic Advisors in 1962 set a ratio between permissible wage and price increases and productivity. The trade unions have faulted this guideposts policy for: (1) the lack of effective consultation, (2) the arbitrariness and inflexibility of the productivity standard, (3) assuming as given the existing distribution of income, (4) the "disparate treatment of wages and prices,"[6] and (5) the scapegoating of wage increases as the source of inflationary pressure. The guideposts were abolished with the settlement of the 1966 airline machinists' strike when stability via guideposts became incompatible with industrial peace, and the choice was made for the latter. The strike made the essential point, which dominated the labor scene for several years thereafter, that wage-restraint policy could not stand up against the rank-and-file's discontent with a worsening real wage position.

The current trade union position on wages and prices takes the form of a defense against the scapegoating of wages as the prime mover in inflation and an attack on the Nixon administration's "blunderbuss, general form of restrictive economic policies, tight money and sky-high interest rates." The AFL-CIO favors "selective measures aimed at restraining the specific causes of inflationary pressures . . . since the inflation of 1969 was largely a profit inflation."[7] It has indicated its willingness to cooperate in an incomes policy as it has "reiterated on many occasions, if the President determines that the situation warrants extraordinary over-all stabilization measures . . . so long as such restraints are equitably placed on all costs, prices and incomes—including all prices, profits, dividends, rents and executive compensation, as well as employees' wages and salaries. 'We are prepared to sacrifice,' the AFL-CIO Executive Council has repeated, 'as

[3]*New York Times,* December 29, 1946.

[4]Report of UAW President Walter P. Reuther, United Automobile Workers Constitutional Convention, 1959, p. 12.

[5]Nat Weinberg, "The Death of the United States Guideposts," in *The Labour Market and Inflation,* ed. Anthony D. Smith (New York: St. Martin's Press, 1968), p. 44.

[6]*Ibid.,* p. 28: Circular, AFL-CIO Department of Research, June 22, 1970.

[7]AFL-CIO, *The National Economy* (Washington, D.C., 1969), p. 6.

much as anyone else, for as long as anyone else—so long as there is equality of sacrifice.' " The federation specifically rejects "a voluntary guideline approach . . . as an unfair and one-sided pressure on workers' wages, as well as unenforceable in a country of continental size, with no nationally centralized business or labor institutions."[8]

III

The trade unions have had a major impact on policies for adjustments to technological change through both collective bargaining and legislation. By common practice rather than by concerted policy, collective bargaining seems to have established the general principle that employees have an equitable interest in the stability of the job situation; in the event of material impairment of that stability due to technological change, the employer is obligated to offset in some degree the losses attributable to that change.

Union obstruction of technological change is the exception rather than the rule. A more characteristic union strategy is first to slow down the pace of displacement. When displacement inevitably occurs, the union acts to ease the burden of change on the displaced worker. Job and income protection for current employees is a characteristic first line of union defense. In one form, unions negotiate explicit productivity gain-sharing; for example, an "annual improvement factor" where wage rates rise in line with a predetermined rate of productivity increase. More broadly, any increase in real wages and wage supplements (such as negotiated health, welfare, and pension programs and supplementary unemployment benefits) and reduction in hours without loss in earnings may represent an explicit sharing in the gains of productivity.

Layoffs due to technological change are frequently slowed down by contract requirements (1) prohibiting reduction in the manning schedule for the performance of a given task, (2) guaranteeing current employees against job and income loss so that the displacement operates to reduce future job opportunities, and (3) offsetting net job and income losses through job and income gains as in the reduc-

tion of weekly hours and in increases in paid leaves (holidays, vacations, "sabbaticals," etc.) of one sort or another.

When worker displacement does come, specific provisions act to (1) induce voluntary separations by raising pensions for early retirees, (2) authorize dismissal or separation allowances to tide workers over to the next job, (3) aid the displaced worker to find another job in the same company by enlarging the seniority unit within which the worker can legitimately claim employment rights or by a relocation allowance to permit the displaced worker to move to a company plant in another area, and (4) provide effective retraining opportunities. Procedures to encourage advance planning of technological change have been incorporated in contract provisions requiring (variously) advance notice of major labor-saving changes and consultation between unions and management in planning the displacement. Joint study committees, with participation by neutral outsiders, have been negotiated to explore the problems of work displacement long before the climate of crisis sets in.

This sort of bargaining policy for adjustment to technological change is "programmatic bargaining . . . characterized by agreement on limited mutual goals and the willingness to bring in a sufficient number of variables to insure mutual commitment." This is distinguished from "concessionary" bargaining which "is characterized by unilateral goal-setting and concessions. Because neither party is committed to the other's goal, it is fair game to seek to minimize the costs of the concessions. Concessionary bargaining elicits a series of adaptations, mainly via variables outside the bargaining, which erode the other party's gains" and "tend to frustrate problem-solving."[9] The limitation of collective bargaining under any circumstance has led the unions to legislation as a method of dealing with the disemployment effects of technological change.

IV

The trade union movement continues to be a prime mover in manpower legislation as it has evolved from one dominant theme to the next,

---

[8]*Ibid.*, p. 7.

[9]Melvin Rothbaum, "Economic Dilemmas of Collective Bargaining," in *The Crisis in the American Trade Union Movement,* ed. Solomon R. Barkin, The Annals

specifically; depressed areas, technological unemployment, youth, the "competitively disadvantaged, and the need to coordinate and consolidate our manpower programs."[10]

The trade unions have been under great pressure to make a more intensive effort in behalf of the disadvantaged low-wage worker, especially the ethnic disadvantaged (here the strongest pressure is exerted in behalf of the Negro worker, somewhat less urgent concern is shown for the Puerto Rican and Mexican-American worker). The pressure on the craft unions, particularly the construction trades, has come from civil rights activists and the federal government. The pressure on the industrial unions has come not only from these sources but also from the internal union "black caucus" groups. The target of pressure on the craft unions has been their restrictive entry practices with a special emphasis on apprenticeship. In the industrial unions the targets have been post-hiring disadvantages caused by (1) restricted opportunities for advancement under a seniority system, (2) the denial of fair representation, and (3) an unfavorable imbalance of Negro participation in union leadership.

The methods of pressure have consisted of threats of disruption by civil rights activists and the threat of litigation by the federal government under the Civil Rights Act of 1964 and federal contract compliance standards. The remedies sought against the craft unions and construction trades contractors have been commitments to employ specified numbers of Negro workers by crafts in a fairer proportion to their numbers. Against the industrial union the main thrust of the government has been to modify restrictive seniority and promotion systems to allow fuller participation by Negro workers in promotion opportunities. A more representative distribution of Negro members in the union leadership has been the objective of the "black power" groups in and around the trade union movement.

The trade union response to the pressures begins with the emergence of viewpoints which come to grips with the critical problem. Nowhere is this more apparent than in the building trades unions which have moved from what

amounted to denial that discrimination exists to "affirmative action" and "outreach" programs where "a more intensive effort [is exerted] by paid personnel to recruit, train and place minority youth."[11] Symbolic of the new level of perception is the so-called Chicago Plan which commits an operations committee composed of representatives from the craft unions, contractors, and a coalition speaking for civil rights activist groups "to obtain employment at once for 1,000 qualified journeymen who possess the necessary skills of their respective trades and look to the coalition to supply ... such journeymen. Each respective craft union will accept such journeymen within the time period called for in the pertinent collective bargaining agreement, and each craft union will accept its initiation fee or required fees on a partial payment plan. ..."[12] Standard apprenticeship requirements as a condition of entry are relaxed in the Chicago Plan and supplanted by the standard of "journeymen who possess the necessary skills." Those with less skill or no skill may work up to journeymen status through combinations of apprenticeship and training substantially below conventional standards.

The Chicago Plan makes, as noted, the Coalition for United Community Action a party to the agreement and thereby recognizes the legitimacy of a third party, civil rights interest. The Philadelphia Plan is the prototype of the Chicago Plan but with the difference that the federal government, relying on its procurement authority, is the immediate third party.

Trade union involvement in the administration of manpower programs for the disadvantaged have included: (1) on-the-job training contracts with the U.S. Department of Labor, Manpower Administration, under which "the unions agree to recruit, train and place men and women who are unemployed and who meet the Labor Department's specifications as hardcore"; (2) the "buddy-system" component of the National Association of Businessmen's JOBS program (Job Opportunities in the Busi-

---

of the American Academy of Political and Social Science, Philadelphia, November 1963, pp. 95, 103.

[10]*Studies by the Staff of the Cabinet Committee on Price Stability* (Washington, D.C.: Government Printing Office, 1969), p. 24.

[11]Statement of Policy on Equal Employment Opportunity, AFL-CIO Building and Construction Trades Department, Washington, D.C. September 22, 1969, pp. 1-10 *passim.*

[12]The Chicago Plan, An Agreement for the Implementation of Employment of Minorities in the Chicago Building and Construction Industry, AFL-CIO Building and Construction Trades Department, Washington, D.C., January 12, 1970.

ness Sector) which trains union workers to act as "buddies" to hard-core workers; (3) upgrading programs "to encourage workers hired at entry-level jobs" to move up the ladder; (4) Job Corps training, as in the Operating Engineers, to train for heavy equipment maintenance and to undertake to place those who have completed training; (5) "outreach" programs "to develop special programs to recruit, motivate and prepare minority-group youngsters to become apprentices in skilled trades."[13]

The method of "social enterprise" is meant to describe the establishment of union-sponsored organizations outside of the union structure which engage in research, education, training, and community organization to improve the conditions of life for the disadvantaged. The AFL-CIO's Human Resources Development Institute, financed largely by government grants and trade union contributions, aims to "mobilize and utilize the vast resources of skilled talent and experience available within the labor movement to plan, develop, coordinate and operate manpower programs for the hard-core unemployed . . . with emphasis on developing necessary support and problem solving services to obtain and maintain sound employment for such workers."[14] The Center for Community Change, manned and conceived by former staff of the Industrial Union Department of the AFL-CIO and financed by the Ford Foundation, aims to "provide technical assistance, leadership training and interpretation of legal and governmental rights necessary for local residents to negotiate social change."[15] The A. Philip Randolph Institute aims at "the preparation of far-reaching social and economic programs, serious school integration plans, nonviolent strategy, community organizing . . . to extend the basis for united mass action by the civil rights organizations on the national level."[16] The distinguishing marks of the social enterprise method in its current settings

are (1) the commitment to social rather than to particular union or class interests, (2) the organizational separateness from the union, (3) the reliance on expert personnel rather than on trade union leadership, and (4) the collaboration with government, employer groups, and private foundations.

V

The trade unions have relied on interest representation in government as the major vehicle for involvement in public policy. Interest representation is used in the sense of a pressure group "acting in concert to influence public attitudes or to obtain specific policy decisions from legislative bodies and administrative officials."[17] The leverage for interest representation is general electoral activity made possible by trade union manpower, money, and activity.

Interest representation operates outside and inside the government. The personnel outside the government consists of full-time legislative representatives—"lobbyists"—and technical policy specialists of the AFL-CIO and the national unions who work directly with sympathetic legislators and their staffs for or against specific pieces of legislation. Under mandates established by the governing bodies of the respective unions, this corps participates at all stages of the legislative process and follow-up, including the influencing of public attitudes, bill and speech drafting, lobbying, research, compromise, grass roots pressure, and surveillance of administration.

A variety of methods is utilized to achieve interest representation *within* government. The Department of Labor is viewed "as a department for labor [which] looks to its labor constituency to provide it with continuing sustenance."[18] Appointments to policy-making posts in the department, including the Secretary, have in recent years been made in consultation with the AFL-CIO—more typical in a Democratic administration—or on the basis of a

[13]Julius Rothman, "A New Look at Manpower Policy," *American Federationist* (AFL-CIO), August 1969, pp. 4-6 *passim.*

[14]AFL-CIO, *Executive Council Report, 1969,* pp. 132-33.

[15]Jack Conway, "Challenges to Union Leadership," *Proceedings of the IRRA* (December 1968), p. 185.

[16]"Randolph Forms Institute to End Negro Poverty," *New York Times,* March 12, 1965.

[17]Avery Leiserson, "Organized Labor as a Pressure Group," *Labor in the American Economy,* The Annals of the American Academy of Political and Social Science, Philadelphia, March 1951, p. 111.

[18]*Ibid.,* p. 166.

general sympathy for worker interests. It is customary for one assistant secretary to be chosen from unions ranks—in Democratic administrations, by nomination from the trade union movement. Where an agency's activities impinge directly on union and labor interests, special units or personnel are recruited from union ranks or with union approval to assert union viewpoints. The advisory committee method is widely utilized to secure counsel from unions and other interest groups on specific programs which are affected with a strong labor interest. When advisory committee participation is supported by a substantial research effort, union viewpoints can be highly influential in molding the administration of programs and new legislation. There is also the "window dressing" type of advisory committee participation in which all there is, is a union presence. Interest representation is most influential when union participation is integral to the administration of policy, as in the tripartite disputes settlement procedures during World War II and the Korean War. . . .

The union in America employs law and its administration mainly as an auxiliary strategy. It is subordinate to collective bargaining because, by comparison, (a) its effects on the terms of the employment relationship are less clearly perceived by union people, (b) it is necessarily not as responsive to union influence, and (c) it is not as adaptible to *particular* union interests. Strategy of law and its administration represents a species of bargaining because effective utilization requires the union to engage in negotiations with politicians, legislators, and administrators based on the union's ability to give or withhold material and moral support.